Text and Materials on the Criminal Justice Process

Highlighting key issues in Criminal Justice that students need to consider, the Fifth Edition of this popular text contains a wide and varied selection of materials which help to explain the evolution of the criminal justice process in England and Wales since the early 1990s. Statutes, case law, empirical research and official and unofficial reports, as well as theoretical perspectives and academic comment, are woven together and contextualised by the accompanying narrative to provide an authoritative account of the recent development of the criminal justice system.

Fully updated, this Fifth Edition explores the issues around:

● the introduction of Police and Crime Commissioners;
● the contracting out of probation services;
● the significant reforms to legal aid funding;
● the challenges to trial by jury posed by the internet.

This book also helpfully directs students to further reading by chapter to provide next steps for research. Written in an accessible style, *Text and Materials on the Criminal Justice Process* is a valuable resource for students of criminal justice.

Nicola Padfield is a Reader in Criminal and Penal Justice at the Faculty of Law and Master of Fitzwilliam College, University of Cambridge, UK. A qualified barrister, she has published widely on criminal law and criminal justice and is a Bencher of the Middle Temple.

Jonathan Bild is a Teaching Associate and Affiliated Lecturer at the Faculty of Law, University of Cambridge, UK.

Text and Materials on the Criminal Justice Process

FIFTH EDITION

Nicola Padfield and Jonathan Bild

LONDON AND NEW YORK

Fifth edition published 2016
by Routledge
2 Park Square, Milton Park, Abingdon, Oxon, OX14 4RN

and by Routledge
711 Third Avenue, New York, NY 10017

Routledge is an imprint of the Taylor & Francis Group, an informa business

First edition published by Butterworths Law in 1995
Fourth edition published by Oxford University Press in 2008

British Library Cataloguing-in-Publication Data
A catalogue record for this book is available from the British Library
Library of Congress Cataloging-in-Publication Data
Padfield, Nicola, author.
    Text and materials on the criminal justice process / Nicola Padfield and
Jonathan Bild. — Fifth edition.
        pages cm
    1. Criminal justice, Administration of—Great Britain.   I. Bild, Jonathan,
author.   II. Title.
    KD7876.P33 2015
    345.41'05—dc23
    2015014586

ISBN: 978-1-138-91833-7 (hbk)
ISBN: 978-1-138-91834-4 (pbk)
ISBN: 978-1-315-68857-2 (ebk)

Typeset in Joanna
by Apex CoVantage, LLC

Outline Contents

Detailed Contents

Preface

Since the first edition of this book, the pace of change in the criminal justice system has not slowed. Nor has the quality of justice obviously improved. In the seven years since the publication of the last edition, cost-saving has become a hugely important issue in English criminal justice: the 20 per cent reduction in the Ministry of Justice's budget over the course of the 2010–15 Parliament has impacted on all of the players in the criminal justice process. Everyone, it seems, is expected to do more with less. It is perhaps too early to assess comprehensively the impact of (even more) straitened finances across the whole 'system' but certainly the anecdotal evidence suggests a criminal justice system under great strain. Can we really expect this not to have an effect on substantive outcomes? We must be as vigilant as ever to ensure that the criminal justice process does not deliver injustice.

The shape of the book continues to emphasise each discrete part of the decision-making process, whereas successive governments appear to have been committed to 'team working', 'joined-up' criminal justice and inter-agency co-operation in criminal justice. It might therefore be argued that a book divided as this one is, is out of date. We would argue that the opposite is true. The reality is that there are several very different players within the criminal justice process. We should not be seduced into thinking that they all sing from the same songbook. The working relationships between the various agencies must be explored, as must the legal framework within which they function. As 'Big Brother' tightens his grip, are there enough checks and balances within the process?

There are no easy answers to the dilemmas facing the criminal justice system today. In fact, you may find that this book raises as many questions as it answers. This is not accidental: we want to encourage you to think as well as learn!

Nicola Padfield and Jonathan Bild
March 2015

Acknowledgements

Grateful acknowledgement is made to all the authors and publishers of copyright material which appears in this book, and in particular to the following for permission to reprint material from the sources indicated:

Sheila Brown for the extract from S Brown, *Magistrates at Work: Sentencing and Social Structure* (1991)

Incorporated Council of Law Reporting for extracts from: *Law Reports: Appeal Cases* (AC); *Court of Appeal of England and Wales Criminal Division* (EWCA Crim); *Queen's Bench Division* (QB); and *Weekly Law Reports* (WLR)

Michael King for the extract from M King, *The Framework of Criminal Justice* (1981)

Oxford Centre for Criminological Research and the authors for the extract from A Ashworth, E Genders, G Mansfield, J Peay and E Player, *Sentencing in the Crown Court: Report of an Exploratory Study* (1984) Oxford Centre for Criminological Research Occasional Paper No 10

Oxford University Press for extracts from R Hood, *Race and Sentencing: a Study in the Crown Court* (1992); and M McConville, J Hodgson, L Bridges and A Pavlovic, *Standing Accused: The Organisation and Practice of Criminal Defence Lawyers* (1994)

Oxford University Press Journals for extracts from *The British Journal of Criminology*: C Jones, 'Auditing Criminal Justice' (1993) 33 *British Journal of Criminology* 187; and R Morgan, Review of M Drakeford, K Haines, B Cotton and M Octigan, 'Pre-trial Services and the Future of Probation' (2002) *British Journal of Criminology* 224

Palgrave Macmillan for extract from T Skryme, *The Changing Image of the Magistracy* (2nd edition, 1983)

Pearson Education for extract from A James and J Raine, *The New Politics of Criminal Justice* (1998)

Reed Elsevier (UK) Ltd trading as LexisNexis for extracts from *All England Law Reports* (All ER); and extract from Simon's Tax Cases

Stanford University Press for extract from H Packer, *The Limits of the Criminal Sanction* (1968)

Sweet and Maxwell Ltd for extract from *Archbold News*: *HM Attorney General v Scotcher* [2005] UKHL 36 (as reported at (2005) 6 *Archbold News* 3); extracts from *Archbold Review*: N Padfield, 'Deferred prosecution agreements' (2012) 7 *Archbold Review* 4; *R v Maxwell* [2010] UKSC 48 (as reported at (2011) 8 *Archbold Review* 4); J R Spencer, 'Squaring up to Strasbourg: Horncastle in the Supreme Court' (2010) 1 *Archbold Review* 6; J R Spencer, 'Hearsay evidence at Strasbourg: a further skirmish, or the final round? A comment on *Al-Khawaja and Tahery v UK* in the Grand Chamber' (2012) 1 *Archbold Review* 5; extracts from Criminal Appeal Reports (Cr App R): *R v McIlkenny* (1992) 93 Cr App Rep 287; *R v Mullen* [1999]

2 Cr App Rep 143; *R v Newton* (1982) 77 Cr App Rep 13; *R v Paris, Abdullahi and Miller* (1993) 97 Cr App Rep 99; extracts from *Criminal Law Review* (Crim LR): A Bailin and E Craven, 'Compensation for miscarriages of justice – who now qualifies?' [2014] Crim LR 511; B Block, C Corbett and J Peay, 'Ordered and Directed Acquittals in the Crown Court: A Time of Change?' [1993] Crim LR 95; P Darbyshire, 'The Lamp that Shows that Freedom Lives – is it Worth the Candle?' [1991] Crim LR 740; A Hoyano, L Hoyano, G David and S Goldie, 'A Study of the Impact of the Revised Code for Crown Prosecutors' [1997] Crim LR 556; V Kemp, '"No time for a solicitor": implications for delays on the take-up of legal advice' [2013] Crim LR 184; V Kemp, 'PACE, performance targets and legal protections' [2014] Crim LR 278; *R v Abdroikov* [2008] Crim LR 134; *R v Looseley; A-G's Reference (No 3 of 2000)* [2002] Crim LR 301; *R v McDonald* [2007] Crim LR 737; *R (Mondelly) v Commissioner of Police of the Metropolis* [2007] Crim LR 298; G Richardson, 'Strict Liability for Regulatory Crime: the Empirical Research' [1987] Crim LR 295; J Roording, 'The Punishment of Tax Fraud' [1996] Crim LR 240; P Seago, C Walker and D Wall, 'The Development of the Professional Magistracy in England and Wales' [2000] Crim LR 631; extracts from European Human Rights Reports: *Monnell and Morris v United Kingdom* (1988) 10 EHRR 205; *Stafford v United Kingdom* (2002) 35 EHRR 1121; *Thynne, Wilson and Gunnell v United Kingdom* (1991) 13 EHRR 666; and extracts from *Law Quarterly Review* (LQR): A Ashworth, 'Should the police be allowed to use deception?' (1998) 114 LQR 108; P Devlin, 'The Conscience of the Jury' (1991) 107 LQR 398

Taylor & Francis for extracts from A E Bottoms and J D McClean, *Defendants in the Criminal Process* (1976); K Holloway and A Grounds, 'Discretion and the Release of Mentally Disordered Offenders' in L Gelsthorpe and N Padfield (eds), *Exercising Discretion: Decision-making in the criminal justice system and beyond* (2003); M McConville, A Sanders and R Leng, *The Case for the Prosecution* (1991); M Tonry, *Punishment and Politics: Evidence and emulation in the making of English crime control policy* (2004); A Worrall and C Hoy, *Punishment in the Community: Managing Offenders and Making Choices* (2nd edition, 2005)

Taylor & Francis Journals for extract from *Criminal Justice Matters*: R Reiner, 'Success or statistics? New Labour and crime control: What has happened to crime under New Labour?' (2007) 67 *Criminal Justice Matters* 4

Wiley-Blackwell Publishing Ltd for extracts from *Modern Law Review* (MLR): Lord Hoffmann, 'Human Rights and the House of Lords' (1999) 62 MLR 159; L C H Hoyano, 'Policing Flawed Police Investigations: Unravelling the Blanket' (1999) 62 MLR 912; and extract from *Journal of Law and Society*: R Morgan, 'Magistrates: The Future According to Auld' (2002) 29 J of Law and Society 308

Contains public sector information licensed under the Open Government Licence v2.0

Table of Cases

Table of Legislation and Conventions

*(references in **bold** indicate where material has been reproduced)*

Table of Statutory Instruments

Table of European Legislation

Treaties

Decisions

Table of Foreign Statutes

Table of International Conventions

Chapter 1

Introduction

(i) About this book

Imagine walking home one evening, when you come across a young woman lying on the pavement, moaning. On closer inspection, you see that she looks a little drunk, and she is bleeding through her jacket. What do you do? You telephone the emergency services, dial 999? Do you ask for the police or an ambulance? Whatever you do, the matter will soon be safely out of your hands, and the National Health Service and/or the criminal justice system will take over. This book follows the processes that a case such as this will pass through in the criminal justice system.

In our fictional case, you contacted the ambulance service, who then called for the police to attend. Of course, in many circumstances, the police never hear about a crime. Probably less than half of all crimes are reported to the police and reporting rates vary enormously between different types of offences. The factors which influence victims in their decision whether or not to report a crime were analysed by Clarkson et al (1994). They include victims' habituation to violence, their reluctance to have their own behaviour scrutinised, their fear of reprisals, their own criminality and hostility toward the police, and the social costs associated with reporting crime. And Walby and Allen (2004) found that high numbers of men and women do not report even the worst incidents of domestic violence they suffered to the police: because they thought it was too trivial, or a family private matter, or because they did not want more humiliation, or because they feared more violence or that the situation would get worse if they involved the police. How many times have you witnessed a crime, or indeed been a victim of crime, and not reported it to the police?

Nor do the police record all incidents reported to them: they may not believe the complainant or they may not consider that the reported behaviour constitutes a criminal act. The Crime Survey for England and Wales (CSEW) (formerly the British Crime Survey), which measures crimes against people living in private households by carrying out face-to-face interviews, has been conducted regularly since 1982, and it became an annual event in 2001 (approximately 50,000 households, chosen at random, have been selected to take part in the 2014/15 survey). The CSEW has found that crime has been falling significantly in recent years. It estimated that there were 7.0 million incidents of crime against households and resident adults (aged 16 and over) in England and Wales for the year ending September 2014 (down 11 per cent on the previous year and the lowest estimate since the survey began; it peaked at 19.1 million in 1995). And yet, in the same year, the police recorded only 3.7 million offences – just over half the number of offences estimated by the CSEW. The first document included at [1:1] of this chapter is the summary of the Office for National Statistics Statistical Bulletin for the year to September 2014 which combines findings from the CSEW and police recorded figures.

Of course, it is very difficult to know how much crime there is: readers should explore the Office for National Statistics' website: www.ons.gov.uk/ons/publications/index.html for the latest statistical data. Rising or falling incidents of recorded and reported crime can be influenced by a range of factors beyond there simply being a greater or smaller number of offences being committed. For example, it is difficult to establish whether the rising number of sexual offences recorded by the police (up 22 per cent in the year to September 2014) reflects increasing numbers of these offences being committed or, rather, improvements in recording and less reluctance on the part of victims to come forward to report such crimes. At [1:2] is an extract from an article by Robert Reiner which considers whether or not statistical crime trends are attributable to the Government's criminal justice policy. It focuses on the inevitable unreliability of national crime data. You might like to consider what data you think should be collected: police recorded crime figures will never paint a 'true' figure of crime (and we will see in Chapter 2 that the UK Statistics Authority 'de-designated' police recorded crime as an approved measure of crime statistics in January 2014); offender surveys give different results from victim surveys, but raise significant ethical and practical problems; local data may be more useful than national trends, and so on.

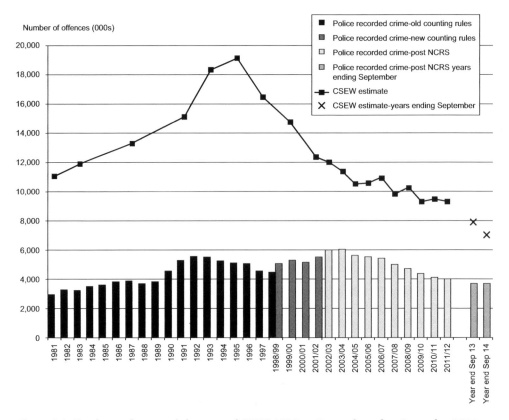

Number of offences (000s)

- ■ Police recorded crime-old counting rules
- ▨ Police recorded crime-new counting rules
- □ Police recorded crime-post NCRS
- ▨ Police recorded crime-post NCRS years ending September
- ━■━ CSEW estimate
- ✕ CSEW estimate-years ending September

Figure 1.1 Trends in police recorded crime and CSEW, 1981 to 12 months ending September 2014

Despite the real challenges of measuring 'crime', what is clear is that, as we move through the process – and as we move through the chapters of this book – we are dealing with an ever-decreasing proportion of cases. Of those cases which are reported to the police, not all result in a prosecution; and not all prosecutions end in convictions – perhaps two in every hundred offences committed result in a conviction. There is a huge amount of statistical information on criminal justice available to the public, but it is presented in an increasingly fragmented manner, split between the (quarterly) Criminal Justice Statistics, Court Statistics and Offender Management Statistics. Why some statistics are in one set of data rather than another is not always obvious. Clearly, it is welcome that so much information is made available – but shouldn't thought also be given to ensure that it is readily accessible to the public? In addition to the fragmentation of the statistics, the process of moving (some previously excellent) websites onto the (not particularly user-friendly) Gov.uk site has left a trail of broken links across the internet: increasingly, it feels like what you are looking for is 'out there somewhere' but it can be a real test of one's patience actually to find it! However, the Criminal Justice Statistics Quarterly Update can be relied upon to provide a useful flowchart of flows through the criminal justice system.

Once an alleged offence is reported, or comes to the attention of the police in some other way, then, as we shall see in Chapter 2, the police have wide discretionary powers. They may record it or they may decide it was just an accident; they may investigate the crime further, using wide common law and statutory powers under the Police and Criminal Evidence Act 1984 (PACE); they (or the Crown Prosecution Service) may eventually charge an arrested person with an offence. Many

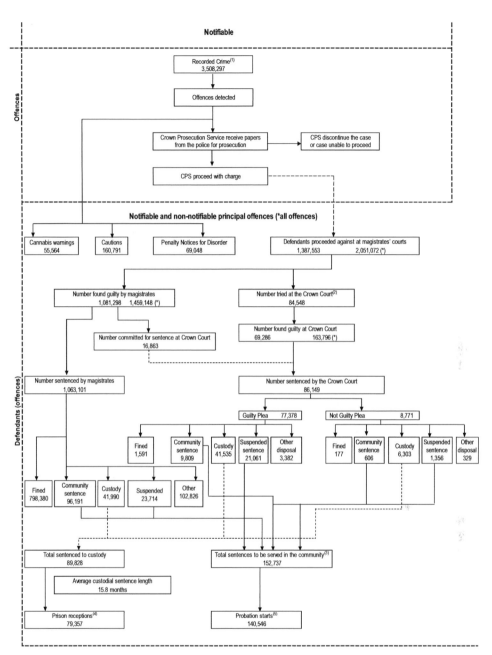

(1) Covers all indictable offences, including triable either way, plus a few closely associated summary offences.
(2) Defendants tried at the Crown Court in a given year may have been committed for trial by a magistrate in a previous year.
(3) Includes community sentences and suspended sentence orders.
(4) Receptions for offenders given a custodial sentence (figures include fine defaulters).
(5) Offenders starting Community Order or Suspended Sentence Order supervision by the Probation Service.
* Total number of all offences in comparison with the total number of defendants on a principal offence basis.

Figure 1.2 Flows through the Criminal Justice System, 12 months ending September 2014

criminals are never charged: they will either be summonsed to appear before a magistrates' court or be cautioned. We shall see in Chapter 2 how an enormous proportion of offenders were dealt with out-of-court in the mid- to late-2000s, although this has fallen significantly in recent years.

Let us go back to our story. Our victim recovers from the attack and tells the police that her name is Rosa Bottles. She says she went to the pub with the usual group of friends, they all drank heavily, and on the way home she was involved in a fight with a man with whom she had earlier had an argument, Gerry Good. She is prepared to see the police proceed against him. The next day Gerry is arrested. What goes on in the police station between the time he is arrested and the time he is charged is perhaps the most crucial to a successful prosecution. It is also in the police station that the seeds of most miscarriages of justice are likely to be sown. In Chapter 2 we examine police powers and the safeguards for the suspect held in a police station. The Crown Prosecution Service (CPS), working in partnership with the police, may give pre-charge advice, and now make the decision whether Gerry should be charged with a minor assault or a more serious wounding offence, and are responsible for the conduct of the prosecution. We will discuss the complex relationship between the police and the CPS in Chapter 3.

But not all prosecutions are initiated by the police. Non-police and non-CPS agencies, such as HM Revenue and Customs, the Environment Agency and the Health and Safety Executive, deal with many criminal offences, often in very different ways. Chapter 4 thus offers a rather different perspective on the criminal justice process.

Another influence which is often neglected is that of the lawyer. The suspect's solicitor and barrister, in particular, may play a significant role in the process, since their advice about such matters as to whether a defendant should plead guilty or not guilty, whether to give evidence and whether to appeal may have a significant impact on the way in which the case is finally proceeded with. Chapter 5, on the role of defence lawyers, will attempt to assess the appropriateness of the legal advice given to suspects at all stages in the criminal process and the very real (and growing) problem of legal costs.

All criminal prosecutions start in the magistrates' court. When the alleged offender reaches the magistrates' court, more decisions are taken. The court may have to decide whether the accused should be remanded in custody or released on bail, or whether the accused should be tried on indictment by a judge and jury in the Crown Court or summarily before the magistrates. If the case remains before the magistrates, they may have to decide on sentence as well as on guilt. Since most prosecutions begin and end in the magistrates' court, they clearly merit a chapter (Chapter 6).

Our fictional case is a serious one and Gerry is charged with an indictable crime, one which can only be tried in the Crown Court by judge and jury. The roles of judge and jury at the trial stage are clearly different, and each merits separate examination (Chapters 7 and 8).

If convicted, Gerry will be sentenced. The role of the judge or magistrate in sentencing (why does the jury have no role here?) will be examined in their respective chapters (see above). But the story, of course, does not end there – perhaps Gerry will appeal or seek some other review of his sentence and/or conviction, so the powers of appellate bodies must be considered (Chapter 9). In any event, the process continues beyond Gerry's conviction – he has a sentence to serve – and in Chapter 10 we look at how various criminal justice agencies exercise their wide discretionary powers in relation to sentenced offenders.

The emphasis of the book is on the decisions made by the key actors in the process, stressing the wide discretionary powers exercised. As Davis (1969) pointed out, the greatest and most frequent injustices occur where discretion is unfettered, where rules and principles provide little or no guidance. Since consistency and certainty are important objectives of the criminal justice system, it might seem that the system should be governed by clearer, pre-determined rules. Why have such wide discretionary powers been delegated to different individuals and bodies? The answer is simple: rules can be inflexible, and decisions based on purely legal criteria would be unduly rigid and harsh. The legal philosopher Ronald Dworkin (1977) famously pointed out that 'discretion, like the hole in a doughnut, does not exist except as an area left open by a surrounding belt of restriction. It is therefore a relative concept' (at page 31). In this book, we encourage you to think about this surrounding belt of restriction, the doughnut, the socio-legal context of decision-making. For a fuller introduction to the literature on discretionary decision making, see Gelsthorpe and Padfield (2003).

If we agree that a certain degree of flexibility is necessary, has the English criminal justice system gone too far? We have moved into an age of 'multi-agency co-operation' (see in particular Chapter 10, but the other agencies described in other chapters of course co-operate closely). 'Agencies' merge, separate and conflate to a confusing extent. Can shared decision-making work in practice? The danger is that as decision-making passes away from the courts, control is lost. Decisions are difficult to challenge and lines of accountability are often blurred. Much of this book is descriptive, painting a picture of decision-making in the criminal process today. There have, of course, been many important changes since the first edition of this book was published in 1995 and yet most of the key issues and tensions remain unresolved (and, in the context of finite resources, are perhaps unresolvable?). Shortly before the first edition was published, the Royal Commission on Criminal Justice **[1:3]** had reported and this remains the 'starting point' for this book. It is the view of the authors that students of today's criminal justice system should have an appreciation of how it has developed – without knowing how we got here makes where we are today even harder to comprehend! We continue to include extracts from research conducted for the Royal Commission as the research and the findings remain relevant today.

This book does not seek to concentrate on the principles behind the process, but the student should nonetheless consider a number of preliminary issues.

(ii) Is there a criminal justice *system*?

Since different parts of the criminal justice system often appear to pull in different directions, working within different (and competing) budgets, it probably should not be called a system at all. For example, the police and the CPS do not necessarily have the same ambitions, and probation services and the prison service compete for a limited budget. But a system is simply, according to the Oxford Reference Dictionary, a 'set of connected things or parts that form a whole or work together'. Remember, too, that we are looking at a 'snapshot' of the system taken at one particular moment in time and that the different elements in the process are constantly evolving. This can help you digest some of the inconsistencies. Norrie (2014) puts English criminal law in its nineteenth-century context, and a similar historical approach to criminal procedure and evidence is also useful. No central planning at one point in history went into drawing up the skeleton of the system. Indeed, if you were inventing a criminal justice system from scratch today, how closely would it resemble our present system?

Feeney **[1:4]** explains clearly the way in which 'systems concepts' came to be applied to criminal justice. Perhaps because the different parts may clash and sometimes work against each other, we should call it a process and not a system, but even this might imply a neat 'conveyor belt' operation. Is this system really little more than a series of decisions? Each actor or agency is interdependent, as Feeney makes clear, but each is not necessarily working consistently with the others. It is one of the purposes of this book to look at the different stages of the criminal justice process in order to see the impact on the process as a whole of different decisions taken at different stages.

(iii) Identifying characteristics of the English criminal justice process

The criminal justice system is not just a stream of unrelated decisions – there are some central themes. Two key characteristics have traditionally been singled out as running throughout the English criminal justice system. Particularly important at the trial stage in the process, they necessarily affect decision-making at all stages.

(i) The system is accusatorial, or adversarial, rather than inquisitorial. Much has been made of the differences between different legal systems, but the differences can be exaggerated. The brief discussion of the differences in the Report of the Royal Commission on Criminal Justice (1993) provides a helpful summary **[1:3]**. This Royal Commission recommended no fundamental change to the accusatorial system in this country. But of course, the number of cases which end up with a 'full-blown' accusatorial trial is small. Look again at Figure 1.2.

The Royal Commission regarded the principle of the presumption of innocence as fundamental. What does this mean in practice? It certainly doesn't mean that the police actually presume that all suspects are innocent! A visit to a police station – or even to a magistrates' court where the court officials may seem to bark out 'Stand up', 'Sit down' – can give the clear impression of a presumption of guilt. Even the substantive criminal law does not always respect the presumption of innocence: strict liability offences are committed without proof of a guilty mind; and defendants are often required to prove elements of specific defences (see Ashworth and Blake (1996)). Reverse burdens of proof are not rare: the House of Lords accepted, for example, in *Sheldrake v DPP* [2004] UKHL 43 that it was proper for a person charged with being in charge of a motor vehicle having consumed excess alcohol, under section 5(1)(b) of the Road Traffic Act 1988, to have the burden of proving the defence that there was no likelihood of him driving. The presumption of innocence is a vitally important procedural safeguard: but do not misunderstand the extent to which it protects the citizen.

Attention should be paid too to the resources available to the defence in an adversarial system: the 'equality of arms' argument. After all, a heavyweight boxer is not permitted to box professionally against a puny opponent. Are the dice loaded too heavily in one direction? In an adversarial system, convictions are achieved either by proof (beyond reasonable doubt) or by an admission of guilt. There is strong pressure on defendants to plead guilty, and on the police to secure guilty pleas. If somebody admits his or her guilt, there may be little 'process' at all. Where does this leave the presumption of innocence? You should also consider the concept of 'adversarialism' in Chapter 7 where we consider the recent trend to encourage judges to 'manage' cases in a more 'hands on' manner. Clearly, a judge must be wary of too great an involvement – a difficult line to draw.

(ii) There is a strong lay element. Two chapters in this book are devoted to non-legally qualified participants in the criminal justice process: juries and magistrates (although we shall see in Chapter 6 that there has been a significant decline in the number of lay magistrates in recent years). Many foreign lawyers are astonished that the powers of a judge are entrusted to lay magistrates and that lay juries are entrusted to reach verdicts without giving reasons or explanations. Increasing inter-agency co-operation at all levels also means a wider range of non-lawyer involvement. The Royal Commission on Criminal Justice (1993) **[1:3]**, in recommending the creation of a Criminal Cases Review Authority (now the Criminal Cases Review Commission – see Chapter 9), suggested that 'both lawyers and lay persons should be represented. We recommend that the Chairman should be chosen for his or her personal qualities rather than for any particular qualifications or background that he or she may have' (page 184). The first chairman was indeed a non-lawyer (an engineer), yet the same report concluded that more use should be made of stipendiary (legally qualified) magistrates, thus recognising the strengths of lay involvement at one point and ignoring them at another.

Unfortunately the Report made no attempt to value the lay element in our criminal justice system. Lord Justice Auld's detailed *Review of the Criminal Courts* (2001) **[1:5]** recommended that the Crown Court and magistrates' courts should be replaced by a unified Criminal Court consisting of three divisions: the Crown Division, the District Division and the Magistrates' Division. Within these three divisions lay juries and lay magistrates would have continued to play an important role. But what is the value of lay involvement, and is it worth striving to keep it? For these authors, the value of trial by jury is diminished by the fact they do not give reasons for their decisions (see Chapter 8), but that is not to deny the importance of involving the ordinary citizen in important criminal justice decisions. We also see increasing use of voluntary organisations in the delivery of sentences (see Chapter 10): is this a commitment to citizen engagement, or simply a way to save money?

A third characteristic has appeared in recent decades:

(iii) 'Managerialism'. The language of management and of audit punctuates the criminal justice system. Much of the Government's agenda for reform has been led by what are often called the 'three Es' – economy, efficiency and effectiveness (see Jones **[1:6]**). In that article, written in 1993, she writes that 'the 1980s saw the "ascendancy of economy" over efficiency and effectiveness, resulting in a "managerial myopia" and a concern with short-term management innovation at the expense of a long-term focus'. The ascendancy of economy remains all too obvious: saving money is at the heart of many initiatives. Would the Coalition Government have been so keen on 'Transforming Rehabilitation' (see Chapter 10) if they were not simultaneously cutting 20 per cent from the Ministry of Justice's budget? Concerns with efficiency and indeed also effectiveness lie behind many recent changes. Tonry **[1:7]** is deeply sceptical of the previous Labour Government's commitment to effectiveness. They paid lip-service, he suggests, to what the evidence tells us, but self-interest often won the day. For Tonry (an American professor who was Director of the Institute of Criminology in Cambridge from 1999–2004), New Labour put on a sorry performance. If you read Government business plans, or the annual reports of key criminal justice agencies, over this period you will see, even before the advent of the enormous budget cut, key performance indicators and measures of success, which put great emphasis on financial savings. But the need to find more subtle measures of success has also been recognised. See, for example, Liebling (2004) on assessing the 'moral' performance of prisons.

It is worth exploring the large number of 'official' reports on criminal justice in recent years to assess their priorities: do they suffer from 'managerial myopia' or do they have a principled focus? Look at who wrote them, and at their terms of reference as well as their conclusions. A starting point might be the Royal Commission on Criminal Justice, set up in 1991 after the Court of Appeal quashed the convictions of the 'Birmingham Six', six Irishmen convicted of murder following a pub bombing in Birmingham in 1974. Its terms of reference are set out at **[1:3]** and it reported in 1993. Many critics have suggested that the Royal Commission wasted its opportunity to suggest a radical overhaul. Thus, Bridges (1994) described its report as 'a sham. It is a document that is slip-shod in its use of empirical evidence, slippery in its argumentation, and shameful in its underlying political purposes'. Is he unduly harsh? The Royal Commission was severely limited by its brief. But note too Professor Zander's dissent, which you will find quoted at greater length at **[9:1]**, where he says:

> At the heart of the criminal justice system there is a fundamental principle that the process must itself have integrity. The majority suggest that the answer to prosecution wrongdoing in the investigation of crime is to deal with the wrongdoers through prosecution or disciplinary proceedings . . . the approach is not merely insufficient, it is irrelevant to the point of principle. The more serious the case, the greater the need that the system upholds the values in the name of which it claims to act . . . The integrity of the criminal justice system is a higher objective than the conviction of any individual.

So, you might conclude that the Royal Commission failed to take an adequate principled approach.

Another influential report – *Review of Delay in the Criminal Justice System* – was produced in 1997 by a Home Office team led by civil servant Martin Narey (later the Chief Executive of the National Offender Management Service), many of whose recommendations were enacted in the Crime and Disorder Act 1998. This emphasis on reducing delays became a key election pledge of the Labour Party in 1997: its manifesto, for example, committed it to halving the time from arrest to sentence for persistent young offenders. Was this emphasis misplaced? Some delays may, after all, be necessary and in the interests of justice.

A flurry of further reports appeared in 2001. There was the Government's White Paper, *Criminal Justice: The Way Ahead* (February 2001), followed by another Home Office report, *Review of the Sentencing Framework* (the Halliday Report), published in July 2001, and the much longer and fuller *Review of the Criminal Courts of England and Wales* by Lord Justice Auld (October 2001) **[1:5]**. Lord Justice Auld's terms of reference were:

> A review into the practices and procedures of, and the rules of evidence applied by, the criminal courts at every level, with a view to ensuring that they deliver justice fairly, by streamlining all their processes, increasing their efficiency and strengthening the effectiveness of their relationships with others across the whole of the criminal justice system, and having regard to the interests of all parties including victims and witnesses, thereby promoting public confidence in the rule of law.

Next came the Audit Commission's *Route to Justice: Improving the pathway of offenders through the criminal justice system* (2002), and the White Paper *Justice for All* (2002) Cm 5563, which led to the very important Criminal Justice Act 2003, which made fundamental changes to the rules of criminal procedure and criminal evidence, and which will be mentioned throughout this book.

After the enactment of the Criminal Justice Act 2003, the pace of change did not slow down. For example, there were two Government papers in 2006: *Delivering simple, speedy, summary justice* (from the Department for Constitutional Affairs) and *Rebalancing the criminal justice system in favour of the law abiding majority* (from the Home Office), both clearly designed to improve public confidence in the criminal justice system. And Lord Carter was commissioned to write three influential 'market-based' reports: first, *Managing Offenders: Reducing Crime* (2003), which resulted in the creation of the National Offender Management Service (see Chapter 10, and **[10:1]**); secondly, his *Review of Legal Aid Procurement* (2006) which influenced the Legal Services Act 2007 (see Chapter 5) and then the *Review of Prisons: Securing the Future: Proposals for the Efficient and Sustainable use of Custody in England and Wales* (2007). Carter, who after a career in business was made a Labour peer in 2004, clearly takes a 'business-like' approach to the criminal justice system: this approach seems to have been accepted unquestioningly by the Government.

In the post-2010 'age of austerity', this efficiency-drive has not gone away. Most recently, in January 2015, Sir Brian Leveson, the President of the Queen's Bench Division, published a *Review of Efficiency in Criminal Proceedings* **[1:8]** in which he recommended: the greater use of video and other conferencing technology across the system (particularly in the Crown Court); more flexible opening hours in magistrates' courts to accommodate those who cannot attend hearings during normal office hours; tighter case management by judges, including, in appropriate cases, the provision of timetables for evidence and speeches; that contracts awarded to those responsible for delivering prisoners to court should require greater efficiency so that prisoners appear on time and do not delay proceedings; and (perhaps optimistically!) that there should be funding available to pay for the inevitable cost of changing from the current systems to the more efficient ones. When he announced the report's publication, Sir Brian Leveson stated that '[o]ur conduct of criminal trials was designed in the 19th century with many changes and reforms bolted on, especially over the last 30 years'. Keep this thought in mind when reading this book: so much change is 'bolted on' that it is perhaps impossible for any new approach to begin with a blank page. And also, of course, when reading anything (including this book!), students should keep an eye on the author (and their perspective) and on their terms of reference or aims in writing.

Running through many of these reports is the shift towards managerialism (or better management?), which can be seen in many of the recent changes. Jones **[1:6]** suggests that the shift towards managerial justice has led not to more public accountability but to increased central control of criminal justice practice. For Bottoms (1995), there are four themes which lie behind many of the recent changes in criminal justice: just deserts, managerialism (he singles out its systematic, consumerist and actuarial dimensions), community, and popular punitiveness. He explains the rise of these in the context of various aspects of theories of modernity: 'the relative erosion of class and its partial replacement by interest-group and lifestyle differentiators; the decline in intermediate-level social groups and a general disembedding of social relations; and the subjective concomitants of living in a technological world'.

These themes remained relevant to the criminal justice system being 'managed' by New Labour between 1997 and 2010. 'Tough on crime, tough on the causes of crime' was a successful election message. The Crime and Disorder Act 1998, the Youth Justice and Criminal Evidence Act 1999, the Criminal Justice and Court Services Act 2000, the Police Reform Act 2002, the Proceeds of Crime Act 2002, the Criminal Justice Act 2003, and the Offender Management Act 2007 are all examples of attempts to 'tighten up' the criminal justice system. One advantage of managerialist practices might be better case management: a better ordering of the 'system'. But the greater the 'order' within the system, the greater the need for checks and balances and for accountability: the more the system appears to join-up 'against' the suspect or offender, the more vigilant we must be to ensure that the aims of the criminal justice system are not forgotten. James and Raine offer a useful reminder of the need to focus on the purpose of the criminal justice system **[1:9]**. For them it has the ancient purpose of providing security in exchange for allegiance as well as a modern purpose of protecting individual human rights. For these authors, justice and fairness must lie at the heart of the process. Let us move on to evaluating the process.

(iv) Evaluating the criminal justice process

So, before evaluating the criminal justice system, we have to identify what the system is seeking to achieve. At one level the answer is easy: it seeks to reduce the incidence of crime in society. But it is not obvious that the criminal justice system itself is (or is even capable of) actually doing that. Perhaps it seeks merely to convict the guilty and to acquit the innocent. We should then question why, and with what justification, we punish those deemed guilty. Ashworth and Redmayne (2010), Walker and Padfield (1996) and von Hirsch and Ashworth (2005) provide some answers to these 'big' questions on crime and punishment.

A useful starting point is Packer's (1968) classic exposition of two models of the criminal process: the Due Process Model and the Crime Control Model **[1:10]**. No one would suggest today that these models are entirely satisfactory, but they do allow us to recognise the value choices that underlie the details of the criminal process. The assumptions that underlie competing policy claims have to be recognised. McConville and Baldwin (1981) suggested that the English system conforms to the Crime Control Model, pointing out, for example, the lack of due process safeguards in a system where 90 per cent of all defendants plead guilty and trial by jury is so rarely used. Their concerns are as valid today as they were then (or is the situation even 'worse' now defendants are more transparently 'bribed' by sentence discounts to plead guilty?).

But Packer's models are not enough. There are not just two clear-cut alternative value systems competing for priority in the criminal process. Bottoms and Maclean **[1:11]** identified a third model – the Liberal Bureaucratic Model – and King **[1:12]** preferred six models, three based on the perspective of the typical participants and three based on the work of social theorists. Students may well find it useful to keep these different perspectives in mind as they attempt to evaluate the different processes at work.

Other writers have sought to move away from the 'model' perspective, to identify other fundamental values and principles. Cavadino, Dignan and Mair (2013) argue that the key to what they see as a penal crisis is one of legitimacy. The penal process needs to be reconstructed around the principle of respect for human rights. Ashworth and Redmayne (2010) concentrate on the need to identify fundamental values and principles. They single out, for example, the right of an innocent person not to be convicted and the right to consistent treatment within declared policies. Ashworth's insistence on a principled approach is particularly important at a time when, as was discussed above, governments are putting increasing emphasis on managerialism and auditing, perhaps at the expense of justice (see also his *Sentencing and Criminal Justice* (2010)).

International and European standards play an increasing role in helping to identify basic principles. Thus, the European Court of Human Rights (ECtHR), applying the European Convention for the Protection of Human Rights and Fundamental Freedoms, is frequently asked to rule on criminal justice matters. There are frequent references in this book to judgments of the ECtHR, illustrating the way in which the court applies the Convention in practice. Since the Human Rights Act 1998 **[1:13]** incorporated the Convention into domestic law, the Convention has been used in domestic courts to challenge, for example, police surveillance techniques and Parole Board decision-making. It is often cases involving prisoners, such as over voting rights (*Hirst v United Kingdom (No 2)* (2006) 42 EHRR 41), the Government's policy on artificial insemination for prisoners (*Dickson v United Kingdom* (2008) 46 EHRR 41), and whole life sentences (*Vinter and others v United Kingdom* [2013] ECHR 645), which tend to capture most public (and political) attention. However, the relationship between the ECtHR, the domestic courts and Parliament is a complicated one. Increasingly, the ECtHR and the domestic courts are engaging in what they refer to as 'dialogue'. The 'dialogue' between the two over hearsay evidence is discussed at **[1:14]** and **[1:15]**.

The 'other' Europe, the European Union, has only involved itself in criminal justice matters more recently. Most importantly, the Amsterdam Treaty of 1997 gave the Council of Ministers of the European Union the power to draw up a variety of legal instruments to help create an 'area of freedom, security and justice'. The most important legal instruments in this area are Framework Decisions, such as the Framework Decision on the European Arrest Warrant, which led to a degree of harmonisation in the laws on extradition (see the Extradition Act 2003). Driven by concerns for security, many of the Brussels-led initiatives seem authoritarian and prosecution-minded. By the time the Treaty of Lisbon came into force in December 2009, there were approximately 130 police and criminal justice measures which had been adopted by EU Member States and the United Kingdom (alone) negotiated the power to opt out of all of these measures before the expiry of the transitional period on 1 December 2014. If the Government did not opt out, these measures would have become subject to the jurisdiction of the Court of Justice of the European Union and the enforcement powers of the European Commission. As with so much of the United Kingdom's relationship with 'Europe' this issue has become deeply political: the Government has exercised its opt-out and, at the time of writing, is deliberating about which of the individual measures it wishes to opt back into – much of the debate is on the most controversial measure, the European Arrest Warrant.

At an international level, the Universal Declaration of Human Rights was adopted in December 1948 by the General Assembly of the United Nations. As significant, and perhaps with potentially more impact, is the International Covenant on Civil and Political Rights (ICCPR), which came into force in 1976. The body set up by the ICCPR to monitor compliance is the Human Rights Committee. The United Kingdom has not ratified the Optional Protocol to the ICCPR, which provides for written applications to the Human Rights Committee by individuals who have been victims of violations of the Covenant's provisions. However, the United Kingdom is coming under increasing pressure to recognise a right of individual petition, which it will eventually have to do if it wishes to play a significant role in enhancing the protection of human rights around the world.

One measure of whether the system is working well is whether there is evidence of bias. Section 95 of the Criminal Justice Act 1991 **[1:16]** put the official seal of approval on the detection of discrimination. The statistics are very worrying: for example, black people are six times more likely to be stopped and searched by the police than white people; and, whereas 3 per cent of the general population of England and Wales in 2012 was estimated to be black, 13 per cent of the prison population was black **[1:17]**. At several points in this book we will review the evidence as to whether 'the system' in its many parts is biased against, for example, women or people from ethnic minorities. But the over-representation of black people in the criminal justice system cannot simply be explained away by racism. The evidence is far from clear, since the causes of crime are many and complex. Poverty, unemployment, poor education and environmental deprivation may all lead to a higher rate of crime. Since many people from ethnic minority backgrounds are poorer than the average citizen, it is difficult to identify whether any bias is the result of the criminal justice system or merely a reflection of society generally. Whilst there has been a steady trickle of equality legislation over the years (such as the Equality Act 2006, which created the Equality and Human Rights Commission), we have yet to see significant improvements. **[10:8]** is a summary of the Corston Report, published in 2007, which suggested that this was the right time to adopt a new approach to women in the criminal justice system. Yet a House of Commons Justice Committee report, *Women offenders: after the Corston Report* (2013) (see **[10:9]**), found that

> There is little evidence that the equality duty – in so far as it relates to gender – has been used robustly to hold providers to account. In particular, the duty does not appear to have had the desired impact on systematically encouraging local mainstream commissioners to provide gender specific services tackling the underlying causes of women's offending, or on consistently informing broader policy initiatives within [the Ministry of Justice] and [National Offender Management Service]. For too long, while the needs of female offenders have been recognised as different from those of males, the criminal justice system generally and the National Offender Management Service in particular have struggled to reflect these differences fully in the services it provides. A key lesson still to be learnt is that tackling women's offending is not just a matter for the justice system (at paragraph 41).

The law seeks to impose a universal framework on diverse groups of people: but can there be justice in an economically unjust society? As Phillips and Bowling (2012) suggest, we need more sophisticated qualitative research, as well as quantitative measures, in order to understand changing patterns in criminal justice. Other forms of bias, defined by wealth and class, and which may reflect either prejudice or merely statistical imbalance, are even more difficult to detect. Hood, Shute and Seemungal **[1:18]** note an important 'cultural shift' in the treatment of ethnic minorities in recent years but also raise important questions about perceptions of fairness.

A final word of warning: in this book we are following a relatively straightforward case study in order to understand how the system works in practice. Even if the system works quite appropriately in the case of Gerry Good, you should remain alert. Notice when the system fails – a fundamental aim of the criminal justice system must be to reduce injustice.

Further reading

Ashworth, A, *Sentencing and Criminal Justice* (5th edition, 2010) Cambridge University Press
Ashworth, A and Blake, M, 'The presumption of innocence in English law' [1996] Crim LR 306
Ashworth, A and Redmayne, M, *The Criminal Process* (4th edition, 2010) Oxford University Press

Bottoms, A E, 'The philosophy and politics of punishment and sentencing' in Clarkson, C and Morgan, R (eds), *The Politics of Sentencing Reform* (1995) Oxford University Press

Bridges, L, 'Normalising Injustice: the Royal Commission on Criminal Justice' (1994) 21 *Journal of Law and Society* 20

Cavadino, M, Dignan, J and Mair, G, *The Penal System: An Introduction* (5th edition, 2013) Sage

Clarkson, C, Cretney, A, Davis, G and Shepherd, J, 'Assaults: the relationship between seriousness, criminalisation and punishment' [1994] Crim LR 4

Davis, K C, *Discretionary Justice: A Preliminary Inquiry* (1969) Louisiana State University Press

Dworkin, R, *Taking Rights Seriously* (1977) Harvard University Press

Gelsthorpe, L and Padfield, N (eds), *Exercising Discretion: Decision-making in the criminal justice system and beyond* (2003) Willan

Hedderman, C, 'Government policy on women offenders: Labour's legacy and the Coalition's challenge' (2010) *Punishment & Society* 12(4): 485

Hobbs, S and Hamerton, C, *The Making of Criminal Justice Policy* (2014) Routledge

House of Commons Justice Committee, *Women offenders: after the Corston Report* (2013) The Stationery Office

Liebling, A, *Prisons and their Moral Performance* (2004) Oxford University Press

McConville, M and Baldwin, J, *Courts, Prosecution and Conviction* (1981) Oxford University Press

Maguire, M, 'Crime statistics and the construction of crime' in Maguire, M, Morgan, R and Reiner, R (eds), *The Oxford Handbook of Criminology* (5th edition, 2012) Oxford University Press

Norrie, A, *Crime, Reason and History* (3rd edition, 2014) Cambridge University Press

Phillips, C and Bowling, B, 'Ethnicities, racism, crime, and criminal justice' in Maguire, M, Morgan, R and Reiner, R (eds), *The Oxford Handbook of Criminology* (5th edition, 2012) Oxford University Press

Silvestri, A (ed), *Lessons for the Coalition: an end of term report on New Labour and criminal justice* (2011) Centre for Crime and Justice Studies

Shute, S, Hood, R and Seemungal, F, *A Fair Hearing? Ethnic Minorities in the Criminal Courts* (2005) Willan

von Hirsch, A and Ashworth, A, *Proportionate Sentencing: Exploring the principles* (2005) Oxford University Press

Walby, S and Allen J, 'Domestic Violence, sexual assault and stalking: findings from the British Crime Survey' (2004) HORS No 276, HMSO

Walker, N, *Why Punish?* (1991) Oxford Paperbacks

Walker, N and Padfield, N, *Sentencing Theory, Law and Practice* (2nd edition, 1996) Butterworths

Young, J, *The Vertigo of Late Modernity* (2007) Sage

A note on free resources

The internet is a wonderful resource. For government websites, good starting points are www.gov.uk/government/organisations/ministry-of-justice and www.gov.uk/government/organisations/home-office

It is worth looking at Parliament's website too: www.parliament.uk. Remember that whilst Parliament (the legislature) and the Government (the executive) are very different players in our political system, the notes on clauses available on Bills going through Parliament are written by Government civil servants.

A useful website monitoring developments in the EU include http://curia.europa.eu/ and www.cer.org.uk

Annual reports are available online (or may be bought for a hefty fee). For example, you might like to keep an eye on:

- Report of Her Majesty's Chief Inspector of Prisons for England and Wales
- Report of the Parole Board
- Report of the National Offender Management Service (NOMS)
- Report of the Crown Prosecution Service
- Report of Her Majesty's Chief Inspector of Constabulary.

Documents

[1:1] Office for National Statistics, *Crime in England and Wales, Year Ending September 2014*

(At page 2):

Understanding Crime Statistics

This quarterly release presents the most recent crime statistics from two main sources: the Crime Survey for England and Wales (CSEW; previously known as the British Crime Survey), and police recorded crime. Neither of these sources can provide a picture of total crime.

Crime Survey for England and Wales

The CSEW is a face-to-face victimisation survey in which people resident in households in England and Wales are asked about their experiences of a selected number of offences in the 12 months prior to the interview. It covers both children aged 10–15 and adults aged 16 and over, but does not cover those living in group residences (such as care homes, student halls of residence and prisons), or crimes against commercial or public sector bodies. For the population and offence types it covers, the CSEW is a valuable source for providing robust estimates on a consistent basis over time.

It is able to capture all offences experienced by those interviewed, not just those that have been reported to, and recorded by, the police. It covers a broad range of victim-based crimes experienced by the resident household population. However, there are some serious but relatively low volume offences, such as homicide and sexual offences, that are not included in its main estimates. The survey also currently excludes fraud and cyber crime though there is ongoing development work to address this gap.

Police recorded crime

Police recorded crime figures cover selected offences that have been reported to and recorded by the police. They are supplied by the 43 territorial police forces of England and Wales, plus the British Transport Police, via the Home Office, to the Office for National Statistics (ONS). The coverage of police recorded crime is defined by the Notifiable Offence List (NOL), which includes a broad range of offences, from murder to minor criminal damage, theft and public order offences. The NOL excludes less serious offences that are dealt with exclusively at magistrates' courts.

Police recorded crime is the primary source of sub-national crime statistics and for relatively serious, but low volume, crimes that are not well measured by a sample survey. It covers victims (including, for example, residents of institutions and tourists) and sectors (for example commercial bodies) excluded from the CSEW sample. While the police recorded crime series covers a wider population and a broader set of offences than the CSEW, it does not include crimes which do not come to the attention of the police or that are not recorded by them.

Statistics based on police recorded crime data do not currently meet the required standard for designation as National Statistics.

(At page 5):

Summary

Latest headline figures from the CSEW and police recorded crime

The Crime Survey for England and Wales (CSEW) covers a broad range of victim-based crimes experienced by the resident household population although there are some serious but relatively low volume offences, such as homicide and sexual offences, that are not included in its headline estimates. The survey also currently excludes fraud and cyber crime though there is ongoing development work to address this gap.

Latest figures from the CSEW show there were an estimated 7.0 million incidents of crime against households and resident adults (aged 16 and over) in England and Wales for the year ending September 2014. This represents an 11% decrease from 7.9 million incidents compared with the previous year's survey and continues the long downward trend seen since the mid-1990s. The latest estimate is the lowest since the survey began in 1981. The total number of CSEW incidents is estimated to be 32% lower than the 2008/09 survey, and 63% lower than its peak level in 1995.

Crime covered by the CSEW rose steadily from 1981, before peaking in 1995. After peaking, the CSEW showed marked falls up until the 2004/05 survey year. Since then, the underlying trend has continued downwards, but with some fluctuation from year to year

. . .

Police recorded crime is restricted to offences that have been reported to and recorded by the police and thus does not provide a total count of all crimes that take place. The police recorded 3.7 million offences in the year ending September 2014, a similar number to that recorded in the previous year. This is a change from the downward trend seen since 2003/04 in police recorded crime figures. Although the rate of reduction has slowed over the last three years, the latest figures are 21% lower than in 2008/09 and 38% lower than the peak in 2003/04.

Like CSEW crime, police recorded crime also increased during most of the 1980s, reaching a peak in 1992, and then fell each year until 1998/99. Expanded coverage of offences in the recorded crime collection, following changes to the Home Office Counting Rules (HOCR) in 1998, and the introduction of the National Crime Recording Standard (NCRS) in April 2002, saw increases in the number of crimes recorded by the police while the CSEW count fell. Following the bedding in of these changes, trends from the two series tracked each other well from 2002/03 until 2006/07. While both series continued to show a downward trend between 2007/08 and 2012/13, the gap between the two series widened with police recorded crime showing a faster rate of reduction (32% compared with 19% for the CSEW for a comparable basket of crimes). However, for the most recent year this pattern has changed with the recorded crime series showing no percentage change while the survey estimates have continued to fall.

A likely factor behind the changing trend in recorded crime is the recent renewed focus on the quality of recording by the police in the light of the inspections of forces by Her Majesty's Inspectorate of Constabulary (HMIC), the Public Administration Select Committee (PASC) inquiry into crime statistics, and the UK Statistics Authority's decision to remove the National Statistics designation from recorded crime. This renewed focus is thought to have led to improved compliance with the NCRS leading to a greater proportion of crimes reported to the police being recorded than previously.

Victim-based crime accounted for 84% of all police recorded crime and fell by 1% in the year ending September 2014 compared with the previous year, with 3.1 million offences recorded. Within victim-based crime, there were decreases across most of the police recorded crime categories. The notable exceptions to this were violence against the person, which was up by 16% (an additional 96,000 offences), sexual offences up by 22% (13,000 offences) and shoplifting up by 3% (9,000 offences).

Other crimes against society accounted for 11% of all police recorded crime (with 399,469 offences recorded) and showed an increase of 1% compared with the previous year. Trends in such offences often reflect changes in police workload and activity rather than levels of criminality. Within this crime type, offences involving possession of weapons rose by 4%, public order offences rose by 10% and miscellaneous crimes against society rose by 12%. Drug offences decreased by 7% to 186,657 offences. Public order offences account for the largest volume rise and anecdotal evidence from forces suggests that this is being driven by a tightening of recording practices.

The remaining 6% of recorded crimes were fraud offences. There were 212,699 fraud offences recorded by the police and Action Fraud in the year ending September 2014 (an increase of 5% on the previous year). However, trends in fraud should be interpreted with caution. It is unclear to what extent there has been a genuine increase in such crimes or whether the move to the centralised recording of such offences has led to improved reporting and recording of fraud offences.

In addition, fraud data are also collected from industry bodies by the National Fraud Intelligence Bureau (NFIB). In the year ending September 2014, there were 391,221 reports of fraud to the NFIB from industry bodies, the vast majority of which were related to banking and credit industry fraud. For more information on these data sources, see the 'Fraud' section of this bulletin.

Overall level of crime – Other sources of crime statistics

Around 2.0 million incidents of anti-social behaviour (ASB) were recorded by the police for the year ending September 2014. These are incidents which were not judged to require recording as a notifiable offence within the Home Office Counting Rules for recorded crime. The number of ASB incidents in the year ending September 2014 decreased by 10% compared with the previous year. However, it should be noted that a review by Her Majesty's Inspectorate of Constabulary (HMIC, 2012) found that there was a wide variation in the quality of decision-making associated with the recording of ASB. As a result, ASB incident data should be interpreted with caution.

In the year ending June 2014 (the latest period for which data are available) there were 957,000 convictions in magistrates' courts for non-notifiable offences (down 5% from the year ending June 2013), which are not covered in police recorded crime or the CSEW (for example: being drunk and disorderly; committing a speeding offence). There were 31,000 Penalty Notices for Disorder issued in relation to non-notifiable offences.

The CSEW does not cover crimes against businesses and police recorded crime can only provide a partial picture (as not all offences come to the attention of the police). The 2012 and 2013 Commercial Victimisation Surveys, respectively, estimated that there were 9.2 million and 6.8 million incidents of crime against businesses in England and Wales in the four sectors covered by each of the two surveys. The sectors covered in the two surveys differed ('Wholesale and retail', 'Accommodation and food', 'Manufacturing' and 'Transportation and storage' in 2012; 'Wholesale and retail', 'Accommodation and food', 'Arts, entertainment and recreation' and 'Agriculture, forestry and fishing' in 2013); thus the two estimates are not directly comparable.

Trends in victim-based crime – CSEW

The CSEW provides coverage of most victim-based crimes, although there are necessary exclusions from its main estimates, such as homicide and sexual offences.

Estimates of violent crime from the CSEW have shown large falls between 1995 and the 2004/05 survey. In recent years the rate of reduction has slowed and while the latest estimate is 11% lower compared with the previous year, it was not statistically significant.

CSEW domestic burglary follows a similar pattern to that seen for overall crime, peaking in the mid-1990s survey and then falling steeply until the 2004/05 CSEW. The underlying trend in domestic burglary remained fairly flat between the 2004/05 and 2010/11 surveys. Since then estimates have fallen and incidents of domestic burglary for the year ending September 2014 are 40% lower than those in the 2003/04 survey. The apparent year on year fall of 8% was not statistically significant.

Levels of vehicle-related theft estimated by the CSEW show a 15% fall compared with the previous year, and follow a consistent downward trend since the mid-1990s, explained in-part by improvements in vehicle security. The latest estimates indicate that a vehicle-owning household was around five times less likely to become a victim of such crime than in 1995.

There was a 9% decrease in CSEW other household theft compared with the previous year. This decrease sees estimated levels of other household theft return to levels similar to that seen in the 2007/08 survey, following a period of year on year increases between the 2007/08 and 2011/12 surveys. Peak levels of other household theft were recorded in the mid-1990s and the latest estimate is half the level seen in 1995.

The CSEW estimates that there were around 848,000 incidents of other theft of personal property in the survey year ending September 2014. The apparent 9% decrease, was not statistically significant. The underlying trend has been fairly flat since 2004/05 following marked declines from the mid-1990s; the current estimate is under half the level seen in 1995.

Latest CSEW findings for bicycle theft show little change in the level of incidents in the year ending September 2014 compared with the previous year (the apparent 1% increase was not statistically significant). Over the long term, incidents of bicycle theft are now 40% lower than in 1995.

Criminal damage estimated by the CSEW decreased by 15% in the year ending September 2014 compared with the previous year, continuing the downward trend seen since 2008/09.

CSEW estimates for robbery and theft from the person were not significantly different from the previous year (the apparent respective 27% and 9% decreases were not statistically significant). However these must be treated with caution and interpreted alongside police recorded crime as short term trends in these CSEW crimes are typically prone to fluctuation due to a small number of victims interviewed in any one year. Further information on these crimes is provided in the relevant sections of this bulletin.

Trends in victim-based crime – Police recorded crime

There was a 1% decrease in victim-based crimes in the year ending September 2014 to 3.1 million offences. To put this volume into context, this is equivalent to 55 recorded offences per 1,000 population (though this should not be read as a victimisation rate as multiple offences could be reported by the same victim). There were decreases in theft from the person (down 24%), vehicle offences (down 6%), criminal damage and arson (down 4%) and robbery (down 14%). There were increases in violence against the person (up 16%), sexual offences (up 22%) and shoplifting (up 3%).

The 16% increase in violence against the person offences recorded by the police is likely to be driven by improved compliance with the NCRS; the CSEW, for example, showed an 11%

decrease over the same period. The volume of crimes (699,832 offences) equates to approximately 12 offences recorded per 1,000 population in the year ending September 2014. The increase in total violence against the person offences was largest in the subcategory violence without injury, which showed an increase of 20% compared with the previous year. The violence with injury subcategory showed a smaller increase of 12% over the same period.

In the year ending September 2014 the police recorded 507 homicides, 47 fewer than in the previous year. This latest annual count of homicides is at its lowest since 1977 (482 offences). The number of homicides increased from around 300 per year in the early 1960s to over 800 per year in the early years of this century, which was at a faster rate than population growth over that period. Over the past decade however, the volume of homicides has decreased while the population of England and Wales has continued to grow.

Offences involving firearms have fallen 7% in the year ending September 2014 compared with the previous year, continuing the falls seen since their peak in 2005/06. The number of offences that involved a knife or sharp instrument fell by 2% over the same period.

Robberies fell 14% in the year ending September 2014 compared with the previous year, from 61,843 offences to 53,080 offences. This is equivalent to around 1 offence recorded per 1,000 population and is the lowest level since the introduction of the NCRS in 2002/03 (when 110,271 offences were recorded). With the exception of a notable rise in the number of robberies in 2005/06 and 2006/07, there has been a general downward trend in robbery offences since 2002/03. The overall decrease has been driven by falls in most of the large metropolitan force areas, where robbery offences tend to be concentrated (nearly half of all robbery offences were recorded in London alone). In volume-terms, the most notable drop in robbery offences over the last year was in the Metropolitan Police force area (25%; 8,116 offences).

Sexual offences recorded by the police increased by 22% in the year ending September 2014 compared with the previous year, to a total of 72,977 across England and Wales, the highest level since the introduction of the NCRS in 2002/03. Within this, the number of offences of rape increased by 31% and the number of other sexual offences increased by 19%. These increases are likely to be due to an improvement in crime recording by the police for these offences and an increase in the willingness of victims to come forward and report these crimes to the police; see the 'Sexual offences' section for more information.

While previous releases have showed that the rise in sexual offences was being largely driven by a rise in the number of historical offences, additional analysis of data supplied by around half the forces show recent offences now account for the majority of the increase (78% of the increase was due to offences committed within the last 12 months).

Total theft offences recorded by the police in the year ending September 2014 showed a 5% decrease compared with the previous year, continuing the year on year decrease seen since 2002/03. The majority of the categories in this offence group ('Burglary', 'Vehicle offences', 'Theft from the person', 'Bicycle theft' and 'All other theft offences') showed decreases compared with the previous year. The only exception to this was shoplifting, which increased by 3% compared with the previous year (from 313,700 offences to 322,904).

Theft from the person offences recorded by the police in the year ending September 2014 showed a 24% decrease compared with the previous year. This is a reversal of recent trends, which showed year-on-year increases between 2008/09 and 2012/13. This decrease is driven by a large drop in offences from December 2013 onwards, thought to be associated with improved mobile phone security features.

Fraud offences

Responsibility for recording fraud offences has transferred from individual police forces to Action Fraud. This transfer occurred between April 2011 and March 2013. In the year ending

September 2014, there were 212,699 fraud offences recorded by Action Fraud in England and Wales. This represents a volume increase of 5% compared with the previous year and an increase of 194% compared with 2008/09. These reported increases over the past 12 months should be seen in the context of the recent move to centralised recording of fraud. During the transition to Action Fraud, level of recorded fraud showed steady increases. It should be noted that since all forces completed the transfer of recording to Action Fraud (April 2013), the levels of fraud have remained fairly steady.

In addition, there were 391,221 reports of fraud to the National Fraud Intelligence Bureau from industry bodies.

CSEW data on plastic card fraud show that, for the year ending September 2014 survey, 5.2% of plastic card owners were victims of card fraud in the last year, an increase on 4.6% in the year ending September 2013. Before that, there had been small reductions in levels of plastic card fraud over the last few years, following a rise between the 2005/06 and 2008/09 surveys.

[1:2] Reiner, R, 'Success or statistics? New Labour and crime control: What has happened to crime under New Labour?'

(2007) *Criminal Justice Matters*, No 67 (at page 4)

Tony Blair's capture of the issue of law and order from the Tories with his trademark slogan tough on crime, tough on the causes of crime was one of New Labour's most surprising and characteristic political coups en route to its 1997 general election victory. During the 2005 election campaign that gave New Labour its record third win, its literature made much of a supposed triumph in the war against crime. 'When Labour came to power in 1997 we inherited a grim legacy. Crime had doubled [since the 1970s] . . . Overall crime is down by 30 per cent on 1997 . . . violent crime by 26 per cent' (Labour Party, 2005). Michael Howard attacked with directly contradictory figures: 'When I was Home Secretary crime fell by 18 per cent . . . Under Mr Blair . . . Overall crime is up by 16 per cent. Violent crime is up by over 80 per cent' (Conservative Party, 2005). Neither the Labour nor the contradictory Conservative claims quoted above are based on lies: just different damned statistics. Labour's success story cites the *British Crime Survey* (BCS), the Conservative rebuttal uses the police recorded statistics. The BCS trends suggest that Tony Blair might be the greatest crime buster since Batman tamed Gotham City; the police figures give that mantle to Michael Howard. Not surprisingly the issue of the validity of these different data sets has become sharply politicised. Survey evidence suggests that the public are not buying either good news story. The BCS regularly finds that some two-thirds of the population believe crime is rising nationally. No wonder the government agonises over the reassurance gap.

So what has happened to crime under New Labour? Nobody who has studied even a few weeks of Criminology 101 will be unaware of the pitfalls of interpreting official crime statistics. Almost from their inception, the limitations of the crime figures collated nationally by the Home Office from local police records since the 1850s were well known. Because victims may not report crimes to the police and the police may not record them, and because an unknowable number of crimes occur that have no individual victims who could report them, there is a vast, incalculable dark figure of unrecorded offences. So apparent trends in the statistics may reflect changes in recording crime rather than in offending. Until quite recently not much more could be said with confidence about crime patterns although much was! The key change has been the development of victim surveys, in particular the BCS since the early 1980s. As it is not subject to the reporting and recording vicissitudes of the police data, the

BCS is generally seen as a more reliable estimate of trends. It also sheds light on changes in reporting and recording patterns, making interpretation of the police recorded statistics safer.

Putting together the implications of both police recorded statistics and victim surveys suggests that there have been at least three distinct phases within what otherwise appears as a pretty unbroken story of remorseless and huge rise in the recorded rate since the mid-1950s (Reiner, 2007, ch. 3). Until the 1970s there was no other measurement of trends apart from the police statistics. But during the 1970s the General Household Survey (GHS) began to ask about burglary victimisation. Its data suggest that most of the increase in recorded burglary in that decade was due to more reporting by victims. This cannot be extrapolated necessarily to other crimes, or even for burglary to previous decades. But certainly the GHS suggests that much of the rise in the rate for this highly significant volume crime was a recording phenomenon, up to the early 1980s, and it is plausible that this applies to volume property crimes more generally.

The BCS in its first decade showed the reverse: although recorded crime rose more rapidly between 1981–1993 than BCS crime, the trends were very similar. By both measures crime rose at an explosive rate in the 1980s and early 90s. From the early 1990s, however, the police statistics and the BCS began to show different trends. The BCS continued to chart a rise until 1995, but the police data fell from 1992 to 1997. This was because the proportion of offences reported by victims and recorded by the police decreased as victimisation rose. Insurance companies made claiming more onerous, discouraging reporting by victims, and a more business-like managerial accountability structure for policing implicitly introduced incentives to keep the recorded crime rate down. So Michael Howard's success in bringing the crime rate down was in large part a recording phenomenon.

After New Labour came to power in 1997 the two measures continued to diverge – but in the opposite direction. The BCS fell continuously from 1995 to 2005, since when it has remained roughly at the level of the first BCS conducted in 1981 before the crime boom of the 1980s. The police recorded statistics, however, began to rise again in 1998 up to 2004, since when they have begun to decline a little.

The rise in the recorded rate was due overwhelmingly to two major changes in the procedures for counting crimes used by the police: new Home Office Counting Rules in 1998, and the 2002 National Crime Recording Standard (NCRS). These two reforms clearly boosted the recorded rate substantially compared to what would have been measured previously (as shown by the alternative calculations by both methods in Walker *et al*, 2006, figure 2.6). This was a predictable consequence of the changes, because the 1998 rules made notifiable a number of offences (such as common assault and assault on a constable) that hitherto had not been included in the recorded rate, whilst the NCRS sought to make universal the *prima facie* rather than evidential criterion for recording offences, whereby police were required to record "any notifiable offence which comes to the attention of the police" (Burrows *et al*, 2000, p.31), even in the absence of evidence supporting the victim's report. Whatever the reasons for these reforms, keeping the crime rate down for political reasons cannot have been amongst them! This cannot be said of a further recent revision in 2006 that restores some discretion to the police not to record offences reported to them in the absence of supporting evidence. The rules as amended in 2006 specify that: "An incident will be recorded as a crime (notifiable offence) if, on the balance of probability: (a) the circumstances as reported amount to a crime defined by law; and (b) there is no credible evidence to the contrary" (Home Office, 2006).

The BCS is free from the particular problems that make the police figures particularly unreliable as a measure of trends. However, it is not (and has never claimed to be) the authoritative index that many journalists now regularly refer to it as. It is conducted with exemplary rigour and thoughtfully reflexive scrutiny of its own methods. But as a survey of individuals to ascertain their victimisation it necessarily omits many types of offences: the supreme example of personal victimisation, homicide; crimes with individual victims who are not aware of what happened (such as successful frauds); crimes with institutional victims such as businesses, or where the victim is the public at large; consensual offences such as drug-taking, and many other serious examples. Its sampling frame excludes certain highly victimised groups such as children under 16 and the homeless. So the government's tendency to treat the BCS as the key measure is as problematic as the earlier exclusive reliance of policy-makers on the police statistics.

Nonetheless, it seems clear that overall crime and volume property crime have gone down under New Labour. This is indicated clearly by the BCS, and the contrary impression given by the police statistics is primarily due to the altered counting procedures. The omissions from the BCS, however, are arguably of increasing significance, and can only be estimated by the police statistics, or indirect measures. Murder and other serious crimes of violence have gone up, but are either not measured at all by the BCS or particularly inadequately. Drug offences are not tapped by it. Crimes against young people and the homeless are probably increasing. So the trends of the last ten years are certainly not as rosy as the BCS suggests. It is also questionable how far the reduction of overall crime is attributable to the success of New Labour criminal justice policy.

Has crime fallen because of New Labour criminal justice policy?

As far as the overall level of crime is concerned, Labour's period in office since 1997 has been a success, with victimisation returning to the levels of a quarter of a century ago. But it has got things right for the wrong reasons as Richard Garside argues (Garside, 2006). Labour captured the issue of law and order from the Conservatives in the early 1990s with the pledge to be "tough on crime, tough on the causes of crime". Over the years its rhetoric and practice have increasingly concentrated on the former, sidelining the significance of causes, especially root causes in terms of political economy (Reiner, 2007, ch. 5). In the recent panic over gun crime, it is the Conservative leader David Cameron who talks about society being badly broken (conveniently neglecting to mention that it was his party that broke it in the 1980s). Tony Blair sees the problem as having very specific causes, with policing as the main solution.

Yet as a recent comprehensive audit of Labour's criminal justice record shows, its success in boosting the resources and powers of the system bears at best little relation to the crime decline (Solomon *et al*, 2007 and see Solomon in this CJM). A review by the Prime Minister's Strategy Unit itself concluded that 80% of the crime reduction was attributable to economic factors, although it concentrates its attention almost entirely on criminal justice solutions, and this estimate is somehow omitted from the version of the report currently on the Cabinet website (Solomon *et al*, 2007, p.14).

The rise in crime up to the early 1990s, and the subsequent decline, are primarily driven by changes in political economy and culture (Reiner, 2007, ch. 4 is a detailed overview of the evidence). The decline that began in the mid-1990s was a paradoxical result of the failure of Conservative economic policy when it was driven out of the ERM, thus ending the deep recession. But as David Downes has pointed out in these pages (Downes, 2004), neither party can espouse this account. Both are locked into the law and order political auction of anything you can do, I can do tougher. So Labour's relative economic success (less long-term unemployment, less family and child poverty) has mitigated the causes of crime a little, but by stealth. And overall inequality, a major factor in generating *anomie* and crime, is something it is explicitly relaxed about.

In so far as crime control specifically has had a major impact, it is through the vastly improved security of the targets of volume property crime, especially cars and buildings. This is a great success, but has its downsides as long as the fundamental causes of crime are unabated. There is some evidence of displacement to more serious crimes such as robbery, and rising homicide is attributable in large part to economic exclusion and inequality (Dorling, 2004). Crime reduction through better physical security, desirable in itself, paradoxically feeds a sense of insecurity as its paraphernalia and routines act as constant signs of threat (Zedner, 2003). These are major factors in the reassurance gap, the failure of public opinion to recognise the declining overall levels of crime. In short, New Labour has largely delivered on its pledge to be tough on crime overall, but it needs to get tough on the economic and social causes of crime, especially more serious crimes, if it is to achieve security and a public sense of security.

References

Burrows, J, Tarling, R, Mackie A., Lewis, R, and Taylor, G (2000) Review of Police Forces' Crime *Recording Practices*, Home Office Research Study 204. London: Home Office Research, Development and Statistics Directorate.

Conservative Party (2005) *Conservative Election Manifesto 2005*. London: Conservative Party.

Dorling, D (2004) 'Prime Suspect: Murder in Britain' in P. Hillyard, C. Pantazis, S. Tombs and D. Gordon (eds.) *Beyond Criminology*. London: Pluto.

Downes, D (2004) 'New Labour and the Lost Causes of Crime', *Criminal Justice Matters*, 55: 4–5. London: CCJS.

Home Office (2006) Counting Rules for Recording *Crime, General Rule A.*

Garside, R (2006) *Right For the Wrong Reasons: Making Sense of Criminal Justice Failure*. London: Crime and Society Foundation.

Labour Party (2005) *Tackling Crime, Forward not Back*. March 2005, p. 2. London: Labour Party.

Reiner, R (2007) *Law and Order: An Honest Citizen's Guide to Crime and Control*. Cambridge: Polity.

Solomon, E, Eades, C, Garside, R, and Rutherford, M (2007) *Ten Years of Criminal Justice Under Labour: An Independent Audit*. London: Centre for Crime and Justice Studies.

Walker, A, Kershaw, C, and Nicholas, S (2006) *Crime in England and Wales 2005/06*. London: Home Office.

Zedner, L (2003) 'Too Much Security?' *International Journal of the Sociology of Law* 31/1: 155–184.

[1:3] *Report of the Royal Commission on Criminal Justice*
(1993) Cm 2263, HMSO (at page iii)

Terms of reference

To examine the effectiveness of the criminal justice system in England and Wales in securing the conviction of those guilty of criminal offences and the acquittal of those who are innocent, having regard to the efficient use of resources, and in particular to consider whether changes are needed in:

(i) the conduct of police investigations and their supervision by senior police officers, and in particular the degree of control that is exercised by those officers over the conduct of the investigation and the gathering and preparation of evidence;

(ii) the role of the prosecutor in supervising the gathering of evidence and deciding whether to proceed with a case, and the arrangements for the disclosure of material, including unused material, to the defence;

(iii) the role of experts in criminal proceedings, their responsibilities to the court, prosecution, and defence, and the relationship between the forensic science services and the police;

(iv)   the arrangement for the defence of accused persons, access to legal advice, and access to expert evidence;

(v)   the opportunities available for an accused person to state his position on the matters charged and the extent to which the courts might draw proper inferences from primary facts, the conduct of the accused and any failure on his part to take advantage of an opportunity to state his position;

(vi)   the powers of the court in directing proceedings, the possibility of their having an investigative role both before and during the trial, and the role of pre-trial reviews, the courts' duty in considering evidence, including uncorroborated confession evidence;

(vii) the role of the Court of Appeal in considering new evidence on appeal, including directing the investigation of allegations;

(viii) the arrangements for considering and investigating allegations of miscarriages of justice when appeal rights have been exhausted.

(At page 3):

Adversarial or inquisitorial?

11 The criminal justice system of England and Wales, in common with other jurisdictions which have evolved with the 'Anglo-Saxon' or 'common law' tradition, is often categorised as 'adversarial'. This is in contrast to the so-called 'inquisitorial' system based on the 'Continental' or 'civil law' tradition. In this context, the term 'adversarial' is usually taken to mean the system which has the judge as an umpire who leaves the presentation of the case to the parties (prosecution and defence) on each side. These separately prepare their case and call, examine and cross-examine their witnesses. The term 'inquisitorial' describes the systems where judges may supervise the pre-trial preparation of the evidence by the police[1] and, more important, play a major part in the presentation of the evidence at trial. The judge in 'inquisitorial' systems typically calls and examines the defendant and the witnesses while the lawyers for the prosecution and the defence ask supplementary questions.

12 It is important not to overstate the differences between the two systems; all adversarial systems contain inquisitorial elements, and vice versa. But it is implicit in our terms of reference that we should consider whether a change in the direction of more inquisitorial procedures might not reduce the risks of mistaken verdicts and the need for subsequent re-examination of convictions which may be unsafe. For the reasons set out below we do not recommend the adoption of a thoroughgoing inquisitorial system. But we do recognise the force of the criticisms which can be directed at a thoroughgoing adversarial system which seems to turn a search for the truth into a contest played between opposing lawyers according to a set of rules which the jury does not necessarily accept or even understand. In some instances, such as our approach to forensic science evidence, our recommendations can fairly be interpreted as seeking to move the system in an inquisitorial direction, or at least as seeking to minimise the danger of adversarial practices being taken too far. But we have not arrived at our proposals through a theoretical assessment of the relative merits of the two legal traditions. On the contrary, we have been guided throughout by practical considerations in proposing changes which will, in our view, make our existing system more capable of serving the interests of both justice and efficiency.

---

1   Although in practice this is rare. For example, in France the *juge d'instruction* plays a part in only some 10% of cases. See the Report of the French Commission Justice Penale et Droits de l'Homme, La Mise en Etat des Affairs Penales, Paris 1991.

13 We have sought information from a wide range of other countries' criminal jurisdictions (both adversarial and inquisitorial) in order to see whether there are lessons to be learned from them that might be applied with advantage to the criminal justice system in England and Wales. In particular, we have during two visits to Scotland looked in some depth at the Scottish system. We have not, however, found, either in Scotland or anywhere else, a set of practices which has so clearly succeeded in resolving the problems which arise in any system of criminal justice that it furnishes the obvious model which all the others should therefore adopt. Every system is the product of a distinctive history and culture, and the more different the history and culture from our own the greater must be the danger that an attempted transplant will fail. Hardly any of those who gave evidence to the Commission suggested that the system in another jurisdiction should be adopted in England and Wales; and of those who did, not argued for it in any depth or with any supporting detail. We have, accordingly, no evidence to suggest that there is somewhere a jurisdiction in which the rights and interests of the various parties involved are so uniquely well balanced as to give the system the best of all worlds. In the relevant chapters of this report, we make occasional reference to the features of other jurisdictions by which we have been influenced in arriving at our conclusions. But we make no attempt to give them either an 'adversarial' or an 'inquisitorial' label.

14 Our reason for not recommending a change to an inquisitorial system as such is not simply fear of the consequences of an unsuccessful cultural transplant. It is also that we ourselves doubt whether the fusion of the functions of investigation and prosecution, and the direct involvement of judges in both, are more likely to serve the interests of justice than a system in which the roles of police, prosecutors, and judges are as far as possible kept separate and the judge who is responsible for the conduct of the trial is the arbiter of law but not of fact. We believe that a system in which the critical roles are kept separate offers a better protection for the innocent defendant, including protection against the risk of unnecessarily prolonged detention prior to trial. Moreover, there are 'inquisitorial' jurisdictions in which the system is moving, or being urged to move in an 'adversarial' direction. For example, Italy has sought to introduce a more adversarial approach, and in France there has been widespread criticism of the role of the *juge d'instruction*.

15 We in no way suggest, as is sometimes done, that 'Inquisitorial' systems presume suspects to be guilty until they are proved innocent. Nor do we suggest, as is also sometimes done, that 'Adversarial' systems are not concerned to unearth the facts on which the guilt or innocence of the suspect depends. Both recognise the principle of the 'burden of proof' – that is, the obligation on the prosecution to establish the defendant's guilt on the basis of evidence which the defence is entitled to contest. We regard this principle as fundamental. This, as will become apparent in later chapters, is not incompatible with changes to our system which would require the defence to disclose the outline of whatever case it intends to put forward at an earlier stage than at present, or remove from the defendant charged with an 'either way' offence the right to choose the mode of trial, or permit the judge to rule before the jury is empanelled on questions of admissibility of evidence or the production of statements of agreed facts. But defendants are always to be presumed to be innocent unless and until the prosecution has satisfied the magistrates or jury of their guilt beyond reasonable doubt.

[1:4] Feeney, F, 'Interdependence as a working concept'

In Moxon, D (ed), *Managing Criminal Justice* (1985) HMSO (at page 8)

There may well have been a time when criminal justice was viewed as a series of separate processes connected neither with each other nor anything else. These times have long since passed, however, and today there is widespread agreement that the work of the various criminal justice agencies is closely related and that together these agencies form some kind of 'system'. There is much less agreement, however, about the nature of this system and the implications of such related concepts as interdependence of the criminal justice system.

The general idea of a system dates back at least to the ancient Greeks, who saw systems as some kind of organised whole. By the eighteenth century the system concept had already assumed great importance in branches of theoretical physics such as mechanics where it appeared in full mathematical garb. In the nineteenth century the term began to be applied to biology, and has since been extended to a wide variety of fields including engineering, physiology, international affairs, political affairs and even language. In the late 1950s and early 1960s the concept was further refined and systems analysis appeared as an 'in' method for analysing complex problems. It became common at this time to think of systems in almost every field of human and scientific endeavour. While some earlier criminal justice studies had taken something of a systems-type approach, it was not until this era that the term 'criminal justice system' first began to be used.

The application of systems concepts to criminal justice which followed these developments bore almost immediate fruit, leading to a much better understanding of the linkages among the various parts of the system and the way that the work of each agency affected the work of the other agencies involved. This knowledge proved to be very useful in thinking about criminal justice problems and 'criminal justice system' rapidly became a standard part of the criminal justice vocabulary.

The explicit application of systems concepts to criminal justice produced a number of other results as well. It exposed a great deal of divergence in the way that agencies approach particular problems and showed that the policies followed by one agency often undermined or were at cross-purposes with those followed by other agencies. It also demonstrated just how complex and interdependent the various parts of the system actually are.

Public drunkenness was an early example used to illustrate the kind of divergences that systems analysis could expose. Enforcement efforts for this crime at this time typically involved a large number of police arrests followed in America by short jail sentences and in England by fines. In both countries the offenders were rapidly back on the street, and the whole process started over again. Calculating the enormous waste of police and court effort in this revolving-door situation, systems analysts sought to devise treatment approaches that would make more productive use of the resources expended. They argued explicitly that there were benefits to be gained in overall system accomplishment by transferring resources from the police and the courts to the treatment end of the system. Experiments with detoxification programmes for street alcoholics were one result of their efforts.

Some of those who first sought to apply systems concepts to criminal justice were less impressed with the linkages among criminal justice agencies, however, than with their fragmentation. They argued that criminal justice was in reality not a system but a 'non-system'. Judged strictly by the formal definitions developed by theorists these analysts made a persuasive case.

A very broad definition, used by some general systems theorists, for example, views a system as a set of entities whose relations are specified so that deductions may be made from some relations to others or from the relations among the entities to the behaviour or history of the system. A more detailed formulation requires that the system under investigation be explicitly distinguished from its environment, the internal elements of the system be explicitly stated, the relationships between the elements of the system and between the system and its environment be explicitly stated, the use of canons of logical or mathematical reasoning in deductions relating to these relationships, and the confirmation of assertions about these relationships through scientific methods.

Even the strongest proponents of the systems approach would be hard-pressed to claim that their efforts meet the precision required by these standards. Despite this, however, most of those involved in criminal justice have come to think of it as a system. There is also considerable agreement that the system includes: the police and the prosecution; the defence; the courts; and corrections, including probation and the prisons. The medical, mental health, welfare, education and private security systems are all seen as closely related systems but not as part of the criminal justice system. As the criminal justice system receives not only clients but also political guidance, financial support, information and personnel from the larger society, it obviously is part of the general political, economic and social systems of the larger society.

One of the central features of all systems is the interdependence of the various system parts. The concept of interdependence is therefore a natural part of the systems idea. In recent years, however, interdependence has taken on special meaning in the criminal justice system, particularly in Great Britain. As this special meaning has a considerable overlap with the more general systems approach, it cannot be defined in ways that sharply distinguish the two concepts. It is perhaps best understood, however, as meaning that what one criminal justice agency does is likely to affect and be affected by other agencies and that a detailed knowledge of the kinds of interactions that are likely to take place is essential for undertaking system improvements. The idea is thus explicitly concerned with the development of improved performance in functions that cross agency lines.

In the criminal justice system interdependence occurs at many different levels – national and local; agency head and working officer; strategic, tactical and mechanical. Strategic level choices include large questions of system design or structure, and in Great Britain are generally made at the national level. Included in such choices would be issues such as whether there should be an independent prosecution service, whether probation resources should be increased in order to provide more sentencing alternatives to prison, and whether the police should receive a much larger share of the system's resources than the courts. Questions such as how the defence function is to be organised and financed and whether greater efforts should be expended on prevention as opposed to apprehension and punishment also involve strategic issues likely to be decided at the national level.

Tactical level choices generally concern use of the resources available to particular criminal justice agencies. Whilst these choices can be made at many different levels within a given organisation, they are generally made locally rather than nationally. Decisions of this kind include such things as the deployment of police forces, the hours of service provided by the courts, and how the duty solicitor rota is to function.

Perhaps the most fundamental sense in which criminal justice agencies are linked together at the tactical level lies in the process of discretionary decision-making by which cases are adjudicated and transferred from one agency to another. Cases typically begin with the discovery of a crime and the apprehension of a suspected offender by the police. After deciding whether to prosecute, the police pass the case on to the courts for adjudication. The courts in turn often secure the services of the probation service to assist in the sentencing decision, and in this decision may pass the case on either to probation or the prison service. This process is rather like an assembly line in which each agency's workload is essentially controlled by the actions of the previous agency. In most instances the decision of the transmitting agency is largely discretionary, but the receiving agency generally has little or no say in the decisions made. Probably the most important of these discretionary decisions are the decisions to arrest, to prosecute and to sentence. Obviously policies such as cautioning and non-charging by the prosecution are of major importance in this system of discretionary decision-making.

[1:5] Auld, LJ, *Review of the Criminal Courts of England and Wales*
(2001) The Stationery Office (at page 23)

Summary and Recommendations

Introduction (Chapter 1 – pages 7–22, rec 1)

2. The criminal law should be codified under the general oversight of a new Criminal Justice Council and by or with the support as necessary of the Law Commission. There should be codes of offences, procedure, evidence and sentencing (paras 35–36, rec 1). See also: as to a code of criminal procedure, (Chapter 10 paras 271–280, recs 228–234); as to a code of criminal evidence, (Chapter 11, paras 76–77); and as to a sentencing code, (Chapter 11, para 198, and Chapter 12, paras 110–111).

The Criminal Justice System (Chapter 8 – pages 315–336, recs 121–139)

3. A national Criminal Justice Board should replace all the existing national planning and 'operational' bodies, including the Strategic Planning Group, and the Trial Issues Group. The new Board should be the means by which the criminal justice departments and agencies provide over-all direction of the criminal justice system (paras 37–66, recs 121–122). It should have an independent chairman and include senior departmental representatives and chief executives of the main criminal justice agencies (including the Youth Justice Board) and a small number of non-executive members (paras 67–72, recs 123–125). At local level, Local Criminal Justice Boards should be responsible for giving effect to the national Board's directions and objectives and for management of the criminal justice system in their areas. Both the national and local Boards should be supported by a centrally managed secretariat and should consult regularly with the judiciary (paras 73–77, recs 126–129). The national Board should be responsible for introducing an integrated technology system for the whole of the criminal justice system based upon a common language and common case files, the implementation and maintenance of which should be the task of a Criminal Case Management Agency accountable to the Board. (paras 92–114, recs 137–139).

4. A Criminal Justice Council, chaired by the Lord Chief Justice or senior Justice of Appeal, should be established to replace existing advisory and consultative bodies, including the Criminal Justice Consultative Council and the Area Strategy Committees. It should have a statutory power and duty to keep the criminal justice system under review, to advise the Government on all proposed reforms, to make proposals for reform and to exercise general oversight of codification of the criminal law. The Council should be supported by a properly resourced secretariat and research staff (paras 78–88, recs 130–135).

A unified Criminal Court (Chapter 7 – pages 269–314, recs 83–120)

5. The Crown Court and magistrates' courts should be replaced by a unified Criminal Court consisting of three Divisions: the Crown Division, constituted as the Crown Court now is, to exercise jurisdiction over all indictable-only matters and more serious 'either-way' offences allocated to it; the District Division, constituted by a judge, normally a District Judge or Recorder, and at least two magistrates, to exercise jurisdiction over a mid range of 'either-way' matters of sufficient seriousness to merit up to two years' custody; and the Magistrates' Division, constituted by a District Judge or magistrates, as magistrates' courts now are, to exercise

their present jurisdiction over all summary matters and the less serious 'either-way' cases allocated to them (paras 2–35, recs 83–87). The courts, that is those of the Magistrates' Division, would allocate all 'either-way' cases according to the seriousness of the alleged offence and the circumstances of the defendant, looking at the possible outcome of the case at its worst from the point of view of the defendant and bearing in mind the jurisdiction of each division. In the event of a dispute as to venue, a District Judge would determine the matter after hearing representations from the prosecution and the defendant. The defendant would have no right of election to be tried in any division (paras 36–40, recs 88–95). (In the event of the present court structure continuing, the defendant should lose his present elective right to trial by jury in 'either-way' cases; see paragraph 10 below.)

6. Whether or not the Crown Court and magistrates' courts are replaced with a unified Criminal Court, there should be a single centrally funded executive agency as part of the Lord Chancellor's Department responsible for the administration of all courts, civil, criminal and family (save for the Appellate Committee of the House of Lords), replacing the present Court Service and the Magistrates' Courts' Committees. For the foreseeable future, circuit boundaries and administrations should remain broadly as they are and the courts should be locally managed within the circuits and the 42 criminal justice areas (paras 41–73, recs 96–103). Justices' clerks and legal advisers responsible to them should continue to be responsible for the legal advice provided to the magistrates (para 74, rec 104; see also Chapter 4 – Magistrates paras 50–58, recs 6–7).

Magistrates (Chapter 4 – pages 94–134, recs 2–15)

7. Magistrates and District Judges should continue to exercise their established summary jurisdiction and the work should continue to be allocated between them as much as at present (paras 1–49, recs 2–5). If my recommendation for the establishment of a new unified Criminal Court with a District Division is adopted, they should also sit together in that division exercising its higher jurisdiction. I do not recommend any further extension of justices' clerks' case management jurisdiction (paras 50–58, rec 7). Steps should be taken to provide benches of magistrates that more broadly reflect the communities they serve (paras 59–86, recs 8–9). In order to strengthen the training of magistrates, the Judicial Studies Board should be made responsible, and be adequately resourced, for devising and securing the content and manner of their training (paras 91–100, recs 11–15).

Juries (Chapter 5 – pages 135–225, recs 16–60)

8. Jurors should be more widely representative than they are of the national and local communities from which they are drawn. Qualification for jury service should remain the same, save that entitlement to, rather than actual, entry on an electoral role should be the criterion. Potential jurors should be identified from a combination of public registers and lists (paras 21–24, recs 17–18). While those with criminal convictions and mental disorder should continue to be disqualified from service, no one in future should be ineligible for or excusable as of right from it. Any claimed inability to serve should be a matter for discretionary deferral or excusal (paras 27–40, recs 20–24). Provision should be made to enable ethnic minority representation on juries where race is likely to be relevant to an important issue in the case (paras 52–62, rec 25).

9. The law should not be amended to permit more intrusive research than is already possible in the workings of juries, though in appropriate case trial judges and/or the Court of Appeal should be entitled to examine alleged improprieties in the jury room (paras 76–98, recs 26–29). The law should be declared, by statute if need be, that juries have no right to acquit defendants in defiance of the law or disregard of the evidence (paras 99–107, rec 30).

10. The defendant should no longer have an elective right to trial by judge and jury in 'either-way' cases. The allocation should be the responsibility of the magistrates' court alone and exercisable where there is an issue as to venue by a District Judge. The procedures of committal for trial and for sentence in 'either-way' cases should be abolished. Under my recommendation for a unified Criminal Court with three divisions, matters too serious for the Magistrates' Division would go direct either to the District or Crown Division depending on the seriousness. In the meantime 'either-way' cases for the Crown Court should be "sent" there in the same way as indictable-only cases (paras 119–172, recs 32–36). Trial by judge and jury should remain the main form of trial of the more serious offences triable on indictment, that is, those that would go to the Crown Division, subject to four exceptions. First, defendants in the Crown Court or, if my recommendations for a unified Court with three divisions is accepted, in the Crown and District Divisions, should be entitled with the court's consent to opt for trial by judge alone (paras 110–118, rec 31). Second, in serious and complex frauds the nominated trial judge should have the power to direct trial by himself and two lay members drawn from a panel established by the Lord Chancellor for the purpose (or, if the defendant requests, by himself alone) (paras 173–206, recs 37–47). Third, a youth court, constituted by a judge of an appropriate level and at least two experienced youth panel magistrates, should be given jurisdiction to hear all grave cases against young defendants unless the charges are inseparably linked to those against adults (paras 207–211, recs 48–50). Fourth, legislation should be introduced to require a judge, not a jury, to determine the issue of fitness to plead. (paras 212–213, rec 51).

The Judiciary (Chapter 6 – pages 226–268, recs 61–82)

11. The current hierarchy of judges and their jurisdictions should continue, subject to my recommendations for the establishment of a District Division of a new unified Criminal Court and extension of the powers of District Judges and magistrates when sitting in it (paras 1–18). Systems of judicial management and deployment should be strengthened and also made more flexible to enable a better match of High Court and Circuit Judges to criminal cases, proper regard also being given to the arrangements for civil and family justice. In particular, there should be a significant shift in heavy work from High Court Judges to the Circuit Bench, coupled with greater flexibility in the system for allocating work between them. Save in the case of Circuit Presiding Judges, the present rigid circuiteering pattern of High Court Judges should be replaced by one in which they travel out to hear only the most serious of cases (paras 19–56, recs 63–70). In implementing the recent recommendations for reforms in the system of appointing judges, the Lord Chancellor's Department should exercise vigilance to root out any indirect discrimination, hurry forward the substitution of assessment exercises for short interviews and establish and publish a clear policy for the appointment of disabled persons to judicial office (paras 65–88, recs 76–78). There should be a strengthening in the training provided to judges, appropriately enlarging the Judicial Studies Board's role for the purpose (paras 89–97, rec 79). There should be a system of appraisal for all part-time judges, and consideration should be given to the appraisal of full-time judges (paras 98–104, recs 80–82).

Decriminalisation and alternatives to conventional trial
(Chapter 9 – pages 367–394, recs 140–151)

12. I have found little scope or justification for decriminalisation of conduct that Parliament has made subject to penal sanctions (paras 1–6). There should, however, be greater use of a system of fixed penalty notices subject to a right of challenge in court, for example for television licence evasion and the existing provisions for road traffic offences (paras 7–25, recs 140–142). There is no compelling case at present for the creation of any specialist courts, in

particular, drugs or domestic violence courts (paras 26–40). Consideration should be given to the wider use of conditional cautioning or 'caution-plus' alongside existing and future restorative justice schemes, for which a national strategy should be devised (paras 41–47 and 58–69, recs 143–144 and 150). Once the Financial Services Authority has assumed full responsibility for supervision in the financial services field, consideration should be given to transferring appropriate financial and market infringements from the criminal justice process to the Authority's regulatory and disciplinary control. Consideration should also be given in this field for combining parallel criminal and regulatory proceedings (paras 48–57, recs 145–149). Preparatory work should be undertaken with a view to removal of all civil debt enforcement from courts exercising a criminal jurisdiction (paras 70–77, rec 151).

Preparing for trial (Chapter 10 – pages 395–513, recs 152–235)

13. The key to better preparation for, and efficient and effective disposal of, criminal cases is early identification of the issues. Four essentials are: strong and independent prosecutors; efficient and properly paid defence lawyers; ready access by defence lawyers to their clients in custody; and a modern communications system (paras 1–34, recs 152–153). All public prosecutions should take the form of a charge, issued without reference to the courts but for which the prosecutor in all but minor, routine or urgent cases, would have initial responsibility. It should remain the basis of the case against a defendant regardless of the court which ultimately deals with his case, thus replacing the present mix of charges, summonses and indictments (paras 35–63, recs 154–170). A graduated scheme of sentencing discounts should be introduced so that the earlier the plea of guilty the higher the discount for it. This should be coupled with a system of advance indication of sentence for a defendant considering pleading guilty (paras 91–114, recs 186–193).

14. The scheme of mutual disclosure established by the Criminal Procedure and Investigations Act 1996 should remain, but subject to the following reforms: its expression in a single and simply expressed instrument; a single and simple test of materiality for both stages of prosecution disclosure; automatic prosecution disclosure of certain documents; removal from the police to the prosecutor of such responsibility as the police have for identifying all potentially disclosable material; and encouragement, through professional conduct rules and otherwise, of the provision of adequate defence statements (paras 115–184, recs 194–205). There should be a new statutory scheme for third party disclosure (paras 185–190, rec 206) and for instruction by the court of special independent counsel in public interest immunity cases where the court considers prosecution applications in the absence of the defendant (paras 191–197, rec 207).

15. In the preparation for trial in all criminal courts, there should be a move away from plea and directions hearings and other forms of pre-trial hearings to cooperation between the parties according to standard time-tables, wherever necessary, seeking written directions from the court. In the Crown and District Divisions and, where necessary, in the Magistrates' Division, there should then be a written or electronic 'pre-trial assessment' by the court of the parties' readiness for trial. Only if the court or the parties are unable to resolve all matters in this way should there be a pre-trial hearing before or at the stage of the pre-trial assessment. The courts should have a general power to give binding directions and rulings either in writing or at pre-trial hearings (paras 198–234, recs 208–221). In the Crown and District Divisions and, where necessary, in the Magistrates' Division, following the pre-trial assessment and in good time before hearing, the parties should prepare, for the approval of the judge and use by him, them, and the jury in the hearing, a written case and issues summary setting out in brief the substances of charge(s) and the issues to be resolved by the court (para 235; see also Chapter 11, paras 15–24, recs 235–236).

The Trial: procedures and evidence (Chapter 11 – pages 514–610, recs 236–300)

16. In trials by judge and jury, the judge, by reference to the case and issues summary, copies of which should be provided to the jury, should give them fuller introduction to the case than is now conventional (paras 14–24, recs 235–236). The trial should broadly take the same form as at present, though with greater use of electronic aids in appropriate cases. The judge should sum up and direct the jury, making reference as appropriate to the case and issues summary. So far as possible, he should 'filter out' the law and fashion factual questions to the issues and the law as he knows it to be. Where he considers it appropriate, he should require the jury publicly to answer each of the questions and to declare a verdict in accordance with those answers (paras 25–55, recs 237–250).

17. In trials by judge and magistrates in the District Division, the judge should be the sole judge of law, but he and the magistrates should together be the judges of fact, each having an equal vote. The order of proceedings would be broadly the same as in the Crown Division. The judge should rule on matters of law, procedure and inadmissibility of evidence in the absence of the magistrates where it would be potentially unfair to the defendant to do so in their presence. The judge should not sum up the case to the magistrates, but should retire with them to consider the court's decision, which he would give and publicly reason as a judgment of the court. The judge should be solely responsible for sentence (paras 57–61, rec 251).

18. There should be a comprehensive review of the law of criminal evidence to identify and establish over-all and coherent principles and to make it an efficient and simple agent for securing justice. Subject to such review, I consider that the law should, in general, move away from technical rules of inadmissibility to trusting judicial and lay fact finders to give relevant evidence the weight it deserves. In particular, consideration should be given to the reform of the rules as to refreshing memory, the use of witness statements, hearsay, unfair evidence, previous misconduct of the dependant, similar fact evidence and the evidence of children (paras 76–128, recs 254–261). There should be reforms to strengthen the quality and objectivity of expert evidence and improve the manner of its presentation both from the point of view of the court and experts, following in some respects reforms made in the civil sphere by the Civil Procedure Rules (paras 129–151, recs 262–275). Urgent steps should be taken to increase the numbers and strengthen the quality of interpreters serving the criminal courts and to improve their working conditions (paras 155–162, recs 276–286). There are a number of ways in which the facilities and procedures of the courts should or could be modernised and better serve the public (paras 163–196, recs 287–295). The criminal courts should be equipped with an on-line sentencing information system (paras 200–211, recs 296–299).

Appeals (Chapter 12 – pages 611–658, recs 301–328)

19. There should be the same tests for appeal against conviction and sentence respectively at all levels of appeal, namely those applicable for appeal to the Court of Appeal (paras 5–13, and 45–46, recs 300–301). There should be a single line of appeal from the Magistrates' Division (Magistrates' Courts) and above to the Court of Appeal in all criminal matters. This would involve: 1) abolition of appeal from magistrates' courts to the Crown Court by way of rehearing and its replacement by an appeal to the Crown Division (Crown Court) constituted by a judge alone; and 2) abolition of appeal from magistrates' courts and/or the Crown Court to the High Court by way of a case stated or claim for judicial review and their replacement by appeal to the Court of Appeal under its general appellate jurisdiction enlarged if and to the extent necessary (paras 14–44, recs 302–307).

20. I support the general thrust of the Law Commission's recommendations for the intro-duction of statutory exceptions to the double jeopardy rule, save that a prosecutor's right of appeal against acquittal should not be limited to cases of murder and allied offences, but should extend to other grave offences punishable with life or long terms of imprisonment (paras 47–65, recs 308–309). There should be provision for appeal by the defence or the pros-ecution against a special verdict of a jury which on its terms is perverse; see para 16 above (paras 66–67, rec 310).

21. The Court of Appeal should be reconstituted and its procedures should be improved to enable it to deal more efficiently with, on the one hand appeals involving matters of general public importance or of particular complexity and, on the other, with 'straightforward' appeals (paras 73–101, recs 311–321). The law should be amended: to widen the remit of the Sentenc-ing Advisory Panel to include general principles of sentencing, regardless of the category of offence; and to enable the Court of Appeal to issue guidelines without having to tie them to a specific appeal before it (paras 108–111, recs 324–325).

[1:6] Jones, C, 'Auditing Criminal Justice'
(1993) 33 BJ of Criminology 187 (at page 199)

I have argued that the auditing process has had a profound impact upon the practice of crim-inal justice in Britain. Clearly, the process has a good side in so far as it has made more explicit the value preferences underlying the criminal justice system. It has also subjected criminal justice agencies to an unprecedented degree of scrutiny – the hearings of the Public Accounts Committee, which summons top civil servants and officials to answer criticisms made by the National Audit Office, have provided parliamentary accountability of a particularly robust kind.

Officials are frequently placed in 'the hot seat'. Senior law officers have been brought for the first time before a Committee of Parliament to answer criticisms, and their evidence has been published. Arguably, the National Audit Office, the Audit Commission, and the Public Accounts Committee are fulfilling the promise of 'social accounting' to render key organisa-tions more open to public scrutiny.

At first sight, therefore, the traditional structures of accountability appear to be reinforced by the new system. The contrary view argues that auditing undermines these traditional structures. Instead of officials being responsible to ministers for their decisions, ministers are forced to rely upon the professional values of accountants and auditors. Accountants are no longer simply providers of financial information: they are in the forefront of decision-making. Policy-making thus moves outside recognised political channels.

The National Audit Office recommendation of greater liaison between all agencies of the criminal justice system (courts, police, prosecution) also weakens traditional constitu-tional boundaries. The pursuit of economy and effectiveness thus encourages a more intri-cate meshing of criminal justice agencies, whose efficiency and effectiveness are increasingly defined in terms of their 'success rate': i.e. convictions. The auditing process itself also ena-bles central government to penetrate criminal justice agencies more effectively and less obtrusively. Standardisation creeps through the system via a new route. National application of the 'three Es' undercuts local distinctiveness and professional autonomy. It may also cut across national boundaries. For example, procurators fiscal in Scotland were literally 'called to account' because their practices did not accord with a set of criteria formulated in another legal system. What is marketed as a 'hands off' policy may thus actually result in a 'receding locus of power' which masks a more intricate realignment of the forces of law and order and removes existing – if imperfect – channels of accountability.

Cumulatively, there has also been a shift away from a formal commitment to rational justice and 'rule of law' to 'managerial justice'. While managerialism may pay lip-service to all the 'three Es', the 1980s saw the 'ascendancy of economy' over efficiency and effectiveness, resulting in a 'managerial myopia' and a concern with short-term managerial innovation at the expense of a long-term focus. 'Value for money' translated not only into a greater emphasis upon crime control but also into 'more crime control with fewer resources'. This produced a new definition of what the criminal justice system was for; the rights of accused persons were inefficient and uneconomic 'trappings'; due process of law was too expensive, too inefficient, and too ineffective – it 'let too many guilty persons go free'. Thus the tenets of auditing, allied to those of managerialism and devolved control, came to underpin an increasingly 'crime control'-oriented legal system.

I have argued that the construction of the consumer as a participant in the management of his or her own life served as a useful ideological strategy for stabilising this increasing focus on 'law and order' in society. This was particularly crucial at a time when the 'post-war consensus' appeared to be breaking down, where the policy was 'not to integrate the poor and underprivileged but to manage their protest'.[1] I have also argued that despite the rhetoric of consumer power there has in fact been a greater centralisation of control over criminal justice practices. This undercuts the notion of consumers being able to make strategic choices among competitors in a free market.

The increase in managerial discretion is also quite at odds with the tenets of 'rule of law' ideology, though the rhetoric of freely contracting consumers is the epitome of that bourgeois individualism found in rule of law ideology. It provides a gloss of equality where none exists. It legitimises a system of settled – or emerging – inequalities. Managerialism undercuts the distinction between formal legal rationality and technocratic rationality. It also undercuts the 'traditional apparatuses of justice' and increasingly legitimises a 'relatively naked emphasis within the criminal justice system upon criminalisation and the suppression of resistance, and a relative de-emphasising of the formal norms and values of individual justice. Typically, sociologists have predicted that a move away from formal legal rationality will result in a move towards technocratic justice. Managerialism is a hybrid form which intercepts these boundaries. It is pragmatic and instrumentalist but it is also flexible and informal, substituting discretion and 'the right of management to manage' for explicit legal rules, formal procedural norms, the principle of precedent, and due process of law. In this respect, managerialism shares what Heydebrand has termed the 'tendencies of de-juridification and de-stratification' which characterise technocratic decision-making. The 'virtue' of managerialism is that it is divorced from any substantive normative or political value. Indeed, it transforms the absence of principled policy (for example, along lines of justice and fairness) from a vice into a virtue.

[1:7] Tonry, M, *Punishment and Politics: Evidence and emulation in the making of English crime control policy*
(2004) Willan (at page 22)

In the Preface, Tonry 'puzzles' over why England is the only major Western country whose government has chosen to emulate American crime-control policies and politics of the past quarter century, when 'many of the most notorious American innovations, including some that

---

1   Norrie and Adelman (1989) Journal of Law and Society 16/1 112, at page 123.

England has embraced and others it has considered, have been conspicuously unsuccessful, and at devastating social and economic cost'.

In Chapter 1, Tonry reviews seven features of the Criminal Justice Act 2003 (charging, community punishment orders, custody plus and minus, the Sentencing Guidelines Council, mandatory minimum sentences, preventive detention, protections against wrongful convictions) and concludes (at page 22):

The seven features of the Criminal Justice Act that I have discussed were not entirely arbitrarily chosen; others could have been selected, but they are among the most substantial and politically contentious of the Act's provisions. They demonstrate an inverse relation between the government's reliance on evidence and the political salience of a subject. In relation to the changed roles of police and prosecutors in formulating criminal charges, and the design of the new community punishment order, evidence has been considered and taken into account. These however are technical and intra-institutional issues that provoke little political or public controversy. At the spectrum's other end, in relation to defendants' procedural protections and dangerous offenders – issues about which the tabloids bray- evidence seems nether neither to have been consulted nor to have played a role.

Where there was no powerful constituency to be faced down, as with changing in the charging rules, evidence mattered. Where a powerful constituency was affronted, as with development of sentencing guidelines, the government backed down.

The Labour government's has been a sorry performance. If the principal drivers of crime-control policy proposals are evidence, ignorance and ideology or self-interest, ideology and self-interest won the day . . .

[1:8] Leveson, B, *Review of Efficiency in Criminal Proceedings*

(2015) Judiciary of England and Wales (at page 96)

Summary of Recommendations

Chapter 2: Overarching Principles

Getting it Right First Time

1. This is particularly important for the police and the CPS who are the gatekeepers of the entry into the criminal justice process. If they make appropriate charging decisions, based on fair appraisal of sufficient evidence, with proportionate disclosure of material to the defence, considerable delay can be eradicated. [Paragraph 25]

Case Ownership

2. For each case, in the police, the CPS and for the defence, to maximise the opportunities for case management, there must be one person who is (and is identified to be) responsible for the conduct of the case. [Paragraph 26]

3. In order for case ownership to work in practice, the Legal Aid Agency (LAA) should change the definition of 'instructed advocate' to the advocate who conducts the main hearing. [Paragraph 31]

Duty of Direct Engagement

4. The Criminal Procedure Rules (and Practice Directions, as appropriate) should:

    4.1 place a duty of direct engagement between identified representatives who have case ownership responsibilities; [Paragraph 33]

4.2 require that engagement to be at the first available opportunity before the first hearing; [Paragraph 34]

4.3 place an obligation on any party to justify the need for an interlocutory hearing to take the form of a formal court hearing with all parties present. [Paragraph 37]

Consistent judicial case management

5. Effective and consistent judicial case management require the court robustly to manage its work. To that end, all parties must be required to comply with the Criminal Procedure Rules and to work to identify the issues so as to ensure that court time is deployed to maximum effectiveness and efficiency. [Paragraph 38]

6. To assist the courts in consistent decision-making statistical information should be more readily available, tailored to the needs of the court specifically to assist with allocation and sentencing decisions. [Paragraph 39]

Chapter 3 The role of IT

7. Essential prerequisites for remote hearings are high quality equipment; digital recording and access; a mechanism for cases to be queued; involvement of advocates instructed for the substantive hearing; video facilities in prison (both for participation in court proceedings and out of court conferences); a mechanism for showing exhibits; training. [Paragraph 47]

8. A committee should be constituted of representatives from the relevant participants in the criminal justice system to determine best practice in the conduct of such hearings which should then be included in Criminal Practice Rules or Directions. [Paragraph 47]

9. Moving to a position where interlocutory hearings occur out of court, the utilisation of audio and video hearings, with a view to countrywide implementation, should be made a priority within the work of the CJS Efficiency Programme. [Paragraph 49]

10. Within the prison estate, appropriately locked-down computers linking lawyers and in-custody clients via internet-based video conferencing would allow instructions to be obtained far more efficiently and with considerable saving of time and public money. Similar facilities would also be of value in police stations. [Paragraph 50]

11. Part of the work of the CJS Efficiency Programme and the enhancement of IT within the courts must be to ensure that digital evidence (in whatever form) can be presented easily and without the delay or complications associated with present attempts to do so. [Paragraph 51]

12. Further testing and pilots involving the use of body worn video should be encouraged and mechanisms developed to ensure that this evidence can be deployed in court without disruption to the business of the court. [Paragraph 57]

Chapter 4 Allocation

13. Those who make charging decisions must be appropriately trained in the law (including the evidential requirements of specific offences) and the CPS standards and practice relating to appropriate levels of charge depending on the specific facts. There must also be a mechanism for review of inappropriate charges and a proper line of accountability to the Director of Public Prosecutions. [Paragraph 63]

14. The allocation procedure could be conducted more quickly if the defence was invited to indicate at the outset if the accused intends to elect Crown Court trial. If so, there would be

little to be gained from hearing sometimes lengthy representations about whether the case is suitable for summary trial. A Criminal Practice Direction allowing for this change in approach should suffice. [Paragraph 77]

15. Magistrates' Courts must be encouraged to be far more robust in their application of the allocation guideline which mandates that either way offences should be tried summarily unless it is likely that the court's sentencing powers will be insufficient. The word 'likely' does not mean 'possible' and permits the court to take account of potential mitigation and guilty plea, so can encompass cases where the discount for a guilty plea is the feature that brings the case into the Magistrates' jurisdiction. It is important to underline that, provided the option to commit for sentence is publicly identified, the decision to retain jurisdiction does not fetter discretion to commit for sentence even after requesting a pre-sentence report. [Paragraph 78]

16. Local Resident and other Circuit Judges should be encouraged to engage with Magistrates' training to assist in the approach to allocation decisions and to highlight the extent to which sentences imposed in the local Crown Court are within the sentencing powers of magistrates. This training can supplement training of legal advisors and magistrates which should incorporate analysis of some of the common errors which impact on the current allocation process. The Judicial Business Group responsible for the management of the Magistrates' Court must monitor allocation decisions with the benefit of feedback from the Crown Court and be accountable for training in this area. [Paragraph 79]

17. The Sentencing Council should reconsider the Allocation Guideline and the Magistrates' Courts Sentencing Guidelines in the light of the amendments brought about by the implementation of Schedule 3 of the Criminal Justice Act 2003 (bringing committals to an end) and further to encourage the retention of jurisdiction in cases where a combination of lack of complexity and gravity point to the conclusion that summary trial is justified and does not satisfy the test that it is likely that the court's sentencing powers will be insufficient even if, after full examination of the circumstances, it then becomes appropriate to commit for sentence. [Paragraph 80]

18. The Sentencing Guideline on Allocation should be construed such that, in cases where magistrates are uncertain about the adequacy of their powers (short of it being likely that they are not), they can retain the case and commit for sentence if they later take the view that the case falls outside their sentencing powers. This possibility needs to be made clear to the accused. [Paragraph 81]

19. The judiciary should investigate the reasons for differences in allocation in different parts of the country for which purpose HM Courts & Tribunals Service (HMCTS) should collect and provide the appropriate statistics; feedback should be available for local Magistrates' Courts on the comparative information. Part of the training and refresher training for Magistrates should revolve around the significance and impact of allocation decisions. [Paragraph 82]

Chapter 5 The Magistrates' Court

20. I fully support the principles behind Transforming Summary Justice (TSJ). The ten key characteristics which TSJ identifies are the essential building blocks for a simple summary process and echo earlier drives for efficiency. The scheme will require substantial commitment from all agencies and those working in the Magistrates' Courts whose cooperation, engagement and collaboration will be vital if TSJ is to have the success that is necessary to improve summary justice. [Paragraph 86]

21. Given the nature of the TSJ process at the pre first hearing stage (bail cases having a 14 or 28 day lead in time), I strongly encourage the parties to take advantage of this period and enter into early discussion in order that the first hearing is as effective as possible. [Paragraph 92]

22. In such offence types characterised by high guilty plea rate and simple file build, I would urge those implementing TSJ to examine ways in which a fast track approach to first hearing for some offences could be achieved. [Paragraph 94]

23. I would therefore recommend that the LAA work with the CPS and the defence community in order to introduce a process by which details of the named lawyers for prosecution and defence in any particular case can be matched and exchanged, thereby facilitating the early disclosure of Initial Disclosure of the Prosecution Case (IDPC). [Paragraph 96]

24. When the above is in place the Criminal Procedure Rules Committee should consider rule amendments, first to create a firm responsibility on the prosecution to provide the IDPC to the identified defence representative at the earliest opportunity and secondly for the identified defence representative and CPS advocate to engage in discussions about the case at the earliest opportunity. [Paragraph 97]

25. The LAA should examine the possibilities of a redistribution of the money available for defence lawyers, to support the efforts required for early engagement with clients so as to resolve the case or identify the true issues. [Paragraph 99]

26. HMCTS should establish a single Case Progression Officer and develop processes which move case progression into the hands of appropriate legal or other teams within HMCTS, using currently available technology where it is appropriate and of value. [Paragraph 107]

27. A Justices' Legal Advisor should have power to extend time pursuant to the Criminal Procedure Rules subject only to the trial date remaining unaffected. To support a more focused approach to out of court case progression consideration should be given to extending case progression powers of Justices Legal Advisers. [Paragraph 114 and 117]

28. To assist with the management and efficient disposal of cases, the recommendations of the Disclosure Reviews should be implemented. The role of Magistrates within the Early Guilty Plea scheme should also be emphasised. Both should be incorporated into local bench training events/updates so appropriate intervention is effective and timely. The Judicial Business Group responsible for the management of the Magistrates' Court must monitor performance in these areas with the benefit of liaison with the local circuit judiciary to ensure consistency. This will both provide a degree of accountability but will also highlight possible differences in approach which can then be the subject of further consideration. [Paragraph 122]

Chapter 6 Listing

29. I suggest that if there has been a 'not guilty' indication at the Magistrates' Court and a 'guilty' plea entered at the first Crown Court hearing, it should be open to the judge, exercising his discretion, to reduce the credit for that plea, it not having been tendered at the first available opportunity. [Paragraph 142]

30. The present approach to multiple listing, while it provides an immediate solution to the twin problems of optimum court utilisation and timely hearings, is also an inefficient means of organising the court's work and it frequently leads to dissatisfaction on the part of victims, witnesses, the general public and the professions. I therefore recommend that steps are taken

to enable the courts to move towards single/fixed listing. The Judicial Business Group for the Magistrates' Court and the Resident Judge for the Crown Court should monitor the operation of listing and be accountable for its development best to meet the needs of the court and its users. [Paragraph 144]

31. Consideration should be given to an increased use of thematic listing. [Paragraph 145]

32. Changes should be considered to the traditional opening and closing hours of the Magistrates' Courts as a means of tackling some of the inefficiencies identified in this Review. However, the views of the public and all court users should be taken into account when deciding on a new model. [Paragraph 150]

33. There should be a reduction in the number of orders that are made for pre-sentence reports (with legislative change considered) and greater consistency in the presence of probation officers at court to ensure that oral and stand down reports can be provided. [Paragraph 156]

34. A judge should be involved in the National Improvement Board (responsible for setting performance standards) so that the judicial perspective of what is being measured is fully understood and relevant statistics kept accordingly. [Paragraph 162]

35. A small cross-circuit working party of Presiding Judges and Resident Judges should be created to consider the HMCTS Data Envelopment Analysis tool and to identify measures which assist in assessing the true effectiveness of the Crown Court. A similar approach should also be adopted for the development of the data collection for the CJS Common Platform. [Paragraph 163]

36. Whilst accepting that the creation of CJS-wide performance measures may take some time to establish, I consider they would provide important tool as part of the endeavour to raise standards. [Paragraph 164]

Chapter 7 Crown Court Pre Trial

37. I wholeheartedly endorse the EGP scheme. My support is based upon a number of factors not least of which is the extensive work carried out over the last 12 months and, importantly, the undertakings given by all parties in the associated work on the TSJ scheme upon which the anticipated benefits of the scheme are founded. [Paragraph 183]

38. I would recommend that the LAA examine a fee mechanism that rewards early significant engagement with the prosecution that results in the more effective and efficient early disposal of cases. [Paragraph 190]

39. I recommend that the Committee and the Judicial College consider ways of improving the extent to which criminal practitioners and judges understand, engage with and put into daily practice the requirements of the Criminal Procedure Rules. [Paragraph 193]

40. I recommend that there should be one case progression officer, responsible to the judge whose role will be to ensure that all the participants have complied with their obligations at each stage of the case, and especially as regards judicial orders. [Paragraph 195]

41. The police, CPS and defence practitioners must be held accountable for repeated default. Courts should therefore maintain a record of failures to comply with the Criminal Procedure Rules and insist on a compliance court appearance once a pattern of failure is identified: Presiding and Resident Judges should consider how best this can be achieved locally, ensuring that the focus of this mechanism addresses the real problem of delay and non-disclosure and

is not a means by which tactical advantage may be taken by one party from technical failures to comply that are inconsequential to the real issue. [Paragraph 202]

Chapter 8 Crown Court Trial

Maximising available time in the Crown Court

42. In relation to prisoners arriving at court on time. I would urge those responsible to reconsider the terms of any future contract with prisoner movement providers. They must demand greater efficiency and properly manage performance of the contract. NOMS must also focus to a greater extent on re-organising the way that remand prisoners are processed and on ensuring that they are held in custodial institutions that are near to the court before which they are appearing, so that long journeys are avoided. [Paragraph 210]

43. There must be provision in any future contract to benefit financially from the increasing efficiencies which will be derived from technological advances and improved working practices. [Paragraph 212]

44. With immediate effect, constructive dialogue must take place between resident judges, senior prison staff and prisoner movement providers as to how best to adapt the existing arrangements to achieve maximum efficiency. I know that in some areas engagement of this sort takes place. I endorse it, and encourage others to follow suit. [Paragraph 213]

45. In relation to court sitting hours and flexible court arrangements, it would certainly be of value to time table case management or other hearings which can be conducted either by joint conference telephone or by some form of video conferencing outside court sitting hours so that instructed advocates can take part without disrupting trials which they are then undertaking. [Paragraph 217]

46. The number of cases in which the 'Maxwell' approach could be adopted is likely to be very limited, for example, to lengthy, complex trials where defendants are on bail or, perhaps, for certain terrorism trials at Woolwich Crown Court: before adopting this procedure in any case, the consent of a Presiding Judge must be obtained. The broader principle operating in such arrangements is also worth emphasising: there must be a willingness and commitment on the part of everyone involved to work flexibly to achieve greater efficiency. I encourage judges actively to consider ways in which – appropriate to local conditions – they may adapt this principle. [Paragraph 222]

47. Expert evidence

47.1 In relation to the more esoteric areas of science, more research as to its validity is needed. This is so in particular in relation to those disciplines where there is very little peer reviewed, published evidence. [Paragraph 228]

47.2 There are differing views on the question of statutory powers for a Forensic Science Regulator, but my view is that such powers are now necessary to ensure and if necessary enforce compliance with quality standards. [Paragraph 229]

47.3 Courts must use more frequently their power (pursuant to CPR 33.6(2) of the Criminal Procedure Rules) to direct a discussion between experts and jointly agree at the earliest possible stage before trial those issues on which they agree and those on which they do not, and to prepare a joint statement for use in evidence indicating the measure of their agreement and a summary of the reasons for their disagreement. [Paragraph 236]

47.4 I firmly support the development of suitable mechanisms whether in the form of 'primer' documents or electronic presentation aids relating to the most common forms of forensic evidence. [Paragraph 237]

47.5 The Criminal Procedure Rules Committee should consider the terms of the certificate required as part of the standard assurance that every expert report must carry. [Paragraph 242]

47.6 When it is appropriate, in a publicly funded case, at an early hearing or in writing, a fully explained application should be made for expert evidence and, bearing in mind the impact on public funds and the obligation to deploy limited resources proportionately, the court should be prepared to provide a reasoned decision as to whether it is justified: this could be done by email or following a video hearing. If it is, that direction should be regarded by the Legal Aid Agency as strong evidence to support the application such that if it decides not to grant funding, it must provide full reasons which must be passed to the relevant court. [Paragraph 244]

47.7 The Criminal Procedure Rules should encourage greater use by legal practitioners of video-conferencing and other similar technology for communicating and conferring with experts in preparation for trial. [Paragraph 245]

47.8 The law and the provision of facilities on a national basis should be developed to encourage experts to give evidence by video link or other similar technology in appropriate cases. [Paragraph 246]

48. Achieving Best Evidence

48.1 After a first general investigative interview conducted in accordance with best practice (taken from the ABE practice guide), in most cases, there should be a second, far shorter interview, ordered, chronologically presented and directed only to the relevant material. It is this interview that should be presented as examination in chief. [Paragraph 250]

49. Use of remote witness links/video testimony

49.1 I recommend that a review of training for court staff on the efficient use of court technology is undertaken and refresher training implemented as appropriate to ensure that in each court centre, there are is always at least one member of staff with sufficient knowledge to ensure that courts are deriving as much benefit as possible from existing technology. As the technology is improved, that training should be further extended. [Paragraph 254]

49.2 I recommend that there is a greater involvement by judges and court staff on a local level in the manner in which future technological developments are implemented. [Paragraph 255]

50. Ground rules approach

50.1 I accordingly recommend that consideration be given to specifically and unambiguously extending the power of the court to prevent repetitious or otherwise unnecessary evidence and to control prolix, irrelevant or oppressive questioning of witnesses. For clarity, if approved, a Practice Direction or decision of the Court of Appeal (Criminal Division) would be necessary: the alternative would be legislation. [Paragraph 264]

50.2 Ground Rules arrangements ought to be extended to all categories of 'vulnerable' witness. In due course, consideration should be given to whether or not this approach may sensibly be extended to other areas of cross-examination in which it may take place (for example, with expert witnesses). [Paragraph 267]

50.3 I would encourage the ATC to expand the range of toolkits to encompass as many areas of criminal practice as practicable, and encourage the judiciary to promote the use of such toolkits as a means of raising – and then maintaining – standards of advocacy. [Paragraph 271]

51. Opening Speeches

51.1 I recommend that the jury should not be overloaded by an opening which provides greater detail of the proposed evidence or the law than is demonstrably appropriate to their understanding of the case and the issues. [Paragraph 274]

51.2 I recommend that the Criminal Procedure Rules be amended so as to require, immediately following the prosecution opening, a public identification by the defence of the issues in the case. [Paragraph 279]

51.3 A change of culture so as to use the Criminal Procedure Rules to ensure that trials proceed expeditiously and commensurately with the issues in the case is essential. Trial judges should approach each case with these principles in mind actively manage the case accordingly; the Court of Appeal (Criminal Division) should support judges in this endeavour. [Paragraph 281]

52. Route to verdict

52.1 When appropriate, a judge should be prepared to provide such directions as will assist the jury to evaluate the evidence either after the opening of the case or prior to it being given. Directions on the approach to identification evidence provide one example. [Paragraph 306]

52.2 The judge should devise and put to the jury a series of written factual questions, the answers to which logically lead to an appropriate verdict in the case. Each question should be tailored to the law as the judge understands it to be and to the issues and evidence in the case. [Paragraph 307]

52.3 These questions – the 'route to verdict' – should be clear enough that the defendant (and the public) may understand the basis for the verdict that has been reached. [Paragraph 308]

52.4 These directions, along with the standard generic directions relevant to all criminal trials should be provided before speeches so that advocates can tailor their remarks to the law as the judge has propounded it and so avoid repetition (frequently in slightly different language) of the legal principles. [Paragraph 309]

52.5 The judge should remind the jury of the salient issues in the case and (save in the simplest of cases) the nature of the evidence relevant to each issue. This need be only in summary form to bring the detail back to the minds of the jury, including a balanced account of the issues raised by the defence. It is not necessary to recount all relevant evidence. Appropriate training on the constituents of an effective summing up should be a standard part of the Crime seminars provided by the Judicial College. [Paragraph 310]

Chapter 9 Transition

53. The Treasury should be asked to fund the transition period for the CPS to ensure that the necessary work can be completed and the new systems implemented: although it would need detailed consideration, I anticipate that the period involved could be 12–18 months depending on the CPS area involved. [Paragraph 316]

54. HMCTS will require transitional funding to provide additional sitting days and available judges to dispose of the legacy work while at the same time processing new cases earlier and with greater efficacy and efficiency. [Paragraph 319]

55. Negotiations (and, if necessary, contractual modifications) are required to improve the problems arising from the ways in which PECS operates both in relation to timely delivery to court (so as not to hold up the court) and the provision of dock officers leading to delay and steps put in place to ensure that remand prisoners are held close to their court of trial. [Paragraph 320]

56. Funding appropriate internet based video conferencing at remand prisons will form an integral part of the package aimed at improving efficiency and reducing costs with positive benefits to the administration of justice. [Paragraph 321]

[1:9] James, A and Raine, J, *The New Politics of Criminal Justice*
(1998) Longmans (at page 44)

The story of the public service managerialist reforms as they affected criminal justice is one of inconsistent and piecemeal direction on the part of ministers and reluctant participation on the part of most agencies. First, in the absence of an agreed purpose for the reform of criminal justice itself (see Chapter 2), the intermediate goals of cost efficiency and service effectiveness became pre-eminent. In the absence of an agreed strategy for change, intervention by government was influenced by size of budget, ease of pickings and ministerial preference. The effort put into resisting the reforms by agencies, perhaps with only the Crown Prosecution Service as the exception, hampered any real potential for imaginative and innovative change driven by services themselves.

Second, it is arguable that the reforms could never have worked in criminal justice in any case where the three prerequisites for their success were absent. There was no market and hence no real consumer in criminal justice, and no real prospect of creating one given the special character of the key 'customer' (the offender) and difficulties for providers around market entry and exit. Without even a quasi-market in place, there was no real basis for competition between providers (Le Grand, 1990).

Together, it is argued, these two factors resulted in managerialism; that is, the introduction of a variety of methods and techniques into practice without a meaningful context. They were management tools introduced without a broad understanding, a theory or a praxis of management, and without consent to or support for the change process within agencies.

Managerialism can be, and was, heavily criticised. Its characteristically extreme rationalism in decision-making was arguably inappropriate within a complex and pluralistic setting; its simplistic conversion of service users into consumers made no sense when the service user was an offender; the use of false competition created inequality and artificiality in the contracting process which, in turn, created a paper-chase of new administrative demands.

At the same time, wrapped up in the reforms were a number of important ideas and developments which had, and have, the potential to progress criminal justice, and which can be all too easily overlooked. Among these was the impetus to needs-driven rather than provider-driven services, propelled by a formulae basis for budget calculation. Important, too, was the demand for transparency and the provision of public information in services and service performance as part of a revised approach to public accountability. There was also an emphasis on service quality which, though not necessarily realised, was to persist. Of on-going significance was the focus on service efficiency and practice effectiveness, known within criminal justice as the 'what works' debate. Above all, the identification of purchasers (or commissioners) and providers of service, though never converted into structural reform in most criminal justice settings, facilitated the realisation that public services did not necessarily need to be publicly provided. This made explicit the potential for a mixed economy of provision (public, private and voluntary).

The immediate effect of the imposition of managerial reforms on a reluctant audience was, first, to drive a deep division between government and agencies normally characterised by their conservatism. Second was the deleterious effect on staff morale, particularly among professional groups. The longer term effect is more difficult to estimate. Certainly at the end of the 1990s, variations on managerialism were embedded in criminal justice, as in the wider public service sector, in the UK and abroad, suggesting a continuing influence. At the same time, Labour's commitment to end the introduction of markets into public services, if implemented, must affect the shape of future reform. Rather than dismantling what limited markets currently exist, a more successful way forward might be to concentrate on growing the mixed economy for which the market was itself simply a tool in a transition process from a paternalistic and bureaucratic model of social welfare to a model more appropriate for the future (James, 1997). Getting beyond the market means getting beyond means to ends in criminal justice. It means actively pump-priming private and voluntary sector initiatives to generate a mixed economy; identifying the needs of offenders in addition to the needs of service providers; and, above all, agreeing an overall purpose and change strategy in criminal justice such that strategy drives behaviour and not the other way around.

(At page 116):

In discussing the influences which have shaped criminal justice in recent years, Part I of this volume (Chapters 2–5) has argued the presence and interplay of four dynamics (politicisation, managerialism, administrative processing and public voice and participation). In thinking about criminal justice for the future, Part II has rehearsed the key features of a revised approach (Chapter 6) and a set of priorities: informing and educating public voice and participation; addressing the reality of crime as it affects the public; addressing the totality of crime, not just that small proportion which reaches the courts; and redesigning and rebalancing the organisation of criminal justice to address the requirements of an informed public rather than those of the official agencies and government departments. Finally, Chapter 7 has gone on to present a possible way forward in the interests of dialogue and discussion.

The extent to which a revised approach emerges for criminal justice depends on developments with regard to each of the four dynamics. Each has the potential to (a) contribute towards the realisation of a more effective criminal justice process and (b) address the crime problem.

The dynamic of *politicisation* is clearly important; fresh direction from political leaders is necessary to move on from the narrow preoccupation with sentencing and punishment of recent years towards a new vision for tackling crime and for relocating criminal justice firmly in its social policy context. It is also vital in the renegotiation of the 'contract' between the State and its people about a shared responsibility for crime.

The dynamic of *managerialism* – though problematic because of the tendency for management to become regarded as an end in itself rather than part of the means by which criminal justice is done better – is also important for the future. Significant weaknesses about the pre-managerial way of doing things have been highlighted and challenged. Much of the complacency and inertia of the past, particularly regarding the way the agencies have approached their responsibilities, has been driven out. The momentum for change that managerialism has created will remain an important attribute underpinning a revised approach to criminal justice. In particular, a revised approach depends on sustaining and developing those legacies of managerialism: needs-driven rather than provider-driven services, more transparency and stronger public accountability, and a focus on effectiveness and outcomes (on 'what works').

The *administrative processing* dynamic, though also in some ways associated with negative attributes of inertia and resistance to change, of organisational fragmentation, and of undue provider-orientation, is important to the revised approach. It provides the key to the translation of policy into practice. Its focus on the practitioners and on how criminal justice works in practice means that it is potentially a very important dynamic in relation to local communities being empowered to take responsibility for crime and encouraged to participate more actively in tackling the problem. The challenge is for practitioners to reorient their work and their organisational and administrative processes so that a stronger relationship with, and accountability to, local communities is achieved.

This brings us to the *public voice and participation* dynamic, which is perhaps the most important key to realisation of the revised approach. Above all, the revised approach builds upon the notion that tackling crime should begin with the reality of crime as it is experienced by the public and as it affects them. The challenge here is to find ways of capturing and engaging the full complexity of public voice and participation in appropriate ways within the criminal justice policy-making process and in its practice.

What, then, is the contemporary purpose of criminal justice? The conclusion from this volume is that first, it remains that identified in the ancient contract between the people and the State – namely, the provision of security in exchange for allegiance. Second, and relevant to the position of the UK in Europe, it is the protection of individual human rights (as presently represented in the European Convention on Human Rights, and endorsed by the Labour Government in 1997).

Recapturing that ancient purpose, and making explicit that new purpose, is the fundamental prerequisite to the rebuilding of trust in the criminal justice agencies and in government on law and order. It is also a prerequisite to public confidence in the view that crime is not, after all, out of control and that there are constructive approaches to be pursued, based on a partnership between the State and its people, which will make a difference.

[1:10] Packer, H, *The Limits of the Criminal Sanction*
(1968) Oxford University Press (at page 153)

Two models of the criminal process will let us perceive the normative antinomy at the heart of the criminal law. These models are not labeled 'Is' and 'Ought', nor are they to be taken in that sense. Rather, they represent an attempt to abstract two separate value systems that compete for priority in the operation of the criminal process. Neither is presented as either corresponding to reality or representing the ideal to the exclusion of the other. The two models merely afford a convenient way to talk about the operation of a process whose day-to-day functioning involves a constant series of minute adjustments between the competing demands of two value systems and whose normative future likewise involves a series of resolutions of the tensions between competing claims.

Crime control values

(At page 158):

The value system that underlies the Crime Control Model is based on the proposition that the repression of criminal conduct is by far the most important function to be performed by the criminal process. The failure of law enforcement to bring criminal conduct under tight control is viewed as leading to the breakdown of public order and thence to the disappearance of an important condition of human freedom. If the laws go unenforced – which is to say, if it is perceived that there is a high percentage of failure to apprehend and convict in the criminal process – a general disregard for legal controls tends to develop. The law-abiding citizen then becomes the victim of all sorts of unjustifiable invasions of this interests. His security of person and property is sharply diminished, and, therefore, so is his liberty to function as a member of society. The claim ultimately is that the criminal process is a positive guarantor of social freedom. In order to achieve this high purpose, the Crime Control Model requires that primary attention be paid to the efficiency with which the criminal process operates to screen suspects, determine guilt, and secure appropriate dispositions of persons convicted of crime.

The model, in order to operate successfully, must produce a high rate of apprehension and conviction, and must do so in a context where the magnitudes being dealt with are very large and the resources for dealing with them are very limited. There must then be a premium on speed and finality. Speed, in turn, depends on informality and on uniformity; finality depends on minimising the occasions for challenge. The process must not be cluttered up with ceremonious rituals that do not advance the progress of a case. Facts can be established more quickly through interrogation in a police station than through the formal process of examination and cross-examination in a court. It follows that extrajudicial processes should be preferred to judicial processes, informal operations to formal ones. But informality is not enough; there must also be uniformity. Routine, stereotyped procedures are essential if large numbers are being handled. The model that will operate successfully on these presuppositions must be an administrative, almost a managerial, model. The image that comes to mind is an assembly-conveyor belt down which moves an endless stream of cases, never stopping, carrying the cases to workers who stand at fixed stations and who perform on each case as it comes by the same small but essential operation and brings it one step closer to being a finished product, or, to exchange the metaphor for the reality, a closed file. The criminal process, in this model, is seen as a screening process in which each successive stage – pre-arrest investigation, arrest, post-arrest investigation, preparation for trial, trial or entry of plea, conviction, disposition – involves a series of routinised operations whose success is gauged primarily by their tendency to pass the case alone to a successful conclusion.

What is a successful conclusion? One that throws off at an early stage those cases in which it appears unlikely that the person apprehended is an offender and then secures, as expeditiously as possible, the conviction of the rest, with a minimum of occasions for challenge, let alone post-audit. By the application of administrative expertness, primarily that of the police and prosecutors, an early determination of probable innocence or guilt emerges. Those who are probably innocent are screened out. Those who are probably guilty are passed quickly through the remaining stages of the process. The key to the operation of the model regarding those who are not screened out is what I shall call a presumption of guilt. The concept requires some explanation, since it may appear startling to assert that what appears to be the precise converse of our generally accepted ideology of a presumption of innocence can be an essential element of a model that does correspond in some respects to the actual operation of the criminal process.

The presumption of guilt is what makes it possible for the system to deal efficiently with large numbers, as the Crime Control Model demands. The supposition is that the screening processes operated by police and prosecutors are reliable indicators of probable guilt. Once a man has been arrested and investigated without being found to be probably innocent, or, to put it differently, once a determination has been made that there is enough evidence of guilt to permit holding him for further action, then all subsequent activity directed toward him is based on the view that he is probably guilty. The precise point at which this occurs will vary from case to case; in many cases it will occur as soon as the suspect is arrested, or even before, if the evidence of probable guilt that has come to the attention of the authorities is sufficiently strong. But in any case the presumption of guilt will begin to operate well before the 'suspect' becomes a 'defendant'.

The presumption of guilt is not, of course, a thing. Nor is it even a rule of law in the usual sense. It simply is the consequence of a complex of attitudes, a mood.

If there is confidence in the reliability of informal administrative fact-finding activities that take place in the early stages of the criminal process, the remaining stages of the process can be relatively perfunctory without any loss in operating efficiency. The presumption of guilt, as it operates in the Crime Control Model, is the operational expression of that confidence.

Due process values

(At page 163):

If the Crime Control Model resembles an assembly line, the Due Process Model looks very much like an obstacle course. Each of its successive stages is designed to present formidable impediments to carrying the accused any further along in the process. Its ideology is not the converse of that underlying the Crime Control Model. It does not rest on the idea that it is not socially desirable to repress crime, although critics of its application have been known to claim so. Its ideology is composed of a complex of ideas, some of them based on judgments about the efficacy of crime control devices, others having to do with quite difference considerations. The ideology of due process is far more deeply impressed on the formal structure of the law than is the ideology of crime control; yet an accurate tracing of the strands that make it up is strangely difficult. What follows is only an attempt at an approximation.

The Due Process Model encounters its rival on the Crime Control Model's own ground in respect to the reliability of fact-finding processes. The Crime Control Model, as we have suggested, places heavy reliance on the ability of investigative and prosecutorial officers, acting in an informal setting in which their distinctive skills are given full sway, to elicit and reconstruct a tolerably accurate account of what actually took place in an alleged criminal event. The Due Process Model rejects this premise and substitutes for it a view of informal, non-adjudicative fact-finding that stresses the possibility of error. People are notoriously poor observers of disturbing events – the more emotion-arousing the context, the greater the possibility that recollection will be incorrect; confessions and admissions by persons in police custody may be induced by physical or psychological coercion so that the police end up hearing what the suspect thinks they want to hear rather than the truth; witnesses may be animated by a bias or interest that no one would trouble to discover except one specially charged with protecting the interests of the accused (as the police are not). Considerations of this kind all lead to a rejection of informal fact-finding processes as definitive of factual guilt and to an insistence on formal, adjudicative, adversary fact-finding processes in which the factual case against the accused is publicly heard by an impartial tribunal and is evaluated only after the accused has had a full opportunity to discredit the case against him. Even then, the distrust of fact-finding processes that animates the Due Process Model is not dissipated. The possibilities of human error being what they are, further scrutiny is necessary, or at least must be available, in case facts have been over-looked or suppressed in the heat of battle. How far this subsequent scrutiny must be available is a hotly controverted issue today. In the pure Due Process Model the answer would be: at least as long as there is an allegation of factual error that has not received an adjudicative hearing in a fact-finding context. The demand for finality is thus very low in the Due Process Model.

This strand of due process ideology is not enough to sustain the model. If all that were at issue between the two models was a series of questions about the reliability of fact-finding processes, we would have but one model of the criminal process, the nature of whose constituent elements would pose questions of fact not of value. Even if the discussion is confined, for the moment, to the question of reliability, it is apparent that more is at stake than simply an evaluation of what kinds of fact-finding processes, alone or in combination, are likely to produce the most nearly reliable results. The stumbling block is this: how much reliability is compatible with efficiency?

Granted that informal fact-finding will make some mistakes that can be remedied if backed up by adjudicative fact-finding, the desirability of providing this backup is not affirmed or negated by factual demonstrations or predictions that the increase in reliability will be x per cent or x plus n per cent. It still remains to ask how much weight is to be given to the competing demands of reliability (a high degree of probability in each case that factual guilt has been accurately determined) and efficiency (expeditious handling of the large numbers of cases that the process ingests). The Crime Control Model is more optimistic about the improbability of error in a significant number of cases; but it is also, though only in part therefore, more tolerant about the amount of error that it will put up with. The Due Process Model insists on the prevention and elimination of mistakes to the extent possible; the Crime Control Model accepts the probability of mistakes up to the level at which they interfere with the goal of repressing crime, either because too many guilty people are escaping or, more subtly, because general awareness of the unreliability of the process leads to a decrease in the deterrent efficacy of the criminal law. In this view, reliability and efficiency are not polar opposites but rather complementary characteristics. The system is reliable because efficient reliability becomes a matter of independent concern only when it becomes so attenuated as to impair efficiency. All of this the Due Process Model rejects. If efficiency demands short-cuts around reliability, then absolute efficiency must be rejected. The aim of the process is at least as much to protect the factually innocent as it is to convict the factually guilty. It is a little like quality control in industrial technology: tolerable deviation from standard varies with the importance of conformity to standard in the destined uses of the product. The Due Process Model resembles a factory that has to devote a substantial part of its input to quality control. This necessarily cuts down on quantitative output.

[1:11] Bottoms, A E and McClean, J D, *Defendants in the Criminal Process*
(1976) Routledge and Kegan Paul (at page 228)

The Liberal Bureaucratic Model is the model of the criminal justice process typically held by humane and enlightened clerks to the justices and Crown Court administrators in this country – as well as by many others. It differs substantially from the Crime Control Model, the model typically held by the police, since it dissents from its underlying central value-position: 'The value-system that underlies the Crime Control Model is based on the proposition that the repression of criminal conduct is by far the most important function to be performed by the criminal process' (Packer, 1969, p 158).

The Liberal Bureaucratic Model holds, rather, that the protection of individual liberty, and the need for justice to be done and to be seen to be done, must ultimately override the importance of the repression of criminal conduct. The liberal bureaucrat here joins with the advocate of Due Process in agreeing that formal adjudicative processes are very important, and moreover that – in the conventional phrase – 'it is better for ten guilty men to go free than for one innocent man to be convicted'.

But the Liberal Bureaucratic Model also differs substantially from the Due Process Model. For the Due Process Model looks very much like an obstacle course. Each of its successive stages is designed to present formidable impediments to carry the accused any further along in the process . . . [It] resembled a factory that has to devote a substantial part of its input to quality control. *This necessarily cuts down on quantitative output* (Packer, 1969, pp 163, 165; italics added).

It is precisely this restriction on quantitative output which offends the liberal bureaucrat about the Due Process Model. The liberal bureaucrat is a practical man; he realises that things have to get done, systems have to be run. It is right that the defendant shall have substantial protections; crime control is not the overriding value of the criminal justice system. But these protections must have a limit. If it were not so, then the whole system of criminal justice, with its value to the community in the form of liberal and humane crime control, would collapse. Moreover, it is right to build in sanctions to deter those who might otherwise use their 'Due Process' rights frivolously, or to 'try it on'; an administrative system at State expense should not exist for this kind of time-wasting.

[1:12] King, M, *The Framework of Criminal Justice*
(1981) Croom Helm (at page 13)

Theoretical Models and Their Features

I Social Function	II Process Model	III Features of Court
1. Justice	Due Process Model	(a) Equality between parties
		(b) Rules protecting defendant against error
		(c) Restraint of arbitrary power
		(d) Presumption of innocence
2. Punishment	Crime Control Model	(a) Disregard of legal controls
		(b) Implicit presumption of guilt
		(c) High conviction rate
		(d) Unpleasantness of experience
		(e) Support for police
3. Rehabilitation	Medical Model (diagnosis, prediction and treatment selection)	(a) Information collecting procedures
		(b) Individualisation
		(c) Treatment of presumption
		(d) Discretion of decision-makers
		(e) Expertise of decision-makers or advisers
		(f) Relaxation of formal rules

(Continued)

(Continued)

I Social Function	II Process Model	III Features of Court
4. Management of crime and criminals	Bureaucratic Model	(a) Independence from political considerations (b) Speed and efficiency (c) Importance of and acceptance of records (d) Minimisation of conflict (e) Minimisation of expense (f) Economical division of labour
5. Denunciation and degradation	Status Passage Model	(a) Public shaming of defendant (b) Court values reflecting community values (c) Agents' control over the process
6. Maintenance of class domination	Power Model	(a) Reinforcement of class values (b) Alienation and suppression of defendant (c) Deflection of attention from issues of class conflict (d) Differences between judges and judged (e) Paradoxes and contradictions between rhetoric and performance

[1:13] Human Rights Act 1998 (as amended)

Sections 1–6; 8; Schedule 1 (European Convention on Human Rights)

1 The Convention Rights

(1) In this Act "the Convention rights" means the rights and fundamental freedoms set out in –

(a) Articles 2 to 12 and 14 of the Convention,
(b) Articles 1 to 3 of the First Protocol, and
(c) Article 1 of the Thirteenth Protocol,

as read with Articles 16 to 18 of the Convention.

(2) Those Articles are to have effect for the purposes of this Act subject to any designated derogation or reservation (as to which see sections 14 and 15).

(3) The Articles are set out in Schedule 1.

(4) The Secretary of State may by order make such amendments to this Act as he considers appropriate to reflect the effect, in relation to the United Kingdom, of a protocol.

(5) In subsection (4) "protocol" means a protocol to the Convention –

(a) which the United Kingdom has ratified; or
(b) which the United Kingdom has signed with a view to ratification.

(6) No amendment may be made by an order under subsection (4) so as to come into force before the protocol concerned is in force in relation to the United Kingdom.

2 Interpretation of Convention rights

(1) A court or tribunal determining a question which has arisen in connection with a Convention right must take into account any –

(a) judgment, decision, declaration or advisory opinion of the European Court of Human Rights,
(b) opinion of the Commission given in a report adopted under Article 31 of the Convention,
(c) decision of the Commission in connection with Article 26 or 27(2) of the Convention, or
(d) decision of the Committee of Ministers taken under Article 46 of the Convention,

whenever made or given, so far as, in the opinion of the court or tribunal, it is relevant to the proceedings in which that question has arisen.

(2) Evidence of any judgment, decision, declaration or opinion of which account may have to be taken under this section is to be given in proceedings before any court or tribunal in such manner as may be provided by rules.

(3) In this section "rules" means rules of court or, in the case of proceedings before a tribunal, rules made for the purposes of this section –

(a) by the Lord Chancellor or the Secretary of State, in relation to any proceedings outside Scotland;
(b) by the Secretary of State, in relation to proceedings in Scotland; or
(c) by a Northern Ireland department, in relation to proceedings before a tribunal in Northern Ireland –
 (i) which deals with transferred matters; and
 (ii) for which no rules made under paragraph (a) are in force.

Legislation

3 Interpretation of legislation

(1) So far as it is possible to do so, primary legislation and subordinate legislation must be read and given effect in a way which is compatible with the Convention rights.

(2) This section –

(a) applies to primary legislation and subordinate legislation whenever enacted;
(b) does not affect the validity, continuing operation or enforcement of any incompatible primary legislation; and
(c) does not affect the validity, continuing operation or enforcement of any incompatible subordinate legislation if (disregarding any possibility of revocation) primary legislation prevents removal of the incompatibility.

4 Declaration of incompatibility

(1) Subsection (2) applies in any proceedings in which a court determines whether a provision of primary legislation is compatible with a Convention right.

(2) If the court is satisfied that the provision is incompatible with a Convention right, it may make a declaration of that incompatibility.

(3) Subsection (4) applies in any proceedings in which a court determines whether a provision of subordinate legislation, made in the exercise of a power conferred by primary legislation, is compatible with a Convention right.

(4) If the court is satisfied –

(a) that the provision is incompatible with a Convention right, and
(b) that (disregarding any possibility of revocation) the primary legislation concerned prevents removal of the incompatibility,

it may make a declaration of that incompatibility.

(5) In this section "court" means –

(a) the Supreme Court;
(b) the Judicial Committee of the Privy Council;
(c) the Court Martial Appeal Court;
(d) in Scotland, the High Court of Justiciary sitting otherwise than as a trial court or the Court of Session;
(e) in England and Wales or Northern Ireland, the High Court or the Court of Appeal;
(f) the Court of Protection, in any matter being dealt with by the President of the Family Division, the Chancellor of the High Court or a puisne judge of the High Court.

(6) A declaration under this section ("a declaration of incompatibility")—

(a) does not affect the validity, continuing operation or enforcement of the provision in respect of which it is given; and
(b) is not binding on the parties to the proceedings in which it is made.

5 Right of Crown to intervene

(1) Where a court is considering whether to make a declaration of incompatibility, the Crown is entitled to notice in accordance with rules of court.

(2) In any case to which subsection (1) applies –

(a) a Minister of the Crown (or a person nominated by him),
(b) a member of the Scottish Executive,
(c) a Northern Ireland Minister,
(d) a Northern Ireland department,

is entitled, on giving notice in accordance with rules of court, to be joined as a party to the proceedings.

(3) Notice under subsection (2) may be given at any time during the proceedings.

(4) A person who has been made a party to criminal proceedings (other than in Scotland) as the result of a notice under subsection (2) may, with leave, appeal to the Supreme Court against any declaration of incompatibility made in the proceedings.

(5) In subsection (4)—

"criminal proceedings" includes all proceedings before the Court Martial Appeal Court; and
"leave" means leave granted by the court making the declaration of incompatibility or by the Supreme Court.

Public authorities

6 Acts of public authorities

(1) It is unlawful for a public authority to act in a way which is incompatible with a Convention right.

(2) Subsection (1) does not apply to an act if –

- (a)   as the result of one or more provisions of primary legislation, the authority could not have acted differently; or
- (b)   in the case of one or more provisions of, or made under, primary legislation which cannot be read or given effect in a way which is compatible with the Convention rights, the authority was acting so as to give effect to or enforce those provisions.

(3) In this section "public authority" includes –

- (a)   a court or tribunal, and
- (b)   any person certain of whose functions are functions of a public nature,

but does not include either House of Parliament or a person exercising functions in connection with proceedings in Parliament.

(5) In relation to a particular act, a person is not a public authority by virtue only of subsection (3)(b) if the nature of the act is private.

(6) "An act" includes a failure to act but does not include a failure to –

- (a)   introduce in, or lay before, Parliament a proposal for legislation; or
- (b)   make any primary legislation or remedial order.

8 Judicial remedies

(1) In relation to any act (or proposed act) of a public authority which the court finds is (or would be) unlawful, it may grant such relief or remedy, or make such order, within its powers as it considers just and appropriate.

(2) But damages may be awarded only by a court which has power to award damages, or to order the payment of compensation, in civil proceedings.

(3) No award of damages is to be made unless, taking account of all the circumstances of the case, including –

- (a)   any other relief or remedy granted, or order made, in relation to the act in question (by that or any other court), and
- (b)   the consequences of any decision (of that or any other court) in respect of that act,

the court is satisfied that the award is necessary to afford just satisfaction to the person in whose favour it is made.

(4) In determining –

- (a)   whether to award damages, or
- (b)   the amount of an award,

the court must take into account the principles applied by the European Court of Human Rights in relation to the award of compensation under Article 41 of the Convention.

(5) A public authority against which damages are awarded is to be treated –

(a) in Scotland, for the purposes of section 3 of the Law Reform (Miscellaneous Provisions) (Scotland) Act 1940 as if the award were made in an action of damages in which the authority has been found liable in respect of loss or damage to the person to whom the award is made;

(b) for the purposes of the Civil Liability (Contribution) Act 1978 as liable in respect of damage suffered by the person to whom the award is made.

(6) In this section –

"court" includes a tribunal;
"damages" means damages for an unlawful act of a public authority; and
"unlawful" means unlawful under section 6(1).

SCHEDULE 1

The Articles

Section 1(3)

Part I The Convention
Rights and Freedoms

Article 2

Right to life

1 Everyone's right to life shall be protected by law. No one shall be deprived of his life intentionally save in the execution of a sentence of a court following his conviction of a crime for which this penalty is provided by law.

2 Deprivation of life shall not be regarded as inflicted in contravention of this Article when it results from the use of force which is no more than absolutely necessary:

(a) in defence of any person from unlawful violence;
(b) in order to effect a lawful arrest or to prevent the escape of a person lawfully detained;
(c) in action lawfully taken for the purpose of quelling a riot or insurrection.

Article 3

Prohibition of torture

No one shall be subjected to torture or to inhuman or degrading treatment or punishment.

Article 4

Prohibition of slavery and forced labour

1 No one shall be held in slavery or servitude.

2 No one shall be required to perform forced or compulsory labour.

3 For the purpose of this Article the term "forced or compulsory labour" shall not include:

(a) any work required to be done in the ordinary course of detention imposed according to the provisions of Article 5 of this Convention or during conditional release from such detention;
(b) any service of a military character or, in case of conscientious objectors in countries where they are recognised, service exacted instead of compulsory military service;
(c) any service exacted in case of an emergency or calamity threatening the life or well-being of the community;
(d) any work or service which forms part of normal civic obligations.

Article 5

Right to liberty and security

1 Everyone has the right to liberty and security of person. No one shall be deprived of his liberty save in the following cases and in accordance with a procedure prescribed by law:

(a) the lawful detention of a person after conviction by a competent court;
(b) the lawful arrest or detention of a person for non-compliance with the lawful order of a court or in order to secure the fulfilment of any obligation prescribed by law;
(c) the lawful arrest or detention of a person effected for the purpose of bringing him before the competent legal authority on reasonable suspicion of having committed an offence or when it is reasonably considered necessary to prevent his committing an offence or fleeing after having done so;
(d) the detention of a minor by lawful order for the purpose of educational supervision or his lawful detention for the purpose of bringing him before the competent legal authority;
(e) the lawful detention of persons for the prevention of the spreading of infectious diseases, of persons of unsound mind, alcoholics or drug addicts or vagrants;
(f) the lawful arrest or detention of a person to prevent his effecting an unauthorised entry into the country or of a person against whom action is being taken with a view to deportation or extradition.

2 Everyone who is arrested shall be informed promptly, in a language which he understands, of the reasons for his arrest and of any charge against him.

3 Everyone arrested or detained in accordance with the provisions of paragraph 1(c) of this Article shall be brought promptly before a judge or other officer authorised by law to exercise judicial power and shall be entitled to trial within a reasonable time or to release pending trial. Release may be conditioned by guarantees to appear for trial.

4 Everyone who is deprived of his liberty by arrest or detention shall be entitled to take proceedings by which the lawfulness of his detention shall be decided speedily by a court and his release ordered if the detention is not lawful.

5 Everyone who has been the victim of arrest or detention in contravention of the provisions of this Article shall have an enforceable right to compensation.

Article 6

Right to a fair trial

1 In the determination of his civil rights and obligations or of any criminal charge against him, everyone is entitled to a fair and public hearing within a reasonable time by an independent and impartial tribunal established by law. Judgment shall be pronounced publicly but the press and public may be excluded from all or part of the trial in the interest of morals, public order or national security in a democratic society, where the interests of juveniles or the protection of the private life of the parties so require, or to the extent strictly necessary in the opinion of the court in special circumstances where publicity would prejudice the interests of justice.

2 Everyone charged with a criminal offence shall be presumed innocent until proved guilty according to law.

3 Everyone charged with a criminal offence has the following minimum rights:

(a) to be informed promptly, in a language which he understands and in detail, of the nature and cause of the accusation against him;
(b) to have adequate time and facilities for the preparation of his defence;
(c) to defend himself in person or through legal assistance of his own choosing or, if he has not sufficient means to pay for legal assistance, to be given it free when the interests of justice so require;
(d) to examine or have examined witnesses against him and to obtain the attendance and examination of witnesses on his behalf under the same conditions as witnesses against him;
(e) to have the free assistance of an interpreter if he cannot understand or speak the language used in court.

Article 7

No punishment without law

1 No one shall be held guilty of any criminal offence on account of any act or omission which did not constitute a criminal offence under national or international law at the time when it was committed. Nor shall a heavier penalty be imposed than the one that was applicable at the time the criminal offence was committed.

2 This Article shall not prejudice the trial and punishment of any person for any act or omission which, at the time when it was committed, was criminal according to the general principles of law recognised by civilised nations.

Article 8

Right to respect for private and family life

1 Everyone has the right to respect for his private and family life, his home and his correspondence.

2 There shall be no interference by a public authority with the exercise of this right except such as is in accordance with the law and is necessary in a democratic society in the interests of national security, public safety or the economic well-being of the country, for the prevention

of disorder or crime, for the protection of health or morals, or for the protection of the rights and freedoms of others.

Article 9

Freedom of thought, conscience and religion

1 Everyone has the right to freedom of thought, conscience and religion; this right includes freedom to change his religion or belief and freedom, either alone or in community with others and in public or private, to manifest his religion or belief, in worship, teaching, practice and observance.

2 Freedom to manifest one's religion or beliefs shall be subject only to such limitations as are prescribed by law and are necessary in a democratic society in the interests of public safety, for the protection of public order, health or morals, or for the protection of the rights and freedoms of others.

Article 10

Freedom of expression

1 Everyone has the right to freedom of expression. This right shall include freedom to hold opinions and to receive and impart information and ideas without interference by public authority and regardless of frontiers. This Article shall not prevent States from requiring the licensing of broadcasting, television or cinema enterprises.

2 The exercise of these freedoms, since it carries with it duties and responsibilities, may be subject to such formalities, conditions, restrictions or penalties as are prescribed by law and are necessary in a democratic society, in the interests of national security, territorial integrity or public safety, for the prevention of disorder or crime, for the protection of health or morals, for the protection of the reputation or rights of others, for preventing the disclosure of information received in confidence, or for maintaining the authority and impartiality of the judiciary.

Article 11

Freedom of assembly and association

1 Everyone has the right to freedom of peaceful assembly and to freedom of association with others, including the right to form and to join trade unions for the protection of his interests.

2 No restrictions shall be placed on the exercise of these rights other than such as are prescribed by law and are necessary in a democratic society in the interests of national security or public safety, for the prevention of disorder or crime, for the protection of health or morals or for the protection of the rights and freedoms of others. This Article shall not prevent the imposition of lawful restrictions on the exercise of these rights by members of the armed forces, of the police or of the administration of the State.

Article 12

Right to marry

Men and women of marriageable age have the right to marry and to found a family, according to the national laws governing the exercise of this right.

Article 14

Prohibition of discrimination

The enjoyment of the rights and freedoms set forth in this Convention shall be secured without discrimination on any ground such as sex, race, colour, language, religion, political or other opinion, national or social origin, association with a national minority, property, birth or other status.

Article 16

Restrictions on political activity of aliens

Nothing in Articles 10, 11 and 14 shall be regarded as preventing the High Contracting Parties from imposing restrictions on the political activity of aliens.

Article 17

Prohibition of abuse of rights

Nothing in this Convention may be interpreted as implying for any State, group or person any right to engage in any activity or perform any act aimed at the destruction of any of the rights and freedoms set forth herein or at their limitation to a greater extent than is provided for in the Convention.

Article 18

Limitation on use of restrictions on rights

The restrictions permitted under this Convention to the said rights and freedoms shall not be applied for any purpose other than those for which they have been prescribed.

Part II

The First Protocol

Article 1

Protection of property

Every natural or legal person is entitled to the peaceful enjoyment of his possessions. No one shall be deprived of his possessions except in the public interest and subject to the conditions provided for by law and by the general principles of international law.

The preceding provisions shall not, however, in any way impair the right of a State to enforce such laws as it deems necessary to control the use of property in accordance with the general interest or to secure the payment of taxes or other contributions or penalties.

Article 2

Right to education

No person shall be denied the right to education. In the exercise of any functions which it assumes in relation to education and to teaching, the State shall respect the right of parents to ensure such education and teaching in conformity with their own religious and philosophical convictions.

Article 3

Right to free elections

The High Contracting Parties undertake to hold free elections at reasonable intervals by secret ballot, under conditions which will ensure the free expression of the opinion of the people in the choice of the legislature.

Part III
The Sixth Protocol

Article 1

Abolition of the death penalty

The death penalty shall be abolished. No one shall be condemned to such penalty or executed.

Article 2

Death penalty in time of war

A State may make provision in its law for the death penalty in respect of acts committed in time of war or of imminent threat of war; such penalty shall be applied only in the instances laid down in the law and in accordance with its provisions. The State shall communicate to the Secretary General of the Council of Europe the relevant provisions of that law.

[1:14] Spencer, J R, 'Squaring up to Strasbourg: *Horncastle* in the Supreme Court'
(2010) 1 *Archbold Review* 6

On December 9 the Supreme Court gave its long-awaited judgment in *Horncastle* [2009] UKSC 14; [2010] 2 W.L.R. 47 on the compatibility of the hearsay provisions of the Criminal Justice Act 2003 with the defendant's right to question prosecution witnesses guaranteed by Article 6 of the European Convention of Human Rights. Rejecting the reasoning of the Strasbourg Court in a line of cases culminating in *Al-Khawaja and Tahery v UK* (2009) 49 E.H.R.R. 1 – in which the UK was condemned – the Supreme Court unanimously held that the reformed hearsay rule is compatible with the Convention. For the purpose of ongoing criminal proceedings in the courts of the United Kingdom this means the matter is now settled. But further developments in Strasbourg are awaited, and in the light of these, it is conceivable that the issue will come before the Supreme Court again. The nub of the matter is that Art.6(3) of the European Convention guarantees defendants in criminal proceedings a list of "minimum rights", including among other things the right

    (d) *to examine or have examined witnesses against him. . .*

    As interpreted by the Strasbourg Court, this means that a defendant cannot properly be convicted if the "sole or decisive" evidence against him is a statement fed into the criminal justice system by a potential witness if the defendant had no chance to put his questions to him, either at trial or during the preliminary stages. This overriding limitation on the use of hearsay evidence was not, however, incorporated in the reform of the hearsay rules contained in Pt 11 of the Criminal Justice Act 2003. Section 125 of the Act does require a judge at a jury trial to stop the case if it largely consists of hearsay evidence that is "unconvincing" – but if the evidence is convincing the judge is not required to stop the case simply because the key pieces of evidence come from a source that the defendant has been unable to challenge by questioning.

On January 20, 2009 the resulting tension led the Fourth Section of the Strasbourg Court to condemn the UK in *Al-Khawaja and Tahery v UK*, two conjoined cases in which defendants had been convicted on the basis of statements – admitted under statutory exceptions to the hearsay rule – made to the police by witnesses who were "unavailable" to testify at trial. In the first case the witness had died before the trial, and in the second case, the witness was excused from court appearance because he was "in fear".

This *Al-Khawaja* decision was unwelcome to the UK government, which in April requested the decision to be referred to the Grand Chamber. It was also unwelcome to the Court of Appeal. In March, sitting as panel of five instead of the usual three, it heard appeals from a group of defendants, headed by Horncastle, who had been convicted in similar circumstances to Al-Khawaja and Tahery; and in May it delivered a resounding judgment in which it refused to follow the decision of the Strasbourg Court and upheld the convictions [2009] EWCA Crim 964; [2009] 2 Cr. App. R. 15 (230). In taking what might be called "the UKIP line" it said (in essence) that the Strasbourg Court had failed to appreciate the safeguards against wrongful conviction that the hearsay provisions of the Criminal Justice Act 2003 provide, which ensure that a conviction based on hearsay admitted under the statutory scheme is fair.

Leave was given to the defendants to appeal to the House of Lords – as it then was – and in June Strasbourg adjourned consideration of the UK's request for the case to be reheard before the Grand Chamber until the House of Lords had decided the appeal. Sitting as a panel of seven, the Law Lords heard the appeal early in July and it was widely expected that the decision would follow shortly after. But it did not, and judgment was reserved until the autumn, to be given by the same judges, now in their new capacity as Justices of the Supreme Court. As autumn turned to winter, so speculation grew that the justices were deeply divided on the issue, and the result, when it eventually came, would be "a close run thing". But as we now know, this was not the case. The cause of the delay, it seems, was that the Justices, having decided to defy Strasbourg, were preparing a block-buster of a judgment which – to change the metaphor from aerial warfare to fox-hunting – would "stop up all the earths".

And the resulting judgment is indeed impressive. Unusually, it consists of three distinct elements. First there is long and thorough judgment delivered by the President, Lord Phillips, in which all the other members of the court concurred; then there is a collection of four Annexes – one examining the treatment of hearsay in Canada, Australia and New Zealand, two examining some of the Strasbourg caselaw in greater detail, and a fourth, prepared by Lord Judge C.J., explaining how, in England, the prosecutions at the end of which Strasbourg had condemned other contracting states for breaches of Art.6(3)(d) would have ended in acquittal, or more radically, have failed to get off the ground. And finally there are some extra remarks from Lord Brown, saying (in effect) that the Supreme Court might, against its better judgement, bend before a decision of the Strasbourg Grand Chamber that it inwardly believed to be unwise or wrong, but that it would not do so in the face of such a decision coming from a Section.

Conveniently for readers, Lord Phillips began his judgment by summarising his main conclusions, which in his own words were as follows.

1. Long before 1953 when the Convention came into force the common law had, by reason of the hearsay rule, addressed that aspect of a fair trial that article 6(3)(d) was designed to ensure.

2. Parliament has since enacted exceptions to the hearsay rule that are required in the interests of justice. Those exceptions are not subject to the 'sole or decisive' rule. The regime enacted by parliament contains safeguards that render the sole or decisive rule unnecessary.
3. The continental procedure had not addressed that aspect of a fair trial that article 6(3)(d) was designed to cure.
4. The Strasbourg Court has recognised that exceptions to article 6(3)(d) are required in the interests of justice.
5. The manner in which the Strasbourg Court has approved those exceptions has resulted in a jurisprudence that lacks clarity.
6. The 'sole or decisive' rule has been introduced into the Strasbourg jurisprudence without discussion of the principle underlying it or full consideration of whether there was justification for imposing the rule as an overriding principle applicable equally to the continental and common law jurisdictions.
7. Although English law does not include the 'sole or decisive' rule it would, in almost all cases, have reached the same result in those cases where the Strasbourg Court has invoked the rule.
8. The 'sole or decisive' rule would create severe practical difficulties if applied to English criminal procedure.
9. *Al-Khawaja* does not establish that it is necessary to apply the "sole or decisive" rule in this jurisdiction.

In the rest of his judgment Lord Phillips elaborated each of these points, with cogency and eloquence; and his conclusions are fortified by the material he and his judicial brethren had assembled in the Annexes.

Much of his judgment was devoted to explaining why the "sole and decisive" rule is unsatisfactory. It is unsatisfactory, he said, because it produces a paradox. The more cogent the piece of hearsay evidence is, the more likely it is to be "decisive" – and the more decisive it is, the less the court will be able to act upon it.

The test is also unsatisfactory, he said, because in practice it would be difficult to apply. The duty not to treat a particular piece of evidence as "decisive", he said, would be "hard enough for a professional judge". And for a lay tribunal, the use of which in contested cases is seen by common lawyers as one of the basic ingredients of fair trial, it would "involve them in mental gymnastics that few would be equipped to perform." And anyway, he asked, what is meant by evidence that is "decisive"? "If 'decisive' means capable of making the difference between a finding of guilt and innocence, then all hearsay evidence will have to be excluded."

But, said Lord Phillips, his most important objection to rule forbidding courts to act on hearsay as the "sole or decisive" evidence is that "If applied rigorously it will in some cases result in the acquittal, or failure to prosecute, defendants where there is cogent evidence of their guilt". This, he said, "will be to the detriment of their victims and will result in defendants being left free to add to the number of those victims".

To underline this point, he gave the following example.

A visitor to London witnesses a hit and run road accident in which a cyclist is killed. He memorises the number of the car, and makes a statement to the police in which he includes not merely the number, but the make and colour of the car and the fact that the driver was a man with a beard. He . . . is then himself killed in a road accident. The police find that the car with the registration number that he provided is the make and colour that he reported and that it is owned by a man with a beard. The owner declines to answer questions as to his whereabouts at the time of the accident. It seems hard to justify a rule that would preclude the conviction of the owner of the car on the basis of the statement of the deceased witness, yet that is the effect of the sole or decisive test.

Other examples were given by the Court of Appeal in their judgment, and others can be imagined that are equally telling: for example, where the key eye-witness gives a convincing account of the crime in his evidence in-chief, but then drops dead in the witness-box just as defence counsel is rising to his feet to cross-examine.

In *Al-Khawaja*, said Lord Phillips, the Strasbourg Court had accepted that the "sole or decisive" rule was subject to one exception, namely where the reason the defence were unable to put questions to the key witness was that the defendant had intimidated him, so keeping him away from the court of trial. If one exception were possible, said Lord Phillips, so too were others: and of these the Criminal Justice Act 2003 created a scheme that is both orderly and consistent with the need to ensure the defendant is given a fair trial.

By way of a digression – though an important one – Lord Phillips also discussed the law relating to anonymous witnesses. He pointed out that the Strasbourg Court had also applied the "sole or decisive" rule to limit the power of a criminal court to convict on evidence from an anonymous witness (whether subject to cross-examination or not) whose identity is not disclosed to the defence. Following the decision of the House of Lords in *Davis* [2008] UKHL 36; [2008] 1 A.C. 1128, Parliament had enacted a statutory scheme setting the limits within which anonymous evidence could be used in criminal proceedings. These limits, like the limits on hearsay evidence set out in the Criminal Justice Act 2003, contain no overriding principle that anonymous evidence may not constitute the "sole or decisive" element in the case. And in his view, the English statutory scheme for anonymous evidence, like the English statutory scheme for hearsay evidence, is satisfactory and not open to attack because it is in conflict with the defendant's rights as guaranteed by the European Convention.

The intended consumer of this important judgment was undoubtedly Grand Chamber of the Court at Strasbourg; which the Supreme Court hopes to influence, if and when it rehears the *Al-Khawaja* case. As a practical matter, the decision in *Horncastle* is eminently sensible; but will the Grand Chamber be convinced by the arguments contained in it? The basic issue in this case is the status of the right to question prosecution witnesses that is conferred on defendants by Art.6(3)(d) of the Convention. Is this a purely *instrumental* right, meant merely as a part of a package of protections the overall aim of which is to see that trials are "fair", in the sense of avoiding the conviction of the innocent? Or is it an *absolute* right, in the absence of which no trial can ever be considered fair, however obvious the defendant's guilt may be at the end of it?

The Criminal Justice Act 2003 is constructed on the assumption that it is purely instrumental, and with that in mind it assumes that the inability of the defendant to question a key prosecution witness is something which can be compensated for by "other measures". And that, of course, is the way in which the Court of Appeal and the Supreme Court interpret it, and hope to persuade the Grand Chamber to view it too. But the Grand Chamber may or may not feel able accept this, because if Art.6 of the Convention is read with the eye of a textual fundamentalist, the right to question prosecution witnesses, like other rights set out in subs. (3), is set out in terms suggesting it is absolute, and not merely instrumental.

The scheme set out in Art.6, it will be remembered, is as follows. Article 6(1) guarantees the general right of every citizen to a "fair trial" for the determination of his civil rights and any criminal charge against him. Article 6(2) proclaims the presumption of innocence. And then descending to specifics, Art.6(3) provides that "Everyone charged with a criminal offence has the following minimum rights", among which appears in subsection (d) the right "to examine or have examined witnesses against him". By labelling the contents of this list "minimum rights" Art.6(3) does not tell us that they are mere suggestions, to be recognised when this is convenient, and to be ignored by contracting states with impunity so long as the trial, when viewed in the round, can be considered to be in some nebulous sense "fair". On the contrary, it appears to tell us that they are rights that have to be respected in each and every case. If the right to question witnesses is indeed one that is absolute – on a par, for example, with the right to a tribunal that is independent – the result is indeed practically inconvenient, for all reasons given by the Court of Appeal and now by the Supreme Court as well. But for good or ill, this is the meaning the plain wording of the article suggests.

If this construction were adopted, a criminal court could presumably still hear and act upon the evidence of an absent witness whom the defendant had intimidated, because by scaring the witness away the defendant could be said to have waived his right to question him: just as if, knowing of his right to require the witness to attend for cross-examination, he had expressly agreed to allow the statement of an absent witness to be read. But on this view it would not be possible to adduce against a defendant the statement of any witness to whom he was unable to put questions, where he had not brought this impossibility about: for example, statements from a key witness who has died without his intervention, or who is too ill to come to court, or who is "unavailable" for any of the other reasons listed in s.116 of the Criminal Justice Act 2003.

Up to now, the Strasbourg Court, as we have seen, has avoided taking a strictly fundamentalist line with the right to question witnesses contained in Art.6(3)(d), to the limited extent of restricting it to those main witnesses whose evidence will be "sole or decisive". But it would be a significantly greater derogation from the right were it to say, as the Supreme Court hopes that it will say, that wherever sufficient "counterbalancing measures" are present, it can be disregarded altogether. And the eloquence and learning of Lord Phillips and his colleagues may or may not be enough to persuade them to accept this.

A reason why the Grand Chamber may possibly be unsympathetic to the Supreme Court's arguments about the practical inconveniences of a strict interpretation of the defendant's right to question witnesses in Art.6(3)(d) is that it feels that the UK is, at least so some extent, complaining of a self-inflicted wound. In many parts of continental Europe the problem of vulnerable witnesses who die, fall ill, disappear or otherwise become unavailable to testify at trial is eased (if not completely solved) by the existence of machinery enabling the prosecution to have the evidence of such witnesses taken "on commission" (as common lawyers call it) ahead of trial, at a hearing where the defence are present and able to put questions. Where the witness has been heard in this way there is no difficulty about Art.6(3) (d), because the Strasbourg Court has said, repeatedly, that the defendant's right to question the witnesses against him is properly respected by giving him either the chance to question the prosecution witnesses at trial, or the chance to do so at an earlier stage in the proceedings.

In *Kostovski v The Netherlands* it said:

> In principle, all the evidence must be produced in the presence of the accused at a public hearing with a view to adversarial argument. . . This does not mean, however, that in order to be used as evidence statements of witnesses should always be made at a public hearing in court: to use as evidence such statements obtained at a pre-trial stage is not in itself inconsistent with paragraphs 3(d) and 1 of Article 6, provided the rights of the defence have been respected.

> As a rule, these rights require that an accused should be given an adequate and proper opportunity to challenge and question a witness against him, either at the time the witness was making his statement or at some later stage in the proceedings. . . ([1990] 12 E.H.R.R. 434 at [41]).

And this remark has been repeated in many cases since. As older readers will remember, formerly such mechanisms existed in English criminal procedure too. A preliminary step towards a trial on indictment used to be "committal proceedings" at which the prosecution witnesses gave their evidence orally in the presence of the defence – and if the witness then failed to attend trial the depositions given at committal could be used if he or she was "proved by the oath of a credible witness to be dead or insane, or so ill as not to be able to travel, or to be kept out of the way by means of the procurement of the accused or on his behalf." And this general provision was supplemented by other statutory provisions under which formal depositions could be taken from merchant seamen, witnesses to offences committed on aircraft, young children, and persons who were dangerously ill. But in recent years it has been the policy of the government to abolish these procedures, whilst at the same time promoting changes to the hearsay rule to make admissible, by way of an exception to the hearsay rule, the statements absent witnesses gave to the police: statements made, of course, without the safeguard of a judicial figure, or any opportunity for the defence to put their questions to the accuser.

When reform of the hearsay rule was being mooted, some commentators (including this one) argued the case for the creation of a modernised version of these now-abandoned formal procedures for taking evidence ahead of trial. But to this the Law Commission was opposed, saying – inaccurately, in the light of relatively recent history – that this would "constitute a radical change to English criminal procedure". And so the Law Commission argued, and the government accepted, that the problem would be met by the new exceptions to the hearsay rule which they had in mind, and which were eventually enacted in the Criminal Justice Act 2003. In view of all this, the Strasbourg Grand Chamber could take the view that the proper solution to the problems the Supreme Court identified is not for them to water down the guarantee contained in Art.6(3)(d), but for the UK to modify its laws.

It is to be hoped that the Grand Chamber does not take a strictly fundamentalist approach to Art.6(3)(d), because, as both the Court of Appeal and the Supreme Court have correctly pointed out in *Horncastle*, this would lead to outcomes that are practically unjust: namely, the acquittal of persons whose guilt can be shown beyond all reasonable doubt; and this would be so, even allowing for the possibility of hearing certain vulnerable witnesses ahead of trial. It would mean, for example, that there could be no conviction in a case where, immediately after being fatally wounded and just before his death, a murder victim convincingly identified the defendant as his attacker; or again the case previously mentioned where, having given overwhelmingly convincing evidence in chief, the key prosecution witness drops dead just as the defence begin their cross-examination.

To make sense of the situation, in other words, Art.6(3)(d) must be read as subject to some implied qualification or qualifications, and the Supreme Court was entirely right to challenge Strasbourg with vigour on this point. Personally, however, I question whether it can properly be read subject to a general limitation that the defendant can only insist on it where depriving him of it would make the resulting trial in some wider sense "unfair", because this risks watering a valuable safeguard down too far. But I think a sensible, and workable, qualification would be to say that it only applies to those witnesses whom, by taking reasonable efforts, the State could make available for the defence to question. Under this interpretation, the defendant would have no valid complaint if, for example, he were convicted on the statement of a person who had died just after making a statement to the police, or someone who died in the witness-box just as he was about to be cross-examined. However, he might have a valid complaint if he were convicted on the out-of-court statement of a witness to whom, if the State had constructed its criminal justice system more intelligently, or had operated it more conscientiously, he could have put his questions ahead of trial.

[1:15] Spencer, J R, 'Hearsay evidence at Strasbourg: a further skirmish, or the final round? A comment on *Al-Khawaja and Tahery v UK* in the Grand Chamber'
(2012) 1 *Archbold Review* 5

On December 15, 2011 the Grand Chamber at Strasbourg delivered its long-awaited judgment in *Al-Khawaja and Tahery v UK* (Applications Nos 26766/05 and 22228/06). The hearing took place in May 2010, 20 months earlier: a delay surprising in a court which, at regular intervals, condemns contracting States for failing to render justice within a "reasonable time". However, if it was a long time coming, the judgment was—at least in this commentator's view—well worth the wait. The majority judgment is clearly reasoned, clearly expressed and provides a solution to the legal issues that seems both just and workable. And for good measure, in terms of "judicial politics" it defuses a quarrel between London and Strasbourg that risked getting out of hand.

The previous instalment of this long-running legal soap-opera was the decision of the UK Supreme Court in *Horncastle* [2009] UKSC 14, delivered even further back in December 2009. The lapse of time between instalments means that a brief synopsis of the background is now required.

The plot so far

Once upon a time, the hearsay rule rendered inadmissible almost any account of an incident other than one delivered in oral evidence by a witness live at trial. The Criminal Justice Act 1988 made some important new exceptions to this rule and the Criminal Justice Act 2003 created a new and longer list, so making the out-of-court statements of absent witnesses generally admissible in cases where the maker of the statement was "unavailable" to give evidence at trial. The 2003 Act creates various safeguards but does not in principle restrict the use that may be made of hearsay evidence. Broadly speaking, if one of the exceptions renders a piece of hearsay evidence legally admissible the court is entitled to convict on it, even if it is the central piece of evidence in the case. To this extent there is a possible conflict between English law and Art.6(3)(d) of the European Convention on Human Rights, which lists as one of the basic rights for criminal defendants "the right to examine or have examined the witnesses against him".

In 2004 Al-Khawaja, a doctor, was convicted of indecently assaulting a patient, who had died before the trial, on the basis of the statement she had earlier made to the police—admitted under the hearsay provisions of the CJA 1988, which were then still in force. In 2005 Tahery was convicted of a stabbing on the basis of the police witness statement of a frightened witness, admitted under the provisions of the CJA 2003, which had by then replaced the 1988 provisions. In January 2009 the UK was condemned by the Fourth Section of the Strasbourg Court on the ground that the convictions in both cases infringed the convicted defendants' right to a fair trial under Art.6—the problem being the use of hearsay evidence, which the Court considered to infringe Art.6(3)(d).

The decision was ill-received in the UK and in March 2010 the government successfully applied to have the cases referred to the Grand Chamber. Meanwhile in March 2009 the Court of Appeal, in *Horncastle* [2009] EWCA Crim 964, had refused to follow the decision. The rebellion spread further in December of that year when the Supreme Court upheld the Court of Appeal, delivering a long judgment trenchantly criticising the reasoning of the Fourth Section:

a judgment evidently written with the Grand Chamber as its intended readership. The arguments it contained were summarised in an earlier number of *Archbold Review*.

The legal issue in a nutshell

So far as relevant for present purposes, Art.6 of the European Convention on Human Rights is as follows:

(1) In the determination of his civil rights and obligations or of any criminal charge against him, everyone is entitled to a fair and public hearing . . .

(2) . . .

(3) Everyone charged with a criminal offence has the following minimum rights:

. . .

(d) to examine or have examined witnesses against him and to obtain the attendance and examination of witnesses on his behalf under the same conditions as witnesses against him.

The key question at the centre of this litigation was this: will there invariably be a violation of Art.6(3)(d) if a defendant is convicted in a case where some part of the evidence came from a witness to whom he was unable to put questions? Or only sometimes? And if only sometimes, when?

On a literal reading of the Article, the answer would be "invariably". Article 6(3) sets out a list of what it describes as "minimum rights". On the face of it, "minimum rights" means rights that must always be respected—essential components of a fair trial, not rights that can be disregarded if the proceedings would be in some vague sense "fair" without them. However, such a fundamentalist reading would be inconvenient and result in manifestly guilty people getting off. In consequence, the previous case-law of the Strasbourg Court has watered Art.6(3)(d) down to a limited extent; and in the UK, the hearsay provisions of the Criminal Justice Acts of 1988 and 2003 were enacted on the assumption that it can be watered down still further.

The Strasbourg dilution of Art.6(3)(d) was achieved by reading it as subject to a qualification that the right only applies in respect of those witnesses who provide the sole or decisive evidence in the case. On this view there is no infringement of Art.6(3)(d), and hence of the defendant's wider right to a fair trial, if some small or incidental part of the total evidence comes from witnesses whom the defendant has no opportunity to question; but there is an infringement if such evidence forms the centrepiece of the prosecution case. By contrast, the English hearsay reforms of 1988 and 2003 proceeded on the assumption that there is no violation even where the witness or witnesses whom the defendant was unable to question supply the sole or decisive evidence in the case, provided sufficient "counterbalancing factors" are present to offset any disadvantage this might cause him.

Put another way, the difference between the Strasbourg interpretation of Art.6(3)(d) and the interpretation underlying the English reforms to the hearsay rule in 1988 and 2003 was as to whether Art.6(3)(d) exists to protect some higher procedural value, or is purely instrumental: i.e. just one of a number of tools designed to protect the innocent from conviction, able to be left in the legal toolbox when other tools can be used to do the job as well. And behind this difference of opinion lies two subtly different conceptions of what constitutes a "fair trial". Is a "fair trial" simply one that is conducted in such a way as to avoid those features which tend to produce convictions of the innocent? Or does a "fair trial" also mean one in which certain procedural values are observed, whether or not their observance is required in order to eliminate this risk? (The same difference of conception underlies the divergent approaches of different people at different times in England as to whether, in the context of s.2 of the Criminal Appeal Act 1968, a conviction is "unsafe".)

Though it did not formulate the issue in these explicit terms, it was the broader conception of "fair trial" that underlay the decision of the Strasbourg Fourth Chamber in January 2009, and the narrower one that underlay the decision of the UK Supreme Court in December of that year. According to the UK Supreme Court there is no problem about a trial being "unfair" where the "sole or decisive" evidence all comes from sources to which the defence has been unable to put questions, provided sufficient "counterbalancing factors" are present; and in their view, such "counterbalancing factors" are provided by the new scheme for hearsay evidence set out in Pt 11 of the Criminal Justice Act 2003.

The decision of the Grand Chamber

The Grand Chamber, by an overwhelming majority of 15 to two, conceded the essential point that the Court of Appeal and the Supreme Court were making: in certain cases it *is* possible for the defendant to have a "fair trial" as required by Art.6 where the main body of the prosecution evidence comes from witnesses he was unable to question or have questioned. However, said the judges, a fair trial is possible in such circumstances only provided two conditions have been met.

The first is that there should be a really good reason for the witness's absence from the trial. Good reasons, said the Grand Chamber, could take various forms, of which it was at present necessary to examine only those put forward in the two cases that were before them. Death, they said, was obviously a good reason. So too in principle was fear. Fear would obviously be a sufficient reason if the defendant or his associates had directly caused it by threatening the witness with reprisals; but even in the absence of explicit threats, general fear would be a sufficient reason if, for example, it was "attributable to the notoriety of a defendant or his associates". Furthermore, "fear of death or injury of another person or of financial loss are all relevant considerations in determining whether a witness should not be required to give oral evidence".

The second condition is that sufficient safeguards are provided to guard against a miscarriage of justice resulting from the defendant's inability to question his accusers. Here the key paragraph in the majority judgment is as follows:

> [147] The Court therefore concludes that, where a hearsay statement is the sole or decisive evidence against a defendant, its admission as evidence will not automatically result in a breach of Article 6 § 1. At the same time where a conviction is based solely or decisively on the evidence of absent witnesses, the Court must subject the proceedings to the most searching scrutiny. . . The question in each case is whether there are sufficient counterbalancing factors in place, including measures that permit a fair and proper assessment of the reliability of that evidence to take place. That would permit a conviction to be based on such evidence only if it is sufficiently reliable given its importance in that case.

The Grand Chamber then examined the procedural safeguards surrounding the admission of hearsay evidence in the reformed law contained in the CJA 2003 and in the hearsay provisions of the CJA 1988 which the 2003 Act had replaced, and concluded that, properly applied, they were capable of "delivering the goods".

Viewed from the perspective of the Court of Appeal and the Supreme Court, so far so good; but the English judicial team did not achieve a total victory.

First, the Grand Chamber then decided to examine in detail the facts of the two cases before them, to see whether the applicants had in fact received a "fair trial" according to the Grand Chamber's perception of the concept; and they held that whereas Al-Khawaja had received a fair trial, Tahery had not—and in respect of Tahery's case the UK was condemned. In Al-Khawaja's case the complainant had died, so to produce her as a live witness at the trial was obviously impossible. Though there was some other evidence in the case, her police witness-statement complaining of the offence was the "sole or decisive" evidence in the case, in the sense that, unless it could be put before the court, there would have been no chance of convicting the defendant of indecently assaulting her. But her evidence was supported by the fact that, immediately after the alleged incident, she had complained about it to two friends, both of whom gave evidence at the trial, and more importantly, it was also corroborated by the fact that another patient, who also gave live evidence and was cross-examined, claimed to be the victim of a very similar assault. All that, taken together with the fact that the judge had warned the jury that the defendant's inability to cross-examine the complainant rendered her evidence less cogent, meant that the Al-Khawaja's trial had been a fair one.

Tahery's case arose out of a street fight in the early hours of morning between a group of Kurds and a group of Iranians in the course of which an Iranian, Sadeghi, had been twice stabbed in the back. Tahery was not at first the obvious suspect because he had administered first aid to Sadeghi and accompanied him to hospital. However another participant in the disturbance, one Takhtshami, later told the police that he had seen Tahery wield the knife. No other person identified Tahery as the attacker; though in the immediate aftermath of the stabbing Tahery drew suspicion on himself by claiming—falsely as he then admitted—that the stabbing was the work of two fictitious blacks. Before the trial began, Takhtshami told the judge that he had been threatened (though he refused to say by whom), and on hearing this, the judge excused him from giving oral evidence and allowed the prosecution to put his police witness-statement in evidence instead. Tahery then gave evidence denying the offence, though admitting the lie about the blacks. On this evidence he was convicted. The Court of Appeal reduced his sentence from nine years' imprisonment to seven, but dismissed his appeal against conviction. However, if the Court of Appeal was satisfied that Tahery's conviction was "safe", the Grand Chamber was not satisfied that the proceedings leading up to it were a "fair trial". First, Takhtschami's evidence—unlike some of the examples of hearsay given by the Supreme Court and the Court of Appeal in *Horncastle*—was not "demonstrably reliable". And secondly, it stood alone: no other evidence in the case corroborated the key parts of it. In the light of these two factors, the judge's warning to the jury about the dangers of untested evidence were insufficient to counter the disadvantage to Tahery in his ability to conduct a cross-examination.

(With this assessment of the two cases it is surely hard to disagree. The complainant in *Al-Khawaja* was unlikely to have been honestly mistaken about what the doctor did to her, and had no obvious motive for telling lies. But Takhtshami, like any other witness to a street fight, could easily have been honestly mistaken in what he thought he saw, and as a participant in the disturbance himself there were obvious reasons why he might wish to lie. He was, in fact, the very sort of witness whose evidence is sometimes dramatically demolished by a cross-examination—which may indeed have been the real reason why he was so anxious to avoid the witness-box. And whereas the complaint's evidence in *Al-Khawaja* was corroborated, Takhtshami's evidence was not. In retrospect, it seems surprising that the Court of Appeal pronounced the resulting conviction "safe".)

Secondly, the Supreme Court's victory was qualified by the fact that Grand Chamber refused to accept several key elements of its reasoning.

One was the Supreme Court's argument that the "sole or decisive" test is irrational, inflexible and unworkable. This might be so, the Grand Chamber said, if the three words were to be read narrowly and literally. But there was no real problem if the phrase is interpreted, as it should be, in a broader sense as meaning the central corpus of evidence, without which the case could not proceed. As such, the concept was one with which the English law of evidence was already quite familiar. Among other places, they pointed out, it occurs in s.125 of the

Criminal Justice Act 2003, which requires the judge to stop a case which depends "wholly or partly" on hearsay evidence which "is so unconvincing that, considering its importance to the case against the defendant", a conviction on it would be unsafe.

The Supreme Court had also argued that the "sole or decisive" test is misconceived, because it is based on the false notion that all hearsay evidence which is crucial to a case is unreliable or incapable of proper assessment unless tested by cross-examination. This too the Grand Chamber rejected.

Rather, it is predicated on the principle that the greater the importance of the evidence, the greater the unfairness to the defendant in allowing the witness to remain anonymous or to be absent from the trial and the greater the need for safeguards to ensure that the evidence is demonstrably reliable or that its reliability can be properly tested and assessed.

The Supreme Court's judgment in *Horncastle* opened with remarks suggesting that common law systems such as ours should be exempted from the "sole or decisive" rule because the Strasbourg case-law which created it was developed in order to sensitise the systems of continental Europe to the risks involved in hearsay evidence: risks of which the common law systems were already well aware, having internalised them centuries before (remarks which I suspect some continental lawyers will have read as "Don't preach to us about fair trials—we invented them!") This line of argument the Grand Chamber also pointedly rejected:

The Court accepts that the sole or decisive rule may have been developed in the context of legal systems which permitted a defendant to be convicted on evidence of witnesses whom he did not have an opportunity to challenge. . . However, the Court notes that the present cases have arisen precisely because the legal system in England and Wales has abandoned the strict common law rule against hearsay evidence.

So where does all this leave us?

The most obvious result of this decision is that the looming conflict between Strasbourg and the English legal system over hearsay evidence has been averted. In its judgment the Grand Chamber conceded the essential point that the Court of Appeal and the Supreme Court wished to make. This means that English judges and practitioners, who would have been bound to follow the decision in *Horncastle* whatever the Grand Chamber had said, can now do so without the worry that this will precipitate another condemnation for the UK at Strasbourg.

That said, however, the condemnation of the UK over *Tahery* should sound a note of caution. A court which applies the hearsay provisions of the Criminal Justice Act 2003 in such a way as to permit a defendant to be convicted on the basis of a piece of hearsay evidence which stands alone, and which emanated from a witness who might well have lied or been honestly mistaken, and whose lies or honest errors—had there been any—would probably have been exposed in cross-examination, should be aware that a successful application to Strasbourg could well be the result.

A further and more worrying point that emerges from the decision concerns hearsay from a source that is anonymous. In listing the counterbalancing measures that English law currently applies the Grand Chamber mentioned, with apparent approval, the rule that "the admission of statements of a witness who is not only absent but anonymous is not admissible" [at 148]. If the Grand Chamber was endorsing a rule that English law will not tolerate attempts by prosecutors to put before the court a statement obtained from a witness whom they wish to protect not only from the ordeal of giving evidence in court but also from having their identities disclosed, then this is welcome. But insofar as it appears to endorse an overriding rule to the effect that no piece of hearsay evidence, however demonstrably reliable, is ever admissible in evidence if the identity of the original maker of the statement is unknown, it is not. Such a rule would have disastrous consequences. (It would, for example, resurrect the extraordinary decision of the House of Lords in *Myers v DPP* [1965] A.C. 1001, which held that a prosecutor could not establish which engine had been originally fitted into which car by producing microfilms of record-cards filled in by the factory workers, now unidentified, who routinely noted the chassis and the engine numbers when working on the assembly-line some years before.)

A final point is one which this author has already made, at greater length, in his commentary on *Horncastle*. The problem of squaring the defendant's Art.6 right to question his accusers with the fact that it is sometimes impossible to produce key witnesses at trial would be reduced, if not completely removed, if English criminal procedure provided a mechanism for the examination and cross-examination ahead of trial of witnesses whose inability or reluctance to testify at trial can be foreseen. Procedures of this sort exist in many other legal systems; and indeed a general one formerly existed in this country in the days of "old style" committals. A new mechanism for the pre-trial cross-examination of vulnerable witnesses was created 13 years ago by s.28 of the Youth Justice and Criminal Evidence Act 1999, but never implemented. In recent years, serious pressure has been building for its belated implementation. At the time of writing the government is said to be considering this—though with nervousness about cost implications. Let us hope that before long the money as well as the will is to be found.

[1:16] Criminal Justice Act 1991 (as amended)
Section 95

95 Information for financial and other purposes

(1) The Secretary of State shall in each year publish such information as he considers expedient for the purpose of –

    (a)   enabling persons engaged in the administration of criminal justice to become aware of the financial implications of their decisions;
        (aa) enabling such persons to become aware of the relative effectiveness of different sentences –
           (i)   in preventing re-offending, and
           (ii) in promoting public confidence in the criminal justice system; or
    (b)   facilitating the performance by such persons of their duty to avoid discriminating against any persons on the ground of race or sex or any other improper ground.

(2) Publication under subsection (1) above shall be effected in such manner as the Secretary of State considers appropriate for the purpose of bringing the information to the attention of the persons concerned.

[1:17] *Statistics on Race and the Criminal Justice System 2012*
(2013) Ministry of Justice

Executive summary

This report provides information about how members of all ethnic groups, including those from Black, Asian and Minority Ethnic (BAME) groups, were represented in the Criminal Justice System (CJS) in England and Wales in the most recent years for which data were available, and, wherever possible, in the preceding four years. However, the identification of differences should not be equated with discrimination, as there are many reasons why apparent disparities may exist.

Victims of Crime

The 2012/13 Crime Survey for England and Wales (CSEW) shows that adults from self-identified Mixed, Black and Asian ethnic groups were more at risk of being a victim of personal crime than adults from the White ethnic group. This has been consistent since 2008/09 for adults from a Mixed or Black ethnic group; and since 2010/11 for adults from an Asian ethnic group. Adults from a Mixed ethnic group had the highest risk of being a victim of personal crime in each year between 2008/09 and 2012/13

Homicide Victims

Homicide is a rare event, therefore, homicide victims data are presented aggregated in three-year periods in order to be able to analyse the data by ethnic appearance. The most recent period for which data are available is 2009/10 to 2011/12.

The overall number of homicides has decreased over the past three three-year periods. The number of homicide victims of White and Other ethnic appearance decreased during each of these three-year periods. However the number of victims of Black ethnic appearance increased in 2006/07 to 2008/09 before falling again in 2009/10 to 2011/12.

For those homicides where there is a known suspect, the majority of victims were of the same ethnic group as the principal suspect. However, the relationship between victim and principal suspect varied across ethnic groups. In the three-year period from 2009/10 to 2011/12, for victims of White ethnic appearance the largest proportion of principal suspects were from the victim's own family; for victims of Black ethnic appearance, the largest proportion of principal suspects were a friend or acquaintance of the victim; while for victims of Asian ethnic appearance, the largest proportion of principal suspects were strangers.

Homicide by sharp instrument was the most common method of killing for victims of White, Black and Asian ethnic appearance in the three most recent three-year periods. However, for homicide victims of White ethnic appearance hitting and kicking represented the second most common method of killing compared with shooting for victims of Black ethnic appearance, and other methods of killing for victims of Asian ethnic appearance.

Suspects

In 2011/12, a person aged ten or older, who self-identified as belonging to the Black ethnic group was six times more likely than a White person to be stopped and searched under section 1 (s1) of the Police and Criminal Evidence Act 1984 and other legislation in England and Wales; persons from the Asian or Mixed ethnic group were just over two times more likely to be stopped and searched than a White person.

Despite an increase across all ethnic groups in the number of stops and searches conducted under s1 powers between 2007/08 and 2011/12, the number of resultant arrests decreased across most ethnic groups. Just under one in ten stop and searches in 2011/12 under s1 powers resulted in an arrest in the White and Black self-identified ethnic groups, compared with 12% in 2007/08. The proportion of resultant arrests has been consistently lower for the Asian self-identified ethnic group.

In 2011/12, for those aged 10 or older, a Black person was nearly three times more likely to be arrested per 1,000 population than a White person, while a person from the Mixed ethnic group was twice as likely. There was no difference in the rate of arrests between Asian and White persons.

The number of arrests decreased in each year between 2008/09 and 2011/12, consistent with a downward trend in police recorded crime since 2004/05. Overall, the number of arrests decreased for all ethnic groups between 2008/09 and 2011/12, however arrests of suspects from the Black, Asian and Mixed ethnic groups peaked in 2010/11.

Arrests for drug offences and sexual offences increased for suspects in all ethnic groups except the Chinese or Other ethnic group between 2008/09 and 2011/12. In addition, there were increases in arrests for burglary, robbery and the other offences category for suspects from the Black and Asian ethnic groups.

Defendants

The use of out of court disposals (Penalty Notices for Disorder and cautions) decreased each year across all ethnic groups between 2008 and 2012. This decline coincided with the replacement, in April 2008, of a target to increase offences brought to justice, with one placing more emphasis on bringing serious crime to justice. The later target was subsequently removed in May 2010.

Black persons were less likely to receive an out of court disposal for an indictable offence, and more likely to be proceeded against at magistrates' court, than all other ethnic groups. This remained consistent between 2009 and 2012 despite the overall decrease in the proportion of out of court disposals of those formally dealt with by the CJS.

Fewer offenders entered the court system in 2012 compared with 2009, which is consistent with the decrease in the number of arrests across all ethnic groups. As a result, fewer offenders were sentenced overall.

The conviction ratio (the number of convictions divided by the number of people proceeded against) for indictable offences increased across all ethnic groups between 2009 and 2012, but has generally been higher for the White ethnic group compared with any other ethnic group during this period. These figures do not necessarily relate to the same persons, as someone can be convicted in a different year to that in which they were proceeded against.

Between 2009 and 2012, for indictable offences, there was a decrease across all ethnic groups in the proportion receiving community sentences. In contrast there was an increase for most ethnic groups in the proportion receiving an immediate custodial sentence for an indictable offence. The most common sentence outcome for White and Mixed ethnic group offenders was a community sentence, whilst for Black, Asian and Chinese or Other offenders the most common sentence outcome was immediate custody.

There are differences in the offence profile for which different ethnic groups are sentenced, reflecting differences in the patterns of proceedings. For offenders from the White and Mixed ethnic groups sentenced to immediate custody, the most common offence group between 2009 and 2012 was theft and handling stolen goods, while for Black and Asian offenders it was drug offences. For offenders from the Chinese or Other ethnic group, the most common offence up to 2010 was drug offences, and since 2011, has been theft and handling stolen goods.

The Average Custodial Sentence Length (ACSL) for indictable offences has been higher in all years between 2009 and 2012 for offenders from a BAME group compared with those from a White ethnic group. However, there are differences by offence group. For example, between 2009 and 2012, offenders from the Asian ethnic group had a consistently higher ACSL for theft and handling stolen goods and a consistently lower ACSL for sexual offences than offenders from both the White and Black ethnic groups. A range of offences of varying levels of seriousness are included within each offence group and differences in the ACSL may to a large extent be due to the different offences committed by different ethnic groups.

While the ACSL for drug offences decreased between 2009 and 2012, the number of offenders sentenced to immediate custody for drug offences has increased. This has coincided with a decrease in the use of cautions for drug offences over the same time period. The decline in the number of cautions for drug offences varied across ethnic groups, ranging from a decrease of 13% for the White ethnic group to a decrease of 29% for the Asian ethnic group. Since their introduction in 2009, the number of PNDs issued for the possession of cannabis2 increased across all ethnic groups. For example, there was a 29% increase to persons who self-identified as Asian.

Offenders

On 30 June 2012, the proportion of White offenders in the British national prison population was more than twice as high than in the foreign nationals prison population. Conversely, the proportion of Black and Asian offenders in the foreign national prison population was nearly three times as high as those in the British national prison population.

The proportion of offenders sentenced for particular offence groups do not always represent the prison population in the same way, as it does not reflect the length of sentence each offender must serve. For example, although in 2012 similar proportions of offenders of White and Black ethnicity were sentenced to immediate custody for sexual offences, on the 30 June 2012, the proportion of White prisoners serving a sentence for sexual offences was higher than for Black prisoners.

There were 192 deaths in prison in 2012, the same as in 2011, approximately 2.2 deaths per 1,000 prisoners in both years. There were differences across the ethnic groups; a higher rate of White offenders died in prison compared with the other ethnic groups. White offenders also represent the majority of self-harm incidents. Despite an overall decrease in the number of such incidents, in 2012 nearly nine out of ten self-harm incidents involved a White offender, while less than three quarters of the prison population self-identified as being White. In contrast, less than one in ten self-harm incidents in 2012 were by a BAME prisoner, despite this group representing one quarter of the prison population.

Practitioners

For police officers, staff and practitioners in the Crown Prosecution Service (CPS), National Offender Management Service (NOMS) and Ministry of Justice, there has been an overall reduction in the number of officers, staff or practitioners over the most recent five years (four years for the CPS). However, during this period the ethnic breakdown of staff has remained relatively stable.

[1:18] Hood, R, Shute, S and Seemungal, F, *Ethnic Minorities in the Criminal Courts: Perceptions of Fairness and Equality of Treatment*
(2003) Lord Chancellor's Department Research Series No 2/03

Executive Summary

. . .

A substantial number (778) of ethnic minority and (for comparative purposes) white defendants were interviewed at the conclusion of the criminal proceedings against them.

The study was conducted at both the Crown Court and magistrates' courts in three urban areas with high concentrations of ethnic minority citizens – Manchester, Birmingham, and South-East London. In addition, 150 witnesses were interviewed at the same courts, as well as 112 solicitors and barristers, 125 magistrates, 61 court staff, and 26 judges in the Crown Court. Those working in the courts were asked about their perceptions of how the courts deal with persons from ethnic minorities, and in particular whether this has changed over time. Altogether, 1,252 people were interviewed and the proceedings in more than 500 cases were observed.

Respondents were asked to classify their ethnicity according to the categories used in the national census of 2001 but, so as to make the findings comparable with official data on race and criminal justice, persons have, for most purposes, been classified as black, Asian or white.

It is important to emphasise that this is a study of how defendants and witnesses *interpreted* their experiences in the criminal courts. It is not an *objective* study of whether or not racial discrimination had actually taken place.

The Defendants' Perspective:

- Most of the defendants who were interviewed had just been convicted and sentenced, many to imprisonment, so their feelings may well have been running high. Very few had been acquitted. The sample therefore probably over-represented the kind of defendant who might be most likely to complain of unfair or racially biased treatment. The majority were interviewed by ethnic minority researchers. Defendants were given several opportunities to express any concerns about racial bias. For these reasons it is likely that the findings reflect 'a worst case scenario.'

- Leaving aside complaints which turned out *not* to be directed at the courts (i.e. mainly at the police and to a lesser extent the Crown Prosecution Service), the proportion of defendants who said their treatment had been unfair in court was *nearly a third* (31 per cent) in the Crown Court, with little difference between the ethnic minority and white defendants (33 per cent of black, 27 per cent of Asian and 29 per cent of white defendants).

- In the magistrates' courts *a quarter* of defendants (26 per cent) said they felt unfairly treated, a rather higher proportion among ethnic minority than among white defendants (26 per cent of black, 31 per cent of Asian and 19 per cent of white defendants).

- However, when ethnic minority defendants were asked whether they thought that their unfair treatment in court had *anything to do with their ethnicity*, a lower proportion said definitely 'YES': *one in five* of black defendants in the Crown Court and *one in ten* in the magistrates' courts, and *one in eight* Asian defendants in both the Crown Court and the magistrates' courts.

- Most of the defendants' complaints about racial bias concerned sentences perceived to be more severe than those they thought would have been imposed on a similarly placed white defendant. Very few perceived explicit racial bias in the conduct or attitude of judges or magistrates – only *three per cent* in the Crown Court and *one per cent* in the magistrates' courts. The majority thought the remarks made when their sentence had been imposed had been fair, and no complaints were made about racist remarks from the Bench.

- Neither age, country of birth, nor previous court appearances affected the propensity of defendants to complain of racial bias. But there were substantial variations between the court areas. These were not explained by the proportion sentenced to custody or the proportion of ethnic minority staff employed in the particular court.

The Witnesses' Perspective:

- *Sixteen per cent* of witnesses in the Crown Court complained of unfair treatment, almost the same proportion amongst black, white and Asian witnesses. But *none* of the 68 ethnic minority witnesses complained of *racial* bias. There were more complaints (mostly about inconvenience and feeling intimidated) in the magistrates' courts: one in five of white and Asian and 45 per cent of black witnesses; but *only seven per cent* of the 41 ethnic minority witnesses perceived the unfairness to have been *racially* motivated.
- *None* of the witnesses in either court complained of ill treatment by a judge or magistrate.

Issues of Confidence:

- In the Crown Court, black (38 per cent) and Asian defendants (34 per cent) were just as likely as white defendants (40 per cent) to say that they would *not* expect to be fairly treated next time they came to court. In the magistrates' courts, a higher proportion of black (39 per cent) and Asian (35 per cent) than white defendants (15%) said this.
- However, a much smaller proportion of *all* black and Asian defendants (seven per cent in the Crown Court and nine per cent in the magistrates' courts) believed they would be disadvantaged in the future *because of their ethnic origin*.
- Nevertheless, a considerably higher proportion of black (44 per cent in the Crown Court; 49 per cent in the magistrates' courts) than either Asian (33 per cent and 26 per cent) or white defendants (30 per cent and 16 per cent) believed that generally there was *not always* equal treatment of ethnic minority defendants by the courts.

The Perspective of Informed Observers – Court Officials and Lawyers:

- Most white (98 per cent) and Asian (71 per cent) clerks and ushers and white (69 per cent) and Asian (63 per cent) lawyers thought that there was *nowadays always* equal treatment of ethnic minorities by the courts. But the proportion was much lower among the black lawyers (43 per cent) and black staff (28 per cent).
- A higher proportion of black (30 per cent) and either white (13 per cent) or Asian (11 per cent) lawyers said they had personally witnessed incidents in court that they regarded as 'racist.'

The Judicial and Magisterial Perspective:

- All the judges and two-thirds of the magistrates interviewed had received training in ethnic awareness. Only two of the 26 judges and three of the 125 magistrates said that it had 'added nothing' or been 'unhelpful.' Yet only a few (2 judges and 11 magistrates) thought there was a need for further such training.

A Cultural Change?

- Judges mentioned that judicial attitudes and behaviour towards ethnic minority defendants had changed markedly in recent years for the better, and magistrates also reported a substantial decline in the frequency of racially inappropriate remarks. Many lawyers reported that racial bias or inappropriate language in court was becoming 'a thing of the past.'

- These positive findings, taken together with the much lower than expected proportion of defendants complaining of racial bias, may be a reflection of both general social improvements in the treatment of ethnic minorities and the specific efforts begun by the Lord Chancellor's Department in the early 1990s to heighten the awareness of all involved in the system of the need to be aware of, and guard against, racial bias.

What Still Needs to be Done?

- Although this study has revealed that the perceptions of racial bias amongst ethnic minority persons who appear before the criminal courts appear to be less widely held than in the past, the findings should not lead to complacency. The fact that one in five black and one in eight Asian defendants definitely perceived racial bias in the Crown Court, and at least one in ten in the magistrates courts, combined with the fact that black lawyers and staff were more likely to perceive racial bias than others, is sufficient cause to continue the efforts towards eliminating the vestiges of perceived unequal treatment.
- Perceptions of racial bias, more frequently held by black defendants in the Crown Court, may well arise from a belief that the disproportionately large number of black people caught up by the criminal justice and prison systems must, at least to some extent, be a reflection of racism. Every effort therefore should be made when passing sentence to demonstrate and convince defendants that no element of racial stereotyping or bias has entered into the decision.
- Among black defendants and lawyers in particular there was a belief that the authority and legitimacy of the courts, and confidence in them, would be strengthened if more personnel from ethnic minorities were seen to be playing a part in the administration of criminal justice. Indeed, in the Crown Court 31 per cent ethnic minority defendants, and in the magistrates' courts 48 per cent, said they would like more people from ethnic minorities sitting in judgment and amongst the staff of the courts. Many judges shared this view that more could be done to avoid the impression of the courts as 'white dominated institutions.'
- It should be emphasised that this research has been directed at revealing *perceptions of and beliefs about* equal treatment held by ethnic minorities who have found themselves subject to the jurisdiction of the criminal courts. It has shown that the main concern amongst the *minority* who perceived racial bias in their treatment arose from their view that the sentence imposed was more severe than a similarly placed white defendant would have received. Very few complained that they had been subjected by any court official to racist language or conduct. However, given the changing circumstances since an objective study of sentencing practices in the West Midlands in 1989 was carried out (Roger Hood, *Race and Sentencing* 1992), it is not possible to say whether that perception of differential racially biased sentencing has any basis in objective evidence.
- The findings of this study may go some way to dispelling the view that most minority ethnic defendants believe that their treatment by the courts has been racially biased. But, if it could be shown that the 'cultural change' which this study has identified has had a real impact on eliminating differential sentencing of white and ethnic minority defendants, this would further encourage the confidence of ethnic minorities in the criminal courts.

Chapter 2

The Police

Chapter Contents

In our case study, you rang the ambulance service to tell them that you had found an injured woman in the street. The ambulance crew radioed for the police to attend. This is a fairly typical scenario: in the majority of cases the police rely heavily on members of the public, and in particular on victims, to tell them about crimes. Between 75 per cent and 90 per cent of offences are brought to the attention of the police by victims, bystanders or other members of the public. The preliminary decision of the victim to report a crime may be influenced by many factors, as was mentioned in Chapter 1.

The police officer who arrives on the scene has to make several decisions. Wide discretionary powers are exercised by those at the very lowest level in the organisation: in the vast majority of cases, if a police officer chooses not to act, not to intervene, this decision will not be subject to any review. Police officers decide whether to record a crime, whether to arrest someone, whether to initiate a prosecution (or refer the case to the Crown Prosecution Service (CPS) in more serious cases), whether to release a suspect on bail, whether informally to warn or formally to caution or to issue another out-of-court disposal to an offender. Much fieldwork has been carried out in recent years to assess 'police culture' and policing in practice. A review of some of this research, and an analysis of the efficacy of the statutory and common law limits on this discretion, will be explored later in this chapter, but it may be useful to start by looking briefly at the accountability of the police in constitutional terms.

There were 127,909 full-time equivalent police officers in England and Wales in March 2014 (this is down from 143,770 in March 2009). As well as police 'officers', the Police Reform Act 2002 introduced police community support officers (PCSOs). In March 2014, there were 13,066 PCSOs in England and Wales (this, too, reflects a fall in numbers: there were 16,918 in March 2010). Their role is to provide visible reassurance as part of 'neighbourhood policing'. Originally, the Government made it clear that PCSOs would have many fewer powers than police officers, but unsurprisingly, this has now changed: section 7 of the Police and Justice Act 2006 amended the Police Reform Act to enable the Secretary of State to introduce an Order establishing a standard set of powers and duties that apply to all PCSOs. As well as these powers, PCSOs may be given additional powers by their chief constables. So the differences between PCSOs and police officers are beginning to shrink.

Far more people are employed in private security firms than are employed as police officers. As Newburn and Reiner (2004) put it, 'the police, the state financed and organised body that specialises in policing, is only one aspect – and possibly a diminishing aspect – of an ensemble of policing institutions and processes' (at page 601). What used to be seen as 'public' spaces (shopping malls, courts and nightclubs, for example) are guarded by private companies. As well, private companies provide many investigative and forensic services, and of course CCTV is largely provided by private companies. Whilst the focus of this chapter is on the role of the 'classic' police officer, students should be well aware of the extent of privatisation of policing in this country.

(i) Police accountability

The police as we know them are a modern development. Whether you conclude that they have evolved out of community-based consensus policing, or rather as agents of state control, depends on your interpretation of history. Not until the late-eighteenth century did the need for a paid police force become widely accepted. The Metropolitan Police Act 1829 gave London its first police force, nicknamed 'Peelers' or 'Bobbies' after Robert Peel, the Home Secretary. In 1856 it became compulsory for every county to have a police force. Today there are still 43 separate police forces in England and Wales. Their function continually evolves: concepts such as community policing, zero-tolerance policing, intelligence-led policing, and problem-oriented policing reflect changing police priorities (see Newburn and Reiner (2004) and (2012)), but our concern here is the governance of the police.

Their 'independence' has traditionally been valued as reflecting the fact that the police are not an arm of government. Strong 'security police' are a feature of dictatorships and totalitarian states; democratic government is seen to require something less centrally controlled. Yet the downside of this independence may be that the police are both inadequately powerful and inadequately accountable. Until 2012, they were governed by a curious tripartite structure – what Laws LJ called (in *R v DPP, ex p Duckenfield* [1999] 2 All ER 873) the 'interlocking roles' of three key players: the chief constable, the police authority and the Home Secretary.

A police force was under the direction and control of the chief constable and each police area had a police authority comprising of local councillors, magistrates and 'independent members'. The authority appointed the chief constable and had a duty under section 6 of the Police Act 1996 to 'secure the maintenance of an efficient and effective' force for its area. The elected councillor element on police authorities had been reduced from two-thirds to 'a number which is greater by one' than half, which reflected the increasingly centralised control, and five members, or up to one-third of the authority, were 'independent', but appointed from a short-list prepared by the Secretary of State.

In their manifestos for the 2010 General Election, both the Conservatives and the Liberal Democrats committed to introducing a directly elected element to police accountability (the Conservatives proposed the abolition of police authorities and their replacement with a single, elected, Police and Crime Commissioner whilst the Liberal Democrats advocated the direct election of police authorities, which would also be given greater powers). After the formation of the Coalition Government, the Home Office issued a consultation paper, *Policing in the 21st Century: Reconnecting Police and the People*, which led ultimately to the Police Reform and Social Responsibility Act 2011 **[2:1]**. This enacted the Conservatives' manifesto proposal: directly elected Police and Crime Commissioners (PCCs) were introduced to replace the police authorities (with the exception of London, where the Mayor has responsibility for policing). Under section 1, the PCC is responsible for securing 'the maintenance of the police force for that area' and ensuring that 'the police force is efficient and effective' – thus taking over the role of the old police authorities.

The first elections for PCCs, in November 2012, saw a (predictably) low turnout of just 15.1 per cent (the lowest turnout of any election in British peacetime history). However, PCCs wield real power: they are the recipient of all funding for policing in their area and have responsibility for appointing, and dismissing, the chief constable. They are responsible for delivering a five-year police and crime plan, based on local priorities developed in consultation with the chief constable, 'communities' and other partners. Yet, despite this, Lister and Rowe (2014) suggest that democratically governed policing depends on a much wider range of social, economic and political factors that do not rest on the election of a PCC alone. Whether 'democratised' policing benefits from an injection of party politics (29 out of the 41 successful candidates in 2012 were running under either a Conservative or Labour banner) is questionable and even the existence of PCCs remains highly political: Labour had proposed the abolition of PCCs in their 2015 General Election manifesto.

As we shall see, the police enjoy huge discretionary powers, and clearly this discretion needs to be controlled. What are the mechanisms of accountability? In addition to the direct line of accountability running between the PCC and the electorate, PCCs are also accountable to their local Police and Crime Panel (PCP) which is made up of elected councillors representing each local authority in the police area and at least two co-opted members. The PCP scrutinises the actions and decisions of their PCC (by, for example, reviewing the PCC's proposals for the amount of council tax people pay towards policing and considering whether they have achieved the aims in their police and crime plan) and also has a power of veto over the PCC's appointment of a new chief constable.

Another important side to police accountability is the way in which individual officers can be held to account for their decisions. This may be by the courts (criminal courts may refuse to accept evidence unlawfully obtained, for example: see **[2:13]**; or in civil courts, officers may be sued) or by internal disciplinary measures. If police priority is to catch criminals (or, to go back to Packer **[1:10]**, if they give a high priority to crime control at the expense of due process), it is vital that an internal disciplinary procedure effectively fights malpractice. The Police Act 1964 required chief officers of police to supervise all serious complaints against the police made by members of the public, and to cause them to be investigated. This procedure was widely criticised, largely for having no independent elements in the investigation process. The Police and Criminal Evidence Act 1984 (commonly known as PACE) replaced the Police Complaints Board with the Police Complaints Authority, in order that internal police investigations should be externally supervised. Nevertheless, public disquiet with a system that was both secret and not wholly independent of the police, and whereby many police officers were able to take early retirement when facing the prospect of disciplinary action, continued. The Home Affairs Select Committee Inquiry into Police Disciplinary and Complaints Procedures (1998) concluded, depressingly, that 'police complaints and disciplinary procedures are inadequate both to ensure effective management and to command public confidence'. New police discipline procedures took effect in April 1999, incorporating: the civil standard of proof; a 'fast-track' dismissal system for the most serious cases; and measures to prevent the misuse of retirements 'on medical grounds' to evade disciplinary action. This was followed by the creation, in the Police Reform Act 2002, of a new 'independent' Police Complaints Commission (IPCC), which replaced the Police Complaints Authority in 2004. Any body which is 'independent' merits careful exploration: study the reports on the IPCC website. After a considerable rise in the number of complaints in the early years of the IPCC (from 22,898 in 2004/05 to 34,310 in 2009/10), the total number of complaints has fallen more recently (down to 30,143 in 2011/12).

Complainants who prefer to bring civil proceedings against the police frequently find this route problematic. First, there is the problem of cost. Although (civil) legal aid may be available, this has been squeezed hugely in recent years (even more fiercely than criminal legal aid, discussed in Chapter 5). And then, although police authorities are vicariously liable for the wrongful actions of police constables, civil proceedings do nothing to reprimand the individual police officer. And even here, as *Hill v Chief Constable of West Yorkshire* **[2:2]** revealed, the courts remain reluctant to fetter police discretion in policing matters. There the House of Lords held that the police did not owe a general duty of care, under the tort of negligence, to individual members of the public to apprehend an unknown criminal. This attitude may change slowly over time: in *Osman v United Kingdom* (2000) 29 EHRR 245 the European Court of Human Rights (ECtHR) stated that police immunity from negligence claims was only one aspect of the public interest. Note that each of the applicants was awarded £10,000 by way of compensation. Rather than extract the decision itself, the materials at **[2:3]** and **[2:4]** reveal two very different interpretations of the ECtHR's decision. Are you convinced by Hoyano's criticisms of Lord Hoffman's analysis? More recent decisions in the domestic courts, whilst recognising that the liability of the police is not set in stone, give little encouragement to sue. In *Brooks v Commissioner of Police of the Metropolis* at **[2:5]** the House of Lords is unanimous that the police owe no duty in the law of negligence to take reasonable steps to assess whether the friend of a murder victim was a victim of crime and to accord him reasonably appropriate protection, support, assistance and treatment if he was so assessed. Do you agree with this decision? Eventually in 2006 Mr Brooks was paid £100,000 plus costs in settlement of his other claims (of false imprisonment and under the Race Relations Acts) against the police. That the police do not generally owe a duty of care in negligence was upheld again recently in *Michael and others v The Chief Constable of South Wales Police and another* [2015] UKSC 2 where the Supreme Court held that the police could not be sued for negligence when they responded with inadequate haste to a 999 call in which a woman reported that her ex-partner was going to return and kill her. Gwent Police graded the call 'G1' (meaning it required an immediate response) but this was subsequently downgraded to 'G2' by South Wales Police (meaning officers should respond within 60 minutes). In the gap between when the call would have been responded to if it had remained 'G1' and the time when the police actually arrived, the victim had been murdered.

(ii) Recording and enforcing crime

In theory, all laws are enforced, but in practice clearly some are enforced more than others. With limited operational resources, particularly in view of a 20 per cent reduction in the police budget between 2010 and 2015, the police are selective in which crimes they pursue. Thus, for example, the police give a fairly low priority to enforcing laws about obscenity – but without going so far as to refuse to act in this area – largely because the law itself is unsatisfactory, and the police choose not to waste their resources in an area where they are particularly ineffective. In other areas, the police may choose not to enforce laws which they perceive to be outdated. In effect, this gives them a power to decriminalise. A case brought over 40 years ago is still useful in illustrating the extent of police discretion **[2:6]**. Although he lost several cases, Blackburn achieved a certain publicity for his causes by initiating judicial review proceedings, and this 'political' side-effect of judicial review may sometimes be as useful to applicants as the decision itself. A more recent example is R v *Chief Constable of Sussex, ex p International Trader's Ferry Ltd* [1999] 2 AC 418, in which exporters of live animals were unsuccessful in their attempts to force the police to give them greater police protection. The case was, in the words of Lord Nolan, 'an acceptance of the plain fact that there are limits to the extent to which the police can control unlawful violence in any given situation. If those limits are felt to be too narrow, the remedy lies in increasing the resources of the police. It does not lie in the imposition of further restrictions upon the discretion which the law allows to a chief constable to decide upon the best use of the resources which are in fact available to him'. Another example is provided by R *(Mondelly) v Commissioner of the Police of the Metropolis*, decided in 2006 but cited here at **[2:7]** from the report in the Criminal Law Review in 2007 with Andrew Roberts' commentary. Given the police guidance in 2004 on arrests for simple possession of cannabis (which was reclassified as a Class C drug in 2004 before being returned to Class B in 2009), would you have taken the line of the dissenting judge?

To revert to the story with which this book began, PC Jane Green, the police officer called to the scene where the woman is found bleeding in the street, has to decide whether to record this as a crime. Here, she will undoubtedly record the incident. Individual police officers affect crime statistics by their decision to record an incident as an offence or not. A reported theft may be recorded as an incidence of lost property, or not recorded at all. Maybe the police officer does not believe the person who is reporting the crime, or perhaps it happened a long time ago or is considered insufficiently serious. A broken window might be an accident, but it might be recorded as criminal damage or even attempted burglary. The divergence between actual, reported and recorded crime was noted in Chapter 1.

What guidance does the police officer have? The police have a statutory obligation to record 'notifiable offences', which broadly cover the most serious offences. The study by Farrington and Dowds **[2:8]** shows how different police practices can have astonishing results. They established that the high official crime rate in Nottingham in the 1980s resulted largely from differential police recording of crimes. Although much has been done to try to standardise the rules for the recording of crimes by the police, different practices will inevitably continue. As politicians (and funders) use the figures as measures of police performance, and to inform the distribution of resources, a certain degree of scepticism in your approach to these figures may be warranted. Indeed, concerns with the reliability of police-recorded crime led the UK Statistics Authority, in January 2014, to 'de-designate' it as an approved measure of crime statistics.

Once reported and recorded, the likelihood of an offender being caught will be affected by the decision as to how much time and money is spent on an inquiry. Thus, in our case study, if resources allow, a police car will immediately drive around looking for a suspect escaping the scene of the crime. A suspect carrying a knife and wearing bloodied clothes, arrested on the day of the incident, will provide more compelling evidence than one arrested three days later!

(iii) Police powers

The statutory powers of the police in the investigation of crime were largely codified by the Police and Criminal Evidence Act 1984 (PACE) **[2:9]**, which was enacted as a result of the 1981 Report of the Royal Commission on Criminal Procedure. Whilst PACE has achieved some uniformity in police practice, widespread powers have been given to the police by subsequent Acts, such as the Public Order Act 1986, the Criminal Justice and Public Order Act (CJPOA) 1994, the Proceeds of Crime Act 2002, the Criminal Justice Act 2003, the Serious Organised Crime and Police Act 2005 and other statutes. Thus, PACE cannot be seen as the only code of police powers. PACE has also been amended many, many times.

PACE authorised the Secretary of State to issue Codes of Practice in connection with the exercise by police officers of their various statutory duties. The Criminal Justice Act 2003 abolished the necessity for revisions of the codes to be approved by an affirmative resolution of both Houses of Parliament: now they are simply laid before Parliament. Revised codes were brought into force in 1991 and then in 1995 to take account of new police powers contained in the CJPOA 1994. Further revisions have been made to at least one of the Codes every year in recent years. There are currently eight Codes (and all are available online):

- Code A: on the exercise of statutory powers of stop and search, and the requirements to record public encounters
- Code B: on searches of premises and the seizure of property found on premises and persons
- Code C: on the detention, treatment and questioning of suspects (not related to terrorism) in police custody by police officers
- Code D: on the identification of persons by police officers
- Code E: on audio recording of interviews
- Code F: on visual recording with sound of interviews with suspects. (There is no statutory requirement on police officers to visually record interviews. However, the contents of this code should be considered if an interviewing officer decides to make a visual recording with sound of an interview with a suspect.)
- Code G: on the statutory power of arrest by police officers
- Code H: on the detention, treatment and questioning of suspects related to terrorism in police custody by police officers.

Brown **[2:10]** reviewed the research into the first 10 years of life with PACE, concluding that PACE 'has not yet produced a system in balance'. Bucke and Brown **[2:11]** researched the 1995 changes: note in particular their comments on the quality of legal advice.

There has been considerable debate not only about the constitutional status of these Codes, but also about the capacity of legal rules to influence police conduct (see Zander (2012)). Chapter 7 includes a discussion of the trial judge's discretion to exclude evidence which was unfairly obtained. Proof of a breach of a code of practice does not necessarily lead to the exclusion of the evidence. In *Christou* **[7:11]** the Court of Appeal held that the appellants' admissions had been rightly admitted in evidence even though they had not been cautioned or informed of their rights – was the Court correct in concluding that the relevant Code was 'simply not intended to apply in such a context'? Ashworth **[2:12]** seeks to test the justifications for the use of deceptive practices by the police. (His article was published before the Human Rights Act 1998 came into force in 2000.) Since then, there have been a number of important rulings applying the Human Rights Act to police practice. *R v Loosely; A-G's Reference No 3 of 2000* **[2:13]** is one such important example. It is extracted not from the full judgment but from the Criminal Law Review summary, which includes the brief commentary by Professor David Ormerod.

Covert and intrusive surveillance are obviously important police 'tools', and tools which must be carefully monitored. They are governed by Part III of the Police Act 1997 and by the Regulation of Investigatory Powers Act 2000, which distinguishes 'directed surveillance', 'intrusive surveillance' and the use of covert human intelligence sources. The Office of Surveillance Commissioners oversees this hugely important but largely invisible area of police activity: see Chief Surveillance Commissioner Annual Reports on https://osc.independent.gov.uk. Hyland and Walker (2014) note how recent controversies regarding the infiltration and targeting of political activists have dented confidence in the police and raised legitimate public concerns – but, nonetheless, conclude that such powers are vital in the fight against serious crime and terrorism.

As well as Codes of Practice, Home Office circulars are used to control police discretion. These advise chief constables as to how particular policing tasks should be performed. For example, *R v Secretary of State for the Home Department, ex p Northumbria Police Authority* [1989] QB 26 concerned the lawfulness of a circular on the use of plastic bullets. Another example, is the practice of cautioning, which until 1999 was governed solely by Home Office circulars. It is important to recognise that such circulars do not have the force of law. Nearly 30 years ago, Baldwin and Houghton (1986) painted a highly critical picture of the growth of 'government by informal decree'. If the 'informal decree' is not obeyed, no sanction for disobedience necessarily follows. Do such documents have any effect on individual police officers? 'Police culture' is not easily changed, certainly not just by a new document from the Home Office.

Let us look at some examples of police powers. Before 1984, there were a variety of laws granting powers of stop and search. Most notorious was the Vagrancy Act 1824, which gave parish constables powers to arrest vagabonds, trespassers and loiterers. This 'sus' law was repealed in 1981, largely as a result of increasing evidence that it was being used disproportionately towards black people. The dangers of bias and prejudice within the system are clear – if police officers expect more trouble from certain individuals, the expectation can become self-fulfilling; if more attention is given to a particular section of the community, it is hardly surprising if more offences are detected amongst that group (see the data on race and criminal justice at **[1:17]**). Also, innocent people within that group will be more frequently stopped and searched. Part I of PACE **[2:9]** gave the police wide powers to stop and search, and to carry out road-checks, both of which are forms of detention short of arrest. Section 60 of CJPOA 1994 gave the police a wide new power to stop and search for offensive weapons in anticipation of violence – officers do not need to have grounds for suspicion against an individual before searching him under this power: a huge discretion to be exercised by junior officers out of the sight of senior officers. Section 1 of the Criminal Justice Act 2003 further extended the powers to stop and search by widening the definition of prohibited articles.

Many police powers are dependent upon proof of 'reasonable suspicion'. The classic definition of suspicion is that of Lord Devlin in *Hussein v Choong Fook Kam* [1970] AC 942: 'Suspicion in its ordinary meaning is a state of conjecture or surmise where proof is lacking: I suspect but I cannot prove.' The Royal Commission on Criminal Procedure (1981) concluded that it would be impracticable to formulate standards of reasonable suspicion in a statute or code of practice. It concluded (at page 29) that the requirements of notifying reasons, making records and the monitoring of such records by superior officers would be the most effective way of reducing the risk of random action. For a less complacent view, see Clayton and Tomlinson's comments on the case of *Castorina v Chief Constable of*

Surrey (1988) 138 NLJ Rep 180: 'If the police are justified in arresting a middle-aged woman of good character on such flimsy grounds, without even questioning her as to her alibi or possible motives, then the law provides very scant protection for those suspected of crime' (at page 26).

A concept so vague as 'reasonable suspicion' is almost impossible to challenge. Constables are under a duty, imposed by section 3 of PACE, to make comprehensive records of searches, and chief constables are obliged to report annually on how many, and what kinds of, stops and searches have been carried out in their force areas. Yet these figures are not a totally accurate record of how many people are being stopped, since not all searches will have been recorded (see Code A). There is also a concern that, because the exercise of stop-and-search powers can be used as a measure of a constable's industry, the pressure on officers to stop and search poorer/disadvantaged people – rather than the more affluent, who are less likely to be out in the street – will increase. In 2014, all 43 police forces in England and Wales signed up to a new Government initiative: a 'Best Use of Stop and Search Scheme' **[2:14]** which is, in part, a response to long-held concerns that ethnic minorities are disproportionately targeted by stop and search. Although it is too early to comment on the effectiveness of the scheme, it is important that the Government has acknowledged – and taken action on – something that has eroded trust between some communities and the police.

A detailed analysis of the powers of entry, search and seizure (Part II of PACE), the powers of arrest (Part III), the powers of detention (Part IV) and the powers of questioning and treatment of persons by the police (Part V) is beyond the scope of this book. However, let us apply the rules to our story. It seemed obvious to the ambulance crew that the victim had suffered four or five knife wounds to various parts of her upper body, arms and chest, which necessitated many stitches and a stay in hospital. PC Green was not able to carry out a detailed interview since the ambulance crew wanted to take the woman straight to hospital, but she did establish that the woman's name is Rosa Bottles. She was drinking in the Black Bull pub with a group of friends, and at closing time there had been a fight. She mentions a few names, and says it was Gerry Good who stabbed her. PC Green goes straight to the pub, and asks the landlord, who is just going to bed, some questions. Meanwhile, two other officers in a police car are looking for Gerry Good. However, neither the landlord nor Rosa's friends seem to have witnessed the stabbing. They seem to agree that Rosa and Gerry, two regulars at the pub, had had an argument, and that Gerry had been seen following Rosa home in a fury. Rosa has a reputation as a heavy drinker, and as a 'tough cookie' capable of looking after herself.

The next day the police are able to interview Rosa at length in hospital. They also find Gerry Good, who spent the night with friends. Rather than ask him questions, they arrest him straight away and take him to the police station for questioning. For the power to arrest, see section 24 of PACE **[2:9]**, which was radically amended by section 110 of the Serious Organised Crime and Police Act 2005. The power of arrest, like the power to stop and search, is drafted in such vague terms that it is very difficult to challenge, and attempts through the courts to challenge the legality of arrests are rarely successful. The police inform Gerry that he is under arrest on suspicion of having committed a wounding. He may be searched on arrest only as authorised within section 17 of PACE **[2:9]**. If the police are still looking for the knife used in the attack, they may well wish to search Gerry's home under section 18 or 32 **[2:9]**. If so, since Gerry has not been at his home for some hours, the police officers should obtain authority from an officer of the rank of inspector or above before entering his house.

What sort of conversation will go on in the police car taking him to the police station? There has been some concern, especially since the introduction of taped interviews at police stations, about so-called 'car-seat' confessions. In Moston and Stephenson's study **[2:15]** arresting officers reported having interviewed suspects before arrival at the station in 8 per cent of cases in the sample. In addition, 31 per cent of suspects were reported to have been questioned before their arrest. They saw strong arguments in favour of the provision of portable tape recorders, and the Royal Commission (1993) recommended that a PACE code of practice should cover what is and is not permissible between the time of arrest and arrival at the police station. Brown, Ellis and Larcombe (1992) found that, although the rewording of Code of Practice C in 1991 to discourage interviews outside police stations had had some effect, such interviews still took place in 10 per cent of cases. Do you think that interviews should only happen at police stations? And what should happen when, as the result of an interrogation (not under caution) in a police car, a suspect guides police to the remains of a woman with whom he was not previously suspected of any connection, and with whom there is no other evidence against him? This happened in the case of Christopher Halliwell in 2011 and, as this evidence was inadmissible, the CPS was unable to proceed with the prosecution for the murder (although he was convicted of a separate murder – the one for which he was being investigated when he made his surprise 'admission' to the other offence). Returning to Packer's models **[1:10]**, this outcome would clearly be anathema to the crime control model as a (presumably) guilty person escapes conviction on due process principles.

As soon as Gerry is brought to the police station, the police must open a custody record. However, the reception area at the police station is a busy, sometimes chaotic, place and he may have to wait before being booked in. The custody officer, a sergeant, is responsible for the accuracy and completeness of the custody record, and all entries must be timed and signed by the maker. It is the custody officer who has the main responsibility for upholding the suspect's rights. Is it appropriate that this person should be a serving police officer? Is there a viable alternative? When Gerry eventually leaves the police station, he (or his solicitor) will be given a copy of the custody record, if he requests it.

The custody officer will inform Gerry of his rights: he has the right to consult a solicitor; the right to ask the police to notify his arrest to a relative or other named person likely to take an interest in his welfare; and the right to consult the PACE codes of practice. Sanders, Young and Burton (2010) comment that giving the police the job of 'triggering' legal advice appears to be a major obstacle to the success of the scheme: 'if suspects need protection from the police, by what logic can custody officers be expected to provide that protection?' (at page 252). The right to legal advice is, in the words of the Court of Appeal in *Samuel* [1988] QB 615, clear and unambiguous, but it is only effective if the legal profession provides the advice adequately, and we will return to this subject in Chapter 5.

The arrangements for supervising police inquiries were criticised by the Royal Commission on Criminal Justice (1993). In a research study conducted for the Royal Commission, Baldwin and Moloney (1993) found that supervision as such was rare in most of the cases they studied. In the general run of cases, supervision and investigation were inextricably blurred, with supervising officers doing much of the interviewing. As Maguire and Norris (1993) comment, 'In a sense, the actual extent of malpractice, even if it is minuscule, is irrelevant . . . what is important is the potential for it to occur, should any officer or group of officers fail to do their job properly, and the soundness of any system designed to prevent it' (at page 3). The Royal Commission (1993) **([1:3]** and **[2:16]**) concluded that a new approach to supervision was needed throughout the police service, with improved training in the supervision of inquiries at all levels. The need for close quality control over investigations and effective supervision remains: see Brown **[2:10]**, though even this is now sadly dated: are you surprised that there is not more empirical data in this area?

The length of time that a suspect can be held in custody without charge is strictly regulated by Part IV of PACE. Detention beyond an initial 24 hours can only be authorised by a police officer of at least the rank of superintendent and detention beyond 36 hours must be authorised by a magistrate (up to a total of 96 hours). The rules are controversially different for those suspected of offences of terrorism. (The Terrorism Act 2000 allowed for seven days of pre-charge detention but this was increased to 14 days by the Criminal Justice Act 2003, then 28 days by the Terrorism Act 2006 – this in itself was a compromise as the Government initially sought to increase the maximum period of pre-charge detention in terrorism cases to 90 days. It was reduced back to 14 days by the Protection of Freedoms Act 2012.) Kemp, Balmer and Pleasence (2012) found from an analysis of custody records across 44 police stations that the average length of detention for suspects was eight hours and 55 minutes. Their findings also suggested that the time detainees spend in the police station has been increasing in recent years. A review by the custody officer to check whether the criteria for detention are still satisfied must be made at regular intervals: six hours after initial detention and then at least every nine hours. In any 24-hour period a detained person must be allowed a continuous period of at least eight hours for rest, free from questioning, travel or other interruption arising out of the investigation concerned. Police cells accommodating detainees must be adequately lit, heated, cleaned and ventilated (see Code C: The Detention, Treatment and Questioning of Persons by Police Officers). Access to toilet facilities must be provided, as well as suitable food and clothing. Despite these provisions, the student must remember that police cells and custody blocks are often dismal places.

Gerry tells the custody officer that he wants to see his solicitor, and so the custody officer rings Shaw and Co, the solicitors who have represented him in the past, and they agree to send someone. There is often no facility for private telephone calls by suspects. Ian Brown, a paralegal from Shaw and Co, arrives soon after 1pm. In a private interview, Gerry admits that he was in the Black Bull that night, that he had been involved in a fight, but that he hadn't used a knife and hadn't seen anyone else use one either. At 3pm Gerry is formally interviewed by a different police officer, since the arresting officer has now gone off duty. Ian Brown is present throughout, but says nothing. Detailed rules governing the questioning of persons held in custody are set out in Code C. The suspect must be cautioned before any questions are put for the purpose of obtaining evidence. The current caution says:

> **You do not have to say anything. But it may harm your defence if you do not mention when questioned something which you later rely on in court. Anything you do say may be given in evidence.**

False confessions and police misconduct are two of the main causes of miscarriages of justice, and much of the Report of the Royal Commission on Criminal Justice (1993) looked at ways to improve safeguards inside the police station. A whole chapter was given over to the 'right of silence' and confession evidence. The discussion of the right to silence is reproduced at **[2:16]**. The Royal Commission concluded that, because it is the less experienced and more vulnerable suspects against whom the threat of adverse comment at trial would be likely to be more damaging, there should be no adverse comments if they do not answer police questions. In reality, few suspects exercise their right to silence, and Leng's research (1993) found no evidence that the abolition of the right to silence would lead to more convictions. Zuckerman (1994) doubted that the right to silence ever protected the weak or confused: they have always been more likely to succumb to police demands for answers despite the right. Sections 34–39 of the CJPOA 1994 **[2:17]** controversially changed the law on the right to silence, setting out the circumstances when the court or the jury may draw adverse inferences from the fact that a person did not give evidence at his trial or answer questions put to him by the police. In response to the ECtHR decision in *Murray v United Kingdom* (1996) 22 EHRR 29, section 58 of the Youth Justice and Criminal Evidence Act 1999 prevents such an inference being drawn against a silent suspect who has not yet consulted a solicitor.

An important challenge to the new rules was made in the case of the Condrons, who were convicted of drug-related offences following a direction by the trial judge stating that the jury had the option of drawing an adverse inference from silence during police interviews. Their solicitor, believing them to be suffering from heroin withdrawal symptoms, had advised them to say nothing. They were found guilty and whilst the Court of Appeal in *Condron* [1997] 1 Cr App Rep 185 considered the judge's direction to be flawed, it did not find the conviction to be unsafe. However, the Condrons complained to the ECtHR, contending that they had not received a fair trial within the meaning of Article 6(1) of the European Convention on Human Rights. The ECtHR in *Condron v United Kingdom* (2001) 31 EHRR 1 allowed their application, stating that they had not received a fair trial under Article 6(1) as the jury should have been directed that, if the silence could not be attributed to the Condrons having no answer, or none that would stand up in cross-examination, no adverse inference should be drawn. The reason for the silence, if one is proffered, and its plausibility, should have been taken into account. However, this ruling has not prevented the domestic courts from taking a tough line: a series of cases from the Court of Appeal has confirmed that legal advice to remain silent cannot prevent an adverse inference being drawn under section 34 of the CJPOA 1994. Whilst at one level this makes sense (to have held otherwise would have given solicitors *carte blanche* to advise silence on all occasions, so undermining the change in the law), the current position can be highly problematic. In *Howell* [2003] EWCA Crim 1, the Court of Appeal confirmed that there must always be 'soundly based objective reasons' for silence, which makes the advisory role of the solicitor very difficult. As Lord Woolf put it in *Beckles* (No 2) [2004] EWCA Crim 2766:

> Where the reason put forward by a defendant for not answering questions is that he is acting on legal advice, the position is singularly delicate. On the one hand the Courts have not unreasonably wanted to avoid defendants driving a coach and horses through section 34 and by so doing defeating the statutory objective. Such an explanation is very easy for a defence to advance and difficult to investigate because of legal professional privilege. On the other hand, it is of the greatest importance that defendants should be able to be advised by their lawyer without their having to reveal the terms of that advice if they act in accordance with that advice (at paragraph 43).

In our case, Gerry Good is reminded of the caution, and makes admissions to the police similar to those he made earlier to the paralegal. He admits that he had an argument with Rosa Bottles earlier in the evening, when she had refused to go home with him, but continued to deny using a knife. He is very irritated at the tone of the police questioning, insisting that he is being set up. What is acceptable police practice in interviews remains unclear. There is a classic dilemma here between crime control and due process (see **[1:10]**) – tactics that will often effectively uncover the truth will elicit false confessions in other cases. However many due process safeguards are imposed on the police, 'cop culture acts as a powerful crime control engine at the heart of the machinery of criminal justice' (Sanders, Young and Burton (2010) at page 70).

It has been standard practice to tape-record interviews since 1991, but the custody officer, who in Gerry's case will decide whether to refer the case to the CPS for a charging decision, will not listen to the tape. He will rely on the version of events reported to him by the police officer who conducted the interview. At 6pm, after consultation with the CPS, Gerry is charged. The CPS accept the interviewing officer's view that there is enough evidence that it was Gerry who stabbed Rosa Bottles. As it is a serious offence, it is for the CPS to decide what Gerry should be charged with. He could be charged with an offence under section 18 (grievous bodily harm with intent), section 20 (reckless grievous bodily harm) or section 47 (actual bodily harm) of the Offences Against the Person Act 1861. There may be a degree of 'over-charging': he may be charged with section 18, in the knowledge that a lower charge can be bargained in return for a guilty plea. The Code for Crown Prosecutors **[3:5]** sets out in paragraph 6 that the charges selected should reflect the seriousness of the offending, give the court adequate sentencing powers, and enable the case to be presented in a clear and simple way.

Charging standards were introduced in 1994 in order to bring more consistency to police charging practice, but it has remained a thorny issue. There had long been concern that the police selected inappropriate charges. Auld's *Review of the Criminal Courts* **[1:5]** recommended that the CPS should assume from the police a greater responsibility for determining the charges at the outset of criminal proceedings, and this was adopted in the Criminal Justice Act 2003. The police may now only charge summary offences and either way offences anticipated as a guilty plea and suitable for sentence in a magistrates' court (except for cases involving death, terrorist activity or official secrets, hate crimes or domestic violence, and certain violent and sexual offences). All other cases must be referred to the CPS. We return to this subject in the next chapter, on the CPS.

Gerry is charged with an offence under section 18 of the Offences Against the Person Act 1861. Once he has been charged, the police may no longer ask him any questions relating to the offence, and will have to decide whether to grant him bail, discussed in section (v) below.

(iv) Out-of-court disposals

The police have a number of options when dealing with a suspect: they can take no further action (NFA); they can issue an informal warning (when no official record is made); they can issue a penalty notice for disorder (PND); they can give a simple or a 'conditional' caution; or they can charge (or discuss a prosecution with the CPS). (In the case of possession of a small amount of cannabis, consistent with personal use, they may also issue a cannabis warning – although only one such warning should be issued against any particular person.) The use of these 'out-of-court' disposals (OOCDs) has risen and then fallen dramatically in recent years. A Criminal Justice Joint Inspection (2011) report found that in 2009, 38 per cent of the 1.29 million offences 'solved' by the police were dealt with by a disposal outside the court system (which was actually a fall from 40 per cent in 2008) and they also noted that in a five-year period from 2003, the number of OOCDs administered each year increased by 135 per cent, from 241,000 in 2003 to 567,000 in 2008 (at page 9). This was despite the number of court convictions remaining stable over this period – suggesting that OOCDs were not diverting offenders from court but rather were being used to bring formal sanctions against people who would otherwise have been dealt with informally. Why would the police use OOCDs against people they might previously have dealt with informally? This brings us back to the growth of managerialism discussed in Chapter 1: the increase in the use of OOCDs in the 2000s coincided with the introduction in 2001 of a target to increase the number of offences brought to justice (someone who receives an OOCD is deemed to have been 'brought to justice' whereas those dealt with informally are not). When this target was replaced in 2008 with one focused on serious offences (which was later removed in 2010), the number of OOCDs began to decrease. Having peaked at a total of 625,229 OOCDs issued in 2007, this figured had more than halved in the year to June 2014, with 301,800 OOCDs issued (Criminal Justice Statistics Quarterly Update to June 2014 at page 9). Kemp [2:18] argues that the target had 'encouraged the police to take formal action in relation to minor offences and other "easy hits"' (at page 283).

There is relatively clear guidance issued by the Ministry of Justice relating to when the three main OOCDs (PNDs, simple cautions and conditional cautions) should be issued by the police. OOCDs are deemed to be a 'proportionate response to low level offending'. For either a simple or a conditional caution to be issued, there must be an admission of guilt by the offender and they must consent to the caution (and any conditions attached to it in the case of conditional cautions). However, for a PND to be issued (which involves the payment of a charge of £60 or £90 depending on the offence) no admission of guilt needs to be made and the payment of the fine does not amount to an admission of guilt; yet if it is for a recordable offence, an entry may be made on the Police National Computer which may be disclosed as part of an enhanced Disclosure and Barring Service check. People should always think very carefully before accepting an OOCD as they are very difficult to undo at a later date. As Hynes and Elkins (2013) note, '[f]or professionals and regulated industry workers, a caution can end a career' (at page 966) – and they rightly point out that these potentially life changing decisions are being made in highly pressured environments.

The introduction of conditional cautions by Part 3 of the Criminal Justice Act 2003 (sections 22–27) has been perhaps the most controversial development in OOCDs. These originated in the Auld Report [1:5], which proposed a 'discretionary power . . . not to prosecute, or to withdraw a prosecution, on condition (for example) that the offender submitted to some form of penalty or supervision of his conduct and/or offered some form of redress and/or submitted to medical or other treatment' (at page 381). However, in allowing a police officer to select the conditions attached to the caution (and liability for prosecution for the offence is not discharged until all conditions have been fulfilled) the concern is that the police have been handed quasi-sentencing powers. This is particularly the case since section 17 of the Police and Justice Act 2006 came into force in 2009. Originally, the conditions attached to a conditional caution had to be rehabilitative and/or reparative but the Police and Justice Act 2006 amended section 22 of the Criminal Justice Act 2003 to allow the condition to have the 'object' of 'punishing the offender'. Should the police have the power to 'punish' offenders like this – even with the person's consent? And yet, at the time of writing, we seem to be heading even farther down the road towards 'punishing' people out-of-court. In November 2014, the Ministry of Justice announced plans to end what it referred to as 'soft option' cautions and proposes replacing simple cautions with a 'community resolution' (which could include making reparation or paying financial compensation). Huge concerns also remain about the use of OOCDs in inappropriate cases – see R (Guest) v DPP [2:19] for a notable example.

PNDs were introduced by sections 1–11 of the Criminal Justice and Police Act 2001, and were rolled out nationally in 2004. In the 12 months to June 2005, 104,701 PNDs were issued: the majority for 'causing harassment, alarm or distress' (47,758 issued) or being 'drunk and disorderly' (32,925 issued). The number of PNDs issued rose steeply in the year to June 2007 (during which 192,585 were issued) before falling steadily down to 71,697 in the year to June 2014 (Criminal Justice Statistics Quarterly Update to June 2014, Table 2.1). 'Causing harassment, alarm or distress' and being 'drunk and disorderly' remain the primary offences for which PNDs are issued.

A detailed consideration of the merits and demerits of OOCDs falls beyond the scope of this book (see Padfield, Morgan and Maguire (2012)) but it is important for the student to appreciate that a large number of offenders are dealt with outside the court system and this inevitably places significant discretionary powers in the hands of police and prosecutors. Concerns about due process are no less important (indeed are probably more important) when sanctions are being applied outside the public court system.

(v) Bail

Will Gerry be granted bail? His case will not be tried for many weeks. The police will have to decide whether it will be enough merely to give him a date on which he is to appear before the court. The Bail Act 1976 [6:6] provides a statutory presumption in favour of bail, but section 38 of PACE (as amended by CJPOA 1994, section 28) [2:9] sets out the grounds on which the custody officer may keep Gerry in custody. This involves him in the impossible task of predicting risk. Until section 27 of the CJPOA 1994 inserted a new section 3A in the Bail Act 1976, the custody officer could not release someone on bail subject to conditions. This section adopted the Royal Commission on Criminal Justice (1993) recommendation that the police should have the power to release a suspect on bail subject to conditions (though not a condition that they reside at a bail hostel). This power should have reduced the suspect's liability to attend court, and a person bailed by the police in this way whom it is later decided not to charge or to prosecute may thus avoid altogether a court appearance and its attendant publicity. He is also spared the unpleasant experience of a night in the cells. The disadvantage for the suspect is that he may agree to unwarranted conditions just to get away from the police station. Bucke and Brown [2:11] found that the power to attach conditions to police bail was being used in roughly one-fifth of cases in which suspects were bailed after charge, but that there had been little reduction in the proportion detained for court. Rather, conditions are often imposed where the suspect would formerly have been given unconditional bail. The impact of these conditions on levels of offending whilst on bail are difficult to measure. In Gerry Good's case, the police are concerned that he will go back to the Black Bull and 'have a go' at all those who have mentioned him to the police. They decide, to Gerry's fury, to keep him in the cells until the morning and take him to the magistrates' court for a remand hearing. Bail applications are discussed in Chapter 6.

As far as Gerry is concerned, he has now been 'set up' by the police. He does not think they have any evidence against him. What goes on in the early stages of an investigation is clearly vital to the satisfactory conviction of offenders, but also at the root of many apparently unsafe convictions. The courts have a vital role in preventing inappropriate policing: see Chapter 7, and Ashworth (1998). It was partly a recognition of the wide discretionary powers that are wielded by the police which led to the creation in 1985 of the CPS. In the next chapter, we examine the role of the CPS and the friction that has been generated between it and the police. With decreasing resources, the police are working under increasing pressure. It is clearly essential that legal safeguards are present in the police station and not just in the courtroom: should there be greater independent scrutiny of what goes on in the police station?

Further reading

Ashworth, A, 'Should the police be allowed to use deceptive practices?' (1998) 114 *Law Quarterly Review* 108

Ashworth, A and Redmayne, M, *The Criminal Process* (4th edition, 2010) Oxford University Press

Baldwin, J and Moloney, T, *Supervision of Police Investigations in Serious Criminal Cases* (1993) RCCJ Research Study No 4, HMSO

Baldwin, R and Houghton, J, 'Circular arguments: the status and legitimacy of administrative rules' [1986] *Public Law* 239

Brown, D, Ellis, T and Larcombe, K, *Changing the Code: Police Detention under the Revised Codes of Practice* (1992) HORS No 129, HMSO

Bucke, T, Street, R and Brown, D, 'The Right to Silence: The Impact of the Criminal Justice and Public Order Act 1994' (2000) HORS No 199, HMSO

Cape, E, 'PACE then and now: Twenty-one years of "rebalancing"' in Cape, E and Young, R (eds), *Regulating Policing: The Police and Criminal Evidence Act 1984 Past, Present and Future* (2008) Hart Publishing

Cooper, C, Anscombe, J, Avenell, J, McLean, F and Morris, J, 'A national evaluation of Community Support Officers' (2006) HORS No 297

Cotton, J and Povey, D, 'Police Complaints and Discipline, England and Wales, April 1997 to March 1998' (1998) HORS Issue 20/1998, HMSO

Criminal Justice Joint Inspection (2011) *Exercising Discretion: The Gateway to Justice*

Gleeson, E and Grace, K, 'Police complaints: statistics for England and Wales 2006/07', IPCC Research and Statistics Series: Paper 8

Hyland, K and Walker, C, 'Undercover policing and underwhelming laws' [2014] Crim LR 555

Hynes, P and Elkins, M, 'Suggestions for reform to the police cautioning procedure' [2013] Crim LR 966

Kemp, V, Balmer, N J and Pleasence, P, 'Whose time is it anyway? Factors associated with duration in police custody' [2012] Crim LR 736

Leng, R, 'The right to silence in police interrogation' (1993) RCCJ Research Study No 10, HMSO

Lister, S and Rowe, M, 'Electing police and crime commissioners in England and Wales: prospecting for the democratisation of policing (2014) *Policing and Society*, Online Access

Macpherson, W, 'The Stephen Lawrence Inquiry' (1999) Cm 4262–1, HMSO

Maguire, M and Corbett, C, *A Study of the Police Complaints System* (1991) HMSO

Maguire, M and Norris, C, 'The conduct and supervision of criminal investigations' (1993) RCCJ Research Study No 5, HMSO

Morgan, D and Stephenson, G, *Suspicion and Silence: the Right to Silence in Criminal Investigations* (1994) Blackstone

Newburn, T, *Handbook of Policing* (2nd edition, 2008) Willan

Newburn, T and Reiner, R, 'PC Dixon to Dixon PLC: policing and policing powers since 1954' [2004] Crim LR 601

Newburn, T and Reiner, R, 'Policing and the police' in Maguire, M, Morgan, R and Reiner, R (eds), *The Oxford Handbook of Criminology* (5th edition, 2012) Oxford University Press

Office of Surveillance Commissioners Annual Reports, HMSO

Padfield, N, Morgan, R and Maguire, M, 'Out of court, out of sight? Criminal sanctions and non-judicial decision-making' in Maguire, M, Morgan, R and Reiner, R (eds), *The Oxford Handbook of Criminology* (5th edition, 2012) Oxford University Press

Report of the Royal Commission on Criminal Procedure (1981) Cmnd 8092

Rowe, M (ed), *Policing beyond Macpherson* (2007) Willan

Sanders, A, Young, R and Burton, M, *Criminal Justice* (4th edition, 2010) Oxford University Press

Walker, C and Starmer, K, *Justice in Error* (Chapters 1–4) (1993) Blackstone

Zander, M, 'The Revised PACE Codes' (2003) 3 *Archbold News* 5

Zander, M, 'If the PACE Codes are not law, why do they have to be followed?' (2012) *Criminal Law and Justice Weekly*, 30 November

Zander, M, *The Police and Criminal Evidence Act 1984* (6th edition, 2013) Sweet & Maxwell

Zuckerman, A, 'The inevitable demise of the right to silence' (1994) 144 *New Law Journal* 1104

Documents

[2:1] Police Reform and Social Responsibility Act 2011
Sections 1–8

Part 1 Police reform

Chapter 1 Police areas outside London

1 Police and crime commissioners

(1) There is to be a police and crime commissioner for each police area listed in Schedule 1 to the Police Act 1996 (police areas outside London).

(2) A police and crime commissioner is a corporation sole.

(3) The name of the police and crime commissioner for a police area is "the Police and Crime Commissioner for" with the addition of the name of the police area.

(4) The police and crime commissioner for a police area is to be elected, and hold office, in accordance with Chapter 6.

(5) A police and crime commissioner has –

    (a) the functions conferred by this section,

    (b) the functions relating to community safety and crime prevention conferred by Chapter 3, and

    (c) the other functions conferred by this Act and other enactments.

(6) The police and crime commissioner for a police area must –

(a) secure the maintenance of the police force for that area, and
(b) secure that the police force is efficient and effective.

(7) The police and crime commissioner for a police area must hold the relevant chief constable to account for the exercise of –

(a) the functions of the chief constable, and
(b) the functions of persons under the direction and control of the chief constable.

(8) The police and crime commissioner must, in particular, hold the chief constable to account for –

(a) the exercise of the duty under section 8(2) (duty to have regard to police and crime plan);
(b) the exercise of the duty under section 37A(2) of the Police Act 1996 (duty to have regard to strategic policing requirement);
(c) the exercise of the duty under section 39A(7) of the Police Act 1996 (duty to have regard to codes of practice issued by Secretary of State);
(d) the effectiveness and efficiency of the chief constable's arrangements for co-operating with other persons in the exercise of the chief constable's functions (whether under section 22A of the Police Act 1996 or otherwise);
(e) the effectiveness and efficiency of the chief constable's arrangements under section 34 (engagement with local people);
(f) the extent to which the chief constable has complied with section 35 (value for money);
(g) the exercise of duties relating to equality and diversity that are imposed on the chief constable by any enactment;
(h) the exercise of duties in relation to the safeguarding of children and the promotion of child welfare that are imposed on the chief constable by sections 10 and 11 of the Children Act 2004.

(9) The police authorities established for police areas under section 3 of the Police Act 1996 are abolished.

(10) Schedule 1 (police and crime commissioners) has effect.

2 Chief constables

(1) Each police force is to have a chief constable.

(2) The chief constable of a police force is to be appointed, and hold office, in accordance with –

(a) section 38, and
(b) the terms and conditions of the appointment.

(3) A police force, and the civilian staff of a police force, are under the direction and control of the chief constable of the force.

(4) A chief constable has the other functions conferred by this Act and by other enactments.

(5) A chief constable must exercise the power of direction and control conferred by subsection (3) in such a way as is reasonable to assist the relevant police and crime commissioner to exercise the commissioner's functions.

(6) Subsection (3) is subject to any provision included in a collaboration agreement (see section 22A of the Police Act 1996).

(7) Schedule 2 (chief constables) has effect.

(8) In this section "police force" means the police force for a police area listed in Schedule 1 to the Police Act 1996 (see section 2 of that Act).

Chapter 2 Metropolitan police district

3 Mayor's Office for Policing and Crime

(1) There is to be a body with the name "The Mayor's Office for Policing and Crime" for the metropolitan police district.

(2) The Mayor's Office for Policing and Crime is a corporation sole.

(3) The person who is Mayor of London for the time being is to be the occupant for the time being of the Mayor's Office for Policing and Crime.

(4) Accordingly, where a person is the occupant of the Mayor's Office for Policing and Crime by virtue of a particular term of office as Mayor of London (the "relevant mayoral term"), the person's term as the occupant of the Mayor's Office for Policing and Crime –

  (a)   begins at the same time as the relevant mayoral term, and
  (b)   ends at the same time as the relevant mayoral term.

(5) The Mayor's Office for Policing and Crime has –

  (a)   the functions conferred by this section,
  (b)   the functions relating to community safety and crime prevention conferred by Chapter 3, and
  (c)   the other functions conferred by this Act and other enactments.

(6) The Mayor's Office for Policing and Crime must –

  (a)   secure the maintenance of the metropolitan police force, and
  (b)   secure that the metropolitan police force is efficient and effective.

(7) The Mayor's Office for Policing and Crime must hold the Commissioner of Police of the Metropolis to account for the exercise of –

  (a)   the functions of the Commissioner, and
  (b)   the functions of persons under the direction and control of the Commissioner.

(8) The Mayor's Office for Policing and Crime must, in particular, hold the Commissioner to account for –

(a) the exercise of the duty imposed by section 8(4) (duty to have regard to police and crime plan);
(b) the exercise of the duty under section 37A(2) of the Police Act 1996 (duty to have regard to strategic policing requirement);
(c) the exercise of the duty imposed by section 39A(7) of the Police Act 1996 (duty to have regard to codes of practice issued by Secretary of State);
(d) the effectiveness and efficiency of the Commissioner's arrangements for co-operating with other persons in the exercise of the Commissioner's functions (whether under section 22A of the Police Act 1996 or otherwise);
(e) the effectiveness and efficiency of the Commissioner's arrangements under section 34 (engagement with local people);
(f) the extent to which the Commissioner has complied with section 35 (value for money);
(g) the exercise of duties relating to equality and diversity imposed on the Commissioner by any enactment;
(h) the exercise of duties in relation to the safeguarding of children and the promotion of child welfare that are imposed on the Commissioner by sections 10 and 11 of the Children Act 2004.

4 Commissioner of Police of the Metropolis

(1) There is to be a corporation sole with the name "the Commissioner of Police of the Metropolis".

(2) The Commissioner of Police of the Metropolis is to be appointed, and hold office, in accordance with –

(a) sections 42 and 48, and
(b) the terms and conditions of the appointment.

(3) The metropolitan police force, and the civilian staff of the metropolitan police force, are under the direction and control of the Commissioner of Police of the Metropolis.

(4) The Commissioner of Police of the Metropolis has the other functions conferred by this Act and by other enactments.

(5) The Commissioner of Police of the Metropolis must exercise the power of direction and control conferred by subsection (3) in such a way as is reasonable to assist the Mayor's Office for Policing and Crime to exercise that Office's functions.

(6) Subsection (3) is subject to any provision included in a collaboration agreement (see section 22A of the Police Act 1996).

(7) Schedule 4 (Commissioner of Police of the Metropolis) has effect.

Chapter 3 Functions of elected local policing bodies etc

5 Police and crime commissioners to issue police and crime plans

(1) The police and crime commissioner for a police area must issue a police and crime plan within the financial year in which each ordinary election is held.

(2) A police and crime commissioner must comply with the duty under subsection (1) as soon as practicable after the commissioner takes office.

(3) A police and crime commissioner may, at any time, issue a police and crime plan.

(4) A police and crime commissioner may vary a police and crime plan.

(5) In issuing or varying a police and crime plan, a police and crime commissioner must have regard to the strategic policing requirement issued by the Secretary of State under section 37A of the Police Act 1996.

(6) Before issuing or varying a police and crime plan, a police and crime commissioner must –

    (a)   prepare a draft of the plan or variation,
    (b)   consult the relevant chief constable in preparing the draft plan or variation,
    (c)   send the draft plan or variation to the relevant police and crime panel,
    (d)   have regard to any report or recommendations made by the panel in relation to the draft plan or variation (see section 28(3)),
    (e)   give the panel a response to any such report or recommendations, and
    (f)   publish any such response.

(7) In complying with subsection (6)(c), the police and crime commissioner must ensure that the relevant police and crime panel has a reasonable amount of time to exercise its functions under section 28(3).

(8) A police and crime commissioner must consult the relevant chief constable before issuing or varying a police and crime plan if, and to the extent that, the plan or variation is different from the draft prepared in accordance with subsection (6).

(9) A police and crime commissioner must –

    (a)   keep the police and crime plan under review, and
    (b)   in particular, review the police and crime plan in the light of –
        (i)   any report or recommendations made to the commissioner by the relevant police and crime panel under section 28(4), and
        (ii)   any changes in the strategic policing requirement issued by the Secretary of State under section 37A of the Police Act 1996;

and exercise the powers under subsection (3) or (4) accordingly.

(10) A police and crime commissioner who issues or varies a police and crime plan must –

    (a)   send a copy of the issued plan, or the variation, to the relevant chief constable and to each of the other persons and bodies that are, for the purposes of section 5 of the Crime and Disorder Act 1998, responsible authorities in relation to local government areas that are wholly or partly within the relevant police area, and
    (b)   publish a copy of the issued plan, or the variation.

(11) The duty under subsection (10) to send or publish a copy of the variation may instead be satisfied by sending or publishing a copy of the plan as varied.

(12) It is for the commissioner to determine the manner in which –

    (a)   a response to a report or recommendations is to be published in accordance with subsection (6)(f), and
    (b)   a copy of the plan or variation is to be published in accordance with subsection (10)(b).

(13) In this section –

"financial year" means the financial year of the police and crime commissioner;

"ordinary election", in relation to the police and crime commissioner for a police area, means an election held under section 50 in relation to that area.

6 Mayor's Office for Policing and Crime to issue police and crime plans

(1) The Mayor's Office for Policing and Crime must issue a police and crime plan within the financial year in which each ordinary election is held.

(2) The Mayor's Office for Policing and Crime must comply with the duty under subsection (1) as soon as practicable after the person elected in the ordinary election takes office.

(3) The Mayor's Office for Policing and Crime may, at any time, issue a police and crime plan.

(4) The Mayor's Office for Policing and Crime may vary a police and crime plan.

(5) In issuing or varying a police and crime plan, the Mayor's Office for Policing and Crime must have regard to the strategic policing requirement issued by the Secretary of State under section 37A of the Police Act 1996.

(6) Before issuing or varying a police and crime plan, the Mayor's Office for Policing and Crime must –

   (a) prepare a draft of the plan or variation,
   (b) consult the Commissioner of Police of the Metropolis in preparing the draft plan or variation,
   (c) send the draft plan or variation to the police and crime panel of the London Assembly (see section 32),
   (d) have regard to any report or recommendations made by the panel in relation to the draft plan or variation (see section 33(1)),
   (e) give the panel a response to any such report or recommendations, and
   (f) publish any such response.

(7) In complying with subsection (6)(c), the Mayor's Office for Policing and Crime must ensure that the police and crime panel has a reasonable amount of time to exercise its functions under section 33(1).

(8) The Mayor's Office for Policing and Crime must consult the Commissioner of Police of the Metropolis before issuing or varying a police and crime plan if, and to the extent that, the plan or variation is different from the draft prepared in accordance with subsection (6).

(9) The Mayor's Office for Policing and Crime must –

   (a) keep the police and crime plan under review, and
   (b) in particular, review the police and crime plan in the light of any changes in the strategic policing requirement issued by the Secretary of State under section 37A of the Police Act 1996;

and exercise the powers under subsection (3) or (4) accordingly.

7 Police and crime plans

(1) A police and crime plan is a plan which sets out, in relation to the planning period, the following matters –

(a) the elected local policing body's police and crime objectives;
(b) the policing of the police area which the chief officer of police is to provide;
(c) the financial and other resources which the elected local policing body is to provide to the chief officer of police for the chief officer to exercise the functions of chief officer;
(d) the means by which the chief officer of police will report to the elected local policing body on the chief officer's provision of policing;
(e) the means by which the chief officer of police's performance in providing policing will be measured;
(f) any grants which the elected local policing body is to make under that section, and the conditions (if any) subject to which any such grants are to be made.

(2) The elected local policing body's police and crime objectives are the body's objectives for –

(a) the policing of the body's area,
(b) crime and disorder reduction in that area, and
(c) the discharge by the relevant police force of its national or international functions.

(3) A police and crime plan has effect from the start of the planning period until –

(a) the end of that planning period, or
(b) if another police and crime plan is issued in relation to the elected local policing body's area before the end of that planning period, the day when that other plan first has effect.

(4) The Secretary of State may give guidance to elected local policing bodies about the matters to be dealt with in police and crime plans.

(5) An elected local policing body must have regard to such guidance.

(6) Before giving guidance under subsection (4) the Secretary of State must consult –

(a) such persons as appear to the Secretary of State to represent the views of police and crime commissioners,
(b) the Mayor's Office for Policing and Crime,
(c) such persons as appear to the Secretary of State to represent the views of chief officers of police, and
(d) such other persons as the Secretary of State thinks fit.

8 Duty to have regard to police and crime plan

(1) A police and crime commissioner must, in exercising the functions of commissioner, have regard to the police and crime plan issued by the commissioner.

(2) The chief constable of the police force for a police area listed in Schedule 1 to the Police Act 1996 must, in exercising the functions of chief constable, have regard to the police and crime plan issued by the police and crime commissioner for that police area.

(3) The Mayor's Office for Policing and Crime must, in exercising the functions of the Office, have regard to the police and crime plan issued by the Office.

(4) The Commissioner of Police of the Metropolis must, in exercising the functions of Commissioner, have regard to the police and crime plan issued by the Mayor's Office for Policing and Crime.

(5) The Secretary of State may give guidance to a person subject to a duty under this section about how that duty is to be complied with.

(6) A person given such guidance must have regard to the guidance.

(7) Before giving guidance under subsection (5) the Secretary of State must consult –

(a) such persons as appear to the Secretary of State to represent the views of police and crime commissioners,
(b) the Mayor's Office for Policing and Crime,
(c) such persons as appear to the Secretary of State to represent the views of chief officers of police, and
(d) such other persons as the Secretary of State thinks fit.

[2:2] *Hill v Chief Constable of West Yorkshire*
[1988] 2 All ER 238

Between 1969 and 1980 Peter Sutcliffe (the 'Yorkshire Ripper') committed a series of 13 murders and eight attempted murders. The mother of his last murder victim sued under section 48(1) of the Police Act 1964, claiming damages against the chief constable in whose area most of the offences took place. Her claim was struck out on the ground that the police owed no duty of care to a member of the public who suffered injury through the activities of a criminal.

The House of Lords dismissed her appeal. Having held that no duty of care was owed to members of the public, Lord Keith stated (at page 243):

In my opinion there is another reason why an action for damages in negligence should not lie against the police in circumstances such as those of the present case, and that is public policy.

The general sense of public duty which motivates police forces is unlikely to be appreciably reinforced by the imposition of such liability so far as concerns their function in the investigation and suppression of crime. From time to time they make mistakes in the exercise of that function, but it is not to be doubted that they apply their best endeavours to the performance of it. In some instances the imposition of liability may lead to the exercise of a function being carried on in a detrimentally defensive frame of mind. The possibility of this happening in relation to the investigative operations of the police cannot be excluded. Further, it would be reasonable to expect that if potential liability were to be imposed it would be not uncommon for actions to be raised against police forces on the result that he went on to commit further crimes. Whilst such actions might involve allegations of a simple and straightforward types of failure, for example that a police officer negligently tripped and fell while pursuing a burglar, others would be likely to enter deeply into the general nature of a police investigation, as indeed the present action would seek to do. The manner of conduct of such an investigation must necessarily involve a variety of decisions to be made on matters of policy and discretion, for example as to which particular line of inquiry is most advantageously to be pursued and what is the most advantageous way to deploy the available resources. Many such decisions would not be regarded by the courts as appropriate to be called in question, yet elaborate investigation of the facts might be necessary to ascertain whether or not this was so. A great deal of police time, trouble and expense might be expected to have to be put into the preparation of the defence to the action and the attendance of witnesses at the trial. The result would be a significant diversion of police manpower and attention from their most important function, that of the suppression of crime. Closed investigations would require to be reopened and retraversed not with the object of bringing any criminal to justice but to ascertain whether or not they had been competently conducted. I therefore consider that Glidewell LJ, in his judgment in the Court of Appeal in the present case, was right to take the view that the police were immune from an action of this kind on grounds similar to those which in *Rondel v Worsley* were held to render a barrister immune from actions for negligence in his conduct of proceedings in court (see [1987] 1 All ER at 1183, [1988] QB 60 at 76). My Lords, for these reasons I would dismiss the appeal.

Lord Templeman (at page 244):

My Lords, the appellant, Mrs Hill, is tormented with the unshakeable belief that her daughter would be alive today if the respondent, the West Yorkshire police force, had been more efficient. That belief is entitled to respect and understanding. Damages cannot compensate for the brutal extinction of a young life and the appellant proposes that any damages awarded shall be devoted to an appropriate charity. Damages awarded by the court would not be paid by any policeman found wanting in the performance of his duty but would be paid by the public. The appellant therefore brings these proceedings with the object of obtaining an investigation into the conduct of the West Yorkshire police force so that lives shall not be lost in the future by avoidable delay in the identification and arrest of a murderer.

The question for determination in this appeal is whether an action for damages is an appropriate vehicle for investigating the efficiency of a police force. The present action will be confined to narrow albeit perplexing questions, for example whether, discounting hindsight, it should have been obvious to a senior police officer that Sutcliffe was a prime suspect, whether a senior police officer should not have been deceived by an evil hoaxer, whether an officer interviewing Sutcliffe should have been better briefed and whether a report on Sutcliffe should have been given greater attention. The court would have to consider the conduct of each police officer, to decide whether the policeman failed to attain the standard of care of a hypothetical average policeman. The court would have to decide whether an inspector is to be condemned for being as obtuse as Dr Watson. The appellant will presumably seek evidence, for what it is worth, from retired police inspectors, who would be asked whether they would have been misled by the hoaxer and whether they would have identified Sutcliffe at an earlier stage. At the end of the day the court might or might not find that there had been negligence by one or more.

It may be, and we all hope that the lessons of the Yorkshire Ripper case have been learned, that the methods of handling information and handling the press have been improved, and that co-operation between different police officers is now more highly organised. The present action would not serve any useful purpose in that regard. The present action could not consider whether the training of the West Yorkshire police force is sufficiently thorough, whether the selection of candidates for appointment or promotion is defective, whether rates of pay are sufficient to attract recruits of the required calibre, whether financial restrictions prevent the provision of modern equipment and facilities or whether the Yorkshire police force is clever enough and, if not, what can and ought to be done about it. The present action could only investigate whether an individual member of the police force conscientiously carrying out his duty was negligent when he was bemused by contradictory information or overlooked significant information or failed to draw inferences which later appeared to be obvious. That kind of investigation would not achieve the object which the appellant desires. The efficiency of a police force can only be investigated by an inquiry instituted by the national or local authorities which are responsible to the electorate for that efficiency.

Moreover, if this action lies, every citizen will be able to require the court to investigate the performance of every policeman. If the policeman concentrates on one crime, he may be accused of neglecting others. If the policeman does not arrest on suspicion a suspect with previous convictions, the police force may be held liable for subsequent crimes. The threat of litigation against a police force would not make a policeman more efficient. The necessity for defending proceedings, successfully or unsuccessfully, would distract the policeman from his duties.

This action is in my opinion misconceived and will do more harm than good. A policeman is a servant of the public and is liable to be dismissed for incompetence. A police force serves the public, and the elected representatives of the public must ensure that the public get the police force they deserve. It may be that the West Yorkshire police force was in 1980 in some respects better and in some respects worse than the public deserve. An action for damages for alleged acts of negligence by individual police officers in 1980 could not determine whether and in what respect the West Yorkshire police force can be improved in 1988. I would dismiss the appeal.

[2:3] Lord Hoffman, 'Human Rights and the House of Lords'
(1999) 62 MLR 159 (at page 162)

We have had a very recent example of a decision of the Strasbourg court giving an interpretation to the Convention which, I venture to suggest, it is inconceivable that any domestic court in this country would have adopted. I want to use this decision as an example of the potential conflict between our legal system under the new regime and the jurisprudence emanating from Strasbourg.

On 28 October 1998, judgment was given in the case of *Osman v United Kingdom*. Mrs Osman's husband had been shot and killed by an insane teacher who had formed an obsessional attachment to their young son at school. She sued the police for damages, alleging that they had been warned that the man was a danger to her family but had not taken adequate steps to protect them. The Court of Appeal struck out the action on the ground that the police could not be made liable in negligence for failing to take action in the investigation or suppression of crime. The decision was based upon the Yorkshire Ripper case, *Hill v Chief Constable of West Yorkshire*, in which the House of Lords held that the imposition of a duty of care in such circumstances would be contrary to public policy. The maintenance of police efficiency was better secured by other methods than having the question of whether they had acted reasonably in a given case expensively investigated in civil proceedings at the instance of a private litigant, with the possibility of compensation having to be paid out of the police budget. The prospect of such an investigation and the payment of compensation might in fact be detrimental to good policing, since it might make the police defensively unwilling to take risks. Furthermore, the efficiency with which the police handled a particular investigation often depended upon the share of their resources which was devoted to that kind of investigation and questions about the allocation of resources by public authorities such as the police were not suitable for determination by judges.

Persons who suffer criminal damage have no claim to compensation solely on the ground that it could have been prevented by more efficient policing. This decision is in line with a number of recent cases on the failure of public authorities to deliver services which could have prevented loss, such as *X (Minors) v Bedford County Council* on social services, *Stovin v Wise* on highway improvements, *Capital and Counties plc v Hampshire County Council* on fire services, *O'Rourke v Camden LBC* on housing the homeless, and *Murphy v Brentwood LBS* on building inspection services. The theme which runs through these cases is that the fact that public services are provided at the public expense to confer benefits or protection on members of the public does not mean that a person who fails to receive those benefits or protection will be entitled to sue for compensation on the ground that the authority acted negligently in failing to provide them. The social justification for such a rule is that, on the one hand, the person who has failed to receive the benefit is no worse off than if it had not been provided in the first place, and on the other hand, the budgetary and efficiency grounds discussed in *Hill v Chief Constable of West Yorkshire*.

Not everyone would agree with such a rule. Some might think that it shows a somewhat niggardly attitude to people who have suffered loss because they had the misfortune not to receive some public benefit which they were reasonably entitled to expect, and that the allocation of funds for public services should budget not merely for providing the services but also for compensating those who did not receive them. It might also be said that the law is inconsistent in excluding liability in such cases but making public authorities liable when they enter into relationships which have long been recognised as giving rise to a duty of care in private law, such as between a doctor or hospital and a patient. For my part, I see no inconsistency, but I recognise that the merits of the rule are open to political debate, the question being essentially one about the obligations of the welfare state.

Mrs Osman, however, petitioned the European Court of Human Rights on the ground that the rejection of her claim was a denial of her fundamental human right under Article 6(1) of the Convention, which provides that 'in the determination of his civil rights and obligations, everyone is entitled to a hearing by a tribunal'. One might be forgiven for thinking that Mrs Osman's rights had been determined, rightly or wrongly, by a tribunal. She had been before the Court of Appeal and they had decided that even if all the allegations in her statement of claim were proved at the trial to be true, she would not be entitled under English domestic law to compensation from the police. But the Court, consisting of 17 judges including one from the United Kingdom, decided unanimously that because her action had not been allowed to proceed to trial, she had not had a hearing. What, you may ask, would be the point of a hearing which, under English law, was bound to end in the claim being dismissed? The answer, according to the European Court, was that it should not have been treated as bound to be dismissed. There should have been the possibility that on the facts alleged, Mrs Osman would win. A rule that in no circumstances should a person be able to claim compensation on the ground that the police failed to protect him from criminal injury was not proportionate to the public policy grounds advanced in its support. In other words, English domestic law failed to provide compensation out of public funds in cases in which the Strasbourg court thought it should do so.

I am not sure, on a reading of the judgment of the court and the concurring judgment of the British judge, whether they had persuaded themselves that they were really dealing with the right to a hearing rather than the merits of the substantive tort law under which the Court of Appeal had held that Mrs Osman was bound to lose. In my view, there is no disguising the fact that the case was about the latter.

I am bound to say that this decision fills me with apprehension. Under the cover of an Article which says that everyone is entitled to have his civil rights and obligations determined by a tribunal, the European Court of Human Rights is taking upon itself to decide what the content of those civil rights should be. In so doing, it is challenging the autonomy of the courts and indeed the Parliament of the United Kingdom to deal with what are essentially social welfare questions involving budgetary limits and efficient public administration. I say the Parliament of the United Kingdom because it must follow from the decision of the Strasbourg court that even if the rule in *Hill v Chief Constable of West Yorkshire* had formed part of the Police Act 1996, it would have been held to contravene the right in art. 6(1) to a hearing before a tribunal. I understand that a petition by the unsuccessful plaintiffs in *X (Minors) v Bedfordshire County Council* is already on its way and no doubt there are other cases in which the same general principle will be challenged. The whole English jurisprudence on the liability of public authorities for failure to deliver public services is open to attack on the grounds that it violates the right to a hearing before a tribunal. And although the Strasbourg court appears to contemplate the possibility that after a hearing of the facts, the court might still come to the conclusion that on grounds of public policy the claim should be dismissed, it ignores one of the principle reasons for the present doctrine, which is to avoid a trial altogether, to avoid the waste of public resources involved in a judicial investigation, usually on legal aid, as to whether the public authority should reasonably have provided the benefit or not.

It may be that the court did not understand the rather formulaic reasoning by which English courts say that no duty of care exists when they mean that the case is one in which the law does not recognise a right to compensation. It may be that they did not understand the principle by which an action is struck out without going to trial if proof of all the facts alleged would not sustain a cause of action. Either way, the case serves to reinforce the doubts I have had for a long time about the suitability, at least for this country, of having questions of human rights determined by an international tribunal made up of judges from many countries.

I would not like anyone to think that this view reflected a vulgar Euroscepticism. When it comes to questions of a common currency and a large number of other economic and social issues, the advantages and disadvantages of a common European position are matters for pragmatic decision on which one has to weigh up the evidence as best one can. I do not regard national sovereignty on every issue as either possible or desirable. But the international adjudication of questions of human rights goes much deeper because it raises an ancient question about the universality of human values. It brings into focus the conflict between the universalist philosophy of the French enlightenment, who thought that French concepts of *liberté, égalité, fraternité* were derived from our common humanity and could therefore be applied world-wide, and pluralist views such as those of that each community had its own set of values, different but not better or worse than those of other communities.

Voltaire said that morality was the same in all civilised nations. This is a half truth; of course we share a common humanity and there are some forms of behaviour such as torture which we all either reject or are unwilling to acknowledge. But even this is not inherent in civilisation: in the law of ancient Rome, the evidence of slaves was always taken under torture and none of the great Roman lawyers who developed the elaborate and sophisticated system, which forms the basis of law through so much of the world, seems to have thought this inhuman. Of course, I applaud the patient efforts of the human rights movement since the Second World War to promote the acceptance of basic human rights throughout the world. I am well aware that there are countries which deny their citizens basic human rights and which claim to be justified on grounds of cultural diversity, when the true reasons are the power and greed of their rulers. Nevertheless, I say that Voltaire's remark was only half true and that in a confident democracy such as the United Kingdom the other half is important. We do have our own hierarchy of moral values, our own culturally-determined sense of what is fair and unfair, and I think it would be wrong to submerge this under a pan-European jurisprudence of human rights.

The problem about the hierarchy of rights is not the conflict between good and evil but the conflict between good and good. Free speech is a good thing; justice is a good thing, but there are cases in which free speech and justice come into conflict with each other. For example, the law that preserves the anonymity of rape victims is an infringement of the freedom of the press, but it assists justice by encouraging women to make complaints against rapists. How then are these two desirable objectives – free speech and justice – to be reconciled with each other? There is no right answer to that question; any choice involves some degree of sacrifice. But in my view, the specific answers, the degree to which weight is given to one desirable objectives rather than another, will be culturally determined. Different communities will, through their legislatures and judges, adopt the answers which they think suit them. So the Supreme Court of the United States has ruled a State law which gave anonymity to rape victims to be unconstitutional as infringing the First Amendment right to freedom of the press, whereas such laws exist in the United Kingdom and other countries. The Supreme Court of the United States attaches what other communities may regard as an exaggerated value to the First Amendment and no doubt they think we do not respect it enough. But the difference in the answers given to the perennial conflict between goals which everyone accepts to be good shows how impractical it would be to subject the United States and the United Kingdom to a common court of human rights. If this is true of two countries so closely bound together in culture, law and history, how much more true must it be of the disparate collection of states, some old democracies, some former police states, which belong to the Council of Europe.

Of course it is true that to some extent the Strasbourg court acknowledges the fact that often there is no right answer by allowing what it calls a 'margin of appreciation' to the legislature or courts of a member State. Within limits, they are allowed to differ. And, as I have said, I accept that there is an irreducible minimum of human rights which must be universally true. But most of the jurisprudence which comes out of Strasbourg is not about the irreducible minimum. These questions tend to come into play at a point when civil society itself is called into question; they are far from the normal currency of dispute over competing values in a democracy like the United Kingdom. The *Osman* case, dealing with the substantive civil law right to financial compensation for not receiving the benefit of a social service, is as far as one can imagine from basic human rights. And I have taken it only as a very recent example: it is by no means unusual. It is often said that the tendency of every court is to increase its jurisdiction and the Strasbourg court is no exception. So far as the margin of appreciation accommodates national choices, the jurisdiction of the European court is unnecessary; so far as it does not, it is undesirable.

[2:4] Hoyano, L C H, 'Policing Flawed Police Investigations: Unravelling the Blanket'
(1999) 62 MLR 912 (at page 920)

Lord Hoffmann's critique of the intersection of tort law and the European Convention

Lord Hoffmann has stated in this journal that the *Osman* decision 'fills me with apprehension'. His Lordship contends that the ECHR, under the guise of Article 6 which says everyone is entitled to have his civil rights and obligations decided by a tribunal, has taken it upon itself to decide the content of those civil rights, which here meant the merits of the substantive tort rules governing duty of care. In so doing, His Lordship maintains, the ECHR is 'challenging the autonomy of the courts and indeed the Parliament of the United Kingdom to deal with what are essentially social welfare questions involving budgetary limits and efficient public administration'.

Is this criticism justified? Parliament, exercising its autonomy, has seen fit to require the British courts to adjudicate issues arising under the Convention, and in so doing to take into account any judgment of the ECHR. Parliament has bound neither itself nor the British courts to act on any declaration of incompatibility by the ECHR. If this amounts to an unjustifiable surrender of parliamentary autonomy, then that is a political, not a legal, issue.

The ECHR had also given due warning that while Article 6§1 does not in itself guarantee any particular content for civil rights and obligations in the substantive law of the Contracting States, and so cannot provide a vehicle for their creation by the Convention enforcement bodies, the State does not enjoy unlimited scope to remove issues of civil liability from the jurisdiction of the courts. In *Fayed v UK*, the ECHR observed:

> [It] would not be consistent with the rule of law and democratic society or with the basic principle underlying Article 6(1) – namely that civil claims must be capable of being submitted to a judge for adjudication – if, for example, a State could, without restraint or control by the Convention enforcement bodies, remove from the jurisdiction of the courts a whole range of civil claims or confer immunities from civil liability on large groups or categories of persons.

Parliament must be taken to have known of this interpretation of Article 6(1) prior to incorporating the Convention into English domestic law.

Lord Hoffman argues that the case was really about the merits of the substantive tort law under which the Osmans were 'bound to lose', rather than about the right to a hearing; viewed from this perspective, the *Osman* case 'is as far as one can imagine from basic human rights'. However, a close examination of the Court's reasoning suggests that this criticism is less persuasive than it may initially appear.

Interestingly, at several points in his critique His Lordship treats *Hill* as conferring blanket immunity upon the police, without addressing the ECHR's crucial point that the English courts themselves had already torn some holes in that blanket, particularly through the recently resurrected 'assumption of responsibility' justification for duty of care, but then had denied the Osman plaintiffs the opportunity or prove that their case fitted within any of these exceptions or justified unravelling the blanket further.

It is of vital importance to note that the ECHR did not require English courts to rescind public policy immunity from tort liability; rather, it said that the courts must permit litigants an opportunity to contend that countervailing public policy considerations dictate that immunity should not apply to their case. This does not mean that defendants can no longer bring cost-efficient interlocutory applications to strike out pleadings on the ground that they are immune from negligence suits, as Lord Hoffmann suggests; it does mean that the court hearing such an application must approach the issue from the perspective that public policy immunity does not automatically provide a 'watertight defence'. The factors which the ECHR indicated might be relevant to an English court in deciding whether to apply the immunity rule in *Hill* – the alleged failure by an agent of the state to protect the life of a vulnerable child due to a catalogue of gravely negligent acts and omissions – brings Ahmet Osman's case much closer to 'basic human rights' as they are commonly conceptualised.

Thus it is strongly arguable that the *ratio* of *Osman* is quite narrow. Viewed in this way, the ECHR has not taken it upon itself to dictate to domestic courts the content of tort law rules but rather, in the best common law tradition, has upheld the principle that the categories of negligence are not closed, and that tort law must be allowed the flexibility to develop incrementally.

Lord Hoffmann stoutly defends the immunity conferred by *Hill* as being in line with other recent cases refusing to permit plaintiffs to sue public authorities for failure to deliver services which could have prevented their loss. But given the extensive police involvement responding to multiple complaints about the activities of Paget-Lewis over a period of 14 months, is *Osman* simply a case of nonfeasance? As the plaintiffs alleged that they, the school and the ILEA had the Osman and Perkins families, can it fairly be said in their case that 'the person who has failed to receive the benefit [of public services] is no worse off than if it had not been provided in the first place', as Lord Hoffmann asserts? Without such assurances, the Osmans might well have left the locality or made other arrangements to provide for their security; without a trial, it cannot be assumed that they did not rely upon the police to their detriment.

His Lordship contends that public authorities are currently exposed to negligence actions only when they enter into relationships which have long been recognised as giving rise to a duty of care in private law, such as between a doctor or hospital and patient. While there may be an emerging trend in that direction, such reasoning does not appear in the seminal cases delineating the applicability of negligence law to public authorities. Indeed the House of Lords expressly eschewed such a limitation in *Dorset Yacht Co Ltd v Home Office*; Lord Diplock pointed out:

To relinquish intentionally or inadvertently the custody and control of a person responsible in law for his own acts is not an act or omission which, independently of any statute, would give rise to a cause of action at common law against the custodian on the part of another person who subsequently sustained tortious damage at the hands of the person released.

It would have been impossible to establish the existence of a free-standing duty of care absent the statutory power to imprison which, at least until the recent advent of privately managed prisons, was vested solely in public authorities. *Dorset Yacht* thus cannot be explained on the basis of Lord Hoffmann's private/public distinction.

Furthermore, it is unlikely that the ECHR ruling in *Osman* will force the English courts to adjudicate policy issues involving the efficiency of public administration and the allocation of limited public resources, as Lord Hoffmann fears . . .

In *Osman*, there was no suggestion that the police's failure to arrest Paget-Lewis was due to a paucity of resources to dedicate to the investigation or to a policy decision not to act on the numerous complaints. While the policy/operational divide may sometimes be difficult to discern, it should have been relatively straightforward to apply here: even if the decision to arrest a suspect might conceivably fall within the realm of non-justifiable discretion, surely the inexplicable failure to implement that decision with any zeal would fall at the operational end of the spectrum.

(At page 934):

Conclusion

I have argued that it is possible to construe *Osman v UK* as standing for no broader proposition than that where the domestic courts have carved out some exceptions to a general rule conferring immunity upon a class of decision-makers, litigants must be afforded the opportunity to bring their cases within those exceptions or (in the case of a judge-made immunity rule) to develop new exceptions. However, some dicta in the ECHR's lead judgment point to a wider implication, that blanket immunity for any class of potential tortfeasors is likely to violate Article 6(1), as the courts must leave themselves free to examine the merits of each case and to weigh the public policy considerations for and against the existence of the duty of care in a particular case . . .

The Human Rights Act 1998 may signal a return to the spirit of flexibility which infused *Donoghue v Stevenson*, and to the robust view of the Court of Appeal in *Dorset Yacht* about the salutary effects of negligence law unless, that is, other English judges share the apprehension of Lord Hoffmann, and lack the confidence of Lord Nicholls in their ability to adjudicate duty of care issues on a case-by-case basis . . .

How much better it would be if negligence law could draw on these common law concepts to retain its original vigour and flexibility rather than forcing human rights law to do its work.

[2:5] *Brooks v Commissioner of Police of the Metropolis*
[2005] UKHL 24

Lord Bingham (all five judges agreed that this claim failed)
1 My Lords, Duwayne Brooks, the respondent, was present when his friend Stephen Lawrence was abused and murdered in the most notorious racist killing which our country has ever known. He also was abused and attacked. However well this crime had been investigated by the police and however sensitively he had himself been treated by the police, the respondent would inevitably have been deeply traumatised by his experience on the night of the murder and in the days and weeks which followed. But unfortunately, as established by the public inquiry into the killing (The Stephen Lawrence Inquiry: Report of an Inquiry by Sir William Macpherson of Cluny (1999) (Cm 4262-I), the investigation was very badly conducted and the respondent himself was not treated as he should have been. He issued proceedings against the Metropolitan Police Commissioner and a number of other parties, all but one of whom were police officers . . .

2 . . . the only issue before the House is whether, assuming the facts pleaded by the respondent to be true, the Commissioner and the officers for whom he is responsible arguably owed the respondent a common law duty sounding in damages to (1) take reasonable steps to assess whether the respondent was a victim of crime and then to accord him reasonably appropriate protection, support, assistance and treatment if he was so assessed; (2) take reasonable steps to afford the respondent the protection, assistance and support commonly afforded to a key eye-witness to a serious crime of violence; (3) afford reasonable weight to the account that the respondent gave and to act upon it accordingly.

3 . . . Two considerations, however, persuade me that this appeal should be allowed and the respondent's claims in common law negligence struck out.

4 The first is that the facts of this case have been exhaustively investigated. While theoretically the facts are only to be assumed, and have not been proved, it seems most unlikely that there are factual discoveries to be made or that there will be any substantial challenge to the facts as pleaded. If the case went to trial, the judge would base his decision on essentially the same facts as are now before the House. The second consideration is that the three duties pleaded are not, in my opinion, duties which could even arguably be imposed on police officers charged in the public interest with the investigation of a very serious crime and the appre-hension of those responsible. Even if it were to be thought, for reasons such as those touched on by Lord Steyn, in paras 27–29 of his opinion, that the ratio of *Hill*'s case called for some modification, I cannot conceive that any modification would be such as would accommodate the three pleaded duties. This conclusion imports no criticism at all of the respondent's expert advisers, who have plainly pleaded the strongest duties available on the facts. But these are not duties which could be imposed on police officers without potentially undermining the officers' performance of their functions, effective performance of which serves an important public interest. That is, in my opinion, a conclusive argument in the Commissioner's favour. Fortunately, the respondent has other causes of action which he is free to pursue.

[2:6] *R v Metropolitan Police Commissioner, ex p Blackburn (No 3)*
[1973] QB 241

The applicant sought an order of mandamus to require the Metropolitan Police Commissioner to secure the enforcement of the law against the illegal publishing and selling of pornography. The Court of Appeal held that, although the evidence disclosed that obscene material was widely available for sale in shops, the applicant had not established that it was a case for the court to interfere with the discretion of the police in carrying out their duties.

Lord Denning MR (at page 254):

> In *R v Commissioner of Police of the Metropolis, ex p Blackburn* [1968] 2 QB 118, 136, 138, 148–149, we made it clear that, in the carrying out of their duty of enforcing the law, the police have a discretion with which the courts will not interfere. There might, however, be extreme cases in which he was not carrying out his duty. And then we would. I do not think this is a case for our interference. In the past the commissioner has done what he could under the existing system and with the available manpower. The new commissioner is doing more. He is increasing the number of the Obscene Publications Squad to 18 and he is reforming it and its administration. No more can reasonably be expected.

> The plain fact is, however, that the efforts of the police have hitherto been largely ineffective. Mr Blackburn amply demonstrated it by going out from this court and buying these pornographic magazines – hard and soft – at shops all over the place. I do not accede to the suggestion that the police turn a blind eye to pornography or that shops get a 'tip-off' before the police arrive. The cause of the ineffectiveness lies with the system and the framework in which the police have to operate. The Obscene Publications Act 1959 does not provide a sound foundation. It fails to provide a satisfactory test of obscenity: and it allows a defence of public good which has got out of hand. There is also considerable uncertainty as to the powers and duties of the police when they seize articles.

> If the people of this country want pornography to be stamped out, the legislature must amend the Obscene Publications Act 1959 so as to make it strike unmistakably at pornography: and it must define the powers and duties of the police so as to enable them to take effective measures for the purpose. The police may well say to Parliament: 'Give us the tools and we will finish the job'. But, without efficient tools, they cannot be expected to stamp it out. Mr Blackburn has served a useful purpose in drawing the matter to our attention: but I do not think it is a case for mandamus. I would, therefore, dismiss the appeal.

[2:7] *R (Mondelly) v Commissioner of Police of the Metropolis*
[2007] Crim LR 298

M was arrested for permitting his premises to be used for the smoking of cannabis (the Misuse of Drugs Act 1971, s.8(d)). Subsequently, he was cautioned for simple possession of cannabis. He applied for the decision to caution him to be judicially reviewed in the light of the policy adopted by the Metropolitan Police in connection with the offence of simple possession. The policy relied on was that which was contained in Metropolitan Police Service Notice 3/2004, issued on the day that cannabis was reclassified as a Class C drug and entitled "Policing of Cannabis as a Class C Drug". The notice was available on the internet. The notice laid down a general policy that an officer should not arrest a person found to be in possession of cannabis for personal use unless an aggravating factor applied, but the drug should be seized. The notice stated that the policy was not intended to interfere with the discretion of a police officer. Its aim was to ensure that the least amount of time possible was spent on policing simple possession of the drug. The notice included a cross-reference to the Standard Operating Procedure as identifying the aggravating factors where an officer may consider arrest. That document (disclosed for the purposes of the case) identified various potential aggravating factors, including where the offender was a young person. None applied to M's case. M argued that, on public law principles, the police were obliged to follow the policy described in the notice unless a departure could be justified. In the absence of any of the aggravating features identified in the Standard Operating Procedure, there was no such justification.

Held, dismissing the application, that M's argument was misconceived. (1) The court considered the authorities on judicial review of decisions to caution or to prosecute (*R. v Commissioner of Police of the Metropolis Ex p. Blackburn (No.1)* [1968] Q.B. 118; *R. v Chief Constable of the Kent County Constabulary Ex p. L (A Minor)* [1993] 1 All E.R. 756; *R. v Commissioner of Police of the Metropolis Ex p. P* (1996) 8 Admin. L.R. 6; *R. v Commissioner of Police of the Metropolis Ex p. Thompson* [1997] 1 W.L.R. 1519; *R. v Adaway* [2004] EWCA Crim 2831). These authorities established (a) that generally the courts were reluctant to intervene in relation to decisions to prosecute, even in the case of juveniles; (b) that the courts were reluctant to intervene in relation to the administration of cautions; (c) the courts would refuse to intervene save where the policy which it was suggested had been breached was clear and settled; and (d) that the breach itself was established.

(2) It was wrong to extend the policy on arrest contained in the notice and apply it to the administration of cautions. M accepted that it was a necessary consequence of the submission that the arrest policy made the administration of the caution unlawful, that any prosecution of M would have been unlawful as well. So the policy on arrest when read across to cautions, as M contended, would also become a prohibition on prosecution. That was an utterly misconceived approach to the meaning and effect of the policy. It took the policy several steps beyond its stated confines and purpose. There was nothing to suggest that the authors thought they were creating such a policy. Were there to be a police and CPS policy that no one should be prosecuted for simple possession of cannabis (unless the exceptions in the Standard Operating Procedures applied), that policy itself would be unlawful. It was not for executive prosecution policy to change the law. The implication of M's argument was that the police could suspend or dispense with part of the law.

(3) Even if it were possible to contemplate a policy having the effect for which M contended, M would have to establish that there was in fact a clear policy not to administer a caution for simple possession, departure from which must be justified. There was no such clear policy. The notice expressly provided that it was not intended to interfere with the discretion of a police officer. There was nothing in the policy that stated that it was applicable to cautioning or prosecution after arrest. The purpose of the notice was stated to be about ensuring that the least amount of police time possible was spent on simple possession of cannabis for reasons of resources and policing priorities. A person choosing to break the law by possessing cannabis could not rely on such a policy to avoid prosecution or a caution; and the policy itself was not clear (it did not state that "no further action" precluded a caution, and there was no cross-referencing between it and the guidance in the Home Office Circular 18/1994 on cautioning). There was therefore no clear and settled policy not to arrest or prosecute for simple possession.

(4) In any event, there had been no breach of the Standard Operating Procedures. M relied on a passage asserting that there should be no re-arrest for simple possession following an initial arrest for another offence. But M had not been rearrested for simple possession and there was no non-compliance with that Standard Operating Procedure. The Standard Operating Procedure said that if arrest were not appropriate, the simple possession offence should

be recorded but that was not a criminal record. The Standard Operating Procedure does not deal with whether or not there should be any further prosecution or caution in express terms, although it would appear to be the expectation that that would be the end of the matter. (per Moses L.J., with whom Ouseley J. agreed, Walker J. dissenting)

. . .

Commentary (by Andrew Roberts): If the applicant suffered any procedural unfairness it did not arise from the fact that he might have been treated differently from others whom the police discovered to be in possession of cannabis. The policy concerning arrest for this offence had been widely reported in the news media. More significantly the police had published the policy in some detail. The basis of a claim of unfairness in such circumstances is that the publication of the policy creates a legitimate expectation that the applicant would be treated in a particular manner and that deviation from the policy constitutes a failure to provide the applicant with what he is due (see generally D. Galligan, *Due Process and Fair Procedures* (Oxford University Press, 1996), pp.56–60).

The question on which the application turned was whether, in addition to creating an expectation as to arrest for possession of cannabis, the policy could also be said to have created an expectation as to the use of cautions for that offence. The basis of the application was that implicit in the policy relating to arrest was a corresponding stance in relation to the use of cautions for possession of cannabis, i.e. those individuals who would not be subject to arrest by application of the arrest policy would neither be cautioned (nor prosecuted).

Where the enforcement of substantive criminal law is subject to operational policy difficult issues of the weight that ought to be attached to the competing considerations arise. Failure on the part of the authority issuing the policy to implement it in particular cases provides the foundation of a claim of procedural unfairness described above. However, were decision-makers not permitted to deviate from the authority's policy, there is a danger of ossification of what originally constituted a "rule of thumb", offering guidance to the decision-maker, so that in effect it becomes a prescriptive rule which imposes an impermissible limitation on the scope of the substantive criminal law (see *R. v Commissioner of Police of the Metropolis Ex p. Blackburn (No.1)* [1968] Q.B. 118, per Lord Denning at p.136e-f: "Suppose a Chief Constable were to issue a directive to his men that no person should be prosecuted for stealing any goods less than £100 in value. I should have thought that the court could countermand it. He would be failing in his duty to enforce the law.")

Policies must necessarily leave scope for the exercise of discretion. While recognising that any failure to follow such policies is open to judicial review the courts have generally shown reluctance to interfere with operational decisions in which a decision-maker has declined to apply a policy. In light of this, it is unsurprising that the court in the present case disposed of the application on the grounds that one of the preconditions for judicial review was a clearly stated policy, and no such policy existed in relation to the use of cautions for possession of cannabis.

In a persuasive dissenting opinion Walker J. adopted a rather more functional approach, recognising the procedural injustice which resulted from the mistaken thinking on the part of the arresting officers. Had this not occurred the applicant would have benefited from the arrest policy, and would also have been spared a criminal record and having to surrender a sample of his DNA. It was further pointed out that administering a caution was inconsistent with the underlying purposes of the arrest policy. These included the macro-consideration of achieving consistency with an enforcement policy which takes account of the Government's reasons for reclassifying cannabis, and more specific considerations of achieving transparency and consistency in enforcement of the law between individuals.

[2:8] Farrington, D and Dowds, E, 'Why does crime decrease?'
(1984) Justice of the Peace 506 (at page 507)

We do not know why recorded crime in the whole country decreased between 1982 and 1983, but we do know why it has been decreasing in one county – Nottinghamshire. Taken at face value, the Criminal Statistics for 1981 showed that Nottinghamshire was the most criminal area in the country. For several years, Nottingham, the Metropolitan Police area and Merseyside had the three highest recorded crime rates in the country, and in 1981 Nottinghamshire regained the top position it had last held in 1977. Our research into the puzzling case of the high Nottinghamshire crime rate began in 1982. Between 1981 and 1982, whereas recorded crime in the whole country increased by 10%, in Nottinghamshire is stayed virtually unchanged, leading to a decline in Nottinghamshire's position in the 'league table' of crime rates from first to fifth. In 1983, whereas recorded crime in the whole country fell by 0.5%, the decrease in Nottinghamshire was 5%, and in the first quarter of 1984, when crime increased by 5% overall, it decreased in Nottinghamshire by 6%. These decreases will lead to a further decline in Nottinghamshire's relative standing.

The aim of our research was to compare Nottinghamshire with two other counties which were similar in many respects – Staffordshire and Leicestershire. According to the chief constables' reports, there were 87 recorded crimes per 100 population in Nottinghamshire in 1981, in comparison with 44 in Leicestershire and 40 in Staffordshire. We wanted to explain why Nottinghamshire was roughly twice as high as the other two counties.

There were basically four possible explanations:

(a)   more crimes were committed (in relation to population) in Nottinghamshire;
(b)   members of the public were more likely to report crimes to the police in Nottinghamshire;
(c)   the police were more likely to discover crimes in Nottinghamshire; and
(d)   an alleged crime which was discovered by or reported to the police was more likely to be recorded in Nottinghamshire.

In order to investigate (a) and (b), a random sample of about 1,000 adults in each county was interviewed and asked about crimes committed against them in the previous year and about whether these crimes were reported to the police. In order to investigate (c) and (d), police discovery and recording practices in the three counties were studied.

The crime survey (whose methodology was based on the British Crime Survey) indicated that the number of crimes committed in each county was far greater than the number recorded by the police: 405 per 1,000 in Nottinghamshire, in comparison with 326 in Leicestershire and 262 in Staffordshire. (These estimates include crimes against organisations and against persons under 16). The proportion of crimes reported to the police was almost exactly the same in each county, at about 40%. This led to an estimate of crimes reported to the police per 1,000 population of 162 in Nottinghamshire, 136 in Leicestershire and 102 in Staffordshire.

Comparing these figures with the recorded crime rates of 87, 44 and 40 (respectively) led to the conclusion that the ratio of recorded to reported crime was far higher in Nottinghamshire (53%) than in Leicestershire (32%) or Staffordshire (39%). If the probability of a crime known to the police being recorded had been 35% in all counties (the average of the Leicestershire and Staffordshire figures), the recorded crime rates per 1,000 population would have been 57 in Nottinghamshire, 48 in Leicestershire and 36 in Staffordshire. The police figures for Nottinghamshire were therefore about 30 crimes per 1,000 population higher than expected on the basis of the other two counties.

The study of police recording practices analysed a 1% random sample of 1981 crime reports in each county (over 1,600 in all). The main aims of this analysis were to investigate the origin of each recorded crime (e.g. from citizen reports or police investigatory practices) and the characteristics of each (e.g. the value of property stolen). The types of crimes recorded in the three counties were quite similar.

Differences – admissions

One major difference between the counties was in crimes arising from admissions, where a person apprehended for one crime admitted others which had not previously been reported to or recorded by the police. About a quarter of Nottinghamshire's crime reports originated in this way, in comparison with 4% in Leicestershire and 8% in Staffordshire. The difference between the counties in crimes arising from admissions amounted to a difference of 18–20 crimes per 1,000 population.

Differences – crime seriousness

The second major difference between the counties was in the seriousness of recorded crimes. Nearly half of the crimes of dishonesty in Nottinghamshire involved property worth £10 or less, in comparison with 29% in Leicestershire and 36% in Staffordshire. Crimes arising from admissions were especially likely to involve property worth £10 or less (72%). It seemed likely that the Nottinghamshire police were more willing to record relatively trivial crimes than the other two forces.

Adding together crimes arising from admissions and those involving property worth £10 or less, the rate in Nottinghamshire for crimes in one or both of these categories was 43 per 1,000 population, or about half the country's crime rate. The corresponding figure for the other two counties was 12 in both cases. Therefore, these two effects together accounted for a difference of 31 crimes per 1,000 population between Nottinghamshire and the other two counties – almost exactly the excess identified in the crime survey.

We therefore concluded that, of the difference in recorded crime rates between Nottinghamshire and the other two counties of about 45 offences per 1,000 population, about two-thirds reflected differences in police recording practices, while about one-third reflected real differences in crimes committed.

Since our research began, and possibly in the light of our results, the Nottinghamshire police have changed their recording practices. In particular, they decided to spend less time questioning apprehended offenders about all their crimes, and so nowadays do not record so many trivial crimes arising on admission. This is one of the major reasons why recorded crime in Nottinghamshire decreased between 1981 and 1984. Police practices in Nottinghamshire are now come comparable to those in Leicestershire and Staffordshire.

[2:9] Police and Criminal Evidence Act 1984 (as amended)
Sections 17–19; 24; 25; 28–32; 36–38; 56; 58; 66; 76; 78

17 Entry for purpose of arrest etc

(1) Subject to the following provisions of this section, and without prejudice to any other enactment, a constable may enter and search any premises for the purpose –

   (a) of executing –
      (i) a warrant of arrest issued in connection with or arising out of criminal proceedings; or

      (ii)   a warrant of commitment issued under section 76 of the Magistrates' Courts Act 1980;

(b)   of arresting a person for an indictable offence;

(c)   of arresting a person for an offence under –

      (i)   section 1 (prohibition of uniforms in connection with political objects) of the Public Order Act 1936;

      (ii)   any enactment contained in sections 6 to 8 or 10 of the Criminal Law Act 1977 (offences relating to entering and remaining on property);

      (iii)   section 4 of the Public Order Act 1986 (fear or provocation of violence);

      (iiia) section 4 (driving etc when under influence of drink or drugs) or 163 (failure to stop when required to do so by constable in uniform) of the Road Traffic Act 1988;

      (iiib) section 27 of the Transport and Works Act 1992 (which relates to offences involving drink or drugs);

      (iv)   section 76 of the Criminal Justice and Public Order Act 1994 (failure to comply with interim possession order);

      (v)   any of sections 4, 5, 6(1) and (2), 7 and 8(1) and (2) of the Animal Welfare Act 2006 (offences relating to the prevention of harm to animals);

      (vi)   section 144 of the Legal Aid, Sentencing and Punishment of Offenders Act 2012 (squatting in a residential building);

(ca) of arresting, in pursuance of section 32(1A) of the Children and Young Persons Act 1969, any child or young person who has been remanded to local authority accommodation or youth detention accommodation under section 91 of the Legal Aid, Sentencing and Punishment of Offenders Act 2012;

(caa) of arresting a person for an offence to which section 61 of the Animal Health Act 1981 applies;

(cb) of recapturing any person who is, or is deemed for any purpose to be, unlawfully at large while liable to be detained –

      (i)   in a prison, remand centre, young offender institution or secure training centre, or

      (ii)   in pursuance of section 92 of the Powers of Criminal Courts (Sentencing) Act 2000 (dealing with children and young persons guilty of grave crimes), in any other place;

(d)   of recapturing any person whatever who is unlawfully at large and whom he is pursuing; or

(e)   of saving life or limb or preventing serious damage to property.

(2) Except for the purpose specified in paragraph (e) of subsection (1) above, the powers of entry and search conferred by this section –

(a) are only exercisable if the constable has reasonable grounds for believing that the person whom he is seeking is on the premises; and

(b) are limited, in relation to premises consisting of two or more separate dwellings, to powers to enter and search –

      (i)   any parts of the premises which the occupiers of any dwelling comprised in the premises use in common with the occupiers of any other such dwelling; and

      (ii)   any such dwelling in which the constable has reasonable grounds for believing that the person whom he is seeking may be.

(3) The powers of entry and search conferred by this section are only exercisable for the purposes specified in subsection (1)(c)(ii), (iv) or (vi) above by a constable in uniform.

(4) The power of search conferred by this section is only a power to search to the extent that is reasonably required for the purpose for which the power of entry is exercised.

(5) Subject to subsection (6) below, all the rules of common law under which a constable has power to enter premises without a warrant are hereby abolished.

(6) Nothing in subsection (5) above affects any power of entry to deal with or prevent a breach of the peace.

18 Entry and search after arrest

(1) Subject to the following provisions of this section, a constable may enter and search any premises occupied or controlled by a person who is under arrest for an indictable offence, if he has reasonable grounds for suspecting that there is on the premises evidence, other than items subject to legal privilege, that relates –

    (a) to that offence; or
    (b) to some other indictable offence which is connected with or similar to that offence.

(2) A constable may seize and retain anything for which he may search under subsection (1) above.

(3) The power to search conferred by subsection (1) above is only a power to search to the extent that is reasonably required for the purpose of discovering such evidence.

(4) Subject to subsection (5) below, the powers conferred by this section may not be exercised unless an officer of the rank of inspector or above has authorised them in writing.

(5) A constable may conduct a search under subsection (1)—

    (a) before the person is taken to a police station or released on bail under section 30A, and
    (b) without obtaining an authorisation under subsection (4),

if the condition in subsection (5A) is satisfied.

(5A) The condition is that the presence of the person at a place (other than a police station) is necessary for the effective investigation of the offence.

(6) If a constable conducts a search by virtue of subsection (5) above, he shall inform an officer of the rank of inspector or above that he has made the search as soon as practicable after he has made it.

(7) An officer who –

    (a) authorises a search; or
    (b) is informed of a search under subsection (6) above, shall make a record in writing –

        (i)   of the grounds for the search; and
        (ii) of the nature of the evidence that was sought.

(8) If the person who was in occupation or control of the premises at the time of the search is in police detention at the time the record is to be made, the officer shall make the record as part of his custody record.

19 General power of seizure etc.

(1) The powers conferred by subsections (2), (3) and (4) below are exercisable by a constable who is lawfully on any premises.

(2) The constable may seize anything which is on the premises if he has reasonable grounds for believing –

(a) that it has been obtained in consequence of the commission of an offence; and
(b) that it is necessary to seize it in order to prevent it being concealed, lost, damaged, altered or destroyed.

(3) The constable may seize anything which is on the premises if he has reasonable grounds for believing –

(a) that it is evidence in relation to an offence which he is investigating or any other offence; and
(b) that it is necessary to seize it in order to prevent the evidence being concealed, lost, altered or destroyed.

(4) The constable may require any information which is stored in any electronic form and is accessible from the premises to be produced in a form in which it can be taken away and in which it is visible and legible or from which it can readily be produced in a visible and legible form if he has reasonable grounds for believing –

(a) that –
  (i)   it is evidence in relation to an offence which he is investigating or any other offence; or
  (ii) it has been obtained in consequence of the commission of an offence; and
(b) that it is necessary to do so in order to prevent it being concealed, lost, tampered with or destroyed.

(5) The powers conferred by this section are in addition to any power otherwise conferred.

(6) No power of seizure conferred on a constable under any enactment (including an enactment contained in an Act passed after this Act) is to be taken to authorise the seizure of an item which the constable exercising the power has reasonable grounds for believing to be subject to legal privilege.

24 Arrest without warrant: constables

(1) A constable may arrest without a warrant –

(a) anyone who is about to commit an offence;
(b) anyone who is in the act of committing an offence;
(c) anyone whom he has reasonable grounds for suspecting to be about to commit an offence;
(d) anyone whom he has reasonable grounds for suspecting to be committing an offence.

(2) If a constable has reasonable grounds for suspecting that an offence has been committed, he may arrest without a warrant anyone whom he has reasonable grounds to suspect of being guilty of it.

(3) If an offence has been committed, a constable may arrest without a warrant –

(a) anyone who is guilty of the offence;
(b) anyone whom he has reasonable grounds for suspecting to be guilty of it.

(4) But the power of summary arrest conferred by subsection (1), (2) or (3) is exercisable only if the constable has reasonable grounds for believing that for any of the reasons mentioned in subsection (5) it is necessary to arrest the person in question.

(5) The reasons are –

(a) to enable the name of the person in question to be ascertained (in the case where the constable does not know, and cannot readily ascertain, the person's name, or has reasonable grounds for doubting whether a name given by the person as his name is his real name);
(b) correspondingly as regards the person's address;
(c) to prevent the person in question –
    (i) causing physical injury to himself or any other person;
    (ii) suffering physical injury;
    (iii) causing loss of or damage to property;
    (iv) committing an offence against public decency (subject to subsection (6)); or
    (v) causing an unlawful obstruction of the highway;
(d) to protect a child or other vulnerable person from the person in question;
(e) to allow the prompt and effective investigation of the offence or of the conduct of the person in question;
(f) to prevent any prosecution for the offence from being hindered by the disappearance of the person in question.

(6) Subsection (5)(c)(iv) applies only where members of the public going about their normal business cannot reasonably be expected to avoid the person in question.

24A Arrest without warrant: other persons

(1) A person other than a constable may arrest without a warrant –

(a) anyone who is in the act of committing an indictable offence;
(b) anyone whom he has reasonable grounds for suspecting to be committing an indictable offence.

(2) Where an indictable offence has been committed, a person other than a constable may arrest without a warrant –

(a) anyone who is guilty of the offence;
(b) anyone whom he has reasonable grounds for suspecting to be guilty of it.

(3) But the power of summary arrest conferred by subsection (1) or (2) is exercisable only if –

(a) the person making the arrest has reasonable grounds for believing that for any of the reasons mentioned in subsection (4) it is necessary to arrest the person in question; and
(b) it appears to the person making the arrest that it is not reasonably practicable for a constable to make it instead.

(4) The reasons are to prevent the person in question –

(a) causing physical injury to himself or any other person;
(b) suffering physical injury;
(c) causing loss of or damage to property; or
(d) making off before a constable can assume responsibility for him.

(5) This section does not apply in relation to an offence under Part 3 or 3A of the Public Order Act 1986.

28 Information to be given on arrest

(1) Subject to subsection (5) below, where a person is arrested, otherwise than by being informed that he is under arrest, the arrest is not lawful unless the person arrested is informed that he is under arrest as soon as is practicable after his arrest.

(2) Where a person is arrested by a constable, subsection (1) above applies regardless of whether the fact of the arrest is obvious.

(3) Subject to subsection (5) below, no arrest is lawful unless the person arrested is informed of the ground for the arrest at the time of, or as soon as is practicable after, the arrest.

(4) Where a person is arrested by a constable, subsection (3) above applies regardless of whether the ground for the arrest is obvious.

(5) Nothing in this section is to be taken to require a person to be informed –

(a) that he is under arrest; or
(b) of the ground for the arrest,

if it was not reasonably practicable for him to be so informed by reason of his having escaped from arrest before the information could be given.

29 Voluntary attendance at police station etc.

Where for the purpose of assisting with an investigation a person attends voluntarily at a police station or at any other place where a constable is present or accompanies a constable to a police station or any such other place without having been arrested –

(a) he shall be entitled to leave at will unless he is placed under arrest;
(b) he shall be informed at once that he is under arrest if a decision is taken by a constable to prevent him from leaving at will.

30 Arrest elsewhere than at police station

(1) Subsection (1A) applies where a person is, at any place other than a police station –

(a) arrested by a constable for an offence, or
(b) taken into custody by a constable after being arrested for an offence by a person other than a constable.

(1A) The person must be taken by a constable to a police station as soon as practicable after the arrest.

(1B) Subsection (1A) has effect subject to section 30A (release on bail) and subsection (7) (release without bail).

(2) Subject to subsections (3) and (5) below, the police station to which an arrested person is taken under subsection (1A) above shall be a designated police station.

(3) A constable to whom this subsection applies may take an arrested person to any police station unless it appears to the constable that it may be necessary to keep the arrested person in police detention for more than six hours.

(4) Subsection (3) above applies –

(a) to a constable who is working in a locality covered by a police station which is not a designated police station; and
(b) to a constable belonging to a body of constables maintained by an authority other than a local policing body.

(5) Any constable may take an arrested person to any police station if –

(a) either of the following conditions is satisfied –
   (i) the constable has arrested him without the assistance of any other constable and no other constable is available to assist him;
   (ii) the constable has taken him into custody from a person other than a constable without the assistance of any other constable and no other constable is available to assist him; and
(b) it appears to the constable that he will be unable to take the arrested person to a designated police station without the arrested person injuring himself, the constable or some other person.

(6) If the first police station to which an arrested person is taken after his arrest is not a designated police station, he shall be taken to a designated police station not more than six hours after his arrival at the first police station unless he is released previously.

(7) A person arrested by a constable at any place other than a police station must be released without bail if the condition in subsection (7A) is satisfied.

(7A) The condition is that, at any time before the person arrested reaches a police station, a constable is satisfied that there are no grounds for keeping him under arrest or releasing him on bail under section 30A.

(8) A constable who releases a person under subsection (7) above shall record the fact that he has done so.

(9) The constable shall make the record as soon as is practicable after the release.

(10) Nothing in subsection (1A) or in section 30A prevents a constable delaying taking a person to a police station or releasing him on bail if the condition in subsection (10A) is satisfied.

(10A) The condition is that the presence of the person at a place (other than a police station) is necessary in order to carry out such investigations as it is reasonable to carry out immediately.

(11) Where there is any such delay the reasons for the delay must be recorded when the person first arrives at the police station or (as the case may be) is released on bail.

(12) Nothing in subsection (1A) or section 30A above shall be taken to affect –

(a) paragraphs 16(3) or 18(1) of Schedule 2 to the Immigration Act 1971;
(b) section 34(1) of the Criminal Justice Act 1972; or
(c) any provision of the Terrorism Act 2000.

(13) Nothing in subsection (10) above shall be taken to affect paragraph 18(3) of Schedule 2 to the Immigration Act 1971.

30A Bail elsewhere than at police station

(1) A constable may release on bail a person who is arrested or taken into custody in the circumstances mentioned in section 30(1).

(2) A person may be released on bail under subsection (1) at any time before he arrives at a police station.

(3) A person released on bail under subsection (1) must be required to attend a police station.

(3A) Where a constable releases a person on bail under subsection (1)–

(a)   no recognizance for the person's surrender to custody shall be taken from the person,
(b)   no security for the person's surrender to custody shall be taken from the person or from anyone else on the person's behalf,
(c)   the person shall not be required to provide a surety or sureties for his surrender to custody, and
(d)   no requirement to reside in a bail hostel may be imposed as a condition of bail.

(3B) Subject to subsection (3A), where a constable releases a person on bail under subsection (1) the constable may impose, as conditions of the bail, such requirements as appear to the constable to be necessary–

(a)   to secure that the person surrenders to custody,
(b)   to secure that the person does not commit an offence while on bail,
(c)   to secure that the person does not interfere with witnesses or otherwise obstruct the course of justice, whether in relation to himself or any other person, or
(d)   for the person's own protection or, if the person is under the age of 17, for the person's own welfare or in the person's own interests.

(4) Where a person is released on bail under subsection (1), a requirement may be imposed on the person as a condition of bail only under the preceding provisions of this section.

(5) The police station which the person is required to attend may be any police station.

31 Arrest for further offence

Where –

(a)   a person –
    (i)   has been arrested for an offence; and
    (ii)   is at a police station in consequence of that arrest; and
(b)   it appears to a constable that, if he were released from that arrest, he would be liable to arrest for some other offence,

he shall be arrested for that other offence.

32 Search upon arrest

(1) A constable may search an arrested person, in any case where the person to be searched has been arrested at a place other than a police station, if the constable has reasonable grounds for believing that the arrested person may present a danger to himself or others.

(2) Subject to subsections (3) to (5) below, a constable shall also have power in any such case –

- (a) to search the arrested person for anything –
  - (i)   which he might use to assist him to escape from lawful custody; or
  - (ii) which might be evidence relating to an offence; and
- (b) if the offence for which he has been arrested is an indictable offence, to enter and search any premises in which he was when arrested or immediately before he was arrested for evidence relating to the offence.

(3) The power to search conferred by subsection (2) above is only a power to search to the extent that is reasonably required for the purpose of discovering any such thing or any such evidence.

(4) The powers conferred by this section to search a person are not to be construed as author-ising a constable to require a person to remove any of his clothing in public other than an outer coat, jacket or gloves but they do authorise a search of a person's mouth.

(5) A constable may not search a person in the exercise of the power conferred by subsection (2)(a) above unless he has reasonable grounds for believing that the person to be searched may have concealed on him anything for which a search is permitted under that paragraph.

(6) A constable may not search premises in the exercise of the power conferred by subsection (2)(b) above unless he has reasonable grounds for believing that there is evidence for which a search is permitted under that paragraph on the premises.

(7) In so far as the power of search conferred by subsection (2)(b) above relates to premises consisting of two or more separate dwellings, it is limited to a power to search –

- (a) any dwelling in which the arrest took place or in which the person arrested was imme-diately before his arrest; and
- (b) any parts of the premises which the occupier of any such dwelling uses in common with the occupiers of any other dwellings comprised in the premises.

(8) A constable searching a person in the exercise of the power conferred by subsection (1) above may seize and retain anything he finds, if he has reasonable grounds for believing that the person searched might use it to cause physical injury to himself or to any other person.

(9) A constable searching a person in the exercise of the power conferred by subsection (2)(a) above may seize and retain anything he finds, other than an item subject to legal privilege, if he has reasonable grounds for believing –

- (a) that he might use it to assist him to escape from lawful custody; or
- (b) that it is evidence of an offence or has been obtained in consequence of the commis-sion of an offence.

(10) Nothing in this section shall be taken to affect the power conferred by section 43 of the Terrorism Act 2000.

36 Custody officers at police stations

(1) One or more custody officers shall be appointed for each designated police station.

(2) A custody officer for a police station designated under section 35(1) above shall be appointed –

   (a) by the chief officer of police for the area in which the designated police station is situated; or

   (b) by such other police officer as the chief officer of police for that area may direct.

(2A) A custody officer for a police station designated under section 35(2A) above shall be appointed –

   (a) by the Chief Constable of the British Transport Police Force; or

   (b) by such other member of that Force as that Chief Constable may direct.

(3) No officer may be appointed a custody officer unless the officer is of at least the rank of sergeant.

(4) An officer of any rank may perform the functions of a custody officer at a designated police station if a custody officer is not readily available to perform them.

(5) Subject to the following provisions of this section and to section 39(2) below, none of the functions of a custody officer in relation to a person shall be performed by an officer who at the time when the function falls to be performed is involved in the investigation of an offence for which that person is in police detention at that time.

(6) Nothing in subsection (5) above is to be taken to prevent a custody officer –

   (a) performing any function assigned to custody officers –
      (i) by this Act; or
      (ii) by a code of practice issued under this Act;

   (b) carrying out the duty imposed on custody officers by section 39 below;

   (c) doing anything in connection with the identification of a suspect; or

   (d) doing anything under sections 7 and 8 of the Road Traffic Act 1988.

(7) Where an arrested person is taken to a police station which is not a designated police station, the functions in relation to him which at a designated police station would be the functions of a custody officer shall be performed –

   (a) by an officer who is not involved in the investigation of an offence for which he is in police detention, if such an officer is readily available; and

   (b) if no such officer is readily available, by the officer who took him to the station or any other officer.

(7A) Subject to subsection (7B), subsection (7) applies where a person attends a police station which is not a designated station to answer to bail granted under section 30A as it applies where a person is taken to such a station.

(7B) Where subsection (7) applies because of subsection (7A), the reference in subsection (7)(b) to the officer who took him to the station is to be read as a reference to the officer who granted him bail.

(8) References to a custody officer in section 34 above or in the following provisions of this Act include references to an officer other than a custody officer who is performing the functions of a custody officer by virtue of subsection (4) or (7) above.

(9) Where by virtue of subsection (7) above an officer of a force maintained by a local policing body who took an arrested person to a police station is to perform the functions of a custody officer in relation to him, the officer shall inform an officer who –

    (a)   is attached to a designated police station; and
    (b)   is of at least the rank of inspector,

that he is to do so.

(10) The duty imposed by subsection (9) above shall be performed as soon as it is practicable to perform it.

37 Duties of custody officer before charge

(1) Where –

    (a)   a person is arrested for an offence –
        (i)   without a warrant; or
        (ii)   under a warrant not endorsed for bail,
the custody officer at each police station where he is detained after his arrest shall determine whether he has before him sufficient evidence to charge that person with the offence for which he was arrested and may detain him at the police station for such period as is necessary to enable him to do so.

(2) If the custody officer determines that he does not have such evidence before him, the person arrested shall be released either on bail or without bail, unless the custody officer has reasonable grounds for believing that his detention without being charged is necessary to secure or preserve evidence relating to an offence for which he is under arrest or to obtain such evidence by questioning him.

(3) If the custody officer has reasonable grounds for so believing, he may authorise the person arrested to be kept in police detention.

(4) Where a custody officer authorises a person who has not been charged to be kept in police detention, he shall, as soon as is practicable, make a written record of the grounds for the detention.

(5) Subject to subsection (6) below, the written record shall be made in the presence of the person arrested who shall at that time be informed by the custody officer of the grounds for his detention.

(6) Subsection (5) above shall not apply where the person arrested is, at the time when the written record is made –

    (a) incapable of understanding what is said to him;
    (b) violent or likely to become violent; or
    (c) in urgent need of medical attention.

(7) Subject to section 41(7) below, if the custody officer determines that he has before him sufficient evidence to charge the person arrested with the offence for which he was arrested, the person arrested –

(a) shall be–
  (i) released without charge and on bail, or
  (ii) kept in police detention, for the purpose of enabling the Director of Public Prosecutions to make a decision under section 37B below,
(b) shall be released without charge and on bail but not for that purpose,
(c) shall be released without charge and without bail, or
(d) shall be charged.

(7A) The decision as to how a person is to be dealt with under subsection (7) above shall be that of the custody officer.

(7B) Where a person is dealt with under subsection (7)(a) 5 above, it shall be the duty of the custody officer to inform him that he is being released, or (as the case may be) detained, to enable the Director of Public Prosecutions to make a decision under section 37B below.

(8) Where –

(a) a person is released under subsection (7)(b) or (c) above; and
(b) at the time of his release a decision whether he should be prosecuted for the offence for which he was arrested has not been taken,

it shall be the duty of the custody officer so to inform him.

(8A) Subsection (8B) applies if the offence for which the person is arrested is one in relation to which a sample could be taken under section 63B below and the custody officer–

(a) is required in pursuance of subsection (2) above to release the person arrested and decides to release him on bail, or
(b) decides in pursuance of subsection (7)(a) or (b) above to release the person without charge and on bail.

(8B) The detention of the person may be continued to enable a sample to be taken under section 63B, but this subsection does not permit a person to be detained for a period of more than 24 hours after the relevant time.

(9) If the person arrested is not in a fit state to be dealt with under subsection (7) above, he may be kept in police detention until he is.

(10) The duty imposed on the custody officer under subsection (1) above shall be carried out by him as soon as practicable after the person arrested arrives at the police station or, in the case of a person arrested at the police station, as soon as practicable after the arrest.

(15) In this Part of this Act –

"arrested juvenile" means a person arrested with or without a warrant who appears to be under the age of 17;

"endorsed for bail" means endorsed with a direction for bail in accordance with section 117(2) of the Magistrates' Courts Act 1980.

38 Duties of custody officer after charge

(1) Where a person arrested for an offence otherwise than under a warrant endorsed for bail is charged with an offence, the custody officer shall, subject to section 25 of the Criminal Justice

and Public Order Act 1994, order his release from police detention, either on bail or without bail, unless –

    (a) if the person arrested is not an arrested juvenile –
- (i) his name or address cannot be ascertained or the custody officer has reasonable grounds for doubting whether a name or address furnished by him as his name or address is his real name or address;
- (ii) the custody officer has reasonable grounds for believing that the person arrested will fail to appear in court to answer to bail;
- (iii) in the case of a person arrested for an imprisonable offence, the custody officer has reasonable grounds for believing that the detention of the person arrested is necessary to prevent him from committing an offence;
- (iiia) in a case where a sample may be taken from the person under section 63B below, the custody officer has reasonable grounds for believing that the detention of the person is necessary to enable the sample to be taken from him;
- (iv) in the case of a person arrested for an offence which is not an imprisonable offence, the custody officer has reasonable grounds for believing that the detention of the person arrested is necessary to prevent him from causing physical injury to any other person or from causing loss of or damage to property;
- (v) the custody officer has reasonable grounds for believing that the detention of the person arrested is necessary to prevent him from interfering with the administration of justice or with the investigation of offences or of a particular offence; or
- (vi) the custody officer has reasonable grounds for believing that the detention of the person arrested is necessary for his own protection;

    (b) if he is an arrested juvenile –
- (i) any of the requirements of paragraph (a) above is satisfied (but, in the case of paragraph (a)(iiia) above, only if the arrested juvenile has attained the minimum age); or
- (ii) the custody officer has reasonable grounds for believing that he ought to be detained in his own interests;

    (c) the offence with which the person is charged is murder.

(2) If the release of a person arrested is not required by subsection (1) above, the custody officer may authorise him to be kept in police detention but may not authorise a person to be kept in police detention by virtue of subsection (1)(a)(iiia) after the end of the period of six hours beginning when he was charged with the offence.

(2A) The custody officer, in taking the decisions required by subsection (1)(a) and (b) above (except (a)(i) and (vi) and (b)(ii)), shall have regard to the same considerations as those which a court is required to have regard to in taking the corresponding decisions under paragraph 2(1) of Part I of Schedule 1 to the Bail Act 1976 (disregarding paragraphs 1A and 2(2) of that Part).

(3) Where a custody officer authorises a person who has been charged to be kept in police detention, he shall, as soon as practicable, make a written record of the grounds for the detention.

(4) Subject to subsection (5) below, the written record shall be made in the presence of the person charged who shall at that time be informed by the custody officer of the grounds for his detention.

(5) Subsection (4) above shall not apply where the person charged is, at the time when the written record is made –

(a) incapable of understanding what is said to him;
(b) violent or likely to become violent; or
(c) in urgent need of medical attention.

(6) Where a custody officer authorises an arrested juvenile to be kept in police detention under subsection (1) above, the custody officer shall, unless he certifies –

(a) that, by reason of such circumstances as are specified in the certificate, it is impracticable for him to do so; or
(b) in the case of an arrested juvenile who has attained the age of 12 years, that no secure accommodation is available and that keeping him in other local authority accommodation would not be adequate to protect the public from serious harm from him,

secure that the arrested juvenile is moved to local authority accommodation.

(6A) In this section –

"local authority accommodation" means accommodation provided by or on behalf of a local authority (within the meaning of the Children Act 1989);
"minimum age" means the age specified in section 63B(3)(b) below;
"secure accommodation" means accommodation provided for the purpose of restricting liberty;
"sexual offence" means an offence specified in Part 2 of Schedule 15 to the Criminal Justice Act 2003; "violent offence" means murder or an offence specified in Part 1 of that Schedule;

and any reference, in relation to an arrested juvenile charged with a violent or sexual offence, to protecting the public from serious harm from him shall be construed as a reference to protecting members of the public from death or serious personal injury, whether physical or psychological, occasioned by further such offences committed by him.

(6B) Where an arrested juvenile is moved to local authority accommodation under subsection (6) above, it shall be lawful for any person acting on behalf of the authority to detain him.

(7) A certificate made under subsection (6) above in respect of an arrested juvenile shall be produced to the court before which he is first brought thereafter.

(7A) In this section "imprisonable offence" has the same meaning as in Schedule 1 to the Bail Act 1976.

(8) In this Part of this Act "local authority" has the same meaning as in the Children Act 1989.

56 Right to have someone informed when arrested

(1) Where a person has been arrested and is being held in custody in a police station or other premises, he shall be entitled, if he so requests, to have one friend or relative or other person who is known to him or who is likely to take an interest in his welfare told, as soon as is practicable except to the extent that delay is permitted by this section, that he has been arrested and is being detained there.

(2) Delay is only permitted –

    (a)   in the case of a person who is in police detention for an indictable offence; and

    (b)   if an officer of at least the rank of inspector authorises it.

(3) In any case the person in custody must be permitted to exercise the right conferred by subsection (1) above within 36 hours from the relevant time, as defined in section 41(2) above.

(4) An officer may give an authorisation under subsection (2) above orally or in writing but, if he gives it orally, he shall confirm it in writing as soon as is practicable.

(5) Subject to sub-section (5A) below an officer may only authorise delay where he has reasonable grounds for believing that telling the named person of the arrest –

    (a)   will lead to interference with or harm to evidence connected with an indictable offence or interference with or physical injury to other persons; or

    (b)   will lead to the alerting of other persons suspected of having committed such an offence but not yet arrested for it; or

    (c)   will hinder the recovery of any property obtained as a result of such an offence.

(5A) An officer may also authorise delay where he has reasonable grounds for believing that –

    (a)   the person detained for the indictable offence has benefited from his criminal conduct, and

    (b)   the recovery of the value of the property constituting the benefit will be hindered by telling the named person of the arrest.

(5B) For the purposes of subsection (5A) above the question whether a person has benefited from his criminal conduct is to be decided in accordance with Part 2 of the Proceeds of Crime Act 2002.

(6) If a delay is authorised –

    (a)   the detained person shall be told the reason for it; and

    (b)   the reason shall be noted on his custody record.

(7) The duties imposed by subsection (6) above shall be performed as soon as is practicable.

(8) The rights conferred by this section on a person detained at a police station or other premises are exercisable whenever he is transferred from one place to another; and this section applies to each subsequent occasion on which they are exercisable as it applies to the first such occasion.

(9) There may be no further delay in permitting the exercise of the right conferred by subsection (1) above once the reason for authorising delay ceases to subsist.

(10) Nothing in this section applies to a person arrested or detained under the terrorism provisions.

58 Access to legal advice

(1) A person arrested and held in custody in a police station or other premises shall be entitled, if he so requests, to consult a solicitor privately at any time.

(2) Subject to subsection (3) below, a request under subsection (1) above and the time at which it was made shall be recorded in the custody record.

(3) Such a request need not be recorded in the custody record of a person who makes it at a time while he is at a court after being charged with an offence.

(4) If a person makes such a request, he must be permitted to consult a solicitor as soon as is practicable except to the extent that delay is permitted by this section.

(5) In any case he must be permitted to consult a solicitor within 36 hours from the relevant time, as defined in section 41(2) above.

(6) Delay in compliance with a request is only permitted –

   (a)   in the case of a person who is in police detention for an indictable offence; and
   (b)   if an officer of at least the rank of superintendent authorises it.

(7) An officer may give an authorisation under subsection (6) above orally or in writing but, if he gives it orally, he shall confirm it in writing as soon as is practicable.

(8) Subject to sub-section (8A) below an officer may only authorise delay where he has reasonable grounds for believing that the exercise of the right conferred by subsection (1) above at the time when the person detained desires to exercise it –

   (a)   will lead to interference with or harm to evidence connected with an indictable offence or interference with or physical injury to other persons; or
   (b)   will lead to the alerting of other persons suspected of having committed such an offence but not yet arrested for it; or
   (c)   will hinder the recovery of any property obtained as a result of such an offence.

(8A) An officer may also authorise delay where he has reasonable grounds for believing that –

   (a)   the person detained for the indictable offence has benefited from his criminal conduct, and
   (b)   the recovery of the value of the property constituting the benefit will be hindered by the exercise of the right conferred by subsection (1) above.

(8B) For the purposes of subsection (8A) above the question whether a person has benefited from his criminal conduct is to be decided in accordance with Part 2 of the Proceeds of Crime Act 2002.

(9) If delay is authorised –

   (a)   the detained person shall be told the reason for it; and
   (b)   the reason shall be noted on his custody record.

(10) The duties imposed by subsection (9) above shall be performed as soon as is practicable.

(11) There may be no further delay in permitting the exercise of the right conferred by subsection (1) above once the reason for authorising delay ceases to subsist.

(12) Nothing in this section applies to a person arrested or detained under the terrorism provisions.

66 Codes of practice

(1) The Secretary of State shall issue codes of practice in connection with –

- (a) the exercise by police officers of statutory powers –
    - (i) to search a person without first arresting him;
    - (ii) to search a vehicle without making an arrest; or
    - (iii) to arrest a person;

- (b) the detention, treatment, questioning and identification of persons by police officers;
- (c) searches of premises by police officers; and
- (d) the seizure of property found by police officers on persons or premises.

(2) Codes shall (in particular) include provision in connection with the exercise by police officers of powers under section 63B above.

(3) Nothing in this section requires the Secretary of State to issue a code of practice in relation to any matter falling within the code of practice issued under section 47AB(2) of the Terrorism Act 2000 (as that code is altered or replaced from time to time) (code of practice in relation to terrorism powers to search persons and vehicles and to stop and search in specified locations).

76 Confessions

(1) In any proceedings a confession made by an accused person may be given in evidence against him in so far as it is relevant to any matter in issue in the proceedings and is not excluded by the court in pursuance of this section.

(2) If, in any proceedings where the prosecution proposes to give in evidence a confession made by an accused person, it is represented to the court that the confession was or may have been obtained –

- (a) by oppression of the person who made it; or
- (b) in consequence of anything said or done which was likely, in the circumstances existing at the time, to render unreliable any confession which might be made by him in consequence thereof,

the court shall not allow the confession to be given in evidence against him except in so far as the prosecution proves to the court beyond reasonable doubt that the confession (notwithstanding that it may be true) was not obtained as aforesaid.

(3) In any proceedings where the prosecution proposes to give in evidence a confession made by an accused person, the court may of its own motion require the prosecution, as a condition of allowing it to do so, to prove that the confession was not obtained as mentioned in subsection (2) above.

(4) The fact that a confession is wholly or partly excluded in pursuance of this section shall not affect the admissibility in evidence –

- (a) of any facts discovered as a result of the confession; or
- (b) where the confession is relevant as showing that the accused speaks, writes or expresses himself in a particular way, of so much of the confession as is necessary to show that he does so.

(5) Evidence that a fact to which this subsection applies was discovered as a result of a statement made by an accused person shall not be admissible unless evidence of how it was discovered is given by him or on his behalf.

(6) Subsection (5) above applies –

   (a)   to any fact discovered as a result of a confession which is wholly excluded in pursuance of this section; and
   (b)   to any fact discovered as a result of a confession which is partly so excluded, if the fact is discovered as a result of the excluded part of the confession.

(7) Nothing in Part VII of this Act shall prejudice the admissibility of a confession made by an accused person.

(8) In this section "oppression" includes torture, inhuman or degrading treatment, and the use or threat of violence (whether or not amounting to torture).

78 Exclusion of unfair evidence

(1) In any proceedings the court may refuse to allow evidence on which the prosecution proposes to rely to be given if it appears to the court that, having regard to all the circumstances, including the circumstances in which the evidence was obtained, the admission of the evidence would have such an adverse effect on the fairness of the proceedings that the court ought not to admit it.

(2) Nothing in this section shall prejudice any rule of law requiring a court to exclude evidence.

[2:10] Brown, D, 'PACE ten years on: a review of the research'
(1997) HORS No 155, HMSO (at page ix)

The Police and Criminal Evidence Act 1984 (PACE) is the direct outcome of the Royal Commission on Criminal Procedure's (RCCP) recommendations for systematic reform in the investigative process. The provisions of the Act are designed to match up to principles of fairness (for both police and suspect), openness and workability. Overall, they are intended to strike a balance between the public interest in solving crime and the rights and liberties of suspects.

A considerable body of research on the operation of the Act now exists, and this is reviewed in this report. The main areas examined are as follows.

Stop and search: PACE introduced a general power to stop and search persons or vehicles for stolen or prohibited articles. The safeguards include the requirement to keep records and to inform the person stopped of the reasons for police action.

Entry, search and seizure: PACE provides powers to search premises for evidence, to search premises in connection with making an arrest and to seize evidence. Safeguards relate to the level of authority required to search, the keeping of records and provisions of reasons for searches.

Arrest: PACE rationalises police arrest powers. The basis for arrest is reasonable grounds for suspicion. In less serious offences, arrests may only be made where service of a summons is impracticable.

Detention: detention is only permissible where necessary to secure or preserve evidence, or obtain evidence by questioning. Custody officers, independent from the investigation, decide on the necessity of detention and look after the suspect's welfare while in custody. An upper limit of 24 hours is put on detention without charge, other than in a limited group of 'serious arrestable offences'. Officers of inspector rank or above review the need for further detention at specified intervals.

Questioning and treatment of suspects: suspects have statutory rights to legal advice and to have someone informed of their detention under PACE. They may not generally be interviewed until they have received legal advice, if requested. Accurate records of interviews must be made. Juveniles and the mentally disordered or handicapped must not be interviewed in the absence of an 'appropriate adult'. PACE defines circumstances in which interview evidence is liable to be excluded.

Accountability and supervision: PACE emphasises the need for the reviewability of police actions and the importance of internal police supervision. Custody records for each prisoner must record events occurring during detention. Certain decisions – delaying access to legal advice, for example – must be made by senior officers independent from the investigation. External accountability is enhanced through changes to the police complaints procedure, including the formation of the independent Police Complaints Authority, which supervises the investigation of serious allegations. The Act also provides for arrangements to be made to obtain the views of the community about policing.

The main findings of research are summarised below.

Stop and search

Pre-PACE research points to considerable under-recording of stops and suggests that the decision to stop was often based on hunch or stereotyping, with Afro-Caribbeans more likely to be stopped than white people. Records of stops were rarely inspected by supervisors. Only a small minority of stops led to arrest.

Frequency of stop and search has increased under PACE, although to some extent this may be an artefact of better recording. Stop/searches occur most frequently in the Metropolitan Police. Around one in eight searches lead to an arrest.

It is doubtful if stops are always made on the basis of reasonable suspicion. Where the suspect's consent is obtained, this may not always be fully informed.

Afro-Caribbeans are more likely to be stopped than white people or Asians, more likely to be repeatedly stopped, and more likely to be searched following a stop.

Entry, search and seizure

Stemming from clearer statutory powers, there has been a rise in the proportion of searches of premises authorised by the police rather than under court warrants. The most frequently used powers are those to search premises upon or after arrest. Around 15% of searches are conducted with the occupant's consent.

Around three-quarters of searches on warrant and about half of other searches lead to the seizure of property, usually stolen goods. However, it is doubtful whether all searches are conducted on the basis of reasonable suspicion.

Around half of those whose premises are searched are satisfied with the conduct of the search. Where there is dissatisfaction it is caused by officers' failures to identify themselves, provide a copy of the search warrant or state their search powers.

PACE powers to obtain access to confidential information are proving a valuable asset, although problems may arise where large volumes of material are sought or where some explanation of the material found is required.

Arrest and detention

Although PACE was intended to restrict arrest to situations in which it was strictly necessary, suspects are very rarely summonsed instead. However, there are indications of increased police professionalism and that arrests are now made on a firmer evidential basis. Fewer than before are made without independent evidence.

Black people are arrested at a higher rate than white people, but this does not appear to be because weaker evidence is used to justify their arrest.

Custody officers rarely scrutinise the necessity for a suspect's detention in any detail and almost all those arrested are detained. Similarly, reviews of detention after 6 and 15 hours are largely routinised procedures lacking any substantial enquiry.

Under PACE, those arrested for serious offences are generally held for shorter periods than before but in less serious cases several factors (such as waiting for legal advice or the arrival of appropriate adults) have pushed the length of detention up.

PACE limits on length of detention have not generally created problems for investigating officers.

There is considerable regional variation in the bailing of suspects after charge, probably reflecting different interpretations of the PACE bail criteria, particularly in relation to the risks of re-offending.

Treatment of suspects

The effectiveness of custody officers in looking after the suspect's welfare is constrained by pressure of work and lack of direct oversight of some aspects of the detention process. However, they appear able to maintain a viewpoint independent of that of investigating officers.

Detainees are generally given written and spoken information about their rights, although not always clearly. There is little evidence that rights are systematically denied.

A large and increasing proportion of suspects are aware of their basic rights although some confusions remain and the written information provided is not always found to be helpful.

Nearly 20% of detainees ask to have someone informed of their arrest and implementation of requests is rarely formally delayed. Only around 12% of detainees ask to make a telephone call, and only five receive visitors.

Doctors are called to examine prisoners in about 7% of cases (although in the Metropolitan Police this rises to 25%), usually where detainees are believed to be drunk, but also where mental disorder or mental handicap is suspected.

Legal advice

The great majority of suspects are given information about their right to legal advice. Improved information has been provided since the first revised PACE Codes of Practice were introduced, raising awareness among suspects that legal advice is free. Custody officers may exercise considerable influence over whether legal advice is sought.

Requests for legal advice have more than doubled under PACE and have increased further since. Nearly 40% of suspects now request advice, although there are large regional variations.

Over 80% of those who request legal advice eventually receive it. Cancellation of requests often occur where the chosen adviser is unavailable or where the parents of juveniles consider a lawyer unnecessary.

In around 70% of cases in which legal advice is given, the adviser attends the police station, but in the remainder advice is given solely over the telephone. A significant proportion of advice is provided by non-qualified solicitors' representatives.

Legal advisers often obtain only sketchy information about cases from the police, either because they do not ask for it or because the police withhold it. Generally, consultations with clients prior to police interviews are brief. The advice given is usually either neutral in character or to co-operate with police questions. Advice to remain silent is given in around a fifth of legal advice cases.

In most police interviews legal advisers are passive and do not always intervene to curtail oppressive or repetitive questioning or to allow suspects to present their version of events.

Access to legal advice was occasionally delayed when PACE was first introduced but this now occurs only exceptionally.

Interviews with suspects

Under PACE, interviews are rarely conducted with those who are unfit to be questioned. Suspects are also interviewed less frequently. Interviews do sometimes occur with those suffering from psychological conditions due to the difficulties in identifying such disorders.

Securing a confession remains an important aim of interviewing suspects, although this is now probably more to supplement other evidence.

Interviewing officers continue to use tactics designed to secure a confession, although unacceptable tactics (for example, exploiting police control over bail and charge decisions) are now used less often.

Some forms of questioning raise concerns about false confessions. These concerns are mitigated – although not entirely removed – by the fact that in over 90% of cases preceded with by the police independent corroborative evidence is obtained.

Between 55% and 60% of those interviewed confess – little different from pre-PACE estimates. Confessions are less likely where suspects are legally advised or the evidence is weak; they are more likely in cases involving juveniles or strong evidence.

Audio-taping of interviews has led to fewer disputes in court about what was said and has improved the flow of questioning. However, there are considerable problems with written records of taped interview prepared by police officers, with up to half suffering from the omission of salient points, prolixity or prosecution bias. Records prepared by civilians are significantly better in terms of quality and cost.

Video-taping of interviews has raised some technical problems but has proved its value as a supervisory and training tool. It also appears to offer advantages over audio-taping in a significant minority of cases – some very serious – by clarifying what was taking place in the interview room. However, few videos are presently played at court.

Little supervision or monitoring of interviewing takes place. One reason is that supervisory responsibility often rests with those who conduct interviews; another is supervisors' reluctance to risk injuring the professional pride of interviewing officers.

Some questioning of suspects occurs outside of formal police station interviews. Up to 10% of suspects are interviewed after arrest and prior to arrival at the station; up to a third of suspects who are charged may have made admissions prior to reaching the station. Once at the station, a certain amount of unregulated questioning by case officers still occurs.

Right of silence

Research has provided widely varying estimates of the use by suspects of the right of silence but it would appear that, under PACE, initially around 5% of suspects outside London and up to 9% in London refused to answer all questions, while 5% and 7% respectively refused to answer some questions of significance. This represents little change from the pre-PACE situation.

Data from recent studies (albeit pre-dating the implementation of the Criminal Justice and Public Order Act 1994) suggest that increasing numbers of suspects are staying silent and that 10% are refusing all questions and 13% some significant questions.

Suspects detained for more serious offences, those with previous convictions and those who have taken legal advice are more likely to refuse police questions. In the latter instance, this a direct result of legal advice in only a minority of cases. More often, advisers either proffer no such advice, go along with their client's wishes or urge the opposite course.

Some interviewing officers abandon interviews with silent suspects but others have various techniques – such as increasing the pressure by revealing further incriminating information – to elicit answers.

Police decisions to take no further action are largely unrelated to whether suspects have exercised their right of silence. There also appears to be no link with CPS decisions to discontinue cases.

Those who plead not guilty at court are more likely to have refused to answer police questions than those who plead guilty. However, those pleading not guilty who have exercised their right of silence are less likely to be acquitted than other defendants.

Significant minorities of defendants who plead not guilty raise defences not previously mentioned during questioning. However, few such defences genuinely amount to 'ambushes' because, for example, they relate to matters the suspect could not have raised during police interviews.

Juveniles

Up to a fifth of suspects detained by the police are aged 16 or under. In around two-thirds of cases parents or relatives act as appropriate adults but, in 20% or more, social workers fulfil this function.

Parents are often not well-equipped to act as appropriate adults because they may know little about police procedures or what is acceptable in police interviews, may be emotionally upset at their child's predicament, or may take sides with or against the police. Their role is often not explained to them by the police. They tend to play little part in police interviews.

Social workers also often lack training in the appropriate adult's role. The quality of their response is related to the organisation of juvenile justice work in social services departments and the extent to which staff specialise in this area. Like parents, they generally remain passive during police interviews.

Around 60% of juveniles' time in custody is spent waiting for an appropriate adult to attend. Demands on social services mean that waits are often longer for social worker than relatives. On average, however, juveniles are detained for shorter periods than adults.

Juveniles are given full information about their rights less often than adults and in some cases information is either not given at all or not until an adult is present. There have been recent improvements in this situation.

Juveniles are less likely than adults to request legal advice and there is far more variation between areas in request rates than for adults. There is evidence that the police sometimes delay or avoid taking forward requests by juveniles for legal advice.

There is some evidence that juveniles are more likely than adults to provide admissions, although questioning is not often oppressive. Admissions are most often provided where there is strong evidence, the juvenile has no previous convictions and the offence is less serious.

PACE and the mentally disordered and mentally handicapped

Up to 2% of detainees are treated by the police as mentally disordered or mentally handicapped. Up to one-third are brought to the police station as a place of safety rather than on suspicion of committing an offence. Identifying detainees with mental health problems presents difficulties for custody officers and substantially more detainees may in fact need an appropriate adult.

Custody officers often summon the police surgeon in the first instance and in many cases, acting on the doctor's advice, do not then call for an appropriate adult.

Ensuring that detainees with mental health problems understand their rights is problematic. Experiments with simplified versions of the notices currently provided to all suspects have had some success in raising levels of understanding.

The role of the appropriate adult raises a number of problems. Firstly, there is sometimes confusion as to whether social workers are acting in this role or making an assessment under the Mental Health Act. Secondly, custody officers may not always be right in assuming that professionals know what is expected of them as appropriate adults. Thirdly, there is a lack of clarity about the status of information confided in appropriate adults by detainees.

The interviewing of those with mental health problems raises dangers of generating false confessions and of over-ready compliance, leading to inaccurate replies. Police officers tend to over-estimate the reliability of the information provided.

Appropriate adults seldom intervene during interviews with mentally disordered or mentally handicapped suspects and may not always constitute an adequate safeguard against the production of unreliable interview evidence.

Supervision and accountability

Supervision

Detectives receive relatively little training in the supervision of investigations; in consequence, investigative errors or shortcomings may be overlooked.

Effective supervision of investigations is impeded by the low visibility of much detective work, issues of professional pride (especially in relation to interviewing skills) and an emphasis on quantity rather than quality of clear-ups.

The bulk of investigations are supervised by lower-ranking officers, who have their own caseloads to cope with, and not by senior officers. This carried the risk that malpractice or incompetence may pass unnoticed.

There is tighter supervision by senior officers in major inquiries and in special squads. In major inquiries, supervision is more directive, there are quality control procedures and teams are comprised of officers without established loyalties to each other. In special squads, there is rigorous scrutiny of the evidence before offenders are targeted and tight managerial control over dealings with informants.

Complaints

No recent research has been carried out in this area. Work carried out in 1987 suggested that, at that time, the Police Complaints Authority (PCA) was less likely to select assault cases than others for supervision. Complaints of assault tend to be particularly difficult to prove and this may have had a bearing on the PCA's decision.

PCA supervision varied from passive, active or directive, depending on how complex and how high profile cases were. Where investigations were supervised, action was more frequently taken against officers, complaints were less often withdrawn, reports were of better quality and investigation was speedier.

Most complainants were dissatisfied with the outcome of supervised cases, although they were more likely than other complainants to feel their case had been treated seriously and to receive good feedback and less likely to have experienced pressure to withdraw. Investigating officers felt that the PCA had little impact on the outcome of investigations, although its attention to the case put them on their mettle.

Informal resolution of complaints were generally not popular with officers subject to complaint since they felt that accepting it was seen as admitting guilt. Officers did not view meetings between officer and complainant as productive.

Where complaints were informally resolved, most complainants accepted this outcome as satisfactory, despite persuasion to take this course in some cases. Complainants were dissatisfied at not meeting officers subject to complaint and with lack of feedback.

A third of complainants reported attempts to dissuade them registering a complaint. Of those withdrawing and proceeding, a majority reported attempts to secure a withdrawal.

Over two-thirds of complainants were dissatisfied with the outcome of their complaint, usually due to the lack of an apology or of an explanation for decisions reached. Those whose complaints were informally resolved were the most satisfied.

Investigating officers were concerned to be seen by complainants to be taking their grievances seriously, although they accepted that the low chances of substantiation meant that many complainants would ultimately be dissatisfied. The thoroughness of investigations meant that they tended to be slow, and this was the subject of considerable criticism by officers subject to complaint.

Public attitude surveys show that up to two-thirds of the public know of the PCA, although rather fewer are aware that it is impartial and independent from the police. Levels of awareness are far lower among members of ethnic minority groups.

Police community consultative committees

Consultation arrangements now exist in most parts of the country. However, there have been difficulties recruiting members representative of local communities, particularly those from minority ethnic groups and younger people. Meetings are infrequent in some areas and, where public, have tended to be poorly attended.

Agenda are sometimes dominated by police authorities. For their part, the police have not always been willing to share information, especially where it relates to operational matters.

The effectiveness of consultative groups appears to be constrained by several factors including: lack of formal authority; absence of hard-edged information; ignorance of policing issues; pro-police orientation; and non-representativeness. However, some groups are notably successful in actively involving local people. Others, which contain influential coalitions of representatives from political parties, local government and statutory and voluntary agencies are effective in raising their agendas with the police.

Conclusions

Fairness, openness and workability

The review concludes that PACE has introduced a greater element of fairness into pre-charge procedures, in that suspects are now more aware of their rights and given the chance to exercise them, although there remain areas in which improvement is required. There are also benefits for the police in terms of clearer and more certain powers, particularly at the station.

However, both police and suspect may suffer from the lack of clarity in relation to powers outside the station, particularly stop, search and entry powers, while, at the station, the suspect may be at a disadvantage due to the lack of clear delineation of what interview tactics are permissible.

The extent to which the exercise of police powers outside the police station can be reviewed after the event is limited where officers act with the apparent consent of the suspect.

Reviewability of police action, both at the station and outside, is also constrained by dependence on official records, which may be incomplete, unreliable or unverifiable.

PACE powers are generally more workable than their predecessors, because they provide clarification and certainty, particularly in relation to detention at the station. However, the use of stop and search and entry and search powers remains problematic, and officers often prefer to operate with the subject's consent.

Legal regulation of policing

Police behaviour appears to be more strongly influenced by PACE rules inside the police station than out. The reason for this difference is probably that insufficient account was taken of the strong informal working rules which determine how the police behave on the street.

The lessons to be drawn from the experience of implementing PACE are that new legal rules can alter existing working practices provided that: they are clear; their introduction is accompanied by adequate training; there are effective sanctions and supervision; and the public are aware of their rights and of police powers.

Balance in the investigative process

The review concludes that PACE has not yet produced a system in balance, in the sense that police powers and safe guards for the suspect are generally well matched in key areas.

In relation to the exercise of stop and search and entry and search powers and the treatment of at risk groups, suspects may be at a relative disadvantage. However, at the police station suspects may be benefiting considerably from the availability of legal advice and use of the right of silence, to the detriment of the public interest in bringing criminals to account.

The picture is a shifting one, and current initiatives in the criminal justice field may go some way towards producing a balanced pre-charge process.

[2:11] Bucke, T and Brown, D, 'In police custody: police powers and suspects' rights under the revised PACE Codes of Practice'
(1997) HORS No 174 HMSO (at page 69)

The main aim of this study was to examine changes in the revised PACE Codes of Practice concerning those in police detention. It also sought to investigate other related changes arising from the CJPOA and to monitor a number of aspects in the operation of PACE. In this concluding chapter the main findings of the research are discussed along with their implications.

Appropriate adults

In line with the Codes of Practice appropriate adults were provided in the majority of cases involving juvenile and mentally disordered or handicapped detainees. However, shortcomings were found in the level of guidance provided to appropriate adults. Custody officers rarely gave advice to those acting as appropriate adults about the role, and were unlikely to be asked for any. The implication of this lack of guidance is that a large proportion of those acting as appropriate adults, particular those other than social workers, probably do not know what their role actually is, and could be said to be acting as appropriate adults in name only.

The research also examined the suitability of those acting as appropriate adults for juvenile detainees. Here the reactions of family members on finding a child in police custody could undermine their ability to be an appropriate adult. Notable proportions of family members were found to be distressed or hostile to the juvenile, leading to various reactions including remoteness, antagonism and, in some cases, violence. In slightly more cases family members were described as either supportive or calm. However, such demeanours did not mean that the appropriate adult role was adequately fulfilled. As revealed by other research (see Palmer and Hart, 1996; Evans, 1993) many parents were simply passive observers, making few or no interventions and providing little advice or assistance to the juvenile. The actions of those who became involved revealed their confusion about the role, with some parents advising their children to remain silent and others encouraging them to confess. The effectiveness of parents acting as appropriate adults and providing a safeguard is an important issue. Juveniles represent around *one in five detainees* and parents act as appropriate adults in the majority of cases. The research also raised questions about the suitability of those other than family members acting as appropriate adults.

Concerns about the role of appropriate adults led the RCCJ to recommend a comprehensive review of the role, functions, qualifications, training and availability of appropriate adults. This review was instituted by the Home Office in 1994. The resulting Appropriate Adults Working Group was also asked to consider three other issues. Firstly, the changes to Code C needed to give effect to any recommendations. Secondly, whether the police required clearer guidance about the criteria to be used in considering the need for an appropriate adult. Thirdly, and following another RCCJ recommendation, whether there was a need for a rule governing the status of information passed by suspects to appropriate adults. The Working Group reported in mid-1995 and made a series of wide ranging recommendations which are currently under consideration. A future Home Office circular will provide the police with further guidance on appropriate adults, with associated changes possibly being made to the Codes of Practice.

Legal advice

Studies since the introduction of PACE have indicated rises in suspects requesting legal advice. The current study found a further increase, with four out of ten suspects now making requests. One explanation for this is the increase in requests among juvenile suspects. However, the level of legal advice actually received was only slightly higher than in previous studies, indicating a rise in the attrition rate. Reasons given by suspects for refusing legal advice were rarely recorded by custody officers; in those cases where they were, the majority of suspects simply said that the situation did not merit it.

Comparisons with previous research suggest that legal consultations have increased in duration. The changes to the right of silence mean that suspects in custody require sound legal advice on their position when being questioned by officers. As a result legal advisers need to take time to guide their clients on how to respond to police questions in the context of the inferences that may be drawn from silence. The quality of legal advice received by suspects has been the source of some criticism in the past, notably surrounding the use of unqualified legal staff. As a result the Law Society introduced a scheme whereby those passing a series of tests can become 'accredited representatives' and receive the same status as solicitors. The current study indicates that the proportion of unqualified legal staff advising at police stations has declined, due to a rise in solicitors attending and the introduction of 'accredited representatives'. Whether this development has led to any improvement in the legal advice suspects receive remains unclear.

The right of silence

The extent to which suspects used the right of silence was found to have declined compared to estimates from studies conducted before the new provisions. 'No comment' interviews were found to have fallen by just under a half, while the selective answering of questions had fallen by just under a third. Reductions in the use of silence were found to be greatest among those receiving legal advice. However, confessions by suspects during interviews remained at the same level as before the new provisions. Suspects therefore appear to be responding to police questions without making admissions of guilt any more than before. One possibility is that more suspects are providing officers with statements which, while not admissions of guilt, can be tested against other evidence. The full implications of the new provisions will depend on what happens in the prosecution and trial processes; however these will be addressed in a forthcoming report which will provide further information from this research and other work.

Disposal of juvenile suspects

One of the most pronounced developments found in the study concerned juveniles. Probably as a result of a Home Office circular advising against multiple cautions, juveniles were more likely to be charged and less likely to be cautioned. Furthermore decisions on juveniles were made much earlier in the process than in the past. Consequently, there was a decline in juveniles being bailed for inquiries or reported for summons, with disposal decisions being increasingly made at the end of detention. Finally, once charged juveniles were more likely than before to be refused bail and detained for court.

These developments have a number of consequences. First, juveniles are less likely to be diverted away from prosecution than in the past. This is linked to a decline in the role of juvenile bureaux or panels, with decisions on juvenile cases increasingly the sole responsibility of police officers. Second, changes in the disposal of juveniles together with the rise in their requests for legal advice, means that previous divisions in the treatment of juvenile and adult suspects appear much less distinct. Third, these developments mean that a greater number of juveniles will be at liberty having been charged by the police and bailed pending various court appearances. An unintended consequence of this may be a rise in the levels of offending on bail.

DNA sampling

Alterations to the Code of Practice have provided far greater scope for DNA sampling, with officers now able to take samples from a much larger range of suspects than in the past. However, the study found samples to be taken from a relatively small proportion of suspects. Clearly intimate samples were only taken in very specific cases, while non-intimate samples were also taken selectively. This may be due to ACPO and Home Office guidance advising that non-intimate samples should only be taken for certain types of crime (i.e. offences against the person, sexual offences and burglaries). Samples were taken for other forms of crime, although it is likely that the suspects concerned had previous links to the offences in the designated categories. The vast majority of samples were taken in order to build up the DNA database and, while the proportion of suspects sampled appears relatively small, it should be noted that approximately 1.5 million people enter police custody every year. Selective sampling therefore is likely to add a substantial number of people to the database over the forthcoming years.

[2:12] Ashworth, A 'Should the police be allowed to use deception?'
(1998) 114 *Law Quarterly Review* 108 (at page 138)

There is a long line of judicial authority to the effect that a criminal court may properly exclude evidence which has been obtained by means of a trick, sometimes justified by reference to the privilege against self-incrimination. The aim of this article has been to conduct a deeper examination: rather than relying on judicial authority, and not confining the discussion to the reception of evidence by courts, it has set out to articulate and to test the justifications for the use of deceptive practices by the police and other law enforcement agencies. The conclusions, in brief, are as follows:

(i)   that lying in court is absolutely wrong because it compromises the integrity of the crim-inal justice system, and any attempt to justify it in terms of convicting the factually guilty is constitutionally and morally unsustainable;

(ii)   that at any earlier stage in the criminal process 'tricks about rights' are wrong for similar reasons, in so far as the rights are recognised in the European Convention on Human Rights, in domestic legislation or in the Codes of Practice;

(iii) that for this purpose a trick should be defined so as to include any deception, including a failure to inform a suspect when there is a duty to do so; but,

(iv)   that there are distinctly fewer moral objections to the use of disguises, informers or other agents at the investigative stage, so long as this does not involve prompting or questioning a suspect in relation to an incident in a way that undermines rights that should be protected; and

(v)   that there are also fewer moral objections to covert tape recording or electronic surveil-lance, although the moral objections to 'bugging' private premises remain strong and should only be overcome in situations where the justifications for invading privacy are powerful and properly tested.

In relation to undercover policing and the use of electronic devices, the community's interests in the prevention and detection of crime may justify a judicious use of these prac-tices, subject to appropriate safeguards. There is a need for controls for two distinct reasons – to prevent the abuse of power by law enforcement agencies, and to ensure that any relevant rights of citizens are recognised and protected. Questions of accountability and of the criteria on which the deployment of these policing methods should be justified must be tackled more convincingly than they are in the Police Act 1997. The admissibility of evidence obtained in contravention of the principles is a separate issue, although several of the arguments dis-cussed above are relevant.

In respect of undercover policing, operations ought to be approved at a high level of command within the police service. Customs and Excise, or whatever agency in concerned; and they should be subject to scrutiny by, for example, the Chief Inspector of Constabulary. So far as the criteria are concerned, it must be established the normal methods of gathering evi-dence would be 'bound to fail', and the reasons for this must be recorded; the police officer(s) involved in the undercover work must be briefed specifically about the rights of others that must be respected, particularly in terms of not trying to prompt admissions.

Turning to electronic, telephonic and other forms of surveillance, this is likely to involve interference with the privacy and/or the property rights of citizens, and it should therefore be taken far more seriously than it has been hitherto. English law is truly in a lamentable state, and requires both greater consistency and firmer principle. The lack of consistency derives not merely from the variety of separate statutory regimes that exist (e.g. the Interception of Communications Act 1985, the Intelligence Services Act 1994, the Security Services Act 1996, and the Police Act 1997), but also from the failure of these statutes to cover several forms of electronic surveillance and communications equipment. The lack of principle stems from the desire (at least in previous years) to keep to a minimal compliance with the European Conven-tion. Instead, greater attention should be given to principled criteria for determining whether permission should be granted. Five points should be considered. First, the nature of the right of privacy and the reasons for it should be spelt out. Second, there must be a clear and circumscribed indication of the level of seriousness of offence necessary to justify an incursion on the right of privacy: mere references to 'crimes of violence' is much too broad, whereas a criterion of offences serious enough to attract at least three years imprisonment for an adult of good character gives a better indication of the necessary threshold. Third, it must be shown that the use of electronic devices is necessary, and that no less intrusive method would be likely to succeed. Fourth, it must be shown that the electronic device has good prospects of success. Fifth, any curtailment of the right of privacy should be kept to a minimum.

This discussion of accountability and criteria should not distract attention from the central argument that, in principle, the police should recognise a duty not to use deceptive practices in the investigation of crime. In those limited circumstances in which deceptive practices or electronic surveillance can be justified, the reasons for the general duty and the exceptions should form part of police training and re-training, with a view to implanting them in police culture. For so long as the restrictions are regarded as pointless or irritating handicaps to the pursuit of proper goals, law enforcement officers will be tempted to try to circumvent them or simply to ignore them.

[2:13] *R v Looseley; A-G's Reference (No 3 of 2000)*
[2002] Crim LR 301

House of Lords; Lord Nicholls of Birkenhead, Lord Mackay of Clashfern, Lord Hoffmann, Lord Hutton and Lord Scott of Foscote: October 25, 2001; [2001] UKHL 53.

L was charged with supplying or being concerned in the supply of heroin to an undercover police officer known as 'Rob' who was part of an undercover operation mounted by the police in 1999 in Guildford because of their concern about the trade in Class A drugs in that area. Rob's evidence was that a man in a public house had provided him with the appellant's first name and telephone number and suggested he should telephone the appellant if he wished to obtain drugs. Rob telephoned the appellant who agreed that he could 'sort him out a couple of bags' and gave him directions to his flat. The appellant drove Rob from the flat to the supplier's home where the appellant left the car taking £30 from Rob. He returned saying he had the 'stuff'. He kept a small quantity for himself and gave the remainder to Rob. On analysis the package was found to contain 152 milligrams of heroin at 100 per cent purity. Four days later a similar transaction took place and a third transaction took place three days after that. At the trial the defence submitted, as a preliminary issue, that the indictment ought to be stayed as an abuse of the process of the court or, alternatively, that Rob's evidence should be excluded under section 78(1) of the Police and Criminal Evidence Act 1984. The judge ruled against those submissions and the appellant changed his pleas to guilty. His appeal against conviction was dismissed by the Court of Appeal on the grounds that although if a person had been incited or entrapped by a law enforcement officer into committing an offence then the officer's evidence should be excluded under section 78, where the officer, as in this case, had done no more that give the appellant the opportunity to break the law and the appellant had freely taken advantage of that opportunity in circumstances where it appeared he would have behaved in the same way if the opportunity had been offered by anyone else, there was no reason why the officer's evidence should be excluded. The Court of Appeal certified the following point of law of general public importance: 'Should the judge have refused to admit the evidence of the undercover police officer 'Rob' because the role played by 'Rob' went beyond mere observation and involved asking the appellant to supply him with heroin, a request to which, on the judge's findings, the appellant readily agreed?'

In the second case, the Attorney-General referred a point of law to the Court of Appeal after the acquittal of an accused charged with supplying or being concerned in the supply to another of a Class A drug. Undercover police officers had asked S if he wanted to buy some contraband cigarettes. S took them to the accused and after conversations about cigarettes, the police officers asked the accused if he could sort them out some 'brown'. After further conversations the police officers persuaded the accused to provide them with heroin. The accused said at one stage 'I'm not really into heroin myself'. He also said, when interviewed by the police, that the officers 'were getting me cheap fags, so as far as I was concerned a favour for a favour'. At the trial the judge ruled that the police officers went further than was permissible and in fact incited and procured this accused to commit an offence which he would not otherwise have committed. On the accused's acquittal, the Attorney-General referred the following point of law to the Court of Appeal for its opinion: 'In a case involving the commission of offences by an accused at the instigation of undercover police officers, to what extent, if any, have: (i) the judicial discretion conferred by section 78 of the Police and Criminal Evidence Act 1984; and (ii) the power to stay the proceedings as an abuse of the court been modified by Article 6 of the European Convention of the Protection of Human Rights and Fundamental Freedoms and the jurisprudence of the European Court of Human Rights?' The Court of Appeal answered the question in the negative and ruled that the trial judge had erred in staying the proceedings. The question of law was further referred to the House of Lords.

Held, that it was a fundamental principle of the rule of law that every court had an inherent power and duty to prevent abuse of its process. It was simply not acceptable that the State through its agents should lure its citizens into committing acts forbidden by the law and then seek to prosecute them for doing so. That would be entrapment and misuse of State power. The role of the courts was to stand between the State and its citizens and to make sure this did not happen. Although entrapment was not a substantive defence, English law had now developed remedies in respect of entrapment: the court might stay the relevant criminal proceedings or it might exclude evidence pursuant to section 78. The grant of a stay should normally be regarded as the appropriate response in a case of entrapment. Police conduct which brought about State-created crime was unacceptable and improper but if the police conduct preceding the commission of the offence was no more than might have been expected from others in the circumstances it was not to be regarded as inciting or instigating crime, or luring a person into committing a crime. In the latter situation the police did no more than others could be expected to do and did not create the crime artificially. In assessing the propriety of police conduct proportionality had a role to play; the greater the degree of intrusiveness, the closer the court would scrutinise the reasons for using it. Ultimately, the overall consideration was always whether the conduct of the police or other law enforcement agency was so seriously improper as to bring the administration of justice into disrepute. Accordingly, L's appeal would be dismissed since the undercover officer in that case did no more than present himself as an ordinary customer to an active drug dealer. On the Attorney-General's reference, affirming the Court of Appeal's decision in part, the court's power to exclude evidence under section 78 or to stay proceedings were unaffected by article 6. But in this case the trial judge was entitled to stay the proceedings on the ground that the police officer had instigated the drug offence by offering an inducement of a profitable trade in contraband cigarettes, an inducement which would not ordinarily be associated with the commission of that offence.

Sang (1979) 69 Cr.App.R. 282, [1980] A.C. 402, HL; *R. v. Horseferry Road Magistrates' Court, ex p. Bennett* (1994) 98 Cr.App.R. 114, [1994] 1 A.C. 42, HL; *Latif and Shahzad* [1996] 2 Cr.App.R. 92 [1996] 1 W.L.R. 104, HL, *Teixeira de Castro v. Portugal* [1998] 28 E.H.R.R. 101 and *Nottingham City Council v. Amin* [2001] 1 Cr.App.R. 426, [2000] 1 W.L.R. 1071, DC considered.

Decision of the Court of Appeal (Criminal Division) in *Looseley* affirmed.

Decision of the Court of Appeal (Criminal Division) in *Attorney-General's Reference (No. 3 of 2000)* reversed in part.

Commentary (by Professor David Ormerod): For the comment on the decision of the Court of Appeal in the *Attorney-General's Reference (No. 3 of 2000)* see [2001] Crim.L.R. 645, and for a comprehensive analysis of the House of Lords decisions and its broader implications, see A. Ashworth, 'Re-drawing the Boundaries of Entrapment' [2002] Crim.L.R. 249.

As Ashworth observes, at a general level, the decision is to be welcomed for clarifying the rationale of, and remedies available for, entrapment. The unanimous decision that although there is no defence of entrapment, nevertheless the principal remedy for entrapment is a stay for abuse of process, demonstrates how significant that doctrine has become. Although the remedy of a stay for abuse looks like a defence created through the back door, the House of Lords acknowledged that, on this point at least, *Sang* had been 'overtaken': per Lord Nicholls at paragraph 16.

On narrower issues the decision is welcome for some clarification of definitions: 'incitement' in this context is not to be construed in its technical criminal law sense. The House of Lords is also to be commended for emphasising that the predisposition of the accused is not a key factor. Indeed, Lord Hoffmann reasons that since the court's inquiry is about abuse of process and not about whether D has a defence or is blameworthy, any predisposition is 'irrelevant', otherwise than in the police forming a reasonable suspicion. This approach prevents the potential for abuse of this pro-active policing method which the decision of the Court of Appeal left open. With the central question of entrapment now clearly stated to be whether the police conduct was 'unexceptional', and the House of Lords' endorsement of a need for prior suspicion and even possibly authorisation, the decision puts the law in this area on a more acceptable foundation. Inevitably, there is still some room for clarification of the application of the principles in hard cases. Prime candidates for argument will be the relevance of the vulnerability of the accused and precisely what amounts to 'unexceptional' behaviour in organised criminal activity.

[2:14] *Best Use of Stop and Search Scheme*
(2014) Home Office/College of Policing (at page 2)

Summary

The Best Use of Stop and Search Scheme was announced by the Home Secretary in her statement to Parliament on 30th April 2014.

The principal aims of the Scheme are to achieve greater transparency, community involvement in the use of stop and search powers and to support a more intelligence-led approach, leading to better outcomes, for example, an increase in the stop and search to positive outcome ratio.

The features of the Scheme are:

- Data Recording – forces will record the broader range of stop and search outcomes e.g. arrests, cautions, penalty notices for disorder and all other disposal types. Forces will also show the link, or lack of one, between the object of the search and its outcome.
- Lay observation policies – providing the opportunity for members of the local community to accompany police officers on patrol using stop and search.
- Stop and search complaints 'community trigger' – a local complaint policy requiring the police to explain to local community scrutiny groups how the powers are being used where there is a large volume of complaints.

- Reducing section 60 'no-suspicion' stop and searches by –
  - Raising the level of authorisation to senior officer (above the rank of chief superintendent);
  - Ensuring that section 60 stop and search is only used where it is deemed necessary – and making this clear to the public;
  - In anticipation of serious violence, the authorising officer must reasonably believe that an incident involving serious violence will take place rather than may;
  - Limiting the duration of initial authorisations to no more than 15 hours (down from 24); and
  - Communicating to local communities when there is a section 60 authorisation in advance (where practicable) and afterwards, so that the public is kept informed of the purpose and success of the operation.

By adopting the Scheme, forces will use stop and search strategically, which will improve public confidence and trust.

[2:15] Moston, S and Stephenson, G M, 'The Questioning and Interviewing of Suspects Outside the Police Station'
(1993) RCCJ Research Study No 22, HMSO (at page 46)

This study has shown that in a large number of cases suspects are questioned, interviewed, or have other conversations with police officers prior to their arrival at the police station. In most cases there is no record of the content of these exchanges and even when records are ostensibly kept, they are typically inadequate. Even under ideal circumstances, contemporaneous notes are not suited for encounters outside the police station and there are strong arguments in favour of the provision of portable recorders.

Encounters outside the police station are important for understanding why suspects make admissions inside the police station. Interviews inside the police station, either recorded on audio or video tape, contain only one part of the relevant exchanges between the suspect and police officers. The current legislation, by emphasising the importance of interviews inside the police station has resulted in a situation in which evidence gathered outside the station is seemingly of minimal value. It is widely assumed that the use of tape or video recording equipment inside the station gives a complete picture of the interview with a suspect. This assumption appears to be incorrect. The statement made by suspects on tape are the outcome of a series of conversations with police officers. The interview inside the police station is merely the final part of this process.

[2:16] *Report of the Royal Commission on Criminal Justice*
(1993) Cm 2263, HMSO (at page 52)

(iii) Arguments for retaining the right of silence
13 Those opposed to any weakening of the right of silence in response to police questioning include the Bar Council, Law Society and the Criminal Bar Association, who do not accept that it could be right to allow suspects to be threatened with the possibility of adverse comment simply because they refused to answer police questions. They say that not only are the circumstances of police interrogation disorientating and intimidating in themselves, but there can be justification for requiring a suspect to answer questions when he or she may be unclear both about the nature of the offence which he or she is alleged to have committed

and about the legal definitions of intent, dishonesty and so forth on which an indictment may turn. Innocent suspects' reasons for remaining silent may include, for example, the protection of family or friends, a sense of bewilderment, embarrassment or outrage, or a reasoned decision to wait until the allegation against them has been set out in detail and they have had the benefit of considered legal advice. Members of ethnic or other minority groups may have particular reasons of their own for fearing that any answers they give will be unfairly used against them. There is the risk that, if the police were allowed to warn suspects who declined to answer their questions that they faced the prospect of adverse comment at trial, such a power would sometimes be abused. It is now well established that certain people, including some who are not mentally ill or handicapped, will confess to offences they did not commit whether or not there has been impropriety on the part of the police. The threat of adverse comment at trial may increase the risk of confused or vulnerable suspects making false confessions.

14 Those who take this view argue that it would, for all these reasons, be against the interests of justice to weaken the protection afforded to the innocent suspect by the right of silence. They do not agree that the present safeguard against adverse comment necessarily encourages the police to press too hard for confessions. It may indeed be the case that the police do sometimes try too hard and too exclusively to obtain a formal confession; but they maintain that, if silence is not of itself acceptable evidence, the police should thereby be encouraged to look for other evidence by which the prosecution case can be strengthened. If the right not to answer police questions were removed, adverse comment at the trial would enable a prosecution case which was otherwise too weak to secure a conviction to be strengthened in the minds of the jury by the implication that the defendant's silence automatically supported it.

. . .

(v) Our conclusions

20 In the light of all the evidence put before us, we have had to weigh against each other two conflicting considerations. One is the prospect, if adverse comment at trial were to be permissible, of an increase in the number of convictions of guilty defendants who have refused to answer police questions. The other is the risk of an increase in the number of innocent defendants who are convicted because they have made admissions prejudicial to themselves through the fear of adverse comment at trial or whose silence has been taken by the jury to add sufficient weight to the prosecution case to turn a not guilty verdict into one of guilty.

21 Two of us take the view that it would be right for adverse comment (as suggested in paragraph 11 above) to be permitted at the trial and for a consequential amendment (on the lines of the example in paragraph 10 above) to be made to the wording of the caution. In the appropriate case the jury could thus be invited to draw its own conclusions as to whether the silence in the case in question supported the evidence pointing to guilt. The two of us who take this view believe that it is amply justified by the arguments set out in paragraphs 6 to 12 above. They accept that the majority of us are reluctant to take this step for, among other reasons, fear of weakening the safeguards that exist for the vulnerable suspect. The minority would, however, strengthen those safeguards in other ways and in any case believe that the right of silence offers little or no protection to the vulnerable. There is some evidence, as well as the experience of the police service, which in their view implies that it is not the vulnerable but the experienced criminal who shelters behind the right of silence.

22 The majority of us, however, believe that the possibility of an increase in the conviction of the guilty is outweighted by the risk that the extra pressure on suspects to talk in the police

station and the adverse inferences invited if they do not may result in more convictions of the innocent. They recommend retaining the present caution and trial direction unamended. In taking this view, the majority acknowledge the frustration which many police officers feel when confronted with suspects who refuse to offer any explanation whatever of strong prima facie evidence that they have committed an offence. But they doubt whether the possibility of adverse comment at trial would make the difference which the police suppose. The experienced professional criminals who wish to remain silent are likely to continue to do so and will justify their silence by stating at trial that their solicitors have advised them to say nothing at least until the allegations against them have been fully disclosed. It may be that more defendants would be convicted whose refusal to answer police questions had been the subject of adverse comment; but the majority believe that their number would not be nearly as great as it popularly imagined.

23 It is the less experienced and more vulnerable suspects against whom the threat of adverse comment would be likely to be more damaging. There are too many cases of improper pressures being brought to bear on suspects in police custody, even where the safeguards of PACE and the codes of practice have been supposedly in force, for the majority to regard this with equanimity. As far as silence at the police station is concerned, therefore, the majority find themselves taking the same stance as the majority of the Royal Commission on Criminal Procedure (RCCP) which said, at paragraph 4.50 on its Report that, if adverse inferences could be drawn from silence, 'It might put strong (and additional) psychological pressure upon some suspects to answer questions without knowing precisely what was the substance of and evidence for the accusations against them . . . This in our view might well increase the risk of innocent people, particularly those under suspicion for the first time, making damaging statements . . . On the other hand, the guilty person who knew the system would be inclined to sit it out . . . If the police had sufficient evidence to mount a case without a statement from him, it would still be to the guilty suspect's advantage to keep to himself as long as possible a false defence which was capable of being shown to be such by investigation. It might just be believed by the jury despite the fact that the prosecution and the judge would be able to comment.'

24 In the majority's view, therefore, in accordance with the recommendations which are argued more fully in chapter six, it is when, but only when, the prosecution case has been fully disclosed that defendants should be required to offer an answer to the charges made against them at the risk of adverse comment at trial on any new defence they then disclose, or on any departure from the defence which they previously disclosed. They may still choose to run the risk of such comment, or indeed to remain silent throughout their trial. But if they do, it will be in the knowledge that their hope of an acquittal rests on the ability of defending counsel either to convince the jury that there is a reasonable explanation for the departure or, where silence is maintained throughout, to discredit the prosecution evidence in the jury's eyes. As argued below, it should be open to the judge, as now in serious fraud cases, to comment on any new defence or any departure from an earlier line of defence.

25 In reaching this view the majority have considered whether there may be a special category of case where a different approach is needed. This is where a crime may have been committed, more than one person is present, and it is impossible to say who has committed the offence. This typically happens when one of two parents is suspected of injuring or murdering a child but it is impossible to say which one. It must not, however, be supposed that removing the right of silence would be the solution in such cases. It would not enable the prosecution to establish which of them had committed the offence if both nevertheless insisted on remaining silent. Nor would the possibility of adverse comment at the trial enable a court or a jury to determine in respect of which of them the silence should be taken as

corroboration. We have every sympathy with the public concern over such cases but it seems to us that they need approaching in a different way, perhaps, where children are the victims, by extending the concept of absolute liability for a child's safety.

[2:17] Criminal Justice and Public Order Act 1994 (as amended)
Sections 34–38

34 Effect of accused's failure to mention facts when questioned or charged

(1) Where, in any proceedings against a person for an offence, evidence is given that the accused –

(a) at any time before he was charged with the offence, on being questioned under caution by a constable trying to discover whether or by whom the offence had been committed, failed to mention any fact relied on in his defence in those proceedings; or

(b) on being charged with the offence or officially informed that he might be prosecuted for it, failed to mention any such fact;

(c) at any time after being charged with the offence, on being questioned under section 22 of the Counter-Terrorism Act 2008 (post-charge questioning), failed to mention any such fact,

being a fact which in the circumstances existing at the time the accused could reasonably have been expected to mention when so questioned, charged or informed, as the case may be, subsection (2) below applies.

(2) Where this subsection applies –

(a) . . .

(b) a judge, in deciding whether to grant an application made by the accused under paragraph 2 of Schedule 3 to the Crime and Disorder Act 1998;

(c) the court, in determining whether there is a case to answer; and

(d) the court or jury, in determining whether the accused is guilty of the offence charged,

may draw such inferences from the failure as appear proper.

(2A) Where the accused was at an authorised place of detention at the time of the failure, subsections (1) and (2) above do not apply if he had not been allowed an opportunity to consult a solicitor prior to being questioned, charged or informed as mentioned in subsection (1) above.

(3) Subject to any directions by the court, evidence tending to establish the failure may be given before or after evidence tending to establish the fact which the accused is alleged to have failed to mention.

(4) This section applies in relation to questioning by persons (other than constables) charged with the duty of investigating offences or charging offenders as it applies in relation to questioning by constables; and in subsection (1) above "officially informed" means informed by a constable or any such person.

(5) This section does not –

(a) prejudice the admissibility in evidence of the silence or other reaction of the accused in the face of anything said in his presence relating to the conduct in respect of which he is charged, in so far as evidence thereof would be admissible apart from this section; or

(b) preclude the drawing of any inference from any such silence or other reaction of the accused which could properly be drawn apart from this section.

(6) This section does not apply in relation to a failure to mention a fact if the failure occurred before the commencement of this section.

35 Effect of accused's silence at trial

(1) At the trial of any person for an offence, subsections (2) and (3) below apply unless –

(a) the accused's guilt is not in issue; or
(b) it appears to the court that the physical or mental condition of the accused makes it undesirable for him to give evidence;

but subsection (2) below does not apply if, at the conclusion of the evidence for the prosecution, his legal representative informs the court that the accused will give evidence or, where he is unrepresented, the court ascertains from him that he will give evidence.

(2) Where this subsection applies, the court shall, at the conclusion of the evidence for the prosecution, satisfy itself (in the case of proceedings on indictment with a jury, in the presence of the jury) that the accused is aware that the stage has been reached at which evidence can be given for the defence and that he can, if he wishes, give evidence and that, if he chooses not to give evidence, or having been sworn, without good cause refuses to answer any question, it will be permissible for the court or jury to draw such inferences as appear proper from his failure to give evidence or his refusal, without good cause, to answer any question.

(3) Where this subsection applies, the court or jury, in determining whether the accused is guilty of the offence charged, may draw such inferences as appear proper from the failure of the accused to give evidence or his refusal, without good cause, to answer any question.

(4) This section does not render the accused compellable to give evidence on his own behalf, and he shall accordingly not be guilty of contempt of court by reason of a failure to do so.

(5) For the purposes of this section a person who, having been sworn, refuses to answer any question shall be taken to do so without good cause unless –

(a) he is entitled to refuse to answer the question by virtue of any enactment, whenever passed or made, or on the ground of privilege; or
(b) the court in the exercise of its general discretion excuses him from answering it.

(7) This section applies –

(a) in relation to proceedings on indictment for an offence, only if the person charged with the offence is arraigned on or after the commencement of this section;
(b) in relation to proceedings in a magistrates' court, only if the time when the court begins to receive evidence in the proceedings falls after the commencement of this section.

36 Effect of accused's failure or refusal to account for objects, substances or marks

(1) Where –

- (a) a person is arrested by a constable, and there is –
  - (i) on his person; or
  - (ii) in or on his clothing or footwear; or
  - (iii) otherwise in his possession; or
  - (iv) in any place in which he is at the time of his arrest,
    any object, substance or mark, or there is any mark on any such object; and
- (b) that or another constable investigating the case reasonably believes that the presence of the object, substance or mark may be attributable to the participation of the person arrested in the commission of an offence specified by the constable; and
- (c) the constable informs the person arrested that he so believes, and requests him to account for the presence of the object, substance or mark; and
- (d) the person fails or refuses to do so,

then if, in any proceedings against the person for the offence so specified, evidence of those matters is given, subsection (2) below applies.

(2) Where this subsection applies –

- (a) ...
- (b) a judge, in deciding whether to grant an application made by the accused under paragraph 2 of Schedule 3 to the Crime and Disorder Act 1998;
- (c) the court, in determining whether there is a case to answer; and
- (d) the court or jury, in determining whether the accused is guilty of the offence charged,

may draw such inferences from the failure or refusal as appear proper.

(3) Subsections (1) and (2) above apply to the condition of clothing or footwear as they apply to a substance or mark thereon.

(4) Subsections (1) and (2) above do not apply unless the accused was told in ordinary language by the constable when making the request mentioned in subsection (1)(c) above what the effect of this section would be if he failed or refused to comply with the request.

(4A) Where the accused was at an authorised place of detention at the time of the failure or refusal, subsections (1) and (2) above do not apply if he had not been allowed an opportunity to consult a solicitor prior to the request being made.

(5) This section applies in relation to officers of customs and excise as it applies in relation to constables.

(6) This section does not preclude the drawing of any inference from a failure or refusal of the accused to account for the presence of an object, substance or mark or from the condition of clothing or footwear which could properly be drawn apart from this section.

(7) This section does not apply in relation to a failure or refusal which occurred before the commencement of this section.

37 Effect of accused's failure or refusal to account for presence at a particular place

(1) Where –

(a) a person arrested by a constable was found by him at a place at or about the time the offence for which he was arrested is alleged to have been committed; and

(b) that or another constable investigating the offence reasonably believes that the presence of the person at that place and at that time may be attributable to his participation in the commission of the offence; and

(c) the constable informs the person that he so believes, and requests him to account for that presence; and

(d) the person fails or refuses to do so,

then if, in any proceedings against the person for the offence, evidence of those matters is given, subsection (2) below applies.

(2) Where this subsection applies –

(a) ...

(b) a judge, in deciding whether to grant an application made by the accused under paragraph 2 of Schedule 3 to the Crime and Disorder Act 1998;

(c) the court, in determining whether there is a case to answer; and

(d) the court or jury, in determining whether the accused is guilty of the offence charged,

may draw such inferences from the failure or refusal as appear proper.

(3) Subsections (1) and (2) do not apply unless the accused was told in ordinary language by the constable when making the request mentioned in subsection (1)(c) above what the effect of this section would be if he failed or refused to comply with the request.

(3A) Where the accused was at an authorised place of detention at the time of the failure or refusal, subsections (1) and (2) do not apply if he had not been allowed an opportunity to consult a solicitor prior to the request being made.

(4) This section applies in relation to officers of customs and excise as it applies in relation to constables.

(5) This section does not preclude the drawing of any inference from a failure or refusal of the accused to account for his presence at a place which could properly be drawn apart from this section.

(6) This section does not apply in relation to a failure or refusal which occurred before the commencement of this section.

38 Interpretation and savings for sections 34, 35, 36 and 37

(1) In sections 34, 35, 36 and 37 of this Act –

"legal representative" means a person who, for the purposes of the Legal Services Act 2007, is an authorised person in relation to an activity which constitutes the exercise of a right of audience or the conduct of litigation (within the meaning of that Act); and

"place" includes any building or part of a building, any vehicle, vessel, aircraft or hovercraft and any other place whatsoever.

(2) In sections 34(2), 35(3), 36(2) and 37(2), references to an offence charged include references to any other offence of which the accused could lawfully be convicted on that charge.

(2A) In each of sections 34(2A), 36(4A) and 37(3A)"authorised place of detention" means –

(a)   a police station; or
(b)   any other place prescribed for the purposes of that provision by order made by the Secretary of State;

and the power to make an order under this subsection shall be exercisable by statutory instrument which shall be subject to annulment in pursuance of a resolution of either House of Parliament.

(3) A person shall not have the proceedings against him transferred to the Crown Court for trial, have a case to answer or be convicted of an offence solely on an inference drawn from such a failure or refusal as is mentioned in section 34(2), 35(3), 36(2) or 37(2).

(4) A judge shall not refuse to grant such an application as is mentioned in section 34(2)(b), 36(2)(b) and 37(2)(b) solely on an inference drawn from such a failure as is mentioned in section 34(2), 36(2) or 37(2).

(5) Nothing in sections 34, 35, 36 or 37 prejudices the operation of a provision of any enactment which provides (in whatever words) that any answer or evidence given by a person in specified circumstances shall not be admissible in evidence against him or some other person in any proceedings or class of proceedings (however described, and whether civil or criminal).

In this subsection, the reference to giving evidence is a reference to giving evidence in any manner, whether by furnishing information, making discovery, producing documents or otherwise.
(6) Nothing in section 34, 35, 36 or 37 prejudices any power of a court, in any proceedings, to exclude evidence (whether by preventing questions being put or otherwise) at its discretion.

[2:18] Kemp, V, 'PACE, performance targets and legal protections'
[2014] Crim LR 278 (at page 282)

This study involved an examination of the main police station in four different police force areas in late 2010. It included observation of suspects being booked into police custody, interviews with fifty custody sergeants and analysis of police custody records. It was arising out of this study that one of the four stations – Police Station B – was identified with a relatively low take-up of legal advice. The finding prompted the police and the defence in this station to support new arrangements intended to help improve access to legal advice; referred to as the "Bridewell study" [The police station involved has not been named and instead the colloquial term the "Bridewell" has been used].

In an ideal world, the findings arising out of this study of four stations would have been published before the commencement of the new initiative, but this was not possible. Accordingly, and by way of an update, reference is sometimes made to findings arising out of the Bridewell study. The methods in that study included observations of police custody and the police investigation, as well as interviews with suspects, custody sergeants, police investigators and defence practitioners.

"Offences brought to justice": widening the net of social control

The metaphor of "net-widening" is useful when examining the OBTJ [offences brought to justice] target, as this target encouraged the police to take formal action in relation to minor offences and other "easy hits". Despite the target having been withdrawn some months prior to these research interviews, custody sergeants in all four police stations complained about policing strategies which were continuing to pick on children and young people in order to help increase the number of detections. In relation to children, for example, one custody sergeant said, "You get a fight in a school playground – a nothing job. In the old days we would have taken them home and interviewed them in front of their parents but now they are brought into custody" (B:PI) [The first letter identifies the police station involved and the next two letters are the initials of the respondent, coded for reasons of confidentiality]. In a similar vein, another respondent was critical of officers for bringing children into custody for "a kid-on-kid fight in a school playground" (A:JL). There were also concerns raised over the police responding formally to complaints made inappropriately by staff in children's homes. As one respondent put it:

> "We are getting kids who are only 12 or 13 for minor assaults and criminal damage. They might have thrown a cup or something like that. The home should be geared up to deal with incidents like that and not involve the police" (C:PI).

There were also examples given by custody sergeants of where the police would pick on students as "easy hits" for behaviour which would otherwise be ignored, or dealt with informally. The following three comments help to highlight some of the stratagems adopted:

> "We have officers based in a nightclub so they can catch those under-aged who are trying to get in. They picked up a 17-year-old for having a fake ID [identity card] and bailed him back to the police station. What for? I don't get it. The police want a detection so they will put resources into that sort of thing. It's wrong." (A:ES)

> "It's not fair when you get students away from home for the first time. They go out and have a bit to drink. They might be loud and swear at an officer. In the past they would have got a warning and been sent home but now they get arrested because it helps with the figures. It's wrong, as you can have a law student getting a caution and it can affect their lives." (B:PI)

> "Every night the Governor is sending a pair of officers up to the university in order to turn over students for using cannabis. They get a caution and a criminal record and they will probably find that this then comes up on a CRB [criminal records bureau] check when they are looking for a job." (D:SD)

Custody sergeants were critical of other police officers for failing to use their discretion when responding to minor incidents. After making the above comment, for instance, the respondent continued saying:

> "We used to have discretion but it's gone now. If I found a small amount of drugs on someone it didn't mean they'd be arrested. It's nobody's business the amount of cannabis I've chucked down the drains" (D:SD).

The net-widening effect of the OBTJ target was commented on by a number of custody sergeants. One respondent said, for example:

> "The problem is the pressure they [the police] are under. I'm not joking – it's leading to the criminalisation of a section of society who should never have a criminal record" (A:ES).

Another said, "We are criminalising a lot of youngsters who should be sorted out another way" (C:BQ). There were some custody sergeants, particularly the more experienced officers, who said that they would seek to challenge the police when bringing people inappropriately into custody. As one custody sergeant put it:

"There are a lot now where we won't authorise a detention because we think it's a load of rubbish. Like schoolboy fall-outs, minor assaults and shop thefts. They are under pressure to get detections and picking on school kids is easy" (B:QT).

In practice, however, custody sergeants were rarely seen to challenge the police when bringing suspects into custody, even though it was their responsibility under PACE [Police and Criminal Evidence Act 1984] to authorise the detention of suspects.

When it was pointed out to custody sergeants during the research interviews that the OBTJ target had been withdrawn most were surprised that this was the case. Indeed, having referred to such pressure as being a "major problem", when told that there was no longer a national target, one custody sergeant replied: "If it's gone you wouldn't know it here because nothing has changed" (A:ES). It seems that "nothing had changed" in three out of the four police force areas because a target to increase the number of detections had been included in local policing plans for 2010/2011. In Police Station D, on the other hand, a couple of custody sergeants commented on a recent change in policing priorities. As one custody sergeant explained: "Performance here is no longer all about arrests and detections. It's more about victim satisfaction" (D.SE).

With concerns raised over the way in which the OBTJ target encouraged the police to concentrate their efforts on minor offences and other "easy hits", it is interesting that a number of police force areas have adopted OBTJ-type targets as a local performance measurement. Indeed, this was despite strong criticism coming from senior police officers nationally, who felt the OBTJ target was undermining police discretion when responding to minor incidents. This was also an issue raised by Sir Ronnie Flanagan in his Review of Policing. In particular, he stated that:

"My research has consistently highlighted examples where the service could improve its professional judgement and adopt a more proportionate response in responding to lower level crimes. The consequence of poor professional judgement, combined with existing performance management arrangements, is that officers are encouraged to criminalise people for behaviour which may have caused offence but the underlying behaviour would be better dealt with in a different way."

While a substantial proportion of out-of-court disposals were penalties imposed by the police on the streets, increasingly the police were encouraged to bring more minor and trivial offences into custody. There were three main reasons for this change. First, there were incentives within a performance culture for the police to make arrests as well as to increase the number of detections. Secondly, the police were encouraged to convey a suspect into custody so that their identity could be checked through the routine taking of fingerprints and DNA samples. Thirdly, there had been a change in police powers of arrest, which meant that, "the police will be able to arrest anyone without warrant for anything, whether trivial or serious".

The intention of Government in withdrawing the OBTJ target and replacing it with another was to encourage the police to concentrate their efforts on reducing crime. By the first phase of the Bridewell study (February–May 2011), however, there was seen to be little change as the police continued to arrest and detain suspects for minor and trivial offences. Indeed, a key finding at that time was that custody continued to be used inappropriately for low-level offences, which included children and the elderly being detained for a minor first offence. It seems that by the time of the second phase (July–October 2012) there had been a change in police practices because the number of suspects detained had reduced significantly.

While in mid-2012 there had been a reduction in the number of suspects brought into custody in the Bridewell, the police would continue to detain suspects for minor offences. When interviewing police investigators in October 2012, for example, they acknowledged the trivial nature of some of the cases referred to them by front-line officers. Despite the minor nature of some of the offences involved, not one of the investigators said they would refuse to accept a case. On the contrary, one police investigator said: "Drivel is our thing and nothing can be too minor. If it is really minor then we can always use RJ [restorative justice]." Another police investigator said:

> "There's no end of stuff which I think is far too trivial to be dealt with . . . I should say about a third to a quarter of cases we shouldn't even be bothering with. We wouldn't have dealt with them ten years ago."

In Choongh's ethnographic study of police custody in the late 1990s, he noted that a significant minority of people were brought into custody for minor offences, particularly offences of disorder, where the police had no intention of invoking the criminal process. It seems that a change brought about by the OBTJ target has been to put the police under pressure to invoke the criminal process in relation to minor offences in order to increase the number of detections. While the OBTJ target had been withdrawn by June 2010, the police were still seen to be under such pressure in September 2012. In a discussion observed between two officers in the Bridewell study, for example, a police investigator asked a front-line officer how his policing priorities had changed now that he was no longer under pressure to increase the number of detections. The officer replied:

> "You must be joking. That's the biggest load of rubbish I have ever heard. I had a meeting with my Chief Inspector and all he was banging on about was detections, detections, detections."

From recent comments made by government ministers to senior police officers, it is evident that the OBTJ target is not just a local problem in these three police force areas. On the contrary, it seems that other police forces have adopted a local performance target to encourage the police to increase the number of detections. Accordingly, at the Association of Chief Police Officer's annual conference (in September 2013) the Minister for Policing and Justice urged the police to use more judgment and discretion when dealing with low-level crime. He also reminded senior officers that it might be appropriate to simply give someone a "telling off" when called to a relatively minor incident. In a similar vein, at the Superintendents' Association's Annual Conference (also in September 2013) the Home Secretary chastised senior officers for having

> "brought back 'mechanical processes for assessing performance' in the hope that they could 'simply tick boxes' in order to prove that [they were] doing the right thing".

There are not only resource implications for the police when pursuing such a strategy but, as noted above, it can lead to people being criminalised unnecessarily.

[2:19] *R (Guest) v DPP*
[2009] EWHC 594 (Admin)

The claimant applied for judicial review of the decision to offer a conditional caution to a man who had attacked him instead of prosecuting the offender. After the High Court quashed the decision in this case, the attacker, Mr Watts, was subsequently prosecuted and received a suspended prison sentence and was ordered to pay his victim £1,000 in compensation when he pleaded guilty to Assault occasioning Actual Bodily Harm.

(At paragraph 24):

The allegation in this case

24 On Friday, 4 April 2008, following some abusive texts from Mr Guest to Mr Watts, Mr Watts came round to Mr Guest's home. Mr Guest and his partner were asleep in bed. According to Mr Guest's witness statement, which has corroboration from the photographs taken shortly after these events, he was punched several times to the right eye and fell to the floor. When on the floor and crawling towards his bedroom, Mr Watts, it is alleged, continually kicked him in the legs and head. According to Mr Guest, his partner pleaded with Mr Watts to stop kicking and punching. He continued. Mr Guest estimated the length of the incident at about five to ten minutes. He was taken by ambulance to Poole General Hospital. Mr Guest says that he sustained severe bruising to the right eye. He was given some four stitches and butterfly clips by the hospital staff. His nose bled internally. There was bruising to his left outer and inner thigh. Not surprisingly, if the allegations are true, he states he was shocked at what happened.

25 There are, as I have indicated, some photographs which the court has seen. They reveal, among other things, the extent of the bleeding suffered by Mr Guest.

(At paragraph 40)

Judgment

Lord Justice Goldring:

40 It seems to me, on proper analysis, the following is the position:

41 1. As Mr Moores [counsel for the Crown Prosecution Service] ultimately accepted, it is wholly artificial to distinguish between the decision not to prosecute and the decision to administer a conditional caution. The decision not to prosecute and the authority given to the police to administer the caution were part and parcel of the same decision. If the decision, as Mr Moores concedes, not to prosecute was flawed, so too was the decision conditionally to caution. If one falls to be quashed, so too does the other.

42 2. I have no doubt that the decision not to prosecute and to administer a conditional caution was fundamentally flawed.

43 First, it is clear that the assault occasioning actual bodily harm passed both the evidential and public interest limbs of the Code for Crown Prosecutors. The evidence on its face, and I emphasise the words "on its face" for these are allegations, was strong. Mr Watts made admissions. The photographs speak for themselves. Serious violence was not simply threatened; it was used. On the face of it, moreover, although Mr Watts disputes it, there was evidence it was premeditated.

44 Second, the precise terms of the Code for Crown Prosecutors apart, this was a very serious assault. It took place at night, at someone's home, in the presence of that person's partner. It involved, if Mr Guest is right, kicking when someone was on the ground.

45 Third, Annex A of the Director's guidance to conditional cautioning did not permit the administration of a conditional caution in such circumstances. It did not permit conditional cautioning for an offence of assault occasioning actual bodily harm.

46 Fourth, conditional cautioning was not an appropriate and proportionate response to the offending behaviour as required by the Director's guidance.

47 Fifth, Mr Guest was not involved in the decision. Indeed, it was clear that he did not agree with it (although that is not necessarily decisive). Paragraph 5 of Annex B of the Secretary of

State's Code contemplates the victim's involvement. Paragraph 11 of the Director's guidance requires it wherever possible. It also requires consultation where possible on the condition to be imposed as part of the caution.

48 Sixth, in the light of the photographs and the injuries suffered by Mr Guest, there appears to have been only limited consideration of the appropriateness of £200 as compensation.

49 Seventh, the factors taken into account by Mr Clark in arriving at his decision cannot be supported.

50 3. Judicial review is a discretionary remedy. The court has a discretion as to whether or not it makes a quashing order. It will not if to do so would merely be academic. In the context of this case, that means that if an order quashing the decision not to prosecute and to administer the conditional caution were to be academic, because any subsequent decision would be not to prosecute on the basis that there would no reasonable prospect of success on the grounds of abuse of process, no quashing order should be made.

51 4. Speaking for myself, I am far from convinced that such would be the case. Criminal litigation is not a game. Whether in any given situation it can be proved by a defendant that the court's process has been abused is a matter for that court in the light of the facts of that case. All the authorities have to be considered in that light. Mr Watts accepted he was guilty. The caution could not otherwise have been administered. He was given the chance to pay a negligible sum to reflect the offence he admitted he had committed. If the conditional caution were quashed, the sum would be repaid. His admission in the context of the procedure would not stand. He would be in no worse position than had the decision not to prosecute never been taken.

52 It does not seem to me that, in those circumstances, a further prosecution would necessarily amount to an affront to public justice as referred to in some of the authorities. Indeed, many might think that what so far has happened deserves that description.

53 5. Moreover, as Mr Moores has conceded, different considerations could well apply were any private prosecution to be brought by Mr Guest. It was put in argument by Mr Moores in this way: that, as for a private prosecution, the point (i.e. the abuse of process point) is moot. Mr Guest was not part of the flawed decision which was taken by the Crown Prosecution Service.

54 6. Further, while it does not seem to me that in *Jones v Whalley* [2006] UKHL 41] the House of Lords was indicating that invariably an abuse of process argument would not succeed in circumstances such as the present, it is undoubtedly very persuasive authority for the proposition that, given the quashing of a caution, abuse of process would not run. I say that bearing in mind the differences between that case and the present. One thing is clear: in that case, as in the present, a formal, albeit not statutory, caution was administered with the representation to the cautioned person that he would not be prosecuted. The speeches of their Lordships clearly indicate that given a quashing of the caution, a prosecution would lie.

55 7. In short, I have concluded that to quash the decision not to prosecute and administer the conditional caution would not be academic, and the court should order accordingly. If my Lord agrees, we will hear submissions as to the precise form of any order.

A final observation

56 By Part 3 of the Criminal Justice Act 2003, Parliament has decided to place very considerable responsibility on the Crown Prosecution Service. By a decision to offer a conditional

caution to an offender, the court is effectively bypassed. It means that someone who is guilty of committing a criminal offence is not prosecuted, does not appear before the court and is not sentenced by the court. The importance of taking such a decision conscientiously and in accordance with the law can hardly be overstated. The effect on the victim and the damage to the criminal justice system is self-evident if such a decision is taken without proper regard to the relevant guidance.

57 In this case, decisions were taken without regard to the Code for Crown Prosecutors, the Director's guidance on Conditional Cautioning and the Secretary of State's Code of Practice. It seems to me astonishing, as it would no doubt to many members of the public, that the Crown Prosecution Service could seriously contemplate not prosecuting someone who, it was alleged, deliberately went to a person's house at night, attacked him inside that house with some ferocity (including kicking him) in the presence of his (obviously very frightened) partner. I very much hope that this was a one-off aberration and not typical of the manner in which the Crown Prosecution Service discharges its heavy responsibilities in respect of conditional cautioning.

58 MR JUSTICE SWEENEY: The Director of Public Prosecutions rightly concedes that the decision of the Crown Prosecutor is, in law, indefensible. However, the stance of the Director as to the consequences which should flow is, in my judgment, surprising. Abuse of process involves a judgment by a court, based on well-defined principles, on the particular facts of a case. A decision to stay proceedings is a rare outcome. In a case in which, in accordance with the Code for Crown Prosecutors, the evidential and public interest tests are otherwise met, it will thus be in only the most exceptional case, where the Prosecutor can say with a high degree of certainty that a court will rule that a prosecution is proved to be an abuse of its process, that a decision not to prosecute is likely to be valid.

59 On the material before this court, it seems to me that, if the decision to prosecute and the conditional caution are quashed and the £200 returned, this case falls far short of a high degree of certainty that any resultant prosecution would be ruled to be an abuse of process. Rather the reverse. The affront to justice, thus far, of the decision not to prosecute would be put right. It is troubling, to say the least, that the Director, apparently by two senior local lawyers, does not appear to be able to see that.

60 I wholeheartedly agree with the reasoning and observations of my Lord, Goldring LJ, and with his conclusion that both the decision not to prosecute and the conditional caution must be quashed, meaning that the £200 must be returned.

61 For my part, and subject to the further submissions which my Lord has mentioned, I would be minded to order that the case be reconsidered, hopefully at a level at which the abuse of process jurisprudence is properly understood. Subject to that, I would order accordingly.

Chapter 3

The Crown Prosecution Service

Chapter Contents

The police now think they have enough evidence to charge Gerry Good with 'causing grievous bodily harm with intent', contrary to section 18 of the Offences Against the Person Act 1861 (an offence triable on indictment only – i.e. before a judge and jury in the Crown Court). But he will still not necessarily be prosecuted. The Crown Prosecution Service (CPS) has responsibility under the Prosecution of Offences Act 1985 [3:1] for the conduct of all criminal proceedings and, because the CPS may drop or amend charges, they have, in effect, a veto over prosecution. They also advise the police on cases for possible prosecution, review cases submitted by the police and, where the decision is to prosecute, they determine the charge in the more serious cases. They prepare cases for court, thereby possibly having an influence on the distribution of cases between the Crown Courts and magistrates' courts, and in indictable crimes will be involved in the transfer of the case to the Crown Court. In other cases, the CPS may be involved in responding to bail applications and in appeals against decisions by magistrates to grant bail. Increasingly, CPS staff also present cases at court, rather than relying on members of the independent Bar. In others, they prepare the case for trial, and brief counsel (a barrister) to prosecute. They prepare the documents for the Crown in the event of an appeal. Now a key player, the CPS has only been in existence since 1986.

(i) Background

Until 1986, the police were responsible for initiating criminal prosecutions, and bringing cases to court. Of the 43 police forces, 31 had their own prosecution departments, and the rest used private firms of solicitors to carry out prosecutions. The Director of Public Prosecutions Department in London dealt with all murder prosecutions and certain other cases, such as those involving national security or public figures. A Royal Commission on Criminal Procedure (chaired by Sir Cyril Philips), set up in 1977 and reporting in 1981, concluded that the traditional police role in investigating crime was incompatible with the objectivity required in prosecution. The police were not in a position to take a sufficiently broad view when applying public interest criteria to prosecution decisions. They criticised the inconsistent policies pursued by different police forces, especially in relation to the decision whether or not to prosecute, and concluded that too many weak cases were being pursued, resulting in a high percentage of trials in which the judge directed a verdict of not guilty at the close of the prosecution case. They therefore recommended a new prosecution service. In 1983 the Home Office published a White Paper, *The Investigation and Prosecution of Criminal Offences in England and Wales*, which favoured a national organisation with strong local features.

The Prosecution of Offences Act 1985 [3:1], which was brought into force in 1986, still lays down the framework for prosecutions. The CPS is headed by the Director of Public Prosecutions (DPP), under the Attorney General, and has its headquarters in London. They have two main functions: to provide an objective assessment of the results of police investigation; and to prosecute those cases which pass the tests laid down in the Code for Crown Prosecutors. The CPS ran into serious problems at birth. Many of its initial problems were financial: in 1987/88, the CPS cost £134m, almost double the estimated £70m. Moreover, the managerial structure proved unworkable and had to be reorganised in 1989 and again in 1993. Until 1993 the CPS was organised into 31 areas covering England and Wales, usually aligned with one, or sometimes two, police force areas, but in that year the 31 areas were reduced to 13 in order to rationalise area administration and to delegate more responsibility to the areas. The financial problems were exacerbated by the difficulty of recruiting enough well-qualified staff, which meant that the service had to use numerous agency lawyers, who were both expensive and, since they worked only occasional days, unable to see cases through consistently.

The problems did not disappear: in 1998 Sir Iain Glidewell was asked to review the CPS and he produced a detailed report in June 1998 [3:2]. He found that the 1993 reorganisation had been a mistake, and that the CPS should be divided into 42 areas, coterminous with police areas. This reorganisation took place in 1999, and each area was then headed by a Chief Crown Prosecutor, and subdivided into two or more branches. However, despite suggestions that this had improved joint-working between the CPS and the police, the CPS was reorganised in April 2011. This followed the decision in the 2010 Comprehensive Spending Review that the CPS budget would be reduced by 25 per cent over four years. As a consequence, the CPS is once again divided into 13 areas (each still led by a Chief Crown Prosecutor). Charging advice is also given by telephone and email by CPS Direct, 24 hours a day, 365 days a year (CPS Direct was initially established to provide police with overnight charging advice but has since been expanded as it proved to be a more cost-effective way of providing advice).

(ii) The role and legal status of the CPS

It is important to remember that the CPS was a totally new creature to the English legal system in 1986. Its relationship with the police continues to evolve. Until 2004, the police took the decision to charge a suspect and then passed a file to the CPS. However, now the police usually consult the CPS much earlier in the process: the precise rules are complex (see section 28 and Schedule 2 of the Criminal Justice Act 2003), but in reality the relationship between the police and CPS is now governed by the DPP's Guidance on Charging (the current version, available on the CPS website, is the 5th edition, issued in May 2013). Under this guidance, the police may charge summary only and most either way offences (i.e. some of the lower level, 'routine' street crimes, such as shoplifting) which are likely to be dealt with in the magistrates' court (with some exceptions, such as offences which may be classified as hate crimes or domestic violence and certain violent and sexual offences) and the CPS is responsible for all other charging decisions.

We saw in Chapter 2 that there has been a growth in the variety of out-of-court disposals in recent years. In many of these cases, there will be no CPS involvement – although if the offence is indictable only, a simple caution or conditional caution can only be administered with the approval of the CPS. If the police refer any case to the CPS for a charging decision, and the CPS instructs that a simple caution should be offered, then this decision is binding on the police.

How does the citizen challenge decisions taken by the CPS? The first case in which a court had to decide whether CPS decisions were subject to judicial review was R v Chief Constable of Kent, ex p L **[3:3]**, in which the Divisional Court explored the legal relationship between the police and the CPS. Whilst the court held that the police decision (to charge) was not reviewable, in respect of juveniles, the discretion of the CPS to continue or discontinue criminal proceedings may be reviewable in limited circumstances. Watkins LJ was fearful of 'opening too wide the door of review of the discretion', but are the dangers of not opening that door not equally manifest? Despite his warning, there has been no shortage of applications for judicial review of CPS decision-making.

Whilst the decision to prosecute is very difficult to challenge, it may be slightly easier to challenge a decision not to prosecute. In R v DPP, ex p C [1995] 1 Cr App R 136, the Divisional Court allowed an application by a wife for judicial review of a decision by the DPP not to prosecute her husband for buggery, contrary to section 12 of the Sexual Offences Act 1956. The court held that the prosecutor had not followed the Code for Crown Prosecutors, and remitted the case to the DPP for further consideration. The case was cited in the famous decision of the House of Lords (supported by the European Court of Human Rights) in R (Pretty) v DPP [2002] 1 AC 800, upholding the DPP's refusal to undertake not to prosecute Mrs Pretty's husband if he helped her to die. She suffered from motor neurone disease, and was physically unable to end her own life. Her husband was prepared to help her die provided he had an undertaking that he would not be prosecuted. The House of Lords was unanimous that Mrs Pretty could not establish any breach of any Convention right. Beyond that, although the DPP can make statements about prosecuting policy, he had no power to give a 'proleptic grant of immunity from prosecution . . . The power to dispense with and suspend laws and the execution of laws without the consent of Parliament was denied to the crown and its servants by the Bill of Rights 1688' (per Lord Bingham at paragraph 39).

This issue returned to the House of Lords in R (Purdy) v DPP [2009] UKHL 45. Ms Purdy, another motor neurone disease sufferer, sought not immunity from prosecution for her husband if he assisted her suicide, but rather that the DPP should be required to publish a policy outlining the circumstances in which a prosecution would or would not be appropriate. The House of Lords unanimously allowed Ms Purdy's appeal in holding that the Code for Crown Prosecutors alone was insufficient to satisfy the requirements of Article 8 of the European Convention on Human Rights 1950 (see [1:13]) of accessibility and foreseeability in assessing how prosecutorial discretion was likely to be exercised in cases of assisted suicide. It therefore 'require[d] the Director to promulgate an offence-specific policy identifying the facts and circumstances which he will take into account in deciding, in a case such as that which Ms Purdy's case exemplifies, whether or not to consent to a prosecution' (per Lord Hope at paragraph 56). Following this judgment, the then DPP, Keir Starmer, issued the policy for prosecutors in respect of cases of encouraging or assisting suicide in February 2010 (updated by his successor, Alison Saunders, in October 2014 following the Supreme Court's decision in R (Nicklinson) v Ministry of Justice [2014] UKSC 38).

Since June 2013, victims have had an additional avenue to challenge a decision not to prosecute through the Victims' Right to Review Scheme. In R v Killick [2011] EWCA Crim 1608, the Court of Appeal held that '[a]s a decision not to prosecute is in reality a final decision for a victim, there must be a right to seek a review of such a decision' (at paragraph 48) and that victims should not have to have recourse to judicial review in such cases. For 'qualifying' decisions (defined as a decision to either: not charge; discontinue all charges; offer no evidence; or to leave all charges to 'lie on file') made on or after 5 June 2013, a victim can request a review by a different prosecutor from the relevant CPS area ('local resolution') and, if still not satisfied, the process will proceed to an independent review carried out by the Appeals and Review Unit or a Chief Crown Prosecutor depending on the nature of the qualifying decision. Only if this fails to resolve the matter to the victim's satisfaction need they seek recourse to judicial review. This move was welcomed by Starmer (2012), who argues that despite the importance of finality in criminal justice, 'the adjustment to the principle of finality is justified and the result perhaps inevitable once it was recognised that victims are not mere observers in the criminal justice process, but real participants with both interests to protect and rights to enforce' (at page 534). Between 5 June 2013 and 31 March 2014, the CPS reviewed 1,186 cases and decisions under this scheme and overturned 162 decisions.

Even though the courts are reluctant to interfere with the discretionary powers of the CPS, they may discharge or stay a case because of 'abuse of process'. R v Croydon Justices, ex p Dean [3:4] reveals a trial judge's control over the actions of the CPS by their power to discharge a case for abuse of process. This case is an important authority discussed by the House of Lords in their decision in Jones v Whalley [4:10] on the right to bring a private prosecution. It was also cited in the high profile case of Hamza (Abu) [2006] EWCA Crim 2918. Abu Hamza unsuccessfully appealed against his convictions for 'soliciting to murder' (contrary to the Offences against the Person Act 1861, section 4), using threatening, abusive or insulting words or behaviour with intent to stir up racial hatred, possessing threatening, abusive or insulting sound recordings with intent to stir up racial hatred, and possessing a document or record containing information of a kind likely to be useful to a person committing or preparing to commit an act of terrorism. Most of the counts related to speeches given by him between 1997 and 2000; the sound recordings were cassettes of these speeches and the documents were 10 volumes of the Afghani Jihad Encyclopaedia. The cassettes and Encyclopaedia had been seized by police in 1999, following his arrest on suspicion of involvement in a terrorist incident in Yemen, but had been returned to him later in 1999 and he had been informed that no further action would be taken. The Court of Appeal, led by the Lord Chief Justice, rejected the argument that there had been an abuse of process because the returning of his materials gave him a legitimate expectation that he would not later be prosecuted for possession of them. The Court concluded that:

> It is not likely to constitute an abuse of process to proceed with a prosecution unless (i) there has been an unequivocal representation by those with the conduct of the investigation or prosecution of a case that the defendant will not be prosecuted and (ii) that the defendant has acted on that representation to his detriment. Even then, if facts come to light which were not known when the representation was made, these may justify proceeding with the prosecution despite the representation (at paragraph 54).

This case, the Court of Appeal said, fell a long way short of satisfying these criteria. The fact that the police did not prosecute the appellant in 1999 could not be taken as an assurance, let alone an unequivocal assurance, that they would not do so in the future.

The House of Lords decided in *R v Manchester Crown Court, ex p DPP* [1993] 2 All ER 663 that the decision of a Crown Court judge (see Chapter 7) to stay an indictment as an abuse of process was not open to judicial review. This decision may prevent delays, but it also meant that the CPS had no power to challenge a decision to stay which they believed to be wrong. However, this was changed by the Criminal Justice Act 2003, section 58 which gave the prosecution the right to appeal against a 'terminating ruling' (see Chapter 9).

(iii) The Code for Crown Prosecutors

When determining charges, Crown Prosecutors and custody officers must apply the principles contained in the latest edition of the Code for Crown Prosecutors [3:5], i.e. there must be enough evidence to provide a realistic prospect of conviction and it must be in the public interest to proceed. The CPS has a duty to keep the evidence continually under review. Thus, in our case, a Crown Prosecutor will have been consulted by the police before Gerry was charged. At this stage, he can be remanded in custody as long as a 'threshold' test has been passed: this only requires 'reasonable suspicion' that the suspect committed the offence. Someone from the CPS (probably an Associate Prosecutor) will attend the magistrates' court for the bail hearing the morning after Gerry was charged. Any decision to discontinue proceedings can only be taken by a Crown Prosecutor. The basic guidance of the Code for Crown Prosecutors [3:5] is amplified by CPS policy guidance (which is available on the internet at www.cps.gov.uk/prosecution_policy_and_guidance.html). The DPP has a duty under the Prosecution of Offences Act 1985, section 10 [3:1] to issue the code, but this does not mean that the Code amounts to delegated legislation. The DPP's guidance must cover three areas: the decision to prosecute; the selection of the appropriate charges; and the representations to be made to magistrates about where the defendant should face trial in either way offences. The current version of the code, the seventh since the CPS was established, was published in 2013. By simplifying the language, the CPS hoped that it was also clarifying the code. Is it now so simple and lacking in detail that it says very little? Hoyano et al [3:6] interviewed CPS personnel even before this simplification and concluded that the impact of the Code had had a very limited effect on actual case decisions. The reality is that CPS staff followed more sophisticated guidance.

In deciding whether to continue a prosecution, the Crown Prosecutor or Associate Prosecutor considers two questions. First is the question of the sufficiency of the evidence. The evidential threshold is a 'realistic prospect of conviction'. This is an objective test: is it more likely than not that the defendant will be convicted? The evidence must be admissible and reliable. We will see in Chapter 7 that there are no clear rules on admissibility of evidence – the judge has a wide discretion to decide what should be admitted. This element, therefore, is very difficult to predict. It may be even more difficult to predict how the jury or magistrates will decide questions of fact. They will have the benefit of hearing both the prosecution and defence cases before they make their decision. Ashworth and Redmayne (2010) question whether this predictive test is more appropriate than a test of the 'intrinsic merits' of the evidence, and Sanders (1994) was clear that he believed a better test would be whether a particular jury or bench ought to convict. The CPS does not review the case only once, but must keep the decision to carry on with a case continually under review – should a single test of 'a realistic prospect of conviction' be applied at whatever stage in the criminal process? The second task for the Crown Prosecutor is to apply the 'public interest' criterion. Over the years, the Code was revised to list more clearly the factors which tend in favour of, and those which tend against, a prosecution. These have, perhaps surprisingly, been removed from the most recent edition [3:5], which instead guides prosecutors as to the questions – relating to both the offence and the suspect – they should consider.

The CPS relies on the police for its information. This is a particular problem where the defendant intends to plead guilty. The file may be very small and the CPS has little information on which to assess the factors relevant to the public interest criterion. The file may also exaggerate the police construction of the case against the suspect – for example, the extent to which the suspect confessed. One way to alleviate this problem is to provide the CPS with material from other sources. In the early 1990s, the Probation Service (see Chapter 10) introduced Public Interest Case Assessment (PICA) units in a number of areas. These units provided information for the CPS in cases where there might be personal or other circumstances that might justify the discontinuance of a prosecution on the public interest factors in the Code for Crown Prosecutors. Whilst Crisp, Whittaker and Harris (1995) suggested that such schemes were very useful in providing the CPS with verified and relevant information about a defendant's version of events, their research also revealed the difficulty in assessing cost-effectiveness in criminal justice initiatives. In his review of an interesting book by Drakeford, Haines, Cotton and Octigan, Morgan [3:7] uses the decline of PICA units to show how funding issues in a 'non-joined-up' criminal justice system lead to misguided decision-making.

The CPS has a duty to disclose to the defence unused material – this means that prosecutors must disclose to the defence a schedule of any unused material which might reasonably be considered capable of undermining the case for the prosecution against the accused, or of assisting the case for the accused. Clearly, any failure to disclose relevant evidence undermines the right to a fair trial, and it can be argued that if relevant evidence has to be excluded in the public interest, then the prosecution should not be sustained. Where the trial judge rules that the defendant cannot have a fair trial without disclosure, the prosecution have the stark choice: disclosure, or drop the prosecution.

Thus, in Gerry Good's case, the Crown Prosecutor must keep the evidence under review. She believes that the witness statements and Gerry's own unsatisfactory statements to the police are sufficient evidence against him, though she does ask the police to continue their investigations, particularly looking for the knife or evidence of blood stains. After considering the relevant questions set out in the Code [3:5], the CPS decide that the public interest suggests that the prosecution should proceed. This is clearly a serious offence where the harm caused is significant and Gerry's 'culpability', in the wording of the Code, will be increased by the presence of his previous convictions (the proviso that the previous conviction must be 'relevant' has been removed from the most recent edition of the Code). Gerry's case will proceed to trial.

The Crown Prosecutor must also decide what is the right offence with which to charge Gerry. In this case, they may well be uncertain whether to charge under section 18 or section 20 of the Offences Against the Person Act (OAPA) 1861. Section 18 is wounding or grievous bodily harm with intent with a maximum sentence of life imprisonment; section 20 is reckless grievous bodily harm which has a maximum sentence of five years. The distinction is one of intent: the CPS will look for evidence of what Gerry intended when he allegedly hit Rosa. Note that the Code specifically warns against proceeding with a more serious charge simply to encourage the defendant to plead guilty to a lesser charge, an issue we will return to in Chapter 5 when discussing plea bargaining. Let us decide they conclude the evidence supports a charge of an offence under section 18. You will see the indictment at the start of Chapter 7.

In our story, Gerry was granted bail by the magistrates. The Crime and Disorder Act 1998, section 51, provides that indictable cases will be 'sent' automatically for trial at the Crown Court, and Gerry Good will not have to return to the magistrates' court for committal proceedings, although he will be able to apply to have the case dismissed. Before the case is listed for trial, there will be a plea and case management hearing (PCMH) in the Crown Court, within three or four weeks of the transfer. Its purpose is to ensure that all necessary steps have been taken in preparation for trial and sufficient information has been provided for a trial date to be arranged. Not long ago it was right to say that whilst Crown Prosecutors and Associate Prosecutors frequently conducted proceedings in the magistrates' court, they did not generally have 'rights of audience' in the Crown Court and so had to brief counsel (instruct an independent barrister). This was a longstanding sore with the CPS, which has maintained that both recruitment and performance standards would improve if they could conduct its own cases. The tide started to turn in its favour in 1993, when the Lord Chancellor's Advisory Committee on Legal Education and Conduct approved part of the Law Society's application for rights of audience by extending them to suitably qualified solicitors in private practice, but employed barristers and solicitors still did not have the right to appear in the higher courts. The argument against granting the CPS rights of audience is based on the view that the Bar needs to be composed of those who prosecute and those who defend. To give rights of audience to the CPS would fundamentally change the 'independent' Bar. Block, Corbett and Peay [3:10] were critical of counsel's performance in many of their cases, and certainly the current system of last-minute briefing of counsel does suggest that the CPS should have greater responsibility at the trial stage. Block et al recommended that counsel should be obliged in the Bar Code of Practice to give advice to the CPS on receipt of the brief, and that Crown Prosecutors of a certain specified degree of seniority should have rights of audience in the Crown Court and the right of judicial appointment. Now employed solicitors with Higher Rights qualifications present some cases in the Crown Court and employed barristers may have also higher court rights of audience. This has challenged the role of the independent Bar: we return to the subject of the proper role of the CPS in the final section of this chapter.

(iv) The Attorney General and the Director of Public Prosecutions

As the Prosecution of Offences Act 1985 makes clear [3:1], the DPP is appointed by the Attorney General (AG) (section 2) and discharges his functions under the superintendence of the AG (section 3). The AG at the time of writing is Jeremy Wright. The AG and his deputy, the Solicitor General, are the Government's chief legal advisers, advising on domestic and international law. The AG is also a Government Minister. They have, as well, important 'public interest' roles in relation to criminal cases, superintending the work of the Crown Prosecution Service and the Serious Fraud Office. More specifically, the AG's consent is required to prosecute certain offences, and the AG may terminate criminal proceedings on indictment before a judge and jury by the entry of a *nolle prosequi*. This puts an end to the prosecution, rather like a stay on proceedings. Prosecutors can discontinue, withdraw or offer no evidence in their cases, but only the AG may enter a *nolle*. The AG's discretion is extremely wide and cannot be questioned by the courts; it is used where there is no other way of ending proceedings (e.g. on the grounds of the ill health of a defendant). All appeals against unduly lenient sentences are done in the name of the AG, and it is the AG who, under section 36 of the

Criminal Justice Act 1972 **[9:13]**, may seek the opinion of the Court of Appeal on a point of law which has arisen in the case when someone who has been tried on indictment has been acquitted. The role of the AG was reviewed in a consultation paper in 2007 **[3:8]** which resulted in a draft Constitutional Renewal Bill in 2008 which proposed reforms to the role of the AG that would have recast their relationship with the prosecuting authorities by removing the power to give directions to prosecutors in individual cases – including abolishing their right to enter a *nolle prosequi* – save in certain exceptional cases which give rise to issues of national security. However, disappointingly, when the Government brought forward the Constitutional Reform and Governance Bill in 2009, the clauses relating to the office of the AG had been removed – instead a non-statutory *Protocol between the Attorney General and the Prosecuting Departments* was agreed in July 2009 **[3:9]**.

The DPP's post, on the other hand, is less overtly political and controversial. Perhaps the AG should simply 'lose' his criminal justice roles to the DPP who would be answerable to Parliament and to the courts?

(v) Evaluation

For Lord Justice Auld **[1:5]** an essential in preparing for trial is 'a strong, independent and adequately resourced prosecutor in control of the case at least from the point of charge'. How can we measure whether Crown Prosecutors live up to this? Initially, we could consider whether the CPS is inclined to pursue weak cases, or whether they drop too many cases that should have been pursued. Whilst there can be no cut-and-dried measure of success, we can try to measure it in a number of different ways (see Ashworth and Redmayne (2010) for a more detailed analysis).

Firstly, we can look at the conviction rate, which appears to be the preferred method for the CPS. In the Crown Court (according to their Annual Report for 2013/14, page 87), this has risen from 74.3 per cent in 2003/04 to 81.0 per cent in 2013/14. This figure alone, however, does not tell the full story: the vast majority of convictions are not achieved in contested trials but rather are obtained through guilty pleas. Indeed in 2013/14 almost nine convictions were obtained in the Crown Court through a guilty plea for every one obtained after trial by jury. Trial by jury is relatively rare: see Chapter 8. It does not necessarily mean that the 19 per cent who were not convicted in 2013/14 should not have been prosecuted in the first place: it is difficult to predict the outcome of cases, especially without a clear knowledge of the defence case.

Secondly, we can look at the discontinuance rate. Crisp and Moxon (1994) found a termination rate of between 10 per cent and 20 per cent. Glidewell **[3:2]**, pointing out a discontinuation rate of 12 per cent of cases, states that there is evidence that the discontinuance rate varies greatly with types of offence, with (worryingly) the highest discontinuance rates for charges of violence against the person and criminal damage. Since then the discontinuance rate has continued to fall slightly, but the CPS now put more emphasis on 'unsuccessful outcomes', which represent all outcomes other than a conviction, i.e. discontinuances and withdrawals, discharged committals, dismissals and acquittals, and what they call 'administrative finalisations'. The CPS website contains an enormous amount of data on case outcomes, published on a monthly basis, which provides information not only on the overall ratio of 'successful' and 'unsuccessful' cases but also on the outcomes in individual CPS areas and for specific types of offences.

It is not clear whether these 'unsuccessful outcomes' are really 'successes' or 'failures' – is the CPS successfully weeding out weak cases or should they have been weeded out sooner? Since the public interest factors specified for police cautioning are similar to those in the Code for Crown Prosecutors **[3:5]**, it is curious that so many cases remain in the system to be able to be discontinued by the CPS (on average around 15 per cent of cases have been discontinued in recent years). Clearly closer working between the police and the CPS is designed to reduce the discontinuance rate.

A third measure of success (or failure) is the number of judge-directed acquittals in the Crown Court. Here we must distinguish between directed acquittals (where the judge rules that the prosecution has not established a case to answer) and ordered acquittals (where the prosecution offers no evidence). As Block, Corbett and Peay **[3:10]** made clear, neither measure is straightforward. However, they were able to conclude that three-quarters of directed acquittals were definitely or possibly foreseeable, and some criticism of the CPS was clearly merited. According to the CPS Annual Report, during 2013/14, 69 per cent (17,042) of the defendants who pleaded not guilty (24,790) in the Crown Court were acquitted, representing 26 per cent of the total 93,727 dealt with who recorded a plea. Of those 17,042, 63 per cent (10,816) were discharged by the judge, 4 per cent (627) were acquitted on the direction of the judge and just 33 per cent (5,599) were acquitted by a jury. It is quite remarkable that only one-third of acquitted defendants in the Crown Court are acquitted by a jury.

The relationship of the CPS with the police remains problematic. At exactly what point does the CPS take over? Under the Prosecution of Offences Act 1985, section 3(2)(e) **[3:1]** it is the duty of the DPP to give advice to police forces on matters relating to criminal offences. However, the police seem reluctant to seek advice in specific cases. Is it feasible to involve the CPS at the beginning of investigations? Should the CPS have greater control over the provision of information? Should they be able to compel further investigations? The Royal Commission on Criminal Justice (1993) **[1:3]**, with one dissent, fudged the issue by deciding that better and more formal consultation, and earlier liaison with the police, would resolve the problems. The Glidewell Report **[3:2]** recommended a single integrated unit, a 'Criminal Justice Unit' – a CPS unit with some police staff – so that the CPS could assume responsibility for 'the prosecution process immediately following charge'. Yet Auld **[1:5]** recommended that the CPS should determine the charge in all but minor, routine offences. Putting the CPS back into the police station may lead to a more effective system, but it raises other concerns. For example, since the police remain in control of the information that reaches the CPS, will the CPS lose much of the 'independence' which is also crucial? More importantly, to what extent does the CPS working closely with the police limit their role as 'independent' reviewers of police decision-making?

This discussion has concerned the early involvement of the CPS in investigations. It is also interesting to consider its involvement in the later stages of a prosecution. We have seen that the CPS (largely as an economy measure but also in order to create better job-satisfaction for good lawyers) is increasingly presenting cases in the Crown Court. Then there is the question of the prosecution's involvement in the sentencing process. We will see in Chapter 7 that the prosecution currently plays a relatively small role at the sentencing stage. But this is changing: see the sentencing manual on the CPS website. Currently the prosecutor is likely to remind the judge of the facts of the case, check that he or she has the latest version of the defendant's previous convictions, the pre-sentence report, and is aware of relevant law, including, most importantly, the relevant sentencing guidelines and sometimes recent guideline cases from the Court of Appeal. But the prosecution does not call for a particular sentence. If they did, the defence would be able to respond with a more focused plea in mitigation. Would the effect be an increase or a decrease in sentencing levels? Defence lawyers tend to fear that prosecutors would 'talk' up sentencing levels, but it might well be that they would be conscious of the costs of imprisonment and lengths of imprisonment might come down? Perhaps it would make less difference today as all parties focus on the same sentencing guidelines. We return to sentencing issues in Chapter 7.

Since the establishment of the CPS in 1986, there have been many initiatives taken to strengthen its profile in the criminal justice system and there is no doubting that the CPS is now a key player. Yet the CPS cannot breach police control unless they have real powers. As McConville, Sanders and Leng **[3:11]** argued, the CPS is a 'police-dependent body'. Sanders (1987) commented on the difficulties of grafting an inquisitorial element onto an adversarial system. Today, as the police and CPS work ever more closely together, you should consider whether the balance of power is weighted too heavily in favour of prosecutors. We look at this in Chapter 5, when considering the role of defence lawyers.

Meanwhile, in Chapter 4 we look at those prosecutions that are not initiated by the police. This raises the question whether greater consistency would be achieved if prosecutions initiated by such bodies as the Environment Agency were brought under the CPS umbrella.

Further reading

Annual Reports of the Crown Prosecution Service and of HM Inspectorate of the Crown Prosecution Service

Ashworth, A and Fionda, J, 'The New Code for Crown Prosecutors: Prosecution, Accountability and the Public Interest' [1994] Crim LR 894

Ashworth, A and Redmayne, M, *The Criminal Process* (4th edition, 2010) Oxford University Press

Block, B, Corbett, C and Peay, J, 'Ordered and Directed Acquittals in the Crown Court' (1993) RCCJ Research Study No 15, HMSO

Cretney, A and Davis, G, 'Prosecuting "Domestic" Assault' [1996] Crim LR 162

Crisp, D and Moxon, D 'Case screening by the CPS: How and why are cases terminated' (1994) HORS No 137, HMSO

Crisp, D, Whittaker, C and Harris, J, 'Public Interest Case Assessment Schemes' (1995) HORS No 138, HMSO

Hall Williams, J E (ed), *The Role of the Prosecutor* (1988) Avebury

Hilsom, C, 'Discretion to Prosecute and Judicial Review' [1993] Crim LR 739

Home Office, 'An Independent Prosecution Service for England and Wales' (1983) HMSO, Cmnd 9074

Kirk, D, 'Reflections of former prosecutor' (2014) *Journal of Criminal Law* 78(2): 99

Mansfield, G and Peay, J, *The Director of Public Prosecutions: Principles and Practices for the Crown Prosecutor* (1987) Tavistock

Sanders, A, 'Constructing the Case for the Prosecution' (1987) 14 *Journal of Law & Society* 229

Sanders, A, 'The Silent Code' (1994) 144 *New Law Journal* 946

Starmer, K, 'Finality in criminal justice: when should the CPS reopen a case?' [2012] Crim LR 526

Documents

[3:1] Prosecution of Offences Act 1985 (as amended)
Sections 1–3; 10

1 The Crown Prosecution Service

(1) There shall be a prosecuting service for England and Wales (to be known as the "Crown Prosecution Service") consisting of –

(a)   the Director of Public Prosecutions, who shall be head of the Service;
(b)   the Chief Crown Prosecutors, designated under subsection (4) below, each of whom shall be the member of the Service responsible to the Director for supervising the operation of the Service in his area; and
(c)   the other staff appointed by the Director under this section.

(2) The Director shall appoint such staff for the Service as, with the approval of the Treasury as to numbers, remuneration and other terms and conditions of service, he considers necessary for the discharge of his functions.

(3) The Director may designate any member of the Service who has a general qualification (within the meaning of section 71 of the Courts and Legal Services Act 1990 for the purposes of this subsection, and any person so designated shall be known as a Crown Prosecutor.

(4) The Director shall divide England and Wales into areas and, for each of those areas, designate a Crown Prosecutor for the purposes of this subsection and any person so designated shall be known as a Chief Crown Prosecutor.

(5) The Director may, from time to time, vary the division of England and Wales made for the purposes of subsection (4) above.

(6) Without prejudice to any functions which may have been assigned to him in his capacity as a member of the Service, every Crown Prosecutor shall have all the powers of the Director as to the institution and conduct of proceedings but shall exercise those powers under the direction of the Director.

(7) Where any enactment (whenever passed)—

(a) prevents any step from being taken without the consent of the Director or without his consent or the consent of another; or
(b) requires any step to be taken by or in relation to the Director;

any consent given by or, as the case may be, step taken by or in relation to, a Crown Prosecutor shall be treated, for the purposes of that enactment, as given by or, as the case may be, taken by or in relation to the Director.

2 The Director of Public Prosecutions

(1) The Director of Public Prosecutions shall be appointed by the Attorney General.

(2) The Director must be a person who has a ten year general qualification, within the meaning of section 71 of the Courts and Legal Services Act 1990

(3) There shall be paid to the Director such remuneration as the Attorney General may, with the approval of the Treasury, determine.

3 Functions of the Director

(1) The Director shall discharge his functions under this or any other enactment under the superintendence of the Attorney General.

(2) It shall be the duty of the Director, subject to any provisions contained in the Criminal Justice Act 1987—

(a) to take over the conduct of all criminal proceedings, other than specified proceedings, instituted on behalf of a police force (whether by a member of that force or by any other person);
(aa) to take over the conduct of any criminal proceedings instituted by an immigration officer (as defined for the purposes of the Immigration Act 1971) acting in his capacity as such an officer;

(ab) to take over the conduct of any criminal proceedings instituted in England and Wales by the Revenue and Customs;

(ac) to take over the conduct of any criminal proceedings instituted on behalf of the National Crime Agency;

(b) to institute and have the conduct of criminal proceedings in any case where it appears to him that –

   (i) the importance or difficulty of the case makes it appropriate that proceedings should be instituted by him; or

   (ii) it is otherwise appropriate for proceedings to be instituted by him;

(ba) to institute and have the conduct of any criminal proceedings in any case where the proceedings relate to the subject-matter of a report a copy of which has been sent to him under paragraph 23 or 24 of Schedule 3 to the Police Reform Act 2002 (c. 30) (reports on investigations into conduct of persons serving with the police);

(bb) where it appears to him appropriate to do so, to institute and have the conduct of any criminal proceedings in England and Wales relating to a criminal investigation by the Revenue and Customs;

(bc) where it appears to him appropriate to do so, to institute and have the conduct of any criminal proceedings relating to a criminal investigation by the National Crime Agency;

(c) to take over the conduct of all binding over proceedings instituted on behalf of a police force (whether by a member of that force or by any other person);

(d) to take over the conduct of all proceedings begun by summons issued under section 3 of the Obscene Publications Act 1959 (forfeiture of obscene articles);

(e) to give, to such extent as he considers appropriate, advice to police forces on all matters relating to criminal offences;

(ea) to have the conduct of any extradition proceedings;

(eb) to give, to such extent as he considers appropriate, and to such persons as he considers appropriate, advice on any matters relating to extradition proceedings or proposed extradition proceedings;

(ec) to give, to such extent as he considers appropriate, advice to immigration officers on matters relating to criminal offences;

(ed) to give advice, to such extent as he considers appropriate and to such person as he considers appropriate, in relation to –

   (i) criminal investigations by the National Crime Agency, or

   (ii) criminal proceedings arising out of such investigations;

(ee) to give, to such extent as he considers appropriate, and to such persons as he considers appropriate, advice on matters relating to –

   (i) a criminal investigation by the Revenue and Customs; or

   (ii) criminal proceedings instituted in England and Wales relating to a criminal investigation by the Revenue and Customs;

(f) to appear for the prosecution, when directed by the court to do so, on any appeal under –

   (i) section 1 of the Administration of Justice Act 1960 (appeal from the High Court in criminal cases);

   (ii) Part I or Part II of the Criminal Appeal Act 1968 (appeals from the Crown Court to the criminal division of the Court of Appeal and thence to the Supreme Court); or

   (iii) section 108 of the Magistrates' Courts Act 1980 (right of appeal to Crown Court) as it applies, by virtue of subsection (5) of section 12 of the Contempt of Court Act 1981, to orders made under section 12 (contempt of magistrates' courts);

(fa) to have the conduct of applications for orders under section 22 of the Anti-social Behaviour, Crime and Policing Act 2014 (criminal behaviour orders made on conviction) and section 14A of the Football Spectators Act 1989 (banning orders made on conviction of certain offences);

(faa) where it appears to him appropriate to do so, to have the conduct of applications made by him for orders under section 14B of the Football Spectators Act 1989 (banning orders made on complaint);

(fb) where it appears to him appropriate to do so, to have the conduct of applications under section 27 of the Anti-social Behaviour, Crime and Policing Act 2014 for the variation or discharge of orders made under section 22 of that Act;

(fc) where it appears to him appropriate to do so, to appear on any application under section 27 20 of that Act made by a person subject to an order under section 22 of that Act for the variation or discharge of the order;

(ff) to discharge such duties as are conferred on him by, or in relation to, Part 5 or 8 of the Proceeds of Crime Act 2002 (c. 29) (civil recovery of the proceeds etc of unlawful conduct, civil recovery investigations and disclosure orders in relation to confiscation investigations);

(g) to discharge such other functions as may from time to time be assigned to him by the Attorney General in pursuance of this paragraph.

(2A) Subsection (2)(ea) above does not require the Director to have the conduct of any extradition proceedings in respect of a person if he has received a request not to do so and –

(a) in a case where the proceedings are under Part 1 of the Extradition Act 2003, the request is made by the authority which issued the Part 1 warrant in respect of the person;

(b) in a case where the proceedings are under Part 2 of that Act, the request is made on behalf of the territory to which the person's extradition has been requested.

(3) In this section –
"the court" means –

(a) in the case of an appeal to or from the criminal division of the Court of Appeal, that division;

(b) in the case of an appeal from a Divisional Court of the Queen's Bench Division, the Divisional Court; and

(c) in the case of an appeal against an order of a magistrates' court, the Crown Court;

"criminal investigation" means any process –
(i)   for considering whether an offence has been committed;
(ii)   for discovering by whom an offence has been committed; or
(iii) as a result of which an offence is alleged to have been committed;

"police force" means any police force maintained by a local policing body and any other body of constables for the time being specified by order made by the Secretary of State for the purposes of this section; and

"specified proceedings" means proceedings which fall within any category for the time being specified by order made by the Attorney General for the purposes of this section.

(3A) In this section a reference to the Revenue and Customs is a reference to –

(a) the Commissioners for Her Majesty's Revenue and Customs;
(b) an officer of Revenue and Customs; or
(c) a person acting on behalf of the Commissioners or an officer of Revenue and Customs.

(4) The power to make orders under subsection (3) above shall be exercisable by statutory instrument subject to annulment in pursuance of a resolution of either House of Parliament.

10 Guidelines for Crown Prosecutors

(1) The Director shall issue a Code for Crown Prosecutors giving guidance on general principles to be applied by them –

(a) in determining, in any case –
    (i) whether proceedings for an offence should be instituted or, where proceedings have been instituted, whether they should be discontinued; or
    (ii) what charges should be preferred; and
(b) in considering, in any case, representations to be made by them to any magistrates' court about the mode of trial suitable for that case.

(2) The Director may from time to time make alterations in the Code.

(3) The provisions of the Code shall be set out in the Director's report under section 9 of this Act for the year in which the Code is issued; and any alteration in the Code shall be set out in his report under that section for the year in which the alteration is made.

[3:2] *Review of the Crown Prosecution Service*
(1998) Chaired by Sir Iain Glidewell (at page 4 of the summary)

How the prosecution process works at present

13 In order to present the case for the prosecution in court the CPS needs to have a file containing the evidence and other relevant information, including any criminal record the defendant may have. While it is for the police to obtain the evidence as part of the process of investigation, in our view the assembly of the file is part of the conduct of the proceedings for which the CPS is, or should be, responsible. Until now, however, the police have continued to compile prosecution files in a special unit often called an Administrative Support Unit (ASU). The most critical point in the flow of case papers between the investigating officer and the CPS prosecutor in court is at the interface between the ASU and the CPS Branch office.

14 Another cause of discord between the police and the CPS stems from the power of the CPS to discontinue a prosecution. One of a CPS lawyer's most important tasks is to review the evidence in the file in order to decide whether it justifies the charge laid by the police, applying criteria set out in the 'Code for Crown Prosecutors'. If the evidence is not sufficient, the lawyer may either substitute a lesser charge ('downgrading') or discontinue the prosecution altogether. The exercise of this power, which was newly-given in 1986, was resented at that time by some police officers, but most now recognise and accept that it is a valuable provision which should ensure that only those prosecutions proceed to court in which there is an appropriate chance of a conviction in accordance with the Code. This is a safeguard not only for defendants who should not have been charged but also for the public purse.

How the CPS has performed

15 Our Terms of Reference require us to 'assess whether the CPS has contributed to the fall-ing number of convictions for recorded crime'. One thing is clear: the CPS is not concerned with the vast majority of recorded crime. The CPS is responsible for the conduct of all criminal proceedings after there has been a charge by the police or a summons. In 1996, of the crimes recorded by the police (nearly 5 million), only one in every nine (576,000) resulted in a charge or summons. Recorded crimes do not include the large number of motoring offences, so the CPS is concerned with only one out of nine recorded crimes.

16 From there onwards our task becomes more difficult. To carry out such an assessment we have had to examine the available statistics, which has not proved an easy matter. The Home Office, the Court Service and the CPS each produce statistics relating to criminal prosecu-tions and often the figures within apparently similar parameters are inconsistent with each other. It was to be expected that when the CPS came into existence convictions would fall as a proportion of total cases simply as a result of the CPS properly exercising their new power to discontinue some cases. However, figures produced by the CPS have shown that in recent years the proportion of cases in the Crown Court resulting in conviction has increased, but this trend differs from that shown by the figures published in the Judicial Statistics produced by the Court Service, which show a decline in convictions over the period 1985 to 1996. We have tried but failed to find an explanation for the disparity in the two sets of statistics. We cannot therefore say that the CPS figures are wrong. We have recommended that attempts are made to agree one set of figures.

17 Overall the CPS discontinues prosecutions in, on average, 12% of cases where the police have charged. The CPS Inspectorate have found, in their consideration of Branch perfor-mance, few decisions to discontinue which they considered wrong. However, there is some evidence that the average rate of discontinuance varies greatly between types of offence, with the highest discontinuance rates being for charges of violence against the person and criminal damage, and the lowest for motoring offences. This is clearly a matter for concern, the reasons for which must be investigated.

18 We have been specifically asked to comment on the proposal in the Narey Report that the CPS should no longer have the power to discontinue cases on certain public interest grounds, namely that the court is likely to impose a nominal penalty or that the loss involved is small. We have recommended that the proposal should not be adopted but that the incidence of discontinuance on these grounds should be rare. To that end we have also recommended a small amendment to the Code for Crown Prosecutors.

19 Charges are sometimes downgraded and such few statistics as are available seem to show that this happens most frequently with those which relate to serious crime, public order offences and road traffic accidents causing death. We have no evidence which proves that downgrading happens when it should not. Nonetheless, we suspect that inappropriate down-grading does occur and have recommended that cases of downgrading are specifically exam-ined by the Inspectorate during visits to CPS Units. Both the police and the CPS are helped by the existence of guidance in the form of Charging Standards and whilst we approve their existence we have raised questions about the content of some of the standards. More infor-mation is needed about the reasons why charges are downgraded. We have recommended research to consider both this matter and discontinuance.

20 The CPS figures show that the proportion of those pleading Not Guilty in the Crown Court who were convicted increased between 1991–92 and 1996–97 to about 40%. We have,

however, given particular consideration to the statistics relating to acquittals in the Crown Court. Both the CPS statistics and Judicial Statistics agree that in 1996 less than half of these were acquittals by a jury. In other words, more than half of all acquittals in the Crown Court resulted from an order or direction of the judge. There are often good reasons why such an order or direction should be made – a vital witness may not appear to give evidence or may prove unreliable in the witness box – but nevertheless the statistic is a cause for concern. In our view, when the CPS has decided to proceed with a case after review, it is reasonable to expect that, unless a major witness is absent, the case will be strong enough to be put before a jury. We conclude that the performance of some parts of the CPS in this respect is not as good as it should be, and improvement is needed.

21 The overall conclusion from this study of the available statistics is that in various respects there has been the improvement in the effectiveness and efficiency of the prosecution process which was expected to result from the setting up of the CPS in 1986. Where the statistics show a recent improvement, that is often a recovery from a deterioration which took place in the years immediately after 1986. We do not place responsibility for this situation wholly on the CPS; in large part it stems from the failure of the police, the CPS and the courts to set overall objectives and agree the role and the responsibility of each in achieving those objectives.

22 Also under the heading 'How the CPS has performed' the Report contains a chapter describing the present state of the relationships between the CPS and the other agencies with whom it works and to whom it relates in the criminal justice system. The tensions between the police and the CPS which existed in the early years have been greatly eased, but in some places have not disappeared. There is still a tendency for each to blame the other if a prosecution file is incomplete or some other essential document missing, and, as a result, a case has to be adjourned. In order to establish their independence from the police after 1986, many in the CPS became isolationist, creating a rift in communication. In addition, many police ASUs are not functioning as effectively as they did when they were first created. As a result the CPS finds that it has to duplicate some of the work the ASU staff have done, in order to prepare a satisfactory prosecution file. It is important to seek a remedy for both problems.

23 There are frequent complaints by both magistrates and judges of inefficiency in case preparation or delay on the part of the CPS. Often the CPS is not the cause of the delay, but sometimes it properly has to accept the blame. Part of the problem lies with court listing practices, into which the CPS at present has no input. Timeliness is a most important aspect of the fair and effective prosecution of crime, but at present the magistrates' courts and the CPS have different, and often inconsistent, performance indicators for timeliness.

24 In the Crown Court, all cases are at present prosecuted by members of the Bar. Both judges and the Bar raised several issues on which action, either by the CPS or by government departments, is needed. They include a considerable disparity between the higher fees paid to defence counsel under the Legal Aid Scheme and those paid to prosecuting counsel briefed by the CPS; the issue of briefs being returned by counsel; problems arising from a shortage of CPS staff in the Crown Court, and a difficulty in Counsel obtaining fresh instructions while in court. These are all matters we address.

25 Finally in this part of the Report we consider the proper role of the CPS in relation to victims and witnesses, particularly its obligations arising out of the Victim's Charter.

26 Our assessment of the CPS is that it has the potential to become a lively, successful and esteemed part of the criminal justice system, but that, sadly, none of these adjectives applies to the Service as a whole at present. If the Service – by which we mean all the members of its

staff – is to achieve its potential, it faces three challenges. Firstly, there must be a change in the priority given to the various levels of casework; the 'centre of gravity' must move from the bulk of relatively minor cases in the magistrates' court in order to concentrate on more serious crime, particularly the gravest types, in the Crown Court. Secondly, the overall organisation, the structure and the style of management of the CPS will have to change. Government has started this process by deciding that the CPS should in future be divided into 42 Areas, each headed by a Chief Crown Prosecutor. Each of these CCPs should be given as much freedom as possible to run his area in his own way, and he should suggest his staff to enable them to get on with the core job of prosecuting. Thirdly, the CPS must establish more clearly its position as an integral part of the criminal justice process. It is no longer the 'new kid on the block'.

The future of the CPS in the criminal justice system

27 The role of the CPS within the criminal justice system has not until now been spelt out and put into the context of its key objectives and related performance indicators. Nor have the relationships with the police and the courts been properly defined. At present neither the police nor the CPS have overall responsibility for the preparation of the case file. We have therefore recommended that the CPS should take responsibility for:

- the prosecution process immediately following charge;
- arranging the initial hearing in the Magistrates' Court;
- witness availability, witness warning and witness care.

. . .

The future organisation of the CPS

36 On coming into office in 1997 the Government announced that the CPS was to be reorganised into a structure of 42 Areas, each to be coterminous with a police force. Our Terms of Reference include that reorganisation as the basis for our work. It would be possible to make a change to a 42 Area structure with minimal disturbance to the current Branch and Headquarters organisation. However, this would not achieve the devolution which we believe is essential. Our view is that the reorganisation should be taken as an opportunity for a genuinely new start, building on the achievements of the past 12 years but creating a form of management at both national and local levels which is different in both structure and style.
37 The objectives of the changes that we propose are to:

- set up a 'decentralised national service' through the genuine devolution of as much responsibility and accountability as possible to the CCPs in the new Areas;
- redefine the role of the Headquarters organisation;
- ensure that all but the most senior lawyers in the CPS, including CCPs, spend much more of their time prosecuting;
- improve the career structure for all staff;
- give each CCP responsibility for managing the administrative support and services in his Area, subject only to the constraints of nationally based accounting and data processing systems;
- reduce the bureaucracy by prioritising the information flows and limiting the Headquarters' support functions to a few key advisory services.

. . .

63 In the past two years the CPS has established an Inspectorate, which publishes reports both on standards of casework in Areas or Branches, and on specific themes. We are impressed by the quality of these reports, but we believe and recommend that the Inspectorate should be made more independent by having a lay Chairman appointed by the Attorney-General and a number of lay members, and that its remit should be widened. We make proposals to achieve these aims.

[3:3] *R v Chief Constable of Kent County Constabulary, ex p L; R v DPP, ex p B*
[1993] 1 All ER 756

Two separate cases were decided together. The applicant L was a 16-year-old boy who was charged with assault occasioning actual bodily harm. Although the criteria for cautioning were made out in his case, it was decided that the circumstances of the case were too serious for a caution to be appropriate. The applicant B was a 12-year-old girl who was charged with theft. She had not been cautioned as she had not admitted the offence. Both applicants unsuccessfully sought judicial review of the decision to prosecute them.

Watkins LJ (at page 767):

The point has not previously arisen for determination. That probably is because the CPS are comparatively new to the prosecution process. They have unquestionably the sole power to decide whether a prosecution should proceed. They are entirely dominant in that very important respect and all the erstwhile corresponding power of the police has been stripped away. The CPS are the prosecutor and the police are the initiators of criminal proceedings which may, or may not, dependent upon the decision of the CPS, be disposed of by the courts. The power of the CPS includes that of referring a case back to the police for a caution to be substituted for the continuance of proceedings.

I have come to the conclusion that if judicial review lies in relation to current criminal proceedings, in contrast to a failure to take any action against a person suspected of a criminal offence, it lies against the body which has the last and decisive word, the CPS.

A refusal to prosecute or even possibly to caution by the police is another matter. In that event the police may be vulnerable to judicial review, but only upon a basis which, as the cases show, is rather severely circumscribed.

The extent of that basis appears in the well-known judgments of Lord Denning MR, Salmon and Edmund Davies LJJ in *R v Metropolitan Police Comr, ex p Blackburn* [1968] 1 All ER 763, [1968] 2 QB 118. In a later case, *R v Metropolitan Police Comr, ex p Blackburn (No 3)* [1973] 1 All ER 324 at 331, [1973] QB 241 at 254, Lord Denning MR, referring to a failure to enforce the law, stated: ' . . . the police have a discretion with which the courts will not interfere. There might, however, be extreme cases in which he [the commissioner] was not carrying out his duty. And then we would'.

In *R v General Council of the Bar, ex p Percival* [1990] 3 All ER 137 at 152, [1991] 1 QB 212 at 234, in giving the judgment of the court, I stated having quoted from, inter alia, *ex p Blackburn* [1968] 1 All ER 763, [1968] 2 QB 118:

'Reference was also made by counsel . . . to a passage in de Smith's Judicial Review of Administrative Action 94th edn, 1980 pp 549–550, to the effect that the discretion of a prosecuting authority though broad is not unreviewable. In our view such discretion is plainly reviewable but the question is whether the limits of review should be as strict as those contended for by the Bar Council. Much will depend, we think, on the powers of the body subject to review, the procedures which it is required to follow and on the way in which a particular proceeding has been conducted; there is potentially an almost infinite variety of circumstances. We do not think it right that strict defined limits should be set to the judicial review of a body which can broadly be described as a prosecuting authority. Each case must be considered with due regard to the powers, functions and procedures of the body concerned and the manner in which it has dealt (or not dealt) with the particular complaint or application'.

That was obviously not intended to indicate a lesser limitation for judicial review of the police than appears in *ex p Blackburn*. The statement relates to other bodies with very different responsibilities and discretions to which perhaps a less rigorous approach to judicial review might apply.

In the present cases it is not inaction by the police which is complained of but the positive action of charging the two applicants and thus commencing criminal proceedings instead of in L's case cautioning him and in the case of B taking no action against her whatsoever, as well, of course, as the failure of the CPS to discontinue proceedings in both cases.

It seems to me that a decision to discontinue proceedings by the CPS can be equated with a decision by the police not to prosecute and is, therefore, open to judicial review only upon the restricted basis available to someone, assuming he has locus standi, seeking to challenge a decision by the police. Accordingly, that situation does not require further to be addressed in this judgment.

I have come to the conclusion that, in respect of juveniles, the discretion of the CPS to continue or to discontinue criminal proceedings is reviewable by this court but only where it can be demonstrated that the decision was made regardless of or clearly contrary to a settled policy of the Director of Public Prosecutions evolved in the public interest, for example the policy of cautioning juveniles, a policy which the CPS are bound to apply, where appropriate, to the exercise of their discretion to continue or discontinue criminal proceedings. But I envisage that it will be only rarely that a defendant could succeed in showing that a decision was fatally flawed in such a manner as that.

The policy of cautioning, instead of prosecuting, has for some time now been well settled and plays a prominent part in the process of decision-making both by the police and by the CPS when consideration has properly to be given to whether, in any individual case, there should be (a) no action taken or (b) a caution delivered or (c) a prosecution and thereafter (d) a continuance or discontinuance of criminal proceedings.

That policy applied, obviously, to the case of L. It did not apply to the case of B because cautioning was not for her an option. The policy, which can, I think, rightly be so called, which is applicable to her is another. It is that which is far more generally expressed, that is to say that a prosecution should not occur unless it is required in the public interest, regard being given to the stigma of a conviction which can cause irreparable harm to the future prospects of a young person and to his previous character, parental attitude and the likelihood of the offence being repeated: see the Attorney-General's 1983 guidelines.

I find it very difficult to envisage, with regard to that policy, a circumstance, fraud or dishonesty apart possible, which would allow of a challenge to a decision to prosecute or to continue proceedings unless it could be demonstrated, in the case of a juvenile, that there had been either a total disregard of the policy or, contrary to it, a lack of inquiry into the circumstances and background of that person, previous offences and general character and so on, by the prosecutor and later by the CPS. But here too I envisage the possibility of showing that such disregard had happened as unlikely. Therefore, although the CPS decision may in principle be reviewed, in practice it is rarely likely to be successfully reviewed.

I have confined my views as to the availability of judicial review of a CPS decision not to discontinue a prosecution to the position of juveniles because, of course, the present cases involve only juveniles. My view as to the position of adults, on the other hand, in this respect is that judicial review of a decision not to discontinue a prosecution is unlikely to be available.

The danger of opening too wide the door of review of the discretion to continue a prosecution is manifest and such review, if it exists, must, therefore, be confined to very narrow limits. Juveniles and the policy with regard to them are, in my view, in a special position.

[3:4] *R v Croydon Justices, ex p Dean*
[1993] 3 All ER 129

The applicant and two others were arrested on suspicion of murdering a man who had been stabbed and killed in woodland. The applicant did not take part in the actual killing, but after it had taken place, he went to the scene of the crime with the others and helped them destroy the victim's car. He was interviewed by the police, agreed to be a prosecution witness and was released without charge. He was subsequently interviewed again and was told that he was a prosecution witness and had the protection of the police. After a conference with the police, the CPS decided that he should be charged under section 4 of the Criminal Law Act 1967 with assisting in the destruction of the victim's car, knowing it was evidence, with intent to impede the apprehension of the other defendants. He was charged and committed for trial, and then applied for judicial review to quash his committal to the Crown Court.

The Divisional Court held that, whereas ordinarily an application to quash a committal ought to be made to the Crown Court before the start of a trial, exceptionally a committal to stand trial which took place in breach of a promise that the defendant would not be prosecuted could be quashed where there was, as in this case, an abuse of process.

Staughton LJ (at page 135):

It is submitted on behalf of the Crown Prosecution Service that they alone are entitled, and bound, to decide who shall be prosecuted, at any rate in this category of case; and that the police had no authority and no right to tell Dean that he would not be prosecuted for any offence in connection with the murder; see the Prosecution of Offences Act 1985, s 3(2). I can readily accept that. I also accept that the point is one of constitutional importance. But I cannot accept the submission of Mr Collins that, in consequence, no such conduct by the police can ever give rise to an abuse of process. The effect on George Dean, or for that matter on his father, of an undertaking or promise or representation by the police was likely to have been the same in this case whether it was or was not authorised by the Crown Prosecution Service. It is true that they might have asked their solicitor whether an undertaking, promise or representation by the police was binding; and he might have asked the Crown Prosecution Service whether it was made with their authority. But it seems unreasonable to expect that in this case. If the Crown Prosecution Service find that their powers are being usurped by the police, the remedy must surely be a greater degree of liaison at an early stage.

[3:5] Code for Crown Prosecutors
(7th edition, 2013)

Introduction

1.1 The Code for Crown Prosecutors (the Code) is issued by the Director of Public Prosecutions (DPP) under section 10 of the Prosecution of Offences Act 1985. This is the seventh edition of the Code and replaces all earlier versions.

1.2 The DPP is the head of the Crown Prosecution Service (CPS), which is the principal public prosecution service for England and Wales. The DPP operates independently, under the superintendence of the Attorney General who is accountable to Parliament for the work of the CPS.

1.3 The Code gives guidance to prosecutors on the general principles to be applied when making decisions about prosecutions. The Code is issued primarily for prosecutors in the CPS, but other prosecutors follow the Code either through convention or because they are required to do so by law.

1.4 In this Code, the term "suspect" is used to describe a person who is not yet the subject of formal criminal proceedings; the term "defendant" is used to describe a person who has been charged or summonsed; and the term "offender" is used to describe a person who has admitted his or her guilt to a police officer or other investigator or prosecutor, or who has been found guilty in a court of law.

General Principles

2.1 The decision to prosecute or to recommend an out-of-court disposal is a serious step that affects suspects, victims, witnesses and the public at large and must be undertaken with the utmost care.

2.2 It is the duty of prosecutors to make sure that the right person is prosecuted for the right offence and to bring offenders to justice wherever possible. Casework decisions taken fairly, impartially and with integrity help to secure justice for victims, witnesses, defendants and the public. Prosecutors must ensure that the law is properly applied; that relevant evidence is put before the court; and that obligations of disclosure are complied with.

2.3 Although each case must be considered on its own facts and on its own merits, there are general principles that apply in every case.

2.4 Prosecutors must be fair, independent and objective. They must not let any personal views about the ethnic or national origin, gender, disability, age, religion or belief, political views, sexual orientation, or gender identity of the suspect, victim or any witness influence their decisions. Neither must prosecutors be affected by improper or undue pressure from any source. Prosecutors must always act in the interests of justice and not solely for the purpose of obtaining a conviction.

2.5 The CPS is a public authority for the purposes of current, relevant equality legislation. Prosecutors are bound by the duties set out in this legislation.

2.6 Prosecutors must apply the principles of the European Convention on Human Rights, in accordance with the Human Rights Act 1998, at each stage of a case. Prosecutors must also comply with any guidelines issued by the Attorney General; with the Criminal Procedure Rules currently in force; and have regard to the obligations arising from international conventions. They must follow the policies and guidance of the CPS issued on behalf of the DPP and available for the public to view on the CPS website at www.cps.gov.uk

The Decision Whether to Prosecute

3.1 In more serious or complex cases, prosecutors decide whether a person should be charged with a criminal offence and, if so, what that offence should be. They make their decisions in accordance with this Code and the DPP's Guidance on Charging. The police apply the same principles in deciding whether to start criminal proceedings against a person in those cases for which they are responsible.

3.2 The police and other investigators are responsible for conducting enquiries into any alleged crime and for deciding how to deploy their resources. This includes decisions to start or continue an investigation and on the scope of the investigation. Prosecutors often advise the police and other investigators about possible lines of inquiry and evidential requirements, and assist with pre-charge procedures. In large scale investigations the prosecutor may be asked to advise on the overall investigation strategy, including decisions to refine or narrow the scope of the criminal conduct and the number of suspects under investigation. This is to assist the police and other investigators to complete the investigation within a reasonable period of time and to build the most effective prosecution case. However, prosecutors cannot direct the police or other investigators.

3.3 Prosecutors should identify and, where possible, seek to rectify evidential weaknesses, but, subject to the Threshold Test (see section 5), they should swiftly stop cases which do not meet the evidential stage of the Full Code Test (see section 4) and which cannot be strengthened by further investigation, or where the public interest clearly does not require a prosecution (see section 4). Although prosecutors primarily consider the evidence and information supplied by the police and other investigators, the suspect or those acting on his or her behalf may also submit evidence or information to the prosecutor via the police or other investigators, prior to charge, to help inform the prosecutor's decision.

3.4 Prosecutors must only start or continue a prosecution when the case has passed both stages of the Full Code Test (see section 4). The exception is when the Threshold Test (see section 5) may be applied where it is proposed to apply to the court to keep the suspect in custody after charge, and the evidence required to apply the Full Code Test is not yet available.

3.5 Prosecutors should not start or continue a prosecution which would be regarded by the courts as oppressive or unfair and an abuse of the court's process.

3.6 Prosecutors review every case they receive from the police or other investigators. Review is a continuing process and prosecutors must take account of any change in circumstances that occurs as the case develops, including what becomes known of the defence case. Wherever possible, they should talk to the investigator when thinking about changing the charges or stopping the case. Prosecutors and investigators work closely together, but the final responsibility for the decision whether or not a case should go ahead rests with the CPS.

3.7 Parliament has decided that a limited number of offences should only be taken to court with the agreement of the DPP. These are called consent cases. In such cases the DPP, or prosecutors acting on his or her behalf, apply the Code in deciding whether to give consent to a prosecution. There are also certain offences that should only be taken to court with the consent of the Attorney General. Prosecutors must follow current guidance when referring any such cases to the Attorney General. Additionally, the Attorney General will be kept informed of certain cases as part of his or her superintendence of the CPS and accountability to Parliament for its actions.

The Full Code Test

4.1 The Full Code Test has two stages: (i) the evidential stage; followed by (ii) the public interest stage.

4.2 In most cases, prosecutors should only decide whether to prosecute after the investigation has been completed and after all the available evidence has been reviewed. However there will be cases where it is clear, prior to the collection and consideration of all the likely evidence, that the public interest does not require a prosecution. In these instances, prosecutors may decide that the case should not proceed further.

4.3 Prosecutors should only take such a decision when they are satisfied that the broad extent of the criminality has been determined and that they are able to make a fully informed assessment of the public interest. If prosecutors do not have sufficient information to take such a decision, the investigation should proceed and a decision taken later in accordance with the Full Code Test set out in this section.

The Evidential Stage

4.4 Prosecutors must be satisfied that there is sufficient evidence to provide a realistic prospect of conviction against each suspect on each charge. They must consider what the defence case may be, and how it is likely to affect the prospects of conviction. A case which does not pass the evidential stage must not proceed, no matter how serious or sensitive it may be.

4.5 The finding that there is a realistic prospect of conviction is based on the prosecutor's objective assessment of the evidence, including the impact of any defence and any other information that the suspect has put forward or on which he or she might rely. It means that an objective, impartial and reasonable jury or bench of magistrates or judge hearing a case alone, properly directed and acting in accordance with the law, is more likely than not to convict the defendant of the charge alleged. This is a different test from the one that the criminal courts themselves must apply. A court may only convict if it is sure that the defendant is guilty.

4.6 When deciding whether there is sufficient evidence to prosecute, prosecutors should ask themselves the following:
Can the evidence be used in court?
Prosecutors should consider whether there is any question over the admissibility of certain evidence. In doing so, prosecutors should assess:

a) the likelihood of that evidence being held as inadmissible by the court; and
b) the importance of that evidence in relation to the evidence as a whole.

Is the evidence reliable?
Prosecutors should consider whether there are any reasons to question the reliability of the evidence, including its accuracy or integrity.
Is the evidence credible?
Prosecutors should consider whether there are any reasons to doubt the credibility of the evidence.

The Public Interest Stage

4.7 In every case where there is sufficient evidence to justify a prosecution, prosecutors must go on to consider whether a prosecution is required in the public interest.

4.8 It has never been the rule that a prosecution will automatically take place once the evidential stage is met. A prosecution will usually take place unless the prosecutor is satisfied that there are public interest factors tending against prosecution which outweigh those tending in favour. In some cases the prosecutor may be satisfied that the public interest can be properly served by offering the offender the opportunity to have the matter dealt with by an out-of-court disposal rather than bringing a prosecution.

4.9 When deciding the public interest, prosecutors should consider each of the questions set out below in paragraphs 4.12 a) to g) so as to identify and determine the relevant public interest factors tending for and against prosecution. These factors, together with any public interest factors set out in relevant guidance or policy issued by the DPP, should enable prosecutors to form an overall assessment of the public interest.

4.10 The explanatory text below each question in paragraphs 4.12 a) to g) provides guidance to prosecutors when addressing each particular question and determining whether it identifies public interest factors for or against prosecution. The questions identified are not exhaustive, and not all the questions may be relevant in every case. The weight to be attached to each of the questions, and the factors identified, will also vary according to the facts and merits of each case.

4.11 It is quite possible that one public interest factor alone may outweigh a number of other factors which tend in the opposite direction. Although there may be public interest factors tending against prosecution in a particular case, prosecutors should consider whether nonetheless a prosecution should go ahead and those factors put to the court for consideration when sentence is passed.

4.12 Prosecutors should consider each of the following questions:

a) How serious is the offence committed?
The more serious the offence, the more likely it is that a prosecution is required.

When deciding the level of seriousness of the offence committed, prosecutors should include amongst the factors for consideration the suspect's culpability and the harm to the victim by asking themselves the questions at b) and c).

b) What is the level of culpability of the suspect?
The greater the suspect's level of culpability, the more likely it is that a prosecution is required.

Culpability is likely to be determined by the suspect's level of involvement; the extent to which the offending was premeditated and/or planned; whether they have previous criminal convictions and/or out-of-court disposals and any offending whilst on bail or whilst subject to a court order; whether the offending was or is likely to be continued, repeated or escalated; and the suspect's age or maturity (see paragraph d) below for suspects under 18).

Prosecutors should also have regard when considering culpability as to whether the suspect is, or was at the time of the offence, suffering from any significant mental or physical ill health as in some circumstances this may mean that it is less likely that a prosecution is required. However, prosecutors will also need to consider how serious the offence was, whether it is likely to be repeated and the need to safeguard the public or those providing care to such persons.

c) What are the circumstances of and the harm caused to the victim?
The circumstances of the victim are highly relevant. The greater the vulnerability of the victim, the more likely it is that a prosecution is required. This includes where a position of trust or authority exists between the suspect and victim.

A prosecution is also more likely if the offence has been committed against a victim who was at the time a person serving the public.

Prosecutors must also have regard to whether the offence was motivated by any form of discrimination against the victim's ethnic or national origin, gender, disability, age, religion or belief, sexual orientation or gender identity; or the suspect demonstrated hostility towards the victim based on any of those characteristics. The presence of any such motivation or hostility will mean that it is more likely that prosecution is required.

In deciding whether a prosecution is required in the public interest, prosecutors should take into account the views expressed by the victim about the impact that the offence has had. In appropriate cases, this may also include the views of the victim's family.

Prosecutors also need to consider if a prosecution is likely to have an adverse effect on the victim's physical or mental health, always bearing in mind the seriousness of the offence. If there is evidence that prosecution is likely to have an adverse impact on the victim's health it may make a prosecution less likely, taking into account the victim's views.

However, the CPS does not act for victims or their families in the same way as solicitors act for their clients, and prosecutors must form an overall view of the public interest.

d) Was the suspect under the age of 18 at the time of the offence?

The criminal justice system treats children and young people differently from adults and significant weight must be attached to the age of the suspect if they are a child or young person under 18. The best interests and welfare of the child or young person must be considered including whether a prosecution is likely to have an adverse impact on his or her future prospects that is disproportionate to the seriousness of the offending. Prosecutors must have regard to the principal aim of the youth justice system which is to prevent offending by children and young people. Prosecutors must also have regard to the obligations arising under the United Nations 1989 Convention on the Rights of the Child.

As a starting point, the younger the suspect, the less likely it is that a prosecution is required.

However, there may be circumstances which mean that notwithstanding the fact that the suspect is under 18, a prosecution is in the public interest. These include where the offence committed is serious, where the suspect's past record suggests that there are no suitable alternatives to prosecution, or where the absence of an admission means that out-of-court disposals which might have addressed the offending behaviour are not available.

e) What is the impact on the community?

The greater the impact of the offending on the community, the more likely it is that a prosecution is required. In considering this question, prosecutors should have regard to how community is an inclusive term and is not restricted to communities defined by location.

f) Is prosecution a proportionate response?

Prosecutors should also consider whether prosecution is proportionate to the likely outcome, and in so doing the following may be relevant to the case under consideration:

- The cost to the CPS and the wider criminal justice system, especially where it could be regarded as excessive when weighed against any likely penalty. (Prosecutors should not decide the public interest on the basis of this factor alone. It is essential that regard is also given to the public interest factors identified when considering the other questions in paragraphs 4.12 a) to g), but cost is a relevant factor when making an overall assessment of the public interest.)
- Cases should be capable of being prosecuted in a way that is consistent with principles of effective case management. For example, in a case involving multiple suspects, prosecution might be reserved for the main participants in order to avoid excessively long and complex proceedings.

g) Do sources of information require protecting?

In cases where public interest immunity does not apply, special care should be taken when proceeding with a prosecution where details may need to be made public that could harm sources of information, international relations or national security. It is essential that such cases are kept under continuing review.

The Threshold Test

5.1 The Threshold Test may only be applied where the suspect presents a substantial bail risk and not all the evidence is available at the time when he or she must be released from custody unless charged.

When the Threshold Test may be applied

5.2 Prosecutors must determine whether the following conditions are met:

a) there is insufficient evidence currently available to apply the evidential stage of the Full Code Test; and
b) there are reasonable grounds for believing that further evidence will become available within a reasonable period; and
c) the seriousness or the circumstances of the case justifies the making of an immediate charging decision; and
d) there are continuing substantial grounds to object to bail in accordance with the Bail Act 1976 and in all the circumstances of the case it is proper to do so.

5.3 Where any of the above conditions is not met, the Threshold Test cannot be applied and the suspect cannot be charged. The custody officer must determine whether the person may continue to be detained or be released on bail, with or without conditions.

5.4 There are two parts to the evidential consideration of the Threshold Test.

The first part of the Threshold Test – is there reasonable suspicion?

5.5 Prosecutors must be satisfied that there is at least a reasonable suspicion that the person to be charged has committed the offence.

5.6 In determining this, prosecutors must consider the evidence then available. This may take the form of witness statements, material or other information, provided the prosecutor is satisfied that:

a) it is relevant; and
b) it is capable of being put into an admissible format for presentation in court; and
c) it would be used in the case.

5.7 If satisfied on this the prosecutor should then consider the second part of the Threshold Test.
The second part of the Threshold Test – can further evidence be gathered to provide a realistic prospect of conviction?

5.8 Prosecutors must be satisfied that there are reasonable grounds for believing that the continuing investigation will provide further evidence, within a reasonable period of time, so that all the evidence together is capable of establishing a realistic prospect of conviction in accordance with the Full Code Test.

5.9 The further evidence must be identifiable and not merely speculative.

5.10 In reaching this decision prosecutors must consider:

a) the nature, extent and admissibility of any likely further evidence and the impact it will have on the case;
b) the charges that all the evidence will support;
c) the reasons why the evidence is not already available;
d) the time required to obtain the further evidence and whether any consequential delay is reasonable in all the circumstances.

5.11 If both parts of the Threshold Test are satisfied, prosecutors must apply the public interest stage of the Full Code Test based on the information available at that time.

Reviewing the Threshold Test

5.12 A decision to charge under the Threshold Test must be kept under review. The evidence must be regularly assessed to ensure that the charge is still appropriate and that continued objection to bail is justified. The Full Code Test must be applied as soon as is reasonably practicable and in any event before the expiry of any applicable custody time limit.

Selection of Charges

6.1 Prosecutors should select charges which:

a) reflect the seriousness and extent of the offending supported by the evidence;
b) give the court adequate powers to sentence and impose appropriate post-conviction orders; and
c) enable the case to be presented in a clear and simple way.

6.2 This means that prosecutors may not always choose or continue with the most serious charge where there is a choice.

6.3 Prosecutors should never go ahead with more charges than are necessary just to encourage a defendant to plead guilty to a few. In the same way, they should never go ahead with a more serious charge just to encourage a defendant to plead guilty to a less serious one.

6.4 Prosecutors should not change the charge simply because of the decision made by the court or the defendant about where the case will be heard.

6.5 Prosecutors must take account of any relevant change in circumstances as the case progresses after charge.

Out-of-Court Disposals

7.1 An out-of-court disposal may take the place of a prosecution in court if it is an appropriate response to the offender and/or the seriousness and consequences of the offending.

7.2 Prosecutors must follow any relevant guidance when asked to advise on or authorise a simple caution, a conditional caution, any appropriate regulatory proceedings, a punitive or civil penalty, or other disposal. They should ensure that the appropriate evidential standard for the specific out-of-court disposal is met including, where required, a clear admission of guilt, and that the public interest would be properly served by such a disposal.

Mode of Trial

8.1 Prosecutors must have regard to the current guidelines on sentencing and allocation when making submissions to the magistrates' court about where the defendant should be tried.

8.2 Speed must never be the only reason for asking for a case to stay in the magistrates' court. But prosecutors should consider the effect of any likely delay if a case is sent to the Crown Court, and the possible effect on any victim or witness if the case is delayed.

Venue for trial in cases involving youths

8.3 Prosecutors must bear in mind that youths should be tried in the youth court wherever possible. It is the court which is best designed to meet their specific needs. A trial of a youth in the Crown Court should be reserved for the most serious cases or where the interests of justice require a youth to be jointly tried with an adult.

Accepting Guilty Pleas

9.1 Defendants may want to plead guilty to some, but not all, of the charges. Alternatively, they may want to plead guilty to a different, possibly less serious, charge because they are admitting only part of the crime.

9.2 Prosecutors should only accept the defendant's plea if they think the court is able to pass a sentence that matches the seriousness of the offending, particularly where there are aggravating features. Prosecutors must never accept a guilty plea just because it is convenient.

9.3 In considering whether the pleas offered are acceptable, prosecutors should ensure that the interests and, where possible, the views of the victim, or in appropriate cases the views of the victim's family, are taken into account when deciding whether it is in the public interest to accept the plea. However, the decision rests with the prosecutor.

9.4 It must be made clear to the court on what basis any plea is advanced and accepted. In cases where a defendant pleads guilty to the charges but on the basis of facts that are different from the prosecution case, and where this may significantly affect sentence, the court should be invited to hear evidence to determine what happened, and then sentence on that basis.

9.5 Where a defendant has previously indicated that he or she will ask the court to take an offence into consideration when sentencing, but then declines to admit that offence at court, prosecutors will consider whether a prosecution is required for that offence. Prosecutors should explain to the defence advocate and the court that the prosecution of that offence may be subject to further review, in consultation with the police or other investigators wherever possible.

9.6 Particular care must be taken when considering pleas which would enable the defendant to avoid the imposition of a mandatory minimum sentence. When pleas are offered, prosecutors must also bear in mind the fact that ancillary orders can be made with some offences but not with others.

Reconsidering a Prosecution Decision

10.1 People should be able to rely on decisions taken by the CPS. Normally, if the CPS tells a suspect or defendant that there will not be a prosecution, or that the prosecution has been stopped, the case will not start again. But occasionally there are reasons why the CPS will overturn a decision not to prosecute or to deal with the case by way of an out-of-court disposal or when it will restart the prosecution, particularly if the case is serious.

10.2 These reasons include:

a)   cases where a new look at the original decision shows that it was wrong and, in order to maintain confidence in the criminal justice system, a prosecution should be brought despite the earlier decision;

b)   cases which are stopped so that more evidence which is likely to become available in the fairly near future can be collected and prepared. In these cases, the prosecutor will tell the defendant that the prosecution may well start again;

c)   cases which are stopped because of a lack of evidence but where more significant evidence is discovered later; and

d)   cases involving a death in which a review following the findings of an inquest concludes that a prosecution should be brought, notwithstanding any earlier decision not to prosecute.

[3:6] Hoyano, A, Hoyano, L, David, G and Goldie, S, 'A Study of the Impact of the Revised Code for Crown Prosecutors'
[1997] Crim LR 556 (at page 557)

In a detailed critique of the revised Code, published in tandem with a response from the CPS, Andrew Ashworth and Julia Fionda generally welcomed the revisions to the Code, but also expressed a number of concerns. For example, they suggested that there had been a change of emphasis in the direction of a greater propensity to prosecute, particularly in relation to young defendants, and they questioned whether the independence of the CPS may not have been compromised by apparent submission to politically inspired changes of policy.

The CPS commissioned two research studies to gauge the impact of the revised Code. The first of these was conducted 'in-house' and examined police views of the revised Code in terms of its clarity, accessibility, and relevance to their work. Secondly, the CPS commissioned us to ascertain whether the evidential and public interest tests were being implemented in line with the guidance contained in the revised Code, and to discover what impact, if any, the revision had had upon prosecutors' case decisions. The terms of reference provided that the research was to be completed in a six-month period beginning September 1995 and that it was to be conducted by way of 80 interviews with CPS personnel in four CPS areas. Four branch offices were selected from within each area. The interview sample included all grades of personnel, from caseworkers to Branch Crown Prosecutors. The interviews, which were tape-recorded, included discussion of specific case scenarios.

Is the revised Code an improvement?

One aim of the revisions was to make the Code more easily understood outside the CPS. Almost all the prosecutors whom we interviewed considered that the Code had been rendered more accessible to the police and to members of the public. That still of course leaves the question of whether a simplified document is of assistance to prosecutors themselves.

(At page 564):

The role of the CPS as a filter for evidentially weak cases and for cases which it would not be in the public interest to pursue is important and demanding in equal measure. Our impression from meeting prosecutors is that it is a responsibility which they take very seriously; but equally many of them feel that factors limiting their discretion are not understood by the public, and that they are often unfairly criticised as a result.

It is our overall impression, based on this survey, that prosecutors in the four areas which we examined adopt a common approach in terms of the way they view cases and the factors which they consider. There was no discernible variation in response by area to any of the issues and questions which we raised in our interviews. This of course cannot be taken as proof that *case decisions* are consistent on a national basis; that is beyond the scope of a study based on interviews with CPS staff, but such interviews do at least provide an indicator. At the same time one must acknowledge that the Code itself guides decision-making only at a very basic level. It is a signpost rather than a map, indicating a general direction rather than providing a detailed route.

According to the Attorney-General, the review of the Code was designed:

(1) to make it more easily understood by the police and members of the public;
(2) to clarify the evidential criterion and the requirement that there be a realistic prospect of conviction; and
(3) to bring out more clearly the public interest factors in favour of a prosecution.

Our interviewees were almost unanimous in their view that the first aim has been achieved. However it is apparent that the revised Code has not been so successful in achieving the other two objectives. Prosecutors appeared uncertain as to whether the revisions were intended to send a strong signal that they should be prosecuting more cases, whether in fact any change of direction was desired, or whether there was perceived to be some inconsistency in prosecutorial decision-making which needed to be corrected. In particular it would seem that the CPS has not adequately explained to its own prosecutors why the phrase 'more likely than not' was inserted into the evidential criterion in the revised version of the Code.

Whatever the purpose of the changes to the Code, the impact upon prosecutors' decisions seems to have been fairly marginal. This is mainly because the Code tests are not susceptible to precise gradations and so prosecutors rely to a large extent on experience, both their own and that of their colleagues. The clarifications and guidance in the revised Code did not represent, for most prosecutors, a strong enough distinction to override this. Detailed policy directives relating to specific offences and problems *do* however make a difference. If changes in decision-making are required, it is clear that specific directives are more effective than altering the language of the Code in ways which do not convey – or at least, do not convey in forthright terms – a specific change of direction. This does not derogate from the value of the Code as a tool for training prosecutors who have recently joined the CPS.

[3:7] Morgan, R, 'Review of Drakeford, M, Haines, K, Cotton, B and Octigan, M, *Pre-trial Services and the Future of Probation*'
(2002) BJ of Criminology 224

Given the pace of contemporary events, there is seldom an ideal time to write and publish a policy-focused book. Do it before a major structural change and the published analysis is, or appears to be, out of date. Wait to start writing until the new structure is in place and one risks missing the priority-setting tide. Drakeford and his co-authors must have faced this dilemma. They presumably collected most of their data (though their research methodological note is somewhat opaque on chronology) at about the time it became apparent that there was to be a National Probation Service, in place since April 2001 as a result of the Criminal Justice and Court Services Act 2000. But they pressed ahead with their text without waiting to see what form the national service was to take. In retrospect it seems a less than happy choice. One cannot but feel that their core fieldwork material – an account of pre-trial services in three probation areas – and their relatively timeless policy objective – furthering the expansion of probation-led pre-trial services – would have been better served had they waited until they could formulate recommendations welded to the current realities of governance. As it is, we are presented in Chapter 5 with reportage of largely irrelevant outdated opinion as to whether there *should* be a national service, and the reader is offered no guidance as to how the authors' project might best be pursued within the new tripartite framework comprising a National Probation Directorate, and 42 local Probation Boards and Chief Officers. This is a pity. A well-timed and linked article or two would have done the job better. The authors' data and argument are nevertheless worthy of close attention.

Pre-trial probation-led services largely comprise bail information and support (including accommodation) schemes. That is, ways of collecting information about accused persons' community ties, and where a remand in custody might be justified, putting in place arrangements which might satisfy the interests of justice and public protection without resort to custody or excessive restriction. There is a powerful case for linking these efforts with information and support for victims – something Drakeford and his colleagues do not discuss – because, as a good deal of evidence makes clear, victims, particularly victims of violence, are often very concerned as to where 'their' offender is during the pre-trial phase of criminal proceedings.

The authors briefly trace the legal framework for the granting and withholding of bail and describe the expanding remand population and the haphazard history of bail information and support schemes in England and Wales from the 1970s onwards. In the first half of the 1990s bail information schemes were extended to most magistrates' courts and some remand prisons by means of a hypothecated Home Office grant which was withdrawn in 1995. Thereafter the funding of pre-trial services was transferred to mainstream probation budgets, which coincidentally were substantially cut back. It is a feature of an unjoined-up criminal justice system that the principal financial beneficiaries of bail information and support services are the CPS and the courts (who are thereby better able to make informed and speedy decisions) and the Prison Service (who are required to accommodate fewer or more short-term remand prisoners), whereas the bail service provider, the Probation Service, incurs increased costs and pressures. It was no surprise, therefore, that when put under budgetary pressure after 1995, bail information and support services declined in number and in some probation areas disappeared altogether.

Are bail information and support services effective? Drakeford and his colleagues suggest that this question can be answered in a variety of ways. Are accused persons who would otherwise have likely been remanded in custody given conditional or unconditional bail, or accused persons who would otherwise have been granted conditional bail subject to no or fewer bail conditions? If so, do these defendants (a) attend court as required and/or (b) not commit further offences or commit fewer or less serious offences and/or (c) retain their employment or maintain their family and other responsibilities and/or (d) address the criminogenic factors underlying their offending behaviour so as to reduce their offending in the future? The authors' review of the research literature suggests that the answer to the effectiveness question is generally positive and that bail services are cost-effective. Remands in custody are reduced as a result of both court and prison based bail information schemes and re-offending rates among the additional bailees appear to be no higher than among bailees generally. The picture regarding the expensive use of probation hostels for bailees is more equivocal because the evidence suggests that a significant proportion would probably not have been remanded in custody.

The authors' survey of pre-trial services in three probation areas indicates that it is currently very variable in character. It is usually the bottom-up product of enthusiastic local managers, often dependent on partnerships with voluntary agencies and, because focused on unconvicted suspects, reminiscent of 'old' as opposed to 'new' probation – that is, a client-centred focus on individuals' social problems – though there are examples of a more top-down emphasis on targets, crime reduction and cost effectiveness.

The big question, however, is how to take matters forward in the new world of a single minister for probation and prisons, a joint probation and prisons Correctional Services Strategy Board (which the minister chairs), a National Probation Directorate and 42 Probation Boards empowered by s.5 of the CJCSA to ensure that there is sufficient provision (including contracted-out provision) locally to protect the public and reduce offending, including 'giving assistance to persons remanded on bail' and 'providing accommodation in approved premises for persons who have any time been charged with an offence'. The fact that this brave new world does not figure in a book entitled *The Future of Probation* should prompt someone, perhaps the author, to pick up the baton in a mainstream journal article.

[3:8] Ministry of Justice, *The Governance of Britain: A Consultation on the Role of the Attorney General* (2007) Cm 7192

The first section is on the history and role of the law officers. The paper then continues:

2. The Current Role of the Attorney General – Fit For the 21st General?

2.1 The Attorney General's role comprises a complex mixture of common law and statutory functions acquired over the centuries, some of which are exercised in a Governmental capacity and some in an independent public interest capacity.

2.2 Successive holders of the office have made a major contribution to upholding the rule of law and the administration of justice, helping to ensure that the Government acts in accordance with the law and with the highest standards of legal propriety, and enhancing the role of the prosecuting authorities at the heart of the criminal justice system. However it is right now to consider, as part of the programme of constitutional reform set out in The Governance of Britain, how best the role of Attorney General should be configured to meet Britain's needs in the 21st century.

2.3 Reform of the Attorney General's role is proposed in the Government's paper on The Governance of Britain. That consultation paper specifically includes a proposal to seek to surrender or limit the powers to direct prosecutors in individual criminal cases, "which [the Government] considers, should not, in a modern democracy, be exercised exclusively by the executive". This is discussed further below. But the wider implications of proposals in this Green Paper for the Attorney General's role should also be considered. For example:

- Does the proposal to put prerogative executive powers on a statutory basis, subject to Parliamentary scrutiny and control, mean that Parliament should have access to the Attorney General's advice on these issues, or to some other source of legal advice?
- Do new ways need to be found of ensuring that, when Parliament exercises such powers, it does so in accordance with the rule of law?

2.4 In addition, one of the themes of The Governance of Britain is greater involvement of Parliament, and there may be implications for the way in which the Attorney General is accountable to Parliament – for example the use of new mechanisms to provide greater accountability for cases involving sensitive intelligence and security issues (see paragraph 1.36 above).

2.5 The current multi-faceted nature of the Attorney's role has given rise to a debate which has focussed mainly on the tension between the Attorney's political status as a Government Minister and the functions as:

- The Government's chief legal adviser. The question arises how the Attorney General can give independent legal advice to Government when he or she is part of Government. The Attorney would fall with the Government and can be dismissed by the Prime Minister like any other minister. This question was raised particularly in relation to the advice on the legality of military action against Iraq in 2003.
- The independent guardian of the public interest. For example, in the *Gouriet* case the then Attorney General refused consent to the bringing of proceedings to enforce the law against the Union of Post Office Workers, whose members had refused to handle mail between England & Wales and South Africa, in a protest against apartheid. That decision was taken in the Attorney General's independent public interest capacity, though the Government of the day also clearly had a legitimate policy against apartheid. In the area of sensitive prosecutions, the Al-Yamamah arms contract with Saudi Arabia is the most recent example. Some have questioned how the Attorney General can be seen to be impartial in weighing up or advising on the public interest on matters in which the Government may itself have a strong policy interest (for example in the protection of jobs).

Attorney General as Government Minister and legal adviser

2.6 The first area of tension arises between the Attorney General's position as a Government Minister, and the role as the provider of independent and impartial legal advice to Government. Attorneys General have worked on the clear basis that their duty is to give wholly independent and impartial legal advice, and they are bound by professional codes of conduct to that effect.

2.7 However, some believe that the Attorney General cannot truly be (or be seen to be) independent from the Government (or party), with the result that the Attorney General's advice lacks at least the appearance of complete impartiality, or even that the Attorney may come under pressure to slant the advice in a particular way to support the Government or political party in Government.

2.8 On the other hand it has been argued that the advice of the Attorney General is more likely to be accepted by Ministers because it comes from one of their number, who understands the wider political and policy context, rather than being provided externally. Thus it is the Attorney General's membership of the Government that gives the advice to Ministerial colleagues its credibility and authority with them.

2.9 Furthermore, it is argued, the Attorney General's advice, as well as needing of course to be honest and authoritative, is advice to a particular client (the Government) on how its policies may lawfully be achieved, including advice on the legal risks attached, the prospects of successful challenge and so on. It is, like other legal advice, subject to legal professional privilege and is not generally published. In this way, the Attorney General operates like an in-house lawyer. It is generally accepted that in-house lawyers (including those in business or the Government Legal Service) are entirely capable of providing independent legal advice to the highest professional standards.

2.10 However, some commentators have suggested that the Attorney General's advice to Government should not (or not always) be treated in the same way as legal advice given to a private organisation. The Government is not a business and the relationship of the Attorney General to the Government is arguably of a different order to that of other in-house lawyers. This raises the question of whether, at least for some purposes, "the public" (or Parliament), rather than the Government, should be treated as the Attorney General's client. Lord Bingham has said:

> "There seems to me to be room to question whether the ordinary rules of client privilege, appropriate enough in other circumstances, should apply to a law officer's opinion on the lawfulness of war; it is not unrealistic in my view to regard the public, those who are to fight and perhaps die, rather than the government, as the client."

2.11 Concern has similarly been expressed that the legal advice which the Government receives from the Attorney General is not generally disclosed to Parliament or to the public, even where the advice relates to very significant decisions, for example the decision to take military action against Iraq in 2003.

Exercise of public interest functions

2.12 The second area of perceived tension arises between the Attorney General's position as a Government Minister and politician and the post's public interest functions. This has given rise to the suggestion or perception that the Attorney General might come under pressure to exercise those public interest functions in a way which reflects the political or policy interests of the Government or party to which he or she belongs, rather than wholly independently and in the public interest.

(i) Functions in relation to individual prosecutions

2.13 Particular concerns have been expressed about the Attorney General's role in relation to decisions about individual criminal cases, including the granting or withholding of consents to prosecute and in relation to those cases where the Attorney General is consulted by the prosecuting authorities as part of the superintendence role, and where there is perceived to be a risk of conflict of interest. In its recent report the Constitutional Affairs Select Committee commented: "The Attorney General's responsibility for prosecutions has emerged as one of the most problematic aspects of his or her role." To address such concerns, other common law jurisdictions have moved to separate the ministerial role from individual prosecution decisions (Annex B sets out some examples).

2.14 The Attorney General's role in relation to consents to prosecution has been considered by the Law Commission. The Law Commission concluded that the existing functions of the Attorney General to give consent to prosecutions should (if not abolished altogether) be transferred to the DPP except where the offence involved national security or had some international element.

2.15 However, some commentators, including some who gave evidence to the Constitutional Affairs Select Committee, have taken the view that, for all its tensions, the advantages of the current system outweigh the disadvantages.

(ii) Other public interest functions

Much of the comment about potential conflict between the Attorney General's Governmental and public interest functions, as discussed above, relates to the role in relation to individual criminal prosecutions. However the Attorney General has a range of other public interest functions which, similarly, have to be exercised independently of Government. These include:

- The bringing of proceedings for contempt of court
- Intervening in certain family and charity cases to protect the public interest
- Bringing proceedings to restrain vexatious litigants
- Appointment of advocates to the court (neutral advisers to the court) and special advocates (to represent the interests of parties in cases involving sensitive national security issues).

2.17 On occasion, the contempt role can be controversial and (as in relation to prosecutions) give rise to accusations that the Attorney General has (for example) acted to restrain a publication for political motives. Any alternative model for exercising this role would still involve striking a balance between the interests of justice and the freedom of the press, often in the most sensitive of cases, and could therefore sometimes be controversial.

2.18 For the most part the Attorney General's other public interest functions have not attracted controversy or criticism and there is seldom any suggestion that they have been exercised for any political or other improper motive.

[3:9] Protocol between the Attorney General and the Prosecuting Departments (July 2009)

1. Scope

1.1. This protocol sets out how the Attorney General and the Directors of the prosecuting departments, (which are the Crown Prosecution Service (CPS), the Serious Fraud Office (SFO), and the Revenue and Customs Prosecutions Office (RCPO)), ("the Directors") exercise their functions in relation to each other. It covers:

- General responsibilities
- Strategy, planning and performance
- Responsibility for prosecution decisions
- Development of policy
- Dealing with the media
- Dealing with complaints

1.2. Details of the Directors' statutory responsibilities may be found in the relevant legislation. In accordance with the Law Officers Act 1997, any function of the Attorney General under this protocol may be performed by the Solicitor General.

2. General responsibilities

2.1. The Attorney General and the Solicitor General (the "Law Officers") are government Ministers, Law Officers of the Crown and senior practising lawyers. They may act as advocates for the Crown. The Attorney General is not a member of the Cabinet but may attend when his or her responsibilities are on the agenda.

2.2. The Directors exercise their statutory functions subject to the superintendence of the Attorney General.

2.3. The Attorney General is accountable to Parliament for his or her functions in relation to prosecutions and for the work of the Directors and the prosecuting departments, including answering Parliamentary Questions and correspondence from Members of Parliament. The Directors ensure that their Departments support the Attorney General in fulfilling this duty.

2.4. The Attorney General is responsible for safeguarding the independence of prosecutors in taking prosecution decisions.

2.5. The Director of Public Prosecutions (DPP) is required by law to issue a Code for Crown Prosecutors, which is applied also by the Director of the SFO and, by law, by the Director of the RCPO. The Code gives guidance on general principles to be applied in determining whether proceedings for an offence should be instituted or discontinued and which charges should be preferred. The DPP consults the Attorney General and the other Directors about any proposed changes to the Code. The provisions of the Code and any changes are required to be included in the DPP's annual report (see 3.4 below) which is laid before Parliament.

2.6. The Attorney General, acting in the capacity of a Law Officer, independently of government, may issue guidance to prosecutors on the conduct of their functions, after consulting the relevant Director(s).

2.7. The Directors and their staff are civil servants of the Crown and are subject to the Civil Service Code.

2.8. When a Parliamentary Select Committee or other Parliamentary Group seeks evidence from the Attorney General and/or the Directors about the work of the prosecuting departments, the Attorney General and the relevant Director(s) will consult one another about how best to meet the requirements of the Committee.

3. Strategy, planning and performance

3.1. The Attorney General receives the budget for the prosecuting departments and in conjunction with the Directors, sets their strategic direction.

3.2. The Directors agree their high level objectives with the Attorney General in line with the strategic direction.

3.3. The Directors are Accounting Officers. They draw up business plans for their Departments, having due regard to the strategic direction and high level objectives agreed. They organise their Departments in the most effective and efficient way in order to deliver their objectives.

3.4. The Directors are required to report annually on the discharge of their functions, and the Attorney General lays these reports before Parliament. The Directors agree mechanisms for reporting periodically during the year to the Attorney General on their progress against plan and budget, and their performance.

3.5. The Attorney General reports to Parliament annually on his or her actions and those of his or her Office.

3.6. There is a Strategic Board, chaired by the Attorney General and including the Directors, which, among other things, oversees strategy, reviews and monitors financial management and performance, oversees the development and delivery of Spending Review submissions, encourages joint work where appropriate, and identifies and pursues opportunities to achieve maximum efficiency and effectiveness.

4. Responsibility for prosecution decisions

4.1. The decision whether or not to prosecute, (or in the case of the SFO, to investigate and prosecute) and, if so, for what offence, or whether to use an out of court disposal, is a quasi-judicial function which requires the evaluation of the strength of the evidence and also a judgment about whether an investigation and/or prosecution is needed in the public interest. Prosecutors take such decisions in a fair and impartial way, acting at all times in accordance with the highest ethical standards and in the best interests of justice. In this way, prosecutors are central to the maintenance of a just, democratic and fair society based on a scrupulous adherence to the rule of law.

4.2. Prosecutors exercise their powers regarding the institution and conduct of proceedings under the direction of their Director. They take casework decisions and conduct individual cases applying the law and the framework of principles set out in the Code for Crown Prosecutors, together with any supplementary guidance issued by the Directors, or the Attorney General. The Attorney General is not informed of, nor has any involvement in, the conduct of the vast majority of individual cases around the country.

4.3. Other than in the exceptional cases described in 4(a) below, decisions to prosecute or not to prosecute are taken entirely by the prosecutors. The Attorney General will not seek to give a direction in an individual case save very exceptionally where necessary to safeguard national security (4(b)).

4(a) Attorney General's consent to prosecute

4(a)1. For certain offences Parliament has decided that the Attorney General's consent is needed to bring a prosecution.

4(a)2. It is a constitutional principle that when taking a decision whether to consent to a prosecution, the Attorney General acts independently of government, applying well established prosecution principles of evidential sufficiency and public interest.

4(a)3. Where the prosecutor considers that there is sufficient evidence to prosecute for one of these offences and that a prosecution is or may be in the public interest, the prosecutor seeks the Attorney General's consent to bring a prosecution. That decision is taken by the Attorney General.

4(a)4. Once a prosecution is commenced in one of these cases, the prosecutor keeps the Attorney General informed of its progress and whenever practicable, consults the Attorney General if the prosecutor is contemplating either dropping the case on public interest grounds, or accepting pleas.

4(a)5. If the case can no longer proceed for evidential reasons which emerge after a prosecution is started, the prosecutor informs the Attorney General of the decision as soon as it is taken.

4(b) Directions necessary to safeguard national security

4(b)1. The one exceptional category of case in which the Attorney General will consider the possibility that she or he may direct that a prosecution is not started or not continued (or, in the case of the SFO, that an investigation is not to take place or not to continue) is where the Attorney General is satisfied that it is necessary to do so for the purpose of safeguarding national security

4(b)2. The offences most likely to give rise to national security considerations require the Attorney General's consent to a prosecution. But if national security considerations emerge partway through a case or investigation, or in cases which do not require consent, the Director will inform the Attorney General as soon as this becomes evident.

4(b)3. Before considering the possibility that he or she may direct in this way, which will only be in the most exceptional cases, the Attorney General will consult the relevant Director. The possibility of direction does not prevent the Director from taking a decision not to start or continue a prosecution or SFO investigation on national security grounds.

4(b)4. If any such direction were made the Attorney General would make a report to Parliament, so far as was compatible with national security.

4(c) Cases on which the Attorney General will not be consulted

4(c)1. Unless for any reason a decision is required from the Attorney General by law (such as in a consent case) and subject to paragraph 4(d)5, the Attorney General will not be consulted in:

- Prosecution decisions relating to Members of Parliament (including Peers) or Ministers;
- Prosecution decisions in cases relating to political parties or the conduct of elections; or
- Any case in which the relevant Law Officer considers that he or she has a personal or professional conflict of interest in accordance with the relevant professional Codes.

4(d) Superintendence of casework

4(d)1. As set out at the opening of this section, the Attorney General will have no involvement in the vast majority of cases. And as at 2.4 above, the Attorney General is responsible for safeguarding the independence of prosecutors taking decisions whether or not to prosecute in individual cases.

4(d)2. The Attorney General's responsibilities for superintendence and accountability to Parliament mean that he or she, acting in the wider public interest, needs occasionally to engage with a Director about a case because it:

- is particularly sensitive; and/or
- has implications for prosecution or criminal justice policy or practice; and/or
- reveals some systemic issues for the framework of the law, or the operation of the criminal justice system.

4(d)3. In these circumstances the Attorney General will be alerted to a case by the Director at the earliest opportunity, or may call for information about a case, or will discuss the case with the Director. The Director will keep the Attorney General informed as significant developments occur. The Attorney General may express any concerns. The decision in these cases remains the Director's.

4(d)4. Directors may raise with the Attorney General for advice or discussion any cases, except those at 4(c)1. above, at any time. Consultation and discussion between the Director and the Attorney General ensures that the Attorney General can provide public or Parliamentary assurance, as necessary, that all relevant considerations have been taken into account.

4(d)5. The Attorney General may additionally ask for information about an individual case in order to perform another of the Attorney's functions, such as considering potential contempt of court, making references on a point of law, or deciding whether to refer an unduly lenient sentence. This does not involve consultation on any prosecution decision by the Director.

4(d)6. The Attorney General may be called upon to help prosecutors to resolve cases where they have not reached agreement, for example where prosecutors have overlapping remits over the same case or adopt different approaches to the same legal question or where there is concurrent jurisdiction.

4(d)7. The Attorney General's assistance may be needed to secure evidence or disclosure of material by another Government Department which is needed to ensure a fair trial.

4(e) Seeking Ministerial Representations on the Public Interest

4(e)1. The Code for Crown Prosecutors sets out the general public interest considerations which are relevant to prosecution decisions.

4(e)2. In a few very exceptional cases the prosecutor, whether the Attorney General or the Directors, may conclude that it is appropriate to consult relevant Government Ministers as part of the decision-making process. In such a case the Attorney General may seek Ministerial representations in a public interest consultation exercise.

4(e)3. The purpose of the exercise is confined to identifying particular public interest considerations which are relevant to the prosecution decision of the Attorney General or the Director. The weight to be given to such representation is a matter for the Director or the Attorney General. Ministers are not able to dictate what the decision ought to be. The responsibility for the eventual decision rests with the Attorney General or with the Director, depending on the case.

4(e)4. The Attorney General ensures that public interest consultation exercises are conducted with propriety, that Ministers who are consulted are informed that the decision is for the Director or the Attorney General alone; and that where such considerations are said to point away from prosecution, the Attorney General and the Director will probe rigorously the representations made where, and as far as, it appears to them appropriate to do so.

5. Development of policy

5.1. The Attorney General is the Government Minister responsible for prosecution. As such, he or she is responsible, with the Directors, for ensuring that in the development of Government policy, due account is taken of the role of the prosecutors, of the impact of policy proposals on prosecution, (or in the case of the SFO, on investigation and prosecution) and of the contribution which prosecutors can make.

5.2. In their support of the Attorney General in the exercise of this function, the Directors provide the Attorney General with information and advice, and ensure that the knowledge and expertise of prosecutors are made available to those developing Government policy. The Attorney General seeks to keep the Directors informed of developing Government policy so that they are able to give their best advice.

5.3. The Directors are responsible for ensuring that, where appropriate, policies and guidance adopted by their Departments are consistent with and give due effect to relevant Government policy. This does not affect the independence of prosecutors in taking prosecution decisions, which must always be free from any party political or other improper influence.

5.4. The Attorney General is not consulted about the generality of prosecutors' guidance, but is consulted and informed in a timely way about any proposed statement of guidance which raises difficult or sensitive questions of law or public policy.

5.5. The Attorney General is consulted about guidance on matters in which the Attorney General exercises functions by law or as part of the wider constitutional role. Examples may include contempt of court, public interest immunity, unduly lenient sentences and consent cases.

5.6. The Directors co-ordinate their approach to, and their guidance on, cross cutting legal, practice or policy guidance to ensure consistency of approach. The Attorney General oversees and coordinates legal and practice issues, both domestic and international, which cross over departments and affect all prosecutors. To ensure consistency of practice across prosecutors generally the Attorney General may issue guidelines.

5.7. Given the Attorney General's public interest role, the Attorney General's views are accorded particular weight on difficult questions of balancing competing public interest considerations in prosecution guidance.

6. Dealings with the press and other media

6. Recognising that the media have a legitimate interest, on behalf of the public, in the Prosecuting Departments and their activities, the Attorney and the Directors make available appropriate information about them. The relevant Director(s) and their departments and the Attorney General's Office co-operate closely on media-handling issues, including the appropriate approach to briefing the media, or making any other public comment, on any particular issue.

7. Dealing with complaints

7. Without prejudice to the responsibilities and public and parliamentary accountabilities for decisions set out in section 4, there are specific arrangements for dealing with complaints from individuals:

- Each Director has a procedure for dealing with complaints about the way in which particular cases have been dealt with by their Department.
- Where a complaint is not satisfactorily resolved by the relevant Director's Department, the complainant is notified that they may refer the matter to the Attorney General.
- The Director ensures that the Attorney General is provided with all relevant information regarding the complaint and the case to which it refers.
- The Attorney General is able, but is not required in every case, to commission an independent review of the way in which the complaint has been handled.

[3:10] Block, B, Corbett, C and Peay, J, 'Ordered and Directed Acquittals in the Crown Court: A Time of Change?'

[1993] Crim LR 95 (at page 100)

Foreseeability and avoidability: how accountable are the CPS?

Of the sample of 100 non-jury acquittals, there were 71 ordered acquittals, 28 directed acquittals and one mixed acquittal, where there were two indictments and one was acquitted by order and one by direction. Although fewer than half of ordered acquittals were considered definitely or possibly foreseeable, three-quarters of directed acquittals were so classified. This supports our view, derived from the study, that directed acquittals result largely from weak cases that should have been discontinued, whereas ordered acquittals often result from unforeseeable circumstances. This may be considered to challenge Zander's assertion that ordered acquittals represent an even weaker category of case than where the judge directs an acquittal [This includes those acquitted by the judge where no evidence is offered (for example, because of the refusal of a witness to testify). Zander, M 'What the Annual Statistics Tell Us about Pleas and Acquittals' (1991) Crim LR 252]. Our study shows that in fact there are at least two categories of ordered acquittals: those weak cases that are spotted by the CPS immediately after committal, and others – seemingly good cases – which weaken unpredictably before committal or trial. Of all ordered acquittals in our sample (71), 14 were listed for mention (the former category) and 37 weakened nearer or on the day of trial (the latter category).

Use of the term 'weak cases' implies criticism of the CPS, but this is misleading. The real basis for criticism is the distinction between predictably weak cases which the CPS fail to spot and unpredictably weak cases. Of fundamentally weak cases, the CPS may be held responsible for those resulting in ordered acquittals that should have been spotted even before committal, and for those ending in directed acquittals due to weaknesses not spotted at all. Any analysis of the national statistics which is used as a basis for assessing the performance of the CPS needs to take account of these distinctions.

Accordingly, the increase in the proportion of ordered to directed acquittals could be interpreted as reflecting the increasing ability of the CPS to identify weak cases, which then result in ordered rather than directed acquittals. Consistent with this would be the numbers of ordered acquittals due to witnesses or victims not turning up at trial – a feature of the unforeseeably weak ordered acquittal group – possibly being due to police not chasing up witnesses rather than CPS inaction. The results of this study, however, equally suggest that many weak cases could have been identified and discontinued before committal. Such action would have prevented the inclusion of these cases in the national statistics of non-jury acquittals completely. These avoidable non-jury acquittals constitute between 15% and 43% of this sample of cases – the 15% figure representing the lowest level of prosecutorial inefficiency (those cases foreseeably weak pre-committal) and 43% the highest (including all those possibly foreseeable cases which might have been identified at or immediately after committal). Moreover, it is surprising that some weak cases, where the weakness was foreseeable (and agreed as such by the CPS assessor), were allowed to proceed to directed acquittals. Although small in number (five), it is an indictment of the CPS that these cases were not converted into ordered acquittals by earlier CPS action, or prevented from becoming acquittals at all by even earlier discontinuance.

(At page 105):

The results of this inquiry show that of a sample of 100 non-jury acquittals, although 45 were unavoidable due to entirely unforeseen and unforeseeable circumstances, the remainder could or might have been avoided, and in 22 cases even the CPS assessor said that the acquittal was foreseeable and arguably therefore ought to have been avoided. In a minimum of 15%, where it was assessed that a directed or ordered acquittal could have been foreseen prior to committal, the case should have been terminated or manifest deficiencies in the evidence rectified. These acquittals were clearly the responsibility of the CPS in the first instance. Once the case had been committed, blame could more properly be laid with counsel, who did not always advise the CPS that a case was weak or that certain evidence was lacking. Other acquittals too were not attributable to the CPS but stemmed from the intervention of the trial judges, or lack of intervention by counsel.

In view of the limited sample size, it would be unwise to make too many claims on the basis of the findings of the present study. However, as there is no reason to believe that the sample was in any way typical of non-jury acquittals some limited observations and recommendations for change will be advanced. It is suggested that, if implemented, the following modifications to the system could reduce substantially the proportion of non-jury acquittals.

First, the powers of the CPS need enhancing. It is all too easy for a case to seem watertight at committal yet to become manifestly unsafe between committal and trial. A further review of the evidence may reveal it to be not so strong as previously believed, or counsel can point out deficiencies that were missed. Where this occurs, all that the CPS can do at present is to list the case for mention; they cannot discontinue. At the beginning of the trial counsel can offer no evidence and the judge can order an acquittal. Since Grafton, however, the judge cannot interfere with counsel's decision not to offer any further evidence and must direct an acquittal. It is anomalous that the CPS cannot discontinue before trial when they have full discretion to offer no further evidence at the trial up to the end of the prosecution case. Clearly, ordered acquittals of this type could be eliminated if section 23 of the Prosecution of Offences Act 1985 were amended so that the CPS were able to discontinue at any time up to the beginning of Crown Court trial.

[3:11] McConville, M, Sanders, A and Leng, R, *The Case for the Prosecution*
(1991) Routledge (at page 124)

All cases which are either charged or reported for summons are subject to review both within the police and by the Crown Prosecution Service. Since the CPS was superimposed upon the pre-existing policy system rather than replacing any part of it, there is considerable duplication and overlap of functions. For both organisations the grounds of review are the same and involve consideration of whether the public interest is best served by prosecution or some other disposal, whether the evidence establishes a realistic prospect of conviction and whether the proposed charge is appropriate in law. Although the CPS, like the police reviewer, is isolated from operational policing, the prosecutor may seek to influence the investigation process by requesting that specific further inquiries be made. However, certain functions are exclusively the preserve of one or other organisation. The police have total control over which cases enter the system and only the police caution or informally warn an offender. In juvenile cases it is the job of the police to solicit the views of other agencies with responsibility for the welfare of children. On the other hand, the CPS has responsibility for the conduct of the case in court, may drop or amend charges and has ultimate veto of prosecution.

All forces have instituted special procedures to enable agencies with responsibility for the welfare of children to take part in the juvenile decision-making process. The official purpose of these juvenile liaison procedures is to ensure that public interest factors including the welfare of the child are considered on an individual basis. The police are under a statutory duty to notify Social Services if they are going to prosecute a juvenile (s 5(8) Children and Young Persons Act 1969). The systems in operation vary considerably ranging from permanent multi-agency bureaux as pioneered by Northampton to less elaborate systems in which the views of the other agencies are solicited by post or telephone. In the forces which we researched, one force relied upon home visits conducted by specialist police officers to obtain information about the circumstances of juvenile suspects, with the views of the other agencies obtained by post or telephone. One force considered juvenile cases at a regular juvenile liaison meeting convened by the police and attended by representatives of Social Services and the Probation Service. In the third force a specialist juvenile liaison officer collected information and views from the other agencies, with the option of convening a 'panel' in the event of persistent disagreement about a particular case.

Conventional explanations for the development of the CPS and juvenile liaison procedures can be traced to the argument of the objectivity required in prosecution and the need to take a broader view when applying public policy criteria to prosecution decisions. Under this view, CPS and juvenile liaison provide effective scrutiny of earlier police decisions because the individuals involved are independent of the police and operate according to the skills and values of their own professions.

Another interpretation is that such agencies and procedures are simply doing the state's job for it more efficiently than previously, albeit in a 'welfare disguise' – whether by 'winning by appearing to lose' in the case of the CPS or by adopting a 'corporatist approach' in the case of juvenile liaison. Corporatism refers, in Pratt's words, to the tendencies found in advanced welfare societies whereby the capacity for conflict and disruption is reduced by means of the centralisation of police, increased government intervention, and the co-option of various professional and interest groups into a collective whole with homogenous aims and objectives. (Pratt, 1989 ['Corporatism: the third model of juvenile justice', 29 BJ of Criminology 236], citing Unger, 1976).

Under corporatism, the legal process takes on the form of bureaucratic-administrative law, blurring the boundary between the public and private realms, and increasingly concerned to develop routinised criteria in order to enable dispositions to be effected according to an extra-judicial tariff in the most efficient manner. We shall argue, especially in relation to juvenile liaison bureaux, that this corporatist tendency is apparent in the dominant position occupied by the police in all decisions, in the co-option of other professionals into police ideologies and in the routinisation of extra-judicial decision-making.

As we described in earlier chapters, constructing the case is not simply an exercise in collecting together and marshalling all relevant information. Rather the selection, creation and presentation of the evidence is geared towards the objective which the police seek to achieve, and effectively dominates later review procedures. Because the police expect case review and understand the ground rules which govern it, they can anticipate it. Thus, the 'seriousness' of an offence may be manipulated by description: an attack may be 'vicious', 'unprovoked', or premeditated; a shop theft may be 'motivated by pure greed'; a suspected shoplifter may have 'looked round furtively'; emphasis on the suspect's own words may be used to convey the officer's view of the case, as by stressing that a shoplifter said 'it just seemed easy' thereby perhaps negating a doubt the reviewer might have about the offence being rooted in forgetfulness, illness or stress. Construction by omission is equally significant. Thus in one case a store detective had suggested to a suspect that she had forgotten to pay. This was criticised by the CPS reviewer who requested the police to advise the store detective not to make such suggestions when questioning shoplifters in future. Case construction may also be a means of co-opting non-police reviewers into police ideology and values or may convey a more general message about local policing imperatives. Thus, the offence in question may be 'rife' in that part of town, the suspect may be described as a 'football hooligan'.

The rhetoric of prosecution decision-making emphasises objectivity, impartiality and individualisation. Police influence over a case is said to be confined to the investigation and case preparation stages with ultimate decision-making by the prosecutor applying rigorous tests of public interest and evidential sufficiency. The reality is a system of routinised decision-making embodying an overwhelming propensity to prosecute, bolstered by the presumption that earlier decisions were properly made and should not be overturned. The system is dominated throughout it stages by the interests and values of the police, with the CPS playing an essentially subordinate and reactive role.

(At page 147):

In the welfarist rhetoric of the criminal justice process, no individual is charged until after the case has been thoroughly reviewed, not only within the police but also ultimately by an independent and impartial prosecuting agency divorced from the investigatory functions of the police. This review process, it is claimed operates to overcome the danger that 'case commitment' by arresting and case officers may lead to unjustified charging, and, generally, to ensure that individuals are brought to court only where there is a realistic prospect of conviction on the basis of the evidence and where it is also in the public interest to deal with the matter by way of prosecution. The special position of juveniles has led to the creation of juvenile liaison bodies where representatives of the caring agencies can give further impetus to non-prosecution by bringing to the forefront non-police values and ideologies.

In reality, the system of review is corporatist in nature: marked by continued police dominance of decision-making, a propensity to prosecute, extra-judicial tariffs, routinisation rather than individualised judgment and the broad rejection of public interest criteria. Police dominance is primarily secured by their control over how cases are constructed, a function which enables them to anticipate and thus control review. Although the police have been required to involve other agencies in decision-making, this has been done within police structures (juvenile liaison bureaux) and on police terms but surrounded by a welfarist rhetoric which masks a structure whose objectives appear to be the opposite of its rubric. The CPS, far from being an independent agency, is a police-dependent body, confining review to evidence-sufficiency questions, eschewing public interest criteria, utilising the contradictory and malleable nature of the principles in the codes to further narrowly conceived objectives and, at its worst, adopting an uncritical support-the-police mandate.

Chapter 4

Non-Police Investigations

Although defendants are most likely to be introduced to the criminal justice system by the victim and a police investigation, there are other, contrasting, routes to prosecution that merit a separate chapter, since different prosecuting authorities have very different policies and priorities. As much as a quarter of all prosecutions of adults for non-motoring offences are not initiated by the police. Every year people are prosecuted for tax and customs offences, for benefit frauds, for failing to purchase a TV licence, or for failing to hold a valid motor vehicle excise licence (formerly, a tax disc).

Companies as well as individuals are prosecuted by non-police organisations. Every year many people die at work, and many more are severely injured. Disasters such as the sinking of a ferry, a train crash or a fire in a public place can reveal corporate incompetence and criminality. They are likely to be investigated by the Health and Safety Executive (and sometimes by the police as well). Then there is corporate fraud. The amount of tax evaded by companies and individuals every year is huge – although the line between tax avoidance (legal) and tax evasion (illegal) seems increasingly blurred. Over 20 years ago, Levi (1993) estimated that one particular case being investigated by the Serious Fraud Office involved a sum equal to the total annual losses from vehicle-related crime. Quite recently, the Government appeared to have woken up to the problem of serious fraud. A *Fraud Review* was published in 2006, and the Government set up a National Fraud Strategic Authority in 2008 (which almost immediately changed its name to the National Fraud Authority). However, this was closed in March 2014. Identifying the extent of the problem is a good start: the National Fraud Authority (2013) estimated that the loss to the UK economy from fraud that year was £52 billion. Fraud is therefore unsurprisingly a focus of this chapter.

Non-police prosecutions are even more important if we look at the number of offences rather than the number of offenders. In fact, the scale of crimes committed other than by 'ordinary people' on the street is so vast that we often find it easier to ignore it! Lidstone et al **[4:1]** carried out a wide-scale study for the 1981 Royal Commission on Criminal Procedure. Although now more than 30 years old, it is a useful starting point, highlighting the wide range of factors which at that time influenced the number of prosecutions an agency undertook. Although it is difficult to discover a list of the key 'agencies' involved today, the list would surely include those discussed below.

A consideration of each 'agency' raises some common concerns. One is the fine line which exists today between criminal and civil enforcement. Roording **[4:2]** is clearly shocked at what he learns of England when he arrives to research the Inland Revenue in the 1990s: the blurring of civil and criminal penalties, and the failure of academics to take the subject seriously. Add to this the fact that many criminal offences in this area, often unhelpfully known as 'regulatory offences', do not require the prosecution to prove fault. The relevance of this strict liability to enforcement practices is discussed by Richardson **[4:3]**. Although this article is quite old, the concerns raised are just as relevant today. She raises the problem of the usurpation of the criminal trial by administrative discretion.

Another concern is the difficulty in challenging decisions to prosecute. The supermarket chain Tesco failed in its attempt to challenge the decision of a local authority to prosecute only large, nationally recognised stores in respect of Sunday trading contrary to the Shops Act 1950: see *R v Kirklees Metropolitan Borough Council, ex p Tesco Stores Ltd* (1993) Times, 26 October. And the (then) Inland Revenue's policy of selective enforcement was unsuccessfully challenged in *R v IRC, ex p Mead and Cook* **[4:4]** (see also *R v IRC, ex p Allen* [1997] STC 1141, where Allen had offered to settle allegations of tax evasion by paying £1 million but was nonetheless prosecuted: his application to challenge the decision to prosecute him by way of judicial review was unsuccessful). The court appears to accept without difficulty a policy that leaves the discretion to prosecute challengeable only when it is proved to be 'irrational'.

(i) Revenue and Customs frauds

HM Revenue & Customs (HMRC) was formed in April 2005, following the merger of Inland Revenue and HM Customs and Excise (HMCE) Departments. This followed on from the recommendations of Gus O'Donnell's report, *Financing Britain's Future: Review of the Revenue Departments*, published in 2004. Whilst this document discussed the need to ensure 'resources are allocated effectively so as to minimise tax losses to the Exchequer and so ensure public services are well financed' (page 12), it had little to say on enforcement and prosecution policy.

In 2005, the Revenue and Customs Prosecution Office (RCPO) was established as an 'independent' prosecuting authority reporting to the Attorney General. This had resulted from two reviews of a series of spectacular failures in prosecutions: first, the Gower Hammond Review (2000) into the failure of two major drugs prosecutions conducted by Customs in the late 1990s, which urged greater independence of prosecutors from investigators, and secondly, the Butterfield Report (2003) into the mistakes in both investigation and prosecution in the London City Bond cases, which went further, urging 'a complete separation of the prosecuting function for HM Customs and Excise's criminal cases from the organisation itself, through the creation of a separate prosecuting authority'. This Report followed on from the collapse of a high-profile investigation and prosecution of 15 defendants on charges of conspiracy to cheat the public revenue of duty on beer and spirits. The trial judge had ordered not guilty verdicts on day 35 of the trial, expressing particular concern on issues of non-disclosure. Mr Justice Butterfield made a number of recommendations on law enforcement (that HMCE should remain as an independent investigating force, but better procedures for handling human sources were urgently necessary), on prosecution (greater independence) and on the criminal justice system (on disclosure, case management and the retention of intercepted materials within the Regulation of Investigatory Powers Act 2000 regime).

The RCPO, however, did not last long: it was merged with the Crown Prosecution Service in January 2010. Keir Starmer, the then Director of Public Prosecutions, was also appointed as the Director of Revenue and Customs Prosecutions (a post since abolished by the Public Bodies (Merger of the Director of Public Prosecutions and the Director of Revenue and Customs Prosecutions) Order 2014) and the cases investigated by HMRC are now prosecuted by the Specialist Fraud Division of the CPS.

Note carefully HMRC's Criminal Investigation policy [4:5]. It is HMRC's policy to deal with fraud by the use of 'cost effective' Civil Investigation of Fraud (CIF) procedures, where appropriate. Following the report of the Keith Committee, *Report on the Enforcement Powers of the Revenue Departments* (1983) Cmnd 8822, the range of sanctions available to the Revenue Departments was extended. Compounding, which enables them to force compliance as well as a financial penalty, is today widely used as an alternative to taking legal proceedings. Other 'non-judicial penalties' include seizure of goods, vehicles or equipment used in smuggling or revenue offences. Civil fraud procedures were introduced for VAT by the Finance Act 1986 and were extended to excise duty frauds and customs duties frauds by sections 7–14 and Schedules 4 and 5 of the Finance Act 1994. This is part of a process of decriminalisation of many (often strict liability) offences, in stark contrast to the criminalisation of much other anti-social behaviour. Dee Cook's work has been important in highlighting the different approaches taken in benefit frauds. In her book, *Criminal and Social Justice* (2006), she asks (at page 46) 'when it comes to fiddling the state, is there one law for the (relatively) rich and another for the poor in contemporary Britain?' She points out how the taxpayer has historically been valued as a law-abiding and productive citizen and a giver of revenue for state services. She notes a plummeting of the number of Inland Revenue prosecutions and a dramatic reduction in yields from investigation work from the early 1990s to the early 2000s. She argues that the current prosecution policy seems to work well – for the fraudster (see page 52).

The emphasis of this section has been on the prosecution policy of the taxation authorities, which is so much more selective than that of the police. However, McBarnet (1992) goes further, pointing out that social control through law is challenged not just by those who abuse the law but also by those who use it. She stresses the manipulability of the law in this area and the scope for bending it to specific interests so that 'economic elites with the resources to buy legal creativity can also buy immunity from the law' (at page 266). Cook (2006) goes so far as to argue that traditional hatred of personal taxation have led to 'agency investigation and prosecution policies and broader political priorities designed to appeal to middle England' (at page 60). But remember that Roording's (1996) (Dutch) perspective also criticises the 'huge and institutionalised pressure' on taxpayers to confess and to co-operate. Should the system be less informal?

(ii) Benefit frauds

Until recently, the Department of Work and Pensions (DWP) used a Fraud Investigation Service to investigate benefit fraud (estimated by the DWP at around £1.2 billion in 2013/14). However, at the time of writing this is being merged with fraud officers from HMRC and local authorities to create a Single Fraud Investigation Service to investigate and prosecute social security welfare benefits and tax credit fraud across local authorities, HMRC and the DWP. The current sanctions policy of the DWP is included at **[4:6]**. The Department's solicitors are bound by the Code for Crown Prosecutors (see paragraph 4.4.3). Would the next logical step be to bring these prosecutions under the CPS? We return to this question in the final section of this chapter.

Cook, in her books of 1989 and 2006, analysed the different responses to tax and social security frauds. She found that in 1986/87, when 457 tax evaders were prosecuted, 8,000 people were prosecuted for falsely claiming Supplementary Benefit (the predecessor of Income Support). As we have noted above, Cook develops these arguments further in her 2006 book which uses data from the 1990s and early 2000s which suggests that the picture has not improved. She suggests that the differences can be explained in terms of the different histories of taxation and welfare and, subsequently, the ideological construction of taxpayers as 'givers' to, and benefit claimants as 'takers' from, the State. McKeever (1999) also highlights the possibility of fraud arising from claimant confusion rather than dishonesty. The stark difference in the way that benefit fraud is dealt with is still illustrated by the number of prosecutions: according to the Sentencing Council (2013), 6,080 offenders were sentenced for benefit fraud offences in 2011 but only 171 offenders were sentenced for revenue fraud against HMRC that year. Are current policies exaggerating the 'one law for the rich and another for the poor' approach, identified by Dee Cook?

(iii) Health and Safety Executive

In 2013/14, the Health and Safety Executive (HSE) brought 551 prosecutions in England and Wales: 517 of these resulted in a conviction for at least one offence – a conviction rate of 94 per cent (Health and Safety Executive Index of Enforcement tables, Table EF1). As the website (www.hse.gov. uk/enforce/what.htm) explains:

> We don't take enforcement action lightly. Visits from our inspectors give duty holders the opportunity to get expert advice face to face. A proportionate approach is taken to any breaches, so in less serious cases, the inspector will explain how the duty holder is not complying with the law and advise them how to put the problem right. The inspector will explain legal requirements and good practice, as well as confirming the advice in writing if asked. However, failure to follow the advice from our inspectors is often taken into account by courts if that failure results in harm.

Where the breach of the law is more serious, the inspector may serve a notice on the duty holder. The inspector can serve:

- an improvement notice, which requires duty holders to take remedial action on specific breaches of the law within a specified time limit;
- a prohibition notice, which is issued in cases where the inspector believes that a work activity involves, or will involve, a risk of serious personal injury. Prohibition notices can take two forms:
  - immediate prohibition notices, which stop a work activity immediately until a risk is dealt with; and
  - deferred prohibition notices, which stop a work activity within a specified time limit.

When an inspector issues a notice, it is an opportunity for the duty holder to put things right and prevent future incidents. If they fail to comply with the notice, prosecution is likely to follow. Inspectors are guided by the Enforcement Management Model when making enforcement decisions and take into account the Code for Crown Prosecutors [3:5] when considering prosecution.

The policies that lie behind health and safety prosecutions can therefore provide useful comparisons to police decision-making: the HSE do not 'take enforcement action lightly'. Should there be greater flexibility in police enforcement policies? Or should there be more attempts to monitor this flexible (and potentially unfair) HSE approach?

(iv) The Environment Agency

The Environment Agency has five principles for 'firm but fair regulation': proportionality, consistency, transparency, targeting and accountability – and their guidance on enforcement and sanctions is available online (see www.gov.uk/government/uploads/system/uploads/attachment_data/file/389349/LIT_5551.pdf). Their focus is on 'enabling' compliance, but what happens in cases of non-compliance? The first port of call is likely to be the use of civil sanctions which, according to the Environment Agency's Annual Report for 2013/14, gives them 'more flexibility to enforce regulations' (at page 15) but they will prosecute 'when necessary' (at page 16). In 2013/14, eight offenders were imprisoned and a further eight received suspended sentences for waste crimes prosecuted by the Environment Agency and they obtained court orders to recover over £2 million of proceeds of crime from offenders (Annual Report 2013/14 at page 16). Before commencing a prosecution, the case will be assessed in accordance with the requirements of the Code for Crown Prosecutors [3:5].

Are these regulatory bodies right to give priority to compliance over prosecution? For the sake of consistency, should all prosecutions be brought under the CPS umbrella (particularly if they are all guided by the Code for Crown Prosecutors in any case)? But is there a difference in principle between these offences and police cases that explains why they should be treated differently?

(v) Serious Fraud Office

The Serious Fraud Office (SFO) was established by the Criminal Justice Act (CJA) 1987 [4:7], following the report of the Roskill Committee on Fraud Trials (1986). The Committee's most controversial recommendation – that in some complex fraud cases the trial should take place not before a judge and jury but before a 'fraud trials tribunal' comprising a judge and two members with financial expertise – was rejected by the government (though we will see in Chapter 8 how this has, in some measure, been adopted). However, many of its other proposals on fraud trials were acted upon in the CJA 1987.

The SFO investigates and prosecutes the most serious frauds in England, Wales and Northern Ireland, but the numbers are small (e.g. it was responsible for 13 trials in 2009/10, involving 24 defendants: 22 were convicted and 2 acquitted; more recently, in 2012/13, 12 trials were completed, involving 20 defendants: 14 were convicted and 6 acquitted). It is accountable through its director to the Attorney General and so to Parliament. Investigations are conducted by interdisciplinary teams of lawyers, police officers, accountants and IT experts. Most of the police officers are members of the Metropolitan Police or the City of London Police.

Thus, the investigatory and prosecution roles were combined in one office, just after they had been separated in the case of 'standard' criminal offences, by the creation of the CPS in 1985. Does the special and complex nature of some frauds make continuity of investigation and prosecution desirable – is fraud necessarily more difficult than other crime? It is not clear exactly where the line between serious fraud and other fraud is drawn, and many serious frauds continue to be dealt with by the CPS. The SFO states that the key criterion they use when deciding whether to accept a case is that the suspected fraud appears to be so serious or complex that its investigation should be carried out by those responsible for its prosecution. The SFO's website explains:

> The SFO investigates and, where appropriate, prosecutes cases of serious or complex fraud (including cases of domestic or overseas bribery and corruption) which, in the opinion of the Director of the SFO, call for the multi-disciplinary approach and legislative powers available to the SFO. In deciding what cases to adopt, the Director will take into account all the circumstances of the case and consider: cases which undermine UK commercial/financial PLC in general and the City of London in particular; cases where the actual or potential loss involved are high; cases where actual or potential harm is significant; cases where there is a very significant public interest element; and new species of fraud.

Note the CJA 1987, section 2 **[4:7]**: the SFO has wide powers of investigation as well as of prosecution. Its powers to compel a suspect to answer questions or otherwise to furnish information, and to require the production of documents, were examined by the House of Lords in *R v Director of Serious Fraud Office, ex p Smith* **[4:8]**. The European Court of Human Rights in *Saunders v United Kingdom* (1996) 23 EHRR 313 held that the admission in evidence at the applicant's trial of transcripts of interviews with Department of Trade and Industry inspectors violated Article 6(1) of the European Convention on Human Rights (see **[1:13]**). Article 6(1) presupposes that the prosecution must prove its case without resort to evidence obtained through methods of coercion. As a result of this decision, section 59 (together with Schedule 3) of the Youth Justice and Criminal Evidence Act 1999 now restricts the use that can be made of answers obtained under compulsory powers of questioning in legislation such as the Companies Act 2006. Are there implications here for the provisions of the Criminal Justice and Public Order Act 1994 restricting the right to silence?

We saw in Chapter 3 how the CPS is handicapped in providing an independent review of police decisions by not having its own powers of investigation. Since the SFO has its own investigators, it should perhaps have a high record of success. However, as Levi (1993) made clear, measuring the success or otherwise of the SFO is not easy. It is impossible to tell whether non-prosecutions are due to political or other extra-legal factors, and prosecution policies can undergo significant shifts if large funds are made available – this happened, for example, with the special Treasury 'votes' for the Bank of Credit and Commerce International investigation. Levi argued that many prosecutions go ahead despite foreseeable weaknesses in the case, and proposes greater judicial involvement before the trial. On the other hand, he fears that prosecution decisions in cases of white-collar crime will become driven almost entirely by cost considerations, a risk exacerbated by the media and the political tendency to look at the huge costs of the individual trial, ignoring the huge dimensions of the misconduct to which they relate (at page 196). If the prosecution of serious frauds proves so difficult, and so expensive, perhaps there is an argument for leaving these cases to the civil law or to administrative regulation. But would this be letting the affluent, white-collar criminal off too lightly? What price are we prepared to pay?

How far have things moved on since 1993? There is no doubt that there is significant public and governmental concern about the extent of fraud, and its effects on the economy and wider society. An interesting perspective on why people choose to commit white-collar crime is offered by Shover and Hochstetler (2006). They distinguish 'ordinary' and 'upperworld' white-collar crime and present reasons theoretically for believing that both have increased substantially in recent decades. It seems that the criminal law can play only a small part in dealing with this problem – although Padfield **[4:9]** argues that the use of Deferred Prosecution Agreements with companies accused of fraud, bribery and other economic crime may be allowing companies off too readily. The Government sought to secure more convictions through the introduction of the Fraud Act 2006, which repealed the earlier law of fraud and created new broad substantive offences. But the Government's own interdepartmental review into the detection, investigation and prosecution of fraud (2006) recognises that there are many institutional and practical hurdles which go far beyond the law itself if we want to reduce fraud.

(vi) Private prosecutions

Many of the prosecutions mentioned in this chapter might be considered 'private prosecutions'. For example, the Royal Society for the Prevention of Cruelty to Animals (RSPCA) has its own prosecution department, and when it prosecutes uses private lawyers.

Lord Wilberforce in *Gouriet v Union of Post Office Workers* [1978] AC 435 described the right of the individual to institute a private prosecution 'as a valuable constitutional safeguard against inertia or partiality on the part of authority' (at page 477). But the value of this right should not be exaggerated. Legal aid is not available to a private prosecutor, and in any case the right is in effect controlled by the Attorney General (see Chapter 3), who may take over the prosecution and, if he thinks fit, enter a plea of *nolle prosequi* ('we do not wish to prosecute'). It is not unusual for the Attorney General to make clear that if a private prosecution were to be launched, he would stop it. This happened in the case of a priest who threatened to prosecute the doctors who, having sought authority from the House of Lords in *Airedale NHS Trust v Bland* [1993] AC 789, 'killed' Tony Bland, a patient in a persistent vegetative state. Thus the Attorney General in effect has a veto on law enforcement. In *Jones v Whalley* **[4:10]**, Lord Bingham described the right to prosecute privately as:

> a somewhat anomalous historical survival . . . A crime is an offence against the good order of the state. It is for the state by its appropriate agencies to investigate alleged crimes and decide whether offenders should be prosecuted. In times past, with no public prosecution service and ill-organised means of enforcing the law, the prosecution of offenders necessarily depended on the involvement of private individuals, but that is no longer so. The surviving right of private prosecution is of questionable value, and can be exercised in a way damaging to the public interest (at paragraphs 15–16).

Lord Mance in that case quotes the Law Commission's *Report on Consents to Prosecution* (1988, LC 255):

> We . . . do not believe that it is appropriate to consider abolishing the right of private prosecution without specific consideration which has neither been sought nor given in this project. The issues raised on the question of retention of the right of private prosecution are complex and they are not capable of being resolved within the scope of this report (paragraph 5.13). They mention three important issues:

(1) There is always a risk that an individual Crown prosecutor will either misapply the code or – more likely, given the width of the code tests – apply a personal interpretation to the tests which, although not wrong, might differ from that of other prosecutors.

(2) The code itself may, in the eyes of some, fail to achieve a proper balance between the rights of the defendant and the interests of the community.

(3) It should not be assumed that if it is wrong to bring a public prosecution then it is also wrong to bring a private prosecution. If, for example, a case is turned down by the [Crown Prosecution Service] because it fails the evidential sufficiency test, but only just; if the private prosecutor knows that the defendant is guilty (because, say, he or she was the victim and can identify the offender); and if the case is a serious one, then a private prosecution might be thought desirable (at paragraph 41).

So the right lives on in a half-hearted manner. Its applicability has been further eroded since the Supreme Court's decision in R (Gujra) v Crown Prosecution Service [2012] UKSC 52 in which the Court, split 3:2, upheld the Director of Public Prosecutions' new policy to take over and discontinue a private prosecution unless the prosecution was more likely than not to result in a conviction. This policy, introduced in 2009, replaced the previous approach in which the DPP would only take over and discontinue a private prosecution if there was clearly no case for the defendant to answer. By aligning the policy to the CPS's own evidential test for public prosecutions laid down in the Code for Crown Prosecutors [3:5], it would appear that private prosecutions will be limited to cases in which the CPS is content to outsource a prosecution to another body which also applies the Full Code Test.

Private prosecutions, and prosecutions by non-police agencies, raise many questions. Whether getting people to agree not to break the law (compliance) is sometimes a better strategy than prosecution; whether these bodies have too many discretionary powers. It is important to remember that a case like Gerry Good's enters the criminal justice system through the 'normal', police, route, but it is certainly not the only route.

Further reading

Attorney General, Fraud Review (2006)

Braithwaite, V, 'Resistant and dismissive defiance towards tax authorities' in Crawford, A and Hucklesby, A (eds), Legitimacy and Compliance in Criminal Justice (2013) Routledge

Butterfield, Mr Justice, Review of criminal investigations and prosecutions conducted by HM Customs and Excise (2003)

Cook, D, Rich Law, Poor Law (1989) Open University Press

Cook, D, Criminal and Social Justice (2006) Sage

Croall, H, Understanding White Collar Crime (2001) Open University Press

Gower, J and Hammond, A, Report on Customs and Excise prosecutions (2000)

Hungerford-Welch, P, 'R (on the application of Gujra) v Crown Prosecution Service: Prosecution-private prosecution – policy of Director of Public Prosecutions' [2013] Crim LR 337

Levi, M, The Investigation, Prosecution and Trial of Serious Fraud (1993) RCCJ Research Study No 14, HMSO

Levi, M, The Phantom Capitalists (2008) Ashgate

Levi, M, 'Regulating Fraud Revisited' in Davies, P, Francis, P and Wyatt, T (eds), Invisible Crimes and Social Harms (2014) Palgrave Macmillan

Levi, M, Burrows, J, Fleming, M and Hopkins, M, The Nature, Extent and Economic Impact of Fraud in the UK (2007) ACPO

McBarnet, D, 'The Construction of Compliance and the Challenge of Control: The Limits of Noncompliance Research' in Slemrod, J (ed), Why People Pay Taxes: Tax Compliance and Enforcement (1992) University of Michigan Press

McBarnet, D, *Crime, Compliance and Control* (2004) Ashgate

McBarnet, D, 'Questioning the legitimacy of compliance: a case study of the banking crisis' in Crawford, A and Hucklesby, A (eds), *Legitimacy and Compliance in Criminal Justice* (2013) Routledge

McKeever, G, 'Detecting, Prosecuting and Punishing Benefit Fraud: The Social Security Administration (Fraud) Act 1997' (1999) 62 *Modern Law Review* 261

McKeever, G, 'Tackling Benefit Fraud' (2003) 32 *Industrial Law Journal* 326

National Fraud Authority, *Annual Fraud Indicator* (2013)

Nelken, D, 'White-collar and corporate crime' in Maguire, M, Morgan, R and Reiner, R (eds), *The Oxford Handbook of Criminology* (5th edition, 2012) Oxford University Press

O'Donnell, G, *Financing Britain's Future: Review of the Revenue Departments* (2004) HM Treasury

Roskill, E, *Report of the Fraud Trials Committee* (1986) HMSO

Sentencing Council, *Fraud Offences Sentencing Data: Analysis and Research Bulletin* (2013)

Shover, N and Hochstetler, A, *Choosing White Collar Crime* (2006) Cambridge University Press

Documents

[4:1] Lidstone, K W, Hogg, R, Sutcliffe, F, *Prosecutions by Private Individuals and Non-Police Agencies*
(1980) HMSO (at page 180)

The prosecuting policies and statistics of nine agencies were considered in some detail – these were the DHSS, The Post Office, the NTVLRO (television licence evasion), the DVLC (vehicle excise licence cases), the Inland Revenue, Customs and Excise, and Health and Safety Executive, the Department of Trade and the Ministry of Agriculture Fisheries and Food. These agencies were selected on the basis of several considerations: we sought to include those agencies which have a large prosecutorial workload as well as those other agencies which, although prosecuting infrequently, fulfil important public functions within which the investigation and/or prosecution of criminal offences plays a significant part. It was found that there were considerable differences in policy between (and sometimes within) agencies. For example, among the revenue-collecting agencies, NTVLRO and DVLC prosecuted far more readily than did the Inland Revenue; within the DHSS, non-compliance with national insurance payments was treated a great deal more lightly than social security fraud; within the Department of Trade there were important differences in policies and types of arrangements for investigation and prosecution in respect of company registration cases, companies investigations, bankruptcy cases and company frauds. A further marked feature of this study of major agencies was the vast potential for further prosecution clearly available in many instances. This was most obvious in agencies which saw their primary task as securing compliance with legislation through persuasion and education (such as the Health and Safety Executive) or through negotiated settlements and penalties short of prosecution (such as the Inland Revenue). Even agencies which prosecuted relatively frequently, such as NTVLRO and DVLC, had considerable further potential for prosecution. Further investigation showed that in nearly all cases the role and extent of prosecution was related to the perceived primary task of the agency. Only the DHSS (in social security cases) and the Post Office tended to see infractions as unambiguously 'criminal', to be pursued through the deterrent and retributive mechanisms of the criminal law; in the case of the DHSS this policy presented the agency with a problem in reconciling this stance with its primary role as a dispenser of welfare benefits.

In Chapter 4 some of the minor agencies were considered, and a group of particular interest here were the 'voluntary agencies' such as the RSPCA, the RSPB and Friends of the Earth.

In general they tended to be reluctant prosecutors, deploring the relative inactivity of the police and other law enforcement agencies concerning their special area of interest; lacking resources themselves to prosecute to any great extent and therefore largely dependent on the police (though here the RSPCA was something of an exception); and only mounting their own prosecutions where the police were unwilling to act.

The court study had given a picture of prosecutorial activity by non-police bodies in 12 courts. The bulk of these were agency prosecutions, rather than prosecutions by private individuals, firms or voluntary bodies. (Some of the latter, such as retail stores and the RSPCA, were in any case reluctant prosecutors.) Among the agencies, however, further investigation revealed vast differences in the numbers of prosecutions, and in prosecution policy. It may be helpful finally to set out in schematic form some of the factors (not all previously mentioned in this summary) which may influence the number of prosecutions an agency undertakes:

(a) The population at risk of offending. Some agencies (like DVLC, NTVLRO and the Inland Revenue) potentially affect nearly every household in the country; others (like to Law Society and the General Nursing Council) will because of their restricted populations at risk never be major prosecutors. But not all 'large risk' agencies prosecute widely; the Inland Revenue is a notable example.

(b) The availability of alternative measures short of prosecution. Some agencies have such methods as formal alternatives, and tend to use them extensively: examples are Inland Revenue, Customs and Excise, and Health and Safety Executive; and the methods include compounding, seizure of goods, enforcement notices and cautions.

(c) The resources available to investigate offences. Several agencies have to restrict their investigative activities because of lack of resources (for example DVLC, Department of Trade and some local authorities). When one metropolitan Passenger Transport Executive set up a squad of plain clothes inspectors to police fare evasion, it was so successful in discovering evaders that a second squad and set up, and the numbers prosecuted soared on each occasion.

(d) The difficulty of proof. Agencies such as the Inland Revenue and the Department of Trade face severe tests of proof in large-scale fraud cases. The subject matter of the charges is often complex, and the prosecutor has to prove intention or at least recklessness. The defendants are often sophisticated and well advised. If a guilty plea is unlikely then prosecution may well be discouraged, especially if, as in the case of Inland Revenue, other courses are open to the agency. This does not apply to offences of strict liability such as using a motor vehicle without a vehicle excise licence, but even here there is often great difficulty in identifying the user of the vehicle.

(e) Political pressure. Both DHSS (markedly) and the Wages Inspectorate (marginally) have increased their prosecutorial work in recent years, in response to different kinds of direct political pressure.

(f) The perception of the primary task of the agency. Agencies which perceive their primary task as educative and persuasive have particularly low prosecution rates in relation to known offences (for example Health and Safety, local authorities). Even quite extensive prosecutors, like NTVLRO and DVLC, will be found not to prosecute in a sizeable proportion of cases if compliance can be secured through other means: for them, revenue collection, not prosecution, remains the primary goal. Conversely, agencies like the larger special police forces tend to see their activity as primarily law enforcement, and therefore use prosecution as a first rather than last resort.

(g) The perception of the offence. A widespread view in many agencies was that the offences involved were not really crime in the proper sense, and therefore not appropriate for automatic prosecution; such a view obviously encourages the use of other methods to secure compliance. A view of this kind may be challenged by outsiders (as it is, for example, by critics of the minimal prosecution policies of the Inland Revenue and the Health and Safety Executive), but this still may not affect the agency's perception. Varying perceptions of different offences may produce markedly different enforcement policies within a single agency, for example social security fraud as against non-compliance cases within the DHSS.

(h) Police reluctance to be involved. Retail stores and electricity boards in London would not themselves prosecute at all if the police would do so; the voluntary agencies also tend to prosecute only because of the perceived reluctance or of inaction by other law enforcement agencies, especially the police. The DHSS may in future be forced to seek wider investigative powers for its officers, and perhaps take on some cases currently prosecuted by the police, if a projected reduction in police co-operation occurs.

[4:2] Roording, J, 'The Punishment of Tax Fraud'
[1996] Crim LR 240
(At page 240):

In this article I intend to explore the field of punishment of tax fraud in the United Kingdom. I will make use of information I gathered with the Inland Revenue, inter alia through discussions with certain officials. As a Dutch lawyer I will necessarily take a continental view, and I shall introduce a perspective which has gained some popularity in the Netherlands recently. In this perspective the criminal law is seen as a system of punishment (a sanctions system) which, together with other such systems (especially the administrative sanctions system), is part of a wider field of law which could be called the law of sanctions. It is thought that these sanctions systems have much in common (i.e. the same purposes), and that all are governed by the same basic principles (for which reference is often made to Article 6 of the European Convention for the Protection of Human Rights and Fundamental Freedoms (ECHR)), so that a more integrated approach is advisable. This perspective provides a framework which makes possible a critical assessment of law enforcement practices of regulatory agencies from the point of view of the rights of suspects and offenders. At the same time it also focuses on alternative ways of punishment which could relieve the overburdened criminal justice system.

The sanctions systems in the field of tax

This sketch of the sanctions systems in the field of tax is limited to the procedures of the Inland Revenue (IR), which is responsible for the administration of direct taxes, such as income tax and corporation tax, in the United Kingdom. (I do not propose to deal with Customs and Excise, who are responsible for the administration of customs, excise and VAT and to that end have separate enforcement powers at their disposal; Customs and Excise have a fundamentally different approach from that of the Inland Revenue.) Two ways of punishment are open to the Inland Revenue: imposition of a civil penalty, and prosecution. Penalties (see Chapter X of the Taxes Management Act (TMA) 1970) are usually imposed by an officer of the Board of Inland Revenue, but in certain cases by an independent body called the (General or Special) Commissioners and in certain cases by the court. Statute either sets the maximum penalty at a fixed amount (for example in case of a simple failure to deliver a return; TMA 1970, s 93 (1) (a): maximum penalty 300) or at 100 per cent of the tax due (in case of a more serious offence, where there is fraud or negligence; see for example s 95 (incorrect return or account)). From a determination of a penalty by an officer of the Board appeal lies, first, to the Commissioners (s 100B(2)) and then to the High Court (s 100B(3)).

Besides imposing a civil penalty the Inland Revenue can also choose to initiate criminal proceedings. Usually the IR will not leave this to the police and the Crown Prosecution Service but bring a prosecution itself. Several charges are available: offences under the general criminal law, such as false accounting (s 17 of the Theft Act 1968), or cheating the public revenue, an offence under the common law. In contrast with Customs and Excise the Inland Revenue has no power to compound criminal proceedings. Theoretically the IR can impose a civil penalty and at the same time institute a prosecution for the same offence. It is however settled practice not to impose a penalty for an offence which has already been dealt with by the criminal court.

(At page 248):

In my view the way tax fraud is punished in the United Kingdom is not satisfactory. My main criticism concerns the huge and institutionalised pressure which is exerted on taxpayers to make them confess and co-operate. It is true that there will be pressure in any system in which the criminal law operates as an alternative to another, less 'heavy' sanctions system (heavy both in terms of sanctions and in terms of procedures). However, in the English system of punishment of tax fraud the pressure is extra strong, because the Inland Revenue seeks to keep the case in the informal sphere as long as possible. There the IR can dictate its own rules, and the formal procedures become a 'big stick'. By contrast, taxpayers have more protection in the Netherlands. There the tax department must choose between prosecution and the imposition of an administrative penalty. There is no third, informal way. In addition, the criminal and administrative spheres seem to be more clearly demarcated with respect to one another. This will be even more so when a current Bill is enacted which goes so far as to determine that once a prosecution or a penalty procedure has reached a certain point, there is no return; the other way is closed then. Further safeguards, which apply in penalty procedures, are a right of access to court, the right to be informed about the grounds of the accusation, and a duty on the Revenue to prove the mental element of the offence (fraud or negligence). The new Bill mentioned above even acknowledges the right to silence with regard to administrative penalty procedures.

The root of the problem seems to me that in the English legal system, systems of punishment outside the criminal law hardly get any attention, whether from the courts or from academics.1 It is not yet recognised that these sanctions systems show big similarities to the criminal law: in practice they operate as a very important alternative to the criminal sanctions system, with the same purpose, i.e. to enforce the law) and with the same means (e.g. fines). Unless and until this is recognised, grey areas such as that of the settlement of tax fraud will continue to exist and they will be governed by practical rules rather than legal principles.

[4:3] Richardson, G, 'Strict Liability for Regulatory Crime: the Empirical Research'
[1987] Crim LR 295

In an article chiefly concerned with the debate surrounding the use of strict liability in the regulatory context, Richardson raises the thorny issue of the usurpation of the criminal trial by administrative discretion.

(At page 303):

To an extent the empirical data, by emphasising the practical relevance of the offender's intent, might suggest that the concern over the propriety of strict liability is irrelevant. Such a conclusion is not inevitable, however. In the first place, although the data indicate that 'blameless innocents' are rarely prosecuted, the traditionalist is unlikely to be satisfied since the determination of 'blame' is made privately by an administrative agent rather than publicly with the full procedural protection of a criminal trial. Secondly, there is still the argument, referred to briefly above, that the use of strict liability serves both to detract from the significance of regulatory offences and to distinguish them from the main body of the criminal law. The introduction of strict liability into early factory legislation, for example, is thought to have placed a part in the marginalisation of early factory crime. In this sense, strict liability can be said to further the interests of the regulated by reducing the significance of non-compliance.

To some extent the first problem, the usurpation of the criminal trial by administrative discretion, can be met by the introduction of civil penalties in place of strict criminal liability. The device is common in the United States where crimes of strict liability are rare. But the mere removal of the criminal label provides no real solution to the problem of administrative discretion and must serve further to marginalise the prohibited activity. Arguably, the question of liability for corporate offences is not a 'problem' to be tackled in isolation but must be seen as merely one element of the regulatory scheme.

Whether or not regulatory offences constitute 'real' crime, the majority can be readily distinguished from the mass of traditional street crime as currently regarded. The distinction does not, however, rely on the narrow argument that regulatory crime is different because it is less serious and therefore strict liability is acceptable because penalties are low. It springs instead from the nature of the regulatory objective.

Legislative schemes regulating corporate conduct are primarily designed to prevent particular harms and are certainly seen in that light by those responsible for their enforcement. In large part, therefore, the overall legitimacy of any regulatory scheme and of the separate elements within it will flow from their combined ability to prevent harm. Each element will both contribute to and reflect the legitimacy of the whole.

In the first place protective regulation must provide for the proper definition of the prohibited event and the closer the relationship between the event and the harm, the more justifiable will be the prohibition. In addition, the research suggests that the more evidently justifiable or rational the prohibition the more assiduous will be the enforcement. In such a context, if the prohibition event is potentially harmful irrespective of the offender's mental state as classified by current criminal law principles, then there can be little instrumental justification for demanding the presence of fault as defined by those principles. Further, the corporate actor typically behaves in a particular way, installs a certain plant, for example, or markets a given drug, because of the anticipated benefits. To place 'properly' defined restrictions on such 'voluntary' behaviour and to penalise non-compliance is not to persecute the innocent even in the absence of any legally recognised degree of fault.

Secondly, if as is claimed here, the primary justification for regulatory prohibition rests on the need to prevent harm, then arguably the sanctions imposed on non-compliance should be designed with that end in view. This question inevitably raises highly contentious issues within the field of penal theory which go far beyond the scope of this article. Nonetheless, the proper role of the penal sanctions cannot be ignored in any consideration of regulatory crime.

With regard to traditional offences the prevention of future harm as the justification for criminal punishment has been severely challenged. In relation to regulatory offences, however, the argument may carry less weight. In the first place corporate offending is often regarded as less intractable than traditional criminality: the application of criminal sanctions might successfully deter, incapacitate, or even rehabilitate. Secondly, with regard to the problem of inequality of treatment, which is often linked to the preventative use of criminal sanctions, Braithwaite has argued that complete equality for regulatory offenders is beyond the scope of any criminal justice system and that the need to prevent serious harm, Thalidomide or Bhopal for example, should take priority over strict equality of treatment. Finally the rearrangement of a company's practices and procedures in order to ensure that it operates without causing harm is not open to the same moral considerations as the coerced rearranging of a psyche. In the light of these considerations most commentators identify harm prevention constrained by the principles of retribution as the primary rationale for the punishment of corporate offences in general and regulatory offences in particular.

It would appear, therefore, that the sanction has considerable potential to further the objectives of the regulatory scheme, and indeed in the United States a variety of sanctioning options have been tried or considered including: equity fines, adverse publicity, redress facilitation through plea bargaining, the integration of civil and criminal claims, community service orders and corporate probation. However, in the United Kingdom, despite widespread doubts as to its efficacy, the fine remains the most common sanction. Arguably, more effort is required to devise alternatives which effectively exploit the supposed susceptibility of corporate offenders to deterrence, incapacitation and rehabilitation.

In sum, the routine enforcement of regulatory offences typically exposes strict liability as merely one element within a regulatory scheme, the overall thrust of which is preventative. The extent to which the use of strict liability in particular is justified, it is claimed, will depend on the acceptability of the whole scheme which will itself be derived from the outcome of a number of policy choices. The principles of traditional criminal law and penology should not be applied automatically to the regulatory context.

[4:4] *R v IRC, ex p Mead and Cook*
[1992] STC 482

In November 1990, the Commissioners of Inland Revenue ordered the prosecution of the applicants for criminal offences in connection with tax evasion, and in March 1991, summonses were served on them. The prosecution had arisen out of the Revenue's investigation of the tax affairs of an accountant who had acted as the accountant to the applicants and to other taxpayers. The applicants sought judicial review of the decision to prosecute them, claiming that a comparison of the applicants' cases should have been made with those of the other taxpayers and only if there were distinguishing features which made the applicants' cases more serious than the others was the decision to prosecute them justified.

The application was dismissed.

Stuart-Smith LJ (at page 492):

The crucial factor in the present case is that the Revenue operate a selective policy of prosecution. They do so for three main reasons: first their primary objective is the collection of revenue and not the punishment of offenders; second they have inadequate resources to prosecute everyone who dishonestly evades payment of taxes; and third and perhaps most importantly they consider it necessary to prosecute in some cases because of the deterrent effect that this has on the general body of taxpayers, since they know that they behave dishonestly they may be prosecuted. It is inherent in such a policy that there may be inconsistency and unfairness as between one dishonest taxpayer and another who is guilty of a very similar offence. Nevertheless while not challenging the validity of the policy Mr Beloff submits that there must be grafted on to it requirement to treat all dishonest taxpayers guilty of similar offences for two reasons. First it is inconsistent with the policy and cannot be operated consistently with it, you cannot be both selective and treat every case alike. Second it seems to be quite impracticable. How are the Revenue to decide what cases are like? What is to be the basis of the group of cases that has to be considered? Over what period of time are the group to be considered? Are all cases involving forgery to be in one group? Or those involving forgery and false accounting? Are those who make a full disclosure to be in the same group as those who deny that they have acted dishonestly, although the Revenue consider that there is evidence that they have? These questions only have to be posed to demonstrate that it is quite impossible to answer them; and certainly in my judgment Mr Beloff was quite unable to proffer any convincing answer. What he did say was that there is an identifiable group of taxpayers here who were all clients of Mr Scannell. That appears to me to be a wholly adventitious and irrelevant consideration. It does not affect the nature or gravity of the offence; it only arises because in the course of investigation Mr Scannell's tax affairs the Revenue have uncovered alleged dishonest tax evasion on the part of a number of his clients, he is simply the common source from which the inquiry springs and the information flows.

There may be other dishonest taxpayers who have been advised by dishonest accountants and who have embarked on similar schemes; why should they not be part of the group? Does the group consist only of the six other taxpayers referred to in Mr Bunker's affidavit or the much larger number who are still being investigated and may turn out to have indulged in similar practices?

In my judgment the requirement of fairness and consistency in the light of the Revenue's selective policy of prosecution is that each case is considered on its merits fairly and dispassionately to see whether the criteria for prosecution was satisfied; there is no dispute that the applicants' cases were so considered. The decision to prosecute must then be taken in good faith for the purpose of fulfilling the Revenue's objectives of collecting taxes and not for some ulterior, extraneous or improper purpose, such as the pursuit of some racialist bias, political vendetta or corrupt motive. This again is not in dispute.

The principle that a public body must not frustrate a citizen's legitimate expectation takes the case no further. The only legitimate expectation that a dishonest taxpayer can have is that he may be selected for prosecution in accordance with the Revenue's stated policy; and that in considering whether to do so the decision-maker will act fairly in the sense that I have just defined.

Only if that policy could be attacked on the grounds of irrationality could the applicants succeed. They do not attempt to do so. It was a policy that was approved by the Keith Committee and it seems to me, for the three reasons that I have given earlier, not only a rational policy but very probably the only workable policy.

For these reasons, in my judgment, this application must be dismissed.

[4:5] HMRC Criminal Investigation Policy

HMRC's aim is to secure the highest level of compliance with the law and regulations governing direct and indirect taxes and other regimes for which they are responsible. Criminal investigation, with a view to prosecution by the Crown Prosecution Service (CPS) in England and Wales or the Crown Office and Procurator Fiscal Service (COPFS) in Scotland and the Public Prosecution Service Northern Ireland (PPSNI) in Northern Ireland, is an important part of HMRC's overall enforcement strategy.

It is HMRC's policy to deal with fraud by use of the cost effective civil fraud investigation procedures under Code of Practice 9 wherever appropriate. Criminal Investigation will be reserved for cases where HMRC needs to send a strong deterrent message or where the conduct involved is such that only a criminal sanction is appropriate.

However, HMRC reserves complete discretion to conduct a criminal investigation in any case and to carry out these investigations across a range of offences and in all the areas for which the Commissioners of HMRC have responsibility.

Examples of the kind of circumstances in which HMRC will generally consider commencing a criminal, rather than civil investigation are:

- in cases of organised criminal gangs attacking the tax system or systematic frauds where losses represents a serious threat to the tax base, including conspiracy
- where an individual holds a position of trust or responsibility
- where materially false statements are made or materially false documents are provided in the course of a civil investigation
- where, pursuing an avoidance scheme, reliance is placed on a false or altered document or such reliance or material facts are misrepresented to enhance the credibility of a scheme
- where deliberate concealment, deception, conspiracy or corruption is suspected
- in cases involving the use of false or forged documents
- in cases involving importation or exportation breaching prohibitions and restrictions
- in cases involving money laundering with particular focus on advisors, accountants, solicitors and others acting in a 'professional' capacity who provide the means to put tainted money out of reach of law enforcement
- where the perpetrator has committed previous offences / there is a repeated course of unlawful conduct or previous civil action
- in cases involving theft, or the misuse or unlawful destruction of HMRC documents
- where there is evidence of assault on, threats to, or the impersonation of HMRC officials
- where there is a link to suspected wider criminality, whether domestic or international, involving offences not under the administration of HMRC

When considering whether a case should be investigated using the civil fraud investigation procedures under Code of Practice 9 or is the subject of a criminal investigation, one factor will be whether the taxpayer(s) has made a complete and unprompted disclosure of the offences committed.

However, there are certain fiscal offences where HMRC will not usually adopt the civil fraud investigation procedures under Code of Practice 9. Examples of these are:

- Vat 'Bogus' registration repayment fraud
- Organised Tax Credit fraud

[4:6] Sanction Policy of the Department for Work and Pensions
(Version 4 – April 2010)

1. Sanction Policy of the Department for Work and Pensions

1.1 This document sets out the policy of the Department for Work and Pensions (DWP) towards sanctions, including criminal prosecutions, for offences relating to 'National' benefit fraud.

1.2 'Local' benefits (Housing Benefit and Council Tax Benefit) are administered by local authorities as part of their statutory local government functions. The sanctions policy in each local authority is therefore a matter for its members. However in practice local authority sanction policy broadly follows the approach of the DWP.

2. General Principles

2.1 The Department for Work and Pensions is committed to the prevention, detection, correction, investigation and, where appropriate, prosecution of fraudulent benefit claims.

2.2 The aim is to prevent criminal offences occurring by making it clear to our customers that they have a responsibility to provide accurate and timely information about their claims; to punish wrongdoing; and to deter offending.

2.3 This policy supports the new Departmental Strategic Objective (DSO 6) to pay our customers the right benefits at the right time which has replaced the Public Service Agreement (PSA 10) to reduce losses from fraud and error for people in working age, on Income Support and Jobseeker's Allowance. It also demonstrates the Department's determination to drive down fraud across the full range of welfare benefits.

2.4 Each potential fraud referral is assessed against national criteria. This assessment will result either in cases being investigated further under criminal investigation standards as set out within the remainder of this document or referred for customer compliance action.

2.5 Customer compliance action usually comprises a robust interview with the customer where they are questioned about any allegations. Further action depends upon the outcome of the interview but they will be reminded of their responsibilities and may be advised about future conduct and required to rectify or withdraw their claim.

2.6 The evidence obtained in each case that is subject to criminal investigation is considered on its own merits, having regard to all of the facts in deciding the most appropriate sanction.

3. Organisation

3.1 Criminal investigations are undertaken by the Department's Fraud Investigation Service (FIS) in accordance with:

- the Police and Criminal Evidence Act 1984 (PACE) and its codes of practice
- the Criminal Procedures and Investigations Act 1996 (CPIA) and its codes of practice
- all other relevant legislative and common-law rules
- Departmental policy
- advice from the Department's Prosecution Division.

3.2 Fraud Investigation Service investigators receive Professionalism in Security (PINS) training which is accredited by Portsmouth University. Additional guidance is provided by the Fraud Procedures and Instructions Manual which is regularly updated to ensure that:

- investigations are conducted in a legal and professional manner
- policy and legislation is correctly applied, and
- approved working methods are applied.

3.3 In England and Wales the Department's Prosecution Division decides whether cases submitted by FIS are suitable for prosecution and then prosecute the case. Most cases are heard by a Magistrates Court, although the more serious cases are usually referred to Crown Court.

3.4 Prosecution Division provides advice and guidance to investigators throughout the investigative and prosecuting process. They do not conduct any part of the investigation but advise on the investigator's obligations, evidential requirements and any appropriate charges. In deciding which cases are suitable for prosecution, Prosecution Division applies the evidential and public interest tests set out in the Code for Crown Prosecutors.

3.5 The Department's Fraud Expert Domain within Jobcentre Plus' Products and Transformation Division provides guidance to investigators on operational policy and technical matters.

3.6 In Northern Ireland the practice is to refer cases suitable for prosecution to the Public Prosecution Service, whilst in Scotland cases thought suitable for prosecution go to the Procurator Fiscal.

3.7 The Department also works closely with local authorities operating under similar prosecution practices. The Welfare Reform Act (WRA) 2007 provided local authorities with powers to investigate and prosecute offences against certain national social security benefits alongside Housing Benefit and Council Tax Benefit (HB/CTB). It also provided access to such information as is necessary to carry out these activities.

3.8 Prosecution Division also prosecutes benefit fraud cases for local authorities that have signed a Service Level Agreement with it.

4. Sanction Policy

4.1 Where an offence has been committed the Department can consider offering a caution, an administrative penalty, or instigating a prosecution. The choice will depend on the factors below.

4.2 Cautions

4.2.1 A caution is an administrative sanction that the Department in England and Wales is able to offer as an alternative to a prosecution as long as specific criteria are met, and the case is one the Department could take to court if the caution was refused.

4.2.2 Cautions are usually aimed at the less serious benefit frauds and those where the overpayment is under £2,000. It also provides an additional tool for the Fraud Investigation Service to use in those cases where the deterrent effect is considered a sufficient and suitable alternative to prosecution or an administrative penalty.

4.2.3 The offender must make a clear and reliable admission of the offence verbally or in writing and there must be a realistic prospect of conviction if the offender were to be prosecuted in line with the full Code Test of the Code for Crown Prosecutors.

4.2.4 If the customer is subsequently prosecuted for another benefit offence the caution may be cited in court.

4.2.5 In Scotland a caution is known as an administrative caution and cannot be cited in court, but may be referred to in a report submitted to the procurator fiscal for consideration of prosecution of any subsequent offence.

4.3 Administrative penalties

4.3.1 An administrative penalty is the offer to the customer to agree to pay a financial penalty where the customer has caused benefit to be overpaid to them, by either an act or omission. The amount of the penalty is currently stipulated at 30 per cent of the amount of the gross overpayment.

4.3.2 It is current DWP policy to offer these penalties where the case is deemed to be not so serious and the offer of an administrative penalty is considered a suitable alternative to prosecution, and where the gross overpayment is under £2,000. Unlike cautions no admission of guilt is required from the customer before offering an administrative penalty, although there is a statutory requirement for investigators to ensure that there are grounds for instituting criminal proceedings for an offence relating to the overpayment.

4.4 Prosecutions (England & Wales)

4.4.1 If there is sufficient evidence the Department will refer the case to the Department's Prosecution Division for consideration of criminal prosecution where one or more of the following criteria are met:

● The gross adjudicated overpayment (including Housing and Council Tax Benefit) is £2,000 or over
● False identities or other personal details have been used
● False or forged documents have been used
● Official documents have been altered or falsified
● The person concerned occupied a position of trust
● The person concerned assisted or encouraged others to commit offences
● There is evidence of premeditation or organised fraud
● The customer had previously been convicted of benefit fraud
● The amount of the overpayment is under £2,000 and the offer of an administrative penalty or caution is not accepted.

4.4.2 In all cases, including those which do not fall within any of the above criteria, the Department's Prosecution Division retains discretion as to whether criminal proceedings are started.

4.4.3 The Department's Prosecution Division is bound by the Code for Crown Prosecutors. A copy of the Code can be obtained either on the CPS website www.CPS.gov.uk or from the CPS Communications Branch, 50 Ludgate Hill, London EC4M 7EX

5. Proceeds of Crime Act (POCA)

5.1 The Department has an active policy of referring all suitable cases for financial investigation with a view to applying to the courts for restraint and/or confiscation of identified assets. A restraint order prevents a person from dealing with specified assets. A confiscation order enables the Department to seek to recover its losses from assets which are found to be the proceeds of crime.

6. Loss of Benefit Provision

6.1 The Loss of Benefit Provision is designed to be a deterrent against the continued abuse of the benefit system by applying a benefit sanction against those who commit benefit fraud.

6.2 This provision introduced by the Social Security Fraud Act 2001 allows the Department to apply a sanction in the form of a fixed 13 week benefit disqualification period where a person is convicted of benefit fraud in two separate proceedings, which have been committed within a five year period.

6.3 The provision was extended by the Welfare Reform Act 2009 to include a new 4 week loss of benefit sanction for all offences of benefit fraud which result in a criminal sanction (convictions, administrative penalties and cautions).

6.4 The existing 13 week loss of benefit sanction still applies to those who have been convicted of benefit fraud in two separate proceedings, which have been committed within a five year period.

6.5 Benefits can be withdrawn, or reduced by 20 or 40 per cent during the disqualification period.

7. Recovery of Debt

7.1 Where an overpayment arising from fraud is identified the Department takes steps to recover the resultant debt, including taking action in the civil courts if necessary, in addition to any sanction it may impose in respect of that fraud.

[4:7] Criminal Justice Act 1987 (as amended)

Sections 1–3

1 The Serious Fraud Office

(1) A Serious Fraud Office shall be constituted for England and Wales and Northern Ireland.

(2) The Attorney General shall appoint a person to be the Director of the Serious Fraud Office (referred to in this Part of this Act as "the Director"), and he shall discharge his functions under the superintendence of the Attorney General.

(3) The Director may investigate any suspected offence which appears to him on reasonable grounds to involve serious or complex fraud.

(4) The Director may, if he thinks fit, conduct any such investigation in conjunction either with the police or with any other person who is, in the opinion of the Director, a proper person to be concerned in it.

(5) The Director may –

   (a)   institute and have the conduct of any criminal proceedings which appear to him to relate to such fraud; and
   (b)   take over the conduct of any such proceedings at any stage.

(6) The Director shall discharge such other functions in relation to fraud as may from time to time be assigned to him by the Attorney General.

(6A) The Director has the functions conferred on him by, or in relation to, Part 5 or 8 of the Proceeds of Crime Act 2002 (c. 29) (civil recovery of the proceeds etc of unlawful conduct, civil recovery investigations and disclosure orders in relation to confiscation investigations).

(7) The Director may designate for the purposes of subsection (5) above any member of the Serious Fraud Office who is –

   (a)   a barrister in England and Wales or Northern Ireland;
   (b)   a solicitor of the Senior Courts; or
   (c)   a solicitor of the Supreme Court of Judicature of Northern Ireland.

(8) Any member so designated shall, without prejudice to any functions which may have been assigned to him in his capacity as a member of that Office, have all the powers of the Director as to the institution and conduct of proceedings but shall exercise those powers under the direction of the Director.

2 Director's investigation powers

(1) The powers of the Director under this section shall be exercisable, but only for the purposes of an investigation under section 1 above or, on a request made by an authority entitled to make such a request, in any case in which it appears to him that there is good reason to do so for the purpose of investigating the affairs, or any aspect of the affairs, of any person.

(1A) The authorities entitled to request the Director to exercise his powers under this section are –

(a) the Attorney-General of the Isle of Man, Jersey or Guernsey, acting under legislation corresponding to section 1 of this Act and having effect in the Island whose Attorney-General makes the request; and

(b) the Secretary of State acting under section 15(2) of the Crime (International Co-operation) Act 2003, in response to a request received by him from a person mentioned in section 13(2) of that Act (an "overseas authority").

(1B) The Director shall not exercise his powers on a request from the Secretary of State acting in response to a request received from an overseas authority within subsection (1A)(b) above unless it appears to the Director on reasonable grounds that the offence in respect of which he has been requested to obtain evidence involves serious or complex fraud.

(2) The Director may by notice in writing require the person whose affairs are to be investigated ("the person under investigation") or any other person whom he has reason to believe has relevant information to answer questions or otherwise furnish information with respect to any matter relevant to the investigation at a specified place and either at a specified time or forthwith.

(3) The Director may by notice in writing require the person under investigation or any other person to produce at such place as may be specified in the notice and either forthwith or at such time as may be so specified, any specified documents which appear to the Director to relate to any matter relevant to the investigation or any documents of a specified class which appear to him so to relate; and –

(a) if any such documents are produced, the Director may –
(i) take copies or extracts from them;
(ii) require the person producing them to provide an explanation of any of them;
(b) if any such documents are not produced, the Director may require the person who was required to produce them to state, to the best of his knowledge and belief, where they are.

(4) Where, on information on oath laid by a member of the Serious Fraud Office, a justice of the peace is satisfied, in relation to any documents, that there are reasonable grounds for believing –

(a) that –
(i) a person has failed to comply with an obligation under this section to produce them;
(ii) it is not practicable to serve a notice under subsection (3) above in relation to them; or
(iii) the service of such a notice in relation to them might seriously prejudice the investigation; and

(b) that they are on premises specified in the information,

he may issue such a warrant as is mentioned in subsection (5) below.

(5) The warrant referred to above is a warrant authorising any constable –

(a) to enter (using such force as is reasonably necessary for the purpose) and search the premises, and
(b) to take possession of any documents appearing to be documents of the description specified in the information or to take in relation to any documents so appearing any other steps which may appear to be necessary for preserving them and preventing interference with them.

(6) Unless it is not practicable in the circumstances, a constable executing a warrant issued under subsection (4) above shall be accompanied by an appropriate person.

(6A) Where an appropriate person accompanies a constable, he may exercise the powers conferred by subsection (5) but only in the company, and under the supervision, of the constable.

(7) In this section "appropriate person" means –

(a) a member of the Serious Fraud Office; or
(b) some person who is not a member of that Office but whom the Director has authorised to accompany the constable.

(8) A statement by a person in response to a requirement imposed by virtue of this section may only be used in evidence against him –

(a) on a prosecution for an offence under subsection (14) below; or
(b) on a prosecution for some other offence where in giving evidence he makes a statement inconsistent with it.

(8AA) However, the statement may not be used against that person by virtue of paragraph (b) of subsection (8) unless evidence relating to it is adduced, or a question relating to it is asked, by or on behalf of that person in the proceedings arising out of the prosecution.

(8A) Any evidence obtained by the Director for use by an overseas authority shall be given to the overseas authority which requested it or given to the Secretary of State for forwarding to that overseas authority).

(8C) Where any evidence obtained by the Director for use by an overseas authority consists of a document the original or a copy shall be forwarded, and where it consists of any other article the article itself or a description, photograph or other representation of it shall be forwarded, as may be necessary in order to comply with the request of the overseas authority.

(8D) The references in subsections (8A) to (8C) above to evidence obtained by the Director include references to evidence obtained by him by virtue of the exercise by a constable or by an appropriate person, in the course of a search authorised by a warrant issued under subsection (4) above, of powers conferred by section 50 of the Criminal Justice and Police Act 2001.

(9) A person shall not under this section be required to disclose any information or produce any document which he would be entitled to refuse to disclose or produce on grounds of legal professional privilege in proceedings in the High Court, except that a lawyer may be required to furnish the name and address of his client.

(10) A person shall not under this section be required to disclose information or produce a document in respect of which he owes an obligation of confidence by virtue of carrying on any banking business unless –

  (a) the person to whom the obligation of confidence is owed consents to the disclosure or production; or
  (b) the Director has authorised the making of the requirement or, if it is impracticable for him to act personally, a member of the Serious Fraud Office designated by him for the purposes of this subsection has done so.

(11) Without prejudice to the power of the Director to assign functions to members of the Serious Fraud Office, the Director may authorise any competent investigator (other than a constable) who is not a member of that Office to exercise on his behalf all or any of the powers conferred by this section, but no such authority shall be granted except for the purpose of investigating the affairs, or any aspect of the affairs, of a person specified in the authority.

(12) No person shall be bound to comply with any requirement imposed by a person exercising powers by virtue of any authority granted under subsection (11) above unless he has, if required to do so, produced evidence of his authority.

(13) Any person who without reasonable excuse fails to comply with a requirement imposed on him under this section shall be guilty of an offence and liable on summary conviction to imprisonment for a term not exceeding six months or to a fine not exceeding level 5 on the standard scale or to both.

(14) A person who, in purported compliance with a requirement under this section –

  (a) makes a statement which he knows to be false or misleading in a material particular; or
  (b) recklessly makes a statement which is false or misleading in a material particular, shall be guilty of an offence.

(15) A person guilty of an offence under subsection (14) above shall –

  (a) on conviction on indictment, be liable to imprisonment for a term not exceeding two years or to a fine or to both; and
  (b) on summary conviction, be liable to imprisonment for a term not exceeding six months or to a fine not exceeding the statutory maximum, or to both.

(16) Where any person –

  (a) knows or suspects that an investigation by the police or the Serious Fraud Office into serious or complex fraud is being or is likely to be carried out; and
  (b) falsifies, conceals, destroys or otherwise disposes of, or causes or permits the falsification, concealment, destruction or disposal of documents which he knows or suspects are or would be relevant to such an investigation, he shall be guilty of an offence unless

he proves that he had no intention of concealing the facts disclosed by the documents from persons carrying out such an investigation.

(17) A person guilty of an offence under subsection (16) above shall –

    (a) on conviction on indictment, be liable to imprisonment for a term not exceeding 7 years or to a fine or to both; and

    (b) on summary conviction, be liable to imprisonment for a term not exceeding 6 months or to a fine not exceeding the statutory maximum or to both.

(18) In this section, "documents" includes information recorded in any form and, in relation to information recorded otherwise than in legible form, references to its production include references to producing a copy of the information in legible form; and "evidence" (in relation to subsections (1A)(b), (8A) and (8C) above) includes documents and other articles.

(19) In the application of this section to Scotland, the reference to a justice of the peace is to be construed as a reference to the sheriff; and in the application of this section to Northern Ireland, subsection (4) above shall have effect as if for the references to information there were substituted references to a complaint.

3 Disclosure of information

(1) Where any information to which section 18 of the Commissioners for Revenue and Customs Act 2005 would apply but for section 18(2) has been disclosed by Her Majesty's Revenue and Customs to any member of the Serious Fraud Office for the purposes of any prosecution of an offence relating to a former Inland Revenue matter, that information may be disclosed by any member of the Serious Fraud Office –

    (a) for the purposes of any prosecution of which that Office has the conduct;

    (b) to the Crown Prosecution Service for the purposes of any prosecution of an offence relating to a former Inland Revenue matter;

    (c) to the Director of Public Prosecutions for Northern Ireland for the purposes of any prosecution of an offence relating to a former Inland Revenue matter; and

    (d) in order to comply with a requirement imposed under paragraph 7 of the Schedule to the Crown Prosecution Service Inspectorate Act 2000,

but not otherwise.

(2) Where the Serious Fraud Office has the conduct of any prosecution of an offence which does not relate to inland revenue, the court may not prevent the prosecution from relying on any evidence under section 78 of the Police and Criminal Evidence Act 1984 (discretion to exclude unfair evidence) by reason only of the fact that the information concerned was disclosed by Her Majesty's Revenue and Customs for the purposes of any prosecution of an offence relating to a former Inland Revenue matter.

(3) Where any information is subject to an obligation of secrecy imposed by or under any enactment other than an enactment contained in the Taxes Management Act 1970, the obligation shall not have effect to prohibit the disclosure of that information to any person in his capacity as a member of the Serious Fraud Office but any information disclosed by virtue of this subsection may only be disclosed –

(a) for the purposes of any prosecution in England and Wales, Northern Ireland or elsewhere, or

(b) in order to comply with a requirement imposed under paragraph 7 of the Schedule to
the Crown Prosecution Service Inspectorate Act 2000

and may only be disclosed by such a member if he is designated by the Director for the purposes of this subsection.

(4) Without prejudice to his power to enter into agreements apart from this subsection, the
Director may enter into a written agreement for the supply of information to or by him subject, in either case, to an obligation not to disclose the information concerned otherwise than
for a specified purpose.

(5) Subject to subsections (1) and (3) above and to any provision of an agreement for the
supply of information which restricts the disclosure of the information supplied, information obtained by any person in his capacity as a member of the Serious Fraud Office may be
disclosed by any member of that Office designated by the Director for the purposes of this
subsection –

(a) to any government department or Northern Ireland department or other authority or
body discharging its functions on behalf of the Crown (including the Crown in right of
Her Majesty's Government in Northern Ireland);

(b) to any competent authority;

(c) for the purposes of any criminal investigation or criminal proceedings, whether in the
United Kingdom or elsewhere,

(d) for the purposes of assisting any public or other authority for the time being designated for the purposes of this paragraph by an order made by the Secretary of State to
discharge any functions which are specified in the order.

(6) The following are competent authorities for the purposes of subsection (5) above –

(a) an inspector appointed under Part XIV of the Companies Act 1985;

(b) an Official Receiver;

(c) the Accountant in Bankruptcy;

(d) an Official Assignee;

(e) a person appointed under –
   (i) section 167 of the Financial Services and Markets Act 2000 (general investigations),
   (ii) section 168 of that Act (investigations in particular cases),
   (iii) section 169(1)(b) of that Act (investigation in support of overseas regulator),
   (iv) section 284 of that Act (investigations into affairs of certain collective investment
   schemes), or
   (v) regulations made as a result of section 262(2)(k) of that Act (investigations into
   open-ended investment companies), to conduct an investigation;

(f) a body corporate established in accordance with section 212(1) of the Financial Services and Markets Act 2000 (compensation scheme manager);

(l) any body having supervisory, regulatory or disciplinary functions in relation to any profession or any area of commercial activity;

(m) any person or body having, under the law of any country or territory outside the United
Kingdom, functions corresponding to any of the functions of any person or body mentioned in any of the foregoing paragraphs;

(n) any person or body having, under the Treaty on European Union or any other treaty to which the United Kingdom is a party, the function of receiving information of the kind in question; and

(o) any person or body having, under the law of any country or territory outside the United Kingdom, the function of receiving information relating to the proceeds of crime.

(7) An order under subsection (5)(d) above may impose conditions subject to which, and otherwise restrict the circumstances in which, information may be disclosed under that paragraph.

(8) In subsections (1) and (2) "former Inland Revenue matter" means a matter listed in Schedule 1 to the Commissioners for Revenue and Customs Act 2005 except for paragraphs 2, 10, 13, 14, 15, 17, 19, 28, 29 and 30.

[4:8] *R v Director of Serious Fraud Office, ex p Smith*
[1993] AC 1

The applicant had been charged with an offence under the Companies Act 1985. Subsequently he was served with a notice to attend the SFO to answer questions. He sought judicial review of the Director's decision to enforce compliance with the requirements of the notice.

The House of Lords held that although there was a strong presumption against interpreting a statute as taking away the right to silence, it was the plain intention of the Criminal Justice Act 1987 that the powers of the Director of the SFO should not come to an end when the person under investigation had been charged.

Lord Mustill (at page 44):

In conclusion I wish to emphasise that if this appeal is allowed the House will not thereby have chosen to re-establish in relation to a limited class of offence an inquisitorial method of ascertaining the truth in criminal cases which English law has long since repudiated in favour of an adversarial process. We were much pressed in argument with submissions that, although fraudulent conduct has become a serious social evil, there are other evils just as grave, or even graver, which have not attracted any special powers; that if the reason for giving exceptional powers to the Serious Fraud Office is that many frauds involve complicated transactions which are difficult to unravel, then the same could be said of the long and complex trials (for instance arising from charges of affray, or of the importation and supply of prohibited drugs) to which no such powers have been applied; and that, moreover, the powers of the Office are made available even where the transactions in question are not complicated, since the Act applies to 'serious or complex fraud' – not 'serious and complex fraud.'

Now these and similar comments would require careful scrutiny if the thrust of the argument were to the effect that Parliament could not have intended to establish an inquisitorial regime of this kind in relation to serious or complex fraud alone. But in fact no such argument is or could be made, for it is indisputable and undisputed that this is just what Parliament set out to do, and has effectively done. In truth the adverse comments are criticisms, not of the Director's contention that the powers created by the Act apply in the situation now under review, but of the policy and scope of the Act itself. These we may not entertain. As Windeyer J said in *Rees v Kratzmann* (1965) 114 CLR 63, 80:

> 'If the legislature thinks that in this field the public interest overcomes some of the common law's traditional considerations for the individual, then effect must be given to the statute which embodies this policy.'

In the present case the only issue is whether there is something in the language of the Act or by necessary implication, to show that the policy embodied in the Act should not be given effect as regards the questioning of a suspect who has been charged. Being of the opinion that there is not. I would allow this appeal.

[4:9] Padfield, N, 'Deferred prosecution agreements'
(2012) 7 *Archbold Review* 4

As reported in the last issue of *Archbold Review*, the Ministry of Justice is currently consulting on a new "enforcement tool" to deal with economic crime committed by commercial organisations: Deferred prosecution agreements (DPAs); closing date August 9. Astonishingly, the Government believes that "this proposal will overcome many of the current difficulties associated with prosecuting commercial organizations". Currently, they acknowledge, "commercial organisations have little incentive to self-report offending to investigating and prosecuting agencies, especially if such self-reporting may result in a criminal conviction and all that entails".

So what will be different under a DPA? Under the proposal, the prosecutor would lay, but would not immediately proceed with, criminal charges pending successful compliance with agreed terms and conditions stated in the DPA. The terms and conditions "might include", we are told:

- payment of a financial penalty;
- restitution for victims;
- disgorgement of the profits of wrongdoing; and
- measures to prevent future offending (a monitoring or reporting requirement).

So, the DPA would be agreed between the parties and then placed before a judge for consideration and approval. Time limits would be attached to the terms and conditions "so that compliance can be managed and it will be clear when the agreement should cease". Whilst we may all agree that criminals in the business world should not "get away with it", that negotiated settlements save money, and that the "voluntary" payment of large fines and the disgorgement (!) of profits are all attractive propositions, we also need to stand back a minute and ask some awkward questions.

What is it about DPAs that make many people nervous? Partly it is a practical concern: DPAs are yet another criminal justice import from the USA which may well not transfer at all easily. How successful would they actually be? It seems improbable that companies will volunteer to admit their crimes. What would be the real incentive for them to do so? Of course a compliance strategy may in some areas be useful: the Environment Agency has long sought co-operation with offenders—prevention may be deemed more appropriate than punishment. But this is a very different context. Where is the evidence? The consultation comments briefly on civil recovery and compounding, which we are told (at para.55) "works successfully, generally against small commercial organisations in a customs and excise setting". Where is the evidence, and indeed, what is "success" in this area?

But even more important than the practical concerns that DPAs won't actually "work", are the more theoretical and ethical issues. Fraud, bribery, corruption and money-laundering are really serious crimes. Economic crimes by commercial organisations are actually carried out by human beings. The priority should surely be prosecuting those individuals. If DPAs resulted in the prosecution of individuals, by forcing companies to help provide evidence and otherwise to co-operate with criminal investigations, there might be a role for them. But this is not what the Government is proposing.

If reparation to victims is the priority, as the consultation seems to imply (see, for example, para.68), why is this not the case for other crimes? Why should a burglar or a drug dealer not be able to ask for a DPA, if they are prepared to admit their guilt? Or indeed someone who regularly hits his wife? Any encouragement of the perception that there is one law for the rich and another for the poor should not be encouraged. Indeed, this is not merely a perception: it would appear that the Government truly thinks that corporate criminals are not real criminals. The Impact Assessment suggests that with the introduction of DPAs,

> Commercial organisations are estimated to incur some benefits. Some commercial organisations could avoid a full conviction due to the introduction of DPAs. This would result in lower financial penalties and wider benefits such as not losing access to the procurement process for some public sector contracts (p.2).

Extraordinary! Surely we, the people, really do want corporate criminals to be caught and prosecuted, because what they have done is seriously wrong? The thought that companies committing such criminal offences should not lose access to the procurement process for public sector contracts is amazing (and could lead me into a diversion exploring why this Government remains so attached to their "instinct" that privatisation improves quality and saves money). Surely it is time to accept that the resources of those responsible for investigating and prosecuting serious financial crimes need to be improved? The criminal justice system is of course a blunt instrument to deal with corporate crime, but that is a reason to focus too on ethics, good governance, transparency and accountability. . . as well as the prosecution of individuals.

There has (to my knowledge) been little qualitative research into the realities of decision-making in the investigation and prosecution of serious crime. To quote the Impact Assessment again,

Prosecutors tackling economic crime (principally the Serious Fraud Office and Crown Prosecution Service, although we do not propose to limit the use of Deferred Prosecution Agreements to these bodies) currently have two key approaches available to them: criminal prosecution or, where this is not appropriate, pursuing a civil recovery order against the commercial organisation. Both involve lengthy investigation while criminal prosecution involves protracted court proceedings to reach a conclusion, the resource and financial costs for prosecutors can be high, and ultimately the number of cases that can be pursued to an outcome is limited.

We know little about which companies currently "escape" with civil recovery. Who takes the decision, and on what basis? Once again, this is a plea for more evidence, a careful analysis of the problems, not a "knee-jerk" reaction.

A final argument against DPAs is that the courts are unlikely to accept "justice" being meted out by the SFO, nor should they. As the history of such prosecutions as that of *Innospec Ltd* show (see [2010] 4 *Archbold Review* 4, where I commented that it was encouraging to see Thomas L.J. putting the brakes on dubious sentence bargains), judges will be able to block DPAs which they do not think would serve the interests of justice. The Consultation recognises such constitutional concerns (at para.67):

> In practice the extent of judicial involvement generally appears to be limited in the US model, and despite the effectiveness of the process, is unlikely to be at a level suitable for the UK's constitutional arrangements. The advantages of possible greater court involvement include the court's ability to act as an arbiter of disputes, or to handle significant events in the DPA process such as the determination

of a breach. However, this places additional pressures on the time and resources available to judges in the DPA process; and presents concerns over the constitutional appropriateness of judges playing a larger role in the DPA process.

In which case, why not simply prosecute? Can the Government make a principled argument which shows why it is not appropriate, in order to mark the seriousness of the offences of fraud, bribery, corruption and money laundering, to prosecute the individuals concerned? Simply and pragmatically suggesting that DPAs might (possibly) be a cheaper and easier solution (to what?) is no answer.

[4:10] *Jones v Whalley*
[2006] UKHL 41

Whalley admitted having assaulted Jones and had accepted a written police caution in respect of an offence of assault occasioning actual bodily harm. The caution form stated that acceptance of the caution meant that he would not have to go before a criminal court. But Jones subsequently decided to bring a private prosecution against him. When the matter came before the magistrates, they stayed the proceedings as an abuse of process, but the Divisional Court lifted the stay. Whalley submitted that since he had agreed to be cautioned on an express assurance by the police that he would not have to go before a criminal court in connection with the matter, it would be an abuse of process for Jones to bring a private prosecution against him. Jones submitted that the right of private prosecution was expressly preserved by the Prosecution of Offences Act 1985, section 6 and that he should not be deprived of his right by a misstatement in a police form.

The House of Lords unanimously allowed the appeal. Save where the DPP was under a duty to take over the conduct of proceedings or, not being under a duty, chose to do so, Part I of the 1985 Act did not preclude the bringing of a private prosecution. To that extent the right of private prosecution survived. But allowing private prosecutions to proceed, despite an assurance that the offender would not have to go to court, would tend to undermine not only the non-statutory system of cautions, but also the schemes for cautioning young offenders and adult offenders that Parliament had endorsed in the Crime and Disorder Act 1998 and the Criminal Justice Act 2003. A court was entitled to ensure that its process was not misused in that way, There were five speeches in the House but here are extracts from only two of them:

Lord Bingham:

15 The broad lines of the argument may be summarised in this way. The practice of cautioning, originally developed by the police as a pragmatic response to a certain class of case, has grown into something much more sophisticated and specific, as evidenced by the statutory regimes established by the 1998 and 2003 Acts and a series of Home Office Circulars. While there are obvious differences between the young offender, conditional cautioning and simple cautioning regimes, they have shared objectives of seeking to keep people out of the criminal courts and preventing further offending. Underlying a decision to reprimand, warn, caution conditionally or caution simpliciter, and fundamental to each, is a judgment made by a responsible official that prosecution would not be in the public interest, or at least that the public interest would be better served by not prosecuting. Such a judgment, like a decision not to prosecute, is not immune from challenge. If shown to be unlawful on any of the familiar grounds relied on to seek judicial review, it may be quashed and set aside. But so long as the

decision stands the judgment should be respected, and it would be wrong in principle to allow it to be circumvented at the behest of a private prosecutor whose motives may have little or nothing to do with the public interest. The right to prosecute privately is a factor of little weight in the balance, since it is a somewhat anomalous historical survival; it cannot outweigh an extant decision of a responsible official on what will best serve the public interest. On this argument, paradoxically, the statement made in the form given to Mr Whalley, in its reference to going before a criminal court, was accurate, and the statement in the *Hayter* forms was inaccurate.

16 I see very considerable force in this argument. A crime is an offence against the good order of the State. It is for the State by its appropriate agencies to investigate alleged crimes and decide whether offenders should be prosecuted. In times past, with no public prosecution service and ill-organised means of enforcing the law, the prosecution of offenders necessarily depended on the involvement of private individuals, but that is no longer so. The surviving right of private prosecution is of questionable value, and can be exercised in a way damaging to the public interest. I would not, therefore, reject this argument. But nor do I think the House should in this appeal accept it, for reasons which I find, cumulatively, to be compelling. It was not advanced in the Divisional Court, so we lack the benefit of its judgment on it. It was scarcely foreshadowed in Mr Whalley's written case, and there was no hint that the correctness of *Hayter* was to be challenged. Thus Mr Swift had little opportunity to prepare an argument in reply. The question is one of some importance, and should not be resolved in the absence of representation of the Crown or any police force, both of whom might be expected to have views on how the issue should be decided. The question is one which might well benefit from legislative attention. It is not necessary to resolve this question to decide the present appeal.

17 For these reasons and those given by my noble and learned friend Lord Rodger of Earlsferry with which I agree, I would therefore allow the appeal on the narrower ground, set aside the decision of the Divisional Court, uphold the decision of the Justices and dismiss the proceedings. I would invite written submissions on costs within 14 days.

Lord Rodger of Earlsferry:

21 When the police officer cautioned Mr Whalley, he was not acting under a statutory scheme. But nor was he off on a frolic of his own, or on a frolic of the Greater Manchester Police. On the contrary, he was acting in accordance with an officially recognised policy which was intended to be followed by police forces throughout the country in accordance with guidance issued by the Home Office. The current guidance was to be found in Home Office Circular 18/1994, to which was annexed a revised version of the National Standards for Cautioning. Paragraph 1 of the Standards describes the purposes of a formal caution as being to deal quickly and simply with less serious offenders, "to divert them from unnecessary appearance in the criminal courts," and to reduce the chances of their re-offending. All worthwhile policy objectives. Before the police can contemplate administering a caution, there must be sufficient evidence of the offender's guilt and he must admit the offence. Provided these requirements are met, "consideration should be given to whether a caution is in the public interest": para 3. The police are told that they should take into account the public interest principles described in the Code for Crown Prosecutors. In their turn, Crown Prosecutors are told in para 8.3 of the current Code for Crown Prosecutors that a simple caution should only be given if the public interest justifies it and in accordance with Home Office guidelines.

22 What is clear from the National Standards is that a police officer should not decide to administer a caution, rather than to prosecute, unless he is satisfied that cautioning rather than prosecution is in the public interest. Presumably, the officer in this case was so satisfied. If that view was untenable, his decision to caution rather than to prosecute could be set aside on judicial review. But Mr Jones has not challenged the officer's decision. The assumption must be that the police officer was entitled to decide that it was in the public interest for Mr Whalley to be given a caution and so avoid an "unnecessary appearance in the criminal courts". On that basis the officer represented to Mr Whalley that he would not have to go before a criminal court for the offence.

23 In these circumstances, where such an assurance had been given to Mr Whalley, any subsequent decision by the Crown Prosecutor to prosecute him would have been capable of being regarded as an abuse of process: *R v Croydon Justices, Ex p Dean* [1993] QB 769, 778F-G per Staughton LJ. What happened in this case, however, was that Mr Jones, a private individual, unconnected with the police or prosecuting authorities, initiated the prosecution, despite the assurance given to Mr Whalley. Whether or not Mr Jones was consulted before the police officer took the decision to caution rather than to prosecute and to give that assurance, he was certainly not a party to it. So there is no question of Mr Jones being estopped from initiating the prosecution. Nor did he do anything to give Mr Whalley any legitimate expectation that he would not be prosecuted. The question is, rather, whether the magistrates were entitled to stay the proceedings because it offended their sense of justice and propriety to be asked to try the accused in these circumstances: *R v Horseferry Road Magistrates' Court, Ex p Bennett* [1994] 1 AC 42, 74G-H per Lord Lowry.

24 Nowadays public prosecutions are the rule. So, usually, the court will be concerned to prevent its process being misused by a public prosecutor. But, in times gone by, when private prosecutions were the rule, the court must have had the power to guard against the corresponding danger of its process being misused by a private prosecutor. So, in this case the justices had the same power to stay for abuse of process as they would have had in the case of a public prosecution. Having duly considered the matter, the justices came to the view that it would be an abuse of their process to allow Mr Jones to continue with the prosecution of Mr Whalley, after the police had given him an assurance that he would not have to go to court in respect of the offence. Clearly, they considered that it offended their sense of justice and propriety to be asked to try the accused in the face of that assurance, irrespective of the fact that the prosecution was initiated by a private individual rather than by a public official. Not only was that a view which was open to the justices, but it is one which I share.

25 Looking at the matter from a slightly different angle, it seems to me that allowing private prosecutions to proceed, despite an assurance that the offender would not have to go to court, would tend to undermine not only the non-statutory system of cautions, but also the schemes for cautioning young offenders and adult offenders which Parliament has endorsed in the Crime and Disorder Act 1998 and the Criminal Justice Act 2003. A court is entitled to ensure that its process is not misused in this way.

26 In the course of the hearing, the House was referred to the decision of the Divisional Court in *Hayter v L* [1998] 1 WLR 854. In that case the defendants had assaulted and injured a young man. The police cautioned them, but the terms of the caution indicated that it did not preclude the bringing of proceedings by an aggrieved party. The victim's father then initiated a prosecution of the defendants. They contended that the proceedings should be stayed as an abuse of process. The justices dismissed the information, but the Divisional Court allowed the prosecutor's appeal.

27 The qualification in a caution of that type means that the decision in *Hayter* is distinguishable from the present case and, for that reason, the House did not hear full submissions on it. I accordingly agree with my noble and learned friend, Lord Bingham of Cornhill, that it would not be appropriate to express a concluded view about the broader argument relating to it. Accordingly, I make only one tentative observation.

28 Plainly, the *Hayter* type of qualification to the caution would alert the offender to the lingering possibility of a private prosecution. So the reaction of a court to being asked to try the case in such circumstances might well be different from its reaction in a case where the caution was not qualified in that way – although, in Hayter's case, the qualification does not actually seem to have weighed with the justices. The point which concerns me, however, is not the effect of such a qualified caution on the court's sense of propriety and justice, but, rather, whether it is proper for a police officer to insert the qualification in the caution and, if so, in what circumstances.

29 The National Standards indicate that a police officer should not administer a caution unless he concludes that it is in the public interest to divert the offender from an unnecessary appearance in the criminal courts. Prima facie, this would seem to suggest that the officer should have concluded that it is unnecessary for the offender to appear in the criminal courts, whether at the instance of a public or a private prosecutor. Some support for that view might perhaps be found in para 7 of the Home Office circular which contemplates the police giving the victim details of the offender in order to institute civil, but not criminal, proceedings. On that assumption, however, it would be difficult to see how the officer could administer a caution but simultaneously contemplate – by including the *Hayter* qualification – that it could be in the public interest for the offender to be prosecuted by the victim. The inclusion of the qualification suggests, however, that the officer has concluded that, while it would not be in the public interest for a public prosecution to be mounted, it would none the less be legitimate, and not contrary to the public interest, for the victim to prosecute, if so advised. Your Lordships heard no submissions on whether it is appropriate for a police officer to issue a caution, with the various consequences for the offender, on that basis. Nor was counsel in a position to explain whether there is an established practice of issuing such qualified cautions in certain kinds of cases. So I simply draw attention to the point but express no view on it.

30 For these reasons, as well as for those given by Lord Bingham, I would allow the appeal and make the order which he proposes.

Chapter 5

Defence Lawyers

Chapter Contents

The pivotal role of lawyers in the criminal justice system is often overlooked. In an adversarial system, those who assess the criminal justice system too often concentrate on the system weighed against the defendant. Yet the most effective due process safeguard is a strong defence team. Lord Justice Auld [1:5] identified two essentials to balance the prosecution: 'an experienced, motivated defence lawyer or lawyers who are adequately paid for pre-trial preparation' and 'ready access by defence lawyers to clients in custody'. And there is a significant European Court of Human Rights jurisprudence on the right to free and confidential legal advice under Article 6 [1:13]: see, for example, *Brennan v United Kingdom* (2002) 34 EHRR 18. In England most defendants tried for the more serious offences are legally represented, often at taxpayers' expense. We should therefore examine the impact and quality of this legal advice.

The legal profession is still divided into two branches. Solicitors are the first port of call for legal advice, while a barrister may advise on legal problems, usually when briefed by a solicitor, and normally represent defendants at trial in the Crown Court. Of course, many of those who work in solicitors' offices are not legally qualified or may hold other qualifications, such as those of the Chartered Institute of Legal Executives (CILEx). The Courts and Legal Services Act 1990 granted to the Lord Chancellor's Advisory Committee on Legal Education and Conduct (ACLEC) the right to make new rules to allow solicitors rights of audience in the higher courts. The Access to Justice Act 1999 replaced ACLEC by a 'smaller and less expensive' committee, the Legal Services Consultative Panel, with the aim of reducing the barriers between the different branches of the profession. The Lord Chancellor (now the Secretary of State for Justice) was given vast powers to change professional rules and to appoint the members of the Consultative Panel. A discussion of whether or not the public is best served by a divided legal profession is beyond the scope of this book, but Kerridge and Davis (1999) caution against 'the drift towards unification'.

The Legal Services Act 2007 has led to more blurring of the traditional distinctions. It made three important changes: it created a Legal Services Board to regulate the legal professions, as well as a new Office of Legal Complaints (which, in turn, created the Legal Ombudsman which began accepting complaints in October 2010). Most originally, it sought to encourage 'alternative business structures' (ASBs) allowing different types of lawyers and non-lawyers to work together, and enabling non-lawyers to own and invest in law firms. The Solicitors Regulation Authority started accepting applications from prospective ASBs in January 2012 and licensed the first ASBs in March 2012; by February 2014, they had licensed 239 ASBs. However, for the moment, it remains usual for solicitors, who may well present their own cases in the magistrates' courts, to brief counsel to represent their clients in the Crown Court or on appeal – although since 2004, it has been possible for the public to directly access a barrister without having to go through a solicitor. Of more significance than direct access barristers has been the growth in the number of solicitor advocates in recent years. These are solicitors who are qualified to represent clients as an advocate in the higher courts. The review of independent criminal advocacy in England and Wales carried out by Sir Bill Jeffrey [5:1], published in May 2014, found that between 2005–06 and 2012–13, the percentage of publicly funded cases in which the defence was conducted by a solicitor advocate rose from 4 per cent to 24 per cent of contested trials and from 6 per cent to 40 per cent of guilty pleas.

The extract [5:2] from McConville et al's hard-hitting analysis of solicitors' firms in England and Wales in the early 1990s reveals the importance of due process safeguards in an adversarial legal system. The deficiencies highlighted by this research led the authors to question the effectiveness of various reforms, with their emphasis on managerialism and cost-effectiveness. The authors proposed what they called 'a cultural transformation' in criminal defence work and a reassertion of defendants' rights within an adversarial system. The extracts included here reflect the research conclusions rather than the reality which lay ahead. The reality is that the picture has not improved and that things do not always go as they should in the police station. This is transparently clear from the case law as well as the research evidence. For example, *R v Grant* [2005] EWCA Crim 1089 was one of three cases in which the Lincolnshire police placed secret listening devices in the exercise yard of a police station. In each case privileged communications between detained suspects, later defendants, and their legal advisers were recorded. This caused the judges in two of the cases to stay the proceedings as an abuse of process. The Court of Appeal in *Grant*, the third case, allowed the appeal. Laws LJ said:

> We are in no doubt but that in general unlawful acts of the kind done in this case, amounting to a deliberate violation of a suspected person's right to legal professional privilege, are so great an affront to the integrity of the justice system, and therefore the rule of law, that the associated prosecution is rendered abusive and ought not to be countenanced by the court (at paragraph 54).

Although this decision was disapproved by the Privy Council in *Warren and others v Attorney General of Jersey* [2011] UKPC 10, it was surely right to stay the proceedings as an abuse of process in such circumstances. These are not isolated incidents – see also *R v Maxwell* [2010] UKSC 48 (discussed at **[5:3]**), for example. As it is not unknown for the police to break the rules, suspects deserve competent well paid legal representatives.

(i) Legal aid

Recent years have seen a decrease in the number of solicitors' firms accepting criminal work. The decline is revealed in the Legal Services Commission's annual reports: in 2001/02, the number of firms offering criminal defence services declined from 3,500 to 2,909 firms in a year; by 2006/07 it had slipped down to 2,510 and it had fallen to 1,640 by 31 March 2012. Whilst bigger firms may be more efficient, quality assurance and value for money have driven many firms away. The Legal Services Commission (LSC) was abolished by the Legal Aid, Sentencing and Punishment of Offenders Act 2012 with the legal aid functions transferred to the Lord Chancellor. An executive agency within the Ministry of Justice, the Legal Aid Agency (LAA), has been created in its place.

More important than the structure of the legal profession is the provision of adequate funds to enable good lawyers to work in the field of criminal justice. In 2001 the Criminal Defence Service (CDS), originally administered by the LSC, but now administered by the LAA, took over from the Legal Aid Board the provision of public funding for criminal defence work (see the Access to Justice Act 1999). The CDS was created 'for the purpose of securing that individuals involved in criminal investigations or criminal proceedings have access to such advice, assistance and representation as the interests of justice require' (section 12(1)). The most radical innovations have been, first, the Public Defender Service (PDS), established in 2001, where salaried lawyers provide legal representation, employed directly by the LSC (now the LAA). This service has been launched in only in a few pilot sites, and currently has offices in Cardiff, Cheltenham, Darlington, Pontypridd and Swansea. In 2014, the PDS was expanded with the establishment of an Advocacy Unit, based in London, which employs a team of 25 barristers and higher courts advocates. The second innovation is CDS Direct, a telephone helpline that provides non-means tested legal advice direct to suspects detained in a police station, launched in 2005. This service has since been renamed Criminal Defence Direct: and needs careful monitoring. It may well be cheaper and quicker to provide advice by telephone: but can it be as good (and indeed confidential)?

The majority of legal services continue to be provided by private practitioners. Private firms must hold a Standard Crime Contract to carry out publicly funded criminal defence work. Funding issues predominate: not only the level of fees but their structure too. 'Standard fees' for magistrates' court work were introduced in 1993, despite strong opposition from the solicitors' profession. The danger of paying solicitors a standard, or fixed, fee is that they may either cut corners or turn away difficult cases. Auld **[1:5]** argued that the current fee structure was 'fundamentally flawed' in that it did not provide an adequate reward or incentive for preparatory work. The fee structure should instead, he argued, encourage efficient preparation of cases. Lord Carter was asked by the Government in 2005 to carry out a review of legal procurement, and his report was published in July 2006. This was followed by a consultation paper *Legal Aid: a sustainable future*, published jointly by the Department for Constitutional Affairs and the Legal Services Commission and then the White Paper *Legal Aid Reform: The Way Ahead* (Cm 6993, 2006). The Labour Government was committed to what they called a market-based system, which included: fixed fees for legal aid work in police stations; revised fees for magistrates' courts in urban areas; a revised Crown Court graduated fees scheme for advocates; a new litigators' Crown Court graduated fees scheme; and a new panel of providers authorised to provide services in Very High Cost Cases (VHCC) – these are the most substantial, complex and lengthy cases to be tried in the Crown Court.

Who pays for legal aid? The taxpayer, of course. It was, therefore, the target of swingeing cuts by the Coalition Government: changes proposed by the Ministry of Justice in their April 2013 consultation paper *Transforming Legal Aid: Delivering a more credible and efficient system* [5:4] were forecast to save £220 million per year by 2018/19 across the criminal and civil legal aid budgets. With around half of the annual £2 billion legal aid budget being spent on criminal legal aid, it was stated in a September 2013 follow-up consultation paper, *Transforming Legal Aid: Next Steps*, that 'In relation to the procurement of criminal defence services, the Government is clear that further significant efficiencies can be made' (at paragraph 1.12). One of the 'inefficiencies' identified by the Government is the number of providers of legal aided criminal defence services, with the April 2013 consultation paper describing contracting with over 1,600 providers as 'far from being the most efficient way of procuring services' (at paragraph 2.7); instead it was proposed that the number of providers should be approximately 400. The proposals contained in the April 2013 consultation paper were highly controversial and it drew around 16,000 responses. Most controversial of all was the proposed introduction of competitive tendering in nearly all areas of criminal legal aid. This would be price competitive and only the successful bidder would be allowed to provide services in their specific geographical area (and, as a consequence, would remove client choice as defendants would be allocated a provider and be allowed to change only in exceptional circumstances). Crown Court advocacy and VHCCs were excluded from competitive tendering but were to be subject to significant cuts: Crown Court advocacy would move to one fixed fee and fees paid in VHCCs would be reduced by 30 per cent.

The revised proposals in the September 2013 consultation paper responded to some of the fierce criticism which had been directed at the previous proposals. Competitive tendering will apply only to Duty Provider Work (which accounts for around 40 per cent of cases receiving criminal legal aid) – and price would not be used as a criterion; the tendering process for the 527 duty contracts opened in November 2014. However, fees for legal aided criminal defence work have been cut as a result of the package of reforms: there has been a 17.5 per cent reduction in fees for solicitors, to be phased in over two separate 8.75 per cent reductions, and an average 6 per cent reduction for barristers, through the Advocates Graduated Fees Scheme (AGFS). The cuts in fees paid to barristers had provoked two walkouts in early 2014 but a truce was reached between the Criminal Bar Association and the Ministry of Justice in March 2014 with the cuts to the AGFS being delayed until at least the summer of 2015 and agreement reached over VHCCs.

However, suspects, also often have to dig into their own pockets to pay for representation in court. With effect from October 2006, a defendant's right to receive legal aid for a case before a magistrates' court became subject not only to a merits test, but also to a means test. Means testing had been abolished in 1999, but disappointingly it has now been reintroduced. Defendants with a household disposable income of £37,500 or more are not eligible for legal aid for a Crown Court trial; if their disposable income is above £3,398 but less than £37,500, they will have to make a contribution to costs in a Crown Court trial. The precise calculations used for legal aid eligibility are now very complicated but there is an eligibility calculator at www.gov.uk/criminal-legal-aid-means-testing. If a defendant is acquitted then they can apply to recover their costs if they were ineligible for legal aid – but under the provisions of Schedule 7 to the Legal Aid, Sentencing and Punishment of Offenders Act 2012, defendants acquitted in the Crown Court can now only recover costs up to the legal aid limit. In practice, this can leave defendants significantly out of pocket where they have instructed more expensive counsel or experts (e.g. the former House of Commons Deputy Speaker, Nigel Evans, has said that his defence cost him £130,000 in unrecoverable costs when he was acquitted of rape and other sexual offences in April 2014).

In addition to defence costs, under the Prosecution of Offences Act 1985, sections 18–19, at the end of a trial a judge may order defendants, depending on their means, to contribute to the costs of the case. In addition to this, upon conviction a defendant will now also have to pay a Victim Surcharge of up to £120 where the defendant was over the age of 18 at the time of the offence and the offence was committed on or after 1 October 2012.

(ii) Legal advice at police stations

In our scenario, Gerry Good was arrested by the police and taken to the police station. As we saw in Chapter 2, the police have a duty to inform him of his right, under section 58 of the Police and Criminal Evidence Act 1984 (PACE), to obtain legal advice at the police station free of charge regardless of his means. The decision of the Court of Appeal in *Samuel* [1988] QB 615 shows how seriously the courts take this right, though there are other cases, such as *Alladice* (1988) 87 Cr App Rep 380, where the conviction has been upheld despite a breach of section 58. We saw in Chapter 2 that, in response to the European Court of Human Rights decision in *Murray* (1996) 22 EHRR 29, section 58 of the Youth Justice and Criminal Evidence Act 1999 prevents any inference being drawn from a suspect's silence prior to consulting a solicitor. Yet, perhaps surprisingly, this right to free legal advice is not exercised by many suspects. A possible explanation for the low take-up of legal advice is offered by Kemp **[5:5]** who found that, after observing police custody suites in four different police stations and conducting in-depth interviews with custody sergeants, there was 'seen to be a common perception among suspects that having a solicitor would lead to delays' (at page 201). Sanders et al's (1989) study showed that about a quarter of all arrested people asked for a solicitor. Brown, Ellis and Larcombe (1992) suggested that the 1991 revision of PACE Code C (on the detention, treatment and questioning of suspects) led to a small increase in the proportion of suspects receiving legal advice and Pleasence et al (2011) found, in a statistical analysis of over 30,000 police custody records, that this trend has continued, with request rates for legal advice rising from 40 per cent in 1995/96 to 45 per cent in 2009. Brown, Ellis and Larcombe concluded that, in the early 1990s, three-quarters of suspects were being informed of the right, and of the fact that the legal advice was free, and just over half were told that the legal advice was independent, but very few were told that the consultation would be in private. They suggested a scheme under which legally qualified personnel are present at main police stations on a round-the-clock basis to avoid the problem of local variations in the provision of legal advice. The cost implications of this, however, suggest that it is highly unlikely: the way forward, as we have seen, seems to be telephone advice.

At present, where suspects do not choose their 'own' solicitor, they may choose from a list of local solicitors, which the police will provide (or by ringing a centralised telephone number). When a duty solicitor is requested under the '24-hour scheme', a telephone referral service is contacted. The telephone call system to duty solicitors required at police stations has been contracted out since 1994 (the Automobile Association won the first contract!). The current system has been much criticised, not least because the police have to answer the phones (and Kemp (2010) found that between April and November 2009, one in four telephone calls from CDS Direct to police custody suites went unanswered), and because confidential facilities are often not available.

Gerry Good was arrested in the morning and might have found someone from his solicitors less willing to come if he had been arrested at night. As we saw in Chapter 2, he rang the firm of solicitors who had represented him before. It was, as is often the case, an employee with no formal legal qualifications who came to the police station to represent him. The need for good quality legal advice is vital. The most striking point to emerge from Baldwin's recordings of police interviews [5:6] was the general passivity of legal representatives at the interviews. There are striking examples in the case law, such as *Miller, Paris and Abdullahi* [5:7] where judges expressed strong and well-deserved criticism of legal advisers. That case may be over 20 years old, but it should still serve as a 'wake-up' call for sloppy legal advisers.

McConville and Hodgson (1993), too, considered that many advisers lacked adequate legal knowledge and confidence, and that sometimes they seemed to identify more with the police than with the suspect. Their conclusions are all the more striking in view of the removal of the unqualified right to remain silent under police questioning and at trial (by the Criminal Justice and Public Order Act 1994 [2:17], discussed in Chapter 2). Good quality legal advice is essential. For example, McConville and Hodgson (1993) found that many legal advisers left the police station before the formal interview took place, and others only gave advice by telephone. The Law Society introduced regulations in 1995 preventing solicitors' representatives who have not passed an accredited examination in police station skills from giving advice in police stations. It would be interesting to know whether courses such as CILEx's six-week home study Police Station Representatives Accreditation Scheme (now see the Criminal Litigation Accreditation Scheme Police Station Qualification) have led to improvements in the standard of advice offered.

(iii) Role of defence lawyers before and at trial

Let us return to Gerry's case. Ian Brown, an employee of the firm, was present at his interview. Once Gerry had been charged by the police, he was refused bail. The next morning he was represented by Mary Chapman, a solicitor with the firm, at his successful bail application in the magistrates' court. Whilst there he filled in the necessary forms to apply for legal representation, and his application was processed by court staff. In Gerry's case, it is likely that he qualifies for legal aid – he is facing a charge of wounding, his liberty is at stake, and so he falls within the 'interests of justice' criteria. This is still based on the so-called 'Widgery criteria' laid down by a committee chaired by the then Lord Chief Justice, Lord Widgery in 1966. These criteria are complex and imprecise. Factors to be taken into account in deciding 'the interests of justice' include: the likelihood of a custodial sentence; the legal difficulty of the case; the defendant's ability to understand the proceedings; and the nature of the defence case. However, as discussed above, legal aid is also means-tested so Gerry will have to complete the very complex questionnaire on his means to see if he qualifies.

How do solicitors decide what work is necessary in preparing a defence? Clearly, solicitors have an enormous influence on the outcome of a case. Their decisions about interviewing alibi witnesses, checking police summaries or commissioning independent medical or forensic experts can make all the difference to the strength of a defendant's case. But whether defence solicitors take such actions may well depend on whether their pay structure rewards such work (hence the vital importance of a good funding scheme). Although Gerry's solicitor represented him at the bail application, she decides to brief counsel to represent him at his trial (however, the trend in recent years, as noted earlier in this chapter, has been increasingly towards keeping such work 'in-house' through the use of solicitor advocates). Gerry's first meeting with his barrister may well be at the Crown Court shortly before the trial is due to begin. Zander and Henderson (1993) found that 44 per cent of defence barristers said that the brief had previously been returned by someone else. No fewer than 25 per cent of defence barristers in contested cases had received the brief later than 4 pm on the day before the trial. Perhaps this is not so surprising: barristers, being self-employed, are likely to hold onto a brief until the last minute in case their present case finishes earlier than expected. The Royal Commission on Criminal Justice (1993) commented (at page 118) on the need to reconstruct the scale of fees to encourage counsel to give adequate priority to pre-trial preparation. This is the message reinforced by Auld [1:5] and although the Jeffrey Review [5:1] heard evidence that 'returned briefs' are now less of an issue than in the past, it found that it still remained a problem. It is perhaps to be expected that the trend towards keeping both defence and prosecution work 'in-house' will reduce the number of returned briefs in the future.

An accused person has to make two vital decisions pre-trial: first, whether to plead guilty or not guilty; and, secondly, with offences triable either way, whether to opt for trial by jury in the Crown Court. The two will often be considered together (though the Government proposed abolishing a defendant's right to choose trial by jury in 1999) and the advice given first by solicitors and later by barristers may be decisive. Hedderman and Moxon (1992) studied the reasons for the decisions leading to Crown Court trial. Most of those who chose to be tried at the Crown Court were influenced by the prospect of acquittal, although 82 per cent ended up pleading guilty. Again, more than half of those who elected trial by jury said that the possibility of a lighter sentence at the Crown Court influenced their decision, even though judges were three times more likely to impose a custodial sentence and the sentences that they imposed were much longer. Riley and Vennard (1988) suggest that one reason for defendants opting for the Crown Court is that they themselves have greater confidence at a hearing in that court. The fact that 82 per cent ended up pleading guilty, despite having opted for jury trial because of its higher rate of acquittal, is not really surprising: in many cases, the prosecution agrees to accept a guilty plea to a lesser charge only at the last minute. It may well be that it is only when they meet their barrister at the door of the court that defendants finally realise that an acquittal may be unlikely. Note that (the now abolished) HM Inspector of Court Administration stated, very worryingly, in his Annual Report (2006/07) that 'in many courthouses the privacy of defendants' conversations with their legal representative could not be guaranteed' (at page 18).

Zander and Henderson (1993) found that 26 per cent of defendants changed their plea to guilty at a late stage, thus causing trials to 'crack'. Is this because people who want to plead not guilty are persuaded to change their minds, or because people who really always planned to plead guilty 'play the system'? If the defendant is confident that ultimately he will be sent to prison, he may seek to delay the fateful day as long as possible. Narey (1997), in his *Review of Delay in the Criminal Justice System*, commented that 'a substantial proportion of elections are little more than an expensive manipulation of the criminal justice system and are not concerned with any wish to establish innocence in front of a jury' (at page 2).

The substantial sentence discount given for guilty pleas must have a strong influence on many defendants. As we will see in Chapter 7, defendants who plead guilty at the first possible opportunity will usually receive a one-third 'discount' on the usual sentence. Bargains as to plea are often distinguished from bargains as to sentence: sentence bargains necessarily involve the judge, and will therefore be examined in Chapter 7, although the questions concerning the legitimacy of such bargains are the same as those discussed here. The Royal Commission's reasons for recommending that judges should be able to indicate sentence are included at [7:7].

Should there be such pressure on people to plead guilty? Zander and Henderson's Crown Court study for the Royal Commission [7:6] controversially led some to argue that perhaps 1,400 innocent people plead guilty every year. Yet the Royal Commission concluded that as long as people were adequately advised and that they were in fact guilty, there was nothing wrong with a system of inducements to encourage them to plead guilty. Following this, the Criminal Justice and Public Order Act 1994 put the discount for guilty pleas on a statutory footing, and this discount is now governed by section 144 of the Criminal Justice Act 2003 and by the definitive guideline of the

Sentencing Guidelines Council (see Chapter 7). Sanders, Young and Burton (2010), in a chapter which they call 'the mass production of guilty pleas', are highly critical, arguing that a system of plea bargaining undermines the rule of law by allowing the State to secure convictions based on vague and unsubstantiated allegations. Defence lawyers spend more time negotiating away defendants' rights than they do in upholding them. This encouragement of guilty pleas is hard to reconcile with adversarial principles.

In Gerry's case, a bargain as to plea might involve an agreement that, in return for his plead-ing guilty to the less serious charge of section 20 (maximum sentence of 5 years' imprisonment), the prosecution will drop the more serious charge under section 18 (maximum sentence of life imprisonment). This can be done without any involvement on the part of the judge, although it is possible for the judge or magistrates to insist that the prosecution proceeds with the more serious charge. Thus, in the trial of Peter Sutcliffe (the 'Yorkshire Ripper') in 1981 the judge insisted that the charges of murder were proceeded with, even though the Attorney General was willing to accept a plea of guilty to manslaughter by reason of diminished responsibility. Gerry maintains with his solicitor that he will plead not guilty and so she does not attempt to negotiate a pre-trial plea bar-gain. On the morning of the trial, there is some informal negotiation in the robing room between counsel for both sides, but the prosecution decide to continue with the charge under section 18, largely because of the evidence that Rosa Bottles was pursued for half a mile from the pub, which they argue suggests that Gerry intended to wound her. His criminal record may also influence their decision.

Defence counsel's role at the trial itself is, of course, vital. In conjunction with the solicitor, many tactical decisions have to be made: which witnesses to call, whether the defendant should give evidence, exactly what questions to ask, and whether to cross-examine or re-examine. In Gerry's case, the barrister, Tim Moffat, is a fiery young man with whom Gerry feels little sympathy when he meets him briefly in court before the trial, but he seems to know his job. He may or may not have been the barrister who represented (briefly) at the plea and case management hearing (PCMH). The personal performance of counsel is likely to have an impact on the jury. Lawyers may have a split loy-alty: should they argue fully every point in their client's case or should they think of the public inter-est in, for example, a brief trial? Their own career prospects may lead them at times to leave some aspects of their client's case unexplored, especially if they think that the judge is unsympathetic. If a solicitor or barrister considers the client to be undeserving, they may provide a poorer service. The eloquence of counsel inevitably affects the verdict: a persuasive barrister will be more effective than a poor one. The Royal Commission on Criminal Justice (1993) recommended limiting the length of opening and closing speeches to 15 and 30 minutes, respectively. Would this be appropriate? In the event of conviction, defence counsel has the stage again, making a speech in mitigation on behalf of the offender, to give to the court the defendant's explanation of the offence and any other matters going in the defendant's favour.

What happens if lawyers are incompetent? Paying clients may vote with their feet and change solicitors, but when the taxpayer is footing the bill, it is more difficult to keep adequate control over incompetence, and the Government continues to work on ways of monitoring performance. Poor performance by barristers should mean that solicitors do not brief them again, but is this adequate quality control, since solicitors themselves will rarely be in court to carry out effective monitor-ing (often sending less senior members of staff instead)? A controversial recent development has been the proposed introduction of the Quality Assurance Scheme for Advocates (QASA) which will require all advocates wishing to undertake criminal advocacy to register within the Scheme and be fully accredited. All advocates will be accredited at one of four levels (a Level 1 advocate can under-take work in the magistrates' court ranging up to a Level 4 advocate who normally undertakes the most serious cases in the Crown Court). Whilst this may become a desirable form of quality control, a questionable conflict of interest could arise through the nature of the assessment: once advocates have registered, they have two years from that date to obtain two pieces of judicial evaluation which confirm their competence at the level at which they registered. Perhaps surprisingly, there is no requirement for an advocate to inform their client that they are being assessed by the judge in their trial. Might a subconscious desire not to upset the judge influence how your advocate conducts your defence in these cases? And shouldn't the judge be concentrating fully on due process rather than also simultaneously assessing the skills of one of the advocates? The introduction of QASA has been delayed but at the time of going to the press it is anticipated that the Scheme will be implemented in 2015.

The importance of competent representation should not be under-estimated. In Ensor **[5:8]** the Court of Appeal confirmed an earlier ruling to the effect that a mistaken or unwise decision by counsel could not normally be regarded as a proper ground of appeal. The Royal Commission (1993) was critical of this narrow test: 'It cannot possibly be right that there should be defendants serving prison sentences for no other reason than that their lawyers made a decision which later turns out to have been mistaken' (at page 174). Malleson **[5:9]**, in her review of grounds for appeal, found that in nine out of 300 cases, lawyers' errors were cited as grounds of appeal. Not surprisingly, all these defendants were either unrepresented or had changed legal advisers, and none were granted leave to appeal. The Royal Commission concluded that vast improvements were needed in the provision of advice: 'We recommend that both branches of the profession take all necessary steps to ensure that practitioners not only perform their duty to see the client at the end of the case, as most do, but also give preliminary advice both orally and in writing' (at pages 164–165). With the continuing financial squeeze on legal aid there can be little doubt that concerns about incompetent representation are likely to grow, not shrink.

The European Court of Human Rights ruling in Boner v United Kingdom, Maxwell v United Kingdom (1994), that the refusal of legal aid for an appeal was a breach of a prisoner's rights under Article 6(3) of the European Convention on Human Rights **[1:13]**, may have encouraged the authorities to be more ready to grant legal representation. But Plotnikoff and Woolfson's **[5:10]** conclusions on the quality of legal advice confirm the view that, within an adversarial system, good quality representation is essential. The fallacy in the argument that, since defendants are frequently legally represented, there is now less of a need to keep due process safeguards within the system, is obvious. Low pay deters good lawyers moving into publicly funded legal work.

Cape (2004) reviews the rise (and fall?) of the defence lawyer in the English legal system over the previous 50 years. Noting that Government spending on criminal legal aid is almost certainly proportionately greater than in any other jurisdiction, he chides not only the Government (for reducing spending on criminal legal aid, without heeding the clear warning from the LSC that Government policies and new laws are a major contributor to increasing costs) but also the legal profession (who must take seriously its responsibilities for ensuring the development of a competent body of lawyers skilled in an adversarial role).

Further reading

Abel, R L, The Legal Profession in England and Wales (1988) Basil Blackwell

Ashworth, A and Blake, M, 'Some ethical issues in prosecuting and defending criminal cases' [1998] Crim LR 16

Boon, A and Levin J, The Ethics and Conduct of Lawyers in England and Wales (1999) Hart

Brown, D, Ellis, T and Larcombe, K, Changing the Code: Police Detention under the Revised Codes of Practice (1992) HORS No 129, HMSO

Cape, E, 'Incompetent police station advice and the exclusion of evidence' [2002] Crim LR 471

Cape, E, 'The rise (and fall?) of a criminal defence profession' [2004] Crim LR 401

Cape, E, 'Rebalancing the criminal justice process: ethical challenges for criminal defence lawyers' (2006) 9 Legal Ethics 56

Carter, P, Review of the Procurement of Criminal Defence Services: Market-Based Reform (2006) London: DCA

Hedderman, C and Moxon, D, Magistrates' Court or Crown Court? Mode of Trial Decisions and Sentencing (1992) HORS No 125, HMSO

Kerridge, R and Davis, G, 'Reform of the Legal Profession: Alternative Way Ahead' (1999) 62 Modern Law Review 807

Kemp, V, 'Transforming legal aid: Access to criminal defence services' (2010) Legal Services Commission

McConville, M and Hodgson, J, Custodial Legal Advice and the Right to Silence (1993) RCCJ Research Study No 16, HMSO

McConville, M and Mirsky, C, 'Looking through the Guilty Plea Glass: The Structural Framework of English and American State Courts' [1993] 2 Social and Legal Studies 173

Ministry of Justice, Transforming Legal Aid: Next Steps (2013)

Newman, D, Legal Aid Lawyers and the Quest for Justice (2013) Hart Publishing

Pannick, D, Advocates (1993) Oxford Paperbacks

Pleasence, P, Kemp, V and Balmer, N J, 'The justice lottery? Police station advice 25 years on from PACE' [2011] Crim LR 3

Riley, D and Vennard, J, Triable-either-way Offences: Crown Court or Magistrates' Court? (1988) HORS No 98, HMSO

Sanders, A, Bridges, L, Mulvaney, A and Crozier, G, Advice and Assistance at Police Stations and the 24-Hour Duty Solicitor Scheme (1989) Lord Chancellor's Department

Skinns, L, 'The right to legal advice in the police station: past, present and future' [2011] Crim LR 19

Young, R and Wilcox, R, 'The merits of legal aid in the magistrates' courts revisited' [2007] Crim LR 109

Zander, M and Henderson, P, Crown Court Study (1993) RCCJ Research Study No 19, HMSO

Documents

[5:1] *Independent criminal advocacy in England and Wales: A Review by Sir Bill Jeffrey*
(2014) Ministry of Justice (at page 3)

Introduction

Effective advocacy is at the heart of our adversarial system of criminal justice. If prosecution and defence cases are not clearly made and skilfully challenged, injustice can and does result. Effective advocates simplify rather than complicate; can see the wood from the trees and enable others to do so; and thereby can contribute to just outcomes, and save court time and public money.

This review reflects concerns about the quality of advocacy in the English and Welsh criminal courts and the longer term implications of current trends in the way advocacy services are provided. These are matters of legitimate interest to the Government and the public at large, but they also have a strong bearing on the future structure and professional standards of the legal profession. Although this report was commissioned by the Justice Secretary, such conclusions as I have been able to reach are addressed as much to the profession and its regulators as to the Government.

I have had meetings with, and received submissions from, the Council of Circuit Judges, the bodies representing barristers, solicitors and legal executives, the main regulators and the Legal Services Consumer Panel. I have visited Crown Court centres and magistrates' courts in five cities, spent time observing proceedings and had meetings with judges, groups of advocates (including younger practitioners), solicitors' firms, barristers' chambers and several businesses providing advocacy services in less conventional ways. I have taken the views of academics and educators in the legal field, and some who provide continuing professional training for advocates. I have also had helpful meetings in Scotland and New Zealand, and am particularly indebted to those who took time and trouble to explain to me the system in these countries. Finally, I have been much assisted by a small Reference Group, comprising representatives of the judiciary, the Bar Council, the Law Society, and the Chartered Institute of Legal Executives, who have given freely of their views and experience. None bear any responsibility for my conclusions.

There is a full list of those whose views I have taken in annex A. I offer warm thanks to all of them. I also offer a pre-emptive apology to the Chartered Legal Executives. They are an increasingly significant part of the scene, particularly in the magistrates' courts. As yet they provide very few advocates, although those whom I met were distinguished by their enthusiasm. It would have been cumbersome to have mentioned them at every stage of the analysis, and I hope they will forgive phrases such as "the two sides of the profession" where they appear in this report.

My approach has been to attempt to describe the "landscape" of criminal advocacy as it is now and the forces which have moulded it in recent years (particularly those which have a bearing on quality), and to offer a view on the longer term implications. Inevitably, this involves an element of speculation, both because the future is unknowable and because hard facts about the present and the recent past are not easy to come by. I also offer some thoughts on measures that could be taken to improve things in the shorter term, if there were sufficient consensus to do so.

My terms of reference (which can be found at annex B) explicitly excluded consideration of legal aid remuneration rates and the requirement for public funding. These are currently matters of public debate and controversy, and many of those in the profession to whom I have spoken in the last few months have found it difficult to get beyond the legal aid cuts as an explanation for poor advocacy quality and indeed any other shortcomings in the system. My own view is that legal aid fee rates are neither the whole story nor none of it. The income to be derived from doing publicly funded work clearly affects behaviour, but there are, I believe, other factors at work which deserve attention. In a system which is still largely publicly funded, the significance of legal aid fee levels cannot be ignored; but it is to these other factors that this report pays most attention ...

Summary and Main Conclusions

The landscape of criminal advocacy has altered substantially in recent years. Recorded and reported crime are down. Fewer cases reach the criminal courts. More defendants plead guilty, and earlier than in the past. Court procedures are simpler. There is substantially less work for advocates to do. Its character is different, with more straightforward cases and fewer contested trials. In the publicly funded sector (86% of the total), it pays less well (paragraphs 1.3 to 1.6).

There has been a marked shift in the distribution of advocacy work in the Crown Court between the two sides of the profession. There are many more solicitor advocates than there were in the years following the liberalisation of rights of audience. Between 2005–06 and 2012–13, the percentage of publicly funded cases in which the defence was conducted by a solicitor advocate rose from 4% to 24% of contested trials and from 6% to 40% of guilty pleas. Both figures are on a rising trend. In 2012–2013, Crown Prosecution Service (CPS) in-house lawyers led the prosecution in approximately 45% of Crown Court trials (paragraphs 1.8 to 1.10).

Standards, quality and training

There is no hard research evidence on the quality of advocacy, but I found a level of disquiet about current standards among judges (including some with long experience as solicitors) which was remarkable for its consistency and the strength with which it was expressed. It would be a mistake to discount these views (paragraphs 2.1 to 2.9, 4.1 and 4.2).

The disparity in mandatory training requirements expected of barristers and solicitor advocates reflects historic differences in the main focus of the two sides of the profession. But it is no reflection on the many highly capable solicitor advocates to observe that it is so marked as to be almost impossible to defend. To be called to the Bar, a barrister needs to have completed 120 days of specific advocacy training. A qualified solicitor can practise in the Crown Court (subject to accreditation) with as few as 22 hours such training. There are also different expectations of continuous professional development training (CPD) for advocates in the Crown Court, for which there is no rational basis. High quality CPD training has been developed by both sides of the profession. There would be a good deal to be gained from a common approach (Section 3 and paragraphs 4.3 to 4.9).

The Quality Assurance Scheme for Advocates (QASA) has divided the legal profession and its regulators. I find it hard to assess how well-founded the professional concern about judicial assessment in live trials will prove to be. I am more inclined than some to have confidence that judges will in practice be able to distinguish poor advocacy from the carrying out of wrong-headed client instructions. The High Court has suggested some changes to the scheme to help mitigate any risk. I hope these are implemented. I do not doubt the strength of the case for some kind of quality assurance scheme, both to reassure the public that there is a means by which advocates can be denied the opportunity to act beyond their competence, and to encourage continuous professional development (paragraphs 2.10 to 2.15 and 4.15 to 4.17).

The market in defence criminal advocacy

The key decision on the choice of advocate is made, if not directly by the solicitor representing the defendant, then at a point when that solicitor is effectively in charge of the case. Solicitors are under a professional duty to ensure their clients are in a position to take informed decisions about the services they need. In the past this was done by recommending a suitable member of the self-employed Bar. This ensured a strong measure of competition, based on barristers' reputations.

Today, the competitive dividing line is between in-house providers and outsourced specialists. The legal aid system provides a fixed fee for the litigation and advocacy elements of defence representation. It is widely believed that solicitors have a commercial incentive to assign a solicitor advocate to retain the combined value of the fee in-house, especially if a guilty plea is likely. The Bar considers that this creates a potential conflict of interest, which needs to be addressed. Solicitors say that they assign advocates on a judgement of what will be in the best interests of the client. Many clients prefer continuity of representation (paragraphs 5.8 to 5.12).

As it exists now, the market could scarcely be argued to be operating competitively or in such a way as to optimise quality. The group of providers who are manifestly better trained as specialist advocates are taking a diminishing share of the work, and are being beaten neither on price nor on quality (paragraphs 5.22 to 5.24).

Solicitors are bound, for good reason, to be influential in the choice of advocate. The fact that there are now internal commercial interests at stake makes it even more important that the process by which an advocate is assigned should be above reproach. This suggests that there would be advantage in reinforcing and clarifying solicitors' professional responsibilities in this area (paragraphs 5.27 to 5.29).

An alternative, more radical approach would be for the Legal Aid Agency (LAA) to take a more assertive role in the acquisition of advocacy services and act more as a guarantor of quality than they do at the moment. Where public money is being spent – as it is both on legal aid and on avoidably protracted trials – the public has a legitimate interest in advocacy quality. An option would be for the LAA to maintain a list or panel of approved advocates for legally aided defence, on the model of that kept by the CPS. This would need to include both barristers and solicitor advocates, but might be a means by which concerns about over-supply and diversity could be addressed (paragraph 5.30).

It is possible to overstate the argument that advocates who only appear in guilty pleas in the Crown Court cannot effectively give advice on plea. Someone who has experience of defending trials in that jurisdiction will no doubt have a better sense of their dynamics, the likely reaction of juries, and the legal issues likely to arise. But legal advice which amounts to advice on plea is given by solicitors from the earliest stage in the process, based on the facts and the inherent strength of the defence case.

Where it is known that a defendant will plead guilty, I can see no objection in principle to him being represented by a less accomplished advocate than would represent him if he pleaded not guilty. Of more concern are the practical consequences for case management where there is doubt about how the defendant will plead, and the assignment of an advocate is deferred until very late in the day, to keep the advocacy task in-house for an advocate who only appears in pleas (paragraphs 5.13 to 5.17, 5.25 and 5.26).

In principle, there is nothing to prevent the Bar from competing now for criminal legal aid contracts. To do so a set of chambers would need to form a legal entity with whom the LAA could do business. They would also need to be able to provide other elements of representation, including (at present) duty advice at police stations and magistrates' courts and case preparation. There are already a few "alternative business structures" led by barristers, but the overwhelming majority of criminal representation is provided in the traditional way.

Even those barristers who are open to the idea of changing the model to compete for legal aid contracts object that they would have to employ so many people to do the non-advocacy elements of the work as to lose the essential independent character of the self-employed Bar. If the LAA were able to contract separately for duty advice and post-charge work, and if, in more straightforward cases, junior barristers were able to operate as a "single pair of eyes" undertaking case preparation as well as advocacy, this objection would have less force. It might be possible for the Bar to compete effectively without changing their current business model out of all recognition. Their high reputation and low overheads could put them in a strong position. Adjusting the legal aid system as I suggest would not be straightforward, and much would depend on whether there were any signs that the Bar was interested (paragraphs 5.31 to 5.43).

Supply of criminal advocates

The number of practising advocates in all courts appears to have increased over a period when magistrates' courts business reduced substantially and Crown Court business fluctuated in volume, but reduced in complexity. There are now many more criminal advocates than there is work for them to do. Under-utilisation depresses average earnings, and makes it even harder to manage reductions in legal aid fees (paragraphs 6.1 to 6.4).

There are no reliable figures for new entrants to the criminal Bar, but strong signs that it is an ageing profession, with fewer younger members than in the past. It is not well-equipped to undertake work-force planning of the kind undertaken by managed businesses in the public and private sectors (paragraphs 6.5 to 6.8).

There are many more graduates of the Bar Professional Training Course (BPTC) than there are pupillages on offer. I cannot fault the logic on which the Wood Working Group dismissed the idea of a cap on numbers taking the BPTC. But the problem of high levels of debt and disappointed hopes of pupillage persists, and is probably most acute in relation to crime (paragraphs 6.10 to 6.15).

Some of these trends seem likely to tell against progress on diversity. There is a realistic fear that the good work which has been done in this area in the relatively recent past is in danger of being undone, with a reversion to a more socially advantaged, less ethnically diverse profession. This is one of the issues which any radical change in the structure of the profession should seek to address (paragraphs 6.18 to 6.20).

How the system works and its impact on quality

Inadequate preparation is the enemy of good advocacy. A combination of delay in assigning advocates (both prosecution and defence) and uncertainty over trial dates makes the system more hand to mouth than is conducive to good quality advocacy. What is badly needed is the timely assignment in as many cases as possible of an advocate who has a good prospect of actually conducting the trial. There was some consensus among the defence practitioners I consulted that advocates on both sides should be assigned about two weeks before the Plea and Case Management Hearing. This would work only if the CPS played its part, and if there was greater certainty over trial dates. To make best use of court time, some flexibility over the scheduling of trials is inevitable, but the "warned list" system as it operates in most parts of the country makes it very hard for advocates to plan their diaries, and increases the likelihood of changes of representative at the last minute. Sir Brian Leveson's review of practice and procedures in the criminal courts provides an opportunity to consider these issues more fully (section 7).

The longer term

There are longer term trends and forces at work which could have profound implications for the future of criminal practice in the legal profession.

The solicitor side of the profession faces a period of upheaval following the legal aid changes, which will probably involve substantial consolidation and the emergence of fewer, larger criminal practices. This will not be easy, but the general character of the change is reasonably well understood (paragraphs 9.2 and 9.3).

The future of the self-employed Bar is less clear. If the trends described here continue unabated, the Bar will undertake a diminishing share of the available work. The intake of younger barristers will decline further, and they will find it even harder to get the early experience of simpler work necessary to build skills. Against that, there are some signs that the tide away from the self-employed Bar may be turning, or be capable of being turned. But this is by no means assured, and if – as appears to be the case – the Bar itself lacks confidence in the future of criminal work, or willingness to adjust to compete for it, the continuation of recent trends will become a self-fulfilling prophecy. In that case, as the present generation of experienced criminal barristers moves towards retirement, concerns about the future "talent pipeline" for criminal QCs and judges are not, in my view, fanciful (paragraphs 9.4 to 9.11).

This matters, because the particular strengths of the English and Welsh criminal Bar are a substantial national asset, which could not easily be replicated. There is also a distinct national interest in having sufficient top-end advocates to undertake the most complex and serious trials, and senior judges with deep criminal experience.

Attempting to turn the clock back, for example by restoring exclusive rights of audience in the Crown Court, would be neither feasible nor desirable. Solicitor advocates are a valuable and established part of the scene. The sensible approach is to invest in their skills and professionalism (paragraphs 9.12 and 9.13).

It may, however, be worth looking more radically at the future structure of this part of the legal profession. In paragraph 9.18, in the hope that it will stimulate debate within the profession and with its regulators, I describe a possible model in which the decision to become a specialist advocate would be taken later in a lawyer's career; a smaller criminal Bar would concentrate on cases where specialist advocacy skills were most evidently required; and early advocacy experience would be obtained elsewhere.

The potential advantages of such a model are that the distribution of work between the two branches of the profession would be clearer and less contested; young criminal practitioners would be called to the Bar with some previous advocacy experience; and the problem of over-provision on the BPTC and indebtedness among its disappointed graduates might be reduced if not removed altogether.

The Lord Chief Justice has encouraged the criminal Bar to consider where it wishes to be in ten years' time. Such a reappraisal of the future of the criminal Bar is, in my view, urgently needed. The two broad avenues of development described in this report – adjustment of the business model to compete for legal aid work on a more level playing field, and restructuring as a smaller, more specialist resource – may not be the only possibilities. But simply carrying on as at present, in an effort to keep intact, in radically changed conditions, every aspect of the model as it existed many years ago, does not seem to me to be a viable option (paragraphs 9.14 to 9.22).

Recommendations

1. The implications for the legal profession of the trends in advocacy described in this report are potentially profound, and – notwithstanding the strong feelings that they arouse – I would urge the profession to seek consensus on how best to address them (Conclusion).

2. There should, over time, be developed a common training expectation of all those practising as advocates in the Crown Court, which need not be as demanding as the Bar's, but should substantially exceed the current requirement on solicitors seeking higher court rights (paragraph 4.6).

3. In following up the Legal Education and Training Review, the profession and the regulators should consider taking the limited advocacy element out of the existing Legal Practice Course and instead develop a more substantial elective advocacy course for trainee (or indeed qualified) solicitors minded to pursue a career in advocacy, completion of which could in future be mandatory for those seeking higher court accreditation (paragraph 4.7).

4. The SRA and the Law Society should consider proportionate ways of replicating for higher court solicitor advocates the supervised experience which pupillage provides for barristers, including early exposure and practice (paragraph 4.8).

5. The profession should work together, with the regulators, to develop common minimum expectations for continuous professional development training (CPD) for advocates in the Crown Court. A common approach could build on the excellent work already being done by the Advocacy Training Council (ATC), including the ATC's Advocacy Gateway,

the Solicitors Association of Higher Court Advocates (SAHCA) and the Law Society's Advocacy Section (paragraph 4.9).

6. The profession should consider the early adoption for defence advocates of a "ticketing" system, of the kind already in place for the judiciary and the CPS, under which those appearing in rape and sexual abuse cases must demonstrate that they have undertaken relevant training. To go further by extending such a requirement to the generality of cases involving vulnerable witnesses would have wider implications, but would make sense in principle, and is something the judges, the CPS and the profession might wish to consider (paragraph 4.11).

7. The SRA and the Law Society should consider what further regulatory or other steps could be taken to clarify and reinforce the professional responsibilities of solicitors in the assignment of advocates and in giving advice on plea (paragraph 5.29).

8. The Government should consider whether the LAA should maintain a list of approved defence advocates in publicly funded cases, on the model of the CPS's panel of barristers briefed to represent the prosecution (paragraph 5.30).

9. The Government should reflect on the implications for the legal aid system of contracting directly with the Bar for defence representation, including the weight given to capability in advocacy, and consider the desirability and feasibility, in future contracting rounds, of separating police station advice and post-charge representational work (paragraph 5.43).

10. In his review of practice and procedures in the criminal courts, Sir Brian Leveson may wish to consider whether there are changes in Court Rules or judicial direction which would help to ensure the timely assignment of advocates, and the impact of the "warned list" system of scheduling trials on the consistency and quality of advocacy (paragraph 7.12).

11. The Government, the regulators and the representative bodies should consider whether more could be done, without over-elaboration, to develop relevant data on criminal advocates and advocacy (paragraph 10.2).

12. They should also look kindly on the case for research in this area, both on the working of the advocacy market – which would repay rigorous economic analysis – and on the vexed question of quality (paragraph 10.3).

[5:2] McConville, M, Hodgson, J, Bridges, L and Pavlovic, A, *Standing Accused: The Organisation and Practice of Criminal Defence Lawyers*
(1994) Clarendon Press

(From Chapter 5: Advisers at Interrogation, at page 126):

Until recently, routine police interrogation methods were well-hidden from courts, solicitors and researchers. Interrogations were essentially police-citizen encounters with outsiders barred from access, accounts of which were police constructions. The accounts attested to the probity of police character, their honesty of purpose, and the reasonableness of their questioning. Clients' accounts, by contrast, were presumptively illegitimate and the official (police) accounts undermined what little credibility suspects might otherwise have enjoyed. The legal profession accepted an element of wrongdoing by the police and misconduct was sometimes established at court but, by and large, the products of interrogation were under police control and collectively they portrayed a system which operated with correctness, restraint and regularity.

Following PACE, the police are presented with a new problem in that they no longer have exclusive control over accounts of interrogations. This has caused a seismic change in the nature of those accounts, with contemporaneous records bearing practically no relation to the world created by the police in their pre-PACE evidence. Whilst this in itself ought to be a matter of concern, it is clear that police goals remain unchanged, although their capacity to instantiate those goals is now imperfect. None the less, the police continue to try to enhance their own credibility and undermine that of the suspect. In this process, rules relating to admissibility are not of central concern to them and they are prepared to bring to bear dubious methods of inquiry.

Although the police are now more frequently than before forced to carry out interrogations in the presence of defence advisers, this has not proved a major restraint. Despite gaining access, the legal profession has no thought out strategy of how to use that access. In part, this is because they have been socialised into accepting as legitimate methods which are objectionable or dubious. In part, they have such a narrow definition of what they *can* do, that they end up by making no objections to police practices. And in part, there has been such insufficient thought given to interrogation, that they do not know what is or is not proper.

It is not simply a question of know-how and technical competence, however, but rather a question of attitude and values. Looked at as a whole, advisers who attend police stations accept uncritically the propriety and legitimacy of police action, even where what they witness themselves, what they hear from clients, and what they suspect goes on, leaves them convinced that the police break the rules and in other ways are beyond the law. The reason for this is that many advisers, like the police, instinctively believe, without requiring substantiation through evidence, that there is a case to answer, and that it is the client who must give the answer. This in turn springs from a working assumption that the client is probably factually guilty. In line with these ideologies, advisers permit the police free rein in interrogations and thereby legitimate dubious police methodologies.

(From Chapter 8: The Solicitor at Court: Plea and Mitigation, at page 210):

The routine nature of work in most solicitors' offices is more than matched by the routinisation of their plea settlement and mitigation practices. For the most part, solicitors do not see magistrates' courts as trial venues but as places where defendants can be processed through guilty pleas without, in general, any risk of severe sanction. The idea that the prosecution should be 'put to the proof' – required to establish a case against the defendant – is not accepted as 'valid' or 'realistic' by defence solicitors. Whilst it would be misleading and unfair to argue that solicitors do not care about their client, so strong is their presumption of guilt and their faith in the prosecution's case, that they fail to see their own role in the production of pleas, and their implication in ambiguous or inconsistent pleas of guilt. But it is not right to argue that solicitors are socialised, through court and prosecutorial inspired disciplinary mechanisms, into non-adversarial practices: they join hands with prosecutors not out of fear of sanction but because they share similar social and crime control values. Whether they like it or not, solicitors, by routinising pleas and mitigation, invite the State to see them as delivering standard services.

(From Chapter 10: Solicitors, Barristers and the Crown Court, at page 267):

In organisational terms, Crown Court cases occupy a regraded position in the structure of the typical firm of solicitors. One or two firms were exceptional in employing competent and experienced clerks and legal executives. Here, the case was prepared well in advance and a real effort made to engage in proactive defence work. Witnesses were sought and pursued until contacted; enquiry agents were sent to draw up plans of the scene of the crime; and forensic experts were employed in response to the client's assertion of inaccurate or fabricated evidence. However, these individuals were quite exceptional even within the firms in which they were employed. In the majority of practices much preparatory work is undertaken by non-qualified staff, and solicitors themselves have little contact with routine Crown Court cases. Lack of care in the preparation of these cases may be partially remedied if there is a case conference with counsel in advance of the court hearing, but reliance on this risks loss of witnesses and other information, and routinely results in the collection of evidence whose value is reduced by its staleness. In an unacceptably high number of cases, evidence is still being gathered long after the time when it was first available, sometimes during the trial itself.

In these cases, solicitors view the tasks of their staff, particularly in attending court, as undemanding and insignificant. The role definition applied to staff, leads solicitors to employ junior, casual or part-time individuals who are not otherwise involved in the case at all. The fact that the rates of remuneration are so low shows that it is not just solicitors who under-value these tasks but the State itself.

The confidence that solicitors have in the system for handling of Crown Court cases is not based upon a rigorous evaluation of the process. With occasional outstanding exceptions, the average solicitor has little involvement in preparing these cases, and what work is done is often too little and too late. Whilst case conferences can make good some of the earlier shortcomings, these do not occur in most cases. At best, conferences can stimulate clerks to set in train investigative tasks that should have taken place much earlier with the increased risk of loss of information or a reduction in its value. In addition to this, cases are routinely vulnerable to changes of counsel and the late delivery of briefs, in several instances being put into the hands of barristers on the day of the hearing itself. With only inexperienced or casual staff from firms in attendance and without a record of what took place at conferences, solici-tors themselves are in no position to evaluate the performance of counsel or any subsequent complaint from the client. Given this context, the trust the solicitors repose in counsel can be based only in images they have of barristers as experts possessing recipe knowledge revealed to 'insiders' as part of the process of Crown Court decision-making.

Whilst our observations confirmed that some barristers are strongly committed to cases, understanding of the need for a sympathetic approach, and careful to test the underlying basis of a guilty plea, counsel in general do not exhibit these positive characteristics. Strik-ingly, on the hearing day at court, but also in conferences in chambers, barristers evince little interest in scrutinising the evidence or in attempting to convince the defendant of its weight and probative value. Rather, conferences are treated as 'disclosure interviews', the purpose of which is to extract a plea of guilty from the client. In this process, what the prosecution alleges, what witnesses may say, and what the client wishes to say, are not discussed. In place of foren-sic testing, 'the evidence' is reified, set up as a totality, and invested with a force which irre-sistibly points to guilt. In place of evidence, a whole gamut of persuasive tactics is deployed against clients enabling barristers to take control of cases and to prevent most clients from becoming, in any real sense, defendants.

If the logic of this process is towards a guilty plea, the precise details of the final arrange-ments are high contingent. In some cases, barristers act to restrain complaint individuals from pleading to any and all charges, but in other cases the client's will is given free and unsuper-vised rein. A small proportion of defendants may resist pressure to capitulate but, deprived of support from solicitors' representatives, few can successfully hold out for long. Compliance is made more likely by the 'offers' which percolate through following prosecution counsel's review of the worth of the prosecution. Whilst the result of this prosecution review is usually a scaling down of the charges in predictable ways, it sometimes appears to have nothing to do with a rational assessment of the evidence but instead is an attempt to get a plea to *something*. When barristers introduce into discussions sentencing and charge propensities of particular judges and dark suggestions of backstairs' dealings, the contingent nature of the outcome is beyond measurement and can only be stated.

[5:3] *R v Maxwell*
[2010] UKSC 48 (report taken from (2011) 8 *Archbold Review* 4)

The appellant and his brother were convicted of murder and two robberies in 1998. On June 11 and October 13, 1996 violent robberies took place at the home of two elderly brothers. On the second occasion, the elder brother sustained injuries to the head which caused his death. The main prosecution witness was Karl Chapman, a supergrass and a professional criminal, who provided the police with information and witness statements implicating the appellant and his brother. He vigorously denied that he was expecting or receiving any benefits from the police for his evidence. Following the convictions, there were allegations in the local press that the police were planning to pay Chapman a large sum of money upon his release from prison. In 1999, an *ex parte* hearing was held on a public interest immunity application by the prosecution. Senior police officers gave evidence to the effect that a reward of £10,000 had been set aside for Chapman, but that he was not aware of it. The Court of Appeal accepted this evidence and dismissed renewed applications for leave to appeal. Subsequently, a Criminal Cases Review Commission (CCRC) report in 2008 showed that the police had conspired to pervert the course of justice in concealing and lying about a variety of rewards and benefits received by Chapman. It was revealed that the police had paid him sums of money, taken him to brothels, allowed him to consume illegal drugs in their company and not investigated allegations that he had committed serious violent crimes. The CCRC made a reference to the Court of Appeal on the ground that the convictions had been procured by gross prosecutorial misconduct on the part of the police. The appellant and his brother remained in prison during this period. Between 1998 and 2004, whilst in prison, the appellant had made various voluntary admissions of involvement in the murder to various people.

In 2009, the Court of Appeal quashed the convictions of both the appellant and his brother. The findings of the CCRC relating to the gross police misconduct were not challenged. The Court held that, had the findings been revealed during the trial, the trial judge might have stayed the prosecution as an abuse of process or applied s.78 of the Police and Criminal Evidence Act 1984 to exclude Chapman's evidence altogether, in which case the appellant and his brother would have been acquitted. However, the Court also held that the admissions made by the appellant constituted clear and compelling evidence of his guilt. In light of this, the Court of Appeal found that it was in the interests of justice to order a retrial.

The Supreme Court dismissed the appeal by a majority of 3 to 2. The Court handed down its decision in November 2010, but withheld its reasoning until the completion of the appellant's retrial. Judgments were given in July 2011. For the majority (Lord Dyson gave the lead judgment, Lords Rodger and Mance gave short concurring judgments) the fact that the confessions on which the retrial would be based would not have been made but for the prosecutorial misconduct was no more than a relevant factor and it was not determinative of the question whether a retrial was required in the interests of justice.

Lord Dyson started by reviewing the law on abuse of process:

> It is well established that the court has the power to stay proceedings in two categories of case, namely (i) where it will be impossible to give the accused a fair trial, and (ii) where it offends the court's sense of justice and propriety to be asked to try the accused in the particular circumstances of the case. In the first category of case, if the court concludes that an accused cannot receive a fair trial, it will stay the proceedings without more. No question of the balancing of competing interests arises. In the second category of case, the court is concerned to protect the integrity of the criminal justice system. Here a stay will be granted where the court concludes that in all the circumstances a trial will "offend the court's sense of justice and propriety" (per Lord Lowry in *R v Horseferry Road*

Magistrates' Court, Ex p Bennett [1994] 1 AC 42, 74G) or will "undermine public confidence in the criminal justice system and bring it into disrepute" (per Lord Steyn in *R v Latif* [1996] 1 WLR 104, 112F) (para.13).

Turning to the power to order a retrial (s.7 of the Criminal Appeal Act 1968, as amended), he said:

The "interests of justice" is not a hard-edged concept. A decision as to what the interests of justice requires calls for an exercise of judgment in which a number of relevant factors have to be taken into account and weighed in the balance. In difficult borderline cases, there may be scope for legitimate differences of opinion. I do not believe it to be controversial that the gravity of the alleged offence is an important relevant factor for the court to take into account when deciding whether to order a retrial in a case which is not complicated by prosecutorial misconduct (paras 19–20).

The gravity of the alleged offence is plainly a factor of considerable weight for the court to weigh in the balance when deciding whether to stay proceedings on the grounds of abuse of process (para.22).

Acknowledging academic criticism of that approach (citing Professor Ashworth's "Exploring the Integrity Principle in Evidence and Procedure" in *Essays for Colin Tapper*, 2003) he said it was unnecessary to engage with this criticism since:

whatever the position may be in relation to an application to stay proceedings for abuse of process, it seems to me beyond argument that, when the court is deciding whether the interests of justice require a retrial, the gravity of the alleged offence must be a relevant factor. Society has a greater interest in having an accused retried for a grave offence than for a relatively minor one (para.22).

The weighing of the balance is fact-sensitive and ultimately requires an exercise of judgment. The present case was a gross violation of the appellant's right to a fair trial, and there had been appalling misconduct by the police, but the Court of Appeal had carried out the balancing exercise precisely and with great care. They had concluded that the public interest in a re-trial prevailed on the facts of this case, in particular because of the gravity of the alleged offence and the existence of new and compelling evidence untainted by the police misconduct. The fact that a differently constituted Court of Appeal might have come to a different conclusion was not material. The decision of the Court of Appeal was not plainly wrong and its judgment should not be interfered with.

Lord Rodger admitted that at the end of the hearing he was inclined to the view that the appeal should be allowed. But having considered the matter further, he then agreed with Lord Dyson. Lord Mance was "unable to accept that the Court of Appeal erred in any way entitling the Supreme Court to interfere with its decision to order a retrial" (para.60).

Lord Brown, with whom Lord Collins agreed, dissented. His is the lengthiest judgment, setting out the factual background in detail, but summarising it thus:

A large number of police officers involved in the investigation and prosecution of the Smales robbery and murder case, including several of very high rank, engaged in a prolonged, persistent and pervasive conspiracy to pervert the course of justice. They colluded in conferring on Chapman a variety of wholly inappropriate benefits to secure his continuing cooperation in the appellant's prosecution and trial. They then colluded in Chapman's perjury at that trial. . . They ensured that Chapman's police custody records and various other official documents presented a false picture of the facts, on one occasion actually forging a custody record when its enforced disclosure to the defence would otherwise have revealed the truth. They lied in their responses to enquiries made of the CPS after the appellant's conviction and, in the case of the two senior officers who gave evidence to the Court of Appeal, perjured themselves so as to ensure that the appellant's application for leave to appeal against his conviction got nowhere. To describe police misconduct on this scale merely as shocking and disgraceful is to understate the gravity of its impact upon the integrity of the prosecution process. It is hard to imagine a worse case of sustained prosecutorial dishonesty designed to secure and hold a conviction at all costs.

Scarcely less remarkable and deplorable than this catalogue of misconduct, moreover, is the fact that, notwithstanding its emergence through the subsequent investigation, not a single one of the many police officers involved has since been disciplined or prosecuted for what he did (paras 83–84).

Lord Brown points out that the appellant would never have been prosecuted or convicted in the first place without this gross misconduct:

> In a real sense, indeed, this case can be seen to come within the same category of "but for" situations as the wrongful extradition and entrapment cases: but for the prosecutorial misconduct which initially secured the appellant's conviction and then ensured the failure of his appeal, he would never have made the series of admissions upon the basis of which it is now sought to prosecute him afresh. There can be little doubt that these admission statements were made generally with a view to advancing the appellant's interests following conviction. For the most part it seems that he made them in the hope that his murder conviction would be replaced by a conviction for manslaughter, but perhaps also in the hope of appearing contrite and securing his earlier release on parole. Either way, the likelihood is that were a trial now to take place and a conviction to be obtained on the basis of these admissions, those responsible for corrupting the original process would still be seen thereby to have achieved their ends and in the long term to have engineered the appellant's conviction. That to my mind is the critical consideration in this case. The court should be astute to avoid giving the impression that it is prepared, even in this limited way, to condone such unforgivable executive misconduct as occurred here (para.102).

On the facts of this particular case, he suggests that the Court of Appeal might perhaps have attached more countervailing importance to the length of time the appellant had already spent in prison and to the disparity of outcome of the appeal as between the appellant and his brother. And keen to give some general guidance, he said:

> It may however be possible and helpful to summarise the position a little more specifically as follows. (1) Whenever, executive misconduct notwithstanding, it remains possible to ensure that the defendant can be fairly tried (or, as the case may be, retried), this ordinarily is the result for which the court should aim, making whatever orders short of a permanent stay are necessary to achieve it (or as the case may be, by ordering a retrial). (2) In certain particular kinds of case, however, the "but for" cases as I have sought to describe and categorise them, even though it would be possible to try (or retry) the defendant fairly, it will usually be inappropriate to do so. It will be inappropriate essentially because, but for the executive misconduct, either there would never have been a trial at all (as in the wrongful extradition and entrapment cases) or (as in the present case) because the situation would never have arisen whereby the all important incriminating evidence came into existence (which is not, of course, to say that the "fruit of the poison tree" is invariably inadmissible). Obviously this is not an exhaustive definition of the "but for" category of cases and, as the word "usually" is intended to denote, whether in any particular case a trial (or retrial) has in fact become inappropriate may still depend in part on other considerations too. Essentially, however, it is the executive misconduct involved in this category of cases which, I suggest, most obviously threatens the integrity of the criminal justice system and where a trial (or retrial) would be most likely to represent an affront to the public conscience. (3) Exceptionally, even in cases of executive misconduct not within the "but for" category, it may be that the balance will tip in favour of a stay (or, as the case may be, a quashed

conviction with no order for retrial), notwithstanding that a fair trial (retrial) remains possible... only exceptionally will the court regard the system to be morally compromised by a fair trial (retrial) in a case which cannot be slotted into any "but for" categorisation. The risk of the court appearing to condone the misconduct (appearing to adopt the approach that the end justifies the means) prominent in the "but for" category of cases, is simply not present in the great majority of abuse cases (para.108).

Lord Collins agreed with Lord Brown that the appeal should be allowed:

Public confidence that the police will act properly and lawfully is one of the cornerstones of democracy. Without proper police conduct and without public confidence in the honesty of the police, the rule of law and the integrity of the criminal justice system would be seriously undermined (para.110). I would find that the interests of justice demand the application of the integrity principle. In this case it means that there should be no retrial on evidence which would not have been available but for a conviction obtained (and upheld) as a result of conduct so fundamentally wrong that for the criminal process to act on that evidence would compromise its integrity (para.115).

[**Comment**: Despite the fact that these judgments had not been published, they were circulated to the parties in *Warren v AG of Jersey* [2011] UKPC 10 (see [2011] 6 *Archbold Review* 6) and were cited at length in the judgments of the Privy Council in *Warren*. In particular, Lord Brown was "anxious to explain" why he took a "rather different view" about that case, and what he then believed to be the overriding principle now to be derived from the majority judgments in both *Maxwell* and in *Warren* :

The distinction between the two cases is this: the defendant in *Maxwell*, but for the police's misconduct, would never have made the confessions that were to form the basis of his retrial; it was accordingly the misconduct itself which induced *Maxwell* to act to his detriment. By contrast the misconduct here had no effect whatever upon the appellants' conduct. The present case is a "but for" case only in the sense that, but for the unlawfully obtained evidence, the appellants would not have been prosecuted or convicted: the Crown would not have had sufficient evidence.

Jonathan Rodgers dismissed this distinction in [2011] 6 *Archbold Review* 6:

It is respectfully submitted that the misconduct needs only to have enabled the case to be brought to trial. If Lord Brown were right, then the House of Lords would not have held in *Ex p. Bennett* that a trial following an arranged illegal extradition of the suspect could properly be stayed, since here the illegality did not cause D to act to his detriment in any way.

Indeed, the Supreme Court has done little to clarify the precise circumstances in which the Court of Appeal may order a retrial having quashed a conviction on the grounds of serious police misconduct. More importantly, when should they definitely not order a retrial? To quote Rodgers again, in abuse of process applications, "concentrating on the gravity of the official misconduct, and not attaching independent (countervailing) significance to the charges against the accused, should *always* be the correct approach".

The police behaved appallingly in *Maxwell*, and the flouting of French and Dutch law by the police in *Warren* was also shocking: "sustained, deliberate and, one might say, cynical" (Lord Hope, para.63). In *Maxwell*, it is simply breathtaking that that none of the police officers involved was prosecuted or even disciplined (see Lord Rodger, para.41). (This is presumably because their admissions of wrongdoing were only obtained in exchange for a waiver of potential disciplinary action). Particularly given this unsatisfactory position, should the Supreme Court not have gone somewhat further in making it clear that such "unforgiveable police misconduct" is not condoned? It remains, of course, open to the Court when and if such shocking cases recur "to strike the balance decisively in favour of indicating the rule of law, however undeserving the accused" (see Lord Brown, in *Warren*, para.78). The appellant pleaded guilty at his retrial.]

[5:4] *Transforming legal aid: delivering a more credible and efficient system*
(2013) Ministry of Justice Consultation Paper CP14/2013 (at page 3)

Ministerial Foreword

Access to justice should not be determined by your ability to pay, and I am clear that legal aid is the hallmark of a fair, open justice system. Unfortunately, over the past decade, the system has lost much of its credibility with the public. Taxpayers' money has been used to pay for frivolous claims, to foot the legal bills of wealthy criminals, and to cover cases which run on and on racking up large fees for a small number of lawyers, far in excess of what senior public servants are paid. Under the previous government, the cost of the system spiralled out of control, and it became one of the most costly in the world.

Earlier in this Parliament, the Government took significant steps to reform legal aid, to bring costs under control particularly in relation to civil claims. In the current financial climate, it is now necessary to make further savings by embarking on the next phase of reform, mainly focused on criminal cases. The principles which underpin these proposals are simple: to ensure that those who can afford to pay do so; to make certain that legal aid is not funding cases which lack merit or which are better dealt with outside court; and to encourage greater efficiency in the criminal justice system to reduce costs. The hard-working public pay for legal aid, and we must deliver a system which commands their confidence and spends their money wisely.

Under these reforms, those with significantly higher than average incomes will no longer be eligible for financial support in criminal cases; those who have no strong connection with the UK will cease to have their civil legal costs covered too. Prisoners who wish to challenge their treatment in custody will have recourse to the prisoner complaints procedures rather than accessing a lawyer through legal aid; on Judicial Reviews, lawyers who bring weak cases will no longer be reimbursed; and cases with less than a 50% chance of success will no longer be funded. This is a comprehensive package of measures to restore the public's faith in the system.

To deliver real savings, it is necessary to drive greater efficiency in the legal aid system too. For criminal litigation, we are proposing a model of competitive tendering, where solicitors firms must compete to offer the best price they can for work in their local area. This will mean successful firms expanding or joining together, to achieve economies of scale which can be passed onto the taxpayer in savings to the public purse. For criminal advocacy, we intend to reform the fee structure, to ensure that cases are resolved as quickly as possible, which will mean less time required of lawyers, and lower costs to the legal aid bill. The impact of these changes will also help remedy the great disparity which had emerged within the legal profession by reducing the payments to that small number of lawyers earning very high fees whilst protecting the majority of barristers who should not lose out as a result of our proposals. Indeed, some of the lowest fee earners will be better off.

In short, the reforms outlined in this document both boost public confidence in and reduce the cost of the legal aid system. In the medium term, I am keen to explore further ways for convicted criminals to bear a greater proportion of their legal costs themselves, rather than the bill simply falling to the taxpayer. Whether through deductions from future earnings, or by some other means, we should be seeking to ease the burden of legal aid on the public purse, whilst guaranteeing everyone the right to a defence.

Though in Britain today we face serious challenges, this must not undermine our determination for reform or our desire to achieve the best value for the taxpayer. These proposals are bold but fair, and I look forward to hearing your views.

. . .

Chapter 1: Executive Summary

Executive Summary

1.1 This document sets out the Government's proposals for further reform of the legal aid system in England and Wales.

1.2 As set out in Chapter 2 (Introduction), against a backdrop of continuing financial pressure on public finances, we need to continue to bear down on public spending.

1.3 We estimate that the proposals set out in this consultation would, if implemented, deliver savings of £220 million per year by 2018/19.1

1.4 Views are invited on the questions set out below. When expressing views on those questions, respondents are advised to have the overall fiscal context firmly in mind.

Proposals for reform

1.5 Chapter 3 (Eligibility, Scope and Merits) sets out proposals for improving public confidence in the legal aid scheme. It includes reforms to prison law to ensure that legal aid is not available for matters that do not justify the use of public funds such as treatment issues; the introduction of a household disposable income threshold above which defendants would no longer receive criminal legal aid; a residence test for civil legal aid claimants; reforms to reduce the use of legal aid to fund weak judicial reviews; and amendments to the civil merits test to prevent the funding of any cases with less than a 50% chance of success.

1.6 Chapter 4 (Introducing Competition in the Criminal Legal Aid Market) sets out proposals for introducing price competition into the criminal legal aid market, initially for the full range of litigation services (except Very High Cost Cases (Crime) VHCCs) and magistrates' court representation only. It details the main features and elements of the proposed model.

1.7 Chapter 5 (Reforming Fees in Criminal Legal Aid) sets out proposals to reduce the cost of criminal legal aid fees for Crown Court advocacy and VHCCs (both litigation and advocacy), which it is not proposed to include in competition. These include, first a proposal to restructure the current Advocacy Graduated Fees Scheme to encourage earlier resolution and more efficient working through a harmonisation of guilty plea, cracked trial and basic trial fee rates to the cracked trial rate, and a reduction in and tapering of daily trial attendance rates from day 3. Second, there is a proposal to reduce all VHCC rates by 30%. Third, there is a proposal to tighten the rules governing the decision to appoint multiple counsel in a case, changes to litigator contracts to require greater support to counsel from the litigation team, and the introduction of a more robust and consistent system of decision-making.

1.8 Chapter 6 (Reforming Fees in Civil Legal Aid) sets out proposals to reduce solicitor representation fees in family public law cases by 10%, to align the fees for barristers and other advocates in non-family cases, and to remove the 35% uplift in provider legal aid fees in immigration and asylum appeals.

1.9 Chapter 7 (Expert Fees in Civil, Family and Criminal Proceedings) sets out a proposal to reduce fees paid to experts in civil, family and criminal cases by 20%.

[5:5] Kemp, V, '"No time for a solicitor": implications for delays on the take-up of legal advice'

[2013] Crim LR 184
(At page 186):

A study of four police stations: methods

This study involved an examination of the main police station in four police force areas; one in South West England, two in the East Midlands, and one in South East England. The volume of cases managed at these four police stations over a two-month period was high, ranging from around 1,500 to 2,500 cases. The methods adopted included observation of police custody suites and in-depth interviews with fifty custody sergeants. There were eighteen days spent in total observing police custody suites and carrying out the interviews: five days and 12, 13 and 10 interviews in Police Stations A, B and C respectively and three days and 15 interviews in Police Station D. The study was carried out during October to December 2010.

(At page 198):

Suspects' perceptions of delays and police ploys

When observing suspects as they were booked into custody it was evident from comments made that there was a perception that having a solicitor would lead to delays and thereby extend their time in custody. Not surprisingly, such concerns led to some suspects rejecting legal advice. For example, when asked by custody sergeants the reason why legal advice was refused responses observed included, "I've no time for a solicitor" or "Let's get on with it". With solicitors being absent from custody suites in Police Stations A and B they were not in a position to challenge any concerns a suspect might have about legal advice causing delays. Interestingly, in an earlier study I interviewed defence solicitors in Police Station A who were then allowed into the custody suite. At that time there were complaints made by a couple of solicitors that they had overheard the police telling suspects that if they wanted a solicitor they would have to wait for a long time. While the solicitors had then been able to challenge such inappropriate comments, their subsequent exclusion meant that this was no longer the case. It is important, therefore, to consider further the extent to which the police might use delays as a way of discouraging suspects from having legal advice.

When examining the potential use of police ploys designed to discourage the take up of legal advice, Brown has been critical of researchers for adopting a wide definition of "ploys" which include cases where there were seen to be "influences on decisions regarding legal advice" but not "active discouragement". It is this more restricted categorisation of "active discouragement" which has been used in this study when examining the potential use of police ploys.

There were said to be three opportunities that the police have for using the threat of delays as a ploy to discourage suspects from having legal advice. The first opportunity was said to arise following an arrest, when during informal conversations on the way to the station the suspect could be told that they would spend longer in custody if they asked for a solicitor. The potential for police ploys to be used at this early stage was commented on by custody sergeants from all four police stations. In Police Station D, for example, this custody sergeant said:

> "I make it very clear that people are entitled to legal advice and that it shouldn't make much differ-
> ence to the time they are here. It would be naive to think that when someone is arrested that the

officer doesn't tell them that they are ready to go and that having a solicitor will hold things up. I expect that sort of thing does happen" (D:VN).

When being booked into custody, suspects sometimes made reference to earlier conversations in which legal advice had been discussed. On one occasion, for instance, when asked why he had declined legal advice this suspect replied, "I don't want to have to wait for a solicitor" and turning to the arresting officer he said, "We are ready to go now aren't we?" In another station, this custody sergeant said:

"When they come into custody it seems that the cop has already told them that they are ready for the interview. We ask if they want a solicitor but they generally say they won't bother because they just want to get out" (B:VS).

It was only in Police Stations A and B that custody sergeants referred to police ploys being used once a suspect was brought into custody. The second opportunity these custody sergeants referred to of the police trying to discourage a suspect from having legal advice was when they were being booked into custody and the police said they were ready to go ahead with the interview. As this custody sergeant put it:

"If the officers are ready to interview straight away, a suspect who has been in custody before will know that if they ask for a solicitor they will then have to wait for them to get to the station" (A:UT).

Suspects wanting to be dealt with quickly, therefore, were likely to feel under pressure not to have legal advice. This was the comment from one custody sergeant who said:

"There are some cops who will do anything they can to try and get a prisoner in quickly and avoid them having a solicitor. They will often say, 'If you don't want a brief I'll take you in for an interview now'. Unfortunately, I think that is quite common" (B:FX).

The extent to which such pressure might be used as a ploy to discourage legal advice was further explored in a later study of legal advice at Police Station B.

The third opportunity for the police to use the threat of delays to try to discourage legal advice was said to be just before the police interview. As noted above, there were times where the late arrival of a solicitor could delay the interview and this could then encourage suspects to change their mind and proceed without a solicitor. However, custody sergeants in Police Stations A and B acknowledged that police officers could blame the solicitor for delays so as to encourage the suspect to change their mind about having legal advice. For some respondents, pressure coming from the police to decline legal advice because of delays was unintentional. This was what one respondent had to say:

"I don't think the police try to do anything unlawful but sometimes they have a chat with them [the suspect] and say they are ready for the interview but their solicitor hasn't arrived. They can then change their mind because they don't want to have to wait for another 40 minutes for their solicitor to get here" (B:IH).

While a custody sergeant in another station said that police ploys were not used in order to discourage legal advice, he later seemed to unwittingly hint at such practices when commenting on why he felt suspects changed their mind about having legal advice:

"To be honest, I don't know why they change their mind. The inspector has to get involved and ask them questions . . . it is normally when they [the investigating officers] are in the cells with them that they then say they don't want a solicitor" (A:PK).

In the same station, an experienced custody sergeant acknowledged that the investigating officers could actively discourage suspects from having legal advice. When commenting on one particular case he said:

"The solicitor arrived in time for the interview but the two detectives were nowhere to be seen. I found out that they visited the suspect in his cell and he then changed his mind about having a solicitor because he said he didn't want to wait anymore. The detectives went straight to the inspector who confirmed that he had changed his mind. This was completely without my knowledge – I was furious" (A:ES).

There was a similar situation described by custody sergeants in Police Station B. When commenting on the potential for such police ploys this respondent said:

"We caught a DC [detective constable] trying to persuade a detainee not to have a solicitor. He came out of the cells and said he didn't want one [a solicitor] but the inspector got wind of it and said you are having a solicitor. We took a decision as a group then that we wouldn't let officers take detainees to or from the cells. I'm not saying that every shift is the same but that was the decision on ours" (B:VS).

To try and protect suspects from police pressure being used to discourage legal advice, PACE [the Police and Criminal Evidence Act 1984] requires that an inspector has to get involved in cases where someone changes their mind about having a solicitor. However, as custody sergeants pointed out, there were inspectors who were more robust than others when not allowing suspects to change their mind. Accordingly, one custody sergeant suggested the following change which he felt could help to increase protections for detainees:

"If someone wants to change their mind I don't see any reason why we can't pick up the phone and get them to speak to their solicitor. It will only take five minutes. He has to speak to an inspector so he might as well speak to a solicitor. I know they [the solicitor] will say that they are on the way and 25 minutes later they will be here" (B:QT).

This suggestion is important because it provides an opportunity for a solicitor to speak to their client over the telephone and to address any concerns they might have about their involvement causing a delay. It could also help to reduce the opportunity for police ploys to be used at this stage to discourage the take-up of legal advice.

Discussion

The findings arising out of this study have helped to identify unobserved factors which can impact on delays and the take-up of legal advice. Some factors have been found to be common across the four stations, including the long-windedness of the police investigation and the involvement of the CPS in pre-charge decision-making. Factors found to influence variations between police stations include differences in the role and remit of police review teams and also in the arrangements for providing access to legal advice. There was also seen to be a common perception among suspects that having a solicitor would lead to delays. Helping to counteract such a view in one police station was the high visibility of solicitors in the custody suite, which seemed to have a positive effect on increasing requests for legal advice. On the other hand, in two police stations where solicitors had been excluded from waiting around in the custody suite, there was evidence of police ploys using the threat of delays in order to discourage suspects from having legal advice.

An important issue arising out of recent research into police station legal advice is the extent to which suspects held in custody are able to judge whether or not they need a solicitor, particularly if they are in custody for the first time and/or have been arrested for serious offences. The criminal law and procedure is extremely complex and within an adversarial system of justice understanding one's legal rights, and the consequences of decisions made, may be beyond the comprehension of many suspects. Once brought into custody it is the police who are responsible for reading out to suspects their legal rights, but PACE requires them to be impartial so they are not able to influence the decisions made. In practice, particularly when dealing with suspects confused or unsure about what to do, the way in which those rights are presented means that custody sergeants can be either encouraging or discouraging of legal advice. One way of improving access to legal advice would be for custody sergeants to point out to suspects who decline to consult with a solicitor in person that the right includes the opportunity to speak to a legal adviser over the telephone. This is a PACE requirement but it was only in one police station where this choice was routinely offered to suspects.

To help protect the legal rights of those held in police custody PACE provides access to free and independent legal advice, which is to be provided "as soon as practicable" once requested. However, since the introduction of fixed fees for police station legal advice it seems that solicitors are tending to concentrate on the offence rather than on the wider issues concerning their clients' detention. This means that they tend to get involved in cases at the time of the police interview, which can be many hours following a request for legal advice. Having received a request for legal advice solicitors could be more challenging of the police timetable, particularly in cases involving unnecessary and/or unduly long delays. If the police were put under pressure to conduct their investigations expeditiously this would not only help to improve efficiencies but it could also lead to their clients being released earlier from custody. Such interventions, therefore, could have a positive effect on the take-up of legal advice, particularly as suspects currently perceive solicitors to be the main cause of delays.

With concerns raised by custody sergeants in all four police stations over long delays in the pre-charge process this study raises questions about the extent to which PACE provides sufficient legal protections for those held in custody. In particular, it seems that within a 24-hour period of detention PACE safeguards intended to restrict the length of time suspects can be held in custody are ineffective. In addition, with the involvement of police review teams and the CPS in pre-charge decision-making, cases are now being prepared to a higher evidential standard, but with consequent delays. Accordingly, it is important to question whether the right balance has been struck between the administrative and investigative needs of the prosecution and the liberty of those held in police custody.

[5:6] Baldwin, J, *The Role of Legal Representatives at the Police Station*
(1992) RCCJ Research Study No 3 HMSO (at page 52)

As noted earlier in this report, a critical question is whether lawyers should be acting more forcefully on their clients' behalf at the police station. There is a good deal of scope for them to do so, and there were only a few lawyers on the video tapes who demonstrated that they could wield much authority in the interview room if the need arose. Some lawyers were more tolerant than were others of police officers who adopted harrying tactics, who persisted doggedly with certain lines of questioning or who made crude assumptions of guilt. Searching questions need to be asked, therefore, about how far legal representatives – who are in most instances unqualified legal personnel – can be said to be providing adequate protection to their clients in the police station.

The lawyers' view of their role at the police interviews reflects the way that their attitudes have been moulded by the history of their relations with the police. The interview takes place on police territory and it is police officers who are in charge of it. Officers often describe it as 'their' interview, and the lawyers contacted in this study did not commonly see it in other terms. Although police attitudes towards the presence of solicitors have shifted in the course of the past decade – reflecting to a considerable extent the changes brought in by the PACE legislation – lawyers continue to be treated with circumspection and suspicion. While they are no longer regarded as gatecrashers at interviews, they are nonetheless only tolerated at police stations if they behave appropriately. Advising clients not to answer questions or intervening at interviews are not seen by police as reasonable forms of behaviour. It is only if they toe the line that lawyers are regarded as acceptable participants at police interviews.

Passivity and compliance on the part of lawyers are therefore the normal, the expected, almost the required responses at the police station. Solicitors are conditioned by their history, their experience, even their own professional training and guidance, to be passive in the police interview room, and the existing rules reinforce this by giving police officers the upper hand. The lawyers' role in the interview room remains a precarious one, and it is no real surprise to note that the junior staff who mainly turn up to police stations are more inclined to facilitate police questioning than they are to challenge it.

[5:7] *R v Paris, Abdullahi and Miller*
(1993) 97 Cr App Rep 99

The three appellants were convicted of the murder of a Cardiff prostitute. There was no forensic evidence against them. Against Miller, the prosecution case rested on the evidence of two discredited witnesses, Miller's own admissions and admissions he made to two visitors when in prison. After hearing part of the confession evidence on tape, the trial judge ruled it admissible. On appeal, it was contended that Miller's confession was unreliable, having been obtained by oppression.

The Court of Appeal, in quashing the convictions, held that it was undoubtedly oppressive within the meaning of section 76(2) of PACE to shout at a suspect what they wanted him to say after he had denied involvement over 300 times, particularly since the person in question was on the borderline of mental handicap. The Lord Chief Justice was critical of both the police and the suspect's solicitor.

Lord Taylor CJ (at page 109):

Before parting with this case, we should comment on the apparent failure of the provisions in the Police and Criminal Evidence Act 1984, to prevent evidence obtained by oppression and impropriety from being admitted. In our judgment, the circumstances of this case do not indicate flaws in those provisions. They do indicate a combination of human errors.

First, the police officers adopted techniques of interrogation which were wholly contrary to the spirit and in many instances the letter of the codes laid down under the Act. In our view, those responsible for police training and discipline must take all necessary steps to see the guidelines are followed.

Secondly, although we did not hear what his instructions were, the solicitor who sat in on the interviews, seems to have done that and little else. Guidelines for solicitors on 'advising a suspect in the police station' were first published by the Law Society in 1985 with second and third editions in 1988 and 1991. The current edition provides under paragraph 6 as follows, inter alia:

'6.3.2 you may need to intervene if the questions are: . . . (c) oppressive, threatening or insulting;

6.3.3　you should intervene if the officer is not asking questions but only making his/her own comments . . .

6.4.1　if questions are improper or improperly put, you should intervene and be prepared to explain your objections . . .

6.4.2　if improprieties remain uncorrected or continue, advise the suspect of his/her right to remain silent.'

It is of the first importance that a solicitor fulfilling the exacting duty of assisting a suspect during interviews should follow the guidelines and discharge his function responsibly and courageously. Otherwise, his presence may actually render disservice. We can only assume that in the present case the officers took the view that unless and until the solicitor intervened, they could not be criticised for going too far. If that is so, they were wholly wrong.

Finally, it is most regrettable that the worst example of the police excesses (tape 7) was not played in full to the learned judge before he ruled on admissibility.

Despite this combination of errors, it must be pointed out that the record of timings and the tape recordings of the interviews required by the Act, have enabled this Court to review what took place and, albeit belatedly, to allow these appeals. At the conclusion, we now direct the learned Registrar to send copies of tape 7 to the Chief Inspector of Constabulary, to the Director of Public Prosecutions and to the Chairman of the Royal Commission on Criminal Justice.

[5:8] *R v Ensor*
[1989] 1 WLR 497

The appellant was tried on two counts of rape, each of a different woman. He wanted an application for severance to be made. Counsel concluded that an application would fail, and that some advantage would accrue from having the counts tried together and no application for severance was made. The appellant was convicted on both counts. The Court of Appeal dismissed the appeal.

Lord Lane CJ (at pages 501):

We must look a little more closely at the extent to which this court will concern itself with what passes between an accused person and his legal representatives.

Mr Escott Cox contends that in a criminal trial defending counsel is only obliged to seek specific instructions from his client in relation to two matters: first, as to plea; and, secondly, as to whether the client himself wishes to give evidence. All other decisions are for counsel, and it is for him to decide, as a matter of discretion, which matters, if any, needed to be discussed with the accused. The discretion is one, he submits, which this court will not attempt directly to review, although it might, for example, in a wholly exceptional case be prepared to consider whether compelling evidence which was available but which defence counsel for no good reason refused to lead renders the conviction unsafe and unsatisfactory.

Mr Jeffreys relied heavily on *R v Irwin* [1987] 1 WLR 902, decided by another division of this court on 19 February 1987. That was a case in which at a retrial counsel for the defence decided not to call alibi witnesses who had given evidence at the earlier trial which had ended in a disagreement. On appeal it was said, at p 905g, that the question was not whether counsel was right in thinking that the witnesses should not be called but whether he was entitled to bind his client. The court held that he was not entitled to do so, asserting at p 906h, that on this topic there is no authority to be found in any criminal case.

It seems that the court in *R v Irwin* [1987] 1 WLR 902 was not referred to the decision of this court in *R v Novac* (1976) 65 Cr App Rep 107. There the court was concerned with the topic we have to consider in the present case, namely, the question of severance. A number of defendants each faced a conspiracy count and counts alleging specific offences, and one defendant, Raywood, applied for the specific offence count against him to be severed from the conspiracy count. The application was refused but his appeal succeeded on the basis that the application ought to have been allowed, and Bridge LJ giving the judgment of the court, continued at p 112:

> 'It is surprising that no application similar to that made on behalf of Raywood should have been made on behalf of Novac or Andrew-Cohen to sever the specific offence counts against them. [Counsel] for Novac told us that he thought it pointless to make such an application after the application on behalf of Raywood had been refused. But we can see no basis which would have justified him in assuming that the one application must necessarily be determined in the same way as the other. It was for him to make an application to sever on his own client's behalf if thought appropriate. *No such application having been made there can be no basis for complaint in this court that the conspiracy and related counts were heard together in Novac's case with the specific offence counts.*' (Our emphasis).

In *Novac* the court does not seem to have considered it necessary to inquire whether counsel in refraining from making an application to sever acted with or without the express authority of his client, no doubt because generally speaking this court will always proceed upon the basis that what counsel does is done with the authority of the client who has instructed counsel to conduct his case.

In *R v Gaultam*, (1987) Times, 4 March, which was decided by this court on 27 February 1987, a few days after the appeal in *R v Irwin* had been heard, Taylor J said:

> 'It should be clearly understood that if defending counsel in the course of his conduct of the case makes a decision, or takes a course which later appears to have been mistaken or unwise, that generally speaking has never been regarded as a proper ground for an appeal.'

That was a shoplifting case in which counsel, for what were patently good reasons, had declined to lead medical evidence at the trial until after the jury had returned a verdict.

On 12 March 1987 another division of this court heard the appeal of Alan John Swain who contended, with apparent justification, that his counsel, by incompetent cross-examination, had introduced evidence which was prejudicial to his case, which was then amplified by the witness in answer to a question put to him by the judge. In an attempt to circumvent the difficulties which he faced arising out of what was said in *R v Gaultam*, counsel at the hearing of the appeal sought to rely mainly on the intervention of the judge, but the court found that what was said in answer to the judge added nothing to what had already been said by the witness to counsel. Various other points were considered with which we need not now be concerned, but O'Connor LJ, giving the judgment of the court, said that, if the court had any lurking doubt that the appellant might have suffered some injustice as a result of flagrantly incompetent advocacy by his advocate, then it would quash the convictions, but in that particular case it had no such doubts.

We consider the correct approach to be that which was indicated by this court in *R v Gaultam* subject only to the qualification to which O'Connor LJ referred in *R v Swain* (unreported). We consider further that the decision in *R v Irwin* [1987] 1 WLR 902, even if it can be reconciled with *R v Novac* – which we doubt – should be regarded as being confined to its own facts. This ground of appeal accordingly fails, because counsel's carefully considered decision not to apply to sever the charges, even if erroneous, cannot possibly be described as incompetent, let alone flagrantly incompetent, advocacy.

[5:9] Malleson, K, *Review of the Appeal Process*

(1993) RCCJ Research Study No 17, HMSO (at page 38)

Taken together the findings from these two comparative studies indicate that when compared with legally assisted applications unassisted applications are:

(i)   Poorly presented and ill-informed.
(ii) More frequently based on substantive issues concerning the justice of their conviction rather than technical or legal grounds.
(iii) More commonly based on the alleged errors of counsel as grounds for appeal despite the fact that the Court will very rarely hear such an appeal.
(iv) Dealt with in very brief judgments by the single judge and the full Court.
(v)   Very unlikely to be granted leave to appeal.

The findings of this research lend support to the concern that unassisted applications are at a disadvantage in the appeal system so that there may be cases with merit which are not identified. Without a detailed study of a large number of individual unassisted cases it is difficult to estimate how many cases with merit are wrongly weeded out by the present 'two tier' system and how best they could in future be identified.

In addition to concern about the nature and treatment of unassisted applications which enter the system, this research highlights the danger that there may be meritorious cases without legal support which do not enter the system in the first place. An unknown number of unassisted convicted persons whose cases have merit may be deterred from appealing because they are aware that unassisted applications are very rarely successful and because they believe that they will serve a longer sentence if their application fails despite the fact that the single judge and the full Court very rarely apply the time loss rules.

Recommendations

Appellants should have a right to legal assistance in presenting an application for leave to appeal for consideration by the single judge and renewing a refused application to the full court.

The findings of the research are such that consideration should be given as to whether the present 'two tier' system needs to be reformed. It is accepted as a basic principle of justice that persons accused of serious offences with limited resources should have legal assistance to defend themselves however weak that defence may be in the view of their legal advisers. We do not expect counsel to decline to present a person's defence in Court because he has determined that it is unlikely to succeed. On this principle we should expect that each convicted person has a similar right to assistance in preparing and presenting an appeal. Just as an accused person instructs his or her solicitor on a defence or provides information for mitigation in a guilty plea so a convicted person should, if he or she wishes, after receiving legal advice, instruct a solicitor in the preparation of an appeal. Counsel may advise that the grounds will be unlikely to succeed, but that decision should be for the single judge alone.

Under the present system an appellant with a meritorious case but without legal assistance must have substantial financial, intellectual, and psychological resources if their appeal is to succeed. If they are in custody, they are particularly reliant on the support and goodwill of others outside. This means that people with limited abilities and resources, such as mentally disordered or handicapped people, young people, or those whose spoken or written English is poor are most disadvantaged. These are also the people who, as miscarriages of justice cases over the years have highlighted, are most likely to be the victims of injustice in the legal system and thus may have most need of the appeal system. The right to legal assistance on appeal would particularly help these vulnerable groups.

If the single judge was retained, this change would not amount to the introduction of a right to appeal, but rather a right to legal assistance in preparing an application for leave to appeal. If all applications were drafted by counsel and submitted by solicitors we could be confident that they would be judged equally on their merits alone.

This reform should not add any great cost to the legal aid bill because the overall numbers affected would be relatively small. Under the present system counsel must advise on appeal, and will draft grounds of appeal in many cases. The change would only affect those few cases where counsel has not provided advice on appeal or advises against appealing where the convicted person still wishes to appeal and requests that grounds be drafted on his or her behalf. While the cost of this change would be small, the potential benefit would be great in that the appeal system would be seen to be more open, accessible and fair at a time when its public credibility is at a particularly low point.

[See also extract at [9:5]]

[5:10] Plotnikoff, J and Woolfson, R, *Information and Advice for Prisoners about Grounds for Appeal and the Appeal Process*
(1993) RCCJ Research Study No 18, HMSO (at page 115)

This chapter discusses the results of the research and proposes some changes at improving the quality of advice and information provided to potential appellants in custody. The objective of these is to specify the commitment on the part of the legal profession and the prisons to providing a defined level of service to inmates and to ensure that the nature of the service is made known to all.

With one exception, none of the recommendations made lends itself to a simple costing exercise and this has not been attempted.

The legal profession

The nature and extent of the service provided to clients by lawyers in the 28 days following conviction or sentence are very variable. There is widespread ignorance both of some aspects of the law on appeal and of the guidelines to good practice on the responsibilities of legal advisers during this period. The first findings and recommendations relate to the guidelines themselves.

The Bar GGP, Law Society GGP and CACD Guide are inconsistent and contain a number of omissions. Specific areas where inconsistencies occur are the length of time that counsel should take to provide written grounds to the solicitor and the powers that exist to order loss of time in the case of frivolous appeals. None of the guidance documents currently reflects both the legal position relating to loss of time and the actual practice in recent years. The Law Society GGP wrongly states that the maximum that can be forfeited is 90 days and omits to mention that the single judge as well as the full Court has the power to issue such an order. None of the documents reflects the infrequency of time loss awards or that the maximum lost in recent years is 28 days.

Over half the solicitors who responded were unaware that the CACD cannot impose a sentence of greater severity than that awarded by the Crown Court. The legal position is not mentioned in any of the guides.

The CACD Guide stipulates that immediately after the conclusion of the case a client should be given a written note of counsel's view, even if this is only provisional, on the advisability of an appeal. Such a note does not constitute written advice but it does provide the client with a record of counsel's view, however provisional, on the advisability of an appeal. This is not mentioned in either the Bar GGP or the Law Society GGP. Responses to the questionnaires sent out during the study revealed that 89% of solicitors and 99% of counsel never hand over anything written at this meeting. No-one did so as a matter of course.

The Law Society GGP makes no mention of including in the brief to counsel a request to furnish written advice on appeal in the event of a conviction. When solicitors were asked whether counsel provide signed grounds without being specifically asked to do so, only 22% said they always did so. Eight per cent said this never happens.

The duty of solicitors to provide advice and keep clients and their families informed is interpreted in differing ways. One quarter of prisoners said they received no appeals advice from their lawyers at any point during the 28 days following conviction or sentence. Only 39% of inmates claimed to have received appeals advice from a lawyer since coming to prison. This situation may be due, at least in part, to confusion over exactly what costs can reasonably be claimed under the trial legal aid order, an issue not covered in any of the guideline documents. Twenty per cent of solicitors said that they do not charge at all for work done in this period and over a third who do charge said that they had had payments refused or reduced.

Recommendation 1: The appeals sections in The Law Society and Bar Guides to Good Practice produced by the Standing Commission on Efficiency and the Guide to Proceedings in the Court of Appeal Criminal Division need to be revised. The revision process should be co-ordinated to ensure that the recommendations in these documents are harmonised.

The following specific areas need to be addressed during this exercise:

(i)   whether it is realistic to expect the solicitor to be present at call visits at court following conclusion of the case and, if not, the consequences that flow from delegation of this duty to a representative
(ii) the completion and handing over at the end of the case of the form at Appendix 1 in the CACD Guide, indicating counsel's view on the advisability of appeal
(iii) the time limit within which counsel should provide the professional client with written advice on the advisability of an appeal and, where appropriate, signed grounds
(iv) the time limit within a copy of counsel's opinion should be forwarded to the client
(v)   the rules and practice relating to loss of time orders
(vi) the activities and costs, including prison visits, relating to advice and assistance on appeals that it is reasonable to fund under the trial legal aid order.

None of the guides contains any provision for the specific problems of clients who do not speak English. Thirty-nine per cent of solicitors and 23% of barristers indicated in their responses that they did not feel able to provide an adequate service to such clients. The following recommendation is a first step towards improving the situation.

Recommendation 2: All forms and written guidance relating to the appeals process should be translated into other languages. The solicitor should include in the brief to counsel a copy of the check-off from Appendix 1 both in English and in the first language of the client where this is different. Counsel should complete both forms at the conclusion of the case. This practice should be included in the guidance documents.

Although many clients are visited in the cells at court immediately following the case, there is no absolute right to such a visit. Both lawyers and prisoners complained of the consultation being cut short by prison or police authorities keen to transport the convicted person to prison. The defendant is often confused and in a state of shock or distress at this time, it may be the last meeting between lawyer and client and time must be made available to allow a written note on counsel's view of an appeal to be handed over and explained.

Recommendation 3: Convicted or sentenced defendants who are legally represented should have a right to a 15 minute meeting with their lawyers at Crown Court following the end of the case for the purpose of discussing counsel's opinion of prospects for an appeal.

Revision of policy documents can only play a limited part in rectifying practices that deny convicted defendants full access to the appeals process. Only through a process of education can there be any real expectation that best practice will become standard practice. For many criminal practitioners, proceeding with an appeal is a relatively infrequent occurrence. Nevertheless, initial procedures relating to provision of advice on appeals apply to all cases that result in a conviction and should form part of the continuing education for lawyers in criminal practice.

Recommendation 4: The Law Society and the Bar Council should take steps to ensure that the guidance they provide on good practice is reflected in the programmes of continuing education for legal practitioners and their representatives working on criminal cases.

Chapter 6

Magistrates

Chapter Contents

One of the most surprising aspects of the English criminal justice system is the vast role given to lay magistrates. Questions of both guilt and sentence in over 95 per cent of all criminal prosecutions are decided by magistrates.

Table 6.1 Number of offenders sentenced in the magistrates' courts (year to March)

2002	1,272,000
2005	1,434,000
2008	1,326,000
2011	1,257,000
2014	1,071,000

Source: Criminal Justice Statistics Quarterly Update to March 2012 (Table Q1.5), Criminal Justice Statistics Quarterly Update to March 2014 (Table Q1.5)

The bulk of these prosecutions were for purely summary offences, which can only be tried in a magistrates' court, and include many minor motoring offences (though not the most minor, which are dealt with by fixed penalty notices issued by the police). The remainder (perhaps 20 per cent) are offences triable either way, which may be tried either in a magistrates' court or in the Crown Court. Even in a case such as Gerry Good's, where he will eventually be tried before a jury, some key decisions are taken in the magistrates' court. Magistrates' justice is cheap and relatively fast – but is amateur justice fair? This question is all the more important given the general shift towards transferring more serious cases down to the magistrates' courts (and the less serious from the courts altogether). It is also important to note the increasing use of lawyer stipendiary magistrates, now known as district judges (magistrates' courts), who sit alone. Is this fairer than a tribunal of lay magistrates? How can we tell?

(i) Role of the lay magistracy

The approximately 21,500 lay magistrates in England and Wales sit in magistrates' courts. Until 1992 the Home Office controlled the organisation of magistrates' courts, whilst the Lord Chancellor appointed and dismissed magistrates. This inconsistency led to the transfer of the management of magistrates' courts to the Lord Chancellor's Department. Meanwhile, new funding arrangements were introduced, putting cash limits on all courts, in effect penalising those that failed to process cases speedily enough. The reorganisation of Magistrates' Courts Committees (MCCs) proposed in the White Paper *A New Framework for Local Justice* was achieved in the Police and Magistrates' Courts Act 1994. Section 69 gave the Lord Chancellor the power to replace two or more MCCs with a single MCC. Under this arrangement, local MCCs, with a Justices' Chief Executive as chief administrative officer, managed the courts. Then the Access to Justice Act 1999 added more flexibility to the rules, allowing alteration of the various territorial units that make up the magistrates' courts service and allowing summary cases to be heard outside the commission area in which they arose. Lord Justice Auld [1:5] recognised the importance of local justice and indeed suggested that 'all members of the judiciary, whether lay or professional, should be brought within the responsibility of the local Resident Judge and the judicial hierarchy of which he is part' (at page 272). He pointed out the difficulty of identifying what precisely it is that is to be valued in 'local justice': he distinguished geographical locality from the locality of those dispensing justice. These issues are explored in depth by Seago et al [6:1] in their research into the expanded use of district judges. Morgan [6:2] argues for greater use of lay magistrates in the criminal justice process, a view which these authors strongly support.

The Courts Act 2003 fundamentally changed the organisation of magistrates' courts. It imposed on the Lord Chancellor a duty to ensure 'an efficient and effective' system to support the courts. The

Act abolished MCCs and created Courts Boards (made up of at least seven members, to include one judge, two magistrates from within the Courts Board area, two people with knowledge or experience of the courts in the local area, and two people who are representative of the people living in the area) and local justice areas which replaced the old commission areas and petty session areas. However, the Courts Boards were abolished by the Public Bodies (Abolition of Courts Boards) Order 2012 (SI 2012/1206) as a consequence of the Coalition Government's programme of reducing the number of non-departmental public bodies. In the explanatory memorandum accompanying the draft 2012 Order, it was stated rather damningly that '[i]n conducting the review of public bodies, the Ministry of Justice first addressed the overarching question of whether a body needed to exist and its functions needed to be carried out at all. It was considered that the answer was no for Courts Boards'. The Courts Boards have not been replaced and this has led Gibbs (2013) to argue that 'now magistrates have no influence over the running of the courts, despite having many ideas on how they could be run more efficiently'.

Prior to October 2013, lay magistrates were appointed by the Lord Chancellor but this power was transferred by the Crime and Courts Act 2013 to the Lord Chief Justice, who delegates the function to the Senior Presiding Judge for England and Wales. In practice, magistrates are recruited and selected by a network of 47 local advisory committees, made up of serving magistrates and local non-magistrates. Until 1992 the names of those on the committees were usually kept secret, but now they are published (most are senior or recently retired magistrates). Magistrates have to retire at 70. They may be dismissed by the Lord Chancellor, with the concurrence of the Lord Chief Justice. Under the Courts Act 2003, section 11 a lay justice can be removed from office on one of three grounds: incapacity or misbehaviour; persistent failure to meet prescribed competence; or neglect of duty.

The key characteristics of the lay magistracy are that they are unpaid and non-lawyers. Nowadays, they receive expenses, but the possibility of lost earnings inevitably deters many potential applicants. A magistrate is expected to sit for at least 13 days/26 half-days a year (or 35 half-days if they also sit in the youth or family courts). For the self-employed this is a hefty commitment, and for those in employment, job and promotion prospects, as well as pay, may suffer. It is not surprising that the social balance of the bench is often criticised. A classic account of the merits of the lay magistracy is provided by Skyrme [6:3]. It is worth comparing his analysis with, for example, the more critical approach of Gifford (1986), who recommended a much more proactive search for magistrates, and suggested that magistrates should only serve limited terms of office in order that they should not become case-hardened. Unfortunately he did not attempt to evaluate the financial implications of his recommendations. Darbyshire (1997) is critical of the class, political, ethnicity and age profile of the magistracy. Have things changed? Table 6.2 provides data on the make-up of the 21,626 serving magistrates as at 31 March 2014.

Women have been well represented for years on the lay magistracy: the typical magistrate for several decades may have been the middle class woman returning to work after her children went to school and wanting useful, but not necessarily paid, part-time employment. However, Gibbs (2014a) notes that '[p]erhaps surprisingly, the magistracy today is less representative of the population in

Table 6.2 Gender, age and ethnicity of the magistracy

	Gender		Age					Ethnicity	
	Male	Female	Under 30	30–39	40–49	50–59	60 & over	White	BME
Total	10,335	11,291	79	556	2,554	6,079	12,358	19,748	1,878
%	47.79%	52.21%	0.37%	2.57%	11.81%	28.11%	57.14%	91.32%	8.68%

Source: Judicial Diversity Statistics, 2014

terms of age and ethnicity than it was 25 years ago' (at page 1). Furthermore, the socio-economic or class profile of the magistracy also requires adjustment if it is to be representative of society as a whole. One of the significant barriers to addressing this issue is the dramatic reduction in the level of recruitment of new magistrates in recent years: according to Gibbs (2014b) the number of annual new joiners to the magistracy has fallen from 1,768 in 2004 to just 300 in 2013. With over eight times the number of leavers in 2013 as joiners, the number of magistrates has declined by over one-quarter since 2007 (see Gibbs (2014b)). How do you address the clear (and growing) age imbalance with so few annual recruits?

Since 1966 magistrates have had to attend compulsory training courses on law and procedure, and on how to act judicially, but these courses are necessarily brief. The training for new magistrates is now designed and directed by the Judicial College, and lasts for three days. New magistrates are also mentored during their first 12 to 18 months and are appraised at the end of this process; throughout their magisterial career, magistrates undertake continuing training and are appraised every three years. But to criticise them because they are not legally trained is to miss the point: they are chosen as lay people, and advised on the law by a professional clerk. Since they normally sit in benches of three, junior magistrates have plenty of time to learn from their senior colleagues. However, Gibbs (2014a) is critical of the training magistrates receive, describing it as 'incomplete' as it fails to examine the causes of crime, the effectiveness of sentences, and does not include visits to see community sentences in action.

Most of the magistrates' work is done in open court, though they may sign arrest and search warrants and emergency protection orders at home. They also have a role in family law, sitting in the Family Proceedings Court, dealing with maintenance, residence and contact orders, as well as questions concerning children in need of care. Criminal cases involving children (under 14) and young persons (14–17 inclusive) are normally dealt with in the Youth Court, where hearings are in private and should be more informal than those before the adult court. There must be at least one magistrate of each sex sitting on the panel of three in the Youth Court. They exercise very different sentencing powers from those available in the adult court.

Riley and Vennard (1988) suggested that defendants have less faith in the magistrates' courts than they do in jury trials. Even the supposed cost advantages need to be properly evaluated. Of course, minor offences should be processed quickly, cheaply and uniformly. Thus, few object to fixed penalties for minor motoring offences. However, more serious offences such as criminal damage up to a value of £5,000 are now triable only by magistrates. Is the line between summary jurisdiction and trials on indictment drawn in the right place? Do you think that Auld's recommendation **[1:5]** of a third, intermediate, tier (a judge and two lay magistrates) should have been explored further?

(ii) District judges

A significant recent development has been the increasing number of district judges (or stipendiary magistrates as they were until 1999). District judges (DJs) are qualified lawyers, who must have a seven-year general qualification (i.e. have held rights of audience in relation to any class of proceedings for at least seven years).

District judges sit alone. Although in theory they share the workload with lay magistrates, in practice they will hear the cases that are likely to last more than one day or which involve difficult points of law – and district judges are likely to wield a strong influence in their courts. As Rozenburg (1994) pointed out: 'Elsewhere in our criminal justice system the initial finding of guilt or innocence is made by ordinary people – juries or magistrates. But a stipendiary magistrate decides the facts as well as the law: he or she is given less pay than a circuit judge for more responsibility. Any move towards the greater use of stipendiaries should be resisted' (at page 341).

Table 6.3 Numbers of district judges (magistrates' courts)/stipendiary magistrates and deputy district judges (magistrates' courts)

	Full-time	Part-time
1990	64 stipendiaries	–
1994	78 stipendiaries	90 acting stipendiaries
1998	78 stipendiaries	90 acting stipendiaries
2003	105 DJs	150 Deputy DJs
2006	134 DJs	158 Deputy DJs
2010	143 DJs	151 Deputy DJs
2014	142 DJs	125 Deputy DJs

Source: Judicial Statistics; Judicial and Court Statistics 2010; Judicial Diversity Statistics 2014

District judges are also perhaps more likely to become case-hardened and judicially 'burnt out' than lay magistrates. The Lord Chancellor set up a working party in 1994 to produce guidelines identifying more clearly the respective roles of district judges and the lay bench. Narey (1997), in his *Review of Delay in the Criminal Justice System*, whilst noting that stipendiaries were 'vastly more effective' in managing the parties in any given case, rejected the possibility of a substantial increase in the number or proportion of DJs. Morgan and Russell's 2000 report **[6:4]**, commissioned on behalf of the Lord Chancellor's Department and Home Office, explored the relationship between lay and professional magistrates. Do you agree with their emphasis on the importance of 'active citizens in an active community'? This report clearly influenced Auld **[1:5]** in his recommendation that magistrates and district judges should continue to exercise their established summary jurisdiction. More recently, research published by the Ministry of Justice **[6:5]** found that whilst magistrates were perceived to have a greater connection with the local community – and thus were better-placed to dispense 'local justice' – DJs were quicker at transacting cases and more adept at case management. The student of the magistrates' courts should watch closely the evolving relationship between professional and lay magistrates: indeed Donoghue (2014) has suggested that the recent approach taken by successive Governments has called into question the viability of a lay magistracy.

(iii) The justices' clerk

The justices' clerk, a barrister or solicitor of not less than five years standing, also has a somewhat ambiguous role in the magistrates' court. A creature of statute (see the Justices of the Peace Act 1968, and now the Courts Act 2003, sections 27 and 28), their role is to provide legal advice to lay magistrates, to deliver certain judicial functions and to supervise those appointed beneath them.

In reality, the clerk in court will be a legal adviser, who may be a qualified barrister or solicitor or who may have recognised Court Clerk qualifications. Since the line between advice and instruction is a thin one, it is difficult to measure whether clerks overstep their purely advisory role. Clerks should, for example, advise on the admissibility of evidence (a question of law) but not on the credibility of a witness (a question of fact). They should advise on appropriate sentences but not on the actual sentence. In recent years, they have also been granted more administrative powers: Narey (1997) went so far as to suggest that the presumption should be that cases should not be put before magistrates until they are ready to proceed. There are concerns that legal advisers and their legal manager, the justices' clerk, might start to usurp the proper role of the magistrates. In their management role, the clerks already have a great influence, since they control the listing of cases. Under the Justices' Clerks Rules 2005 and the Justices' Clerks Regulations 2006, justices' clerks may perform tasks which are authorised to be done by, to or before a single magistrate (allowing agreed adjournments and giving directions for trials). The justices' clerk may delegate these powers to legal advisers. All parties are bound by the Criminal Procedure Rules: see **[7:2]**. Darbyshire (1999) casts a critical eye over the role of the justices' clerk arguing strongly that judicial responsibility should not be delegated to court clerks.

(iv) Bail decisions

Since the accused is presumed innocent until proved guilty, it is hardly surprising that under the provisions of the Bail Act 1976 **[6:6]** there is a general right to bail. As Raifeartaigh (1997) put it, 'the presumption of innocence forbids liberty depriving measures which are premised on the view that the accused is guilty of a crime unless he has been duly convicted by a court of that offence' (at page 18). Does the Bail Act 1976 pass this test? Look at Schedule 1, which provides three grounds for refusing bail – where the court has substantial grounds for believing that if a defendant were remanded on bail, they would: (i) fail to surrender to custody; (ii) commit an offence while on bail; or (iii) interfere with witnesses or otherwise obstruct the course of justice. All turn on questions of predicting risk. However, Schedule 1 was amended by Schedule 11 to the Legal Aid, Sentencing and Punishment of Offenders Act 2012 to introduce an additional safeguard: now a defendant should not be remanded in custody if 'it appears to the justice of the peace that there is no real prospect that the person will be sentenced to a custodial sentence in the proceedings'.

The Criminal Justice and Public Order Act 1994 curtailed the right to bail by introducing two exceptions. Under section 25, a person charged with, or convicted of, murder or attempted murder, rape or attempted rape, or manslaughter, was to be automatically remanded in custody if they had previous convictions for any of those offences. Similarly, under section 26, those accused or convicted of an indictable offence, or one triable either way which appeared to have been committed when the defendant was on bail, 'need not' be granted bail. Imprisonment without trial sits uncomfortably alongside the presumption of innocence, and the European Court of Human Rights found in *Caballero v United Kingdom* (2000) 30 EHRR 643 (followed in *SBC v United Kingdom* (2001) 34 EHRR 619) that the automatic denial of bail was an infringement of the European Convention on Human Rights, Article 5 **[1:13]**. The Government had already anticipated this finding: section 25 was amended by the Crime and Disorder Act 1998, section 56, and again more significant amendments were made by the Criminal Justice Act 2003. The Coroners and Justice Act 2009, however, placed further restrictions on bail for defendants charged with murder: section 115 removes the power of magistrates to consider bail in murder cases, with such decisions now reserved for judges of the Crown Court; section 114 provides that a defendant who is charged with murder may not be granted bail unless the court is of the opinion that there is no significant risk that, if released on bail, he or she would commit an offence that would be likely to cause physical or mental injury to another person. There is, therefore, in effect a presumption against bail in murder cases.

However, the reality is that many suspects are indeed existing offenders and cannot responsibly be left in the community pending their trial. The right of the public to protection and the rights of the suspect thus clash dramatically.

It should be noted that although the number of remand prisoners has grown since 1992, the proportion of prisoners who are on remand has actually shrunk considerably. This is because of the growing prison population over the past two decades. The 10,100 remand prisoners in 1992 made up almost one-quarter of the overall prison population whereas today, due to the doubling of the prison population since the early 1990s, the 12,322 people on remand account for around one-seventh of those in custody.

Conditions for remand prisoners are some of the worst in English and Welsh prisons. The thematic reviews of conditions for unsentenced prisoners, carried out by HM Chief Inspector of Prisons in 2000 and 2012 (**[6:7]** and **[6:8]**), make uncomfortable reading. Although remand prisoners have

Table 6.4 Numbers of remand prisoners

	Average remand population in prisons
1992	10,100
1998	12,600
2000	11,270
November 2007	12,879
September 2010	12,706
September 2014	12,322

Source: Prison Statistics 1998, 2001; Population in Custody (monthly figures); Offender Management Statistics Quarterly Bulletin

rights and entitlements not available to sentenced prisoners (such as additional visits), the benefits of these may be outweighed by the conditions in which they are likely to be held in crowded local prisons: the 2012 report [6:8] found that 29 per cent of remand prisoners said they had spent less than two hours out of their cells each day, and only 42 per cent had spent more than four hours out of their cell. Whilst unconvicted prisoners should be offered the opportunity to work (although they are entitled to choose not to), a lack of places and/or the prioritisation of sentenced prisoners meant that such opportunities were very limited in practice. Furthermore, only 41 per cent of remand prisoners said they had access to outside exercise three or more times a week. The 2000 report [6:7] noted the enormous social and economic dislocation caused by a period of imprisonment. For example, 41 per cent of unsentenced women are held more than 50 miles from home. This figure rose to 44 per cent for young women. Before custody, one-third of men and one-quarter of women had been in employment, but only 18 per cent of men and 11 per cent of women expected to have a job to go to on release. As a group, remand prisoners tend to be anxious, socially isolated, victimised and disturbed. Shockingly, of the 75 self-inflicted deaths in English and Welsh prisons in 2013, 28 were prisoners on remand. It is obviously a particularly difficult time for prisoners.

Could more of these people have been safely left in the community? Two contrasting figures should be looked at: offending rates by those on bail; and the acquittal rate of those who have been remanded in custody. Morgan (1992) showed the difficulties involved in assessing the rates of offending while on bail, though the proportion of defendants convicted of offences committed whilst on bail is about 10–12 per cent. However, some of those remanded in custody will, of course, be acquitted: in the year to June 2014, 9.1 per cent of those remanded in custody in the magistrates' courts and 11.7 per cent of those remanded in the Crown Court were acquitted or not proceeded with – and even if convicted, not all will receive an immediate custodial sentence. Of those remanded and sentenced in the magistrates' court, 12.5 per cent were ultimately sentenced to either a discharge, a fine, a community sentence, or a suspended sentence; and 12.2 per cent of those sentenced in the Crown Court having been remanded in custody received one of those four disposals (Criminal Justice Statistics Quarterly: June 2014, Table Q3a).

Let us apply the test to Gerry Good. How can we know if he will turn up for trial, or whether he will commit an offence while on bail? He has a criminal record, but he is meant to be presumed innocent of his present offence until proved guilty. Are magistrates adequately equipped to evaluate the risks he presents? We noted in Chapter 3 the lack of information available to the courts in deciding bail applications. In the early 1990s, there were significant efforts to improve the quality of this information. In 1992, Lloyd [6:9] analysed the impact of various bail information schemes and tried to assess whether such information is best presented to the court direct, or via the Crown Prosecution Service or defence solicitors. Morgan and Henderson [6:10] reported on the Bail Process Project, set up in 1992 in five court areas to improve the quality of information available to magistrates. Their conclusion that reducing waiting times for trials would reduce the rate of offending on bail can have come as no surprise!

Funding cuts have meant that much less is being done to provide bail accommodation. To try and reduce the population of unconvicted prisoners, the Government awarded a national contract to ClearSprings Ltd in 2007 to provide privately run bail hostels. In 2010, the contract to run these bail hostels was taken away from ClearSprings Ltd and awarded to another organisation, Stonham, who now run the Bail Accommodation and Support Service (BASS). It is questionable whether giving a large, national contract to one provider is the best way to operate such services.

A key question is whether it is just to remand someone in custody because of a statistical risk that they will re-offend. Eaton (1987) usefully pointed out the added hurdle faced by women who are not tied into typical family models: they are less likely to be granted bail. Her conclusion was stark: 'In applications for bail, we have more than a description of an acceptable model of the family and its associated gender roles: we have an acknowledgement that such a family structure may offer a form of control comparable to that offered by the prison system' (at page 106). Worrall (1987) developed this analysis of women as 'socially constructed within the discourses of domesticity, sexuality and pathology' (at page 122) when she contrasted the attitudes of women magistrates to women defendants with the attitudes of their male colleagues on the bench. With regard to magistrates' treatment of defendants from different ethnic groups, Brown and Hullin (1993) studied contested bail applications in Leeds in 1989 and did not uncover any significant differences in treatment. There is clearly a need for much more current research to test whether the situation has changed.

In Gerry Good's case, the bail application lasts less than 20 minutes. The magistrates grant him bail subject to two conditions: one that he does not go within 500 yards of the Black Bull public house, and the second that he reports to the police station three times a week. They lecture him on the need to avoid his victim, and their decision is clearly influenced by the fact that they are convinced by his solicitor, Mary Chapman, that he has a permanent home. Where the magistrates are doubtful about releasing a defendant on bail, they may attach conditions, or require security or sureties. Security involves the deposit of a thing of value, normally a passport, to stop someone leaving the country. Sureties are people who know the defendant and are prepared to put up a sum of money, a recognisance, against the risk that the defendant will fail to appear. Doubts whether it is just to put this pressure on families and friends to act as informal janitors means that sureties are asked for rarely in English courts, and they do not pay the money over in advance. Motivated by a desire to reduce the number of adjournments in criminal proceedings, the Government introduced three measures in the Crime and Disorder Act 1998, which may have resulted in the increased use of sureties (but data is hard to find):

(1) section 54(1) enabled the police and the courts to require a surety in any case where it is believed that the deposit of a security will 'increase the likelihood of a bailed defendant appearing in court when required'. Thus, the court may take the view that an upfront payment, in the form of a surety, will be more effective in securing the defendant's attendance than the availability of a surety with the means to enter into a recognisance for a more substantial sum;

(2) section 54(2) introduced a new power to require a defendant, as a condition of bail, to seek an interview with a legal representative. This addressed the concern that many adjournments are granted simply for the purpose of sorting out legal representation; and

(3) section 55 strengthened existing procedures for the forfeiture of recognisances in bail cases to encourage sureties to make greater efforts to ensure that the defendant appears in court.

Perhaps the best-known recent use of bail sureties was in the case of WikiLeaks founder Julian Assange, whose breach of bail conditions in seeking political asylum, and taking up residence in the Ecuadorian Embassy in 2012, led to a six-figure forfeiture of the surety put up by a group of supporters.

More important has been the increased use of electronic tagging for adults granted bail (since September 2005). Geoghegan (2012) in his report, *Future of Corrections: Exploring the use of electronic monitoring*, estimated that in 2012, almost 10,000 people on a given day were on an electronic tag whilst on bail. But it is not clear that electronic tagging is reducing the remand population: is it instead being used where otherwise offenders might have received unconditional bail? Again, we need more research (but see Cassidy et al (2005)).

What rights of appeal exist from the bail decisions taken by magistrates? It is perhaps surprising that it was not until the Bail (Amendment) Act 1993 **[6:11]** that the prosecution first gained a right of appeal where a court granted bail to someone charged with a serious offence. The Criminal Justice and Public Order Act (CJPOA) 1994, section 30 also strengthened the courts' powers to reconsider a bail decision at any time in indictable cases if information comes to light that was not available to the police or the court when the original bail decision was taken. The 1993 Act has been amended many times and the version we publish here is the most recent: major changes were introduced in both the Criminal Justice Act 2003 and the Police and Justice Act 2006 to simplify appeal procedures; a further amendment was made by the Legal Aid, Sentencing and Punishment of Offenders Act 2012 to enable the prosecution to appeal to the High Court against a Crown Court decision to grant bail (provided that this decision had not already been made as a result of an appeal to the Crown Court from the magistrates' court).

Under the Magistrates' Courts Act 1980, section 128, a magistrates' court has the power to remand a defendant in custody for up to eight days in the first instance, but thereafter may remand them for up to 28 days, provided that the defendant is present in court and has previously been remanded for the same offence. He may be remanded in custody in his absence if he consents. On conviction but pending appeal, the offender may apply for bail. Part 68 of the Criminal Procedure Rules 2014 deals with Bail Pending Appeal. Whether a person should be kept in custody pending an appeal against conviction, or indeed between conviction and the time sentence is passed, raises similar questions to those discussed above.

(v) Mode of trial

All crimes are either indictable, summary or 'triable either way'. Indictable offences are tried by judge and jury in the Crown Court (see the next two chapters); summary offences in the magistrates' court. In cases involving either way offences, the venue for trial is determined following a procedure laid down by the Magistrates' Courts Act 1980, sections 19–20. If the magistrates decide that the case is suitable to be dealt with summarily, they inform the defendant that they might either consent to be tried in the magistrates' court or elect to be tried before a jury. The list of offences which are triable either way is hardly logical and the categorisation of offences makes sense only if one looks at the nineteenth-century origins of much of the criminal law, and the piecemeal way in which some offences have been re-classified downwards in recent years in order to avoid the costs of trial by jury. National Mode of Trial Guidelines, designed to help magistrates decide whether to commit a case for trial, were issued in 1990 by the Lord Chief Justice (although this has since been superseded by the Sentencing Council's allocation guideline, which came into effect in June 2012 **[6:12]**).

The Home Office consultation paper *Determining Mode of Trial in Either-Way Cases* (1998), had laid the ground for the Home Secretary's announcement in 1999 that magistrates, rather than defendants, should decide whether an either-way case should go to jury trial. The Government introduced in the House of Lords the Criminal Justice (Mode of Trial) Bill 1999, which sought to remove defendants' rights to choose trial by jury, but this was defeated. The Government, undeterred, reintroduced the Bill in the House of Commons but was met by a similar revolt. Consideration of whether the Government's offensive on the defendant's right to elect jury trial is well placed must wait until Chapter 8!

(vi) Pre-trial hearings

It is important that weak cases be filtered out. Until 1967, all cases to be tried by jury went through a preliminary hearing in the magistrates' court (committal proceedings) where the magistrates took oral evidence to decide whether the prosecution had made out a *prima facie* case. From 1967 the vast majority of cases were dealt with as 'paper committals'. Where an accused person was legally represented, magistrates' courts could, with defendants' agreement, commit for trial to the Crown Court without any consideration of the evidence. In other cases, the court examined the strength of the evidence and decided whether it warranted committal for trial. However, the CJPOA 1994 sought to abolish committal proceedings: the prosecution was now simply to give a notice of transfer to the defendant and to the court, and unless the defendant applied to have the case dismissed, the notice of transfer would take effect automatically. These provisions, which were hastily added to the Bill, proved unworkable and were never brought into force. Narey (1997) concluded that indictable-only cases should start their life in the Crown Court rather than starting in the magistrates' courts, and this was enacted in the Crime and Disorder Act 1998, section 51. Offenders charged with indictable offences are simply 'sent' to the Crown Court for trial. How are weak cases to be filtered out? Defendants may apply for the dismissal of any charge at any time before they are arraigned (see Schedule 3 to the 1998 Act).

Meanwhile, the Criminal Procedure and Investigations Act 1996 introduced a new 'plea before venue' system, which meant that defendants who intend to plead guilty to either-way offences are automatically dealt with summarily. Since sentences imposed by magistrates are significantly less severe, this must seem unproblematic for those who wish to take the benefit of this, and of the discount for guilty pleas. But it puts further pressure to plead guilty on those who genuinely wish to contest their guilt, and who have not yet seen or heard the prosecution case against them. It also resulted in an extraordinary increase in the number of people committed by magistrates for sentence in the Crown Court: from 7,303 in 1997 to 19,192 in one year (1998/99), a figure which has remained fairly constant (approximately 19,200 in the year to June 2014) (data from Sentencing Statistics, 2006, Table 1.1 and Criminal Justice Statistics Quarterly: June 2014, Table Q3a). These people have pleaded guilty, but the magistrates decide that the appropriate sentence may well be greater than they have the power to impose.

(vii) Trial and sentencing

In summary trials, if the defendant appears, the court clerk will read out the charge(s) and ask the defendant whether he pleads guilty or not guilty. If the defendant pleads guilty, the court may convict him without hearing the evidence.

In the early 1990s, as more defendants made use of their right to plead not guilty, so greater pressures were put on them to plead guilty, thus further undermining due process safeguards. Thus, discounts for guilty pleas were introduced in section 48 of the Criminal Justice and Public Order Act

Table 6.5 Proportion of defendants in magistrates' courts pleading guilty

2003/04	62.8%
2005/06	62.4%
2007/08	67.5%
2009/10	67.6%
2011/12	68.4%
2013/14	72.2%

Source: Crown Prosecution Service Annual Reports

1994, and are now governed by section 144 of the Criminal Justice Act (CJA) 2003 and the Sentencing Guidelines Council's guideline on *Reduction in Sentence for a Guilty Plea* **[7:4]**. We deal with this in Chapter 7, simply because the one-third discount has a bigger (and therefore more controversial) effect in sentencing decisions made in the Crown Court.

If a defendant pleads not guilty, the magistrates will hear the evidence from both parties, and either convict the defendant or dismiss the case. Many researchers have suggested that magistrates are 'prosecution-minded' and 'conviction-minded'. Thus, Parker, Sumner and Jarvis (1989) concluded that magistrates reinterpret legislation and court reports in order to make a moral assessment of each offender; and that local sentencing traditions are maintained by local training, by the apprenticeship model – whereby a magistrate spends several years as a 'winger' before taking the chair in court – and by the local selection process. Brown **[6:13]** interviewed many magistrates in six different courts, carrying out a 'sociological study in the construction of knowledge in organisational life', leading her to conclude that magistrates deal with cases according to depersonalised routines, which takes away the individuality of defendants.

If the accused fails to appear, the court may, on proof of service of summons, proceed in their absence, or they may adjourn the hearing. The Magistrates' Courts Act 1980, section 12 allows defendants to plead guilty by post for certain minor offences (and since March 2015 defendants are able to enter a plea online to some motoring offences). Where they are convicted, the court may proceed to sentence immediately, or it may adjourn the case if further information is required before sentencing. If magistrates decide that their sentencing powers are inadequate they may commit the convicted offender to the Crown Court for sentence. As a result of the plea before venue introduced in 1997 (see above), there has been a significant increase in the number of cases being committed for sentence. Cases committed to the Crown Court for sentence are heard by a judge sitting with between two and four magistrates. The Access to Justice Act 1999, section 79 removed the requirement for magistrates to sit on committals for sentence. Whilst this change might have been economical, it removed a useful mechanism for developing consistency in magistrates' sentencing practice. In fact, it was not brought into force and was repealed in 2004.

Governments seem to enjoy changing the law on sentencing! Let us start the story with the Powers of Criminal Courts (Sentencing) Act 2000, which was a welcome attempt to codify sentencing law. It built on the Criminal Justice Act 1991, which had introduced a new framework for sentencing. The underlying message of the 1991 Act was that the sentence should be in proportion to the seriousness of the offence of which the offender was convicted. At the time, it was not clear what effect the Act would have on sentencers: at one level, it appeared to reproduce in a convoluted and complicated way much of what sentencers were already doing. However, it was not long before the government panicked and 'toughened up' the message – by means of the Criminal Justice Act 1993 – in what Ashworth and Gibson (1994) called 'one of the most remarkable volte-faces in the history of penal policy in England and Wales' (at page 101).

An example of 'toughening up' was the replacement of the original section 29 of the Criminal Justice Act 1991, which required the court to ignore previous convictions unless they demonstrated aggravating features of the offence for which sentence was being passed. This section made little sense, but probably only meant that a bad record should not lead to a disproportionate sentence. However, the Home Secretary feared that the section might be being interpreted as meaning that courts were no longer allowed to take notice of previous convictions. Less than 12 months after coming into force, section 29 was amended by the Criminal Justice Act 1993 to state that courts 'may' take into account any previous convictions of the offender or 'any failure of his to respond to previous sentences' (currently, under section 143(2) of the CJA 2003, relevant and recent previous convictions 'must' be treated as an aggravating factor).

Many, many Acts of Parliament have tinkered with the sentencing framework since 2000: but the CJA 2003 introduced the most radical changes. Part 12 of this Act concerns sentencing. It starts with general provisions including a section which specifies the 'purposes of sentencing'. Thus, section 142 provides that:

(1) Any court dealing with an offender in respect of his offence must have regard to the following purposes of sentencing–
   (a) the punishment of offenders,
   (b) the reduction of crime (including its reduction by deterrence),
   (c) the reform and rehabilitation of offenders,
   (d) the protection of the public, and
   (e) the making of reparation by offenders to persons affected by their offences.

The Act also sets out principles for determining the seriousness of an offence (section 143), for reductions in sentences for early guilty pleas (section 144), and aggravating factors where the offence was motivated by the offender's race, religion, disability or sexual orientation (sections 145–146). Sections 147–151 set out general restrictions on imposing community sentences and sections 152–153 perform a similar function in relation to custodial sentences. Sections 156–160 set out the procedural requirements for imposing community and custodial sentences. They deal, in particular, with pre-sentence reports and other requirements in the case of mentally disordered offenders. Section 161 provides for pre-sentence drug testing when the court is considering imposing a community sentence or a suspended sentence in order to help the court to decide whether drug treatment and testing is necessary (although this provision has never been brought into force). Sections 162–165 deal with the court's powers to impose and remit fines.

Chapter 2 of Part 12 of the 2003 Act provides for Community Orders for offenders aged 16 or over. For offences committed before the implementation of the Act there were a number of different community orders: Community Rehabilitation Orders (until 2000 known as Probation Orders); Community Punishment Orders (previously Community Service Orders); Community Punishment and Rehabilitation Orders (previously Combination Orders); Curfew Orders; and Drug Treatment and Testing Orders, Drug Abstinence Orders, and Exclusion Orders. This Act created a single generic community sentence, which combines requirements previously available under different community sentences. The requirements available with a generic community sentence are:

- compulsory (unpaid) work;
- participation in any specified activities;
- programmes aimed at changing offending behaviour;
- prohibition from certain activities;
- curfew;
- exclusion from certain areas;
- residence requirement/foreign travel prohibition requirement;
- mental health treatment (with consent of the offender);
- drug treatment and testing (with consent of the offender);
- alcohol treatment (with consent of the offender);
- supervision;
- attendance centre requirements (for those under 25).

Magistrates also have the power to send offenders to prison for up to six months for one offence, or up to 12 months in total. (The CJA 2003 extended this to 12 months for a single offence, but this has not been brought into force.) Because of the short sentences that they serve, whilst those sentenced by magistrates' courts account for only about 10 per cent of the prison population, they account for nearly half of those sent to prison in any one year.

Suspended sentences came back into fashion in the CJA 2003. They were first introduced in 1967, but the Criminal Justice Act 1991, with its emphasis on desert and commensurate sentences, had specified that they could only be imposed in 'exceptional circumstances'. However, under the CJA 2003 (see sections 189–195), a court was empowered to suspend a custodial sentence of up to 12 months for between six months and two years on condition that the offender undertakes activities in the community (these activities are chosen by the court from the list available under the generic community sentence) – and suspended sentences were given a further boost by the Legal Aid, Sentencing and Punishment of Offenders Act 2012, section 68 which doubled, to 24 months, the maximum length of sentence which can be suspended. If the offender breaches the terms of the suspension, the suspended sentence is likely to be activated. The commission of a further offence during the period of suspension also counts as a breach, and the offender's existing suspended sentence is normally activated when the court sentences him for the new offence. The Criminal Justice and Immigration Bill 2007 had proposed removing the power of magistrates to suspend a sentence of imprisonment as the use of suspended sentences for summary offences had increased dramatically after the CJA 2003 provisions came into force in April 2005; the Government was concerned that many people were now receiving suspended sentences who would previously have received community penalties. However, the effect of this change may of course have been to increase the number of immediate sentences of imprisonment and this clause was removed from the Bill before it became the Criminal Justice and Immigration Act 2008. This is a good example of the need for detailed empirical research into magistrates' sentencing decision-making: research evidence which is sadly lacking (although see Mair et al (2007) and (2008)).

The most common penalty in the magistrates' court is a fine. How should these be fixed? Unit fines were introduced in 1992 (by the Criminal Justice Act 1991), designed to enable the court to deprive offenders of a proportion of their disposable weekly income for a number of weeks, and so to be fairer between offenders of different wealth. They were abolished after less than a year, largely because the individual units had been inappropriately valued and because defendants were reluctant to fill in the means form. No attempt was made to improve the unit fines system: it was abruptly dumped. For many years, magistrates simply followed the advice of the Magistrates' Association (a voluntary association to which most magistrates belong): 'if imposing a fine, remember to increase or decrease the amount according to the financial circumstances of the offender' before guidance on how to approach the assessment of fines was issued in the Sentencing Guidelines Council's Magistrates' Court Sentencing Guidelines in 2008. Flood-Page and Mackie (1998), in their study of sentencing practice in magistrates' courts in 1994/95, found a wide range of methods used to calculate the size of a fine. They also found a decline in the use of fines (and compensation orders), concluding that 'if some probation schemes require greater resources but achieve more, as some evidence suggests, then there may be a case for reversing the decline in the use of fines partly in order to release resources for more effective intervention with fewer offenders' (at page 129). The Sentencing Advisory Panel commissioned research in 2007 (see Raine et al (2007)) which concluded that the detailed approach and working practices continued to vary between different courts and indeed different sentencers. Until March 2015, magistrates could only impose a fine of up to £5,000 but they can now impose unlimited fines in certain cases (the limit was removed by the Legal Aid, Sentencing and Punishment of Offenders Act 2012 but there was a significant delay before this provision was brought into force).

The Sentencing Guidelines Council (since abolished along with the Sentencing Advisory Panel by the Coroners and Justice Act 2009 and replaced by the Sentencing Council) issued the Magistrates' Court Sentencing Guidelines in 2008 and all guidelines issued by the Sentencing Council apply also in magistrates' courts. Such guidelines have been available for a number of years. As long ago as 1966, the Magistrates' Association produced 'Suggestions for Road Traffic Penalties', and in

1989 a 'Sentencing Guide for Criminal Offences (other than Road Traffic)', together with a table of suggested compensation levels.

The role of the higher courts in laying down sentencing guidelines for magistrates is minimal, since most appeals are heard by the Crown Court, whose decisions receive little publicity. It is unsurprising therefore that magistrates' sentencing has long been criticised for its inconsistencies and local variations. However, the truth is that we know very little about this important area: there is a huge need for empirical studies of sentencing practices.

Magistrates have the power to correct their errors within 28 days, under the Magistrates' Courts Act 1980, section 142. Until 1990, magistrates, although indemnified out of public funds, were personally liable for acting in excess of jurisdiction. Fear that too many claims would lead to defensive judging, which is not in the public interest, led to the amendment of the Justices of the Peace Act 1979, sections 44 and 45 by the Courts and Legal Services Act 1990, section 108. This put magistrates on the same footing as judges, and they are now only liable where they act in bad faith, even when acting outside their jurisdiction.

A final but important discretionary power of magistrates relates to costs, under the Prosecution of Offences Act 1985, section 16. If a defendant is acquitted, they are not automatically entitled to costs, and even if an order as to costs is made, it may be for a lesser sum than the amount that was actually spent.

A conclusion: we believe that there is an important role for lay magistrates in the criminal justice process. Do you?

Further reading

Ashworth, A, *Sentencing and Criminal Justice* (5th edition, 2010) Cambridge University Press

Ashworth, A and Gibson, B, 'The Criminal Justice Act 1993: Altering the Sentencing Framework' [1994] Crim LR 101

Brown, I and Hullin, R, 'Contested Bail Applications: the treatment of ethnic minority and white offenders' [1993] Crim LR 107

Cassidy, D, Harper, G and Brown, S, *Understanding Electronic Monitoring of Juveniles on Bail or Remand to Local Authority Accommodation* (2005) Home Office Online Report 21/05

Darbyshire, P, 'An Essay on the Importance and Neglect of the Magistracy' [1997] Crim LR 627

Darbyshire, P, 'For the New Lord Chancellor – Some Causes for Concern about Magistrates' [1997] Crim LR 861

Darbyshire, P, 'A Comment on the Powers of Magistrates' Clerks' [1999] Crim LR 377

Donoghue, J C, 'Reforming the Role of Magistrates: Implications for Summary Justice in England and Wales' (2014) *Modern Law Review* 77(6): 928

Eaton, M, 'The Question of Bail' in Carlen, P and Worrall, A (eds), *Gender, Crime and Justice* (1987) Open University Press

Faulkner, D (ed), *The Magistracy at the Crossroads* (2012) Waterside Press

Flood-Page, C and Mackie, A, *Sentencing Practice: an examination of decisions in magistrates' courts and the Crown Court in the mid-1990s* (1998) HORS No 180, HMSO

Gibbs, P, 'Return magistrates' courts to local control' (2013) *The Law Society Gazette*, 3 June

Gibbs, P, *Fit for Purpose: do magistrates get the training and development they need?* (2014a) Transform Justice

Gibbs, P, *Magistrates: Representatives of the People?* (2014b) Transform Justice

Gifford, T, *Where's the Justice?* (1986) Penguin

Grove, T, *A Magistrate's Tale: A Front Line Report from a new JP* (2003) Bloomsbury

Hucklesby, A, 'Bail in Criminal Cases' in McConville, M and Wilson, G (eds), *The Handbook of the Criminal Justice Process* (2002) Oxford University Press

Mair, G, Cross, N and Taylor, S, *The use and impact of the Community Order and the Suspended Sentence Order* (2007) Centre for Crime and Justice Studies

Mair, G, Cross, N and Taylor, S, *The Community Order and the Suspended Sentence Order: The views and attitudes of sentencers* (2008) Centre for Crime and Justice Studies

Morgan, P M, *Offending While on Bail: A Survey of Recent Studies* (1992) HORPU Paper No 65, HMSO

Morgan, R and Russell, N, *The Judiciary in the Magistrates' Courts* (2000) Home Office

Parker, H, Sumner, M and Jarvis, G, *Unmasking the Magistrates* (1989) Open University Press

Raifeartaigh, U N, 'Reconciling bail law with the presumption of innocence' (1997) 17 OJLS 1

Raine, J, et al, *Methods of Calculating Fines in Magistrates' Courts* (2007), Sentencing Advisory Panel

Riley, D and Vennard, J, *Triable-either-way Offences: Crown Court or Magistrates' Court?* (1988) HORS No 98, HMSO

Rozenberg, J, *The Search for Justice* (1994) Hodder & Stoughton

Walker, N and Padfield, N, *Sentencing: Theory, Law and Practice* (2nd edition, 1996) Butterworths

Worrall, A, 'Sisters in Law? Women Defendants and Women Magistrates' in Carlen, P and Worrall, A (eds), *Gender, Crime and Justice* (1987) Open University Press

Documents

[6:1] Seago, P, Walker, C and Wall, D, 'The Development of the Professional Magistracy in England and Wales'
[2000] Crim LR 631 (at page 648)

Stipendiary magistrates as out-of-towners

Judicial independence might be compromised in a third, primarily geographical, sense if power is centralised through the expansion of stipendiaries. On this ground, there is the fear that local justice will erode as the links with local communities, as reflected through the backgrounds, experience and outlooks of lay justices, are diluted. Public confidence in the judiciary, in part generated by the judiciary being identifiable with the society which it judges, might then be dented. According to the Home Affairs Committee Report, the Lord Chancellor's Department makes a clear distinction between lay and professional magistrates in terms of how far they should represent the community, but it accepts that in order to ensure confidence, the public should see people like themselves on the bench.[1]

One might begin to explore this allegation in the same way as the previous allegation, in other words, to consider whether stipendiaries should be viewed as unreflective of local interests and then to consider the ways in which the lay magistracy might avoid this charge. However, the furtherance of local justice may, unlike the previous sites for debate, be itself a contested value, the justifiability of which must also be explored.

The localism of lay and professional magistrates

The concept of geographically sensitive justice is troublingly vague, but such a lay 'bench ethos' can be constructed from what Carlen calls a 'mass of situationally evolved knowledge'.[2] Lay magistrates do seem to view themselves as the 'custodians of the community', representing

---

1   *Home Affairs Committee Report*, para. 11; *Hansard*, H. L. Debs, Vol. 573, col. 1122, June 27, 1998, Lord Irvine.
2   P. Carlen, *Magistrates' Justice* (Martin Robertson, London, 1976), p.75.

and understanding the locality and its customs and values, so that a 'threat to the community becomes a threat to the magistracy and vice versa.'[3] In addition, the rules of appointment expressly state that magistrates must live within 15 miles of the boundary of the commission area.[4] By contrast, as already described, stipendiary magistrates will have a nation-wide commission throughout England and Wales under section 78 (1) of the Access to Justice Act 1999, as opposed to their present appointment to a commission area, although they will still be allocated to a base court. The expectation is that they will become more mobile, which could provide some support for the supposition that stipendiary magistrates are less socially reflexive than lay magistrates.

A counter-argument to the claims of lay localism is that localism is itself much diluted in contemporary times. There are, for example, far fewer magistrates' courts sites than in the past, so that any local attachments will be less strong for all justices, whether lay or professional. This trend was given a boost by a Home Office Consultation Paper on *The Size of Benches*[5] which pressed for both the abolition of benches with fewer than 12 magistrates and also a reduction in the number of petty sessional areas. Consequently, the number of benches has been reduced from nearly 650 to under 400 as a result. The administrative squeeze has also been backed by cash limits from 1992 onwards, all of which prompted the closure of smaller court-houses in favour of larger inner-city court buildings. This combination of changes could be said to remove the physical and symbolic link between localities and magisterial justice,[6] though one might argue that the socio-geographical bounds of 'localities' are now considerably wider, so that the alteration of the court boundaries is in correspondence with the expansion of, for example, manageable drives to work, shops or entertainment. The logical next step would be to rationalise further in terms of the provision of judicial administration. In this way, as justice becomes less localised, why should magistrates' courts buildings be distinct from Crown Court buildings? Why should there be a separation of the staff working within them? And most controversial of all, in the absence of any practical need for, as opposed to abstract ideology of, localism, why is there a need for lay justices to reflect local connections?[7]

Local justice as a desirable justice

Even if local justice is a characteristic of lay magistrates more so than stipendiary magistrates, is it consistent with good quality justice?[8] The arguments for it seem to revolve around concepts such as trial by one's peers, as well as the benefits of local knowledge and sensitivity to local needs. More generally, all recent major studies have supported the continuance of a fundamentally lay and local system as a democratic and educative 'bridge' between the public and the courts.[9]

Yet criticism arises whenever local differences do markedly emerge, on the grounds that localism infringes concepts of justice in the sense of treatment as an equal.[10] For example, the

---

3   S. Brown, *Magistrates at Work* (Open University Press, Buckingham, 1991), pp. 111–112.
4   Justices of the Peace Act 1997, s. 6. The Lord Chancellor requires that candidates should have a reasonable degree of knowledge of the area to which they wish to be appointed and generally expects them to have lived in that area for a minimum of 12 months.
5   (1986). See J.W. Raine and M.J. Wilson, *Managing Criminal Justice* (Harvester Wheatsheaf, Hemel Hempstead, 1993), p. 106.
6   Concern on this ground is expressed by the *Home Affairs Committee Report*, para. 198.
7   J.W. Raine and M.J. Wilson, *Managing Criminal Justice* (Harvester Wheatsheaf, Hemel Hempstead, 1993), p. 116.
8   See Z.K. Bankowski, N.R. Hutton and J.J. McManus, *Lay Justice?* (T & T Clark, Edinburgh, 1987).
9   *Home Affairs Committee Report*, para. 198.
10 C. Alugo, J. Richards, G. Wise and J. Raine, 'The magistrates' court and the community' (1996) 160 J.P. 329.

pressure group Liberty complained in their report, *Unequal Before the Law*, in 1992[11] that like cases were not being treated alike in terms of magisterial custodial sentencing differentials. Disproportionate legal aid grants/refusals are also treated as problematic.[12] The Lord Chancellor adverted to the dilemma in a speech in 1999:

> 'Local diversity is your unique strength – the factor which can take into account the idiosyncrasies of local culture and behaviour. But society can be hard in its judgment on what it perceives as inconsistency. The public, and the media, look critically at the decisions of bench against bench. They can interpret differences as proof that the magistrates are uncertain amongst themselves, and that nature of justice that you get depends on where you live.'[13]

Conversely, a professional, non-local background may actually assist independence by ensuring greater standardisation which will engender consumer confidence in judicial standards. One response has been the introduction of training for lay justices since 1966,[14] which might be said to blur the lay/professional boundary.

Conclusion: judicial independence and local accountabilities

Salaried judges predominate in the summary criminal courts of many other common law jurisdictions – including Scotland, Northern Ireland and the Republic of Ireland, as well as Australia, Canada, New Zealand and the USA.[15] However, the wholesale replacement of the lay magistracy is not, and never has been, government policy for England and Wales. The exclusive employment of stipendiary magistrates would be more expensive, and the fundamental principles of citizenship, democracy and the protection of individual rights call for representative, and therefore predominantly lay and local, involvement at all levels of justice whether achieved by a jury or lay magistrates.[16] Though the Criminal Courts Review being conducted by Lord Justice Auld[17] has the authority to reconsider this balance between lay and professional, there are few signs that the demise of the laity in justice, even if recommended, would be politically acceptable.

Equally, the extinction of stipendiary magistrates seems highly impracticable and improbable. In the first place, a significant number of Benches find it difficult to appoint sufficient lay justices, and our calculations suggest that it would probably require thousands of extra volunteers completely to replace the stipendiary magistrates, which would also mean unwieldy Benches of over 700 in the larger City courts. So, the consensus seems to be a compromise between legality and local laity. A strong rhetorical emphasis at the summary level rests upon 'community', as articulated through lay involvement: lay magistrates are 'a bridge between the public and a court system which might otherwise seem remote'.[18] But the lay judiciary must work within a framework of legal formality and have training and professional assistance through clerks – and so they are turned into, what Burney calls, 'half-baked professionals'.[19]

---

11 Custodial sentences made up 4.96 per cent of the total in 1990, but individual petty sessional divisions varied from 17.44 per cent to 0 per cent. See also: R. Hood, *Sentencing in Magistrates' Courts* (Stevens, London, 1962); R. Tarling, *Sentencing Practice in Magistrates' Courts* (Home Office Research Study 56, London, 1979); D. Acres, 'Consistency and sentencing' (1987) 151 J.P. 343, H. Parker, M Sumner and G. Jarvis, *Unmasking the Magistrate* (Open University Press, Milton Keynes, 1989), p. 16.

12 See R. Young and D. Wall, *Access to Criminal Justice* (Blackstone Press, London, 1996), Chap. 7.

13 Speech to the Council of the Magistrates' Association (www.open.gov.uk/lcd/speeches/1999/25–3–99.htm; 1999).

14 See *The Training of Justices of the Peace in England and Wales* (Cmnd. 2856, HMSO, London, 1965).

15 See Sir T. Skyrme, *History of the Justices of the Peace* (Barry Rose, Chichester, 1991) Vol. 3.

16 See *Hansard*, H. L. Debs. Vol. 582, cols 1066, October 29, 1997, Lord Irvine.

17 www.criminal-courts-review.org.uk/.

18 *Home Affairs Committee Report*, para. 198.

19 E. Burney, J.P: *Magistrate, Court, and Community* (Hutchinson, London, 1979), p. 216.

One might then depict the stipendiary as a further form of complementary compromise to community involvement – dealing with cases or case-loads which lay justices find too hot or too heavy to handle. In order to achieve this supportive role, there seems to be broad support for an 'integrationalist' approach whereby there is a greater presence of stipendiaries, but their function is 'to support rather than supersede lay magistrates'.[20] Consistent with this approach, the increase in the number of stipendiaries has been significant but remains very modest and not enough to ensure continuous national coverage in areas without a permanent stipendiary by 'semi-attached' stipendiaries.[21] Nor has the work of stipendiaries been clearly differentiated from that of the lay bench, despite suggestions along these lines by the *Venne Report*[22] and the *Narey Report*.[23]

Alongside independence, another important agenda for the future is accountability with regard to the magistracy, though the tensions between judicial independence and judicial accountability are here evident. One would expect accountability in a system which vaunts its localism, but in what senses, if any, do local judges make themselves accountable for their judicial work? First, there is legal accountability, such as through the giving of reasons (more by stipendiaries than lay justices),[24] through public access to court-rooms, through appeals to the Crown Court or by legal review in the Divisional Court. But legal decisions are not discussed in advance or endorsed after delivery by the general local public. One might argue that judicial independence would be compromised if they were, but these arguments have been faced down in regard to constabulary independence, in respect of which periodic local liaison committee meetings allow for consultation, report and complaint, though not direction or censure, by the public.[25] So, if handled correctly, 'accountability can in fact enhance the public's respect for independence.'[26] Secondly, there is still little obvious accountability in political terms, from individual clerks to the MCCs and from the MCCs to the 'paying authority'.[27]

Why are these major issues of accountability not addressed in any of the policy papers we have discussed? One might conclude that the genuine motivation for the growth of the professional magistracy is driven by the bureaucratic objectives of the New Public Managerialism, which pictures the public, including local offenders, as consumers of services rather than active citizens. The opposition, from lay magistrates, has been pitched at an ideological level, but it is equally an ideology in which the relationship with the community is one way and paternalistic rather than reflexive. Nevertheless, the insertion of a professional magistracy does call into question the justifiability and working of local justice and may, along with other changes expose at the same time the strength of the ideology as well as the weaknesses of its application. If mechanisms of accountability were to be instituted, then the position of the stipendiary in local justice might actually become less anomalous, for there would be a link between professionals and community not currently provided for. Thus, all justices, both lay and professional, would be able to claim that they represented community wishes, and the harmony of judge and judged could be achieved by a more objective conduit than a feeling in the bones of the magistrate.

---

20 *Home Affairs Committee Report*, para. 196.
21 See *Venne Report*, paras 8.4, 8.6.
22 *Venne Report*, para. 5.3.
23 *Narey Report*, para. 14.
24 *R. V. Harrow Crown Court, ex p. Dawe* (1994) 158 J.P. 250.
25 See the Police and Criminal Evidence Act 1984, s. 106.
26 M. L. Friedland, *A Place Apart* (Canada Communications Group, Ottawa, 1995), p.xiii.
27 In relation to a MCC, the 'paying authority' means any responsible local authority whose area comprises all or part of the area to which the MCC relates. The paying authority provides 20% of MCC funding, with the Lord Chancellor's Department responsible for 80%, subject to a cash limit. See the Justices of the Peace Act 1997, ss. 55, 57.

[6:2] Morgan, R, 'Magistrates: The Future According to Auld'
(2002) 29 J of Law and Society 308 (at page 314)

The problem with Auld's dismissive stance [to public opinion] is that it assumes that the judges, and the politicians they advise, are the best and sole arbiters of what system is fair and efficient and suggests that the public must then be persuaded that what the judges have decided is ideal. I consider that position mistaken.

Of course it might be argued that since Auld has endorsed the jurisdiction and role of the lay magistracy, what is the fuss about? There are three ripostes to this. First, Auld's dismissal of public opinion also underpins some of his more radical proposals (regarding access to jury trial, for example). Secondly, it is not clear to me that Auld has endorsed the position of the lay magistracy. Thirdly, Auld has chosen to ignore what the public, were they aware of the fact, would almost certainly find objectionable about the operation of the magistrates' courts as currently constituted, shortcomings which will be exacerbated if Auld's proposals are implemented. I will consider the latter points in reverse order.

1. An aspect of post-code justice ignored?

It is currently a matter of chance whether a defendant in magistrates' court proceedings has his or her case dealt with by lay magistrates or a district judge. It will depend on the court in which the defendant appears (some courts have a full-time district judge, most do not) and the luck of the draw if the defendant appears in a court in which a full-time district judge does sit. There are no allocational rules. There are only general allocational practices, and they vary. Does it matter whether a defendant appears before a district judge sitting alone or lay magistrates sitting as a panel of two or three? The answer, as we have seen, is yes. We do not know if the chances of acquittal are different: the number of trials in our survey were too small to test the proposition. But it makes a substantial difference when it comes to the likelihood of being remanded in custody or sentenced to immediate imprisonment. In cases where there is a possibility of that outcome our defendant is roughly twice as likely to end up in custody if he or she appears before a district judge.

What has Auld to say on this? Very little, save to say that if there is sentencing disparity between lay magistrates and district judges then the district judges are more likely to have got their decisions right:

> 'I believe that District Judges are more likely to follow national practice and sentencing policy guidelines in this respect than magistrates, with their individual traditions and training, and history of disparate sentencing.'

He fails to point out that disparity may be just as much a feature of sentencing by the professional judiciary, something which the professional judiciary, supported by the Lord Chancellor's Department, has taken care to ensure is not investigated. Further, to ensure that lay magistrates are brought into sentencing line Auld proposes that in future their training be organized by the Judicial Studies Board. But he offers no other remedy. He makes no suggestion that lay magistrates and district judges should do other than continue to sit separately in his proposed Magistrates' Division and, as we have noted, he recommends that lay magistrates be excluded from sentencing decisions in his proposed District Division.

The present situation represents the very opposite of what most people think justice demands should be the case. Provision for panel decision-making in more serious cases where issues of liberty are at stake is a safeguard for which there appears to be widespread support. It is significant that since the Auld Report has been published a minister has described the present arrangement as 'odd' and 'arbitrary'.

2. Endorsement of the role of lay magistrates?

Between and on the lines of the Auld Report are several reasons for doubting that the lay magistracy should feel that their role is to be safeguarded.

First, there is Auld's recommendation that in future 'the Lord Chancellor should be more ready to take the initiative to assign a District Judge to an area where, having consulted as appropriate, he is of the view that local justice in the area requires it.' That is, the initiative should not be left to the localities but seized by the centre. Auld's intervention on this issue was prompted by evidence of local benches successfully delaying the appointment of a district judge where the Magistrates' Courts Inspectorate (MCSI) and the Lord Chancellor's Department thought it desirable:

> 'such parochialism demeans the otherwise worthy contribution magistrates make to the running of
> the criminal justice system, and it should no longer hold sway.'

It seems certain that he had in mind the case of Bristol where the recent appointment of a district judge resulted not from a recommendation from the local Lord Chancellor's Advisory Committee but from the MCSI. Senior lay magistrates locally resented the proposition, and following his appointment, the professional incumbent, an experienced stipendiary who had previously worked in London was reputedly given cases to deal with which his lay colleagues considered to be undemanding and probably beneath his dignity – vehicle parking infractions and the like. That is, the lay magistrates delivered a studied insult and asserted their determination not to relinquish to the judge those more serious cases which we must assume they saw his arrival as intending to cream off.

Whatever the rights and wrongs of the Bristol case, it seems likely that Auld's recommendation will be seized on and additional district judges appointed, particularly in areas where there is evidence of delay, where the lay magistrates prove to be less flexible and where there are difficulties recruiting suitable lay magistrates: these conditions are most likely to arise in the metropolitan centres.

Secondly, though Auld says that he sees no case for altering the present balance of lay magistrates and district judges he also says that 'the position may be different' if his recommendation that there be a unified court with an intermediate tier is adopted. There would then be only a compelling case for retaining 'a sizeable lay magistracy' – how sizeable, Auld does not say, though he notes that having many more district judges would 'require a major programme of change' and would take time. It is significant that the relevant Home Office minister has already stated that:

> 'if the District Division becomes a reality, it will be necessary for District Judges to be available
> throughout the country (which, of course, they are not at the moment). If this happens, there may be
> a case for looking again at the distribution of work within the Magistrates' Division.'

I think it is also clear that, in order to pave the way for his District Division, Auld favours substantially increasing the number of district judges who he observes often sit also as recorders and that appointment as a district judge is 'emerging as the first step on a judicial rung that may lead to a permanent appointment as a Circuit Judge and, possibly, beyond'. The vertical integration of the criminal courts implies the further development of judicial careers, both of which I expect to be encouraged. All these developments would have significant implications for the role of the lay magistracy.

Thirdly, it is for above reasons that I doubt lay magistrates should feel greatly reassured by Auld's recommendation that there be no extension of justice's clerks' case management jurisdiction. What is being safeguarded is less the prerogative of lay magistrates and more the developing role of the professional judiciary. Note, for example, that Auld concludes that district judges have no need of a legally qualified clerk to sit with them in court – an anomalous provision to which we drew attention – and that it will be for district judges, not lay magistrates or justices' clerks, to determine the appropriate venue for the hearing of either-way cases in the event of the defence and prosecution disagreeing.

Fourthly, Auld's report has one or two telling comments to make about costs. Auld has practically nothing to say on costs, which makes it all the more striking that he is prepared to suggest that our attempt to estimate the cost implications of employing more district judges in place of lay magistrates is at best incomplete and at worst flawed. We found that:

- estimates of the direct costs to the LCD alone of using two types of magistrate show, not surprisingly, that lay magistrates are far cheaper. A lay justice: we estimated costs £495 per annum compared to £90,000 for a stipendiary, which translates to £3.59 compared to £20.96 per case;
- however, when overheads are loaded into the equation, the difference is far smaller – £52.10 compared to £61.78 per appearance; and
- if opportunity costs are added – a controversial issue in which fairly courageous assumptions have to be made – we estimated that lay magistrates are more expensive – £70.80 compared to £61.78 per court appearance;
- further, if the cost consequences of current differential decision-making, are added, the calculations pull in different directions. Employing more district judges will lead to fewer court appearances as a result of their more robust examination of applications: this would save money. However, district judges' greater use of custody would significantly increase costs for the Prison Service.

Auld thinks, contrary to the Magistrates' Association, that we were correct to include an estimation of opportunity as well as direct costs, but he judged that our calculations were 'necessarily somewhat theoretical and speculative and . . . open to criticism in a number of respects'. Of our conclusion that more district judges would likely add to the number of custodial decisions and thus costs, he says:

> 'Save as a cynical measure of expediency, it would be wrong to consider whether to change the present sharing of summary jurisdiction on the basis that District Judges are too hard or that magistrates are too soft in their decisions as to custody.'

In fact at no stage did we suggest that policy should be decided on the basis of costs: we simply attempted to estimate the likely cost consequences of different policy scenarios. Nevertheless, as we have seen, by saying that if there are sentencing disparities between judges and lay magistrates the district judges are correct, Auld is implicitly arguing that these are extra costs the criminal justice system *should* bear. By contrast the savings accruing from district judges granted fewer adjournments – which might as easily be challenged – Auld is content to accept. Indeed it is apparently not cynical for him to suggest that in our own research we almost certainly underestimated the savings likely to result under this head. He correctly points out, for example, that we failed to estimate – we do not do so because, as we acknowledged, we could find no firm basis on which to do it – the reduced knock-on costs of having fewer court appearances for the police, the legal aid budget, the CPS, and so on. It seems likely that the fact that savings may arise from making greater use of district judges will inevitably encourage their greater use. Indeed, as we argued in our report, if tougher sentencing is set aside (and that might be addressed in training for district judges), the greater the increase in the number of district judges and the greater the displacement of lay magistrates, the more likely it becomes that step savings (resulting from need for fewer courtrooms and a reduced supporting infrastructure, and possibly fewer courthouses) can be achieved.

The above ingredients in Auld suggest less commitment to the current balance of lay magistrates and district judges in the Magistrates' Division than at first appears. If I am correct, and the proportion of appearances in the magistrates' courts is increased, it will have implications for the relationship between two groups. In our survey of lay and stipendiary magistrates we found, not surprisingly, that whereas the stipendiaries could overwhelmingly think of several reasons for having more stipendiaries – faster, more efficient, better able to deal with legally complicated cases, and so on – the majority of lay magistrates could cite no reasons at all. Conversely whereas one or two stipendiaries conceded that there were arguments against having more stipendiaries – that it is unfair to have one person sitting in judgment, for example, the majority of lay magistrates subscribed to several negative arguments. The two groups do not see eye to eye on the possible futures of their respective contribution and since one group comprises unpaid volunteers, this is a factor to be heeded: lay magistrates might widely withdraw their unpaid labour were they to see their own status being diminished and their role reduced. In coming to the conclusion that the business in the magistrates' courts should be allocated as at present, Auld is endorsing the Venne Report which recommended a 'presumption' in favour of stipendiary magistrates, when available, undertaking 'heavier' work. The corollary of additional district judges doing this, if they sit alone, is that lay magistrates are relegated to dealing with the less interesting and challenging work, of having their lists intellectually asset-stripped. This is what the lay magistracy fears and dislikes. There is a real tension here. If lay magistrates perceive their role to be marginalized, it is doubtful whether their continued and widened recruitment can be assured.

The role of magistrates in the proposed district division

One of Auld's answers to the difficulties in recruiting and retaining the services of a socially representative magistracy is the 'attraction' of the 'opportunity to hear more serious and interesting trials' in his proposed District Division. In answer to the practical difficulty of finding lay magistrates with the time to hear such cases, Auld suggests that the proposals he has for the introduction of more flexible magistrates' sitting patterns, combined with evidence of lay magistrates' current availability, make this problem soluble – an opinion with which the Magistrates' Association apparently agrees:

There are many magistrates who, for one reason or another, are not restricted by their employment or other commitments to sitting for half a day a week and who might well relish the opportunity to sit on longer and more substantial cases.

Setting on one side the major arguments which can be made against Auld's proposals for a District Division – arguments which mostly hinge on the great reduction in access to and consequent number of jury trials involved – how practical and logical is the scheme he proposes in terms of lay magistrates' participation?

The first point to make is that Auld's idea of a mixed (lay and professional judges) tribunal conforms broadly to what in our own survey of other jurisdictions we described as the Germano-Scandinavian model, though the arrangement is found in several jurisdictions outside that European region. Mixed tribunals were commended to auld by Sanders. There is one important difference, however. Whereas mixed tribunals in other jurisdictions, and as proposed by Sanders, collectively determine issues of both fact (though generally not law) and sentence, Auld proposes an arrangement [in which] lay magistrates play no part in sentencing. Auld offers two reasons:

- lay magistrates would, he contends, lack the necessary competence and experience: sentencing at this level of seriousness would be very different from sentencing in the summary court and would become more complicated still were the recommendations of the Halliday Report (which proposes sentence review hearings) implemented;
- it would not be practical to involve lay magistrates: following trial most cases would have to be adjourned for sentence and 'it would often be difficult to reconstitute the same panel for the purpose of passing sentence'.

Auld's objections to lay magistrates' involvement in sentencing do not seem to me to be well grounded. If it is possible to find lay magistrates willing and able to sit on trials for several days, it should hardly be difficult to get them to return for a sentencing hearing. As for the suggestion that they lack the necessary competence and experience to do the task, this is likely to be regarded as insulting by lay magistrates and scarcely squares with Auld's earlier argument that in deciding matters of fact the magistrates would not have to be given directions by the judge because of their competence and experience in structured decision-making.

Indeed so disingenuous is Auld's argument for excluding magistrates from sentencing that one wonders whether it is a smokescreen for a more serious consideration, namely, that to concede panel sentencing in the proposed District Division would throw into stark relief and call into question lone sentencing in the Magistrates' and Crown Divisions, something which, as we have seen, our surveys of the public and of lay magistrates is widely considered objectionable (though I should emphasize that we canvassed opinion on this point only with regard to serious decisions in the magistrates' courts). As regards lone sentencing by judges in the Crown Court, Auld maintains that he received no proposals for change, which is odd because the case for panel decision-making in the Crown Court is clearly set out in one submission from a commentator extensively cited by him. Moreover, during the course of undertaking successive research projects I have repeatedly heard barristers argue the shortcomings of lone decision-making by Crown Court judges. As for lone decision-making by district judges in the magistrates' courts Auld, as we have seen, repeatedly had the objections drawn to his attention, but chose to ignore them. What is clear is that if some lay magistrates have the time to sit on lengthy trials in the District Division, they would clearly have time to sit alongside district judges in the Magistrates Division. There is a gap in Auld's logic here.

Other questions remain, however. Were lay magistrates to sit with district judges in the District Division, which lay magistrates would likely do it? And how would they do it?

I have no doubt that some lay magistrates will welcome the opportunity to try contested cases alongside district judges in the District Division and will find time to do it. Our study showed that a minority of lay magistrates are able and do devote much more of their time to the task than the minimum number of twenty-six sittings a year stipulated by the Lord Chancellor. More than one-fifth of lay magistrates already sit more than once a week – that is more than twice the minimum number of sittings – in addition to attendance at meetings, training sessions, and so on. That so many are able and willing to devote so much unpaid time to the task, generally without claiming loss of earnings (86 per cent) and often without claiming expenses either (23 per cent), reflects that fact that the magistracy is overwhelmingly middle-class, two-fifths of whom are retired. We did not analyse our data to consider the socio-economic characteristics of the frequent-sitters, but it would be surprising were they not even more disproportionately from the retired and professional/managerial ranks.

There is a dilemma to be faced, therefore. If lay magistrates are to sit with professional judges in any division they must have the training, experience, and self-confidence to act as equals to challenge the professional judges. For otherwise they may be no more than what one observer has suggested the lay judiciary are generally considered in Germany, 'decorative flower pots'. Auld recognized the objection to mixed panels that they may be dominated by the professional judges. It is an issue on which there is a great deal of anecdotal but virtually no hard evidence both with regard to practice in the Crown Court (where mixed panels hear appeals from magistrates' courts decisions) and the former Quarter Sessions (where magistrates used often to sit with professional judges). The evidence from other jurisdictions is mixed. But, having reviewed that evidence, Doran and Glenn argue that 'the very presence of the lay members may in itself influence the stance adopted by the professional'. Auld is almost certainly correct, however, to doubt that foreign examples are good indicators of the likely pattern here. English and Welsh magistrates are much more highly trained and experienced than their Scandinavian and German counterparts. They sit frequently and separately from professional judges – which their Continental equivalents do not. It is unlikely that they would defer excessively to their professional colleagues.

But the outcome would be different were the sittings of lay magistrates greatly to change. If Sanders's proposal that lay magistrates sit much less frequently were adopted, for example, them mixed tribunals would probably become participative fig-leafs. By the same token, Auld's suggestion that lay magistrates sit in more flexible patterns and possibly less often so as to broaden their recruitment and social representativeness would likely turn out to be something of a sham were magistrates, once appointed, able freely to choose how often and in what court they sat. The bench might *appear* more socially representative, but it would likely be the case that most sittings, and certainly those involving the more serious cases, would involve magistrates more socially unrepresentative than benches are now. Furthermore, at which point does the frequency of sitting engender a case-hardened approach? Auld observed that the practical distinction between lay magistrates and district judges had diminished. At what point do lay magistrates cease to be lay?

There are no easy answers to this dilemma. The essence of the magistracy is that it should be lay and socially representative. But not so lay that it cannot act with justice and self-confidently challenge the professional judges when sitting with them. My own view is that it is objectionable that serious cases should be tried and sentenced by lone judges in the present magistrates' courts. Further, the question raised by Auld's proposed District Court is whether any serious case should be sentenced by a lone decision maker. Finally, I doubt that participation in serious proceedings should be left to the personal decision of individual magistrates. It is desirable that the social composition of the magistracy be broadened. For the same reason it is equally desirable that all magistrates be involved in the trial and sentencing of serious cases.

[6:3] Skyrme, T, *The Changing Image of the Magistracy*
(2nd edition, 1983) Macmillan (at page 6)

At first sight the system seems not only anomalous but indefensible and, having regard to their powers and vast field of responsibility, it is astonishing that the justices have not only survived but have flourished in an age when established institutions have been subject to ever-increasing denigration, when the amateur has been steadily replaced by the professional and when voluntary service is anachronistic in the prevailing climate of totalitarianism. The Justice of the Peace is the kind of historical legacy that one would have expected to be the first to founder in the revolutionary flood of the post-war years. It could not have survived had it not been acceptable to successive governments and to the public at large. The explanation of its acceptability, despite certain latent defects, is probably threefold: first, the depth of the roots of the lay magistracy in the British social system and the inclination of the people to honour tradition and to preserve ancient institutions; second, the ability of the justices, as evidenced in their previous history, to adjust to changing conditions; and third, the intrinsic merits of the system itself which, if exploited and developed, give it a peculiar attraction not shared by any other form of judicial machinery.

The principal defects usually attributed to lay justices are that they are too ready to accept police evidence and that they rely too much on the advice of the clerk. In some degree both criticisms are still valid, though far less so than they were 30 years and more ago, and neither defect is altogether incurable. As against these disadvantages the justices have certain unique qualities on the credit side. From the point of view of the government they have two advantages; they are cheap and they are flexible. As they received no pay they are more cost-effective than a salaried stipendiary, though the difference is not as great as is sometimes assumed because justices work more slowly than stipendiaries and if they have to sit in two or more courts to dispose of the same amount of work there will be the additional cost of extra staff and accommodation; in addition, although not remunerated, justices are entitled to allowances which can amount to a not inconsiderable sum when several of them are sitting. Nevertheless, justices are on the whole cheaper than any other effective method of administering justice than has so far been devised. In 1965, Lord Gardiner caused inquiries to be made in 20 countries to find out in each case the numbers of whole-time judges and the cost of judicial administration. The cost (excluding police and prisons) expressed as a percentage of the annual national budget ranged from 1.46 at the top of the scale to 0.16 in the case of England, Scotland and Wales, who were at the bottom. As regards the number of judges, several counties had more than 200 per million of population while Scotland with 15 and England and Wales with 8 were again at the bottom. As was to be expected, most Common Law countries were in the lowest bracket because of their single-judge systems; thus the United States had 34 judges per million population; Australia 29 and New Zealand 24. These figures should be treated with reserve as some were based on estimates, but the position of England and Wales at the bottom of the league was generally attributed to the much larger proportion of court work disposed of by their unpaid, part-time lay magistrates compared with other countries.

Justices also appeal to the government because their system is flexible; sudden fluctuations in the volume of work can be handled by calling upon justices to sit more or less often in more or fewer courts as the need arises, whereas a whole-time judge or stipendiary has little scope to expand his output if work increases, and if it diminishes he may be left partially unemployed at public expense.

These are not the only inherent merits of a properly constituted lay justice system. Two, or preferably three, heads are better than one and they are better still if they combine intimate knowledge, experience and understanding of the problems facing different sections of the local community, which can often enable them to deal with cases more justly and efficaciously than the professional courts. The collective views of a cross-section of the population, representing different shades of opinion, can be more effective in dispensing justice acceptable to the public than the decision of a single individual necessarily drawn from a fairly narrow social class and whose experience of local problems may be limited. Justices also act as a check on one another and provide a balanced conclusion, whereas there is nothing to curb the general idiosyncrasy or the spasmodic whim or irritability of a single magistrate. Furthermore, as justices attend court at intervals they approach their task with a freshness and objectivity that is lacking in a professional judge who is wholly engaged in adjudicating day after day.

The system of lay justices reflects, through citizens participation, the traditional English involvement of the layman in the administration of justice. It enables the citizen to see that the law is his law, administered by men and women like himself, and that it is not the esoteric preserve of the lawyers. Lord Hailsham, in a speech made when he was Lord Chancellor, stressed the value of the lay magistracy as a unifying factor in society as a whole, and he described their potential influence, not only on the bench but also out of court, as 'one of the characteristic institutions holding our society together'.

The identification of the ordinary citizen with the administration of justice should therefore have a popular appeal, yet when it comes to the test the average citizen seems to prefer to be tried by a professional magistrate. This is most noticeable where there is a clear choice of tribunal, as in family and adoption proceedings, and where preference is normally shown for the professionalism of the county court rather than the lay justices' court. This may be due at least in part to the erroneous view which much of the population hold of the justices today: that they are prejudiced, prosecution-minded, middle-class bigots, motivated by lust for power and totally lacking in any feeling for those who appear before them. This description might not have been far wrong a century ago, when it could have been directed with equal justification at other institutions, but the vast changes that have occurred since then are not generally realised. The detritus of the past has been washed away and the justices of today are able to exhibit some of the latent advantages of the system which were not revealed under their predecessors. A lay justice cannot equal the professional skill of a stipendiary, but the function of magistrates is largely to decide questions of fact and for this purpose to exercise common sense and sound judgment against a background of knowledge and experience of the world at large. By this criterion the quality of the average lay justice is no less than that of the professional stipendiary.

Provided that justices are carefully chosen in the light of their ability, integrity and understanding, and can be seen to be well qualified for their work, and provided also that they are given adequate training and opportunities to enable them to become and remain proficient in the performance of their duties, then it is possible for the layman, who combines experience as a magistrate with experience in other walks of like, to offer advantages which are not to be found in the professional systems; not least of these advantages being the ability to exercise a stabilising influence within the community in which he lives to an extent not open to the professional judge. It is to this end that the reforms of the past 40 years have been largely directed.

(At page 67):

The controversy over the social composition of the magistracy usually turns upon whether benches are predominantly upper-class to the exclusion of the rest of the population. The Lord Chancellor does not seek to strike a numerical balance between representatives of each social group; there seems to be no good reason why he should do so and it would be impossible to achieve this result because of the movement of individuals from one group to another. The declared policy of each Lord Chancellor since 1945 has been to make sure that each bench is a microcosm of the local community within which it operates, and this amounts to seeing that in every petty sessional division there are at least some justices from each of the principal social and political groups in the area and that the bench is not dominated by any one group. I would claim that we have gone a long way towards attaining this object.

[6:4] Morgan, R and Russell, N, *The Judiciary in the Magistrates' Courts*
(2000) HO RDS Occasional Paper No 66, Home Office (from the summary, at page vii)

This research was jointly commissioned by the Lord Chancellor's Department and the Home Office. The study was undertaken during the first nine months of 2000 by a research team comprising the University of Bristol and two commercial companies, RSGB (a division of Taylor

Nelson Sofres plc) and CRG, Cardiff, specialists in market research and cost benefit analysis respectively.

Methodology

The research comprised seven types of data collection:

- baseline information on the budgets, buildings, court staff and magistrates' characteristics. Data were gathered both nationally and locally, and included information on ten magistrates' courts in London and the provinces, with and without stipendiaries
- 2,019 self-completed magistrates' diaries, spanning three-week sessions, covering activities, timings etc. from the ten courts
- 1,120 self-completed magistrates' questionnaires addressing issues of sitting arrangements, their views on balance between lay and stipendiaries etc. from the ten courts
- observations of 535 court sessions at the ten courts
- 400 telephone interviews with regular court users from the ten courts
- public opinion survey: conducted with a nationally representative sample of 1,753 members of public
- 23 responses to a letter to representatives of the Council of Europe Member States.

Composition and working practices of the magistracy

Composition

At the time of the research the magistracy comprised:

- approximately 30,400 lay magistrates
- 96 full-time stipendiaries
- 146 part-time stipendiaries.

The lay magistracy:

- is gender balanced
- is ethnically representative of the population at a national level
- is overwhelmingly drawn from professional and managerial ranks
- comprises a high proportion (two-fifths) who have retired from full-time employment.

In comparison, stipendiaries:

- are mostly male and white
- tend to be younger.

Sitting patterns

Lay magistrates:

- sit in court an average 41.4 occasions annually (although many sit a good deal more frequently)
- devote (taking holidays into account) an extended morning or afternoon to the post once a week

- additionally spend the equivalent, on average, of a full working week on training and other duties.

The contracts of full-time stipendiaries require them to perform judicial duties five days a week, 44 weeks of the year. However there is some ambiguity as to what this means in terms of court sittings. Provincial stipendiaries sit more often than their colleagues do in London, but both groups sit in court closer to four days per week.

Lay magistrates usually sit in panels of three, but sometimes of two (16% of observed panels). Stipendiaries nearly always sit alone but on rare occasions sit together with lay magistrates.

Caseload allocation

While stipendiaries take on more or less the full range of cases and appearances, they tend to be allocated more complex, prolonged and sensitive cases. Unlike lay magistrates, their time is concentrated on triable-either-way rather than summary cases.

Working methods and decision-making

Speed

Stipendiary magistrates deal with all categories of cases and appearances more quickly than their lay colleagues because they retire from court sessions less often and more briefly (0.2 compared to 1.2 occasions per session, for only 3 compared to 16 minutes). They also deal with cases more quickly on average (9 minutes compared to 10 minutes). This means:

- stipendiaries hear 22 per cent more appearances than lay magistrates per standardised court session (12.2 compared to 10)
- if stipendiaries were allocated an identical caseload to lay magistrates, it is estimated that they would deal with 30 per cent more appearances.

The greater speed of stipendiaries is not achieved at the expense of inquisition and challenge; on the contrary, hearings before stipendiaries typically involve more questions being asked and more challenges being made.

Manner of working: adjournments and bail

Both lay and stipendiary magistrates are invariably judged to meet high standards in dealing with court business (attentiveness, clarity of pronouncements, courtesy, and so on). However, stipendiaries are considered to perform better in relation to those criteria that suggest greater confidence – showing command over the proceedings and challenging parties responsible for delay.

Fewer appearances before stipendiaries lead to adjournments (45% compared to 52%). This is partly because fewer applications are made to stipendiaries but also because they are more likely to resist applications for adjournments (97% compared to 93%). It is therefore likely that the employment of additional stipendiaries would lead to fewer court appearances overall.

Lay magistrates are less likely to:

- refuse defendants bail in cases where to prosecution seeks custody and the defence applies for bail (19% compared to 37%)

- make use of immediate custody as a sentence (12% of triable-either-way cases compared to 25%).

The employment of additional stipendiaries might therefore significantly increase the prison population.

Stipendiaries tend to run their courts themselves and rely very little on their court legal advisors when it comes to making and explaining decisions and announcements. This calls into question whether they need legally qualified court advisors.

The views of regular court practitioners

A sample of 400 court practitioners (court advisors, solicitors, CPS personnel, probation officers) were surveyed by telephone.

Very few court users expressed 'no' or only 'a little' confidence in either type of magistrate, but stipendiaries were more likely to inspire a 'great deal' or a 'lot' of confidence. Users found it harder to generalise about lay magistrates, indicating a greater range in their performance.

The court users expressed very similar views to the court observers when asked to rate dimensions of behaviour. Stipendiaries were widely seen as:

- more efficient, more consistent and more confident in their decision-making
- questioning defence lawyers appropriately
- giving clear reasons for decisions
- showing command over proceedings.

Lay magistrates were more often judged better at:

- showing courtesy to defendants and other court members
- using simple language
- showing concern to distressed victims.

But the majority of respondents did not think lay and stipendiary magistrates differed on these criteria.

Regular court practitioners, particularly lawyers and CPS personnel, said that they and their colleagues behave differently when appearing before lay and stipendiary magistrates. They:

- prepare better for stipendiaries
- try to be more precise and concise in their statements to them
- anticipate that they will be questioned and challenged more.

Court legal advisors on the other hand said that they prepare more for lay magistrates, because they anticipate the need to give legal advice to them.

Public opinions of the magistracy

A nationally representative sample of 1,753 members of the public were interviewed regarding their views on, and knowledge of the magistracy.

Whereas the overwhelming majority of the public is aware of the terms 'magistrate' and 'magistrates' court', only a minority have heard of 'lay' as opposed to 'stipendiary' magistrates.

When the difference between them is explained, almost three-quarters (73%) say that they were not aware of this difference.

Only a bare majority of respondents correctly identify that most criminal cases are dealt with in the magistrates' courts, and that juries do not make decisions there. Knowledge about the qualifications and sitting practices of lay magistrates is even less accurate. Respondents who are more knowledgeable about the system tend to have greater confidence in it.

Having had the differences explained to them, most of the public thinks that:

- lay magistrates represent the views of the community better than stipendiaries (63% compared to 9% – the remaining 28% see no difference or don't know)
- lay magistrates are more likely to be sympathetic to defendants' circumstances (41% compared to 12%)
- stipendiaries are better at making correct judgements of guilt or innocence (36% compared to 11%) and managing court business effectively (48% compared to 9%)
- there is no difference between lay and stipendiaries in awareness of the effect of crimes on victims and approaching each case afresh.

In addition, when comparing single magistrates with panels:

- a small majority of respondents (53%) consider that motoring offences are suitable to be heard by a single magistrate
- a large majority think that the more serious decisions of guilty/not guilty (74%) and sending to prison (76%) should be decided by panels of magistrates.

Most respondents think that the work of the magistrates' courts should be divided equally between the two types of magistrates, or that the type of magistrate does not matter.

The direct and indirect costs of lay and stipendiary magistrates

If only directly attributable costs (salaries, expenses, training) are considered, lay magistrates are much cheaper because they are not paid directly and many do not claim loss of earnings. A sizeable minority does not even claim their allowable travelling expenses. A lay magistrate costs on average £495 per annum compared to the £90,000 per annum total employments costs of a stipendiary. These translate into a cost per appearance before lay and stipendiary magistrates of £3.59 and £20.96 respectively (Table 1). When indirect costs (premises, administration staff, etc.) are brought into the equation the gap between the two groups narrows, to £52.10 and £61.78.

The effect upon costs of substituting stipendiary for lay magistrates

There would have to be a significant increase in the use of the more productive stipendiaries to enable administrative staff and courtroom reductions to be made on any scale.

If blocks of work currently undertaken by lay magistrates were transferred to stipendiaries:

Table 1 The cost of appearing before lay and stipendiary magistrates (per appearance)

	Lay Magistrates	Stipendiary Magistrates
	£	£
Direct costs (salary, expenses, training)	3.59	20.96
Indirect costs (premises, administration staff etc.)	48.51	40.82
Direct & indirect costs	52.10	61.78

- one stipendiary would be needed for every 30 magistrates, if all lay tribunals comprised three justices
- one for every 28, if the present proportion of tribunals comprising only two lay justices were to continue.

Stipendiaries' greater tendency to resist adjournments and their greater use of custody at the pre-trial and sentencing stages means that if the number of stipendiaries were doubled (assuming present patterns were retained):

- there would be a reduction of 10,270 appearances in connection with indictable offences, giving an additional cost of £0.88 million per annum (a net increase because the reduced rates of adjournments do not overcome the higher attributable costs of stipendiaries).
- the number of remands in custody would increase by 6,200 per annum. Assuming an average remand period of 46 days, this has an associated cost of around £24 million (essentially falling on the Prison Service)
- the number of custodial sentences would increase by 2,760 per annum, costing £13.6 million. Set against this is the cost of the type of sentence that the offender would have received in the place of a prison sentence. If this is taken as some form of community penalty then the overall additional cost of this increase in custodial sentences would be around £8.5 million.

The effect upon costs of substituting lay for stipendiary magistrates

Alternatively if there were no stipendiaries, then there would be an increase in the number of appearances of 10,270, the number of remands in custody would decrease by 6,200, and the number of custodial sentences would decrease by 2,760 – with each of the consequent cost savings.

Other jurisdictions

Drawing on the 23 responses from the Council of Europe member states and enquiries to other (mostly Common Law) jurisdictions, it can be seen that there are three principal models of adjudication:

- the *professional*
- the *lay*
- the *hybrid* (mixed lay and professional).

Each of these can be refined in terms of whether decision-making is by single persons or panels, and the number of tiers into which criminal cases and courts are divided.

However there is no straightforward relationship between the degree to which democracy is embedded and lay involvement in judicial decision-making. Many longstanding democracies involve lay persons while other do not. The re-establishment of democracy in a country does not necessarily stimulate the introduction of lay involvement in judicial decision-making, sometimes the reverse occurs, depending on the cultural and political tradition.

The most common arrangements for lay involvement comprise lay persons making decisions in the lowest tier, or sitting alongside professional judges in the middle or higher tiers. However, it is also common that their decisions are restricted to minor non-imprisonable offences. More serious decisions are invariably made by professionals or hybrid panels.

England and Wales is the only jurisdiction identified in this research where such a high proportion of criminal cases, including serious cases, are decided by lay persons. In addition, the allocation of cases to either lay or stipendiary magistrates by chance, rather than by policy, is unique to this jurisdiction.

Conclusion

Though the research does not point in a particular policy direction, the findings do indicate how the public and court users are likely to react to certain proposals for change.

Although the public do not have strong feelings about the precise role of magistrates, they think that summary offences, particularly if not contested, can be dealt with by a single magistrate but that panels should make the more serious judicial decisions. Cost considerations suggest that this could only be achieved (in the short-term at least) by continuing to make extensive use of lay magistrates.

Criminal justice practitioners, while appreciative of the quality of service given by lay magistrates, have greater confidence in professional judges (stipendiaries). Furthermore governmental pressure to make the criminal courts more efficient, and to reduce the time that cases take to complete, will also tend to favour the greater efficiency of stipendiary magistrates. However, this has to be balanced against the potential increase in cost to the Prison Service.

The nature and balance of contributions made by lay and stipendiary magistrates could be altered to better satisfy these wider considerations, but should not prejudice the integrity and support of a system founded on strong traditions. Not only is the office of Justice of the Peace ancient and in an important tradition of voluntary public service, it is also a direct manifestation of government policy which encourages *active citizens* in an *active community*. In no other jurisdiction does the criminal court system depend so heavily on such voluntary unpaid effort. At no stage during the study was it suggested that in most respects the magistrates' courts do not work well or fail to command general confidence. It is our view, therefore, that eliminating or greatly diminishing the role of lay magistrates would not be widely understood or supported.

[6:5] Ipsos MORI/Ministry of Justice, *The strengths and skills of the Judiciary in the Magistrates' Courts*

(2011) Ministry of Justice Research Series 9/11 (at page 1)

Summary

Study objectives and methodology

This report presents the findings from a Ministry of Justice (MoJ) commissioned research study, aimed at examining the strengths and skills of the judiciary in the magistrates' courts for criminal cases.

The research was designed to inform operational and policy decisions on the deployment of the judiciary within the magistrates' courts in England and Wales. Specifically the research objectives were to understand:

● the relative strengths and skills of magistrates and District Judges;
● how magistrates and District Judges were best deployed across different types of cases;
● what the process and disposal costs of using magistrates and District Judges are and, if the balance was changed, what the impact would be;

- what relevant professionals think about magistrates and District Judges taking on more serious cases and sitting together in small panels.

The research programme consisted of three stages:

1) In-depth interviews and discussion groups with 355 respondents, which included members of the judiciary, court staff, and professional and lay court users.
2) Observation of 2,291 court cases from 350 criminal court sessions in 44 magistrates' courts across England and Wales. Given the need to make fair comparisons between magistrates and District Judges in terms of case timings and outcomes, extensive data modelling work (both regression and Propensity Score Matching) was conducted following this data collection).
3) The development of an interactive cost model to examine the process and disposal costs of the judiciary in the magistrates' courts.

Perceptions of the strengths and skills of magistrates and District Judges

A widely perceived strength of magistrates was their greater connection with the local community as compared with District Judges, meaning that they were felt to be better placed to make judgments and dispense appropriate "local justice". Other perceived strengths of magistrates relate to the concept of "fairness". Some associated a bench of three with a greater degree of democracy, while magistrates were also felt by some to be more open-minded and less "case hardened" or "fatigued". A few respondents, in particular magistrates themselves, also noted their cost effectiveness as magistrates are not paid a salary.

For District Judges, the most widely cited benefit was their speed in transacting cases given their legal expertise (and subsequent lower reliance on the Legal Adviser) and the fact that they sit alone (meaning they do not need to retire to consider verdict and sentencing). This was supported by the observation data, which found that average case timings for District Judges were typically shorter. District Judges also felt they were more adept at case management, a view that was shared by a number of the Legal Advisers, Justices' Clerks and defence solicitors.

Relationships/interactions with Legal Advisers and professional users

The observations showed that Legal Advisers provided support to both magistrates and District Judges. However, they also revealed that Legal Advisers provided guidance to magistrates within the court room more frequently than they did for District Judges. This finding was reflected by the interviews where magistrates themselves tended to highlight that Legal Advisers played a more crucial role during proceedings. However, in interviews other stakeholders suggested that magistrates were more reliant on Legal Advisers than the observation data indicated. The interviews also highlighted that Legal Advisers provided a much greater degree of support to magistrates outside of the court room than they did for District Judges.

Crown Prosecution Service (CPS) prosecutors and defence solicitors tended to agree that they presented cases differently depending on which judiciary type was presiding. Some scaled back their arguments for District Judges and felt they provided a more detailed outline of the case for a bench of magistrates (which may be partly reflected in the shorter average case lengths for District Judges). It was also suggested by these groups (and by District Judges) that a lay bench could be more accepting of arguments for adjournments. However, the observation data showed that the proportion of cases adjourned was similar across judiciary types.

Listing practices and case types

There was no consistent approach to listing policies and practices across the 44 courts where the case observations were made. Despite this, listing practices and policies did tend to recommend that District Judges should be used for selected cases, such as complex, lengthy or serious cases. Most respondents, including magistrates, supported the notion that District Judges should be prioritised for these cases when possible.

The observations showed that some selective deployment of cases did appear to be taking place, with District Judges more likely to hear "violence against a person" offences and magistrates more likely to hear motoring cases. Furthermore, three in ten cases heard by District Judges were classified as "either way" offences, compared to only 18% for magistrates' cases. However, despite these variations, the findings illustrated that selective allocation is by no means clear-cut and that the differences in the profiles of cases heard by magistrates and District Judges are not as significant as was suggested in the interviews.

Case timings

Using regression analysis, the results indicate that, on average, District Judges transacted cases more quickly than magistrates. These findings corroborated the views expressed in interviews with the judiciary, court staff and professional users. Most magistrates and District Judges perceived that differences in time reflected the fact that three trained lay people take longer to come to a decision on the verdict and sentencing than a single qualified lawyer. They also corroborated previous research, including that by Morgan and Russell (2000); however, they found the difference in timings was smaller than in Morgan and Russell's study. This may well be a result of differences in the methodologies between the two pieces of research.

Comparative costs of magistrates and District Judges

Despite the relative speed with which they handle cases, the cost model showed that District Judges are typically more costly per case (where key differences are controlled for) than magistrates in terms of the magistrates' court processing costs. This was mainly due to their salary costs. However, the evidence suggests that for "either-way" cases District Judges are less costly when either lawyer or CPS costs are included or when volunteering costs are included for magistrates.

Certain factors (e.g. quality of decision-making) were highly subjective and therefore could not be incorporated in the model. Also, disposal costs and wider Criminal Justice System (CJS) costs could not be factored into the cost modelling. Therefore the impact of any differences in these costs; for example, the suggestion that District Judges had a higher propensity to impose custodial sentences, is not included.

Case outcomes

Findings from the regression analysis suggested some differences in the sentencing patterns between magistrates and District Judges. In particular, there was evidence to suggest that District Judges were more likely to impose custodial sentences, disqualify defendants from driving or remand the defendant on either conditional or unconditional bail.

Across all observed cases, while magistrates and District Judges both adjourned with the same frequency, differences were found in their reasons for doing so. Magistrates were more likely to adjourn because of a prosecution or defendant request, while District Judges were more likely to adjourn due to the absence of a witness.

Extending sentencing powers

The majority of respondents believed that an extension of jurisdiction within the magistrates' courts would be a positive step. District Judges tended to cite the current anomaly between sentencing limits in the adult and youth courts as a key reason for an increase, and also highlighted the potential cost savings that could be made if more cases were retained within the magistrates' courts, as opposed to being sent or committed to the Crown Court.

The majority of magistrates were also in favour of extended sentencing powers, believing this would be beneficial in reducing the burden on the Crown Court. However, some Justices' Clerks voiced concerns, anticipating an increase both in workload in the magistrates' courts and in the prison population, based on the belief that magistrates would impose harsher sentences than are imposed now in the Crown Court. A few defence solicitors also highlighted the need for appropriate magistrate training to cope with such powers.

Mini-panels

The majority of those interviewed were not in favour of mini-panels for most criminal cases in the magistrates' court. District Judges, in particular, questioned the rationale for such panels, believing they would undermine their key strength, that of speed, and would not be cost effective. Respondents tended to react more positively to the notion of a "middle tier" within a unified Criminal Court, as advocated by Lord Justice Auld.

Conclusions and implications

In the interviews, stakeholders described key differences between magistrates and District Judges in terms of their interactions with others in court, their handling of cases and their use of Legal Advisers. Many of these differences were not as marked in the observational data. Despite this, the research did indicate that deployment of magistrates and District Judges could be made more effective and efficient by adopting a more systematic, evidence-based approach, both within and across HMCS areas. Specifically, District Judges could be deployed more exclusively on more difficult or complicated cases (though determining this can be difficult), where their training and experience were widely seen as offering notable advantages. In addition to strengthening guidance on deployment, there could be benefits in reviewing the allocation of resources across different court service areas based on caseload information. The observation data suggested that District Judges may be more likely than magistrates to use custodial sentences for comparable cases. This means that deploying District Judges more strategically may have an impact on sentencing outcomes.

The research also showed that savings could be made to magistrates' court processing costs if full advantage was taken of District Judges' legally qualified status, and if they were supported by "court associates" rather than Legal Advisers as they are currently. However, there was some evidence that court associates may need more training. Further costs savings could be made by taking steps to speed up magistrates' handling of summary motoring cases, taking pointers from District Judges where appropriate (it is these cases that show the largest discrepancy in timings between the two judiciary types).

Both magistrates and District Judges supported moves to extend their sentencing powers, saying that any reservations were likely to be overcome through training and safeguards (though their cost implication would need to be considered before any action was taken). In contrast, mini-panels that mix magistrates and District Judges would need some strong promotion to gain support.

[6:6] Bail Act 1976 (as amended)

Section 4; Schedule 1

4 General right to bail of accused persons and others

(1) A person to whom this section applies shall be granted bail except as provided in Schedule 1 to this Act.

(2) This section applies to a person who is accused of an offence when –

- (a) he appears or is brought before a magistrates' court or the Crown Court in the course of or in connection with proceedings for the offence, or
- (b) he applies to a court for bail or for a variation of the conditions of bail in connection with the proceedings.

This subsection does not apply as respects proceedings on or after a person's conviction of the offence.

(2A) This section also applies to a person whose extradition is sought in respect of an offence, when –

- (a) he appears or is brought before a court in the course of or in connection with extradition proceedings in respect of the offence, or
- (b) he applies to a court for bail or for a variation of the conditions of bail in connection with the proceedings.

(2B) But subsection (2A) above does not apply if the person is alleged to have been convicted of the offence.

(3) This section also applies to a person who, having been convicted of an offence, appears or is brought before a magistrates' court or the Crown Court under –

- (za) Schedule 1 to the Powers of Criminal Courts (Sentencing) Act 2000 (referral orders: referral back to appropriate court),
- (zb) Schedule 8 to that Act (breach of reparation order),

- (a) Schedule 2 to the Criminal Justice and Immigration Act 2008 (breach, revocation or amendment of youth rehabilitation orders),
- (b) Part 2 of Schedule 8 to the Criminal Justice Act 2003 (breach of requirement of community order), or
- (c) the Schedule to the Street Offences Act 1959 (breach of orders under section 1(2A) of that Act).

(4) This section also applies to a person who has been convicted of an offence and whose case is adjourned by the court for the purpose of enabling inquiries or a report to be made to assist the court in dealing with him for the offence.

(5) Schedule 1 to this Act also has effect as respects conditions of bail for a person to whom this section applies.

(6) In Schedule 1 to this Act "the defendant" means a person to whom this section applies and any reference to a defendant whose case is adjourned for inquiries or a report is a reference to a person to whom this section applies by virtue of subsection (4) above.

(7) This section is subject to section 41 of the Magistrates' Courts Act 1980 (restriction of bail by magistrates' court in cases of treason) and section 115(1) of the Coroners and Justice Act 2009 (bail decisions in murder cases to be made by Crown Court judge).

(8) This section is subject to section 25 of the Criminal Justice and Public Order Act 1994 (exclusion of bail in cases of homicide and rape).

(9) In taking any decisions required by Part I or II of Schedule 1 to this Act, the considerations to which the court is to have regard include, so far as relevant, any misuse of controlled drugs by the defendant ("controlled drugs" and "misuse" having the same meanings as in the Misuse of Drugs Act 1971).

Schedule 1 Persons Entitled to Bail: Supplementary Provisions

Part I Defendants Accused or Convicted of Imprisonable Offences

Application of Part I

1 (1) Subject to sub-paragraph (2) and paragraph 1A, the following provisions of this Part of this Schedule apply to the defendant if –

  (a) the offence or one of the offences of which he is accused or convicted in the proceedings is punishable with imprisonment, or
  (b) his extradition is sought in respect of an offence.

(2) But those provisions do not apply by virtue of sub-paragraph (1)(a) if the offence, or each of the offences punishable with imprisonment, is –

  (a) a summary offence; or
  (b) an offence mentioned in Schedule 2 to the Magistrates' Courts Act 1980 (offences for which the value involved is relevant to the mode of trial) in relation to which –
    (i) a determination has been made under section 22(2) of that Act (certain either way offences to be tried summarily if value involved is less than the relevant sum) that it is clear that the value does not exceed the relevant sum for the purposes of that section; or
    (ii) a determination has been made under section 9A(4) of this Act to the same effect.

1A (1) The paragraphs of this Part of this Schedule mentioned in sub-paragraph (2) do not apply in relation to bail in non-extradition proceedings where –

  (a) the defendant has attained the age of 18,
  (b) the defendant has not been convicted of an offence in those proceedings, and
  (c) it appears to the court that there is no real prospect that the defendant will be sentenced to a custodial sentence in the proceedings.

(2) The paragraphs are –

  (a) paragraph 2 (refusal of bail where defendant may fail to surrender to custody, commit offences on bail or interfere with witnesses),

(b) paragraph 2A (refusal of bail where defendant appears to have committed indictable or either way offence while on bail), and

(c) paragraph 6 (refusal of bail where defendant has been arrested under section 7).

Exceptions to right to bail

2 (1) The defendant need not be granted bail if the court is satisfied that there are substantial grounds for believing that the defendant, if released on bail (whether subject to conditions or not) would –

(a) fail to surrender to custody, or

(b) commit an offence while on bail, or

(c) interfere with witnesses or otherwise obstruct the course of justice, whether in relation to himself or any other person.

(2) Where the defendant falls within paragraph 6B, this paragraph does not apply unless –

(a) the court is of the opinion mentioned in paragraph 6A, or

(b) paragraph 6A does not apply by virtue of paragraph 6C.

2ZA (1) The defendant need not be granted bail if the court is satisfied that there are substantial grounds for believing that the defendant, if released on bail (whether subject to conditions or not), would commit an offence while on bail by engaging in conduct that would, or would be likely to, cause –

(a) physical or mental injury to an associated person; or

(b) an associated person to fear physical or mental injury.

(2) In sub-paragraph (1) "associated person" means a person who is associated with the defendant within the meaning of section 62 of the Family Law Act 1996.

2A The defendant need not be granted bail if –

(a) the offence is an indictable offence or an offence triable either way, and

(b) it appears to the court that the defendant was on bail in criminal proceedings on the date of the offence.

2B The defendant need not be granted bail in connection with extradition proceedings if –

(a) the conduct constituting the offence would, if carried out by the defendant in England and Wales, constitute an indictable offence or an offence triable either way; and

(b) it appears to the court that the defendant was on bail on the date of the offence

3 The defendant need not be granted bail if the court is satisfied that the defendant should be kept in custody for his own protection or, if he is a child or young person, for his own welfare.

4 The defendant need not be granted bail if he is in custody in pursuance of a sentence of a court or a sentence imposed by an officer under the Armed Forces Act 2006.

5 The defendant need not be granted bail where the court is satisfied that it has not been practicable to obtain sufficient information for the purpose of taking the decisions required by this Part of this Schedule for want of time since the institution of the proceedings against him.

6 The defendant need not be granted bail if, having previously been released on bail in, or in connection with, the proceedings, the defendant has been arrested in pursuance of section 7.

6ZA If the defendant is charged with murder, the defendant may not be granted bail unless the court is of the opinion that there is no significant risk of the defendant committing, while on bail, an offence that would, or would be likely to, cause physical or mental injury to any person other than the defendant.

Exception applicable to drug users in certain areas

6A Subject to paragraph 6C below, a defendant who falls within paragraph 6B below may not be granted bail unless the court is of the opinion that there is no significant risk of his committing an offence while on bail (whether subject to conditions or not).

6B (1) A defendant falls within this paragraph if –

- (a) he is aged 18 or over;
- (b) a sample taken –
    - (i) under section 63B of the Police and Criminal Evidence Act 1984 (testing for presence of Class A drugs) in connection with the offence; or
    - (ii) under section 161 of the Criminal Justice Act 2003 (drug testing after conviction of an offence but before sentence), has revealed the presence in his body of a specified Class A drug;
- (c) either the offence is one under section 5(2) or (3) of the Misuse of Drugs Act 1971 and relates to a specified Class A drug, or the court is satisfied that there are substantial grounds for believing –
    - (i) that misuse by him of any specified Class A drug caused or contributed to the offence; or
    - (ii) (even if it did not) that the offence was motivated wholly or partly by his intended misuse of such a drug; and
- (d) the condition set out in sub-paragraph (2) below is satisfied or (if the court is considering on a second or subsequent occasion whether or not to grant bail) has been, and continues to be, satisfied.

(2) The condition referred to is that after the taking and analysis of the sample –

- (a) a relevant assessment has been offered to the defendant but he does not agree to undergo it; or
- (b) he has undergone a relevant assessment, and relevant follow-up has been proposed to him, but he does not agree to participate in it.

(3) In this paragraph and paragraph 6C below –

- (a) "Class A drug" and "misuse" have the same meaning as in the Misuse of Drugs Act 1971;
- (b) "relevant assessment" and "relevant follow-up" have the meaning given by section 3(6E) of this Act;
- (c) "specified" (in relation to a Class A drug) has the same meaning as in Part 3 of the Criminal Justice and Court Services Act 2000.

6C Paragraph 6A above does not apply unless –

(a) the court has been notified by the Secretary of State that arrangements for conducting a relevant assessment or, as the case may be, providing relevant follow-up have been made for the local justice area in which it appears to the court that the defendant would reside if granted bail; and
(b) the notice has not been withdrawn.

Exception applicable only to defendant whose case is adjourned for inquiries or a report

7 Where his case is adjourned for inquiries or a report, the defendant need not be granted bail if it appears to the court that it would be impracticable to complete the inquiries or make the report without keeping the defendant in custody.

Restriction of conditions of bail

8 (1) Subject to sub-paragraph (3) below, where the defendant is granted bail, no conditions shall be imposed under subsections (4) to (6B) or (7) (except subsection (6)(d) or (e)) of section 3 of this Act unless it appears to the court that it is necessary to do so –

(a) for the purpose of preventing the occurrence of any of the events mentioned in paragraph 2(1) of this Part of this Schedule, or
(b) for the defendant's own protection or, if he is a child or young person, for his own welfare or in his own interests.

(1A) No condition shall be imposed under section 3(6)(d) of this Act unless it appears to be necessary to do so for the purpose of enabling inquiries or a report to be made.

(2) Sub-paragraphs (1) and (1A) above also apply on any application to the court to vary the conditions of bail or to impose conditions in respect of bail which has been granted unconditionally.

(3) The restriction imposed by sub-paragraph (1A) above shall not apply to the conditions required to be imposed under section 3(6A) of this Act or operate to override the direction in section 11(3) of the Powers of Criminal Courts (Sentencing) Act 2000 to a magistrates' court to impose conditions of bail under section 3(6)(d) of this Act of the description specified in the said section 11(3) in the circumstances so specified.

Decisions under paragraph 2

9 In taking the decisions required by paragraph 2(1), or in deciding whether it is satisfied as mentioned in 2ZA(1) or of the opinion mentioned in paragraph 6ZA or 6A, of this Part of this Schedule, the court shall have regard to such of the following considerations as appear to it to be relevant, that is to say –

(a) the nature and seriousness of the offence or default (and the probable method of dealing with the defendant for it),
(b) the character, antecedents, associations and community ties of the defendant,

   (c)   the defendant's record as respects the fulfilment of his obligations under previous grants of bail in criminal proceedings,

   (d)   except in the case of a defendant whose case is adjourned for inquiries or a report, the strength of the evidence of his having committed the offence or having defaulted,

   (e)   if the court is satisfied that there are substantial grounds for believing that the defendant, if released on bail (whether subject to conditions or not), would commit an offence while on bail, the risk that the defendant may do so by engaging in conduct that would, or would be likely to, cause physical or mental injury to any person other than the defendant,

as well as to any others which appear to be relevant.

9AA (1) This paragraph applies if –

   (a)   the defendant is a child or young person, and

   (b)   it appears to the court that he was on bail in criminal proceedings on the date of the offence.

(2) In deciding for the purposes of paragraph 2(1) of this Part of this Schedule whether it is satisfied that there are substantial grounds for believing that the defendant, if released on bail (whether subject to conditions or not), would commit an offence while on bail, the court shall give particular weight to the fact that the defendant was on bail in criminal proceedings on the date of the offence.

9AB (1) Subject to sub-paragraph (2) below, this paragraph applies if –

   (a)   the defendant is a child or young person, and

   (b)   it appears to the court that, having been released on bail in or in connection with the proceedings for the offence, he failed to surrender to custody.

(2) Where it appears to the court that the defendant had reasonable cause for his failure to surrender to custody, this paragraph does not apply unless it also appears to the court that he failed to surrender to custody at the appointed place as soon as reasonably practicable after the appointed time.

(3) In deciding for the purposes of paragraph 2(1) of this Part of this Schedule whether it is satisfied that there are substantial grounds for believing that the defendant, if released on bail (whether subject to conditions or not), would fail to surrender to custody, the court shall give particular weight to –

   (a)   where the defendant did not have reasonable cause for his failure to surrender to custody, the fact that he failed to surrender to custody, or

   (b)   where he did have reasonable cause for his failure to surrender to custody, the fact that he failed to surrender to custody at the appointed place as soon as reasonably practicable after the appointed time.

(4) For the purposes of this paragraph, a failure to give to the defendant a copy of the record of the decision to grant him bail shall not constitute a reasonable cause for his failure to surrender to custody.

Part II Defendants Accused or Convicted of Non-Imprisonable Offences

Defendants to whom Part II applies

1 Where the offence or every offence of which the defendant is accused or convicted in the proceedings is one which is not punishable with imprisonment the following provisions of this Part of this Schedule apply.

Exceptions to right to bail

2 The defendant need not be granted bail if –

- (za) the defendant –
    - (i) is a child or young person, or
    - (ii) has been convicted in the proceedings of an offence;
- (a) it appears to the court that, having been previously granted bail in criminal proceedings, he has failed to surrender to custody in accordance with his obligations under the grant of bail; and
- (b) the court believes, in view of that failure, that the defendant, if released on bail (whether subject to conditions or not) would fail to surrender to custody.

3 The defendant need not be granted bail if the court is satisfied that the defendant should be kept in custody for his own protection or, if he is a child or young person, for his own welfare.

4 The defendant need not be granted bail if he is in custody in pursuance of a sentence of a court or a sentence imposed by an officer under the Armed Forces Act 2006.

5 The defendant need not be granted bail if –

- (za) the defendant –
    - (i) is a child or young person, or
    - (ii) has been convicted in the proceedings of an offence;
- (a) having been released on bail in or in connection with the proceedings for the offence, he has been arrested in pursuance of section 7 of this Act; and
- (b) the court is satisfied that there are substantial grounds for believing that the defendant, if released on bail (whether subject to conditions or not) would fail to surrender to custody, commit an offence on bail or interfere with witnesses or otherwise obstruct the course of justice (whether in relation to himself or any other person).

6 (1) The defendant need not be granted bail if –

- (a) having been released on bail in, or in connection with, the proceedings for the offence, the defendant has been arrested in pursuance of section 7, and
- (b) the court is satisfied that there are substantial grounds for believing that the defendant, if released on bail (whether subject to conditions or not), would commit an offence while on bail by engaging in conduct that would, or would be likely to, cause –

    - (i) physical or mental injury to an associated person, or
    - (ii) an associated person to fear physical or mental injury.

(2) In sub-paragraph (1) "associated person" means a person who is associated with the defendant within the meaning of section 62 of the Family Law Act 1996.

Part IIA Decisions where Bail Refused on Previous Hearing

1 If the court decides not to grant the defendant bail, it is the court's duty to consider, at each subsequent hearing while the defendant is a person to whom section 4 above applies and remains in custody, whether he ought to be granted bail.

2 At the first hearing after that at which the court decided not to grant the defendant bail he may support an application for bail with any argument as to fact or law that he desires (whether or not he has advanced that argument previously).

3 At subsequent hearings the court need not hear arguments as to fact or law which it has heard previously.

Part III Interpretation

1 For the purposes of this Schedule the question whether an offence is one which is punishable with imprisonment shall be determined without regard to any enactment prohibiting or restricting the imprisonment of young offenders or first offenders.

2 References in this Schedule to previous grants of bail include –

- (a) bail granted before the coming into force of this Act;
- (b) as respects the reference in paragraph 2A of Part 1 of this Schedule (as substituted by paragraph 16 of Schedule 11 to the Legal Aid, Sentencing and Punishment of Offenders Act 2012), bail granted before the coming into force of that paragraph;
- (c) as respects the references in paragraph 6 of Part 1 of this Schedule (as substituted by paragraph 17 of Schedule 11 to the Legal Aid, Sentencing and Punishment of Offenders Act 2012), bail granted before the coming into force of that paragraph;
- (d) as respects the references in paragraph 9AA of Part 1 of this Schedule, bail granted before the coming into force of that paragraph;
- (e) as respects the references in paragraph 9AB of Part 1 of this Schedule, bail granted before the coming into force of that paragraph;
- (f) as respects the reference in paragraph 5 of Part 2 of this Schedule (as substituted by section 13(4) of the Criminal Justice Act 2003), bail granted before the coming into force of that paragraph;
- (g) as respects the reference in paragraph 6 of Part 2 of this Schedule, bail granted before the coming into force of that paragraph.

3 References in this Schedule to a defendant's being kept in custody or being in custody include (where the defendant is a child or young person) references to his being kept or being in accommodation pursuant to a remand under section 91(3) or (4) of the Legal Aid, Sentencing and Punishment of Offenders Act 2012 (remands to local authority accommodation or youth detention accommodation).

4 In this Schedule –

"court", in the expression "sentence of a court", includes a service court as defined in section 12(1) of the Visiting Forces Act 1952 and "sentence", in that expression, shall be construed in accordance with that definition;

"default", in relation to the defendant, means the default for which he is to be dealt with under Part 2 of Schedule 8 to the Criminal Justice Act 2003 (breach of requirement of order).

[6:7] HM Chief Inspector of Prisons, *Unjust Deserts: A Thematic Review of the Treatment and Conditions for Unsentenced Prisoners in England and Wales*
(2000) (at page 123)

Strategic Issues and Recommendations for the Management of Establishments Holding Unsentenced Prisoners

12.01 This review has revealed a startling gap between what the public might reasonably expect to be in place for unsentenced prisoners and what is actually in place. More worryingly however, it also identifies a gap between the official understanding of what is being delivered as described in the replies from the *Governors' survey* and the actual experience of unsentenced prisoners; a gap largely supported by our own observations from fieldwork and inspections.

12.02 The following factors seem to be relevant to this state of affairs:

- Local prisons are overcrowded. The Prison Service has endeavoured, quite rightly, to keep the rising numbers of prisoners sent to them by the courts as close as possible to where they are to appear for trial. Also, for entirely understandable and sensible reasons the Prison Service has chosen to protect training prisons from overcrowding by concentrating this pressure on local prisons. This has resulted in the latter holding a rising number of sentenced prisoners, both short term, who increasingly serve their whole sentences in local prisons, and longer term, who can wait for extended periods to be transferred to training prisons. The sheer pressure of numbers has therefore thwarted the development of proper regimes for unsentenced prisoners.
- Prisoners in local prisons are generally compliant. Most prisoners prefer to be held in local prisons where they are closer to their homes, friends and families than in more distant training prisons. Indeed this has been such a priority for most prisoners that they have been prepared to put up with poor conditions in order to take advantage of being able to stay in their local area. The rate of turnover in the population is also such that most prisoners tolerate their conditions on the basis that they will not have to do so for a long time. Apart from the riots of the early nineties, unsentenced prisoners have not posed serious control problems. Complaints from unsentenced prisoners themselves have not therefore provided a stimulus for change.
- The diversity of prisoner needs presents difficult challenges for staff. All offenders entering the prison system do so through local prisons. Any of these establishments might hold remands awaiting trial, convicted unsentenced and sentenced prisoners, debtors, civil prisoners, deportees or immigration detainees and those on over-crowding drafts from other local prisons. Sentenced prisoners may be short or longer sentenced and include life sentence prisoners both newly sentenced, recalled from training prisons or licence revoked. Among this mixture of prisoners will be those with violent tendencies, those who are vulnerable to attack from others, those who are mentally unwell, those who are drug misusers, those who are drug dealers, those who are depressed and suicidal and, of course those who are subsequently found not guilty. Although some may be familiar to staff from previous periods in custody, many will be unknown and the uncertainty and risk inherent in this mix creates one of the biggest challenges for managers and staff.

- Local prisons have inadequate physical facilities. Many of the old local prisons were constructed for the penal policies of a different age and lack the facilities that are required to support healthy prison regimes. Until some twenty years ago when finances for the maintenance of prison buildings became more readily available, all were in a wretched condition. Improvements have been made, notably in the abolition of 'slopping out', but most are still in need of large capital investment to make them fit for their purpose. For example, in many of the cells designed for one person but used to accommodate two, there is no suitable screen between the toilet and the living space. The Director General and his colleagues are aware of these deficiencies and are as keen as anyone else to rectify them, but do not have the necessary finance to carry out the work.

- Local prisons have a culture of disengagement with prisoners. For many decades the unspoken but unmistakable message to staff from senior Prison Service managers has been that their job is to serve the courts by taking as many prisoners as necessary, and to avoid escapes and disturbances. Given the risks associated with these tasks and the limited resources to manage them, a culture of disengagement with prisoners and risk avoidance has become established.

- Local prisons are able to resist change. The staff of local prisons become the culture carriers as they are longer serving than either the prisoners or their managers. The former pass through on short periods of remand, short sentences or on to training prisons, and the latter pass through on relatively short tours of duty as they build their careers. In these circumstances staff become disproportionately influential and without training, management and leadership for their role in a modern Prison Service, their prime motivation becomes one of making life as comfortable as possible for themselves and their colleagues, and their allegiance and commitment to the Prison Service's Statement of Purpose becomes hard to find. In such prisons there is an absence of justice and fairness in dealing with legitimate requests and complaints from prisoners, Governors appear powerless to introduce even the simplest of changes without disputes, and progress becomes impossible without a clear mandate for change from Ministers and the Prisons Board.

The Way Forward

12.03   At any time there are well over thirty thousand people held in fifty-three local prisons and remand centres in England and Wales. Some of the establishments in which they are held treat unsentenced prisoners with humanity and try to meet their individual needs; the five contracted out local prisons, for example, and most local prisons for women. Few of the suggestions for improvement in this review are entirely original in that many reflect examples of good, indeed outstanding current practice in both directly managed and contracted out establishments. One such example is the recommendation to replace the policy of separating unconvicted from convicted prisoners with an integrated approach that is based on safety and respect which has been tried and tested by at least one former Governor of a local directly managed prison. What is missing, however, is a clear unifying vision for unsentenced prisoners which details how they should be treated and the conditions in which they should be held, and a management system which ensures consistent delivery in all local prisons and remand centres.

12.04   The senior management of the Prison Service has tended to believe that the answer lies in finding capable Governors to take command of these prisons. It is true that without strong leadership nothing will change, but far more than the personal qualities of individual governors are needed if lasting change is to be achieved. I must emphasise that responsibility for this state of affairs does not lie with the current Prisons Board. Indeed, I believe that it is because of the leadership already demonstrated by the Director General that there is now a real opportunity to tackle the culture of those establishments that have been producing poor, and in some cases, unacceptable treatment and conditions for prisoners, including those held on remand, for too many years. There is every reason to be optimistic that staff in the Prison Service will respond positively to the challenge of providing a healthy and needs based regime for unsentenced prisoners as they have done successfully in other parts of the prison estate, notably high security prisons. However, they will need re-training as well as strong leadership if they are to operate in a radically different way. Many, for example, will need help to understand the needs and rights of unsentenced prisoners and the proper role of local prisons within a joined up Criminal Justice System. They will also need to understand the complex mental health problems of unsentenced prisoners and the importance of ensuring that they have access to due process.

Recommendations

12.05 I have detailed throughout this review a number of areas where change needs to be made, and a number of recommendations are included in the text. However, I have two over-riding strategic recommendations which I detail here. Firstly, in view of the physical inadequacy of the facilities and buildings within which many unsentenced prisoners are held.

I recommend that the cost of the work required to ensure that all local prisons and remand centres have the necessary facilities to hold prisoners in decent conditions should be published and that the finance to carry it out should be provided within a five year programme.

12.06 In view of the enormity of the challenge which faces the Prison Service in bringing about cultural change in many of the establishments holding unsentenced prisoners.

I recommend that a strategy is introduced by the Prisons Board, with the full support of Ministers, for a two year programme of change to identify and deliver agreed prisoner focused outcomes as detailed in this review, for all unsentenced prisoners in local prisons and remand centres. This strategy should contain a clear sense of direction for local prisons and remand centres, detail the elements of work which they should undertake and include costed service delivery agreements. The strategy should include the introduction of a mandatory and comprehensive initial and ongoing training programme for new staff and an immediate programme to re-educate current staff. There should also be a remedial element to the strategy to identify those prisons needing to achieve fundamental change in the way that unsentenced prisoners are treated. This information can be readily gathered from inspection reports over recent years. Such identified prisons should be set clear targets, based on the delivery of agreed outcomes for unsentenced prisoners. They should also be given suitable senior managers to carry out this work, which might include nominated 'change managers' with a clear briefing and training for what is to be achieved, and time in post to carry through the required changes. Such senior management teams should also be given both practical and personal support from senior functional managers in Prison Service Headquarters, and opportunities for the regular exchange of experiences through meetings with colleagues in other similar establishments.

12.07 I intend to carry out a follow up to this review in two years' time, and will continue to monitor the treatment and conditions of unsentenced prisoners within my ongoing inspection programme. I look forward to witnessing the improvements which I am confident that the Prison Service can deliver, with the full backing of Ministers.

[6:8] HM Inspectorate of Prisons, *Remand prisoners: A thematic review*
(2012) (at page 11)

1. Summary and recommendations

1.1 The findings in this report come from four main sources: inspection reports for 33 category B local prisons published between January 2009 and June 2011, data from surveys at 33 local prison inspections in this period (with 4,868 prisoner respondents, of whom 1,593 were held on remand), interviews with heads of resettlement and residential units at five establishments, and focus groups with unconvicted and convicted unsentenced prisoners at these same establishments.

1.2 At all prison inspections the establishment's performance is assessed against the four tests of a healthy prison which were first introduced in this inspectorate's thematic review, *Suicide is everyone's concern*, published in 1999. This report is structured and focused on the same criteria. The four criteria of a healthy prison are:

Safety	prisoners, even the most vulnerable, are held safely
Respect	prisoners are treated with respect for their human dignity
Purposeful activity	prisoners are able, and expected, to engage in activity that is likely to benefit them
Resettlement	prisoners are prepared for their release into the community and helped to reduce the likelihood of reoffending.

The characteristics of remand prisoners

1.3 In our survey, a third of respondents said they were on remand – 18% said they were unconvicted and 15% that they were convicted unsentenced. Our survey found that prisoners held on remand had some key demographic features differentiating them from sentenced prisoners. Almost a third of all remand prisoners said they were from a black or other minority ethnic background (compared with just over a quarter in the prison population as a whole), which rose to just over two-fifths in the young adult estate. Similarly, foreign nationals were over-represented, especially in the women's estate where over a quarter said they were foreign nationals.

1.4 As expected, fewer remand than sentenced prisoners said they had been in the prison for over six months; a higher proportion of remand than sentenced prisoners stated that they had been in prison for less than one month. Half of all remand prisoners reported they had been in prison on two or more previous occasions but 34% reported that this was their first time in prison.

Remand prisoners in context

1.5 Remand prisoners are detained in local prisons while awaiting trial or sentencing at court. Local prisons tend to be large and located within confined urban settings, many with old buildings that need modernisation to improve conditions and aid dynamic security. Activity spaces are often insufficient for the population and time out of cell is poor for many. Prisoners in local prisons are often held close to home, which makes it easier to receive visits. However, as there are fewer establishments for young adults and women, these groups may be held far from their home.

Safety

1.6 Some remand prisoners in our groups said they had not expected to be remanded into custody. In our survey, only 73% said they knew where they were being taken when they left court, which fell to 60% for the third of those remand prisoners who had not been in prison before. On returning from a court appearance prisoners normally returned to the same prison and cell they were escorted from. At a prison where this was not the case, prisoners said that the disruption of moving cell after each court appearance, added to the stress of undergoing a trial. Remand prisoners in our groups described long days spent at court, even for short appearances, and having to pack up their belongings each time. Prisoners were generally positive about the use of court video links and felt they should be used more to minimise trips to and from court.

1.7 In our survey, remand prisoners were more likely than sentenced prisoners to report welfare problems on arrival in the prison, although relatively few said they had been asked if they needed support for such problems on the day they arrived. Remand prisoners arriving into custody for the first time were less likely to say they were offered support than those who had been in before.

1.8 Many prisoners in our groups felt there was an over-reliance on the induction process to convey too much information, which they found difficult to process, as it took time to acclimatise and stabilise once they had arrived. Most respondents in our survey said they had attended an induction, although only 58% felt it had covered everything they wished to know – which could reflect insufficient content or an inability to process and retain all the information presented. The content of induction was variable, with some prisoners describing it as only an introduction to the rules and regime of the prison, rather than a means to describe and signpost support services.

1.9 Statistics from the Prisons and Probation Ombudsman (PPO) and National Offender Management Service (NOMS) show that remand prisoners are at a heightened risk of self-harm and suicide. Nearly a quarter (23%) of remand prisoners in our survey said they had felt depressed or suicidal when they arrived, although only half of new arrivals said they had been asked if they needed help with this. Remand prisoners reported poorer access to Listeners (peer supporters).

1.10 In our survey, remand prisoners said they felt less safe than sentenced prisoners, although there was no evidence that they experienced more victimisation – 22% said they had experienced victimisation by other prisoners and a quarter (26%) by staff.

1.11 Fewer remand prisoners said they had gained enhanced status in the incentives and earned privileges (IEP) scheme. Remand prisoners in our groups described obstacles to reaching enhanced status. It could take two to three months to achieve, which could be too long for those detained on remand for relatively short periods, and enhanced status commonly depended on a prisoner working or attending education, which unconvicted prisoners had the right to decline. Unconvicted prisoners in groups said they were treated the same as convicted prisoners in the scheme, irrespective of their rights and entitlements. A small number of inspection reports found that unconvicted prisoners were downgraded to basic level for refusing to engage with activities.

1.12 Fewer remand than sentenced prisoners said they had drug or alcohol problems, although the figures were still high with over a third (35%) reporting a drug problem and over a quarter (27%) an alcohol problem. The introduction of the integrated drug treatment system (IDTS) has meant that prisons have moved away from offering detoxification as the only treatment for remand and short-sentenced prisoners, and instead use maintenance drugs, where appropriate, and offer better support. The short duration programme (SDP) was one of the few programmes available to remand prisoners at the prisons visited. In our survey, two-thirds (66%) of those who reported substance misuse problems said they had received an intervention, although less than half (48%) said they knew who could help to put them in contact with services in the community. Remanded young adults with a substance misuse problem were much less likely than those sentenced to say they had received an intervention – 65% compared with 81%.

Respect

1.13 There was considerable variation in the extent and nature of legal and bail services available to remand prisoners. In our groups, remand prisoners had poor awareness of these services and what they offered and there were indications that services were not always active in seeking out candidates. Where services were implemented well, they had a considerable impact on the success of prisoners' bail applications. Some prisoners had been disinclined to apply for bail as they felt it would not be granted. In our survey, 47% of remand prisoners for whom bail was an issue said they had found it difficult to get bail information.

1.14 Remand prisoners reported difficulties managing their court cases from within the prison, and some felt they were impeded by disorganisation at the prison and restrictions on finance and time to make phone calls. In our survey, 45% of those who needed to said they had found it difficult to contact their solicitors. Prison libraries stocked legal texts, although access to the library was reported as limited.

1.15 The ability of remand prisoners to vote was not promoted or even facilitated by some prisons visited, and the majority of prisoners in our groups were unaware of their right to vote while held on remand. Some felt they might have voted had they been given the opportunity.

1.16 The rights of unconvicted prisoners were often compromised by a lack of staff awareness, or broader prison considerations. The rules for sharing accommodation and cells with convicted prisoners were unclear. The Prison Rules state that unconvicted prisoners should not share accommodation or take part in activities with convicted prisoners, unless explicit consent is given, and can even be interpreted to imply that under no circumstances should an unconvicted prisoner share a cell with a convicted prisoner. However Prison Service and establishment policies and practices were that all sharing was permissible if remand prisoners gave their consent.

1.17 Inspections found that, in practice, remand prisoners often did not have an opportunity to give their informed consent to sharing with convicted prisoners. Unconvicted prisoners shared accommodation and cells with convicted and sentenced prisoners at the establishments visited, although one had attempted to designate a wing for unconvicted prisoners. The majority in groups said they had not been asked or were uncertain whether they had been. Nevertheless, many prisoners said they did not object to sharing with convicted prisoners, although some felt they should be held separately. In our groups, remand prisoners reported receiving fewer facilities and privileges than enhanced sentenced prisoners.

1.18 At all prisons visited there was either a higher or no cap on the amount of money unconvicted prisoners could have sent in. To benefit from this privilege, an unconvicted prisoner relied on support from family and friends outside. Unconvicted prisoners were able to spend more each week than convicted and sentenced prisoners.

1.19 Restrictions on the regime and cost made keeping in contact with families by phone difficult, especially if the prisoner was without financial support outside or a prison job. Over a third (37%) in the survey reported problems accessing phones.

1.20 At all five prisons visited, unconvicted prisoners could send as many letters as they wished and received two free letters a week, although at two prisons they needed to request their free letters.

1.21 The policy of most prisons was that unconvicted prisoners could wear their own clothes. However, many unconvicted prisoners were restricted from exercising this right by overly prescriptive and rigid rules, and a lack of laundering facilities.

1.22 In all five prisons visited, prisoners could have books brought in, but only one allowed other in-cell activity or hobby items to be brought in. At the other four these items had to be bought from the prison shop or catalogue.

1.23 Remand prisoners' access to all support services and activities was often reliant on the applications system. In our survey, perceptions of the applications process were poor across the local prison population, although worse for remand prisoners – only just over half (51%) felt the process was fair and 43% that responses were timely, which was a particular issue for those in custody for only a short time.

1.24 In our survey, a similar proportion of remand as sentenced prisoners said that they had a staff member to turn to if they had a problem (71%). Prisoners in groups described staff as unaware and insensitive to the needs of remand prisoners undergoing a trial. As a consequence of being on mixed wings, some prisoners felt staff were not able to distinguish remand from sentenced prisoners. Fewer than half (44%) of remand prisoners in our survey said they had a personal officer, and in groups they were unclear who their personal officer was and what they were supposed to offer.

1.25 Four out of the five heads of resettlement we spoke with were not aware of the right of unconvicted prisoners to see their own GP if they wished. There was virtually no awareness of this right among unconvicted prisoners in our groups, although some felt it might have been feasible had they known. Some inspections found that remand prisoners had curtailed access to the dentist or optician.

1.26 Over a third (36%) of remand prisoners in our survey indicated that they had an emotional well-being or mental health problem. The number of remand prisoners who said they received treatment was comparable with the sentenced population, although 40% who reported this problem said they had not received any help.

Purposeful activity

1.27 High rates of both unconvicted (40%) and convicted unsentenced prisoners (37%) reported they were not involved in any activities at the time of the survey. Nearly a third (29%) of remand prisoners said they had spent less than two hours out of their cells each day, and only 42% had spent more than four hours out of their cell. In our survey, fewer than half (44%) said they had association more than five times a week.

1.28 Although unconvicted prisoners have the right to choose not to engage with work, training or education, Prison Rules specify that unconvicted prisoners should be offered the opportunity to work. Many in our groups said they wanted the opportunity to work to earn money and to occupy themselves while in prison.

1.29 At all five prisons visited, remand prisoners could take part in work or education. Some prison inspection reports described limited opportunities and a lack of priority for remand prisoners in work and education spaces. This affected their time out of cell and ability to earn money.

1.30 Prisoners in groups said that applying for jobs was a lengthier and more difficult process than applying for education, although this was less so for some because they had been in prison before and were known to staff already. At the time of the survey, just over a third (36%) of remand prisoners said they had a job, fewer than sentenced prisoners (46%).

1.31 There were very few vocational and other skills training spaces across the local prison estate, and only 8% of remand prisoners said that they were currently involved in such training. Prisoners told us that education was easier to get involved in, and in our survey the proportion of remand prisoners (27%) involved in education at the time of the survey was comparable with sentenced prisoners. Just over a third (36%) of both remanded and sentenced prisoners said they went to the library at least once a week.

1.32 More remand than sentenced prisoners, although still only 41%, said they had access to outside exercise three or more times a week, but they reported less access to the gym.

Resettlement

1.33 The resettlement strategies in place rarely took account of the needs of the remand population, and some inspections noted that remand prisoners had been excluded in resettlement strategies or a resettlement needs analysis.

1.34 Charting remand prisoners' period in custody can be difficult as outcomes of court appearances and their release date are unpredictable. This emphasises the need for oversight from a case manager to make best use of the defendant's time in custody.

1.35 Initial individual needs assessments were completed at most establishments inspected, but that was often where the work on the remand prisoner's behalf ended. There were few examples of custody plans produced on the basis of the assessment, and there was weak or no case management to track progress on identified needs. Of the few good examples of effective custody planning noted in inspection reports, most were found at establishments that were piloting layered offender management and the work was undertaken by offender supervisors. NOMS has since removed remand prisoners from the new offender management model to be rolled out.

1.36 Remand prisoners, therefore, often had to find their own way to access services, which was especially difficult for those unfamiliar with prison systems. Remand prisoners in our groups had very little awareness of support services at the prison. Some said it was difficult to source the required support and, beyond the induction, many felt there was no clear and single place or individual to approach for help. In our survey, two-thirds (66%) of remand prisoners said they did not know who to contact for assistance in any area of resettlement.

1.37 Over a quarter (27%) of remand prisoners said they had housing problems on arrival in prison. Despite their entitlements to benefits to help maintain housing while held on remand, only 33% of unconvicted prisoners reported that they had been asked if they needed help in this area. Unconvicted prisoners in groups lacked knowledge of their entitlements to housing benefit, and some complained of a slow applications process to access support – several said they had lost their housing since being remanded.

1.38 In the absence of clear time frames to work towards, housing providers find it difficult to work with remand prisoners who are homeless. In our groups and in inspections, there were examples of housing services that would not work with unsentenced prisoners. In our survey, 39% of remand prisoners thought they would have housing problems on release, but only 20% said they knew who to contact for help.

1.39 In our groups some said they had jobs before custody; those who had said they had received no support and were likely to have lost them. Nearly half (45%) of remand prisoners said finding a job would be a problem when released, but less than one in five (18%) that they knew who to contact for help. Three of the five heads of resettlement interviewed did not have any awareness of unconvicted prisoners' right to support for maintaining their business interests, and this was not promoted at any of the establishments. None of the unconvicted prisoners were aware of this entitlement – some had run their own business before custody and might have benefited from this support.

1.40 Unconvicted prisoners had little knowledge of their benefits entitlements, and a few had been misinformed by staff. In our survey, 30% of both remand and sentenced prisoners said that they would have problems claiming benefits once released, but considerably fewer remand prisoners said they knew who to contact for help (20% compared with 32%).

1.41 Constraints on phone access and a lack of support made it difficult to manage any existing financial commitments. Prisoners in groups described a variety of financial commitments that had been left unresolved and the subsequent accrual of debt. Nearly a third (29%) of remand prisoners expected to have problems with finance on release and only 11% said they knew who to contact for help.

1.42 Few prisoners in local prisons felt they had been helped to maintain contact with family and friends, and fewer remand than sentenced respondents (35% against 38%) reported this. In our survey, nearly half (47%) said they had children under 18. Forty-five per cent of remanded women said they had children, and remanded women in our groups reported considerable obstacles and concern about ensuring the well-being of their children, and little support to deal with this. In our survey, 14% of remanded women said they had problems on arrival ensuring their dependants were looked after.

1.43 Most prisons inspected and all five visited gave unconvicted prisoners the minimum of three visits a week as per Prison Service policy; one exceeded this with the provision of a daily hour-long visit. Despite this entitlement, a quarter of unconvicted prisoners in our survey said they had not received any visits. Convicted unsentenced prisoners, who do not have the extra visits privileges, reported delays in visiting orders being processed.

1.44 Remand prisoners had little or no access to programmes for thinking or behaviour at the inspected prisons or those visited for fieldwork, and no remand specific courses were available. One prison visited granted remand prisoners access to some non-accredited programmes, and another to a family relationship course.

Recommendations

To the National Offender Management Service (NOMS)
1.45 A comprehensive review of strategies and polices for remand prisoners should take place to ensure their treatment and conditions is consistent with their unconvicted and unsentenced status and that they receive interventions and support to resettle successfully after release and do not subsequently offend. The strategy should contain the elements set out below.

1.46 The rights and entitlements for remand prisoners should be clarified to ensure they are in line with national legislation and international standards, and that they are considered and, where mandatory, implemented in full by establishments.

1.47 Except in exceptional circumstances, unconvicted prisoners should be located on discrete wings, separate from convicted prisoners. Unconvicted prisoners should have a status and regime that recognises and facilitates their entitlements, and that is distinct from the incentives and earned privileges scheme.

1.48 A senior manager in each local establishment should have oversight of the remand population to ensure they are aware of and receive their entitlements. Staff working with remand prisoners should be aware of their distinct needs and circumstances.

1.49 Bail services should be sufficiently resourced to meet the needs of their remand population and be promoted and active in ensuring that all remand prisoners have access to them.

1.50 Remand prisoners should be offered the same opportunity to work as sentenced prisoners.

1.51 There should be appropriate resettlement services to meet the needs of remand prisoners, with active case management to support each prisoner's reintegration into the community, and, as far as possible, to ensure that all needs are identified and addressed before release.

1.52 Remand prisoners with substance misuse issues should have access to the short duration programmes (SDP).

[6:9] Lloyd, C, *Bail Information Schemes: Practice and Effect*
(1992) HO RPU Paper No 69, HMSO (at page 65)

How is bail information most effective?

One of the most interesting findings of this research has been the differences in the way in which bail information has its effect in the three courts studied. While the Blackpool scheme seemed to have influenced the remand decision primarily through strengthening the defence's case for bail, at the other extreme, the Manchester scheme's effectiveness relies almost entirely on its influence on the CPS. Both these findings from the data could have been predicted from the interviews with solicitors and probation officers in the field. The Manchester CPS were universally described as an independent agency, keen to make their own decisions rather than act at the bidding of the police. Interviews with prosecutors verified this opinion: they spoke positively of bail information and, for the most part, saw it as a useful adjunct to their decision-making. By contrast the CPS at Blackpool – and to a lesser extent at Hull – were more critical of the local scheme and saw bail information primarily as an aid to the defence.

Which *modus operandi* is the most effective? Taking account of the numbers interviewed, it was the Hull scheme that seemed to divert the highest proportion of interviewed defendants from a remand in custody. It would therefore appear that bail information is most effective when used fully by the CPS and the defence.

Another possible way of influencing the remand decision would be to provide information directly to the court. Jones and Goldkamp (1991)['Judicial Guidelines for Pre-trial Release' (1991) 30 Howard Journal 140] have recently criticised the bail information initiative in the UK for not involving magistrates sufficiently in the development and use of bail information. The possibility of providing bail information directly to magistrates was raised in interviews with court clerks, solicitors and probation staff and received a mixed reception. Interestingly, it was a number of defence and CPS solicitors who were in favour of the provision of information direct to the court, suggesting that information would be more effective if presented in this way. However, various criticisms of this approach was made. First, it was thought possible that some magistrates might confuse bail information sheets with social inquiry reports and assume that the sheets represented probation recommendations for bail. Second, it was pointed out that if magistrates expected bail information sheets to be presented for each defendant, if a sheet was not presented for a defendant they might automatically assume that there was nothing positive to be said, although the reason for the absence of a bail information sheet might simply be that the BIO ran out of time. As long as magistrates were adequately prepared for such a scheme's introduction, the first argument would seem to carry little weight. The second argument is more persuasive. A scheme would have to ensure complete coverage of cases where the police were objecting to bail in order to prevent this process occurring. Nevertheless it seems surprising that there has been no experimentation with a scheme that provides copies of the bail information sheet to the CPS, the defence and the court. There is a sense in which information read out in court by the prosecutor or defending solicitor lacks objectivity. While defence solicitors can refer to the fact that the information was verified by a probation officer or ancillary, the context of the presentation of this information is within the defence's argument for bail, and this may detract from the perceived 'independence' of the information.

(At page 70):

Conclusions

The study reported here has added further support to the growing body of research and monitoring evidence which shows bail information schemes to be successful in diverting defendants from remands in custody. The importance of such work cannot be understated. Remand centres and local prisons remain the most crowded sector of the prison system, with Spartan regimes and high rates of suicide. The avoidance of a potential remand in custody is therefore saving the defendant from a period of imprisonment on remand in overcrowded conditions, and may also contribute to the likelihood of a non-custodial sentence. Moreover, the cost-effectiveness analysis presented here suggests that bail information schemes are also saving the criminal justice system a considerable amount of money.

Perhaps the most interesting part of the research has been the exploration of the different ways in which bail information has its effect in three courts. Unfortunately this issue could not be addressed adequately at Lincoln Prison because of the lack of information about CPS and defence applications. While national policy and previous research have tended to focus on the influence of bail information on the CPS, it is clear from the evidence presented here that bail information can also have a significant effect through influencing the number and strength of defence applications. While the sample of three court-based schemes is admittedly small, it is nevertheless interesting to note that the scheme which had the largest relative effect on remand decision was the one which exploited both paths of influence to the full.

However, it should be emphasised that the probation service and its BIOs have only limited powers in influencing the way in which other agencies utilise bail information: good working relationships can be forged between BIOs and prosecutors and defence solicitors, and senior probation managers can liaise with their counterparts in the other organisations. Nevertheless, perhaps the most important determinant of the way in which bail information works is the particular subculture or dynamics of the local magistrates' court, and in particular, the ethos of the local CPS branch. Bail information will be most effective in a court with a high rate of remanding in custody; a local CPS which is prepared to reconsider police requests and use bail information as a means to achieve more independent decision making; and defence solicitors who are prepared to make a bail application at first appearance.

[6:10] Morgan, P M and Henderson, P, *Remand Decisions and Offending on Bail: Evaluation of the Bail Process Project*

(1998) HORS 184 (at page vii)

The aim of the Bail Process Project was to improve the quality, accuracy and timeliness of the information available to remand decision-makers so that they were better able to assess the risk of offending on bail.

Inter-agency working groups were set up in five court areas in 1992. Each group, chaired by the Justices'Clerk, studied the remand process in its own area, and identified problems that affected the information available to the police custody officers, CPS prosecutors and magistrates when they made a pre-trial decision or recommendation on bail or custody. The groups then set in hand the changes that were possible to solve these problems.

The problems that were identified are described by Burrows et al (1994) and are summarised in Appendix A of this report. The main changes that were introduced by the courts were as follows.

- In most areas, the early *availability of the defendant's criminal record* was a problem. One area was able to extend the hours of direct access to its local records from eight to twenty-four hours a day. Another negotiated access to the more detailed record held by the National Identification Service (as compared with the brief record held on the police national computer). A third area was able to establish a mechanism whereby the court was informed if the defendant was already on bail from a different police station or court within the same police force area.
- All five areas carried out some *training of magistrates in risk assessment*, and ways of improving magistrates' awareness of bail hostel facilities in the area were explored. Three areas set up *training courses for police custody officers* on the same topic to ensure greater uniformity of practice.
- Three areas amended the *wording of bail conditions of residence or curfew*, to oblige the defendant to present himself or herself in person to police officers monitoring his/her compliance. Three areas distributed *simplified bail notices* to make the terms of bail clearer to defendants, that is, the date of the next court appearance and any conditions attached. These were issued to defendants granted unconditional bail as well as those granted bail with conditions.
- In two areas, court clerks started to keep *a record of representations made in remand decisions* so that future benches would know the reasons why earlier decisions had been made.
- Two areas made changes in court listing times to allow more *time for pre-court discussion between the agencies* and, in one area, new arrangements allowed Saturday courts to have access to the probation service.
- In two areas, local steering mechanisms were established under the Court User group to ensure *better liaison between two bail information schemes in the same area*, and to ensure general understanding of how negative information (that which might work against the granting of bail) was handled by the probation service (see Appendix D).
- In single areas, the following changes were made: a *new prison-based bail information scheme* and a *trial bail support scheme* for 18- to 25-year-olds were established; a scheme was set up to provide *volunteers to act as 'appropriate adults'* during police interviews with under-17-year-olds; and arrangements were made for a *review panel for mentally disordered offenders*.

Case tracking data were collected on cases involving bail/custody decisions in the five areas over a period of three months in 1993 and three months in 1994 (before and after the improvements suggested above). Defendants released on bail in the two samples of cases were followed up at the criminal records office to find details of any offences that were committed while they were on bail.

Analyses showed that the *proportion of defendants granted court bail who were convicted of an offence committed while they were on bail* was reduced in two of the court areas, and changed only slightly or not at all in the other three. The clear decreases were in the Horseferry Road court area (from 18% in 1993 to 11% in 1994), and in the Leicester court area (from 20% in 1993 to 12% in 1994). The proportion of persons *charged with offences committed on court bail* showed similar decreases: in Horseferry Road area from 22% to 16%, and in Leicester, from 24% to 16%.

The analyses suggest that offending on bail decreased in the Horseferry Road area because more persons were remanded in custody (the custody rates increased by six percentage points between 1993 and 1994). Leicester showed a different picture in that the custody rates went down by about five percentage points. This suggests that the reduction in offending on bail in Leicester may have been caused by some of the improvements made, such as better access to defendant's bail history, or an increased emphasis on the training of magistrates in the assessment of risk.

The analyses also showed that the rates of offending while on police bail after charge (as measured by convictions) showed a small decrease overall from 9% to 8%. There were small decreases in three areas, between two and three percentage points, no change in Newport and a small increase in Bournemouth. Bournemouth and Salford showed the lowest rates for offending on police bail (between 5% and 8%): for Salford this is probably explained by the fact that this area was found to have a much higher rate of police custody after charge (see Chapter 4).

The rates of offending on police bail as measured by charges showed a similar pattern with slightly higher figures. Over all areas, the rates changed from 12% in 1993 to 11% in 1994.

An exercise was carried out with bail decision-makers in Leicester to explore their approach to assessing risk. This established a set of factors which were held to be important, and explored how these were seen to be related to the assessment of the risk of the defendant failing to appear at court and the risk of offending while on bail (see Tables 3.1 and 3.2).

The case tracking data were analysed to explore which categories of defendant were associated with higher and lower than average rates of offending on court bail. Those with higher rates included defendants:

- with no fixed abode (42% offended on bail)
- charged with car theft or burglary (32%, 29% respectively offended on bail)
- who waited more than six months before trial (32% or more than three months (24%)
- aged 17 and under (29%)
- who had served a previous custodial sentence (28%)
- who had a previous record of breaching bail (27%)
- who were unemployed (21%).

Those with lower rates were those:

- who waited less than a month before trial (4%)
- who were in employment (7%)
- who were charged with assault (7%) or fraud (8%)
- who were 21 or over (13%).

The Bail Process Project arose from concern about the extent of offending on bail. In 1992, there was a great deal of public discussion of the issue when three police forces published a range of figures from surveys carried out in their own areas, and the Home Office published results from its internal research. The then Home Secretary gave an undertaking to Parliament to tackle this issue by setting up pilot projects in selected local areas. The intention was to improve the quality of the information available to the courts to assist them in identifying these defendants who were most likely to offend on bail.

This commitment led to a steering committee being set up which included representatives from all the relevant criminal justice agencies, i.e. the police, the Crown Prosecution Service (CPS), the magistrates' courts, the probation service and the Law Society. The committee was to tackle two main tasks:

- to investigate what information was required by remand decision-makers, and in what ways the information available was judged to be deficient
- to explore ways of remedying these deficiencies and, where possible, to put these remedies into effect.

Background: who makes pre-trial decisions

In England and Wales, the majority of decisions about the granting of bail before trial arise at three points: when a suspect has been arrested by the police but the evidence available is not sufficient for charges to be brought; when a suspect has been arrested and charged with an offence; and when the court has decided to adjourn the hearing of a case to another date. The first two of these decisions are made by the police: the third is made by magistrates.

(At page 60):

To avoid unnecessary remands in custody, and to reduce offending on bail, magistrates must target the two out of three (in the highest risk group) and the one in 16 in the lowest risk group. Such targeting might be based on information over and above the broader categories described: perhaps more detail of the current offence and how it relates to the criminal record to indicate a pattern of offending, an indication of the attitude of the defendant, and any circumstances or influences which may have a positive effect on future behaviour. However, even if such information were available, there is no guarantee that accurate predictions of offending would be possible. Another relevant factor is the waiting time before trial: the research has shown that longer waiting times are related to higher offending on bail. This suggests that, if changes in procedure or practice can be devised to reduce the waiting times for defendants on bail, there should be a corresponding reduction in offending on bail. Broad estimates suggest that a reduction in waiting times of around one month should correspond to a decrease of three per cent in offending on bail.

[6:11] Bail (Amendment) Act 1993 (as amended)

Section 1

1 Prosecution right of appeal

(1) Where a magistrates' court grants bail to a person who is charged with, or convicted of, an offence punishable by imprisonment, the prosecution may appeal to a judge of the Crown Court against the granting of bail.

(1A) Where a magistrates' court grants bail to a person in connection with extradition proceedings, the prosecution may appeal to the High Court against the granting of bail.

(1B) Where a judge of the Crown Court grants bail to a person who is charged with, or convicted of, an offence punishable by imprisonment, the prosecution may appeal to the High Court against the granting of bail.

(1C) An appeal under subsection (1B) may not be made where a judge of the Crown Court has granted bail on an appeal under subsection (1).

(2) Subsections (1) and (1B) above apply only where the prosecution is conducted –

    (a) by or on behalf of the Director of Public Prosecutions; or

    (b) by a person who falls within such class or description of person as may be prescribed for the purposes of this section by order made by the Secretary of State.

(3) An appeal under subsection (1), (1A) or (1B) may be made only if –

    (a) the prosecution made representations that bail should not be granted; and

    (b) the representations were made before it was granted.

(4) In the event of the prosecution wishing to exercise the right of appeal set out in subsection (1), (1A) or (1B) above, oral notice of appeal shall be given to the court which has granted bail at the conclusion of the proceedings in which bail has been granted and before the release from custody of the person concerned.

(5) Written notice of appeal shall thereafter be served on the court which has granted bail and the person concerned within two hours of the conclusion of such proceedings.

(6) Upon receipt from the prosecution of oral notice of appeal from its decision to grant bail the court which has granted bail shall remand in custody the person concerned, until the appeal is determined or otherwise disposed of.

(7) Where the prosecution fails, within the period of two hours mentioned in subsection (5) above, to serve one or both of the notices required by that subsection, the appeal shall be deemed to have been disposed of.

(8) The hearing of an appeal under subsection (1), (1A) or (1B) above against a decision of the court to grant bail shall be commenced within forty-eight hours, excluding weekends and any public holiday (that is to say, Christmas Day, Good Friday or a bank holiday), from the date on which oral notice of appeal is given.

(9) At the hearing of any appeal by the prosecution under this section, such appeal shall be by way of re-hearing, and the judge hearing any such appeal may remand the person concerned in custody or may grant bail subject to such conditions (if any) as he thinks fit.

(10) In relation to a person under the age of 18—

    (a) the references in subsections (1) and (1B) above to an offence punishable by imprisonment are to be read as references to an offence which would be so punishable in the case of an adult; and

    (b) the references in subsections (6) and (9) above to remand in custody are to be read subject to the provisions of Chapter 3 of Part 3 of the Legal Aid, Sentencing and Punishment of Offenders Act 2012 (remands of children otherwise than on bail).

(11) The power to make an order under subsection (2) above shall be exercisable by statutory instrument and any instrument shall be subject to annulment in pursuance of a resolution of either House of Parliament.

(12) In this section –

"extradition proceedings" means proceedings under the Extradition Act 2003;
"magistrates' court" and "court" in relation to extradition proceedings means a District Judge (Magistrates' Courts) designated in accordance with section 67 or section 139 of the Extradition Act 2003;
"prosecution" in relation to extradition proceedings means the person acting on behalf of the territory to which extradition is sought.

[6:12] Sentencing Council, *Allocation Guideline*
(2012) (at page 18b)

Applicability of guideline
In accordance with section 122(2) of the Coroners and Justice Act 2009, the Sentencing Council issues this definitive guideline. It applies to all defendants in the magistrates' court (including youths jointly charged with adults) whose cases are dealt with on or after 11 June 2012. It will not be applicable in the youth court where a separate statutory procedure applies.

Section 125(1) of the Coroners and Justice Act 2009 provides that when sentencing offences committed after 6 April 2010:

"Every court -

(a) must, in sentencing an offender, follow any sentencing guideline which is relevant to the offender's case, and

(b) must, in exercising any other function relating to the sentencing of offenders, follow any sentencing guidelines which are relevant to the exercise of the function,

unless the court is satisfied that it would be contrary to the interests of justice to do so."

Statutory framework
In accordance with section 19 of the Magistrates' Courts Act 1980, where a defendant pleads not guilty or has not indicated an intention to plead guilty to an offence triable either way, a magistrates' court must decide whether the offence should be sent to the Crown Court for trial.

When deciding whether an either way offence is more suitable for summary trial or trial on indictment, section 19 of the Magistrates' Courts Act 1980 provides that the court shall give the prosecutor and the accused the opportunity to make representations as to which court is more suitable for the conduct of the trial.[1]

The court must also have regard to:

a) the nature of the case;
b) whether the circumstances make the offence one of a serious character;
c) whether the punishment which a magistrates' court would have the power to inflict for the offence would be adequate; and
d) any other circumstances which appear to the court to make the offence more suitable for it to be tried in one way rather than the other.[2]

[1] s.19(2) Magistrates' Courts Act 1980
[2] s.19(1) ibid

Guidance

It is important to ensure that all cases are tried at the appropriate level. **In general, either way offences should be tried summarily unless it is likely that the court's sentencing powers will be insufficient.** Its powers will generally be insufficient if the outcome is likely to result in a sentence in excess of six months' imprisonment for a single offence.

The court should assess the likely sentence in the light of the facts alleged by the prosecution case, taking into account all aspects of the case including those advanced by the defence.

The court should refer to definitive guidelines to assess the likely sentence for the offence.

Committal for sentence

There is ordinarily no statutory restriction on committing an either way case for sentence following conviction. The general power of the magistrates' court to commit to the Crown Court for sentence after a finding that a case is suitable for summary trial and/or conviction continues to be available where the court is of the opinion that the offence (and any associated offences) is so serious that greater punishment should be inflicted than the court has power to impose.[3] Where the court decides that the case is suitable to be dealt with in the magistrates' court, it should remind the defendant that all sentencing options remain open, including committal to the Crown Court for sentence at the time it informs the defendant of this decision.

However, where the court proceeds to the summary trial of certain offences relating to criminal damage, upon conviction there is no power to commit to Crown Court for sentence.[4]

Linked cases

Where a youth and an adult are jointly charged, the youth must be tried summarily unless the court considers it to be in the interests of justice for both the youth and the adult to be committed to the Crown Court for trial. Examples of factors that should be considered when deciding whether to separate the youth and adult defendants include:

- whether separate trials can take place without causing undue inconvenience to witnesses or injustice to the case as a whole;
- the young age of the defendant, particularly where the age gap between the adult and youth offender is substantial;
- the immaturity of the youth;
- the relative culpability of the youth compared with the adult and whether or not the role played by the youth was minor; and
- the lack of previous convictions on the part of the youth.

---

[3] s.3 Powers of Criminal Courts (Sentencing) Act 2000
[4] s.2 and s.33 Magistrates' Courts Act 1980

[6:13] Brown, S, *Magistrates at Work: Sentencing and Social Structure*
(1991) Open University Press (at page 81)

The processes of classification and translation themselves both help to create and sustain a rendering of reality in which the individual case may be diagnosed, a pathology created, a 'solution' proposed, and which in its very individuality indicates a relationship with the overall corpus of unruly youth. This offender is situated in relation to that offender; this one is not a lost cause, that one is a hardened offender. Similarly one penalty implies the whole hierarchy of penalties. Through the whole business of processing juveniles, very little attention is paid by participating actors to the *validity* of the social background representations invoked.

No desire is shown to understand the meaning of the offence from the child's point of view; rather the child must account for it in the court's terms (Why did you do it? Did you know it was wrong?). Little interest is shown in whether locking children up in detention centres actually has an effect on behaviour, few questions are asked as to whether or not the whole package of an escalating penalty may not successively reinforce the likelihood of the juvenile's being re-introduced into the 'system'.

The emphasis is on describability. The individual is transposed into a set of knowledge representations which are comprehensible not with reference to the actual lived experience and actions of the individual but rather with reference to the instrumentality of those representations: what it is that they enable, and what it is that they preclude. In this sense, Shaun, and Ian, and Nicola, and Michelle themselves, are irrelevant to the juvenile court; 'social information' does not refer to them as people but to the project of the juvenile court in reconstructing them as information objects, entities amenable to processing. Social information simplifies individuals and reduces them to docile figures on sheets of paper.

Thus classification takes away the actual individuality of defendant and the circumstances of his or her life and replaces it with a spurious individuality consisting of a series of attributes capable of judgment; Law's 'docile figures'. The potentially most unruly of the resources is the juvenile her or himself, hence their particular insertion into the business of sentencing. The simultaneous enrolment and silencing of the child is both an expression of, and necessary to, the effective deployment of power.

(At page 104):

Magistrates control a diffuse and potentially all inclusive discourse through the operation of the socialised tariff. They exercise a real power which is based on their ability to invoke social information categories in support of decisions which in the end rest upon their powers of judgment:

> It's just a question of judgment, really, you learn by experience.
> I think a lot of lady magistrates . . . you do things by your intuition.
> We're not social workers. We have to use our common sense.
> It all comes down to . . . judgment really in the end.

The control over imprecise concepts which the use of social information involves ensures that any challenge to that judgment is particularly difficult. The structure of the bifurcatory tariff is a distinct advantage in the successful exercise of discretionary power, because it creates a facility of categories – a continuum of salvability to incorrigibility – which justifies the use of social data. In providing the heuristic mechanism by which magistrates allocate offenders on that always already existing bifurcatory slope, control indicators are techniques of power.

(Ir)rationality and the problem of decision making in the juvenile court

Ultimately, however, the techniques of power of the socialised tariff are enabled by the fundamental irrationality which characterises the most liberal of juvenile courts. The vagueness of the decision concepts with which justices have to work (good/bad home backgrounds etc) are symptomatic of the lack of substantive rationality in the decision environment within which they work. Strictly speaking, substantive rationality ends the moment when it ceases to be possible to make a computation of the type 'if x, then y' (March and Simon 1970). Even allowing that this is an ideal type rather than something which can be fully realised in most decision situations, it is clear that the magisterial task could never remotely approximate rationality. Rationality demands that goals can be clearly defined, that the means to achieve desired goals can be spelt out and that the means to achieve the desired goals are available to the decision maker.

Magistrates are faced with a highly complex decision environment since ostensibly their goal is to alter the behaviour of human beings. The goal of 'trying to prevent re-offending', 'to protect the public' or 'to help pull him back from the edge' are so diffuse as to create a good deal of uncertainty. This is without even beginning to think about the complexities of not just stopping offending behaviour but reforming a person. Such goals defy clear definition, (What is a 'useful citizen'? What is 'normal'?) let alone the formulation of sensible means to achieve them. There is no possibility of magistrates achieving the kind of global behavioural control which is connoted by such aspirations; there is certainly no 'cure' for juvenile offending which can be achieved through magisterial powers.

Chapter 7

Trial Judges

Chapter Contents

An English judge controls a criminal trial in the Crown Court in some ways as a referee supervises a boxing match. The two sides battle it out, and he (or she, of course) stands by to check that neither side breaks the rules. But this simplistic comparison hides the fact that the judge is a powerful referee, whose decisions may often affect the outcome of the trial. It also misses the point that the two sides are not well balanced as they might be in a boxing match: the defence have fewer powers of investigation, but a great deal at stake. In our case, Gerry Good is charged with an offence under the Offences Against the Person Act (OAPA) 1861, section 18. He is to be tried before a judge and jury. The role of the judge is clearly crucial to the conduct and outcome of the proceedings.

Gerry Good has been on bail. Before the case comes on for trial there will have been a plea and case management hearing (PCMH) at the Crown Court. The indictment was put to him by the clerk, and he lodged a plea of not guilty. The prosecution and defence (perhaps not the lawyers who will appear at trial) will have helped the judge identify key issues in the case and agreed time limits for the disclosure of documents. The case will then have been listed for trial.

On the day the trial is listed to start, Gerry Good arrives at court at 9am in order to meet his barrister, Tim Moffat. Perhaps the judge has to deal with other matters first (a sentencing case adjourned for a pre-sentence report after a trial a few weeks previously, or perhaps another PCMH at 10am), so Gerry's case may not come on until 11am. Between 10am and 11am the lawyers involved may try unsuccessfully to bargain a guilty plea (see Chapter 5: even a late guilty plea wins some discount in sentence). The CPS applies to add an alternative count to the indictment:

Count One
Statement of Offence
Wounding with intent, contrary to section 18 of the Offences Against the Person Act 1861.

Particulars of Offence
Gerry Good on or about the 13th day of June 2014 unlawfully and maliciously wounded Rosa Bottles with intent to do her grievous bodily harm.

Count Two
Statement of Offence
Unlawful wounding, contrary to section 20 of the Offences Against the Person Act 1861.

Particulars of Offence
Gerry Good on or about the 13th day of June 2014 unlawfully and maliciously wounded Rosa Bottles.

Sometimes the defence ask the judge for an advance indication of likely sentence (if a defendant is assured for example that he won't go to prison if he pleads guilty, then he might change his plea even at this late stage: see (ii) below), but in our case Gerry maintains his not guilty plea. The jury is sworn (see Chapter 8). The judge takes a low profile throughout the trial. Counsel for the prosecution outlines his case to the jury and calls his witnesses: Rosa Bottles, the pub landlord and two police officers. Witnesses will be examined by prosecution counsel, cross-examined by Gerry's counsel, and re-examined by prosecution counsel. The judge may interrupt to repeat a question or to ask the witness to go slower. She may intervene to stop inappropriate lines of questioning, but from Gerry Good's point of view, the judge seems unimportant until she makes her summing up to the jury. When she imposes the sentence, she moves to centre stage. However, in reality, she is highly influential on all the actors throughout the courtroom drama.

(i) Who are the trial judges?

The Crown Court sits at 77 centres throughout England and Wales. For trial purposes in the Crown Court, offences are divided into three classes of seriousness. Although all those charged with indictable crimes are tried in the Crown Court, the more serious charges will be tried before a High Court judge, the least serious before a circuit judge or recorder (part-time judges, usually practising barristers or solicitors, who usually sit as a judge for between three and six weeks a year). The Circuit Bench was created by the Courts Act 1971 as part of a major reorganisation of the criminal courts. Most judges were previously practising barristers, although since 1971 it has been possible for solicitors to sit as judges in the Crown Court. A barrister or solicitor of ten years' standing, or a recorder who has held office for at least three years, can be appointed as a circuit judge. The Courts and Legal Services Act 1990 enabled suitably qualified solicitors to become High Court judges, and the first was appointed in 1993.

Until quite recently the appointment of judges was in the hands of the Government, but there have been significant changes in recent years to the selection process. Perhaps a turning point came in 1990 when the Lord Chancellor's Department issued a document explaining the system for the appointment of judges, reflecting an opening up of the recruitment process and indeed a commitment to seeking out a wider pool of applicants. Sir Leonard Peach's *Independent Scrutiny of the Appointment Processes of Judges and QCs* (1999) concluded that the process was thorough and competent, but recommended the creation of a Commissioner for Judicial Appointments with the duties of performing audits of procedures as well as carrying out the role of ombudsman for both judicial and Queen's Counsel appointments, and this was accepted. The Commissioner's post existed from 2001 until 2006, but in 2006 we saw more radical change. Uncertainty about the system of appointment had been reinforced by the Scottish High Court of Justiciary's decision in *Starrs v Procurator Fiscal* [2000] HRLR 191, where it was held that the use of temporary sheriffs, who conducted as many as 25 per cent of Scotland's criminal cases, contravened the European Convention on Human Rights, Article 6 [1:13]. The court held that the appointment system failed to uphold judicial independence because temporary sheriffs' contracts were for only a year. They were hired and fired by the Lord Advocate, who, apart from being a member of the Scottish Government responsible for the legal system, is also head of the Scottish prosecution service. Lord Reed said that that did 'not square with the appearance of independence'. In 2000, the Lord Chancellor announced that 'no useful purpose' was served by having separate offices of recorder and assistant recorder. And in 2003 the Government announced that it would create a new Judicial Appointment Commission (JAC), recognising that it was no longer acceptable for judicial appointments to be in the hands of a Government Minister. This was effected by the Constitutional Reform Act 2005, which heralded a new era in judicial appointments.

The JAC started work in April 2006 and has a statutory duty, under the Constitutional Reform Act 2005, section 64, to 'have regard to the need to encourage diversity in the range of persons available for selection for appointments' (although appointments must be made solely on merit). The JAC publish an Equality Objectives Performance Report on an annual basis and it does appear that a greater proportion of women and ethnic minority candidates are being appointed: see http://jac.judiciary.gov.uk/.

Table 7.1 Numbers of judges

	Circuit judges	Recorders
1994	487 (28 women)	795 (42 women)
2000	561 (39 women)	907 (84 women)
2003	621 (50 women)	1,356 (50 women)
2007	639 (73 women)	1,201 (179 women)
2011	665 (106 women)	1,221 (201 women)
2014	640 (131 women)	1,126 (186 women)

Source: Previous editions; Judicial Diversity Statistics, 2011 and 2014

In 2014, there were 14 (2.4 per cent of known ethnicity) circuit judges of ethnic minority origin, up from nine (1.4 per cent) in 2006 and 66 (7.5 per cent of known ethnicity) recorders from ethnic minorities, up from 54 (4.4 per cent) in 2006. Although the appointment system has been much criticised, it is only partly responsible for the narrow social and educational background of English judges, analysed most famously by Griffith (1997) (see also Pannick (1987)). The conservatism of judges is also partly explained by the conservatism of many of those who choose to become lawyers in the first place.

The holder of the office of part-time judge or circuit judge has no special constitutional protection. Whilst the most senior judges – Justices of the Supreme Court, Lords Justices of Appeal and High Court judges – can only be removed by the Queen after an address from both Houses of Parliament, other judges can be removed by the Lord Chief Justice and Lord Chancellor for incapacity or misbehaviour. This is, however, very rare. Recorders are usually appointed for at least five years, and they may not have their contracts renewed on the following grounds: misbehaviour; incapacity; persistent failure to comply with sitting requirements (without good reason); failure to comply with training requirements; sustained failure to observe the standards reasonably expected from a holder of such office; part of a reduction in numbers because of changes in operational requirements; and part of a structural change to enable recruitment of new appointees.

Defendants have little protection against an incompetent or unfair judge. Complaints about a judge's personal conduct can be made to the Judicial Conduct Investigations Office (formerly the Office for Judicial Complaints) and since 2006 they have been able to complain to the Judicial Appointments and Conduct Ombudsman if they are dissatisfied with the outcome of their complaint to the Judicial Conduct Investigations Office. It remains virtually impossible to sue a judge. Section 2(5) of the Crown Proceedings Act 1947 provides that the Crown cannot be sued for the tortious conduct of any person 'while discharging or purporting to discharge any responsibilities of a judicial nature vested in him'. Lord Denning's statements in *Sirros v Moore* [7:1] illustrate the extent of the judge's immunity from suit. The right of appeal against an incorrect decision is not always an adequate remedy, especially since justice is thereby both delayed and often costly. In *FM (a child) v Singer* [2004] EWHC 793 (QB) an 11-year-old child tried to sue a High Court judge for acting so as to 'harass, threaten or intimidate' him (in the context of a custody dispute between his parents) but the High Court struck out his claim following *Sirros v Moore*. There was no question of bad faith, and the judge was absolutely protected from being sued.

(ii) Case management and sentence bargains

Judges today have an increasingly important 'case management' role (see Darbyshire (2014)). What does this mean in practice? See Part 3 of the Criminal Procedure Rules 2014 [7:2]. The Court of Appeal has also given stern advice to trial judges to try and get them to control proceedings effectively: see this extract from *Jisl* [7:3]. How does this fit in with traditional thoughts about the adversarial process (see [1:3])?

One good example of the way the judge's role is changing is in plea bargaining. Plea and charge bargaining between the parties, prosecution and defence, was examined in Chapter 5. It can be seen as a form of sentence bargaining: if Gerry Good, or rather his solicitor or counsel, had persuaded the prosecution to drop the charge under section 18, he could have been fairly confident that, on a guilty plea to a charge under section 20, he would have received a lighter sentence than if he continued to fight the case and been convicted. But here we are concerned with where the bargaining process goes one stage further, and the judge himself becomes involved in the discussions.

For many years, defendants pleading guilty have been regarded as entitled to a sentence discount of some 20–30 per cent, although the precise amount varied from judge to judge and from case to case (see *Claydon* (1993) 15 Cr App Rep (S) 526 where the Court of Appeal went so far as to say that where an offender voluntarily surrenders and confesses, a sentence discount of 50 per cent was appropriate). Then Parliament made a discount a statutory requirement: section 48 of the Criminal Justice and Public Order Act 1994 required all courts, when passing sentence, to take account of the timing and other circumstances of a plea of guilty. The current formula is found in section 144 of the Criminal Justice Act 2003. It was this Act too which created the now-replaced Sentencing Guidelines Council (SGC) (see (iv) below) and one of the first guidelines issued by the SGC concerned the discount for guilty pleas. The issue remains controversial, and the SGC was asked to revise its guideline in 2007. **[7:4]** is an extract from the revised guideline. In 2010, the Government proposed in a Green Paper to increase the maximum guilty plea discount from one-third to one-half but, after considerable hostility from the tabloid press, this proposal was dropped. Research carried out for the Sentencing Council **[7:5]** also found little public support for increases in discounts beyond the current one-third maximum.

Why is the discount controversial? As **[7:4]** makes clear, the discount is given not to reflect remorse (the defendant may get yet more discount for remorse) but as administrative convenience: the system could not cope if all defendants pleaded not guilty. Is there a danger that this discount may lead those who are not guilty to plead guilty? Zander and Henderson **[7:6]** present their findings without comment or evaluation, yet their question to the legally qualified participants in the trials they studied – on whether innocent people were pleading guilty – led some commentators to argue that perhaps 1,400 innocent people plead guilty in the Crown Court every year. However, the Royal Commission (1993) **[7:7]** believed that there was 'little if any' evidence that innocent people had pleaded guilty because of the sentence discount. But the important question is whether those who believe themselves to be innocent should be penalised for pleading not guilty.

Sentence bargains are particularly important where the defendant stands on the cusp of prison. Often he wants to know if he can be sure that, if he pleads guilty, he will avoid prison. This might well be so in the case of Gerry Good. He has several, relatively minor, previous convictions, and is now to be tried for intentional wounding (contrary to OAPA 1861, section 18). If he pleads guilty to malicious wounding (section 20), will he escape prison? For many years the Court of Appeal made it abundantly clear that there should not be informal discussions with judges on this subject: see *Turner* [1970] 2 QB 321 or *Dosseter* [1999] 2 Cr App R (S) 248 for clear examples of how the Court of Appeal discouraged unnecessary visits to the judge's room. Yet because of the cost, in terms of time and money, of cracked trials (those trials where the case is listed for trial before a jury, but on the day of the trial the defendant pleads guilty), the Royal Commission (1993) **[7:7]** rec-ommended the partial reversal of *Turner*. It suggested that, at the request of defence counsel on instructions from the defendant, judges should be able to indicate the highest sentence that they would impose at that point, on the basis of the facts put to them. A request for such an indication might be made at a preparatory hearing called especially for this purpose, or at the trial itself. Lord Justice Auld **[1:5]** also concluded his analysis of this issue with a complex recommendation for a system of 'advance indication of sentence' for those considering pleading guilty, which should be fully recorded. The Court of Appeal took up this proposal themselves in what might be seen as the 'revolutionary' decision in *Goodyear* in 2005 **[7:8]**. What do you make of this decision? Does it reflect the 'system's' crime control mentality (re-read Packer at **[1:10]**)? The decision in *Goodyear* has been much criticised: an obvious danger with this approach is that the judge is being asked to speak with inadequate information, particularly when a pre-sentence report has not yet been pre-pared. *R v McDonald* **[7:9]** may lead to greater caution as the dangers of advance indications become more obvious. After concerns expressed by the Court of Appeal in *Attorney General's Reference (No 34 of 2010)* [2010] EWCA Crim 2055, the Crown Prosecution Service issued guidance stating that where a judge wishes to indicate his or her view of the viability of the case or the acceptance of pleas, this should be done in open court, in the absence of the jury, with both sides represented and the defendant present. It is surely right that such indications are made in open court. But perhaps the only way to relieve the pressure on the innocent to plead guilty would be to abolish the sentence discount for guilty pleas altogether. A one-third discount for a plea is, after all, the equivalent of a 50 per cent increase in sentence for unsuccessfully maintaining a plea of not guilty. But for cost reasons, if no other, this proposal is highly improbable!

Another problem with both formal and informal systems of sentence discounting is that it is likely to be applied unevenly. The Royal Commission supported the policy recommended by Hood [7:10] of ethnic monitoring of all court outcomes. Hood provided evidence that the system of sentence discounts, combined with the tendency of black defendants to plead not guilty, put them at risk of being sentenced to longer sentences than their white peers. There is little reason to think that things are different today (see [1:17]).

(iii) The judge's discretion to exclude evidence

Most evidence in court is given orally, although agreed written statements are increasingly admitted. This section only discusses the wide discretionary power of the trial judge to exclude evidence, but it should be noted that the law of evidence is deeply complex, even more so since the reforms of the Criminal Justice Act 2003. Auld [1:5] called for the codification of the law of evidence. But, sadly, all that was offered in the Criminal Justice Act 2003 was a number of hugely complex amendments to the existing law.

Judges rarely call witnesses themselves: Zander and Henderson's Crown Court study (see [7:6]) found that in 19 per cent of cases judges reported that they knew of one or more important witnesses who had not been called by either side. It is a reflection on the adversarial system (see [1:3]) that they do not see it as their function to call even a useful witness. Perhaps, also, too much weight is given to the performance of individual witnesses, who themselves are dependent on the questions of counsel for the answers they can give.

Decisions to exclude evidence may be taken at a pre-trial hearing to avoid the waste of time and money which occurs when the jury have to be sent out during the trial for a voir dire ('trial within a trial'), but usually the question is not dealt with until the trial itself. The common law position (before the Police and Criminal Evidence Act 1984 (PACE)) on the exclusion of evidence was summed up by Lord Goddard CJ in the Privy Council decision Kuruma v R [1955] AC 197, at page 204:

> In their Lordships' opinion, the test to be applied in considering whether evidence is admissible is whether it is relevant to the matters in issue. If it is, it is admissible and the court is not concerned with how the evidence was obtained . . . The judge always has a discretion to exclude evidence if the strict rules of admissibility would operate unfairly against an accused . . . If, for instance, some piece of evidence, e.g., a document, had been obtained from a defendant by a trick, no doubt the judge might properly rule it out.

In that case, the Privy Council upheld the conviction of a man who had been sentenced to death for the unlawful possession of two rounds of ammunition, after having been unlawfully searched by police officers below the authorised rank. Pre-PACE, the courts usually left the disciplining of police officers to be performed through actions for damages, formal complaints procedures or by the occasional prosecution. We saw the inadequacies of these mechanisms of accountability in Chapter 2.

Nowadays the courts are more likely to exclude evidence which has been obtained improperly or illegally. The present law on the exclusion of evidence is to be found in sections 76(2) and 78 of PACE [2:9]. Read the sections carefully: at first sight, these sections appear to be contradictory, one being mandatory, and the other discretionary. Examples of excluded unfairly obtained evidence were given earlier in this book in *Loosely* **[2:13]** and in *Paris, Abdullahi and Miller* **[5:7]** and also discussed in *Maxwell* **[5:3]**. The courts are involved in a difficult balancing act: supporting the police in the investigation of crime, yet upholding the integrity of the criminal justice system. In *Christou* **[7:11]** the evidence gained by the police officers in an undercover operation was acceptable and in *Bryce* **[7:12]** it was not. Can the cases be distinguished? The law reports contain many other striking examples: in *Khan* **[7:13]** the House of Lords upheld the trial judge's decision to admit evidence, despite the fact that the police were guilty of a civil trespass and may have infringed the defendant's right to privacy by using an electronic listening device (a decision upheld by the European Court of Human Rights in *Khan v United Kingdom* (2001) 31 EHRR 1016). See also *Chalkley and Jeffries* **[9:6]**. We also saw the difficulty of hearsay evidence in the case of absent witnesses in *Horncastle* **[1:14]** and *Al-Khawaja and Tahery* **[1:15]**. Think hard about how you would decide these cases.

The Royal Commission on Criminal Justice (1993) was satisfied with the way that the law was working, though Professor Zander's powerful dissent **[9:1]** is worth noting here. The majority of the Royal Commission thought that the Court of Appeal's power to quash convictions after breaches of PACE should be limited to cases where the jury's verdict was unsafe. But Zander stressed that the role of the Court of Appeal in promoting the observation of the crucial and complex network of the PACE rules is of the greatest importance. He believes that 'the majority would in effect be encouraging the Court of Appeal to undercut a part of [section 78]'s moral force by saying that the issue of "unfairness" can be ignored where there is sufficient evidence to show that the defendant is actually guilty' (at page 235). In Chapter 9 we return to the changes made to the powers of the Court of Appeal by the Criminal Appeal Act 1995 and the current debates.

The Royal Commission was unanimous in recommending the introduction of a rule similar to Rule 403 of the United States Federal Rules of Evidence, which empowers the judge to 'exclude relevant evidence if its probative value is substantially outweighed by a danger of one or more of the following: unfair prejudice, confusing the issues, misleading the jury, undue delay, wasting time, or needlessly presenting cumulative evidence'. The Commission believed that the introduction of such a rule would allow judges to be more 'robust' in preventing juries from having to sit through evidence that adds little or nothing to what is already before them. Thus, the power of the judge to control the issues that would go before the jury would be increased. Auld **[1:5]** on the other hand urged not only a codification of the law of evidence but also a simplification of the rules for excluding evidence on the grounds of its unfairness. What has happened since Auld is the codification not of the rules of evidence but of the secondary rules of criminal procedure (see the Criminal Procedure Rules at **[7:2]**). But we are still a long way from a general code of criminal procedure: a mass of different statutes apply.

(iv) The summing up

After the evidence has been presented, and after the prosecution and defence have made their closing speeches, the judge sums up the case in order to help the jury in their task of reaching a verdict. Until recently, the Judicial Studies Board (now the Judicial College) issued model directions to help judges to craft their summing ups but this was replaced in the 2010 *Crown Court Bench Book – Directing the Jury* with more general guidance designed to move away from what had been perceived as a rigid approach to summing up: the Bench Book is available online (www.judiciary.gov.uk/publications/crown-court-bench-book-directing-the-jury-2/) and a useful student exercise is to have a go writing a summing up!

Thus, the judge in Gerry Good's case, for example, will explain to the jury the burden and standard of proof and the respective roles of judge and jury. She will state that they may only convict if they are sure, or satisfied beyond reasonable doubt, of Gerry's guilt. She will then summarise the facts on which their decision is required, and give directions on relevant points of law. She will have to define to the jury the legal meaning of 'intent' in OAPA 1861, section 18 and explain the effect of Gerry's intoxication (if indeed he was intoxicated) on his 'intent'. She has to describe the relationship of section 18 with section 20 and explain the circumstances when the jury may bring in an alternative verdict. None of these factors are straightforward in English law: indeed, there has been a loud lobby for many years calling for a codification of the substantive criminal law (as well as of procedure and evidence), but this does not catch the politicians' imagination. Even in this simple case, the summing up is likely to last at least an hour. Should the jury be given a written copy? Judge Madge (2006) argues that written directions would help juries understand their task: it is difficult to disagree.

Should the judge be allowed to refer to the facts of the case? Even in a short case like Gerry Good's, the facts are rarely straightforward. Here, Gerry's account of his police interviews does not accord with that of the police. The jury have heard both sides of the case: can the judge present a balanced perspective to the jury? In the United States, where the summing up is known as the 'jury charge', the judge only gives the jury an explanation of the law, without reference to the facts. In England, the extent to which the judge comments on the facts is left to the discretion of the individual judge. In Gerry's case, the jury retire for a little over two hours, and return a verdict of not guilty to the section 18 offence, but guilty to the section 20 offence. Had they taken much longer, the judge would have had a discretion to allow a majority verdict (see Chapter 8).

(v) Sentencing

After a jury brings in a verdict of guilty, the question of sentence is entirely decided by the judge. Where the defendant has pleaded not guilty, the facts will have been explored fully before the jury, before they reached their verdict. More difficult may be the case where the defendant has pleaded guilty, but where there is a wide divergence between the prosecution and defence on the facts. This is dramatically illustrated by the facts of *Newton* **[7:14]**, where the Lord Chief Justice explained the proper approach to be taken by a trial judge when dealing with the task of sentencing such a defendant. The facts of *Newton* will not arise again since consensual buggery is no longer a crime, but the issue is important. The trial judge may feel a pressure to accept the defendant's view of the facts, in order to save the added costs and delays of a 'trial within a trial' to establish contested facts. This can lead to a defendant being substantially under-sentenced. The guidance in *Newton* was 'updated' in *Underwood* **[7:15]**, in 2004, in which the Court of Appeal dealt with four different cases.

The statutory maximum for the offence in question is normally laid down in the statute creating the offence. Gerry was charged with an offence under section 18, but convicted of an offence under section 20, of the OAPA 1861. The Act originally laid down punishments of penal servitude, but it has been amended such that the maximum penalty for wounding with intent (contrary to section 18) is life imprisonment and the maximum penalty for wounding (contrary to section 20) is five years' imprisonment.

The statutory framework of judges' sentencing powers is similar to that discussed in the last chapter on magistrates' powers – consolidated in the Powers of Criminal Courts (Sentencing) Act 2000 but massively changed by the Criminal Justice Act (CJA) 2003. We noted there the role of sentencing guidelines. The Sentencing Guidelines Council (SGC) arose out of a proposal of the *Halliday Report* (2001), which recommended a statutory guideline-setting body that would produce 'structured' and 'accessible' guidelines across the whole range of English sentencing law. It was chaired by the Lord Chief Justice and made up of seven further judicial members and four non-judicial members. It produced a wealth of sentencing guidelines for all criminal courts and, under the CJA 2003, section 172, courts had a duty to have regard to any relevant guidelines when sentencing.

Lord Carter was asked to investigate the long-term supply and demand for prison places and his Report (2007) recommended that a working group be set up to investigate further a 'structured sentencing framework and a permanent Sentencing Commission' (for a critical summary of this Report, see Padfield, 2007). The Secretary of State for Justice established this working group, under the chairmanship of Lord Justice Gage, and it reported in 2008. One of its main conclusions was that having two separate bodies, the Sentencing Advisory Panel and the Sentencing Guidelines Council, was inefficient and it recommended that the two be combined into a single body. Perhaps of more significance though was its recommendation in relation to the role of sentencing guidelines: it concluded that a more 'robust' test for departures from the guidelines should be introduced and that instead of sentencing judges merely having to have regard to the guidelines, courts should only impose sentences outside the guideline if it is in the interests of justice to do so.

The Coroners and Justice Act 2009 put these two main recommendations into practice. The Sentencing Advisory Panel and Sentencing Guidelines Council were both abolished and were replaced, from April 2010, by the Sentencing Council, which consists of 14 members: eight judicial and six non-judicial and is chaired by one of the judicial members. The significance of the guidelines has also changed: for offences committed on or after 6 April 2010, a court 'must, in sentencing an offender, follow any sentencing guidelines which are relevant to the offender's case . . . unless the court is satisfied that it would be contrary to the interests of justice to do so' (Coroners and Justice Act 2009, section 125).

Perhaps the most controversial changes of the CJA 2003 concerned the sentencing of 'dangerous' offenders. First, the Act laid down controversial provisions which established a new scheme (at long last!) under which the court, rather than the Secretary of State, determines the minimum term to be served in prison by a person convicted of murder in order to comply with the judgment of the European Court of Human Rights in *Stafford v UK* (2002) 35 EHRR 1121 **[10:14]**, and the judgment of the House of Lords in R (*Anderson*) v Secretary of State for the Home Department [2003] 1 AC 837. But the Home Secretary seemed determined to have the last word: the length of this minimum term is determined by reference to the framework set out in Schedule 21. When setting a minimum term, the court must take into account four categories of starting point: a whole life order, 30 years, 25 years and 15 years. (Those aged between 18 and 21 years old may only be subject to the 30-, 25- and 15-year starting points and juveniles may only be subject to a 12-year starting point.) Once an offender has been allocated a starting point, the court must then consider aggravating and mitigating factors to arrive at a minimum term. The offender must serve the entirety of this minimum term before being considered for release by the Parole Board. This has greatly increased the length of time that murderers will serve: the average length of a minimum term for murder has risen from 12.5 years in 2003 to 21.1 years in 2013 as a consequence of the CJA 2003 reforms. It has also had a knock-on effect on sentences for other serious offences such as manslaughter and attempted murder (see Jeremy (2010)). Once the minimum term has expired, the Parole Board will consider the person's suitability for release, and if appropriate, direct his release (see Chapter 10).

Even more controversial than the sentence for murder was the scheme of sentences for offenders who have been assessed as dangerous and have committed a specified sexual or violent offence. As originally enacted, where there is 'a significant risk' of 'serious harm' from future 'specified offences' likely to be committed by the offender the court had only the choice between imposing a life sentence or imprisonment for public protection (under section 225). Imprisonment for public protection was available even where the defendant had no previous convictions and if the defendant had a previous conviction for a 'relevant offence' (most sexual or violent offences) then the court 'must assume' that there was a significant risk of future serious harm, unless the court considers that it would be 'unreasonable' to conclude that there was such a risk. This led to a large increase in the number of people serving indeterminate sentences over a very short period of time as, under the original wording of section 229, many offenders were assumed 'dangerous' by virtue of previous convictions even if they had never committed a particularly serious offence. The prison system struggled to cope with this influx of prisoners who would have to undertake courses aimed at tackling their risk factors before release through the Parole Board could become a realistic possibility. The failure to provide such courses attracted a significant amount of litigation and a defeat for the Government in the European Court of Human Rights in *James, Wells and Lee v UK* (2012) 56 EHRR 12.

Section 229 was amended by the Criminal Justice and Immigration Act 2008 to remove the statutory 'assumption' of dangerousness where the defendant had a previous conviction for a 'relevant offence'. This gave a sentencing judge more discretion when assessing whether a defendant was 'dangerous' and an amendment to section 225 restricted the imposition of a life sentence or imprisonment for public protection to cases where the defendant had a previous conviction for a serious offence or where the minimum term would be at least two years. The CJA 2003 also introduced a new form of extended sentence: 'dangerous' offenders who have been convicted of a trigger sexual or violent offence (listed in Schedule 15) for which the maximum penalty is between two and 10 years were given an extended sentence. This sentence was a determinate sentence served in custody to the halfway point, with release during the whole of the second half of the sentence being on the recommendation of the Parole Board. In addition, extended supervision periods of up to five years for violent offenders and eight years for sexual offenders were added to the sentence.

Both the imprisonment for public protection sentence and the CJA 2003 extended sentence were abolished by the Legal Aid, Sentencing and Punishment of Offenders Act 2012: in their place is an automatic life sentence for a second serious offence (those listed in Schedule 15B to the CJA 2003 – although this sentence is only available where the current offence merits a custodial sentence of at least 10 years) and a new extended sentence where two-thirds of the sentence must be served in custody followed by an extended licence period after release (people serving an extended sentence imposed for the more serious offences will not be released automatically at the two-thirds stage and will have to apply to the Parole Board for release). The rules around the sentencing and release of 'dangerous' offenders remain extremely complicated and have been amended yet again by the Criminal Justice and Courts Act 2015, section 4 so that all extended sentence prisoners must go through the Parole Board if they are to be released before the expiry of their sentence.

In sentencing an offender, the judge will take account of the facts of the offence, the circumstances of the offender and the plea in mitigation. In Gerry Good's case, the judge decides to adjourn the case for the preparation of a pre-sentence report (PSR). The judge must now decide whether or not to remand Gerry in custody pending sentence (see Chapter 6 for a discussion of bail). In the event, defence counsel having stressed the fact that Gerry has respected the terms of his conditional bail over the past few months, the judge continues his bail but warns him that although she is seeking a PSR, Gerry should anticipate a custodial sentence.

At the resumed hearing, counsel for the prosecution may call a police officer (the 'antecedents officer') to give details of Gerry Good's previous convictions, or may simply read out the previous convictions himself, and he will ensure that the judge has a copy of the PSR. The role of defence counsel in presenting a plea in mitigation, and in deciding whether to call witnesses in support of the defendant's good character, was raised in Chapter 5. A court duty probation officer will be in court to speak, if necessary, to the pre-sentence report. The report on Gerry Good is included in Chapter 10. The judge gives Gerry Good a brief lecture on why she finds it impossible in this case to do other than impose an immediate custodial sentence. Stockdale (1967) questioned the value of such homilies: it is doubtful whether they have any general or particular deterrent effect – 'a far more likely effect is a general and particular resentment, and sometimes a contempt for the court' (at page 34). But the judge does have a duty to explain the sentence, and to give reasons to explain his or her decision-making process. The task is no easy one: the audience is the public, the victim, the media as well as the defendant. In recent years, selected sentencing remarks have been made available on the Judiciary's website and we include those in the case of Vicky Pryce and Chris Huhne at **[7:16]**.

This book is not a textbook on sentencing: several such are mentioned in the Further Reading. But readers should be well aware of the complexity of the law. Gerry Good is eventually sentenced to two years in prison (see the sentencing guideline for this offence at **[7:17]**). Will he appeal? The Court of Appeal will only vary the sentence imposed at trial where it is 'manifestly excessive or wrong in principle', and so the judge's discretion is rarely interfered with.

Table 7.2 Appeals against sentence

	Offenders sentenced in the Crown Court	Applications for leave to appeal against sentence	Successful appeals against sentence
1993	69,500	4,848	1,309
1998	80,400	6,550	1,589
2001	72,100	5,497	1,101
2006	77,000	5,082	1,391
2009/10	100,511	4,110	1,484
2013/14	86,149	3,841	1,016

Source: Judicial Statistics 2001; Table 1.8; Criminal Statistics 2001, Chapter 7; Sentencing Statistics 2006, Chapter 1; Judicial Statistics 2006, page 13; Criminal Justice System Statistics Quarterly: September 2014, Table Q5.3; Court of Appeal (Criminal Division) Annual Report 2013–14, pages 27–28

To gain an appreciation of how the Court of Appeal deals with appeals against sentence, students should browse through electronic databases, or even better, hard copies of the Criminal Appeal Reports (Sentencing). These serve as a useful reminder of the conditions in which many offenders live, and the very repetition of these sad and often tragic pictures of life is a challenge for those who study the criminal justice system: this 'system' is dealing with very real individuals. Judges develop different reputations as sentencers, and doubtless the reputation of the individual judge has an important influence on the decision of the defendant whether to plead guilty. In 1980 Ashworth et al **[7:18]** carried out a 'pilot study' into sentencing policy and practices in the Crown Court. The Lord Chief Justice then refused permission for the work to proceed any further. Although much has changed in the intervening years, the discussion extracted remains a useful summary of the case for academic research in this area. Hood's study **[7:10]** was the first large-scale statistical attempt to try to assess whether defendants of different ethnic origin were treated equally when sentenced in the Crown Courts. Much more research should be carried out into how, in practice, judges actually reach decisions. Between October 2010 and March 2015, the Sentencing Council conducted a Crown Court Sentencing Survey and plenty of information about it can be found on the Sentencing Council's website.

Until 1988, only the defence had the right to appeal against sentence, but since the enactment of the Criminal Justice Act 1988, section 36 **[9:15]** the Attorney General may refer 'unduly lenient' sentences to the Court of Appeal. Chapter 9 raises arguments in support of a wider prosecution right of appeal, to encourage a more thorough review of sentencing decisions. Sentencing law and practice continues to remain very much on the political agenda.

Further reading

Ashworth, A, *Sentencing and Criminal Justice* (5th edition, 2010) Cambridge University Press

Carter, P, *Securing the Future: proposals for the efficient and sustainable use of custody in England and Wales* (2007) Ministry of Justice

Darbyshire, P, *Sitting in Judgment: The Working Lives of Judges* (2011) Hart Publishing

Darbyshire, P, 'Judicial case management in ten Crown courts' [2014] Crim LR 30

Devlin, P, *The Judge* (1979) Oxford University Press

Griffith, J A G, *The Politics of the Judiciary* (5th edition, 1997) Fontana

Halliday, J, *Making Punishments work: a review of the sentencing framework for England and Wales* (2001) Home Office

Jeremy, D, 'Sentencing policy or short-term expediency?' [2010] Crim LR 593

Madge, N, 'Summing up – a judge's perspective' [2006] Crim LR 817

Ministry of Justice, *Statistics on Race and the Criminal Justice System* (biannual)

Padfield, N, 'Securing the Future? Lord Carter's narrow approach' (2007) 50 JP 876

Pannick, D, *Judges* (1987) Oxford University Press

Roberts, J V, 'Structured sentencing: Lessons from England and Wales for common law jurisdictions' (2012) *Punishment & Society* 14(3): 267

Rock, P, *The Social World of the English Crown Court* (1993) Clarendon Press

Stevens, R, *The Independence of the Judiciary* (1993) Oxford University Press

Stevens, R, 'Unpacking the Judges' (1993) *Current Legal Problems* 1

Stockdale, E, *The Court and the Offender* (1967) Gollanz

Thomas, D A, *Current Sentencing Practice* (constantly updated) Sweet & Maxwell

Thomas, D A, 'Criminal Justice Act 2003: Custodial sentences' [2004] Crim LR 702

Thomas, D A, 'The Legal Aid, Sentencing and Punishment of Offenders Act 2012: the sentencing provisions' [2012] Crim LR 572

Walker, N and Padfield, N, *Sentencing:Theory, Law and Practice* (2nd edition, 1996) Butterworths

Documents

[7:1] *Sirros v Moore*

[1975] QB 118

A judge in the Crown Court heard an appeal against the decision of magistrates to recommend to the Home Secretary that the appellant be deported. The magistrates had directed that he should not be detained pending the Home Secretary's decision. Having dismissed the appeal, the judge then ordered that the appellant be held in custody. The Court of Appeal held that because the judge had not adopted the right procedure, the order on which the appellant was taken into custody was invalid and he had rightly been released on habeas corpus. However, the judge was immune from liability in a civil action for damages.

Lord Denning MR (at page 136):

(iii) The modern courts

In the old days, as I have said, there was a sharp distinction between the inferior courts and the superior courts. Whatever may have been the reason for this distinction, it is no longer valid.

There has been no case on the subject for the last one hundred years at least. And during this time our judicial system has changed out of all knowledge. So great is this change that it is now appropriate for us to reconsider the principles which should be applied to judicial acts. In this new age I would take my stand on this: as a matter of principle the judges of superior courts have no greater claim to immunity than the judges of the lower courts. Every judge of the courts of this land – from the highest to the lowest – should be protected to the same degree, and liable to the same degree. If the reason underlying this immunity is to ensure 'that they may be free in thought and independent in judgment,' it applies to every judge, whatever his rank. Each should be protected from liability to damages when he is acting judicially. Each should be able to do his work in complete independence and free from fear. He should not have to turn the pages of his books with trembling fingers, asking himself: 'If I do this, shall I be liable in damages?' So long as he does his work in the honest belief that it is within his jurisdiction, then he is not liable to an action. He may be mistaken in the fact. He may be ignorant of the law. What he does may be outside his jurisdiction – in fact or in law – but so long as he honestly believes it to be within his jurisdiction, he should not be liable. Once he honestly entertains this belief, nothing else will make him liable. He is not to be plagued with allegations of malice or ill-will or bias or anything of the kind. Actions based on such allegations have been struck out and will continue to be struck out. Nothing will make him liable except it be shown that he was not acting judicially, knowing that he had no jurisdiction to do it.

This principle should cover the justices of the peace also. They should no longer be subject to 'strokes of the rodde, or spur'. Aided by their clerks, they do their work with the highest degree of responsibility and competence – to the satisfaction of the entire community. They should have the same protection as other judges.

(iv) The Crown Court

Today we are concerned with judges of a new kind. The judges of the Crown Court. It is, by definition, a superior court of record: see section 4(1) of the Act of 1971. The judges of it should, in principle, have the same immunity as all other judges, high or low. The Crown Court is manned by judges of every rank. Judges of the High Court, circuit judges, recorders, justices of the peace, all sit there. No distinction can or should be drawn between them. Each one shares responsibility for the decisions given by the court. If the High Court judge is not liable to an action, it should be same with the circuit judge, the recorder or the justice of the peace. No distinction can be taken on the seriousness of the case. Any one of them may sit on one day on a case of trifling importance, on the next on a case of the utmost gravity. No distinction can be taken as to the nature of the case. It may be a matter triable only in indictment, or it may be a man up for sentence, or an appeal from magistrates. If they are not liable in trials on indictment, they should not be liable on other matters. But, whatever, it is, the immunity of the judges – and each of them – should rest on the same principle. Not liable for acts done by them in a judicial capacity. Only liable for acting in bad faith, knowing they have no jurisdiction to do it.

Conclusion

The judge had no jurisdiction to detain Sirros in custody. The Divisional Court were right to release him on habeas corpus. Though the judge was mistaken, yet he acted judicially and for that reason no action will lie against him. Likewise, no action will lie against the police officers. They are protected in respect of anything they did at his direction, not knowing it was wrong: see *London Corp v Cox* (1867) LR 2 HL 239, 269. I would therefore dismiss the appeal.

[7:2] Criminal Procedure Rules 2014/1610
Parts 1–3

Part 1 The Overriding Objective

1.1 The overriding objective

(1) The overriding objective of this new code is that criminal cases be dealt with justly.
(2) Dealing with a criminal case justly includes—

(a) acquitting the innocent and convicting the guilty;
(b) dealing with the prosecution and the defence fairly;

(c) recognising the rights of a defendant, particularly those under Article 6 of the European Convention on Human Rights;

(d) respecting the interests of witnesses, victims and jurors and keeping them informed of the progress of the case;

(e) dealing with the case efficiently and expeditiously;

(f) ensuring that appropriate information is available to the court when bail and sentence are considered; and

(g) dealing with the case in ways that take into account—

  (i) the gravity of the offence alleged,

  (ii) the complexity of what is in issue,

  (iii) the severity of the consequences for the defendant and others affected, and

  (iv) the needs of other cases.

1.2 The duty of the participants in a criminal case

(1) Each participant, in the conduct of each case, must—

(a) prepare and conduct the case in accordance with the overriding objective;

(b) comply with these Rules, practice directions and directions made by the court; and

(c) at once inform the court and all parties of any significant failure (whether or not that participant is responsible for that failure) to take any procedural step required by these Rules, any practice direction or any direction of the court. A failure is significant if it might hinder the court in furthering the overriding objective.

(2) Anyone involved in any way with a criminal case is a participant in its conduct for the purposes of this rule.

1.3 The application by the court of the overriding objective

The court must further the overriding objective in particular when—

(a) exercising any power given to it by legislation (including these Rules);

(b) applying any practice direction; or

(c) interpreting any rule or practice direction.

Part 2 Understanding and Applying the Rules
When the Rules apply

2.1 When the Rules apply

(1) In general, Criminal Procedure Rules apply—

(a) in all criminal cases in magistrates' courts and in the Crown Court;

(b) in extradition cases in the High Court; and

(c) in all cases in the criminal division of the Court of Appeal.

(2) If a rule applies only in one or some of those courts, the rule makes that clear.

(3) These Rules apply on and after 6th October, 2014, but—

(a) unless the court otherwise directs, they do not affect a right or duty existing under the Criminal Procedure Rules 2013(1); and

(b) unless the High Court otherwise directs, Section 3 of Part 17 (Extradition – appeal to the High Court) does not apply to a case in which notice of an appeal was given before that date.

(4) In a case in which a request for extradition was received by a relevant authority in the United Kingdom on or before 31st December, 2003—

(a) the rules in Part 17 (Extradition) do not apply; and

(b) the rules in Part 17 of the Criminal Procedure Rules 2012(2) continue to apply as if those rules had not been revoked.

2.2 Definitions

(1) In these Rules, unless the context makes it clear that something different is meant:

'business day' means any day except Saturday, Sunday, Christmas Day, Boxing Day, Good Friday, Easter Monday or a bank holiday;

'court' means a tribunal with jurisdiction over criminal cases. It includes a judge, recorder, District Judge (Magistrates' Court), lay justice and, when exercising their judicial powers, the Registrar of Criminal Appeals, a justices' clerk or assistant clerk;

'court officer' means the appropriate member of the staff of a court;

'justices' legal adviser' means a justices' clerk or an assistant to a justices' clerk;

'live link' means an arrangement by which a person can see and hear, and be seen and heard by, the court when that person is not in court;

'Practice Direction' means the Lord Chief Justice's Criminal Practice Directions, as amended, and 'Criminal Costs Practice Direction' means the Lord Chief Justice's Practice Direction (Costs in Criminal Proceedings), as amended;

'public interest ruling' means a ruling about whether it is in the public interest to disclose prosecution material under sections 3(6), 7A(8) or 8(5) of the Criminal Procedure and Investigations Act 1996(10); and

'Registrar' means the Registrar of Criminal Appeals or a court officer acting with the Registrar's authority.

(2) Definitions of some other expressions are in the rules in which they apply.

2.3 References to Acts of Parliament and to Statutory Instruments

In these Rules, where a rule refers to an Act of Parliament or to subordinate legislation by title and year, subsequent references to that Act or to that legislation in the rule are shortened: so, for example, after a reference to the Criminal Procedure and Investigations Act 1996(11) that Act is called 'the 1996 Act'; and after a reference to the Criminal Procedure and Investigations Act 1996 (Defence Disclosure Time Limits) Regulations 2011(12) those Regulations are called 'the 2011 Regulations'.

2.4 Representatives

(1) Under these Rules, unless the context makes it clear that something different is meant, anything that a party may or must do may be done –

(a) by a legal representative on that party's behalf;
(b) by a person with the corporation's written authority, where that corporation is a defendant;
(c) with the help of a parent, guardian or other suitable supporting adult where that party is a defendant –

   (i) who is under 18, or
   (ii) whose understanding of what the case involves is limited.

(2) A member, officer or employee of a prosecutor may, on the prosecutor's behalf –

(a) serve on the magistrates' court officer, or present to a magistrates' court, an information under section 1 of the Magistrates' Courts Act 1980(13); or
(b) issue a written charge and requisition under section 29 of the Criminal Justice Act 2003(14).

Part 3 Case Management

3.1 When this Part applies

(1) Rules 3.1 to 3.12 apply to the management of each case in a magistrates' court and in the Crown Court (including an appeal to the Crown Court) until the conclusion of that case.
(2) Rules 3.13 to 3.26 apply where—

(a) the defendant is sent to the Crown Court for trial;
(b) a High Court or Crown Court judge gives permission to serve a draft indictment; or
(c) the Court of Appeal orders a retrial.

3.2 The duty of the court

(1) The court must further the overriding objective by actively managing the case.
(2) Active case management includes—

(a) the early identification of the real issues;
(b) the early identification of the needs of witnesses;
(c) achieving certainty as to what must be done, by whom, and when, in particular by the early setting of a timetable for the progress of the case;
(d) monitoring the progress of the case and compliance with directions;
(e) ensuring that evidence, whether disputed or not, is presented in the shortest and clearest way;
(f) discouraging delay, dealing with as many aspects of the case as possible on the same occasion, and avoiding unnecessary hearings;
(g) encouraging the participants to co-operate in the progression of the case; and
(h) making use of technology.

(3) The court must actively manage the case by giving any direction appropriate to the needs of that case as early as possible.

3.3 The duty of the parties

Each party must—

   (a)   actively assist the court in fulfilling its duty under rule 3.2, without or if necessary with a direction; and

   (b)   apply for a direction if needed to further the overriding objective.

3.4 Case progression officers and their duties

(1) At the beginning of the case each party must, unless the court otherwise directs—

   (a)   nominate someone responsible for progressing that case; and

   (b)   tell other parties and the court who that is and how to contact that person.

(2) In fulfilling its duty under rule 3.2, the court must where appropriate—

   (a)   nominate a court officer responsible for progressing the case; and

   (b)   make sure the parties know who that is and how to contact that court officer.

(3) In this Part a person nominated under this rule is called a case progression officer.

(4) A case progression officer must—

   (a)   monitor compliance with directions;

   (b)   make sure that the court is kept informed of events that may affect the progress of that case;

   (c)   make sure that he or she can be contacted promptly about the case during ordinary business hours;

   (d)   act promptly and reasonably in response to communications about the case; and

   (e)   if he or she will be unavailable, appoint a substitute to fulfil his or her duties and inform the other case progression officers.

3.5 The court's case management powers

(1) In fulfilling its duty under rule 3.2 the court may give any direction and take any step actively to manage a case unless that direction or step would be inconsistent with legislation, including these Rules.

(2) In particular, the court may—

   (a)   nominate a judge, magistrate or justices' legal adviser to manage the case;

   (b)   give a direction on its own initiative or on application by a party;

   (c)   ask or allow a party to propose a direction;

   (d)   for the purpose of giving directions, receive applications and representations by letter, by telephone or by any other means of electronic communication, and conduct a hearing by such means;

   (e)   give a direction—

      (i)   at a hearing, in public or in private, or

      (ii)   without a hearing;

   (f)   fix, postpone, bring forward, extend, cancel or adjourn a hearing;

   (g)   shorten or extend (even after it has expired) a time limit fixed by a direction;

   (h)   require that issues in the case should be—

      (i)   identified in writing,

      (ii)   determined separately, and decide in what order they will be determined; and

   (i) specify the consequences of failing to comply with a direction.

(3) A magistrates' court may give a direction that will apply in the Crown Court if the case is to continue there.

(4) The Crown Court may give a direction that will apply in a magistrates' court if the case is to continue there.

(5) Any power to give a direction under this Part includes a power to vary or revoke that direction.

(6) If a party fails to comply with a rule or a direction, the court may –

(a) fix, postpone, bring forward, extend, cancel or adjourn a hearing;
(b) exercise its powers to make a costs order; and
(c) impose such other sanction as may be appropriate.

[7:3] *R v Jisl*
[2004] EWCA Crim 696

Judge LJ finishes his judgement with the following advice:

Case Management

113. After an earlier trial which had taken place in 1998, this trial took place in the summer of 2001. By the time the retrial started we recognise that its management had already been fixed, virtually immutably, into pre-determined patterns. The observations which follow are not intended to be critical of the trial judge. Rather, they are an attempt to explain that since the date of this trial arrangements for case management by trial judges have changed, and to emphasise the urgent necessity that these changes and their potential impact are fully and widely understood.

114. The starting point is simple. Justice must be done. The defendant is entitled to a fair trial: and, which is sometimes overlooked, the prosecution is equally entitled to a reasonable opportunity to present the evidence against the defendant. It is not however a concomitant of the entitlement to a fair trial that either or both sides are further entitled to take as much time as they like, or for that matter, as long as counsel and solicitors or the defendants themselves think appropriate. Resources are limited. The funding for courts and judges, for prosecuting and the vast majority of defence lawyers is dependent on public money, for which there are many competing demands. Time itself is a resource. Every day unnecessarily used, while the trial meanders sluggishly to its eventual conclusion, represents another day's stressful waiting for the remaining witnesses and the jurors in that particular trial, and no less important, continuing and increasing tension and worry for another defendant or defendants, some of whom are remanded in custody, and the witnesses in trials which are waiting their turn to be listed. It follows that the sensible use of time requires judicial management and control.

115. Almost exactly a year ago in *R v Chaaban* [2003] EWCA Crim. 1012 this Court endeavoured to explain the principle:

"35. . . . The trial judge has always been responsible for managing the trial. That is one of his most important functions. To perform it he has to be alert to the needs of everyone involved in the case. That obviously includes, but it is not limited to, the interests of the defendant. It extends to the prosecution, the complainant, to every witness (whichever side is to call the witness), to the jury, or if the jury has not been sworn, to jurors in waiting. Finally, the judge should not overlook the community's interest that justice should be done . . . without unnecessary delay. A fair balance has to be struck between all these interests.

37. . . . nowadays, as part of his responsibility for managing the trial, the judge is expected to control the timetable and to manage the available time. Time is not unlimited. No one should assume that trials can continue to take as long or use up as much time as either or both sides may wish, or think, or assert, they need. The entitlement to a fair trial is not inconsistent with proper judicial control over the use of time. At the risk of stating the obvious, every trial which takes longer than it reasonably should is wasteful of limited resources. It also results in delays to justice in cases still waiting to be tried, adding to the tension and distress of victims, defendants, particularly those in custody awaiting trial, and witnesses. Most important of all it does nothing to assist the jury to reach a true verdict on the evidence.

38. In principle, the trial judge should exercise firm control over the timetable, where necessary, making clear in advance and throughout the trial that the timetable will be subject to appropriate constraints. With such necessary even-handedness and flexibility as the interests of the justice require as the case unfolds, the judge is entitled to direct that the trial is expected to conclude by a specific date and to exercise his powers to see that it does."

116. The principle therefore, is not in doubt. This appeal enables us to re-emphasise that its practical application depends on the determination of trial judges and the co-operation of the legal profession. Active, hands on, case management, both pre-trial and throughout the trial itself, is now regarded as an essential part of the judge's duty. The profession must understand that this has become and will remain part of the normal trial process, and that cases must be prepared and conducted accordingly.

117. The issues in this particular trial were identified at a very early stage, indeed during the course of the previous trial itself. In relation to each of the defendants, in a single word, the issue was knowledge. And indeed, the issue in most trials is equally readily identified.

118. Once the issue has been identified, in a case of any substance at all, (and this particular case was undoubtedly a case of substance and difficulty) the judge should consider whether to direct a timetable to cover pre-trial steps, and eventually the conduct of the trial itself, not rigid, nor immutable, and fully recognising that during the trial at any rate the unexpected must be treated as normal, and making due allowance for it in the interests of justice. To enable the trial judge to manage the case in a way which is fair to every participant, pre-trial, the potential problems as well as the possible areas for time saving, should be canvassed. In short, a sensible informed discussion about the future management of the case and the most convenient way to present the evidence, whether disputed or not, and where appropriate, with admissions by one or other or both sides, should enable the judge to make a fully informed analysis of the future timetable, and the proper conduct of the trial. The objective is not haste and rush, but greater efficiency and better use of limited resources by closer identification of and focus on critical rather than peripheral issues. When trial judges act in accordance with these principles, the directions they give, and where appropriate, the timetables they prescribe in the exercise of their case management responsibilities, will be supported in this Court. Criticism is more likely to be addressed to those who ignore them.

119. If these principles had been applied to this trial, it seems to us inconceivable that it would have taken 70 days before the jury reached its verdict, or given the issue in Tekin's case, that his evidence would have lasted four days in chief, and part of a further ten days in cross-examination by counsel for the Crown, or that Tekin himself should have been permitted without warning, to produce a bundle of documents some four hundred pages long and seek to adduce it in evidence. Equally, we doubt whether the repeated recall of prosecution

witnesses, some twice, several three times, would have taken place, or that the judge would have been invited time after time to break off the hearing of the evidence in order to give legal rulings. We are not seeking to analyse each and every aspect of the present trial where modern case management would have avoided delay. We are simply illustrating some of the more obvious areas where the modern approach would probably have saved time.

120. The proper progress of this case was also interrupted by additional administrative burdens on the judge, performed and eating into the ordinary sitting hours of the court. Experience shows that once the forward impetus has been lost, it becomes extremely difficult to recover it. Imperceptibly at first, drift infiltrates the proceedings and develops into unacceptable delay. Again, we shall simply illustrate the phenomenon by example. If the jury is asked to be ready for the trial to start at 10.00 am or 10.30 am, and the start is delayed by even a few minutes, a pattern of late sitting eventually engulfs everyone. The ten minute break for the jury then lasts fifteen minutes. Counsel or the defendants, or one or other of them, is then not quite ready for the court to sit at 2.00 pm sharp. And so on. Witnesses whose evidence should have been completed on one particular day have to return on the next. Then, as by definition their evidence is not completed, the next day's hearing inevitably involves some repetition of what has already been explored on the previous day – sometimes inadvertently, sometimes to enable a particular forensic point to be repeated. The inconvenience to the witness, and the problem of repetition would both have been avoided if the evidence had been completed by the end of the previous day. The trial judge is responsible for providing the necessary example and leadership to prevent accumulating drift. In the longer cases in particular, the organisation of his administrative and other judicial burdens should, so far as practical, be reduced or organised to start at times which enable him to sit every day for full court days.

121. As already explained, these observations are directed to future arrangements for case management of criminal trials. They do not impinge on the safety of these convictions, or the appropriate levels of sentence.

[7:4] Sentencing Guidelines Council, *Reduction in Sentence for a Guilty Plea: Definitive Guideline*
(Revised 2007)

B. Statement of Purpose

2.1   When imposing a custodial sentence, statute requires that a court must impose the shortest term that is commensurate with the seriousness of the offence(s).[4] Similarly, when imposing a community order, the restrictions on liberty must be commensurate with the seriousness of the offence(s).[5] Once that decision is made, a court is required to give consideration to the reduction for any guilty plea. As a result, the final sentence after the reduction for a guilty plea will be less than the seriousness of the offence requires.

2.2   A reduction in sentence is appropriate because a guilty plea avoids the need for a trial (thus enabling other cases to be disposed of more expeditiously), shortens the gap between charge and sentence, saves considerable cost, and, in the case of an

---

4   Criminal Justice Act 2003, s.153(2)
5   Criminal Justice Act 2003. s.148(2)

early plea, saves victims and witnesses from the concern about having to give evidence. The reduction principle derives from the need for the effective administration of justice and not as an aspect of mitigation.

2.3   Where a sentencer is in doubt as to whether a custodial sentence is appropriate, the reduction attributable to a guilty plea will be a relevant consideration. Where this is amongst the factors leading to the imposition of a non-custodial sentence, there will be no need to apply a further reduction on account of the guilty plea. A similar approach is appropriate where the reduction for a guilty plea is amongst the factors leading to the imposition of a financial penalty or discharge instead of a community order.

2.4   When deciding the most appropriate length of sentence, the sentencer should address separately the issue of remorse, together with any other mitigating features, before calculating the reduction for the guilty plea. Similarly, assistance to the prosecuting or enforcement authorities is a separate issue which may attract a reduction in sentence under other procedures; care will need to be taken to ensure that there is no "double counting".

2.5   The implications of other offences that an offender has asked to be taken into consideration should be reflected in the sentence before the reduction for guilty plea has been applied.

2.6   A reduction in sentence should only be applied to the **punitive elements** of a penalty.[6] The guilty plea reduction has no impact on sentencing decisions in relation to ancillary orders, including orders of disqualification from driving.

C.   Application of the Reduction Principle

3.1   Recommended Approach

The court decides sentence for the offence(s) taking into account aggravating and mitigating factors and any other offences that have been formally admitted (TICs)

⇩

The court selects the amount of the reduction by reference to the sliding scale

⇩

The court applies the reduction

⇩

When pronouncing sentence the court should usually state what the sentence would have been if there had been no reduction as a result of the guilty plea.

---

6   Where a court imposes an indeterminate sentence for public protection, the reduction principle applies in the normal way to the determination of the minimum term (see para. 5.1, footnote and para. 7 below) but release from custody requires the authorisation of the Parole Board once that minimum term has been served.

D. Determining the Level of Reduction

4.1 The level of reduction should be <u>a proportion of the total sentence</u> imposed, with the proportion calculated by reference to the circumstances in which the guilty plea was indicated, in particular the stage in the proceedings. The greatest reduction will be given where the plea was indicated at the "first reasonable opportunity".

4.2 Save where section 144(2) of the 2003 Act applies,[7] the level of the reduction will be gauged on a <u>sliding scale</u> ranging from a recommended <u>one third</u> (where the guilty plea was entered at the first reasonable opportunity in relation to the offence for which sentence is being imposed), reducing to a recommended <u>one quarter</u> (where a trial date has been set) and to a recommended <u>one tenth</u> (for a guilty plea entered at the 'door of the court' or after the trial has begun). *See diagram below.*

4.3 The level of reduction should reflect the stage at which the offender indicated a <u>willingness to admit guilt</u> to the offence for which he is eventually sentenced:

 (i) the largest recommended reduction will not normally be given unless the offender indicated willingness to admit guilt at the **first reasonable opportunity**; when this occurs will vary from case to case (see *Annex 1 for illustrative examples*);
 (ii) where the admission of guilt comes later than the first reasonable opportunity, the reduction for guilty plea will normally be less than one third;
 (iii) where the plea of guilty comes very late, it is still appropriate to give some reduction;
 (iv) if after pleading guilty there is a Newton hearing and the offender's version of the circumstances of the offence is rejected, this should be taken into account in determining the level of reduction;
 (v) if the not guilty plea was entered and maintained for tactical reasons (such as to retain privileges whilst on remand), a late guilty plea should attract very little, if any, discount.

In each category, there is a presumption that the recommended reduction will be given unless there are good reasons for a lower amount.

First reasonable opportunity	After a trial date is set	Door of the court/ after trial has begun

======= | ============= | ============= |

recommended 1/3   **recommended 1/4**   **recommended 1/10**

---

7 See section A above

[7:5] Dawes, W, Harvey, P, McIntosh, B, Nunney, F and Phillips, A, *Attitudes to guilty plea sentence reductions*
(2011) Sentencing Council Research Series 02/11 (at page 1)

Key points

This report presents findings from research Ipsos MORI carried out for the Sentencing Council to examine attitudes towards guilty plea sentence reductions. It consisted of a face-to-face quantitative survey with the general public, discussion groups with the general public, interviews with those who had been a victim of crime or who had witnessed a crime and interviews with offenders. Key findings include:

- The public often perceive sentencing as too lenient. They feel that too often it can work in favour of offenders, rather than providing justice for victims. For the public, sentence lengths given to offenders are an important indicator of justice being served.
- The public in this research had limited knowledge of the workings of the Criminal Justice System (CJS), especially sentencing, and they reported their views as being highly influenced by the media and word of mouth. Whilst the quantitative survey revealed a degree of familiarity with the principles of guilty plea sentence reductions, qualitative discussions indicated awareness was based on the broad concept of sentences receiving reductions, with participants less certain of the role guilty pleas played in determining sentence outcome. Therefore, the public were generally unaware of the nuances of the guilty plea reductions principle and initially tended to be generally unsupportive of reductions in sentencing for those entering a guilty plea.
- Those who had a better understanding of the system and how it works were more likely to report confidence in the system and in sentencing policies. As such those who had been a victim or who had witnessed a crime were more likely to be supportive of sentence reductions than a broader general public audience.
- While the general public's view of justice being served centred largely on the sentence handed down, victims and witnesses tended to have a more holistic view. They gave consideration to offender circumstances and whether the punishment allowed for rehabilitation and support as well as closure for victims and witnesses. For many, re-offending was a key concern and so there was support for punishments that acted as a deterrent and changed offender behaviour. Indeed, both the general public and victims and witnesses thought that persistent offenders, through their actions, have forfeited their right to a reduction.
- The public assume that the key motivation for the guilty plea sentence reduction is to reduce resources (time and money), but they prefer the idea of it as something which helps prevent victims having to give evidence and experiencing emotional trauma whilst doing this. There is a strong sense that the drive for cost savings should not impact on a system effectively delivering justice.
- There is more support for sentence reductions if the guilty plea is entered at an early point. The benefits – both economic and emotional – are more tangible at this point, and both the public and victims and witnesses are less likely to feel that the offender can 'play the system'. On the other hand offenders say they are less likely to enter an early plea, but prefer to weigh up the evidence against them first.
- There is generally little support for a reduction for a guilty plea made at the court door or once the trial has started amongst the public and many victims and witnesses, although the small number of victims of more serious offences included in this study often felt that reductions at this stage could be acceptable. There was an indication that the prospect

and reality of attending court proved more traumatic for this group, and they therefore may be more open to late reductions.

- For the general public, there was weak support for higher levels of reductions beyond the current guideline range of up to 33% and a fifth (20%) felt that there should be no reduction at all. Supporting this, when survey respondents were asked whether the reduction should be increased from a third if an offender pleads guilty at the earliest opportunity, 58% disagreed and only 22% agreed. A small number of victims of more serious offences were, however, more supportive if it spared them having to testify in court.

- The public (and some victims and witnesses) do not like the idea of a universal approach to reductions – in fact, the public in the survey were less likely to say that an offender pleading guilty to an offence should be given a more lenient sentence in most/all cases (21%) and more likely to say it never should result in a more lenient sentence (29%). They instead think that this should depend on certain factors/circumstances relating to the offender or offence type. For instance, views were often much more punitive towards violent crimes as opposed to those against businesses, and likewise towards repeat offenders versus first time offenders.

- The language and discourse of the reductions did not sit well with people. They were very resistant to the idea of an offender being 'rewarded' for admitting they were guilty of an offence; rather they spontaneously suggested that defendants should be further penalised for not admitting guilt if they are subsequently found guilty.

- Offenders in this study were often unsure what their sentence was likely to be when weighing up how to plead, and felt that decisions on sentence lengths were inconsistent. This made it difficult for them to calculate exactly what the impact of a set reduction to their sentence would be. Offenders also questioned the extent to which reductions for early guilty pleas were actually being applied, with a number feeling that it was very difficult to understand exactly how their final sentence had been determined. However, when probed on the level of reductions, offenders in this study were broadly content with the current discount of a third for an early guilty plea, and felt that without the reduction there was little incentive to admit guilt.

- The main factor determining whether or not offenders plead guilty was the likelihood of being found guilty at trial. The key 'tipping point' here was when offenders realised that the chances of them being found guilty were greater than being found not guilty. Weight of evidence and advice from solicitors/barristers were pivotal in offenders' assessments of whether they were likely to be found guilty and therefore crucial in determining when a guilty plea was entered. There was little evidence from the research that increasing the reduction further would encourage more offenders to plead guilty at an earlier stage, given the reduction only becomes a driver of entering a guilty plea at such a point that an offender considers a conviction to be the likely outcome.

Research summary

Context

This report presents findings from research to examine attitudes towards guilty plea sentence reductions. The Sentencing Council commenced a review of the existing guideline on guilty plea sentence reductions shortly after its creation and this research was commissioned to inform this.

Approach

The research examined the attitudes of three key groups towards guilty plea sentence reductions: the general public, victims and witnesses, and offenders. The research consisted of the following fieldwork, conducted between October and December 2010:

- A face-to-face survey with the general public (987 interviews conducted across England and Wales with respondents aged 15 and over);
- Five extended qualitative discussion groups with the general public;
- Thirty-five in-depth qualitative interviews with victims or witnesses. The majority (30) of these were with victims or witnesses of less serious crimes; and,
- Fifteen in-depth qualitative interviews with offenders (12 in custody, and three undertaking sentences in the community; two of these three had, however, previously served part of their sentence in custody).

The quantitative research gained spontaneous responses to issues relating to guilty plea sentence reductions amongst a representative sample of the general population. In contrast, the qualitative research with the public was intended to facilitate more deliberation and a more considered response.

Interviews with victims, witnesses and offenders largely focused on the process and outcomes concerning their own particular case. Amongst offenders this involved understanding potential motivations for entering an early guilty plea. For victims and witnesses this meant examining the impact on their particular case of a guilty plea being made (or not being made) including the point at which the plea was entered. A range of offences were represented in the offender and victim and witness interviews, including a small number of victims and witnesses of more serious crimes (such as sexual assault and murder). Across both sets of interviews, instances where guilty pleas had and had not been entered were included.

It should be highlighted that whilst the quantitative findings are representative of attitudes amongst the general public in England and Wales, the qualitative findings are not statistically representative and should instead be considered more indicative of a range of views. Qualitative research is by its very nature not designed to represent the views of all, more the range of views of some. This is due to sample sizes, which are low for some of the subgroups involved in this research (particularly amongst the victims, witnesses and offenders), and the non-randomised approach taken to sampling. For instance, the majority of offender interviews were with those in custody and as such are not representative of the actual offender population.

Findings

- The public often perceive sentencing as too lenient. They feel that too often it can work in favour of offenders, rather than providing justice for victims. For the public, sentence lengths given to offenders are an important indicator of justice being served.
- The public in this research had limited knowledge of the workings of the Criminal Justice System (CJS), especially sentencing, and they reported their views as being highly influenced by the media and word of mouth. Whilst the quantitative survey revealed a degree of familiarity with the principles of guilty plea sentence reductions, qualitative discussions indicated awareness was based on the broad concept of sentences receiving reductions, with participants less certain of the role guilty pleas played in determining sentence outcome. Therefore, the public were generally unaware of the nuances of the guilty plea reductions principle and initially tended to be generally unsupportive of reductions in sentencing for those entering a guilty plea.
- Those who had a better understanding of the system and how it works were more likely to report confidence in the system and in sentencing policies. As such those who had been a victim or who had witnessed a crime were more likely to be supportive of sentence reductions than a broader general public audience.
- While the general public's view of justice being served centred largely on the sentence handed down, victims and witnesses tended to have a more holistic view. They gave

consideration to offender circumstances and whether the punishment allowed for rehabilitation and support as well as closure for victims and witnesses. For many, re-offending was a key concern and so there was support for punishments that acted as a deterrent and changed offender behaviour. Indeed, both the general public and victims and witnesses thought that persistent offenders, through their actions, have forfeited their right to a reduction.

- The public assume that the key motivation for the guilty plea sentence reduction is to reduce resources (time and money), but they prefer the idea of it as something which helps prevent victims having to give evidence and experiencing emotional trauma whilst doing this. There is a strong sense that the drive for cost savings should not impact on a system effectively delivering justice.
- There is more support for sentence reductions if the guilty plea is entered at an early point. The benefits – both economic and emotional – are more tangible at this point, and both the public and victims and witnesses are less likely to feel that the offender can 'play the system'. On the other hand offenders say they are less likely to enter an early plea, but prefer to weigh up the evidence against them first.
- There is generally little support for a reduction for a guilty plea made at the court door or once the trial has started amongst the public and many victims and witnesses, although the small number of victims of more serious offences included in this study often felt that reductions at this stage could be acceptable. There was an indication that the prospect and reality of attending court proved more traumatic for this group, and they therefore may be more open to late reductions.
- For the general public, there was weak support for higher levels of reductions beyond the current guideline range of up to 33% and a fifth (20%) felt that there should be no reduction at all. Supporting this, when survey respondents were asked whether the reduction should be increased from a third if an offender pleads guilty at the earliest opportunity, 58% disagreed and only 22% agreed. A small number of victims of more serious offences were, however, more supportive if it spared them having to testify in court.
- The public (and some victims and witnesses) do not like the idea of a universal approach to reductions – in fact, the public in the survey were less likely to say that an offender pleading guilty to an offence should be given a more lenient sentence in most/all cases (21%) and more likely to say it **never** should result in a more lenient sentence (29%). They instead think that this should depend on certain factors/circumstances relating to the offender or offence type. For instance, views were often much more punitive towards violent crimes as opposed to those against businesses, and likewise towards repeat offenders versus first time offenders.
- The language and discourse of the reductions did not sit well with people. They were very resistant to the idea of an offender being 'rewarded' for admitting they were guilty of an offence; rather they spontaneously suggested that defendants should be further penalised for not admitting guilt if they are subsequently found guilty.
- Offenders in this study were often unsure what their sentence was likely to be when weighing up how to plead, and felt that decisions on sentence lengths were inconsistent. This made it difficult for them to calculate exactly what the impact of a set reduction to their sentence would be. Offenders also questioned the extent to which reductions for early guilty pleas were actually being applied, with a number feeling that it was very difficult to understand exactly how their final sentence had been determined. However, when probed on the level of reductions, offenders in this study were broadly content with the current discount of a third for an early guilty plea, and felt that without the reduction there was little incentive to admit guilt.

The main factor determining whether or not offenders plead guilty was the likelihood of being found guilty at trial. The key 'tipping point' here was when offenders realised that the chances of them being found guilty were greater than being found not guilty. Weight of evidence and advice from solicitors/barristers were pivotal in offenders' assessments of whether they were likely to be found guilty and therefore crucial in determining when a guilty plea was entered. There was little evidence from the research that increasing the reduction further would encourage more offenders to plead guilty at an earlier stage given the reduction only becomes a driver of entering a guilty plea at such a point that an offender considers a conviction to be the likely outcome.

[7:6] Zander, M and Henderson, P, *The Crown Court Study*
(1993) RCCJ Research Study No 19, HMSO (at page 138)

4.11 'Innocent pleading guilty' cases

4.11.1 Was this a case of an innocent person pleading guilty?

In cases where the defendant pleaded guilty to all charges, defence barristers were asked (Db184): 'An innocent defendant sometimes decided to plead guilty to achieve a sentence discount or reduction in the indictment. Were you concerned that this was such a case?' (According to the Bar's Code of Conduct, counsel's duty in such a situation is to advise his client that he should not plead guilty unless he is guilty. But the decision as to plea is for the client.)

There were 846 substantive replies to this question – not counting 368 non-replies, most probably signifying Don't know or No view. In 793 (94%) the reply was No. But 53 (6% of the 846) the reply was Yes. These 53 cases 'grossed up' represent close to 1,400 cases a year. This appeared to be a cause for concern. It was clear that further analysis of the cases should be undertaken.

The further analysis showed that few (if any) of these cases could safely be characterised as clear examples of what Q184 in the defence barrister's questionnaire was intended to reveal – namely cases where a person, who in the view of his lawyers could have been innocent of all the charges he faced, nevertheless pleaded guilty because of the sentence discount. It was plain that in many of the 53 cases the defence barristers had misunderstood the thrust of the question – no doubt due to the imperfect drafting of the question and the absence of guidance to respondents as to what it was intended to mean.

In regard to 15 of the 53 cases, the defendant also returned a questionnaire. In six of these cases he pleaded guilty though he was not guilty of the offence. In nine he said he had been guilty of the offence(s) charged or similar offences. The other side of the same coin was the response made by defendants themselves to a somewhat similar question we put to them. We did not think we could fairly ask defendants who pleaded not guilty whether they were actually guilty of the offence. But we asked those who pleaded guilty (Def38): 'Did you actually commit the offence(s) for which you pleaded guilty, or a similar offence?'

There were 269 effective replies. Of these, 71% said they had committed the offence as charged and another 17% said they had committed a similar offence.

But there were 31 cases (11%) where the defendant claimed that he had not committed the offence. In 26 of these 31 cases the defence barrister had also returned a questionnaire. In 20 of the 26 cases the barrister gave no indication in answering Q184 that he took the view that his client might have been an innocent person pleading guilty because of the sentence discount.

But in six, as has been seen, the barrister did give this indication. (In none of these six cases did the defendant go to prison.)

- Case No 46 – D, aged 21, no previous convictions, charged with theft from his employer, got a community service order. He had simply helped a friend but had not done much and had not benefited from the crime. Db thought it was too trivial to warrant prosecution. Def. said 'I didn't commit the offence but pleaded guilty because of the credit factor which was explained to me because of the statement of my co-defendant'. He had confessed in a tape-recorded interview.

- Case No 50 – D, no previous convictions, charged with gross indecency, given a conditional discharge. Def. said he did not commit the offence but pleaded guilty 'to get it over as quickly as possible'. He agreed with the advice of his lawyers to plead guilty. Db said the Def. had had no faith that his evidence would be believed.

- Case No 9 – D, aged 22, several previous convictions, charged with assault occasional actual bodily harm and theft, put on probation and ordered to pay compensation of £400. Db said: 'The prosecution was intending to add a charge of blackmail. D refused to run the risk.' Def. said 'I pleaded guilty because of threat to amend the charges to assault with intent to rob and blackmail, theft and actual bodily harm. I was blackmailed into pleading guilty. Disgusting. By the time you read this paper I will probably be in prison for two crimes – one of which I did not commit'.

- Case No 23 – D, female aged 49, three Class B drugs' charges, one of supplying, two of possession. Three previous convictions for similar offences in 1977, 1986, 1987. Given a suspended sentence of 12 months imprisonment. Def. said 'Knew I was guilty of the offences I was accused for. I was lucky to get away with a suspended sentence.' Db said a conference with the client satisfied him that hers was not a case of an innocent person pleading guilty. She was facing her first custodial penalty.

- Case No 24 – D, female aged 25, charged with theft and 1 other offence taken into consideration (TIC). Previous convictions for shoplifting in 1983, 1987 and 1991. Given a suspended sentence of 3 months. Def. said 'I was advised to plead guilty by my barrister to get it over and done with. Otherwise we would of (sic) come back for a hearing.' She agreed with this advice. Db said D's instructions revealed a good defence. Crown offered to drop a further charge currently in the magistrates' court on a similar matter of a guilty plea.'

- Case No 16 – D, male aged 25, no previous convictions, charged with shoplifting from WH Smith's and Woolworth's. His co-defendant had a string of previous convictions for shoplifting. Def. admitted the WH Smith's offence but initially denied the Woolworth's one. Pleaded guilty to both. Given conditional discharge. Def. said 'Pleaded guilty although I was not guilty – to keep myself in one piece. I decided my plea on advice from the barrister and solicitor. I did not agree with the advice. I was only being used.' He had made a confession in the police car and at the police station. He had signed it, but it was not accurate: 'I signed under the influence of drink and drugs.'

In the other 25 cases where the defendant said he was not guilty the following were typical of the reasons or explanations given:

- Case No 0014 'So I did not have to go through a trial. Also because of the advice of my barrister.' (Many previous convictions. Facing nine charges including burglary and assault occasioning actual bodily harm. Received 15 months.)

- Case No 0085 'If I had pleaded not guilty, I would have received a bigger sentence, I think.' (one previous conviction in 1988 for offences against the person. Charged with burglary. (Conditional discharge plus £75 prosecution costs.)

- Case No 0592 'I have been in prison for similar thefts. I was out to steal that day but I never actually attempted to steal what the store detective claimed. I pleaded guilty because my barrister spoke to the judge and got assurance that if I pleaded guilty I would not be sent to prison. However this guarantee did not extend if I pleaded not guilty and was found guilty.' (Many previous convictions. Charged with attempted theft. Conditional discharge.)

- Case No 0125 'Because the police bully you and it is pure hell.' (Many previous convictions. Facing four charges of burglary and theft. 9 months imprisonment.)
- Case No 0183 'I wanted to protect my co-accused.' (Many previous convictions. Charges of theft, taking a conveyance, driving whilst disqualified, driving without insurance, 6 months' imprisonment on each charge concurrent.)
- Case No 0642 'Seemed easier at the time to get it over with.' Agreed with the lawyers' advice to plead guilty. (Many previous convictions. Charged with drugs and vehicle offences. 3 months imprisonment suspended.)
- Case No 0310 'Because my solicitor told me so.' (Several previous convictions. Charged with burglary. Probation.)
- Case No 0352 'To dispence (sic) with the case and lead a normal life.' (many previous convictions. Charged with theft, 3 months' imprisonment, including 1 months for an activated previous conditional discharge.)
- Case No 0418 'To save time and taxpayer's money.' (Many previous convictions. Facing seven charges of burglary and theft. Three sentences of 2 years' imprisonment concurrent and four of 3 months' imprisonment.)
- Case No 0575 'I did not want to put the victim through a court ordeal.' (1 minor previous conviction. Charged with four counts of indecent assaults on a child. Two months' imprisonment.)

[7:7] *Report of the Royal Commission on Criminal Justice*
(1993) Cm 2263, HMSO (at page 111)

45 Against the risk that defendants may be tempted to plead guilty to charges of which they are not guilty must be weighted the benefits to the system and to defendants of encouraging those who are in fact guilty to plead guilty. We believe that the system of sentence discounts should remain. But we do see reason to make the system more effective. In particular we believe that a clearer system of graduated discounts would help to alleviate the problem of 'cracked' trials. The Crown Court Study showed that 'cracked' trials were 26% of all cases or 43% of cases other than those listed as guilty pleas. 'Cracked' trials create serious problems, principally for all the thousands of witnesses each year – police officers, experts and ordinary citizens – who come to court expecting a trial only to find that there is no trial because the defendant has decided to plead guilty at the last minute. This causes in particular unnecessary anxiety for victims whose evidence has up to that point been disputed.

46 At present, the sentence discount is available at any stage until the beginning of the trial but the Court of Appeal has stated in terms that, other things being equal, an earlier plea ought to attract a higher discount and that late tactical pleas should not attract the same discount:

> 'This court has long said that discounts on sentences are appropriate, but everything depends upon the circumstances of each case. If a man is arrested and at once tells the police that he is guilty and co-operates with them in the recovery of property and the identification of others concerned in the offence, he can expect to get a substantial discount. But if a man is arrested in circumstances in which he cannot hope to put forward a defence of not guilty, he cannot expect much by way of a discount. In between come this kind of case, where the court has been put to considerable trouble as a result of a tactical plea. The sooner it is appreciated that defendants are not going to get a full

discount for pleas of guilty in these sort of circumstances, the better it will be for the administration of justice.' [*R v Hollington and Emmens* (1985) 82 Cr App Rep 281]

47 We agree with the view expressed by the Court of Appeal that, other things being equal, the earlier the plea the higher the discount. In broad terms, solicitors and barristers should advise their clients to that effect. Judges must, however, retain their discretion to deal appropriately with the particular circumstances of the individual case. Subject to these points, a system of graduated discounts might work broadly as follows:

(a) The most generous discount should be available to the defendant who indicates a guilty plea in response to the service of the case disclosed by the prosecution.

(b) The next most generous discount should be available to the defendant who indicates a guilty plea in sufficient time to avoid full preparation for trial. The discount might be less if the plea were entered only after a preparatory hearing.

(c) At the bottom of the scale should come the discount for a guilty plea entered on the day of the trial itself. Since resources would be saved by avoiding a contested trial even at this late stage, we think that some discount should continue to be available. But it should be appreciably smaller than for a guilty plea offered at one of the earlier stages.

We do not think that clearer articulation of the long accepted principle that there should be greater sentence discounts for earlier pleas will increase the risk that defendants may plead guilty to offences they did not commit. We would on the other hand expect that it would lead some who would at present plead guilty to do so earlier.

48 We believe, however, that still more could be done to reduce the incidence of 'cracked' trials. As the Seabrook Committee argued, the most common reason for defendants delaying a plea of guilty until the last minute is a reluctance to face the facts until they are at the door of the court. It is often said too that a defendant has a considerable incentive to behave in this way. The longer the delay, the more the likelihood of a witness becoming intimidated or forgetting to turn up or disappearing. And, if the defendant is remanded in custody, he or she will continue to enjoy the privileges of an unconvicted remand prisoner whereas, once a guilty pleas has been entered, the prisoner enters the category of convicted/unsentenced and loses those privileges. Although this last disincentive can be removed, as we recommend below, the problem of last minute changes of plea can never be completely eradicated. We believe, however, that a significant number of those who now plead guilty at the last minute would be more ready to declare their hand at an earlier stage if they were given a reliable early indication of the maximum sentence that they would face if found guilty.

49 The defendant will be interested not so much in the discount on sentence that he or she might receive as the actual sentence and in particular whether it will be custodial or not. It used to be possible for defence counsel to ask the judge for an indication of the sentence that his or her client might receive if found guilty after a contested trial, as opposed to the sentence that might be passed if the plea were changed to guilty. But the discussion of likely sentences with judges is now severely constrained by the Court of Appeal's judgment in *R v Turner* [1970] 2 WLR 1093]. According to this, judges may say that, whether the accused pleads guilty or not guilty, the sentence will or will not take a particular form. They must not, however, state that on a plea of guilty they would impose one sentence while on conviction following a plea of not guilty they would impose a severer sentence. The court took the view that this would be placing undue pressure on defendants, depriving them of that complete freedom of choice which is essential.

50 Many witnesses, particularly from the judiciary and the Bar, urged on us the desirability of reverting, in essence, to the system as it applied before the judgment in the case of *Turner*. The Crown Court Study also showed that, among the judges and barristers who responded, there was overwhelming support for change. We do not support a total reversal of the judgment in *Turner*, since we agree that to face defendants with a choice between what they might get on an immediate plea of guilty and what they might get if found guilty by the jury does amount to unacceptable pressure. But the effect of *Turner* and related judgments appears to have been to make judges reluctant to discuss sentence with counsel at all. We think that there is a case for a change of approach. We recommend that, at the request of defence counsel on instructions from the defendant, judges should be able to indicate the highest sentence that they would impose at that point on the basis of the facts as put to them. A request for such an indication might be made at a preparatory hearing, at a hearing called specially for this purpose, or at the trial itself.

51 We envisage that the procedure which we recommend would be initiated solely by, and for the benefit of, defendants who wish to exercise a right to be told the consequences of a decision which is theirs alone. Where a defendant would need the protection of an appropriate adult during inquiries carried out at a police station, the system must be operated with particular care. The sentence 'canvass', as we have called it, should normally take place in the judge's chambers with both sides being represented by counsel. A shorthand writer should also be present. If none is available a member of the court staff should take a note to be agreed immediately by the judge and both counsel. The judge may give the answer to the question 'what would be the maximum sentence if my client were to plead guilty at this stage?' but to no other. The judge's indication should be based on brief statements from prosecution and defence of all the relevant circumstances, which should include details of the defendant's previous convictions if any and, if available, any pre-sentence report required by the Criminal Justice Act 1991.

[7:8] *R v Goodyear*
[2005] EWCA Crim 888

Lord Woolf, Chief Justice:

1. This is the judgment of the Court prepared by the Deputy Chief Justice, Lord Justice Judge.

2. On first analysis this is an unremarkable appeal against sentence by Karl Goodyear following his plea of guilty to an offence of corruption on 19th April 2004 at the Crown Court at Doncaster before His Honour Judge Jack.

3. In reality, the appeal raises important questions about the continuing applicability of the practice promulgated in *R v Turner* [1970] 2 QB 321, as underlined and applied in subsequent cases, which, save in the most exceptional circumstances, effectively prohibited the judge from giving any indication of sentence in advance of a guilty plea by the defendant. Accordingly, following the procedure adopted in *Attorney General's Reference (No. 1 of 2004)* 1 WLR 2111 and *R v Simpson* [2004] QB 118, a five-judge court, presided over by the Lord Chief Justice, was convened to consider whether what we shall compendiously summarise as the Turner rule of practice may now properly be modified, and if so, to what extent.

    . . .

Guidelines
53. The objective of these Guidelines is to ensure common process and continuing safeguards against the creation or appearance of judicial pressure on the defendant. The potential

advantages include, first and foremost, that the defendant himself would make a better informed decision whether to plead, or not. Experience tends to suggest that this would result in an increased number of early guilty pleas, which a consequent reduction in the number of trials, and the number of cases which are listed for trial, and then, to use current language, "crack" at the last minute, usually at considerable inconvenience to those involved in the intended trial, and in particular, victims and witnesses. Properly applied, too, there may be a reduced number of sentences to be considered by the Attorney General, and where appropriate, referred to this Court as unduly lenient. In short, an increase in the efficient administration of justice will not impinge on the defendant's entitlement to tender a voluntary plea.

54. In our judgment, any advance indication of sentence to be given by the judge should normally be confined to the maximum sentence if a plea of guilty were tendered at the stage at which the indication is sought. In essence we accept the recommendation of the Report of the Royal Commission that the judge should treat the request for a sentence indication, in whatever form it reaches him, as if he were being asked to indicate the maximum sentence on the defendant at that stage. For the process to go further, and the judge to indicate his view of the maximum possible level of sentence following conviction by the jury, as well as its level after a plea of guilty, would have two specific disadvantages. First, by definition, the judge could not be sufficiently informed of the likely impact of the trial on him (or the trial judge) in the sentencing context. It would be unwise for him to bind himself to any indication of the sentence after a trial in advance of it, in effect on a hypothetical basis. If he were to do so, to cover all eventualities he would probably have to indicate a very substantial possible maximum sentence. This would lead to a second problem, arising from the comparison between the two alternatives available to the defendant, that is the maximum level after a trial, and the maximum level following an immediate plea. With some defendants at any rate, the very process of comparing the two alternatives create pressure to tender a guilty plea.

The Judge

55. The judge should not give an advance indication of sentence unless one has been sought by the defendant.

56. He remains entitled, if he sees fit, to exercise the power recognised in Turner to indicate, that the sentence, or type of sentence, on the defendant would be the same, whether the case proceeded as a plea of guilty or went to trial, with a resulting conviction. Nowadays, given the guidance published by the Sentencing Guidelines Council on the credit to be given for a guilty plea, this would be unusual. He is also entitled in an appropriate case to remind the defence advocate that the defendant is entitled to seek an advance indication of sentence.

57. In whatever circumstances an advance indication of sentence is sought, the judge retains an unfettered discretion to refuse to give one. It may indeed be inappropriate for him to give any indication at all. For example, he may consider that for a variety of reasons the defendant is already under pressure (perhaps from a co-accused), or vulnerable, and that to give the requested indication, even in answer to a request, may create additional pressure. Similarly, he may be troubled that the particular defendant may not fully have appreciated that he should not plead guilty unless in fact he is guilty. Again, the judge may believe that if he were to give a sentence indication at the stage when it is sought, he would not properly be able to judge the true culpability of the defendant, or the differing levels of responsibility between defendants. In a case involving a number of defendants, he may be concerned that an indication given to one defendant who seeks it, may itself create pressure on another defendant. Yet again, the judge may consider that the application is no less than a "try on" by a defendant who intends

or would be likely to plead guilty in any event, seeking to take a tactical advantage of the changed process envisaged in this judgment. If so, he would probably refuse to say anything at all, and indeed, a guilty plea tendered after such tactical manoeuvrings may strike the judge as a plea tendered later than the first reasonable opportunity for doing so, with a consequent reduction in the discount for the guilty plea.

58. Just as the judge may refuse to give an indication, he may reserve his position until such time as he feels able to give one, for example, until a pre-sentence report is available. There will be occasions when experience will remind him that in some cases the psychiatric or other reports may provide valuable insight into the level of risk posed by the defendant, and if so, he may justifiably feel disinclined to give an indication at the stage when it is sought. Another problem may simply be that the judge is not sufficiently familiar with the case to give an informed indication, and if so, he may defer doing so until he is.

59. In short, the judge may refuse altogether to give an indication, or may postpone doing so. He may or may not give reasons. In many cases involving an outright refusal, he would probably conclude that it would be inappropriate to give his reasons. If he has in mind to defer an indication, the probability is that he would explain his reasons, and further indicate the circumstances in which, and when, he would be prepared to respond to a request for a sentence indication.

60. If at any stage the judge refuses to give an indication (as opposed to deferring it) it remains open to the defendant to seek a further indication at a later stage. However once the judge has refused to give an indication, he should not normally initiate the process, except, where it arises, to indicate that the circumstances had changed sufficiently for him to be prepared to consider a renewed application for an indication.

61. Once an indication has been given, it is binding and remains binding on the judge who has given it, and it also binds any other judge who becomes responsible for the case. In principle, the judge who has given an indication should, where possible, deal with the case immediately, and if that is not possible, any subsequent hearings should be listed before him. This cannot always apply. We recognise that a new judge has his own sentencing responsibilities, but judicial comity as well as the expectation aroused in a defendant that he will not receive a sentence in excess of whatever the first judge indicated, requires that a later sentencing judge should not exceed the earlier indication. If, after a reasonable opportunity to consider his position in the light of the indication, the defendant does not plead guilty, the indication will cease to have effect. In straightforward cases, once an indication has been sought and given, we do not anticipate an adjournment for the plea to be taken on another day.

62. Later in this judgment we will deal with the obligations of the defence and the prosecution, and to the extent that they may be relevant to the judge's decision, they should be applied. For example, an indication should not be sought on a basis of hypothetical facts. Where appropriate, there must be an agreed, written basis of plea. Unless there is, the judge should refuse to give an indication: otherwise he may become inappropriately involved in negotiations about the acceptance of pleas, and any agreed basis of plea.

The Defence

. . .

65. The advocate is personally responsible for ensuring that his client fully appreciates that:

    (a)   he should not plead guilty unless he is guilty;

(b) any sentence indication given by the judge remains subject to the entitlement of the Attorney General (where it arises) to refer an unduly lenient sentence to the Court of Appeal;

(c) any indication given by the judge reflects the situation at the time when it is given, and that if a "guilty plea" is not tendered in the light of that indication the indication ceases to have effect;

(d) any indication which may be given relates only to the matters about which an indication is sought. Thus, certain steps, like confiscation proceedings, follow automatically, and the judge cannot dispense with them, nor, by giving an indication of sentence, create an expectation that they will be dispensed with.

The Prosecution

...

70. We must expressly identify a number of specific matters for which the advocate for the prosecution is responsible.

(a) If there is no final agreement about the plea to the indictment, or the basis of plea, and the defence nevertheless proceeds to seek an indication, which the judge appears minded to give, prosecuting counsel should remind him of this guidance, that normally speaking an indication of sentence should not be given until the basis of the plea has been agreed, or the judge has concluded that he can properly deal with the case without the need for a Newton hearing.

(b) If an indication is sought, the prosecution should normally enquire whether the judge is in possession of or has had access to all the evidence relied on by the prosecution, including any personal impact statement from the victim of the crime, as well as any information of relevant previous convictions recorded against the defendant.

(c) If the process has been properly followed, it should not normally be necessary for counsel for the prosecution, before the judge gives any indication, to do more than, first, draw the judge's attention to any minimum or mandatory statutory sentencing requirements, and where he would be expected to offer the judge assistance with relevant guideline cases, or the views of the Sentencing Guidelines Council, to invite the judge to allow him to do so, and second, where it applies, to remind the judge that the position of the Attorney General to refer any eventual sentencing decision as unduly lenient is not affected.

(d) In any event, counsel should not say anything which may create the impression that the sentence indication has the support or approval of the Crown.

....

Process

73. We anticipate that any sentence indication would normally be sought at the plea and case management hearing. In cases "sent" to the Crown Court under s 51 of the Crime and Disorder Act 1998, or transferred under s 4 of the Criminal Justice Act 1987 or s 53 of the Criminal Justice Act 1991, this is usually the first opportunity for the defendant to plead guilty and therefore the moment when the maximum discount for the guilty plea will be available to the defendant. For victims and witnesses, too, there is a huge advantage in the earliest possible conclusion to the case. That said, as the judgment makes clear, we do not rule out the

entitlement of a defendant to seek an indication at a later stage, or even, in what we know would be a rare case, during the course of the trial itself.

74. The judge is most unlikely to be able to give an indication, even if it is sought, in complicated or difficult cases, unless issues between the prosecution and the defence have been addressed and resolved. Therefore in such cases, no less than seven days' notice in writing of an intention to seek an indication should normally be given in writing to the prosecution, and the court. If an application is made without notice when it should have been given, the judge may conclude that any inevitable adjournment should have been avoided and that the discount for the guilty plea should be reduced accordingly. It may be that in due course the Criminal Procedure Rules Committee will wish to consider the question of notice, and its length, and indeed whether either of the relevant case progression forms should be amended.

75. The hearing should normally take place in open court, with a full recording of the entire proceedings, and both sides represented, in the defendant's presence.

76. As already indicated, in cases of any complexity or difficulty, proper notice should be given to the Crown that a sentence indication will be sought. The fact that notice has been given, and any reference to a request for a sentence indication, or the circumstances in which it was sought, would be inadmissible in any subsequent trial.

77. If the process we envisage is properly followed, there should be very little need for the judge to involve himself in the discussions with the advocates, although obviously he may wish to seek better information on any aspect of the case which is troubling him. We do not anticipate an opening by the Crown, or a mitigation plea by the defence. That must be postponed until after the defendant has pleaded guilty. Generally speaking, we assume that the process will be very short, the judge bearing in mind that the defendant and the public are present, and that he (the judge) may be the trial judge, and that he is simply deciding whether to respond, and if so how, to a request that he give an indication of the maximum sentence he would pass if the defendant pleaded guilty at that stage. The fact that the case may yet proceed as a trial, and that if it does so, no reference may be made to the request for a sentence indication, leads to the conclusion that reporting restrictions should normally be imposed, to be lifted if and when the defendant pleads or is found guilty.

Magistrates' Court

78. In our judgment it would be impracticable for these new arrangements to be extended to proceedings in the Magistrates' Court. We are not at present satisfied that an advance sentence indication can readily be applied to and processed there. We believe that it would be better for the new arrangements in the Crown Court to settle in for some time before considering whether and, if so how, similar arrangements can be made in the context of summary trials. Accordingly, for the time being, the magistrates should confine themselves to the statutory arrangements in Schedule 3 of the 2003 Act.

[7:9] *R v McDonald*
[2007] Crim LR 737

The appellant pleaded guilty to burglary and to making a threat to kill. The appellant entered an address late at night. When one of the occupiers awoke, he made his way into the kitchen where the appellant grabbed him from behind around the throat and said "don't make a sound or I will kill you". The occupier fought off the appellant, who eventually ran away.

The appellant had 19 previous convictions for 65 offences, including rape and aggravated burglary. Before the appellant entered a plea to the count charging threatening to kill, the appellant's counsel asked the sentencing judge for an advance indication of sentence in accordance with Goodyear. The proceedings were conducted in open court and eventually the sentencing judge indicated that for the two offences of burglary and threatening to kill, the total sentence would involve five years' custody. Following this indication the appellant pleaded guilty to threatening to kill. The case was adjourned for a pre-sentence report to be obtained. The pre-sentence report indicated that the appellant represented a high degree of risk of harm to the public. When the appellant again appeared before the court, prosecuting counsel indicated that the offence of threatening to kill was one in respect of which a court was obliged to consider whether or not to impose a sentence of imprisonment for public protection. Defence counsel did not remind the judge of the advance indication given on the previous appearance. The sentencing judge imposed a sentence of imprisonment for public protection, with a minimum period of 4.5 years, less 213 days.

Held, the appellant submitted that as the judge had given an indication that the maximum sentence he would impose would be a determinate sentence of five years' imprisonment, he ought not to have imposed an indeterminate sentence in the form of a sentence of imprisonment for public protection. Counsel had requested an advance indication of sentence in accordance with Goodyear. The sentencing judge was not bound to give any indication at all and might have reserved his position until such time as he felt able to give one. Once an indication had been given it was binding on the judge and remained binding on the judge who gave it and any other judge who became responsible for the case. The court was confident that if the judge had been reminded by counsel of the indication that he had given, he would not have imposed a sentence of imprisonment for public protection and would have felt himself bound by the indication he had given on the previous appearance. In the court's view it would be unjust for the sentence of imprisonment for public protection to remain. Accordingly, the appropriate course was to quash that sentence and substitute a determinate sentence of 4.5 years.

Commentary (By David Thomas QC): The implication of this decision seems to be that the expectation raised by a Goodyear indication overrides a statutory obligation to impose a sentence of imprisonment for public protection, which is a mandatory sentence where the court is of the opinion that there is a significant risk to the public from future specified offences. The case makes an interesting contrast with Attorney-General's Reference (No. 112 of 2006) [2007] 2 Cr. App. R. (S.) 39 (p.150). There, the offender pleaded guilty to wounding with intent on the morning of the trial following an advance indication of sentence in accordance with Goodyear, and was sentenced to three years' imprisonment. On a reference by the Attorney-General, the court stated that the sentencer was obliged by statute to consider the question whether there was a "significant risk of serious harm" as required by s.224 of the Criminal Justice Act 2003. As there were previous specified offences, s.229(3) required the sentencing judge to assume that there was a significant risk of serious harm from future specified offences unless it was unreasonable to do so. If the judge had addressed the question of risk, he would inevitably have concluded that there was such a risk. The court accordingly substituted a sentence of imprisonment for public protection. What would have happened in McDonald if the sentencing judge had passed a sentence in accordance with the Goodyear indication? Would a reference by the Attorney-General have succeeded? Goodyear states that an indication, although binding on the sentencing judge and other judges in the Crown Court, does not prevent a reference by the Attorney-General. What would have happened in Glover if the sentencing judge had gone back on his indication and passed a sentence of imprisonment for public protection? Presumably it would have been quashed on the same principle as McDonald. The moral seems to be that Goodyear indications should never be given in respect of a specified offence unless the judge is satisfied that there will be no question of the imposition of a sentence of imprisonment for public protection, or at least given in qualified terms which do not exclude the possibility of a sentence of imprisonment for public protection if the information before the court indicates that such a sentence is required.

[7:10] Hood, R, *Race and Sentencing: a Study in the Crown Court*
(1992) Oxford University Press

This study was carried out in the Crown Court Centres which service the region covered by the West Midland Police, and was based on a sample of 2,884 male offenders sentenced in 1989 (886 black, 536 Asian, 1,443 white and 16 from other backgrounds) as well as all 433 women sentenced in these courts over the same period.

The following extracts are taken from Chapter 12: Discrimination in the Courts? (pages 179–192):

This study has confirmed what has for long been suspected, namely that, to a very substantial degree, the over-representation of Afro-Caribbean males and females in the prison system is a product of their over-representation among those convicted of crime and sentenced in the Crown Courts. The best evidence that it is possible to make from this study is that 80% of the over-representation of black male offenders in the prison population was due to their over-representation among those convicted at the Crown Court and to the type and circumstances of the offences of which black men were convicted. The remaining 20%, in the case of males but not females, appeared to be due to differential treatment and other factors which influence the nature and length of the sentences imposed: two thirds of it resulting from the higher proportion of black defendants who pleaded not guilty and who were, as a consequence, more liable on conviction to receive longer custodial sentences.

From Crown Court records it was not possible to shed much light on the circumstances and factors which might produce a higher rate of convictions amongst the black population, but there were some clues which are worthy of further investigation. A higher proportion of black people were charged with offences which could only be dealt with on indictment at the Crown Court: considerably more being charged with robbery, often of the kind normally referred to as 'mugging'. One should not minimise the distress caused by such behaviour, especially when women are the victims, nor the general sense of unease which it breeds, but as a form of violent or property crime it is often not more serious in its consequences than grievous bodily harm or housebreaking, both of which can be dealt with summarily if the court and defendant consent. This would not, of course, have meant that all of these black defendants would have accepted summary trial. The reason is that considerably more of them had, early on in the procedure, signified their intention to plead not guilty: 46% of blacks and Asians compared with 34% of whites charged with robbery. Nevertheless, the unavailability of discretion to deal with these offences either-way inevitably brings more black defendants into the arena of the Crown Court and its greater propensity to inflict a custodial penalty.

Black offenders were also disproportionately involved in the supply of drugs, usually cannabis, and these convictions regularly arose from police activity rather than from a complaint by citizens. This is not the place to open the debate about the seriousness of illegal dealings at street level in cannabis. It is only to say that if these offences were excluded the proportion of black males dealt with at the West Midlands courts would have been 13.7% rather than 17.2%, equivalent to 20% lower. By contrast, excluding such cases amongst white and Asians would have reduced their number by only 0.6% and 0.9% respectively. Of course, it is impossible to say whether these persons would have committed other offences but it is incontrovertible that the continued legal proscription of cannabis and the insistence that trading in it, even on a small or moderate scale, is an offence which should always be committed to the Crown Court for trial, is a substantial factor influencing the number of black persons in the prison population.

Furthermore, black defendants were at a disadvantage both because of decisions they made and decisions made about them during the processing of cases before they appeared for sentence. They were more likely to be remanded in custody by magistrates who committed them for trial, even taking into account the seriousness of the charges against them and other factors which might legitimately have had an effect on the decision whether to give bail. They were much less likely to have had a social inquiry report prepared on their background, mainly because a considerably high proportion of them signified their intention to plead not guilty, but also because fewer who pleaded guilty were reported on, although, the reasons for this are not known.

Being already in custody, pleading not guilty, and not having a report were all associated with a higher probability of receiving a custodial sentence or with a lengthier sentence. And all of them, of course, limit the possibilities for effective pleas in mitigation. Those who have been in custody have less opportunity to show that they have been of exemplary behaviour or have sought to make amends by, say, entering regular employment since they were charged with the offence. Those who deny the offence cannot suddenly, on being found guilty, convincingly express remorse. For those without social inquiry reports there is often insufficient information on hand to put the offence in its social context, and no opportunity to take advantage of a specific proposal from a probation officer for an alternative sentence to custody. It would appear, therefore, that ethnic minority defendants were inadvertently subjected to a form of indirect discrimination at the point of sentence due to the fact that they chose more often to contest the case against them. Because of the way that the system works to encourage guilty pleas through a 'discount' on sentence, which has been shown to produce a substantial reduction, and because it is the policy of the Probation Service not generally to make social inquiry reports on those who intend to contest the case against them, black defendants obviously put themselves at greater risk of custody and longer sentences.

. . .

Black defendants at the Dudley courts got a sentence greater than that recommended by a probation officer much more often than did blacks at Birmingham. Moreover, blacks at the Dudley courts received sentences generally further up the scale of penalties; and if they were recommended for probation or community service they were more likely to get a more severe penalty than was a white defendant.

In attempting to understand what may have produced this divergent pattern, it was at once noticeable that the differences were greatest not in the mid to upper band of cases where difficult decisions were being made about whether to use custody or not, but in the range of cases at the lower end of the scale of severity. There was strong evidence to suggest that factors which would have been regarded as mitigating the seriousness of the case if the defendant was white were not given the same weight if the defendant was black in the cases dealt with at Dudley courts. Yet, they were given a similar weight for black offenders dealt with at Birmingham. For instance, blacks at the Dudley courts were sentenced to custody in a significantly higher proportion of cases whether they were employed or unemployed, whether they were under 21 or over 21, whether they had only one prior conviction or two or more, whether they pleaded guilty or not guilty.

A much higher proportion of the black offenders at the Dudley courts (amongst those in the lower band of seriousness) who had been convicted with at least one other black defendant were sentenced to custody at the Dudley courts. Here the difference between the observed and expected rate, given the nature of the cases, was so big that it explained half of the difference between the observed and expected rate of custody for all black cases at the Dudley courts. An examination of these cases failed to find any distinctive differences between them and the cases where whites had been convicted with other whites. Nor were the black cases at Birmingham, where custody was, in contrast, rarely used, substantially different in character. It appears reasonable to assume that the judges at the Dudley courts viewed these cases in a different light to those involving groups of whites. While it is true that there were slightly more black offenders who were committed with other black offenders at the Dudley courts than at Birmingham, there were substantially more white at the Dudley courts who had been convicted alongside other whites. Furthermore, blacks were sentenced more often to custody than either whites at the Dudley courts or blacks at Birmingham, when they were the sole offender. On the whole, there was nothing to suggest that the judges who dealt with the Dudley courts' cases were confronted with a worse impression of black criminality than were the far more lenient judges at Birmingham. On the contrary, black defendants were a lower proportion of the caseload of the Dudley courts, and the seriousness of the cases dealt with, as measured by their risk of custody score, was no different from the cases in Birmingham.

...

When one contrasts the overall treatment meted out to black Afro-Caribbean males one is left wondering whether it is not a result of different racial stereotypes operating on the perceptions of some judges. The greater involvement of black offenders in street crime and in the trade in cannabis, their higher rate of unemployment, their greater resistance to pressures to plead guilty, and possibly a perception of a different, less deferential, demeanor in court may all appear somewhat more threatening. And, if not threatening, less worthy of mitigation of punishment. It was significant that being unemployed increased the risk of a black male getting a custodial sentence, but not, in general, for a white or an Asian offender. In contrast, the better financial and employment status of the Asians and their more socially integrated households, when judged by white standards, as well as the fact that they were much more likely to be first-time offenders, may have meant that they were probably able to present themselves as less threatening, and more worthy of mitigation than either white or blacks. Only in respect of the length of sentences received by those who were sentenced to prison did Asian adult males fare worse. But without research which would allow the investigation of judicial attitudes towards, and perceptions of, racially related differences in crime patterns and in cultural responses to the criminal justice system, all this for the moment must remain speculation. It cannot be doubted that such a programme of research is now needed.

The findings regarding women will surprise many, especially given the very large over-representation of black women in penal institutions. The evidence in general supports the so-called 'chivalry' or 'paternalistic' hypothesis that judges give much more weight to mitigating features of the case in sentencing women offenders, whether white or black. No differences were found between the use of custody, of alternatives, or in sentence length between white and black women when variables relating to the seriousness of the offences were controlled for. Black women were just as likely as the whites to have had a social inquiry report prepared about them prior to sentence and were no more likely than the white to have been given a sentence greater than that recommended by the probation officer. Furthermore, compared with black men, black women were dealt with relatively leniently just as white women were dealt with leniently compared with white men. Nevertheless, when a particularly disadvantaged group were singled out – those who had various attributes which could be associated with failure to conform to female stereotypes – a relatively high proportion of them were sentenced to custody: yet, no more blacks than whites and no more females than males. One thing is certain. If considerations relating to their gender did not mitigate the punishment of women, and they were treated as men are, there would be many more in custody than at present.

What conclusions of a practical kind can be drawn from this study? First, that the research has revealed a complex picture of the way in which race appears to have affected the pattern of sentencing. In doing so, it has led to some uncomfortable conclusions for those whose duty it is to sentence offenders. It will not be possible any more to make the claim that all the differences in the treatment of black offenders occur elsewhere in the criminal justice system. At least some of it occurs in the courts, and more often in some localities than others. Much will be achieved if judges recognise this. One aim of studying sentencing by empirical methods is to help stimulate reassessment of attitudes and judicial responses. Previous research has shown how unaware judges may be of their own practices, let alone those of their colleagues. It may be that some are not yet sufficiently sensitive to the way in which racial views and beliefs may influence their judgment. If this research can stimulate such self-awareness and re-evaluation it will have made a modest contribution towards the positive self-conscious appreciation of the need to take the question of race seriously which the Judicial Studies Board has now recognised by the setting up of its Ethnic Minorities Advisory Committee.

Secondly, this study draws attention to the way in which the criminal process may contribute to indirect discrimination against black people. There is clearly a need to consider the implications of the policy which favours so strongly those who plead guilty, when ethnic minorities are less willing to let a prosecution go unchallenged. This has implications, in particular, for the range and value of the information available to the courts in deciding whether or not to impose a custodial sentence as well as the type of non-custodial sentence. And, for the reason already mentioned, it will be necessary to monitor carefully the way in which the courts exercise their discretion, under the Criminal Justice Act 1991, to pass sentence without a pre-sentence report when the case is one triable only on indictment.

Thirdly, there are obvious implications relating to the duty placed on the Secretary of State by Section 95(1)(b) to 'publish such information as he considers expedient for the purpose of . . . facilitating the performance . . . [by persons engaged in the administration of criminal justice] . . . of their duty to avoid discriminating against any person on the grounds of race or sex or any other improper ground.' To do this it will be essential for the Crown Courts to monitor the ethnic origin of all persons appearing before them. If the self-reflection on sentencing performance mentioned above is to be achieved, information on sentencing dispositions, analysed by ethnic origin, should be communicated to each judge and to the court as a whole annually. Only then will it be possible to detect whether sentencing patterns which might prove to be unfavourable to any ethnic minority are becoming established.

[7:11] *R v Christou*

[1992] QB 979

In an undercover police operation in London, a shop was set up purportedly to buy and sell jewellery. It was staffed solely by undercover officers purporting to be shady jewellers willing to buy stolen property. Discreetly sited cameras and sound equipment recorded all that occurred over the counter. The appellants who each made repeated sales at the shop pleaded not guilty to indictments charging burglary and handling stolen goods as alternatives. The trial judge ruled that the evidence obtained was not unfairly obtained.

The Court of Appeal dismissed the appeals, and held that the judge had exercised his discretion correctly.

Lord Taylor CJ (at page 989):

. . . the trick was not applied to the appellants; they voluntarily applied themselves to the trick. It is not every trick producing evidence against an accused which results in unfairness. There are, in criminal investigations, a number of situations in which the police adopt ruses or tricks in the public interest to obtain evidence. For example, to trap a blackmailer, the victim may be used as an agent of the police to arrange an appointment and false or marked money may be laid as bait to catch the offender. A trick, certainly; in a sense too, a trick which results in a form of self-incrimination; but not one which could reasonably be thought to involve unfairness.

In our view, although the Code extends beyond the treatment of those in detention, what is clear is that it was intended to protect suspects who are vulnerable to abuse or pressure from police officers or who may believe themselves to be so. Frequently, the suspect will be a detainee. But the Code will also apply where a suspect, not in detention, is being questioned about an offence by a police officer acting as a police officer for the purpose of obtaining evidence. In that situation, the officer and the suspect are not on equal terms. The officer is perceived to be in a position of authority; the suspect may be intimidated or undermined.

The situation at Stardust Jewellers was quite different. The appellants were not being questioned by police officers acting as such. Conversation was on equal terms. There could be no question of pressure or intimidation by Gary or Aggi as persons actually in authority or believed to be so. We agree with the judge that the Code simply was not intended to apply in such a context.

In reaching that conclusion, we should ourselves administer a caution. It would be wrong for police officers to adopt or use an undercover pose or disguise to enable themselves to ask questions about an offence uninhibited by the requirements of the Code and with the effect of circumventing it.

Were they to do so, it would be open to the judge to exclude the questions and answers under section 78 of the Act of 1984. It is therefore necessary here to see whether the questioning by Gary and Aggi was such as to require the judge in his discretion to exclude the conversation. The judge carefully reviewed the evidence on this issue. He concluded that the questions and comments from Gary and Aggi were for the most part simply those necessary to conduct the bartering and maintain their cover. They were not questions 'about the offence.' The only exception was the questioning about which area should be avoided in reselling the goods. However, even that was partly to maintain cover since it was the sort of questioning to be expected from a shady jeweller.

We are of the view that the judge's approach to the aspect of the case concerned with the Code cannot be faulted.

Before parting with the case, we should refer to a further argument mounted by Mr Thornton. He submitted that the undercover exercise, lasting as it did for some three months, was contrary to public policy. The basis for that submission was that the officers ought to have arrested offenders as soon as they had sufficient evidence. Instead, they allowed offenders such as these two appellants to return again and again with further stolen properties. Only when the shop was wound up were charges brought. The mischief alleged is that offenders were allowed to commit further offences which would or may have been obviated had they been arrested earlier. The existence of the shop was therefore facilitating, if not encouraging, the commission of crime.

Clearly, it must be a matter for policy and operational decision by the police as to how they reconcile and balance the need on the one hand to bring an individual offender swiftly to book and deter crime.

[7:12] *R v Bryce*
[1992] 4 All ER 567

The appellant was charged with handling stolen goods and theft. At his trial, the evidence against him included a conversation alleged to have taken place when an undercover police-man using a false name and posing as a potential buyer for a car telephoned the appellant and agreed to buy a stolen car, another conversation which took place when the two later met, and an unrecorded interview which came after a recorded interview in which the appellant had made no comments. The Court of Appeal quashed his conviction.

Lord Taylor CJ (at page 571):

[Counsel for the appellant] submits the evidence that the appellant turned up in a stolen car at Smithfield as a result of a telephone call was admissible. However, the conversation on the telephone and at Smithfield should, he submits, have been excluded because 'Pearson' asked questions which were in the nature of an interrogation. They deprived the appellant of his right not to incriminate himself by answering questions which, had they been put by a police officer acting overtly as such, would have required a caution under the code. In particular, [Counsel] points to the question and answer on the telephone: *'Pearson. How warm it is? Paul. It is a couple days old'* and the question and answer at Smithfield: *'Pearson. How long has it been nicked? Paul. Two or three days.'*

Those questions went to the heart of the vital issue of dishonesty. They were not even necessary to the undercover operation, which was designed to provide evidence of the appellant in possession of a recently stolen car offering it for sale at a knock-down price. Moreover, the second question simply invited the appellant to repeat his answer to the first in more specifically incriminating terms. On the voire dire 'Pearson' was asked in cross-examination what he would have done had the appellant said the car was not stolen. He replied:

> 'If he had said, "It is not stolen", I would have asked other questions, Sir. What are you doing selling a motor car like that? What is wrong with it? Is it an import? Has it come from abroad?'

In our judgment, that series of questions by an undercover officer would clearly offend against the caveat this court stated in *R v Christou*. It would blatantly have been an interrogation with the effect, if not the design, of using an undercover pose to circumvent the code.

The two questions of which [Counsel] makes strongest complaint did not go as far as that. They were single, isolated questions in separate conversations. There was no extended interrogation. However, they did go directly to the critical issue of guilty knowledge. Moreover, they were hotly disputed and there was no contemporary record. In *R v Christou* there were questions from the undercover officers as to the area where it would be unwise to resell the goods, the answers being obliquely an indication that the goods had been or may have been stolen from that area to the knowledge or belief of the suspect. However, in that case the whole interview was recorded both on tape and on film. The circumstances to be considered by the learned judge in that case in deciding whether the admission of the evidence would have an adverse effect on the fairness of the trial and how adverse where therefore quite different from those in the present case. The film and sound record eliminated any question of concoction. Not so here. The questions asked were direct, not oblique, the conversation was challenged and the appellant had no means of showing by a neutral, reliable record what was or was not said. For those reasons we consider that the learned judge erred here in admitting those answers.

We turn to the second ground. At the police station, an interview was properly set up and conducted in accordance with the code. It was tape-recorded, timed and it began with a caution. However, its only yield was a succession of 'No comment's from the appellant. It is submitted that what followed was clearly in breach of the code. The officers assert that after the tape recorder was switched off the appellant said he did not wish anything written down, but then proceeded to volunteer an account which in effect contained an admission.

Mr Thomas submits, first, that the appellant ought to have been cautioned again or reminded of the caution in accordance with para 10.5 of Code C, which provides:

'When there is a break in questioning under caution the interviewing officer must ensure that the person being questioned is aware that he remains under caution. If there is any doubt the caution should be given again in full when the interview resumes.'

The tape-recorded interview had concluded; what followed was therefore at the very least 'a break in questioning'. In our judgment, that submission is unanswerable. The failure to caution the appellant again was not just a technical breach in the circumstances of this case. According to the police, once the recorder was switched off, the appellant said he wanted nothing written down. He repeated that, saying 'If you record it, I won't say anything.' The officer's reply, 'Well, what happened then?' might reasonably have been taken as an acceptance of the appellant's terms. The appellant may well therefore have believed that what was not recorded could not be given in evidence. Hence the importance of a fresh caution or reminder of it. Significantly, as [Counsel] for the Crown fairly pointed out, the officer does not claim to have asked the question, 'Is that everything Paul?' until he was already sealing the tapes. One might have expected the question to have been asked before the recorder was switched off.

Mr Thomas further submits that the alleged admissions by the appellant were not recorded contemporaneously and, for that reason too, they should have been excluded. It was strenuously denied by the appellant that any such admissions were made and indeed that any interview, on or off the record, occurred after the tape recorder was switched off.

If this interview was correctly admitted, the effect would be to set at nought the requirements of the Police and Criminal Evidence Act 1984 and the code in regard to interviews. One of the main purposes of the code is to eliminate the possibility of an interview being concocted or of a true interview being falsely alleged to have been concocted. If it were permissible for an officer simply to assert that, after a properly conducted interview produced a nil return, the suspect confessed off the record and for that confession to be admitted, then the safeguards of the code could readily be bypassed.

In our judgment there would have to be some highly exceptional circumstances, perhaps involving cogent corroboration, before such an interview could be admitted without its having such an adverse effect on the fairness of the trial that it ought to be excluded under s 78.

Here the situation was a classic example of that suspicious sequence – a total denial or refusal to comment, followed by an alleged confession, followed in its turn by a refusal to sign the notes and a denial that the confession was made. We have no doubt that the alleged interview should in the circumstances of this case have been excluded.

Since the conversations and interviews with the police, both undercover and in uniform, formed such a major part of the prosecution case, we were bound to hold that the irregularities identified above rendered the conviction unsafe and unsatisfactory. Accordingly we quashed the conviction.

[7:13] *R v Khan*

[1997] AC 558

The appellant was charged with being knowingly concerned in the fraudulent evasion of the prohibition on the importation of a class A drug, heroin. The evidence included a record of the appellant's conversation with several people in a house to which, unknown to the occupants, the police had attached an electronic surveillance device. He appealed on the grounds that the evidence of his conversation should not have been admitted in evidence.

The appeal was dismissed.

Lord Nicholls (at page 582):

My Lords, I have had the opportunity to read in advance a draft of the speech of my noble and learned friend, Lord Nolan. I agree that this appeal should be dismissed. I add only two observations of my own. First, the appellant contended for a right of privacy in respect of private conversations in private houses. I prefer to express no view, either way, on the existence of such a right. This right, if it exists, can only do so as part of a larger and wider right of privacy. The difficulties attendant on this controversial subject are well known. Equally well known is the continuing, widespread concern at the apparent failure of the law to give individuals a reasonable degree of protection from unwarranted intrusion in many situations. I prefer to leave open for another occasion the important question whether the present, piecemeal protection of privacy has now developed to the extent that a more comprehensive principle can be seen to exist. It is not necessary to pursue this question on this appeal. Even if the right for which the appellant contended does exist, this would not lead to the consequence that obtaining evidence for the purpose of detecting or preventing serious crime was an infringement of the right or, even if it were, that the evidence was inadmissible at the trial.

Second, the discretionary powers of the trial judge to exclude evidence march and in hand with article 6(1) of the European Convention on Human Rights and Fundamental Freedoms. Both are concerned to ensure that those facing criminal charges receive a fair hearing. Accordingly, when considering the common law and statutory discretionary powers under English law the jurisprudence on article 6 can have a valuable role to play. English law relating to the ingredients of a fair trial is highly developed. But every system of law stands to benefit by an awareness of the answers given by other courts and tribunals to similar problems. In the present case the decision of the European Court of Human Rights in *Schenk v Switzerland* 13 EHRR 242 confirms that the use at a criminal trial of material obtained in breach of the rights of privacy enshrined in article 8 does not of itself mean that the trial is unfair. Thus the European Court of Human Rights case law on this issue leads to the same conclusion as English law.

[7:14] *R v Newton*

(1982) 77 Cr App Rep 13

The appellant pleaded guilty to buggery of his wife. The appellant maintained that the acts complained of were consensual, the victim that they were violent and non-consensual. The Court of Appeal allowed his appeal against sentence.

The Lord Chief Justice (at page 15):

There are three ways in which a judge in these circumstances can approach his difficult task of sentencing. It is in certain circumstances possible to obtain the answer to the problem from a jury. For example, when it is a question of whether the conviction should be under section 18 or section 20 of the Offences against the Person Act 1861, the jury can determine the issue on a trial under section 18 by deciding whether or not the necessary intent has been proved by the prosecution.

The second method which could be adopted by the judge in these circumstances is himself to hear the evidence on one side and another, and come to his own conclusion, acting so to speak as his own jury on the issue which is the root of the problem.

The third possibility in these circumstances is for him to hear no evidence but to listen to the submissions of counsel and then come to a conclusion. But if he does that, then, as Judge Argyle himself said in a passage to which reference will be made in a moment, where there is a substantial conflict between the two sides, he must come down on the side of the defendant. In other words where there has been a substantial conflict, the version of the defendant must so far as possible be accepted.

It is plain from what I have read, and indeed as accepted by learned counsel for the Crown, that the judge failed to adopt one of the three courses open to him, or the one that he did adopt was wrongly performed by him. The answer is, so far as the sentence of eight years is concerned, that that must be quashed. It is plain that in the circumstances of this case the appellant has already served too long in prison, and we propose therefore to substitute for the sentence of eight years' imprisonment such sentence as will result in his release today.

[7:15] *R v Underwood, R v Arobieke, R v Khan, R v Connors*
[2004] EWCA Crim 2256; [2005] 1 Cr App R 13; [2005] 1 Cr App R (S) 90

1. In these appeals, which we heard and decided earlier this week, we are concerned with what can compendiously be described as Newton hearings. Although the principle are clear, they are not always fully understood or applied. These appeals have therefore been listed together to enable this Court to repeat and emphasise general guidance about the procedure to be adopted where the defendant pleads guilty on a factual basis different to that which appears from the Crown's case, or, indeed, a study of the papers. In short, we are concerned with the process which will achieve the sentence appropriate to reflect the justice of the case where there is plea of guilty, but some important fact or facts relating to the offence which the defendant is admitting, of potential significance to the sentencing decision, are in dispute.

2. The essential principle is that the sentencing judge must do justice. So far as possible the offender should be sentenced on the basis which accurately reflects the facts of the individual case. . . .

3. The starting point has to be the defendant's instructions. His advocate will appreciate whether any significant facts about the prosecution evidence are disputed and the factual basis on which the defendant intends to plead guilty. If the resolution of the facts in dispute may matter to the sentencing decision, the responsibility for taking any initiative and alerting the prosecutor to the areas of dispute rest with the defence. The Crown should not be taken by surprise, and if it is suddenly faced with a proposed basis of plea of guilty where important facts are disputed, it should, if necessary, take time for proper reflection and consultation to consider its position and the interests of justice. In any event, whatever view may be formed by the Crown on any proposed basis of plea, it is deemed to be conditional on the judge's acceptance of it.

. . .

6. After submissions from the advocates the judge should decide how to proceed. If not already decided, he will address the question whether he should approve the Crown's acceptance of

pleas. Then he will address the proposed basis of plea. We emphasise that whether or not the basis of plea is "agreed", the judge is not bound by any such agreement and is entitled of his own motion to insist that any evidence relevant to the facts in dispute should be called before him. No doubt, before doing so, he will examine any agreement reached by the advocates, paying appropriate regard to it, and any reasons which the Crown, in particular, may advance to justify him proceeding immediately to sentence. At the risk of stating the obvious, the judge is responsible for the sentencing decision and he may therefore order a Newton hearing and to ascertain the truth about disputed facts.

7. The prosecuting advocate should assist him by calling any appropriate evidence and testing the evidence advanced by the defence. The defence advocate should similarly call any relevant evidence and, in particular, where the issue arises from facts which are within the exclusive knowledge of the defendant and the defendant is willing to give evidence in support of his case, be prepared to call him. If he is not, and subject to any explanation which may be proffered, the judge may draw such inferences he thinks fit from that fact. An adjournment for these purposes is often unnecessary. If the plea is tendered late when the case is due to be tried the relevant witnesses for the Crown are likely to be available. The Newton hearing should proceed immediately. In every case, or virtually so, the defendant will be present. It may be sufficient for the judge's purpose to hear the defendant. If so, again, unless it is impracticable for some exceptional reason, the hearing should proceed immediately.

8. The judge must then make up his mind about the facts in dispute. He may, of course, reject evidence called by the prosecution. It is sometimes overlooked that he may equally reject assertions advanced by the defendant, or his witnesses, even if the Crown does not offer positive contradictory evidence.

9. The judge must, of course, direct himself in accordance with ordinary principles, such as, for example, the burden and standard of proof. In short, his self-directions should reflect the relevant directions he would have given to the jury. Having reached his conclusions, he should explain them in a judgment.

10. Again, by way of reminder, we must explain some of the limitations on the Newton hearing procedure.

(a) There will be occasions when the Newton hearing will be inappropriate. Some issues require a verdict from the jury. To take an obvious example, a dispute whether the necessary intent under section 18 of the Offences against the Person Act 1861 has been proved should be decided by the jury. Where the factual issue is not encapsulated in a distinct count in the indictment when it should be, then, again, the indictment should be amended and the issue resolved by the jury. We have in mind, again for example, cases where there is a dispute whether the defendant was carrying a firearm to commit a robbery. In essence, if the defendant is denying that a specific criminal offence has been committed, the tribunal for deciding whether the offence has been proved is the jury.
(b) At the end of the Newton hearing the judge cannot make findings of fact and sentence on a basis which is inconsistent with the pleas to counts which have already been accepted by the Crown and approved by the court. Particular care is needed in relation to a multi-count indictment involving one defendant, or an indictment involving a number of defendants, and to circumstances in which the Crown accepts, and the court approves, a guilty plea to a reduced charge.

(c) Where there are a number of defendants to a joint enterprise, the judge, while reflecting on the individual basis of pleas, should bear in mind the relative seriousness of the joint enterprise on which the defendants were involved. In short, the context is always relevant. He should also take care not to regard a written basis of plea offered by one defendant, without more, as evidence justifying an adverse conclusion against another defendant.

(d) Generally speaking, matters of mitigation are not normally dealt with by way of a Newton hearing. It is, of course, always open to the court to allow a defendant to give evidence of matters of mitigation which are within his own knowledge. From time to time, for example, defendants involved in drug cases will assert that they were acting under some form of duress, not amounting in law to a defence. If there is nothing to support such a contention, the judge is entitled to invite the advocate for the defendant to call his client rather than depend on the unsupported assertions of the advocate.

(e) Where the impact of the dispute on the eventual sentencing decision is minimal, the Newton hearing is unnecessary. The judge is rarely likely to be concerned with minute differences about events on the periphery.

(f) The judge is entitled to decline to hear evidence about disputed facts if the case advanced on the defendant's behalf is, for good reason, to be regarded as absurd or obviously untenable. If so, however, he should explain why he has reached this conclusion.

11. The final matter for guidance is whether the defendant should lose the mitigation available to him for his guilty plea if, having contested facts alleged by the prosecution, the issues are resolved against him. The principles are clear. If the issues at the Newton hearing are wholly resolved in the defendant's favour, the credit due to him should not be reduced. If for example, however, the defendant is disbelieved, or obliges the prosecution to call evidence from the victim, who is then subjected to a cross-examination, which, because it is entirely unfounded, causes unnecessary and inappropriate distress, or if the defendant conveys to the judge that he has no insight into the consequences of his offence and no genuine remorse for it, these are all matters which may lead the judge to reduce the discount which the defendant would otherwise have received for his guilty plea, particularly if that plea is tendered at a very late stage. Accordingly, there may even be exceptional cases in which the normal entitlement to a credit for a plea of guilty is wholly dissipated by the Newton hearing. In such cases, again, the judge should explain his reasons.

[7:16] *R v Pryce and Huhne*

(2013) Sentencing remarks of Mr Justice Sweeney in the Southwark Crown Court

VP and CH in the spring of 2003 you had been married for nearly 20 years. You had, between you, five children. You each had a stellar career, which had already brought you considerable success and wealth.

But you also had a problem. For the fourth time in just over a year you CH had been caught speeding (on this occasion by a camera on the M11 as you were driving home in your BMW), therefore a course of justice had begun by the sending of the necessary forms to you as the registered keeper at the family home, and thus (if you completed the relevant form truthfully as was your duty) you were facing the prospect of being disqualified from driving for at least six months. You CH were, at that time, involved in a contest to gain the Lib Dem nomination for the Eastleigh constituency, and I have no doubt that both of you were concerned that the loss of your licence CH (whoever drove for you during the period of disqualification) might damage your image, and thus your chances of success. Equally I have no doubt that, in any event, you were both concerned as to the inconvenience to you VP – in particular of taking on all the marital and parental driving duties.

Thus it was that, acting together, out of the combination, I have no doubt, of a shared ambition as to the further success of your political career CH, and a shared desire not to suffer inconvenience, you decided not to tell the truth, but instead to pervert the course of justice by pretending that you VP had been driving CH's car at the time of the offence. To that end, the relevant form addressed to you CH was returned to the authorities nominating VP as the driver, and you VP signed the form that was then sent to you to confirm that you were the driver. In the result, in May 2003, you VP were fined £60 and your licence was endorsed with three points. Hence the course of justice was perverted.

No doubt you thought that you would get away with it. After all, only you CH had been in the car at the time of the offence, it had taken place at night, the camera was forward facing, and you could choose who, if anyone, to share the secret with.

And you did get away with it for some eight years, achieving in the result not only your nomination CH, but also your eventual election as the MP for Eastleigh and your eventual rise to a seat in the Cabinet – all, I have no doubt, supported by you VP.

Whilst ironic, it is no mitigation (beyond saving you from disqualification now) that, only five months after the offence, you CH were disqualified from driving for six months under the totting up provisions.

Nor do the circumstances in which your joint offence eventually came to light reflect any credit on either of you.

At some point you CH began an affair, and in June 2010 (when the affair was about to be made public) separated from VP in circumstances which, for you VP, must have been horrendous. However, in November 2010, motivated (I have no doubt) by an implacable desire for revenge, and with little consideration of the position of your wider family, you decided to set about the dual objective of ruining CH whilst protecting your own position and reputation in the process. Your weapon of choice was the revelation of his part in the offence in 2003. But it was a dangerous weapon because it had, in truth, been a joint offence. Thus you did not go to the police, because (as you admitted during your second trial) you appreciated the risk that you would both be prosecuted. Instead you went first to The Mail on Sunday then, when they didn't publish, to the Sunday Times and then, after they published, back to The Mail on Sunday. Hence it was that over the period of six months from November 2010 to May 2011 you, I have no doubt, sought to manipulate and control the Press so as to achieve that dual objective, hoping all the while to be able to hide behind their duty of source confidentiality, which you tried long and hard to do, as well as laying the ground, if that failed, for a false defence of marital coercion.

However, after the publication of a story by the Sunday Times on 8 May 2011, to the effect that you VP had confirmed that CH had persuaded "someone close to him" to take the points, the momentum of the story led to your unmasking as the other person involved and to a police investigation.

During that investigation you VP said nothing throughout your extensive interviews – hoping, I have no doubt, that the Police would not be able to obtain evidence from anyone as to your involvement. But they did.

Despite your high office you CH tried to lie your way out of trouble by claiming that you were innocent, by repeating that lie again and again during your extensive interviews by the police, and by maintaining it in your Defence Case Statement to the Court in which it was asserted that "Mr Huhne. . . can state unequivocally that he has never asked anyone to accept responsibility for a speeding offence and as a consequence take penalty points on his behalf...".

You then compounded those lies by making numerous applications, which the Court heard and determined in good faith, upon the basis that they were required in order for you to be able to pursue your defence that VP had not taken the points for you, and to enable you (if it proved to be the case) to mount an argument that the case should be stayed as an abuse of process because you could not get all the evidence to which you were entitled to support that defence – whereas the truth, as you well knew throughout, was that VP had taken the points for you and you were guilty. Indeed it was only after the refusal of your abuse of process and dismissal applications and the entering of a plea of not guilty that you finally indicated an intention to plead guilty, and did so on what would otherwise have been the first day of your trial.

I make clear that your lies and your endeavour to manipulate the process of the court will not add a day to your sentence, although they are likely in due course be relevant to the issue of costs.

In any event you must receive a discount of 10% to reflect the fact that your late plea took a degree of courage, saved the time and expense of a trial, and may reflect the beginnings of a degree of remorse – albeit that it is easy now to apologise for your wrongdoing.

Once charged, you VP pursued your false defence of marital coercion. In doing so, just as you did in your dealings with the media, you have demonstrated that there is a controlling manipulative and devious side to your nature. However, ultimately, the good sense of the jury saw through you, and you were convicted.

Having presided over your trials I have no doubt that whilst the immediate problem was CH's, and that it was his idea that you should take his points, you were readily persuaded and chose to go along with it to your mutual benefit. Albeit that, to some limited extent, you regretted it afterwards – particularly when he was disqualified anyway and you were put to the inconvenience that you had sought to avoid in the first place.

In your case too I make clear that the way that you have conducted your case will add nothing to your sentence, but (as with CH) is likely in due course be relevant to the issue of costs.

To the extent that anything good has come out of this whole process, it is that now, finally, you have both been brought to justice for your joint offence. Any element of tragedy is entirely your own fault.

The underlying offence was speeding, the points swapping was considered and deliberate and done to gain joint advantage, the perversion of justice which resulted from it lasted for many years, and (as I have already observed) its eventual revelation and correction reflects no credit on either of you.

Offending of this sort strikes at the heart of the criminal justice system. As has been observed before, the purpose of the points system is that those who drive badly eventually have to be punished by way of disqualification, which serves to discourage bad driving and thereby to protect the public from it. The system depends, in relation to those caught on camera, upon the honest completion of the relevant form or forms. The dishonest completion of such forms is all too easy to do, and the consequent points' swapping often goes unnoticed and unchecked.

However, it must be clearly understood that it amounts to the serious criminal offence of doing acts tending and intended to pervert the course of justice and that, save in the most exceptional circumstances, an immediate custodial sentence must follow.

Indeed, in my view, this is the type of offence which requires the court to underline that deterrence is one of the purposes of sentence.

There is no Definitive Guideline in relation to cases of this type, nor (given that the authorities to which I have been referred were each decided on their own facts) any guideline authority as to the appropriate length of sentence. I must however keep the sentence as short as I can.

CH (please stand) I propose to deal with you first, as the offence was your idea and thus you are somewhat, though not greatly in my view, the more culpable of the two of you.

On the one hand you are a man of positive previous good character (about whom others have spoken extremely well) and who has given valuable public service, you have fallen from a great height (albeit that that is only modest mitigation given that it is a height that you would never have achieved if you had not hidden your commission of such a serious offence in the first place), and you have had to wait some time to be sentenced.

On the other hand this was as your counsel accepts a serious offence, indeed as it seems to me a flagrant offence of its type, its effect lasted for many years, and I must give effect to all the purposes of sentence – including deterrence.

There being no exceptional circumstances in your case, it is clear that an immediate custodial sentence must be imposed. You accept that, to some extent, you were the more culpable of the two of you.

Having weighed all the various features, it seems to me that the least possible sentence after a trial in your case would have been one of 9 months' imprisonment.

From that I must deduct the 10% to reflect your late plea, which (rounded down) results in a sentence of 8 months' imprisonment, which is the sentence that I impose upon you.

Unless released earlier under supervision you will serve half that sentence. Your release will not, however, bring the sentence to an end. If after your release and before the end of your sentence you commit any further offence you may be ordered to return to custody to serve the balance of the original sentence outstanding at the date of the new offence, as well as being punished for that offence.

VP (please stand) as I have already indicated I have no doubt, having presided over your trials, that whilst the immediate problem was CH's, and that it was his idea that you should take his points, you were readily persuaded and chose to go along with it to your mutual benefit. Albeit that, to some extent, you regretted it afterwards – particularly when he was disqualified anyway and therefore you suffered the inconvenience that you had sought to avoid. To repeat, he was therefore somewhat, though not greatly in my view, the more culpable of the two of you.

On the one hand you are now in your early sixties and a woman of positive previous good character (about whom others have spoken well) who has also given valuable public service as well as doing other good works, and you too have fallen from a considerable height (albeit that again that is only modest mitigation at best given that, in your case too, it is an eventual height that you would not have achieved if you had not hidden your commission of such a serious offence in the first place). I also take note of the issues raised as to your health and family problems.

On the other hand this was a serious and flagrant offence of its type, its effect lasted for many years, and I must give effect to all the purposes of sentence – including deterrence. Equally to the extent that there have been delays that has been a by-product of your decision to contest the case.

In my view the matters advanced on your behalf do not amount to exceptional circumstances, thus it is clear that an immediate custodial sentence must be imposed in your case as well.

There can be no discount for a plea, nor any for genuine remorse – clearly there is none.

Having weighed all the various features, including the fact that CH was somewhat more culpable than you but his sentence was discounted to reflect his plea, the sentence that I impose on you is also one of 8 months' imprisonment.

Unless released earlier under supervision you will serve half that sentence. Your release will not, however, bring the sentence to an end. If after your release and before the end of your sentence you commit any further offence you may be ordered to return to custody to serve the balance of the original sentence outstanding at the date of the new offence, as well as being punished for that offence.

In both your cases I will adjourn determination of the costs issue until a date to be fixed.

[7:17] Sentencing Council, *Assault: Definitive Guideline*

(2011) (Guideline for Inflicting grievous bodily harm/Unlawful wounding (Offences Against the Person Act 1861, section 20))

> **STEP ONE**
> **Determining the offence category**

The court should determine the offence category using the table below.

Category 1	Greater harm (serious injury must normally be present) **and** higher culpability
Category 2	Greater harm (serious injury must normally be present) **and** lower culpability; **or** lesser harm **and** higher culpability
Category 3	Lesser harm **and** lower culpability

The court should determine the offender's culpability and the harm caused, or intended, by reference **only** to the factors below (as demonstrated by the presence of one or more). These factors comprise the principal factual elements of the offence and should determine the category.

Factors indicating greater harm

Injury (which includes disease transmission and/or psychological harm) which is serious in the context of the offence (must normally be present)

Victim is particularly vulnerable because of personal circumstances

Sustained or repeated assault on the same victim

Factors indicating lesser harm

Injury which is less serious in the context of the offence

Factors indicating higher culpability

Statutory aggravating factors:

Offence motivated by, or demonstrating, hostility to the victim based on his or her sexual orientation (or presumed sexual orientation)

Offence motivated by, or demonstrating, hostility to the victim based on the victim's disability (or presumed disability)

Other aggravating factors:

A significant degree of premeditation

Use of weapon or weapon equivalent (for example, shod foot, headbutting, use of acid, use of animal)

Intention to commit more serious harm than actually resulted from the offence

Deliberately causes more harm than is necessary for commission of offence

Deliberate targeting of vulnerable victim

Leading role in group or gang

Offence motivated by, or demonstrating, hostility based on the victim's age, sex, gender identity (or presumed gender identity)

Factors indicating lower culpability

Subordinate role in a group or gang

A greater degree of provocation than normally expected

Lack of premeditation

Mental disorder or learning disability, where linked to commission of the offence

Excessive self defence

STEP TWO
Starting point and category range

Having determined the category, the court should use the corresponding starting points to reach a sentence within the category range below. The starting point applies to all offenders irrespective of plea or previous convictions. A case of particular gravity, reflected by multiple features of culpability in step one, could merit upward adjustment from the starting point before further adjustment for aggravating or mitigating features, set out below.

Offence Category	Starting Point *(Applicable to all offenders)*	Category Range *(Applicable to all offenders)*
Category 1	3 years' custody	2 years 6 months' – 4 years' custody
Category 2	1 year 6 months' custody	1 – 3 years' custody
Category 3	High level community order	Low level community order – 51 weeks' custody

The table below contains a **non-exhaustive** list of additional factual elements providing the context of the offence and factors relating to the offender. Identify whether any combination of these, or other relevant factors, should result in an upward or downward adjustment from the starting point. In some cases, having considered these factors, it may be appropriate to move outside the identified category range.

When sentencing **category 3** offences, the court should also consider the custody threshold as follows:
- has the custody threshold been passed?
- if so, is it unavoidable that a custodial sentence be imposed?
- if so, can that sentence be suspended?

Factors increasing seriousness
Statutory aggravating factors:
Previous convictions, having regard to a) the nature of the offence to which the conviction relates and its relevance to the current offence; and b) the time that has elapsed since the conviction
Offence committed whilst on bail
Other aggravating factors include:
Location of the offence
Timing of the offence
Ongoing effect upon the victim
Offence committed against those working in the public sector or providing a service to the public
Presence of others including relatives, especially children or partner of the victim
Gratuitous degradation of victim
In domestic violence cases, victim forced to leave their home
Failure to comply with current court orders
Offence committed whilst on licence
An attempt to conceal or dispose of evidence
Failure to respond to warnings or concerns expressed by others about the offender's behaviour
Commission of offence whilst under the influence of alcohol or drugs
Abuse of power and/or position of trust
Exploiting contact arrangements with a child to commit an offence
Established evidence of community impact
Any steps taken to prevent the victim reporting an incident, obtaining assistance and/or from assisting or supporting the prosecution
Offences taken into consideration (TICs)

Factors reducing seriousness or reflecting personal mitigation
No previous convictions **or** no relevant/recent convictions
Single blow
Remorse
Good character and/or exemplary conduct
Determination and/or demonstration of steps taken to address addiction or offending behaviour
Serious medical conditions requiring urgent, intensive or long-term treatment
Isolated incident
Age and/or lack of maturity where it affects the responsibility of the offender
Lapse of time since the offence where this is not the fault of the offender
Mental disorder or learning disability, where **not** linked to the commission of the offence
Sole or primary carer for dependent relatives

Section 29 offences only: The court should determine the appropriate sentence for the offence without taking account of the element of aggravation and then make an addition to the sentence, considering the level of aggravation involved. It may be appropriate to move outside the identified category range, taking into account the increased statutory maximum.

STEP THREE
Consider any other factors which indicate a reduction, such as assistance to the prosecution
The court should take into account sections 73 and 74 of the Serious Organised Crime and Police Act 2005 (assistance by defendants: reduction or review of sentence) and any other rule of law by virtue of which an offender may receive a discounted sentence in consequence of assistance given (or offered) to the prosecutor or investigator.

STEP FOUR
Reduction for guilty pleas
The court should take account of any potential reduction for a guilty plea in accordance with section 144 of the Criminal Justice Act 2003 and the *Guilty Plea* guideline.

STEP FIVE
Dangerousness
Inflicting grievous bodily harm/Unlawful wounding and racially/religiously aggravated GBH/Unlawful wounding are specified offences within the meaning of Chapter 5 of the Criminal Justice Act 2003 and at this stage the court should consider whether having regard to the criteria contained in that Chapter it would be appropriate to award an extended sentence.

STEP SIX
Totality principle
If sentencing an offender for more than one offence, or where the offender is already serving a sentence, consider whether the total sentence is just and proportionate to the offending behaviour.

STEP SEVEN
Compensation and ancillary orders
In all cases, the court should consider whether to make compensation and/or other ancillary orders.

STEP EIGHT
Reasons
Section 174 of the Criminal Justice Act 2003 imposes a duty to give reasons for, and explain the effect of, the sentence.

STEP NINE
Consideration for remand time
Sentencers should take into consideration any remand time served in relation to the final sentence. The court should consider whether to give credit for time spent on remand in custody or on bail in accordance with sections 240 and 240A of the Criminal Justice Act 2003.

[7:18] Ashworth, A, Genders, E, Mansfield, G, Peay, J and Player, E, *Sentencing in the Crown Court: Report of an Exploratory Study*

(1984) Oxford Centre for Criminological Research Occasional Paper No 10 (at page 60)

All the judges whom we consulted insisted that the right to determine the form and length of sentence in each case should be theirs, and firmly opposed any suggestion of 'interference' by

Parliament in the form of legislative restrictions on sentencing. 'The Judges should be trusted', as one judge put it. A wise sentencing discretion was defended as necessary to give proper effect to the varying facts of individual cases. This pre-occupation with variations of facts in individual cases leads many judges to regard sentencing as 'an art rather than a science'. It is generally thought inappropriate to require a judge to give reasons for his choice of sentence, and such 'reasons' as are given tend to consist of general references to factors taken into account rather than a detailed explanation of how the judge weighted those factors in arriving at the precise sentence. There is judicial ambivalence about the implications of the view that sentencing is 'an art rather than a science'. The grip of the maxim that 'each case depends on its own facts' leads many judges to considerable scepticism about the very enterprise of formulating and stating principles of sentencing. Indeed, even if general principles were clearly articulated, a particular judge's interpretation of the material presented to him might lead him to categorise the facts in one way whilst another judge classified them differently. On the other hand, the 'pilot study' found no shortage of judicial requests for more guidance on some issues which seem capable of resolution or which raise particular difficulties. It is elementary to point out that maxims such as 'each case depends on its own facts' do not sit comfortably with a judicial commitment to consistency and to 'uniformity of approach'. The Lord Chief Justice, in his judgment in *R v Bibi* (1980) 71 Cr App Rep 360 and in other judgments since the 'pilot study' was completed, has shown his firm belief that more guidance is necessary and, by implication, that it can be helpful to Crown Court sentencers in dealing with their cases.

Research could go much further than simply showing that the 'facts of the case' are not objective matters but are the result of a subtle reconstruction by the individual judge, and that judges do draw upon general views or propositions when arriving at sentences. It could identify key factors which tend to be interpreted differently by individual judges, and could identify salient variations in the attitudes of judges to certain types of offence, types of offenders and types of sentence. This information could be used in framing the guidance given to sentencers at judicial seminars or by the Court of Appeal. It could make a major contribution to the development of consistency in sentencing, by ensuring not only that the guidance meets and takes account of the needs of sentencers but also that the guidance is likely to be effective. The possibility of judges interpreting similar cases in different ways ought to be reduced if clear guidance on the significance is to be found in *Bibi* (1980), where the Lord Chief Justice identified classes of case in which sentences might be lowered but made no reference to the effect on sentence of the offender's previous record, the number of offences, and so on. Is it realistic to call for 'uniformity of approach' when no reference is made to the effect on sentence of matters which sentencers clearly regard as important? Policy initiatives aimed at altering practice in a particular sphere of sentencing may meet with little success, as did the *Bibi* initiative, or have unintended side-effects, unless they are grounded upon systematic knowledge of judicial approaches to sentencing.

Some might argue that the diversity of approaches we found among the small numbers of 'experienced' judges interviewed in this 'pilot study' raises a powerful case for greater control over the use of sentencing powers by judges, whether by legislative restrictions or otherwise. That might be the correct conclusion, but it need not be. Another possibility would be to use the results of research in framing study programmes for judges. The 'pilot study' found that many judges appeared to have devoted little thought to the principles on which they act. The Judicial Studies Board might be willing to use research findings on judges' awareness of their own sentencing practices, on judges' feelings of constraint, on different interpretations of the facts of cases, and generally on judicial attitudes towards various factors in sentencing. It might be profitable if the divergent practices were discussed and debated at judicial seminars, with a view to formulating general policies on some matters and modifying attitudes. If, as the 'pilot study' suggests, one reason why guidance from Parliament or from the Court of Appeal might have limited effect lies in the resilience of individual judicial attitudes, then it might be best to tackle these individual differences directly in the context of a judicial seminar. Systematic research into Crown Court sentencing could supply the basis for such an approach.

Research findings also have implications for the concept of judicial independence. On the one hand, despite judges' opposition to any encroachment upon their independence by members of the executive such as the Home Office, some judges seem quite unaware of the influence upon the listing of cases exerted by certain administrators. Research which is able to identify influences of this kind may enhance rather than challenge the independence of the judiciary. On the other hand, there are respects in which the concept of judicial independence seems to be used inappropriately: greater contact with the probation service would not necessarily threaten, either apparently or in reality, the impartiality of the judiciary and might well improve understanding of the expectations of each party. Perhaps the most forceful manifestation of judicial independence, however, lies in the substantial autonomy of the individual judge. In theory, of course, each judge is subject to the law, to the appeal process, and to the undertaking in his judicial oath. In practice, the paucity of legal rules and principles on sentencing and the limitations of their enforcement set by the appeal system (with no prosecution appeals, and few defence appeals actually coming before the Court of Appeal) leave the individual judge with considerable room to gall into idiosyncrasies in sentencing. Whilst assistant recorders and recorders will know that their appointment to a higher judicial office may to some extent depend upon reports of their 'performance', there appear to be few controls on the approach to sentencing of a circuit judge. Sentences which are grossly out of line are likely to be corrected if the excess is one of severity rather than leniency, and there is the possibility of a 'word in the ear' from a presiding judge on the circuit, but in general judges have considerable leeway. They appear also to have developed techniques for the neutralisation of criticism. Apparent inconsistencies in sentencing are explained by reference to the facts of the particular case; the press, the public and politicians are believed to be generally ill-informed about the full facts of cases and thus their criticisms are discounted; indeed, individual judges may attempt to neutralise criticism from the Court of Appeal, in a case in which it varies a sentence passed at the trial, by maintaining that the Court is out of touch with current practice. One consequence of all this is that the principle of judicial independence may have become a cloak behind which the idiosyncrasies of an individual judge go substantially unchallenged, thus undermining the 'uniformity of approach' which the Lord Chief Justice has declared to be his aim.

At the end of our report to the Lord Chief Justice on the 'pilot study', we outlined the proposal for a full research project which would continue the attempt 'faithfully to reflect the realities of Crown Court sentencing and the system within which it takes place, and to explore the reasons why judges approach sentencing as they do'. Within the study we propose to pursue certain particular lines of enquiry:

- the attitudes of judges to certain kinds of crime and certain kinds of sentence;
- the interpretations which judges place upon evidence before them, in order to arrive at the 'facts of the case' which they consider relevant for the purpose of sentencing;
- what judges expect of the Court of Appeal and, if permission were given, how the Court of Appeal views its functions in relation to the lower courts;
- what judges seek from social enquiry reports and speeches in mitigation;
- how the practices of probation officers, counsel and court administrators can influence the course which a case takes;

- how it is that judges sometimes feel they have no alternative but to pass a particular sentence, when other judges would pass different sentences;
- how well judges understand their own sentencing practices, and whether it is possible for a judge to believe that he is passing a reduced sentence when, by his own standards, he is not.

In December 1981, the Lord Chief Justice, Lord Lane, informed us that the research would not be allowed to go ahead.

Chapter 8

Juries

Chapter Contents

Since Gerry Good was charged with an offence under the Offences Against the Person Act (OAPA) 1861, section 18, he can be tried only on indictment. He will therefore be tried in the Crown Court before a judge and jury. It is the jury who decide whether or not he is guilty. Juries are often seen as the 'bulwark of our liberty', yet the reality may be very different: there is increasing scepticism about what is clearly an expensive and under-researched method of trial. Perhaps the most interesting question is how juries reach their decisions, but little is known about how juries work in practice. The Contempt of Court Act 1981, section 8 [8:1] was long interpreted as effectively banning any research into jury decision-making, although Thomas (2014) has recently argued that section 8 is not as restrictive on conducting research on juries as many have thought. No action was taken on the recommendation of the Royal Commission on Criminal Justice (1993) that it should be possible for properly authorised research to be carried out into the way in which juries reach their verdicts and that section 8 should be amended (although Lord Justice Auld [1:5] was more ambivalent about the need for this). Some research into how juries actually carry out their task has been done using shadow or mock juries (see, for example, McCabe and Purves (1974) and, more recently, Thomas [8:2]). However, since the mock jury knows that that is all it is, the value of such studies is limited – a conclusion that the Law Commission has also reached. The Law Commission (2013) recommended reforming section 8 (subject to significant safeguards) to provide an exception allowing approved academic research into jury deliberations. Notably, this idea was opposed by the Criminal Bar Association, the Crown Prosecution Service, the Council of Circuit Judges and some senior judges when it was proposed in the earlier consultation paper.

(i) Selecting the jury

The basic rules governing juries are found in the Juries Act 1974 [8:3], though the Criminal Justice Act 1988, section 119 raised the maximum age of jurors to 70 (and the age limit was raised again to 75 by the Criminal Justice and Courts Act 2015 – although this is not yet in force at the time of writing; the cynic might wonder whether the potential cost-savings of having retired jurors might have played a part in this decision). The Criminal Justice and Public Order Act (CJPOA) 1994, sections 40–43, the Courts Act 2003, the Criminal Justice Act (CJA) 2003, section 321 and Schedule 33, the Constitutional Reform Act 2005 and the Electoral Administration Act 2006 have all also amended the rules on disqualification and excusal. Even today, the jury does not necessarily reflect the community as a whole: the initial summoning is done at random from names on the electoral roll, and many people may not be registered on the roll. Of those summoned, it used to be that a high proportion successfully avoided or evaded service (see Darbyshire et al, 2002) – although this may be more difficult today as a consequence of the reforms introduced by the CJA 2003. The Royal Commission on Criminal Justice [1:3] urged electoral registration officers to take every possible step to ensure that electoral rolls are as comprehensive as possible. It pointed out that it is particularly important that efforts are made to persuade people from ethnic minorities to register. How are electoral officers to achieve this? Is there any convincing alternative to using the electoral roll?

Those who are mentally ill are ineligible for jury service. The people disqualified are those on bail; those who have at any time been sentenced to indeterminate, or more than five years', imprisonment; and those who have served any period of imprisonment, suspended sentence or community order within the last 10 years. Those with minor criminal convictions may sit on a jury – but is it right to disqualify those on bail? Until the CJA 2003, judges, those 'concerned with the administration of justice', and the clergy were ineligible for jury service. At [8:4] we discuss *R v Abdroikov* [2007] UKHL 37 where, in three joined appeals, the House of Lords had to decide whether the presence of a police officer or a Crown Prosecution Service solicitor on a jury would lead a fair-minded and informed observer to conclude that there was a real possibility of bias. This issue arose again when the European Court of Human Rights decided in *Hanif and Khan v United Kingdom* (2012) 55 EHRR 16 that the presence of a police officer on the jury, who knew one of the police witnesses, violated the defendants' right to a fair trial under the European Convention on Human Rights, Article 6 **[1:13]**. Spencer (2012) is critical of the decision to allow police officers to serve on juries and concludes that '[i]n practical terms, the need for judges to question police jurors about their relationships (if any) with witnesses adds a new and needless complication to the trial, and where one does serve and the defendant is convicted, a new and needless ground for possible appeal' (at pages 256–257).

Between the ages of 18 and 70 jury service is compulsory: this can be both inconvenient and expensive to the individual juror. When the jury summonses have been issued, many people return them, pleading a wide variety of reasons for being unable to sit on a jury on the dates in question, such as a booked holiday or an important work commitment. The Divisional Court in *R v Guildford Crown Court, ex p Siderfin* [1990] 2 QB 683 held that there was no excusal as of right on religious grounds. However, the Royal Commission's recommendation **[1:3]** that practising members of religious societies or orders who find jury service to be incompatible with their tenets or beliefs should be excused was enacted by CJPOA 1994, section 42. But the CJA 2003 abolished the right to be excused: now anyone who wishes to be excused must show 'good reason'. An important deterrent may well be the risk of loss of earnings. In a typical short case like Gerry Good's, the jury will have been summoned for a two-week period. Several jurors may have sat together on a jury the day before, but much time will have been spent hanging around – the facilities are often poor: uncomfortable chairs, no TV or newspapers, unattractive refreshment facilities (if there are any refreshment facilities at all: the recent cost-cutting drive has led to the closure of canteens in some Crown Courts). It is not surprising that Auld **[1:5]** argued strongly for improved court facilities for jurors, including facilities to enable jurors-in-waiting to conduct their own affairs. In section (iii) below some attempt will be made to assess the value of the lay jury in deciding questions of fact in certain criminal trials. An important associated question is whether 12 is too high a number – fewer people's time would be wasted if the jury had fewer members. Would a jury made up of nine, or even six, people be as satisfactory?

Are jurors truly representative? Zander and Henderson's famous Crown Court study (1993) (and see **[7:6]**) found that neither women nor people from ethnic minorities were badly under-represented. Women made up 47 per cent of all jurors (but only 22 per cent of jury foremen) and non-white jurors made up 5 per cent of jurors, as compared with 5.9 per cent of the total population. Perhaps of more concern is the distribution of non-white jurors in individual cases. In 65 per cent of cases there were no non-whites on the jury (and in one, no white jurors). The Court of Appeal held in *Ford* **[8:5]** that there is no right to a multiracial jury. However, the Royal Commission believed that in some cases race should be taken into account. It accepted the proposal of the Commission for Racial Equality that, before trial, the prosecution or defence should be able to apply to the judge for a multiracial jury, including up to three people from ethnic minorities. This the judge would grant only if the applicant's case was reasonable because of some special feature. Auld **[1:5]** also advocated a scheme for cases in which the court considers that race is likely to be relevant to an important issue in the case, for the selection of a jury consisting of, say, up to three people from any ethnic minority group. But the decision in *Ford* has not been overruled. It is important to emphasise, however, that Thomas **[8:2]** found that the verdicts of all-white juries did not discriminate against non-white defendants.

There are other criticisms of the composition of juries. The longer a trial, the more complicated it is likely to be. Yet the longer the trial, the more jurors will find legitimate grounds for excusal, and the less representative they will be. There are those who suggest that 18 is too young a minimum age for jurors, since they will be too inexperienced. However, Zander and Henderson (1993) found that age had little or no effect on jury verdicts: if anything, older age-group juries were more likely to acquit than the younger. Should there be physical or educational (reading and writing?) tests, as recommended by Lord Denning (1982)?

Those summoned for jury service constitute the jury panel, and from the panel the jury for an individual case will be selected. The parties to the case are entitled to inspect the list, but it contains only names and addresses. From the jury panel, the jury is selected randomly in open court, by the clerk of the court reading out the names from a pile of cards. Thus, in Gerry Good's case, perhaps 20 jurors will be led into the back of the courtroom. The clerk will read out one name at a time. As they enter the jury box, each juror may be challenged by the prosecution or the defence. Probably Gerry Good keeps his eyes down, vaguely irritated and vaguely embarrassed by the whole process. The defence used to have a right of peremptory challenge (the right to challenge prospective jurors without having to give reasons) but this was reduced from seven to three challenges per defendant by the Criminal Law Act 1977 and abolished by the Criminal Justice Act 1988. The main objection to these challenges was that they interfered with the random selection of the jury, but there was no evidence that peremptory challenges had any effect on acquittals, and they were rarely used. What peremptory challenges did allow was the exclusion of those who defendants, or their counsel, felt by their appearance were unlikely to reach a fair verdict.

Thus, today the defence only has the right to 'challenge for cause', which means the right to ask that a prospective juror be dismissed because there is reason to believe that he or she will be biased or incapable. Since, unlike in the United States, potential jurors cannot be questioned in order to discover whether there is any ground for a challenge, challenges for cause are rare. The prosecution has the right to challenge for cause, or to require a juror to 'stand by for the Crown', which is similar to a peremptory challenge. This right was not abolished by the Criminal Justice Act 1988, but the following year the Attorney General issued guidelines (updated in 2012) [8:6] stating that the Crown should assert its right to stand by 'only sparingly and in exceptional circumstances'. The guidelines allow the search of criminal records for the purpose of ascertaining whether or not a member of the panel is a disqualified person, and some further investigations of members of the panel in security or terrorist cases. This practice, known as 'jury vetting', remains controversial, perhaps mainly because it is unclear how widespread the practice is.

(ii) The function of the jury

This is a book on criminal processes, but it is worth remembering that juries have a role elsewhere in the legal system. The Court of Appeal confirmed in H v Ministry of Defence [8:7] that juries are rarely available in civil personal injury cases. Controversy surrounds the use of juries in libel cases, where the jury not only decide liability but also award damages, often in a way which can be both unpredictable and unjust (and the Defamation Act 2013 introduced a presumption against the use of juries). A jury is also summoned in some inquests in coroners' courts (particularly where there has been a death in custody). In criminal cases, the jury's role is limited to determining guilt, and they have no role in sentencing. Juries have to decide issues of fact, and on those facts decide whether or not the defendant is guilty of the crime charged. They give no reasons for their decisions, with the result that it is extremely difficult to challenge a verdict. Does this undermine a defendant's right to a fair trial?

During the course of a trial the jury sit together in the jury box and listen to the evidence. It is widely acknowledged that juries are likely to perform better if they know what to expect and if they receive full, clear guidance and assistance. They therefore receive written notes explaining the procedure of jury service, and usually see an introductory video, before the case begins. Perhaps they should be encouraged by judges to take notes if they want to? At a time when juries are increasingly being asked to study lengthy and complicated written evidence, the Royal Commission (1993) sensibly recommended that the provision of writing materials should be standard, which it now is. Note Madge (2006) – a judge's view that juries should receive more guidance in writing.

In Gerry Good's case, four witnesses for the prosecution are called, and none for the defence. Gerry chooses, as he is entitled to, not to give evidence. It may not be a very wise decision: since 1995, the jury has been entitled to draw 'such inferences as appear proper' from a defendant's failure to testify in court (see CJPOA 1994, section 35 **[2:17]**). Although a person cannot be convicted solely on an inference drawn from silence, this change in the law can be seen to undermine the presumption of innocence. How it works in practice can be seen in *Cowan* [1996] 1 Cr App R 1. A rather harsh example is *Friend* [1997] 2 Cr App R 231, where the jury were entitled to draw adverse inferences from the decision of a mentally disabled 15-year-old not to give evidence. However, the drawing of adverse inferences from silence in the police station is a much greater threat to due process than inferences drawn from silence at trial (see Chapter 2).

After counsel for both sides have made their closing speeches, the judge gives the summing up, the importance of which was discussed in Chapter 7. The jury will be told that they have to reach a unanimous verdict, although they may well know that eventually a majority verdict may be permitted. At the end of the summing up they retire to a jury room to consider their verdict, and will then be kept together privately until either they reach a verdict or they are discharged because they find themselves unable to do so. Sometimes jurors wish to ask the judge questions or to be reminded of a piece of evidence, in which case they will be brought back into open court. Occasionally, when the jury have been unable to reach a verdict swiftly, it has been necessary to keep them in a hotel overnight, but nowadays they will usually be permitted to separate for the night, even once they have retired to consider their verdict. Remember that the verdict is simply 'guilty' or 'not guilty'. Juries do not give reasons for their decisions. How does this stand up to scrutiny in the light of the right to a fair trial in Article 6 of the European Convention on Human Rights **[1:13]**? As Spencer (2001) shows, the European case law is not altogether helpful on the point; however, despite the Belgian jury system being found by the European Court of Human Rights to violate Article 6 in *Taxquet v Belgium* (2012) 54 EHRR 26, the English jury system has thus far survived unscathed. The Belgian response to the decision in *Taxquet* is somewhat curious: juries reach their verdicts alone but, once given, the judge joins them to write their reasons for the verdict. What happens, one wonders, if this process reveals a deficiency in the jury's reasoning?

Majority verdicts, first introduced by the Criminal Justice Act 1967, are now governed by the Juries Act 1974, section 17 **[8:3]**. The jury are sent out to reach a unanimous verdict and it is left to the judge's discretion whether, after at least two hours have passed, they are prepared to accept a majority verdict. If a majority verdict is guilty, the foreman must state in open court the number of jurors who agreed to, and the number who dissented from, the verdict.

Table 8.1 Jury verdicts and majority verdicts

	Defendants convicted after a plea of not guilty	Percentage after a majority verdict
1993	12,460	15%
1997	11,510	20%
2001	16,605	14%
2006	11,839	18%
2009	11,252	18%
2011	12,152	19%

Source: Judicial Statistics 1997–2001, Table 6.11; Judicial Statistics 2006, Table 6.9; Judicial Statistics 2011, Table 4.9

Are majority verdicts a dangerous inroad into the principle that no one should be convicted unless the prosecution has proved their guilt beyond reasonable doubt, or are they a sensible pragmatic compromise? Are there adequate due process safeguards? The main justification for introducing the majority verdict was said at the time to be that a majority verdict would reduce the risk of improper pressure being put on individual jurors and reduce the likelihood of 'jury nobbling'. Today the main justification would probably be the costs saved in avoiding a retrial, but the risks of corrupt influences and jury intimidation remain (although there are now provisions under section 44 of the CJA 2003 to hold a trial without a jury where there is a 'danger of jury tampering').

Is the function of the jury to apply a clearly established legal definition to the facts that they have found to be proved, or do they have an additional function of introducing lay values into the administration of justice? Is it part of their function to prevent the unjust use of the criminal law, exercising what is sometimes called 'jury equity'? Drawing the line between the proper functions of judge and jury can be very difficult. The criminal law reflects an ambivalence: some words – such as, for example, 'insulting' or 'dishonest' – are left for the jury to interpret according to their common sense, while others – such as 'intention' or 'recklessness' – have been rigidly judicially defined such that, at times, as a matter of law, they no longer mean what ordinary English suggests. *Brutus v Cozens* **[8:8]** is a classic example: whilst the House of Lords says that it is for the magistrates (or jury) to decide the meaning of 'insulting behaviour', the real question is whether it should be the judge or the jury who should decide whether the protester was infringing the law set out in the Public Order Act 1936. The meaning of an ordinary word may not be a question of law, but the proper construction of a statute clearly is. Does the distinction between law and fact in this context make sense, or is it just a technique that allows judges to avoid ruling on difficult questions? Another example: a sewage company unknowingly causes pollution, because an unauthorised person had dumped a chemical into the sewers: do they 'cause' the pollution? Should the judge or jury decide this? (An answer to this question can be found in *National Rivers Authority v Yorkshire Water Services Ltd* [1995] 1 AC 444.)

(iii) Assessing the jury

A fundamental question is whether the jury or the judge is better equipped to deal with the meaning of ordinary words (or the ordinary meaning of words, as Guest (1986) prefers to put it). The jury are often said to have an important constitutional role: 'the lamp that shows that freedom lives', as Lord Devlin famously said. Certainly a jury can acquit someone against the evidence, when their conscience leads them so to do. One reason why sheep-stealing stopped being a capital offence was that juries were refusing to convict sheep-stealers, and in the 1930s Parliament was forced to introduce a new offence of causing death by reckless driving when juries showed a marked reluctance to convict for manslaughter those who killed by dangerous driving. The acquittal in 1984 of Clive Ponting – a senior civil servant who passed secret documents to an MP and was prosecuted under the Official Secrets Act 1911 – is said to show the constitutional importance of the jury, with their freedom to disagree with both the judge and the Government. Lord Devlin **[8:9]** describes the jury as a democratic veto on law enforcement.

But this argument is debunked by Darbyshire **[8:10]**. Juries are used in relatively few cases: the Crown Court deals with less than 5 per cent of all criminal cases.

Let us look a bit more closely at the acquittal rate: as we saw in Chapter 3, during 2013/14, 69 per cent (17,042) of the defendants who pleaded not guilty in the Crown Court (24,790) were acquitted, representing 26 per cent of the total 93,727 dealt with who recorded a plea. Of those 17,042, 63 per cent were discharged by the judge, 4 per cent were acquitted on the direction of the judge, and 33 per cent were acquitted by a jury (CPS Annual Report 2013/14, page 87). How can we know if these people were wrongly acquitted? It is very difficult to assess the jury. Are they too

Table 8.2 Acquittals of defendants by juries

	Acquittals (as percentage of those pleading not guilty)	Percentage of those acquitted who are acquitted by jury (as opposed to on direction of judge)
1993	58%	43%
1997	64%	35%
2001	66%	33%
2005	59%	30%
2009/10	72%	31%
2013/14	69%	33%

Source: Judicial Statistics (various years), Chapter 6; CPS Annual Reports 2009/10 and 2013/14, Annex C

easily swayed, susceptible to rhetoric? Are they prone to leniency? Are they too doubtful nowadays of police evidence? The acquittal of Ponting can be seen as inappropriate – the proper means for amending the Official Secrets Act was through the ballot box, not via the jury room – and one has to remember that in all 'miscarriage of justice' cases it was the jury who decided to convict.

And are juries capable of understanding the evidence and making decisions in complex cases? Concerns about juries' levels of understanding came to public attention in February 2013 when the first jury in the high profile trial of Vicky Pryce **[7:16]**, prosecuted for perverting the course of justice, was discharged after submitting a list of 10 questions, some quite bizarre (for example: 'Can a juror come to a verdict based on a reason that was not presented in court and has no facts or evidence to support it either from the prosecution or defence?'), to the judge when they were considering their verdict. On discharging them, Mr Justice Sweeney stated that the jury had 'absolutely fundamental deficits in understanding' of their role and the trial process. Could this be just the tip of the iceberg? Coen and Heffernan (2010) are surely right to argue that there is 'an urgent need for empirical research involving real jurors in order to gauge jury comprehension of expert evidence, especially in complex cases' (at page 211).

Stockdale (1967) questioned why judge and jury are kept so rigorously separated 'and free to make their own mistakes'. Should they have their own legal adviser (or even the judge) present to steer their deliberations? Jackson and Doran (1997) argue that the traditional division of labour between judges and juries should be redrawn in order to enable judges to take greater responsibility for areas where their fact-finding strengths are located (for example, identification and scientific evidence). As we saw in H v *Ministry of Defence* **[8:7]**, juries are now rarely used in civil cases. The Roskill Committee on Fraud Trials (1986) had little difficulty in concluding that juries should be abolished for complex fraud trials, and that trials should take place before a Fraud Trials Tribunal; it relied on a study that cast grave doubts on a jury's fact-finding ability. But if one accepts that some cases are too difficult for a jury, where should the line be drawn? Many cases hang on complicated scientific evidence, and it is difficult to argue that fraud is necessarily more 'difficult' than, say, murder or rape.

There have been a few scandals involving juror misbehaviour. *Young* [1995] QB 324 involved a jury consulting an Ouija board. Then in *Mirza* [2004] 1 AC 1118 the House of Lords had to consider a case where a juror had written to counsel suggesting that there had been a racial element in the jury's verdict; in *Smith* [2005] 1 WLR 704, after the jury had begun their deliberations, the judge received a letter from one juror alleging that certain jurors were disregarding the judge's directions on the law, were indulging in speculation and were engaging in improper bargaining over verdicts on several counts; in *Charnley* [2007] 2 Cr App R 33 a juror alleged that the verdicts had not been unanimous as directed by the judge. What should happen in such cases? The summary and comment on the decision of the House of Lords in *Attorney General v Scotcher* **[8:11]** raises some important questions.

Perhaps the greatest challenge facing trial by jury today is the internet. The amount of extraneous information about defendants or the cases being tried potentially at jurors' fingertips presents a very real problem: can we be sure that jurors are not going home and doing their own research? Thomas [8:2] found that 5 per cent of jurors on standard cases and 12 per cent of those on high profile cases admitted to looking on the internet for information about their cases whilst the trial was going on – and as Thomas notes, 'it should be borne in mind that they were being asked to admit to doing something they may have remembered being told not to do by the judge. As a result [these] figures may reflect the minimum numbers of jurors who looked for information on the internet during cases' (at page 43). Whilst such behaviour already amounts to contempt of court (and these cases are treated very seriously by the courts: see *Attorney General v Dallas* [8:12]) the Law Commission (2013) recommended the creation of a new criminal offence for a sworn juror in a case deliberately searching for extraneous information related to the case that he or she is trying; this offence would be triable only on indictment, with a maximum sentence of two years' imprisonment and/or an unlimited fine. The Government has acted on this recommendation and the Criminal Justice and Courts Act 2015, section 71 has created this new separate criminal offence.

Most discussions of trial by jury conclude by looking at the alternatives – and deciding that no other system is better. Useful discussion of the alternatives are to be found in Cornish (1968), in the Roskill Committee report (1986), and in Levi (1993), which summarises some of the disadvantages of the possible alternatives in fraud trials. One option, which seems to be the one preferred by Governments in recent years, is to limit the number of cases for which trial by jury is available, and to transfer an increasing number of offences to the magistrates' courts by making them summary-only offences. The heated political debate that erupted over the failed Criminal Justice (Mode of Trial) Bill 1999, which was seen by many as an erosion of a fundamental right, recurred when the CJA 2003 changed the law to allow trials without jury on grounds of length or complexity, or where there is a real danger of jury tampering (the first judge-only trial under this provision was heard in 2010 in R v Twomey and others, Central Criminal Court, unreported: the jury in the second re-trial of the defendants had been discharged in December 2008 amidst allegations of attempted jury tampering and the Court of Appeal had authorised a judge-only trial in R v Twomey and others [2009] EWCA Crim 1035).

However, Roberts and Hough [8:13] suggest that there remains strong public support for trial by jury. But is trial by jury in practice all that it is held up to be? What are the jury actually doing when considering their verdict? More research is needed into the methods used by juries to evaluate the evidence, although Professor Sir John Smith (1998) warns:

> Much of our law of evidence is based on assumptions about the behaviour of juries which are mere guesswork and, of course, I recognise that it is highly desirable that we should know whether these assumptions are well founded or not. But I fear that there is a price to be paid – namely the revelation that many cases are decided in consequence of material irregularities in the jury room with the consequent undermining of public confidence in jury trial. If we are to keep jury trial – and there is an overwhelming sentiment in favour of doing so – it is perhaps better not to know. Is this a case where ignorance is bliss? (at page 105).

These authors reject this approach, and indeed hopes were raised when the Department for Constitutional Affairs consulted in 2005 on options for allowing research into jury deliberations. Particularly worrying is, of course, the fact that juries do not have to give reasons for their decisions (unlike most other decision-making bodies). Most disappointingly, the Government decided that, although most respondents were supportive of the idea of further research into jury deliberations, it would support research only 'within the confines of the current law'. Furthermore, the recommendation of the Law Commission to provide an explicit exception to section 8 of the Contempt of Court Act 1981 [8:1] to allow approved academic research into jury deliberations has not been taken forward by the Government; section 8 continues to provide a barrier to understanding jury decision-making.

Further reading

Baldwin, J and McConville, M, *Jury Trials* (1979) Clarendon Press

Coen, M and Heffernan, L, 'Juror comprehension of expert evidence: a reform agenda' [2010] Crim LR 195

Cornish, W R, *The Jury* (1968) Allen Lane

Darbyshire, P, Maugham, A and Stewart, A, 'What can the English Legal System Learn from Jury Research Published up to 2001?' (2002) Research Papers in Law, Kingston University

Denning, Lord, *What Next in the Law?* (1982) Butterworths

Department for Constitutional Affairs, *Jury Research and Impropriety: a consultation* (2005)

Devlin, P, *Trial by Jury* (1956) Stevens

Findlay, M and Duff, P (eds), *The Jury under Attack* (1988) Butterworths

Guest, S, 'Law, Fact and Lay Questions' in Dennis, I H (ed), *Criminal Law and Justice* (1986) Sweet & Maxwell

Haralambous, N, 'Juries and extraneous material: a question of integrity' (2007) *Journal of Criminal Law* 520

Jackson, J and Doran, S, *Judge without Jury: Diplock Trials in the Adversary System* (1995) Clarendon Press

Jackson, J and Doran, S, 'Judge and Jury: Towards a new division of labour in criminal trials' (1997) 60 *Modern Law Review* 759

Law Commission, *Contempt of Court (1): Juror Misconduct and Internet Publications* (2013) Law Com No 340

Levi, M, *The Investigation, Prosecution and Trial of Serious Fraud* (1993) RCCJ Research Study No 14, HMSO

McCabe, S and Purves, R, *The Shadow Jury at Work* (1974) Blackwell: OUP RU Paper No 8

Madge, N, 'Summing up – a judge's perspective' [2006] Crim LR 817

Roskill, E, *Report of the Fraud Trials Committee* (1986) HMSO

Smith, J C, 'Is Ignorance Bliss? Could Jury Trial Survive Investigation?' (1998) 38 *Med Sci Law* 98

Spencer, J R, 'Inscrutable Verdicts, the duty to give reasons and Art. 6 of the European Convention on Human Rights' (2001) 1 *Archbold News* 5

Spencer, J R, 'Police officers on juries' (2012) 71(2) *Cambridge Law Journal* 254

Stockdale, E, *The Court and the Offender* (1967) Gollanz

Taylor, N and Denyer, R, 'Judicial management of juror impropriety' (2014) *Journal of Criminal Law* 43

Thomas, C, 'Avoiding the Perfect Storm of Juror Contempt' [2013] Crim LR 483

Thomas, C, 'Exposing the Myth of Jury Research' (2014) *Criminal Law and Justice Weekly*, 9 December

Vidmar, N (ed), *World Jury Systems* (2000) Oxford University Press

Zander, M and Henderson, P, *The Crown Court Study* (1993) RCCJ Research Study No 19, HMSO

Documents

[8:1] Contempt of Court Act 1981
Section 8

8 Confidentiality of jury's deliberations

(1) Subject to subsection (2) below, it is a contempt of court to obtain, disclose or solicit any particulars of statements made, opinions expressed, arguments advanced or votes cast by members of a jury in the course of their deliberations in any legal proceedings.

(2) This section does not apply to any disclosure of any particulars –

(a) in the proceedings in question for the purpose of enabling the jury to arrive at their verdict, or in connection with the delivery of that verdict, or
(b) in evidence in any subsequent proceedings for an offence alleged to have been committed in relation to the jury in the first mentioned proceedings,

or to the publication of any particulars so disclosed.

(3) Proceedings for a contempt of court under this section (other than Scottish proceedings) shall not be instituted except by or with the consent of the Attorney General or on the motion of a court having jurisdiction to deal with it.

[8:2] Thomas, C, *Are juries fair?*
(2010) Ministry of Justice Research Series 1/10 (at page i)

Summary
This research asks: How fair is the jury decision-making process? It explores a number of aspects of jury fairness for the first time in this country, and asks specifically:

- Do all-White juries discriminate against BME defendants?
- Do jurors racially stereotype defendants?
- Do juries at certain courts rarely convict?
- Do juries rarely convict on certain offences?
- Do jurors understand legal directions?
- Do jurors know what to do about improper conduct in the jury room?
- Are jurors aware of media coverage of their cases?
- How is the internet affecting jury trials?

The research used a multi-method approach to examine these issues:

- case simulation with real juries at Crown Courts (involving 797 jurors on 68 juries);
- large-scale analysis of all actual jury verdicts in 2006–08 (over 68,000 verdicts);
- post-verdict survey of jurors (668 jurors in 62 cases).

The study found little evidence that juries are not fair. However, it identifies several areas where the criminal justice system should better assist jurors in performing this vital role. The study also demonstrates that section 8 of the Contempt of Court Act 1981 does not prevent comprehensive research about how juries reach their verdicts and that research from other jurisdictions should not be relied upon to understand juries in this country.

All-White juries and BME defendants
A key question remained to be answered from a recent jury study: Do all-White juries discriminate against Black and minority ethnic (BME) defendants? A large number of all-White juries tried an identical case in which only the race of defendants and victims was varied. This enabled the study to determine if race actually affects jury decision-making.

The case simulation was conducted with 41 all-White juries at Winchester and Nottingham Crown Courts (478 jurors). It replicated an earlier study of racially mixed juries at Blackfriars Crown Court in London (27 juries with 319 jurors). Earlier research found that juries at Winchester and Nottingham will almost always be all-White. The juror catchment area for Nottingham is predominantly White but includes neighbourhoods with high levels of ethnic diversity; the Winchester juror catchment area is overwhelmingly White throughout.

The study examined decision-making at the jury verdict level:

- The key finding was that verdicts of all-White juries did not discriminate against BME defendants. Jury verdicts at both courts showed no tendency for all-White juries to convict a Black or Asian defendant more than a White defendant.
- All-White juries at Winchester had almost identical verdicts for White and BME defendants, but all-White juries at Nottingham had particular difficulty reaching a verdict involving a BME defendant or BME victim.
- This suggests that local population dynamics may play a role in jury decision-making.

The study also examined the votes of all individual jurors who sat on these juries:

- White jurors serving on racially mixed juries and on all-White juries had similar patterns of decision-making for White, Black and Asian defendants. But White jurors on racially mixed juries had lower conviction rates overall.
- White jurors in a racially diverse area (Nottingham) appeared sensitive to cases involving inter-racial conflict. These jurors were significantly more likely to convict the White defendant when he was accused of assaulting a BME victim compared to a White victim. No similar trend was found with White jurors in Winchester.
- White jurors serving on all-White juries did not racially stereotype defendants as more or less likely to commit certain offences based on race. The same result was found with both White and BME jurors serving on racially mixed juries.

The only other personal characteristic that appeared to affect juror decision-making was gender. Female jurors were more open to persuasion to change their vote in deliberations than male jurors. Male jurors rarely changed their mind.

Jury verdicts in Crown Courts in England and Wales 2006–08

This study analysed a large dataset of all charges in all Crown Courts in England and Wales (551,669) where outcomes occurred between 1 October 2006 and 31 March 2008.

- Such a large dataset enabled a statistically reliable analysis of trends in jury verdicts.
- The study examined whether defendant ethnicity, offence type, court, severity of offence or number of charges in a trial had any correlation to jury verdicts.

Disproportionality for BME defendants in Crown Court trials

It is already known that members of BME groups are disproportionately represented among those stopped, searched, arrested, charged and in prison. This study found that:

- BME defendants are consistently more likely than White defendants to plead not guilty to charges in all of the 12 general offence categories used in this study except one (falsification, forgery and counterfeiting).

- BME defendants are three and half times more likely to face a jury verdict in the Crown Court relative to their representation in the general population.
- However, jury verdicts showed only small differences based on defendant ethnicity. White and Asian defendants both had a 63% jury conviction rate; Black defendants had a 67% jury conviction rate.

This indicates that one stage in the criminal justice system where BME groups do not face persistent disproportionality is when a jury reaches a verdict.

Appearance of jury fairness

While these findings strongly suggest that racially balanced juries are not needed to ensure fair decision-making in jury trials with BME defendants, concerns about the appearance of fairness with all-White juries may still remain.

- The study found that in all Crown Courts, the proportion of BME defendants is greater than the proportion of BME groups in the local population or BME jurors at each court.
- Concerns about the appearance of jury fairness are likely to arise in courts where all-White juries try substantial numbers of BME defendants or try White defendants accused of racial crimes against BME victims.
- To address these concerns, HMCS should ensure that court users understand how jury pools are selected and how representative they are of the locality.

Scope and effectiveness of jury trials

Most charges brought against defendants in the Crown Court are not decided by a jury:

- Only 12% of all charges are decided by jury deliberation.
- 59% of all charges result in a guilty plea by a defendant.
- Of the remaining charges where a defendant pleads not guilty and therefore gives rise to a potential jury trial, 36% are decided by jury deliberation.

Juries overall appear efficient and effective:

- Once a jury is sworn it reaches a verdict by deliberation on 89% of all charges (judges direct jury verdicts on 11% of charges).
- Once juries deliberate they reach verdicts on virtually all charges (only 0.6% of all verdicts are hung juries).
- Juries convict on almost two-thirds (64%) of all charges presented to them.
- Juries are rarely discharged (less than 1% of sworn juries).

Jury conviction rates

Offence type had an impact on the probability of a jury reaching a guilty verdict.

- Falsification, deception, drugs and theft offences are the general offence types most likely to produce a guilty jury verdict.
- Non-fatal offences against the person are least likely to result in a jury conviction, although juries still reach guilty verdicts more often than not here (52% conviction rate).

Conviction rates for specific offences within general offence types can vary substantially.

- The category of homicide-related offences has some of the lowest jury conviction rates (threatening to kill 36%, manslaughter 48%, attempted murder 47%) but also some of the highest jury conviction rates (death by dangerous driving 85%, murder 77%).

Differences in jury conviction rates for different specific offences suggest that juries try defendants on the evidence and the law.

- Offences where the strongest direct evidence is likely to exist against a defendant appear to have the highest conviction rates (making indecent photographs of a child 89%, drugs possession with intent to supply 84%, death by dangerous driving 85%).
- Cases where juries must be sure of the state of mind of a defendant or complainant in order to convict appear to have the lowest conviction rates (threatening to kill 36%, attempted murder 47%, GBH 48%).

Misconceptions about jury verdicts in rape cases

Contrary to popular belief and previous government reports, juries actually convict more often than they acquit in rape cases (55% jury conviction rate).

- Other serious offences (attempted murder, manslaughter, GBH) have lower jury conviction rates than rape.
- A previous Home Office study stating that jury acquittals were more common than convictions was based on a small number of verdicts (181) in a few courts. Current findings cover all jury rape verdicts in all courts in 2006–08 (4,310).
- Jury conviction rates for rape vary according to the gender and age of the complainant, with high conviction rates for some female complainants and low conviction rates for some male complainants. This challenges the view that juries' failure to convict in rape cases is due to juror bias against female complainants.
- Juries are not primarily responsible for the low conviction rate on rape allegations.

Misconceptions about jury verdicts in certain courts

There are variations in jury conviction rates between Crown Courts.

- In courts with over 1,000 jury verdicts in 2006–08, the conviction rate ranged from 69% to 53%. There were no courts with a higher jury acquittal than conviction rate, and this dispels the myth that there are courts where juries rarely convict.
- Variations in court conviction rates could be due to differences in the types of offences presented to juries at different courts; differences in public attitudes to crime and justice in different communities; or variations in police evidence gathering or prosecution or judicial handling of jury trials.
- It is recommended that the underlying reasons for substantial variations in jury conviction rates between Crown Courts be examined further.

Multiple charges

- The number of charges against a defendant affected the likelihood of the jury returning at least one guilty verdict.

- The probability of a guilty jury verdict increased with the number of charges, rising steeply from 40% with one charge to 80% with five charges.

Juror comprehension of judicial directions

This study involved 797 jurors at three courts who all saw the same simulated trial and heard exactly the same judicial directions on the law.

- There is not a consistent view among jurors at all courts about their ability to understand judicial directions. Most jurors at Blackfriars (69%) and Winchester (68%) felt they were able to understand the directions, while most jurors at Nottingham (51%) felt the directions were difficult to understand.

Jurors' actual comprehension of the judge's legal directions was also examined.

- While over half of the jurors perceived the judge's directions as easy to understand, only a minority (31%) actually understood the directions fully in the legal terms used by the judge.
- Younger jurors were better able than older jurors to comprehend the legal instructions, with comprehension of directions on the law declining as the age of the juror increased.

A written summary of the judge's directions on the law given to jurors at the time of the judge's oral instructions improved juror comprehension of the law:

- The proportion of jurors who fully understood the legal questions in the case in the terms used by the judge increased from 31% to 48% with written instructions.
- The judiciary should reconsider implementing the Auld recommendations for issuing jurors with written *aide memoires* on the law in all cases.
- An assessment should also be made of how many judges already use written instructions, when and how often.
- Further research should be conducted as a matter of priority to identify the most effective tools for increasing juror comprehension of judicial directions.

Jury deliberations and impropriety

This study involved 196 jurors at Winchester who had served on a jury and therefore should have been instructed by a judge on improper conduct.

- Almost half (48%) of all jurors said they either did not know or were uncertain what to do if something improper occurred in the jury deliberating room.
- Most of these jurors (67%) also felt they should be given more information about how to conduct deliberations.
- An even larger majority of these jurors (82%) felt it was correct that jurors should not be allowed to speak about what happens in the deliberating room.
- This was only a limited exploration of these issues. The findings indicate that further research should be conducted to determine what jurors understand improper jury behaviour to be; how jurors think they should deal with improper jury conduct; and what type of information jurors want about deliberations.

Media reporting of jury trials and juror use of the internet

The study was conducted in three different locations (Nottingham, Winchester and London) and included 62 cases and 668 jurors. The sample included both long, high profile cases and standard cases lasting less than two weeks with little media coverage.

- Jurors serving on high profile cases were almost seven times more likely to recall media coverage (70%) than jurors serving on standard cases (11%).
- Most jurors who recalled media reports of their case saw or heard reports only during the time their trial was going on. This provides the first empirical evidence in this country of the "fade factor" in jury trials (the further away media reports are from a trial the more likely they are to fade from jurors' memories).
- But a third of jurors (35%) on high profile cases remembered pre-trial coverage.
- In high profile cases, jurors recalled media reports of their cases from a range of media outlets, with television (66%) and national newspapers (53%) the two main sources. This contrasts with jurors' recall of media reports in standard cases, where local newspapers accounted for almost all (77%) coverage recalled.
- Most jurors (66%) in high profile cases who recalled media coverage either did not or could not remember it having any particular slant. Where jurors did recall any emphasis, almost all recalled it suggesting the defendant was guilty.
- In high profile cases, 20% of jurors who recalled media reports of their case said they found it difficult to put these reports out of their mind while serving as a juror.

The findings show that in high profile cases almost three-quarters of jurors will be aware of media coverage of their case. It would be helpful to know how these jurors perceive this media coverage, what particular type of pre-trial coverage jurors' recall and what type of coverage some jurors find difficult to put out of their minds.

The internet

All jurors who looked for information about their case during the trial looked on the internet.

- More jurors said they saw information on the internet than admitted looking for it on the internet. In high profile cases 26% said they saw information on the internet compared to 12% who said they looked. In standard cases 13% said they saw information compared to 5% who said they looked.
- In the study jurors were admitting to doing something they should have been told by the judge not to do. This may explain why more jurors said they saw reports on the internet than said they looked on the internet.
- Among all jurors who said they looked for information on the internet, most (68%) were over 30 years old. Among jurors on high profile cases, an even higher percentage (81%) of those who looked for information on the internet were over 30.

The findings raise a number of questions that should be examined further: do jurors realise they are not supposed to use the internet? How do they use the internet: do they just look for information or do they also discuss the case on social networking sites? What type of judicial instruction would be most effective in preventing jurors from looking for information about their case on the internet?

Recommendations

The jury system imposes a duty on citizens to participate in the criminal justice system and to decide the most serious criminal cases in this country. It is therefore crucially important that jurors are provided with the most effective tools to carry out that responsibility. The findings on juror comprehension of the law, impropriety, internet use and jurors' views about deliberations suggest that jurors want and need new tools to better understand the process. A concerted effort should be made by those responsible for the criminal justice system to identify the most effective means of ensuring the highest levels of juror understanding in criminal jury trials.

Written juror guidelines

To address both jury impropriety in general and juror use of the internet, the judiciary and HMCS should consider issuing every sworn juror with written guidelines clearly outlining the requirements for serving on a trial.

- The written guidelines should acknowledge the value of the juror's role and clearly explain what improper behaviour is, why it is wrong and what to do about it.
- The judge should review the requirements with jurors as soon as they are sworn. This should include a fuller direction to jurors on why they should not use the internet to look for information or discuss their case.
- Jurors should be required to keep the guidelines with them throughout the trial.

Piloting should be carried out to determine what form of written guidelines and judicial directions are most comprehensible to jurors and are most likely to be taken seriously.

[8:3] Juries Act 1974 (as amended)

Sections 1; 3; 9; 17

1 Qualification for jury service

(1) Subject to the provisions of this Act, every person shall be qualified to serve as a juror in the Crown Court, the High Court and the county court and be liable accordingly to attend for jury service when summoned under this Act if –

- (a) he is for the time being registered as a parliamentary or local government elector and is not less than eighteen nor more than seventy years of age;
- (b) he has been ordinarily resident in the United Kingdom, the Channel Islands or the Isle of Man for any period of at least five years since attaining the age of thirteen; and
- (d) he is not disqualified for jury service.

(3) The persons who are disqualified for jury service are those listed in Schedule 1.

3 Electoral register as basis of jury selection

(1) Every electoral registration officer under the Representation of the People Act 1983 shall as soon as practicable after the publication of any register of electors for his area deliver to such officer as the Lord Chancellor may designate such number of copies of the register as the

designated officer may require for the purpose of summoning jurors, and on each copy there shall be indicated those persons on the register whom the registration officer has ascertained to be, or to have been on a date also indicated on the copy, less than eighteen or more than seventy years of age.

(1A) If a register to be delivered under subsection (1) above includes any anonymous entries (within the meaning of that Act of 1983) the registration officer must, at the same time as he delivers the register, also deliver to the designated officer any record prepared in pursuance of provision made as mentioned in paragraph 8A of Schedule 2 to that Act which relates to such anonymous entries.

(2) The reference in subsection (1) above to a register of electors does not include a ward list within the meaning of section 4(1) of the City of London (Various Powers) Act 1957.

9 Excusal for certain persons and discretionary excusal

(2) If any person summoned under this Act shows to the satisfaction of the appropriate officer that there is good reason why he should be excused from attending in pursuance of the summons, the appropriate officer may, subject to section 9A(1A) of this Act, excuse him from so attending.

(2A) Without prejudice to subsection (2) above, the appropriate officer shall excuse a full-time serving member of Her Majesty's naval, military or air forces from attending in pursuance of a summons if –

> (a) that member's commanding officer certifies to the appropriate officer that it would be prejudicial to the efficiency of the service if that member were to be required to be absent from duty, and
> (b) subsection (2A) or (2B) of section 9A of this Act applies.

(2B) Subsection (2A) above does not affect the application of subsection (2) above to a full-time serving member of Her Majesty's naval, military or air forces in a case where he is not entitled to be excused under subsection (2A).

(3) Criminal Procedure Rules shall provide a right of appeal to the court (or one of the courts) before or any failure by the appropriate officer to excuse him as required by subsection (2A) above which the person is summoned to attend against any refusal of the appropriate officer to excuse him under subsection (2) above.

(4) Without prejudice to the preceding provisions of this section, the court (or any of the courts) before which a person is summoned to attend under this Act may excuse that person from so attending.

17 Majority verdicts

(1) Subject to subsections (3) and (4) below, the verdict of a jury in proceedings in the Crown Court or the High Court need not be unanimous if –

> (a) in a case where there are not less than eleven jurors, ten of them agree on the verdict; and
> (b) in a case where there are ten jurors, nine of them agree on the verdict.

(2) Subject to subsection (4) below, the verdict of a jury (that is to say a complete jury of eight) in proceedings in the county court need not be unanimous if seven of them agree on the verdict.

(3) The Crown Court shall not accept a verdict of guilty by virtue of subsection (1) above unless the foreman of the jury has stated in open court the number of jurors who respectively agreed to and dissented from the verdict.

(4) No court shall accept a verdict by virtue of subsection (1) or (2) above unless it appears to the court that the jury have had such period of time for deliberation as the court thinks reasonable having regard to the nature and complexity of the case; and the Crown Court shall in any event not accept such a verdict unless it appears to the court that the jury have had at least two hours for deliberation.

(5) This section is without prejudice to any practice in civil proceedings by which a court may accept a majority verdict with the consent of the parties, or by which the parties may agree to proceed in any case with an incomplete jury.

[8:4] *R v Abdroikov*
[2008] Crim LR 134

Under the Criminal Justice Act 2003, rules formerly governing the qualification and disqualification of jurors were changed so that police officers and employees of the Crown Prosecution Service (the CPS) were no longer exempt from jury service. The three appellants were tried on an indictment in different courts and on unrelated charges and were convicted. In the first case, the appellant was charged with attempted murder and there was a minor issue concerning one aspect of the evidence of a police witness. When the jury were considering their verdicts the foreman of the jury sent a note to the judge revealing that he was a serving police officer. He was concerned that if required to report for duty on the following Bank Holiday Monday, when the court was not sitting, he might meet one or more of the police officers who had been called to give evidence at the trial. With the acquiescence of defending counsel, the juror was directed not to report for duty on the Monday. The second appellant had been stopped by police officers and searched. In the course of the search one of the officers put his hand into the appellant's pocket and was pricked on the finger by a used syringe. The second appellant was charged with assault occasioning actual bodily harm. At trial there was a dispute on the evidence between the second appellant and the police officer concerning the manner in which he had been searched and what he and the officer had subsequently said. He was convicted. Some time after the trial, the appellant's solicitor became aware that a police officer had been a member of the trial jury. That police officer was at the time posted to a station within the operational command unit which committed its work to the Crown Court at which the second appellant had been tried. Moreover, both the juror and the police officer giving evidence were both serving in the same borough at the time of the incident and had once served in the same police station at the same time. The two officers were not, however, known to one another. The third appellant had been charged with two very serious charges of rape. The jury which convicted him included among its members a solicitor who worked for the CPS. Before the trial he had written to the Crown Court, in accordance with the guidance given to those working in the CPS who were to serve on juries, that he had had worked for the CPS since its inception and was a Higher Court Advocate who had practised in many local courts although he had not conducted a trial in the Crown Court where he was to sit as a juror. Defence counsel objected but the judge ruled that he had to operate within the law passed by Parliament and he could see no objection to the solicitor sitting as a juror in the light of the current legislation. The solicitor thereafter became foreman of the jury and the third appellant was convicted. Each appellant appealed and the cases were joined before the

Court of Appeal. The Court of Appeal concluded that the convictions were safe as the fact that there were 12 members of the jury of which at least 10 had to be agreed was a real protection against the prejudices of an individual juror resulting in unfairness to a defendant and that the fair-minded and informed observer would not conclude that there was a real possibility that a jury was biased merely because his occupation was one which meant that he was involved in some capacity or other in the administration of justice. The appellants all appealed.

Held, dismissing the first appeal and (Lord Rodger and Lord Carswell dissenting) allowing the second and third appeals, it had to be accepted that most adult human beings, as a result of their background, education and experience, harboured certain prejudices and predilections of which they might be conscious or unconscious, but that safeguards established to protect the impartiality of the jury, when properly operated, did all that could reasonably be done to neutralise those prejudices and predilections to which everyone was prone. However, it was not possible to dismiss the argument that there was the possibility of bias, possibly unconscious, which inevitably flowed from the presence on a jury of professional persons committed to one side only of an adversarial trial process. Nevertheless, Parliament had declared that in England and Wales police officers were eligible to sit, perhaps envisaging that their identity would be known and any objection would be the subject of judicial decision. The first case did not turn on a contest between the evidence of the police and that of the appellant and, therefore, it was hard to suggest that the case was one in which unconscious prejudice, even if present, would have been likely to operate to the disadvantage of the appellant, and it made no difference that the officer was the foreman of the jury. It followed that the Court of Appeal had reached the right conclusion in that case. The second appellant's case, however, was different as there was a crucial dispute on the evidence between the appellant and the police officer, and the officer and the juror, although not personally known to each other, had shared the same local background. In those circumstances, the instinct of a police officer, even if it was unconscious, to prefer the evidence of a fellow brother officer to that of a drug-addicted defendant would be judged by the fair-minded and informed observer to be a real and possible source of unfairness, beyond the reach of standard judicial warnings and directions. Thus, the second appellant was not tried by a tribunal which was and appeared to be impartial and his conviction would be quashed. In the case of the third appellant, no possible criticism was to be made of the CPS lawyer, but the judge had given no serious consideration to the objection of defence counsel, who himself had little opportunity to review the law. It had to be doubted whether Parliament had contemplated that employed Crown prosecutors would sit as jurors in prosecutions brought by their own authority. It was clear that justice was not seen to be done if one discharging the very important neutral role of juror was a full-time salaried, long-serving employee of the prosecutor. The third appellant had been entitled to be tried by a tribunal that was, and appeared to be, impartial and he had not been. That appeal, therefore, would be allowed and the matter remitted to the Court of Appeal with an invitation to quash the convictions and rule on any application which might be made for a retrial.

(Case considered: Pullar v United Kingdom (1996) 22 E.H.R.R. 391).

Commentary (by Nick Taylor): For many years the position was that serving police officers and those professionally concerned in the administration of law were not eligible to serve as jury members. Their non-qualification under s.1 of the Juries Act 1974 was based on the concern that persons with specialist knowledge of the system, and the prestige attached to their position would unduly influence other jurors (see Report of the Departmental Committee on Jury Service (1965, Cmnd.2627, para.103) (The Morris Report)). The Morris Report stated (at para.103) that: "It seems to us clearly right that such persons . . . should be specifically excluded from juries." The Royal Commission on Criminal Justice (1993, Cm.2263, Ch.8, para.57) recommended no change to this aspect of the exclusionary rule. The Auld Report (Review of the Criminal Courts of England and Wales, Home Office, 2001) argued that it would today be unlikely that jurors simply on the basis of their status or position would influence other jurors (Ch.5, para.30). Auld L.J. suggested that people no longer deferred to professionals as was once the case and to support this point he drew attention to the position in the United States where there was no evidence that criminal justice professionals dominated jury deliberations to which they were a party. As such, Sch.33 to the Criminal Justice Act 2003 provided that both police officers and prosecuting solicitors could qualify for jury service. Whilst the position adopted in the Criminal Justice Act can be defended, it can be argued that as the Morris Report was so clear in its position that it is difficult to see how such a change could be made in the absence of clear tangible evidence that the problem of bias or perceived bias could in future be catered for. As such, there are those who might consider that there will indeed be at least a perception of bias when serving police officers or those professionally concerned in the administration of law sit on juries. Nevertheless, the statute is clear and the courts must give effect to the intention of Parliament. Even so, as Baroness Hale stated:

> "The fact that Parliament has said that they are eligible to serve does not mean that Parliament intended that they should do so in any case to which they were summoned." (at [46])

What this case seeks to clarify is not whether such professionals can sit on juries, that answer is clear, but that there are occasions when it might be inappropriate for them to do so. In considering the legislative change, Auld L.J. anticipated that doubtful cases would be resolved by the trial court judge on a case-by-case basis. This can only be effective if that judge is aware of the presence of such jurors or the exact nature of their links to the case. In the case of the first appellant this clearly did not happen. However, in light of the clear wording of the legislation the House of Lords were unanimous in dismissing the appeal. Lord Bingham recognised that this case did not turn on evidence that was contested between the appellant and the police officer and as such there was no reason to believe that any unconscious prejudice would disadvantage the appellant. The only ground on which a perception of bias could be pinned would be the mere presence of a police officer on the jury and to find prejudice on this ground alone would be clearly contrary to the legislation. Lord Bingham reached this conclusion with a degree of "unease" (at [25]).

The cases relating to the second and third appellants had crucial features that enabled the majority to distinguish them from the first appellant in that there were links between the particular jurors and specific features of the case. These were not particularly direct links and thus differ from the more straightforward scenario in *Pintori* [2007] Crim. L.R. 997 (see also *Pullar v United Kingdom* (1996) 22 E.H.R.R. 391). In the case of the second appellant the police officer on the jury shared the same local service background as a sergeant in the case though they were not personally known to each other. One can see how the appearance of bias might arise here and Parliament cannot have intended that this should be ignored. This falls within the area identified by Baroness Hale that whilst the police officer is eligible that does not mean that he or she must sit in any case to which they are summoned. In the third case it was suggested that neither Auld L.J. nor Parliament could have intended that Crown prosecutors would sit as jurors in cases brought by their own authority. Lord Rodger in a dissenting opinion stated that such indirect links as occurred in these cases suggested a potential for bias that was no greater than in many other situations that would arise and are catered for by the law, for example, through the oath (or affirmation) by the jury that they will, "give a true verdict according to the evidence". Whilst this does focus the mind of the individual juror and requires them to assess the evidence individually, it is difficult to see how this might impact upon subconscious bias or indeed the outside perception that an individual juror might be biased.

The fact that this was a majority decision emphasises that these are relatively fine distinctions that are being drawn. For example, it is well recognised that police officers share a very strong occupational culture. Can it really be said that the potential for bias, or the perception of bias, only arises when a link can be established between the juror and someone involved in the prosecution, albeit one that, in this case, is based merely on the fact that the two individuals concerned were once based at the same station though did not know each other? Is this any stronger than the already strong occupational culture between all officers, or indeed the perception that officers are more likely to favour the prosecution given that their professional lives are served to supporting one particular side in the prosecution process? Such questions are undoubtedly very difficult to answer, particularly for a trial judge who must make the decision. However, the legislation ensures that such difficult questions must be answered and fine distinctions must be made if the plain meaning of the Act is not to be frustrated and the perception of bias is to be avoided.

[8:5] *R v Ford*
[1989] QB 868

The appellant, who was of mixed race and preferred to be called black, was chased and arrested by a police constable, also of mixed race. He was charged with six offences arising from the unlawful use of a motor car and from his subsequent arrest. At the Crown Court he pleaded guilty to one count, and at the outset of the trial he applied to the judge, through counsel, for a multiracial jury. The judge, under the misapprehension that counsel was about to use the case as a platform for racial haranguing, refused the application. The appellant was convicted on two counts.

The Court of Appeal, allowing his appeal on other grounds, confirmed that there is no right to a multiracial jury.

Lord Lane CJ (at page 871):

At common law a judge has a residual discretion to discharge a particular juror who ought not to be serving on the jury. This is part of the judge's duty to ensure that there is a fair trial. It is based on the duty of a judge expressed by Lord Campbell CJ in *R v Mansell* (1857) 8 E & B 54 as a duty 'to prevent scandal and the perversion of justice'. A judge must achieve that for example by preventing a juryman from serving who is completely deaf or blind or otherwise incompetent to give a verdict.

It is important to stress, however, that that is to be exercised to prevent individual jurors who are not competent from serving. it has never been held to include a discretion to discharge a competent juror, or jurors, in an attempt to secure a jury drawn from particular sections of the community, or otherwise to influence the overall composition of the jury. For this latter purpose the law provides that 'fairness' is achieved by the principle of random selection.

The way in which random selection should take place is a matter not for the judge but for the Lord Chancellor, as we endeavoured to point out in the course of argument to Mr. Herbert by citing the relevant portion of the Juries Act 1974, which is section 5(1). That provides:

'The arrangements to be made by the Lord Chancellor under this Act shall include the preparation of lists (called panels) of persons summoned as jurors, and the information to be included in panels, the court sittings for which they are prepared, their division into parts or sets (whether according to the day of first attendance or otherwise), their enlargement or amendment, and all other matters relating to the contents and form of the panels shall be such as the Lord Chancellor may from time to time direct.'

There are several cases which give examples of this residual discretion. It may be exercised even in the absence of any objection by any of the parties. The basic position is that a juror may be discharged on grounds that would found a challenge for cause. In addition jurors who are not likely to be willing or able properly to perform their duties may also be discharged.

The most common cases which this question has arisen have involved questions of ethnic groups where it has been suggested that the jury should consist partly or wholly of members of that same ethnic group. Those applications provide particular difficulty for the judge and the present case is a very good example. They arise without warning and are usually argued without any reference to authority, as indeed was very largely the case in the present instance.

It has never been suggested that the judge has a discretion to discharge a whole panel or part panel on grounds that would not found a valid challenge. Similarly, in the absence of evidence of specific bias, ethnic origins could not found a valid ground for challenge to an individual juror. The alleged discretion of the judge to intervene in the selection of the jury does not therefore fall within any acknowledged category of judicial power or discretion.

There are, moreover, strong reasons why such a discretion should not be recognised. The whole essence of the jury system is random selection, as the passage from *R v Crown Court at Sheffield, ex p Brownlow* [1980] QB 530, from Lord Denning's judgment cited in the course of argument, shows. He said, at p 541: 'Our philosophy is that the jury should be selected at random – from a panel of persons who are nominated at random. We believe that 12 persons selected at random are likely to be a cross-section of the people as a whole – and thus represent the views of the common man ... The parties must take them as they come.'

The judgment was supported by Shaw LJ, sitting with Lord Denning MR.

Secondly, it is worth noting that on occasions in the past when it has been thought desirable that the court should have a power of this kind, it has been expressly granted by statute and equally subsequently abolished by statute.

Thirdly, such an application is in effect a request to the judge either to give directions as to the constitution of the panel or to order some individual jurors to be replaced without assigning a cause, that is peremptorily. It is true that in *R v Bansall* [1985] Crim LR 151, in response to an application of this type, Woolf J did give directions that the jury panel should be selected from a particular area known to contain members of the Asian community, but the judge does not appear to have had the benefit of full argument on the point.

Responsibility for the summoning of jurors to attend for service in the Crown Court and the High Court is by statute clearly laid upon the Lord Chancellor. That is clear from section 2 and section 5 of the Juries Act 1974 which has already been cited in this judgment. It is not the function of the judge to alter the composition of the panel or to give any directions about the district from which it is to be drawn. The summoning of panels is not a judicial function, but it is specifically conferred by statute on an administrative officer. That fact may not have been drawn to the attention of the court in the cases we have cited and others which have suggested that the judge has power to give directions as to the composition of the panel of jurors.

It should also be remembered that the mere fact that a juror is, for instance, of a particular race or holds a particular religious belief cannot be made the basis for a challenge for cause on the grounds of bias or on any other grounds. If therefore a judge were to exercise his discretion to remove a juror on either of these grounds, he would be assuming bias where none was proved, Such a course is not only unjustified in law, but also indeed might be thought to be seriously derogatory of the particular juror. Further, any attempt to influence the composition of the jury on these grounds would conflict with the requirement that the jury to try an issue before a court shall be selected by ballot in open court from the panel as summoned: see Juries Act 1974, section 11.

The conclusion is that, however well-intentioned the judge's motive might be, the judge has no power to influence the composition of the jury, and that it is wrong for him to attempt to do so. If it should ever become desirable that the principle of random selection should be altered, that will have to be done by way of statute and cannot be done by any judicial decision.

[8:6] Attorney General, *The exercise by the Crown of its right of stand by* (2012 update)

In 1988 the defence right to challenge jurors without cause was abolished, the prosecution right to do so was, however, retained. This means that the prosecution can object to a potential juror without giving any reason. It is recognised that this is an exceptional power and so the Attorney General, therefore, issues guidance to prosecutors on its use.

In essence, the use of the right of stand by is limited to those cases which involve national security or terrorism. The guidelines outline the circumstances in which it is appropriate for the prosecution to exercise this power and the procedure which is to be followed. The guidelines make clear that the authority to use this power is limited to the Attorney General.

Previous versions of the guidelines included an annex prepared by the Association of Chief Police Officers (ACPO) on the conduct of inquiries into a juror's previous convictions. This is now done automatically by Her Majesty's Courts Service and therefore the ACPO guidance is no longer relevant and, in consequence, is not included in these 2012 guidelines.

Guidelines

The Attorney General has issued the following guidelines on the exercise by the Crown in England and Wales of its right to stand by. The guidelines update the previous guidelines issued in 1989 to coincide with the implementation of the Criminal Justice Act 1988 s.118, which abolished the right of peremptory challenge. These updated guidelines are to have effect from the 27th November 2012. The Attorney General has also issued amended guidelines on jury checks.

1 Although the law has long recognised the right of the Crown to exclude a member of a jury panel from sitting as a juror by the exercise in open court of the right to request a stand by or, if necessary, by challenge for cause, it has been customary for those instructed to prosecute on behalf of the Crown to assert that right only sparingly and in exceptional circumstances. It is generally accepted that the prosecution should not use its right in order to influence the overall composition of a jury or with a view to tactical advantage.

2 The approach outlined above is founded on the principles that:

   a.   the members of a jury should be selected at random from the panel subject to any rule of law as to right of challenge by the defence, and
   b.   the Juries Act 1974 identifies those classes of persons who alone are disqualified from or ineligible for service on a jury. No other class of person may be treated as disqualified or ineligible.

3 The enactment by Parliament of s.118 of the Criminal Justice Act 1988 abolishing the right of defendants to remove jurors by means of peremptory challenge makes it appropriate that the Crown should assert its right to stand by only on the basis of clearly defined and restrictive

criteria. Derogation from the principle that members of a jury should be selected at random should be permitted only where it is essential.

4 Primary responsibility for ensuring that an individual does not serve on a jury if he is not competent to discharge properly the duties of a juror rests with the appropriate court officer and, ultimately the trial judge. Current legislation provides, in ss.9 to s.10 of the Juries Act 1974, fairly wide discretion to excuse, defer or discharge jurors.

5 The circumstances in which it would be proper for the Crown to exercise its right to stand by a member of a jury panel are:

a.   where a jury check authorised in accordance with the Attorney General's Guidelines on Jury Checks reveals information justifying exercise of the right to stand by in accordance with para.11 of the guidelines below and the Attorney General personally authorises the exercise of the right to stand by; or
b.   where a person is about to be sworn as a juror who is manifestly unsuitable and the defence agree that, accordingly, the exercise by the prosecution of the right to stand by would be appropriate. An example of the sort of exceptional circumstances which might justify stand by is where it becomes apparent that, despite the provisions mentioned in para.4 above, a juror selected for service to try a complex case is in fact illiterate.

Jury checks

1 The principles which are generally to be observed are:

a.   that members of a jury should be selected at random from the panel,
b.   the Juries Act 1974 identifies those classes of persons who alone are either disqualified from or ineligible for service on a jury; no other class of person may be treated as disqualified or ineligible,
c.   the correct way for the Crown to seek to exclude a member of the panel from sitting as a juror is by the exercise in open court of the right to request a stand by or, if necessary, to challenge for cause.

2 Parliament has provided safeguards against jurors who may be corrupt or biased. In addition to the provision for majority verdicts, there is the sanction of a criminal offence for a disqualified person to serve on a jury. The omission of a disqualified person from the panel is a matter for court officials – they will check criminal records for the purpose of ascertaining whether or not a potential juror is a disqualified person.

3 There are, however, certain exceptional types of case of public importance for which the provisions as to majority verdicts and the disqualification of jurors may not be sufficient to ensure the proper administration of justice. In such cases it is in the interests of both justice and the public that there should be further safeguards against the possibility of bias and in such cases checks which go beyond the investigation of criminal records may be necessary.

4 These classes of case may be defined broadly as (a) cases in which national security is involved and part of the evidence is likely to be heard in camera, and (b) security and terrorist cases in which a juror's extreme beliefs could prevent a fair trial.

5 The particular aspects of these cases which may make it desirable to seek extra precautions are:

a. in security cases a danger that a juror, either voluntarily or under pressure, may make an improper use of evidence which, because of its sensitivity, has been given in camera,

b. in both security and terrorist cases the danger that a juror's personal beliefs are so biased as to go beyond normally reflecting the broad spectrum of views and interests in the community to reflect the extreme views of sectarian interest or pressure group to a degree which might interfere with his fair assessment of the facts of the case or lead him to exert improper pressure on his fellow jurors.

6 In order to ascertain whether in exceptional circumstances of the above nature either of these factors might seriously influence a potential juror's impartial performance of his duties or his respecting the secrecy of evidence given in camera, it may be necessary to conduct a limited investigation of the panel. In general, such further investigation beyond one of criminal records made for disqualifications may only be made with the records of the police. However, a check may, additionally be made against the records of the Security Service. No checks other than on these sources and no general inquiries are to be made save to the limited extent that they may be needed to confirm the identity of a juror about whom the initial check has raised serious doubts.

7 No further investigation, as described in para.6 above, should be made save with the personal authority of the Attorney General on the application of the Director of Public Prosecutions and such checks are hereafter referred to as 'authorised checks'. When a chief officer of police or the prosecutor has reason to believe that it is likely that an authorised check may be desirable and proper in accordance with these guidelines, he should refer the matter to the Director of Public Prosecutions. In those cases in which the Director of Public Prosecutions believes authorised checks are both proportionate and necessary, the Director will make an application to the Attorney General.

8 The Director of Public Prosecutions will provide the Attorney General with all relevant information in support of the requested authorised checks. The Attorney General will consider personally the request and, if appropriate, authorise the check.

9 The result of any authorised check will be sent to the Director of Public Prosecutions. The Director will then decide, having regard to the matters set out in para.5 above, what information ought to be brought to the attention of prosecuting counsel. The Director will also provide the Attorney General with the result of the authorised check.

10 Although the right of stand by and the decision to authorise checks are wholly within the discretion of the Attorney General, when the Attorney General has agreed to an authorised check being conducted, the Director of Public Prosecutions will write to the Presiding Judge for the area to advise him that this is being done.

11 No right of stand by should be exercised by counsel for the Crown on the basis of information obtained as a result of an authorised check save with the personal authority of the Attorney General and unless the information is such as, having regard to the facts of the case and the offences charged, to afford strong reason for believing that a particular juror might be a security risk, be susceptible to improper approaches or be influenced in arriving at a verdict for the reasons given above.

12 Information revealed in the course of an authorised check must be considered in line with the normal rules on disclosure.

13 A record is to be kept by the Director of Public Prosecutions of the use made by counsel of the information passed to him and of the jurors stood by or challenged by the parties to

the proceedings. A copy of this record is to be forwarded to the Attorney General for the sole purpose of enabling him to monitor the operation of these guidelines.

14 No use of the information obtained as a result of an authorised check is to be made except as may be necessary in direct relation to or arising out of the trial for which the check was authorised. The information may, however, be used for the prevention of crime or as evidence in a future criminal prosecution, save that material obtained from the Security Service may only be used in those circumstances with the authority of the Security Service.

[8:7] *H v Ministry of Defence*
[1991] 2 All ER 834

The Ministry of Defence admitted liability for personal injuries caused by negligence in the treatment of a 27-year-old soldier, who had had a major part of his penis amputated without his consent. The Court of Appeal allowed the Ministry's appeal against the trial judge's decision that a trial by jury should be allowed.

Lord Donaldson (at page 839):

Finally, Mr Sedley draws attention to the fact that it is not for this court to disturb a discretionary decision of a judge sitting at first instance, unless it is satisfied that he has misdirected himself or his decision is clearly wrong. This, of course, we unreservedly accept.

We have reluctantly, but firmly, come to the conclusion that the judge's discretionary order was wrong and we think that he basis of the error was either a failure to appreciate the significance of the shift in emphasis created by the enactment of section 69 of the 1981 Act in place of section 6 of the 1933 Act or his acceptance of the submission that the retention of a judicial discretion necessarily involved the proposition that there must be some claims for compensatory damages in personal injury cases which were appropriate to be tried by jury or both. It follows that we are entitled, and indeed bound, to exercise a fresh discretion.

There was some discussion in argument as to the propriety of an appellate court declaring a policy or guidelines for the exercise of a judicial discretion, but it was rightly accepted that this could and should be done, provided that it was made clear that every case had to be considered on its own merits and that, if the rationale of the policy was not wholly applicable, even if the case fell within the terms of that policy, a judge was always free to depart from it. This too was unreservedly accept.

The policy should be that stated in *Ward v James* [1965] 1 All ER 563; [1966] 1 QB 273, namely that trial by jury is normally inappropriate for any personal injury action in so far as the jury is required to assess compensatory damages, because the assessment of such damages must be based upon or have regard to conventional scales of damages. the very fact that no jury trial of a claim for damages for personal injuries appears to have taken place for over 25 years affirms how exceptional the circumstances would have to be before it was appropriate to order such a trial and the enactment of section 69 of the 1981 Act strengthens the presumption against making such an order.

[8:8] *Brutus v Cozens*
[1973] AC 854

During a Wimbledon tennis match the appellant ran onto the court blowing a whistle and attempted to distribute leaflets. He sat down on the court and play was disrupted. He was charged with using insulting behaviour whereby a breach of the peace was likely to be occasioned, contrary to section 5 of the Public Order Act 1936. The magistrates held that his behaviour had not been insulting and dismissed the information. The House of Lords upheld this decision, stating that the magistrates' decision was one of fact, and there was no evidence that they had misdirected themselves.

Lord Reid (at page 861):

The meaning of an ordinary word of the English language is not a question of law. The proper construction of a statute is a question of law. If the context shows that a word is used in an unusual sense the court will determine in other words what that unusual sense is. But here there is in my opinion no question of the word 'insulting' being used in any unusual sense. It appears to me, for reasons which I shall give later, to be intended to have its ordinary meaning. It is for the tribunal which decides the case to consider, not as law but as fact, whether in the whole circumstances the words of the statute do or do not as a matter of ordinary usage of the English language cover or apply to the facts which have been proved. If it is alleged that the tribunal has reached a wrong decision then there can be a question of law but only of a limited character. The question would normally be whether their decision was unreasonable in the sense that no tribunal acquainted with the ordinary use of language could reasonably reach that decision.

Were it otherwise we should reach an impossible position. When considering the meaning of a word one often goes to a dictionary. There one finds other words set out. And if one wants to pursue the matter and find the meaning of those other words the dictionary will give the meaning of those other words in still further words which often include the word for whose meaning one is searching.

No doubt the court could act as a dictionary. It could direct the tribunal to take some word or phrase other than the word in the statute and consider whether that word or phrase applied to or covered the facts proved. But we have been warned time and again not to substitute other words for the words of a statute. And there is very good reason for that. Few words have exact synonyms. The overtones are almost always different.

Or the court could frame a definition. But then again the tribunal would be left with words to consider. No doubt a statute may contain a definition – which incidentally often creates more problems than it solves – but the purpose of a definition is to limit or modify the ordinary meaning of a word and the court is not entitled to do that.

So the question of law in this case must be whether it was unreasonable to hold that the appellant's behaviour was not insulting. To that question there could in my view be only one answer – No.

But as the Divisional Court [1972] 1 WLR 484, have expressed their view as to the meaning of 'insulting' I must, I think, consider it. It was said, at p 487:

'The language of section 5, as amended, of the Public Order Act 1936, omitting words which do not matter for our present purpose, is: "Any person who in any public place … uses … insulting … behaviour … with intent to provoke a breach of the peace or whereby a breach of the peace is likely to be occasioned, shall be guilty of an offence." It therefore becomes necessary to consider the meaning of the word "insulting" in its context in that section. In my view it is not necessary, and is probably undesirable, to try to frame an exhaustive definition which will cover every possible set of facts that may arise for consideration under this section. It is, as I think, quite sufficient for the purpose of this case to say that behaviour which affronts other people, and evidence a disrespect or contempt for their rights, behaviour which reasonable persons would foresee is likely to cause resentment or protest such as was aroused in this case, and I rely particularly on the reaction of the crowd as set out in the case stated, is insulting for the purpose of this section.'

I cannot agree with that. Parliament had to solve the difficult question of how far freedom of speech or behaviour must be limited in the general public interest. It would have been going much too far to prohibit all speech or conduct likely to occasion a breach of the peace because determined opponents may not shrink from organising or at least threatening a breach of the peace in order to silence a speaker whose views they detest. Therefore vigorous and it may be distasteful or unmannerly speech or behaviour is permitted so long as it does not go beyond any one of three limits. It must not be threatening. It must not be abusive. It must not be insulting. I see no reason why any of these should be construed as having a specially wide or a specially narrow meaning. They are all limits easily recognisable by the ordinary man. Free speech is not impaired by ruling them out. But before a man can be convicted it must be clearly shown that one or more of them has been disregarded.

We were referred to a number of dictionary meanings of 'insult' such as treating with insolence or contempt or indignity or derision or dishonour or offensive disrespect. Many things otherwise unobjectionable may be said or done in an insulting way. There can be no definition. But an ordinary sensible man knows an insult when he sees or hears it.

Taking the passage which I have quoted, 'affront' is much too vague a word to be helpful; there can often be disrespect without insult, and I do not think that contempt for a person's rights as distinct from contempt of the person himself would generally be held to be insulting. Moreover, there are many grounds other than insult for feeling resentment or protesting. I do not agree that there can be conduct which is not insulting in the ordinary sense of the word but which is 'insulting for the purpose of this section'. If the view of the Divisional Court was that in this section the word 'insulting' has some special or unusually wide meaning, then I do not agree. Parliament has given no indication that the word is to be given any unusual meaning. Insulting means insulting and nothing else.

If I had to decide, which I do not, whether the appellant's conduct insulted the spectators in this case, I would agree with the magistrates. The spectators may have been very angry and justly so. The appellant's conduct was deplorable. Probably it ought to be punishable. But I cannot see how it insulted the spectators.

[8:9] Devlin, P, 'The Conscience of the Jury'

(1991) 107 *Law Quarterly Review* 398 (at page 402)

These are the mundane reasons for preserving trial by jury, especially in crime. It exhibits, especially in the criminal verdict, the element of popularity that is appropriate in a democracy; it will be a long time before the judiciary ceases to be associated in the public mind with the upper classes.

But the paramount reason for it is that in defiance of regularity and of the disapproval of Lord Mansfield it lets the workings of conscience into the system. Judges are sworn to uphold the law; the jury is not. Sooner or later in life a man may be confronted with a struggle between what the law demands and what conscience urges. It is not a struggle that is peculiar to the jury box.

When juries fail to punish those whom they do not believe to deserve it, who is to say that they have not done what Lord Mansfield told them to do and answered to God? It is not they who are being perverse. The perversity is in the judges and bureaucrats who are so slow to see that when a procession of different juries refuses to convict of a particular crime, there is more likely to be something wrong with the law than with the juries.

This is the situation which gives the jury its peculiar place in our Constitution. It gives it what is tantamount to a democratic veto on law enforcement.

It is true that the law is made by Parliament which is a democratic body. But the function of Parliament in modern times is to approve, reject or modify the plans of the Executive. Members of Parliament are made of the same stuff as jurors. But they operate at planning headquarters behind the lines. Juries are in the front line. They see the impact of the law on its subjects and they have to decide when to use its weapons. They exercise the discretion of the man on the spot. This is as far as military analogy can be pushed. Put into constitutional terms, the jury is invested with a dispensing power to be used when their respect for law is overridden by the conviction that to punish would be unjust.

It is not only in individual cases that they act. Though they themselves have no legislative power, they can decisively influence those who have. For it is no use making laws which juries consistently fail to enforce.

It is not our great liberties that are threatened today. If they were, they would be guarded by judges. It is the little liberties which are infringed. Since the infringements are embedded in the statute the judges are powerless; the jury is not. It respects the law but it will not put it above the justice of the case.

Is this a picture of Lord Denning institutionalised? Perhaps so, but with one very big difference. The power that puts the jury above the law can never safely be entrusted to a single person or to an institution, no matter how great or how good. For it is an absolute power and, given time, absolute power corrupts absolutely. But jurors are anonymous characters who meet upon a random and unexpected summons to a single task (or perhaps a few), whose accomplishment is their dissolution. Power lies beneath their feet but they tread on its so swiftly that they are not burnt.

[8:10] Darbyshire, P, 'The Lamp that Shows that Freedom Lives – is it Worth the Candle?'
[1991] Crim LR 740 (at page 741)

The symbolic function of the jury far outweighs its practical significance. I shall argue in this paper that this sentimental attachment to the symbol of the jury is dangerous. Adulation of the jury is based on no justification or spurious justification. It has fed public complacency with the English legal system and distracted attention from its evils; a systematic lack of due process pre-trial and post-trial and certain deficiencies in the trial process itself. It has distorted the truth. The truth is that for most people who pass through a criminal justice system this palladium is simply not available and for those who can and do submit themselves to its verdict, it will not necessarily safeguard their civil liberties.

A 'Constitutional Right' to jury trial

This justification for the jury is perhaps the best known and the most often served up without explanation, as a self-evident truth. Three problems arise under this heading:

(a) the supposed guarantee of a right to jury in Magna Carta;
(b) what is meant by a constitutional right to jury trial in the English legal system; and
(c) what is meant, in jurisprudential terms, by asserting that there is a right to jury trial.

(a) Magna Carta

Many writers claim that jury trial was enshrined as a constitutional right in Magna Carta 1215, clause 39, which provided for a 'trial by peers'. Later authors undoubtedly derived this myth from Devlin, who perpetuated it in 1956, having taken it from Blackstone's Commentaries.

Whilst Blackstone's grandiloquent account of the English legal system in the eighteenth century is of great entertainment value, few later legal historians or constitutional lawyers would accept it as historically accurate. Some of his assertions have been used to quite an alarming extent, however, in establishing the constitutional foundations of newer common law jurisdictions.

The famous clause 39 of Magna Carta reads: 'Nullus liber homo capiatur vel imprisonetur, aut disseisiatur aut utlagetur, aut utlagetur, aut exuletur, aut aliquo modo destruatur, nec super eum ibimus nec super eum mittemus, nisi per legale judicium parium vel per legum terrae'; which Holdsworth translates as: 'No freeman shall be taken or/and imprisoned, or disseised, or exiled, or in any way destroyed, nor will we go upon him nor will we send upon him, except by the lawful judgment of his peers or/and by the law of the land'.

Legal historians have been at pains to point out that clause 39 has nothing to do with trial by jury and, as Cornish said 'It has always been bad history to trace the system back to Magna Carta.' Holdsworth acknowledges that the mis-interpretation of clause 39 has had sweeping effects on English constitutional history but explains: ' . . . it is also clear that the words judicium parium do not refer to trial by jury. A trial by a royal judge and a body of recognitors was exactly what the barons did not want. What they did want was firstly a tribunal of the old type in which all the suitors were judges of both law and fact, and secondly a tribunal in which they would not be judges by their inferiors. Some of them did not consider that the royal judge, none of them would have considered that a body of recognitors, were their peers.'

Earlier, in his History of Trial By Jury Forsyth had said that it was a common but erroneous opinion that judicium parium or trial by one's peers had reference to the jury and had misled many, including Blackstone. He explains that judicium implies the decision of a judge, not a jury verdict. I would add that it is crucial to remember that, in 1215, the jury was still a group of oathswearing witnesses, or compurgators. They did not pronounce judgment. The *pares*, suggests Forsyth, were: 'members of the county and other courts, who discharged the function of judges, and who were the peers or fellows of the parties before them.'

As these and other historians have pointed out, by Magna Carta the barons simply sought to secure a deal from King John, within which they safeguarded their right to be judged by judges of no lesser rank than themselves. Liber homo has been translated as either 'freeman' or 'freeholder' and 'freeman' did not mean what it does today. As we should remember from school history, freemen were a limited class in the feudal system.

(b) A constitutional right?

Even if one were to concede that it has become a constitutional convention, since the fourteenth century, when statute prescribed that jurors be independent, that juries be used in certain criminal trials, I balk at the concept of trial by jury's being 'more than one wheel of the constitution'.6 Devlin and others speak as if there were an entrenched right to jury trial, as there is in the United States Constitution or the Canadian Bill of Rights. The concept of a 'constitutional right; has, historically, been so alien to British constitutional lawyers, that the phrase seldom appeared in textbooks before the 1980s and now it only appears in the context of the debate over the need for a Bill of Rights. Indeed, the call for a Bill of Rights has arisen for this very reason: the sovereignty of parliament dictates that we do not have any entrenched rights, especially in issues beyond the grasp of EC or international law. This is manifest in relation to jury trial. Parliament has almost rendered the civil jury extinct and has continually eroded the use and availability of the jury in the criminal trial.

(c) A right?

There is also a jurisprudential problem with those who justify the use of jury trial as a right. the term 'right' at least to 'will' theorists, implies a choice. When we speak of procedural rights in the criminal justice system, we imply a choice. For example, I do not have to exercise my right of silence. Similarly, if I am charged with an offence which is triable either way, I can choose to be tried by judge and jury or magistrates. This choice can properly be called a 'right' to jury trial. What of indictable offences? Here, I must appear before the Crown Court, where my only choice is as to plea. My only right is as to trial. I cannot choose to be tried by judge alone, as I could in the United States. Thus, it is correct to speak of a 'right to jury trial' in the United States but not to speak of jury trials being a 'right', in general terms, in the English legal system, as so many defenders of the jury are wont to do.

By reasoning thus, I am accepting that the essence of a right must be a power of waiver, MacCormick would take issue with this and argue that restricting my power of waiver does not negate my right. To this, I would repeat Simmonds' reply 'It is doubtful if paternalism of this kind is best interpreted as a protection of the part's rights'.

Not only does the concept of a right to jury trial in indictable offences fail to accord with 'will' theories of rights, it also fails to satisfy classical 'interest' theories of rights and I would extend my argument here to include triable either way offences. According to interest theories, as I would apply them here, jury trial can only be described as a 'right' if the intended beneficiary of the court's duty to provide that right is the defendant. If the purpose of jury trial is primarily ideological, as I argue here, as a symbol to legitimate the criminal justice system, then the defendant is the unintended beneficiary and thus cannot be said to have real right to jury trial.

[8:11] *Attorney General v Scotcher*

[2005] UKHL 36 (this summary is taken from (2005) 6 *Archbold News* 3)

The appellant was convicted of contempt of court. After serving as a juror at a trial in February 2000, he had written to the defendants' mother explaining how, amongst other things, other jurors had changed their votes simply because they wanted to get out of the court room, and wishing her luck in her further efforts to get the conviction of her sons quashed. It was not disputed that the appellant genuinely believed that there had been a miscarriage of justice due to what he perceived to be failings on the part of his fellow jurors. The mother had passed the letter to her solicitors, who passed the letter to the Court of Appeal, who contacted the police. In July 2002 the Attorney General informed the appellant that he had given his consent to proceedings being instituted. In October 2002 the Divisional Court granted the Attorney General permission to apply for a committal order against the appellant. When the matter came before the court again on May 2003, the court decided to hear argument on whether a defence was available to a juror who disclosed the deliberations of the jury if the juror was motivated by a desire to expose a miscarriage of justice. The Divisional Court held that no such defence was available. The appellant then accepted that he had committed a contempt of court in terms of section 8(1), which provides:

> Subject to subsection (2) below, it is a contempt of court to obtain, disclose or solicit any particulars of statements made, opinions expressed, arguments advanced or votes cast by members of a jury in the course of their deliberations in any legal proceedings

The Divisional Court ordered that the appellant should serve a two-month prison sentence suspended for one year and should pay costs of £2500. He appealed.

The House of Lords unanimously dismissed the appeal, Lord Rodger giving the only speech. He explored the reasoning in *Mirza* [2004] 1 AC 1118 at length, including the speech of Lord Steyn, who had dissented in that case. He concluded that the decision in *Mirza* is

> authority for the proposition that section 8(1) of the 1981 Act does not apply to a court when it considers a juror's complaints about misconduct during the jury's deliberations, since a court cannot be in contempt of itself. By necessary implication, the complaint which the court may lawfully consider must itself be lawful. Therefore, as Lord Hobhouse held, a juror who discloses to the court what is said or done during the jury's deliberations with the intention of prompting an investigation is not, without more, e g malice, dishonesty or improper motive, in contempt of court in terms of section 8(1). The subsection no more applies to the juror than to the court. The background to the enactment of the provision is wholly consistent with that interpretation, which can be reached on ordinary principles of statutory construction without resort to section 3 of the 1998 Act. (para 25)

Thus, had the juror written to the court he would not have been guilty of contempt. Lord Rodger accepted that

> frequently, what can be done directly can also be done indirectly and to hold otherwise would be to promote form over substance. For example, if instead of writing to the trial judge or to the appeal court, the appellant had spoken or written to the jury bailiff or to the clerk of court, he would not have been in contempt. Similarly, if he had sent a sealed letter containing his complaint to the defendants' solicitors or counsel, or even to a citizens' advice bureau or similar organisation, and had asked them to forward it unopened to the appropriate court authorities, any disclosures in the letter would have been disclosures to the court and so outside the terms of section 8(1). (para 27)

However, what this juror had done was very different. Section 3 of the Human Rights Act 1998 did not apply as section 8(1) is compatible with Article 10 of the European Convention on Human Rights.

Comment: It would not be surprising if the appellant in this case felt rather sore at Lord Rodger's reasoning. No-one, at the time of the trial in which he served as a juror, had informed him that he could complain to the court. He had simply been told it was a contempt to discuss the jurors' deliberations at all. Now that all jurors should be made well aware of their right (duty?) to bring inappropriate decision-making to the attention of the proper authorities (see *Mirza*), it would be interesting to know if jurors have become more active in this regard.

[8:12] *Attorney General v Dallas*
[2012] EWHC 156 (Admin)

The facts

8 Medlock was charged with two others with causing grievous bodily harm with intent, contrary to section 18 of the Offences against the Person Act 1861. The allegation was that the three men had subjected the victim to torture over an extended period, which left him scarred for life and for which he is still undergoing major surgery. Medlock was not alleged to be the worst of the three offenders, but in particular it was alleged against him that he obtained boiling water which was used as a solvent for caustic soda. The soda was poured over the victim. At some point in the assault he also attacked the victim with a broom handle.

9 The defendant is a native of Greece. She is a woman without previous convictions and of positive good character. These considerations were fully in mind when we evaluated her evidence and whether it was likely that she would have deliberately disobeyed a court order. She

came to England in 1996 when aged 19. She graduated at the University of Luton, as it then was, in 1999 with a degree in psychology. In 2001 she was awarded a Masters Degree in Health Psychology, and a year later she was invited to be a guest lecturer in psychology. She then began to study for a Doctorate of Philosophy in Health Psychology. In 2005 she was appointed a part-time lecturer. In 2008 this appointment became permanent and full-time. She was due to submit her doctoral thesis on 24 June 2011. There were a number of delays. In due course, however, after she had taken a viva voce examination she was successfully admitted to her degree. Throughout all these studies the language of her education, and her written and oral exams from her first degree to her most recent degree, was English. Her teaching and lecturing were also conducted in English.

10 From the evidence of events which occurred when the jury was in retirement she is plainly capable of communicating in English. Her subsequent police interviews underline her skill. In her evidence before us her grasp of the English language and her ability to communicate by comprehending what she was being asked and to respond appropriately was most impressive. Any suggestion that she might have been at a disadvantage during any part of her jury service would be without foundation.

11 When the defendant was first summoned for jury service, she questioned whether, as a non-British citizen, she was eligible for service. She was told that she was. She recollected that none of the written material sent to her made reference to the use of the internet. The trial of Medlock began on 4 July 2011. The defendant was one of the jurors summoned for jury service on that date. It was her first week of service. She told us that she was overwhelmed by the honour.

12 When the defendant arrived at the jury waiting room she was shown a video about the responsibilities of the jury and given verbal instructions by the jury officer of the court. The defendant recollects being shown the introductory video. She again remembers, correctly, that nothing said in the video, suggested that the use of the internet was prohibited. At court the jury officer, speaking after the showing of the video, expressly told the jury in waiting that they must not discuss the case or the evidence with anyone outside the court. She said that this applied to internet and social networking sites. The jurors were instructed in terms that they must not research the case on the internet or research the defendant or any of those involved in the trial. Having concluded these instructions, she asked the jurors whether they understood what had been said and invited questions. On this particular occasion there were questions about expenses and the answer phone service, but none about the video or the instructions she had given. The defendant told us that she could not really remember anything said by the jury officer about the internet. She said that because of the delay in the submission of her doctoral thesis, she was not fully focused on the introductory video. However, she remembered reference to Facebook or Twitter but even now she would not know what she was supposed to do about the internet.

13 Unequivocal notices are posted in the jury retiring room and the jury waiting room. Having alerted the juror to the possibility of proceedings for contempt of court leading to a fine and/or imprisonment for disclosing the contents of jury deliberations, they read:

"You may also be in contempt of court if you use the internet to research details about any cases you hear."

14 At about 2.30 in the afternoon of 4 July, and before the case was opened by the prosecution, the judge gave the jury a number of directions. These underlined the importance of deciding the case only on the basis of what the jury saw and heard in the courtroom. Two

consequences were identified by the judge. The first was that they should not speak about the case to anybody, including their nearest and dearest. He went on:

"The second consequence is a newer one: that you do not go on the internet. You have probably read in the last few weeks about a juror who did go on the internet; went on Facebook and severe problems followed for that juror. I am sure you will not want any of those. So, the rule is – and it is told to every jury – that not only do you not discuss it, but you do not go on the internet; you do not try and do any research of your own; you do not discuss it on Facebook; you do not tweet about it; or anything of that nature. So, simply, once you leave this room you do not talk about it or deal with it in any way with anybody."

The judge continued by informing them that the evidence would be put before them in a "carefully considered way". That, he explained, was why the jury were "not to discuss it with anybody else or do your own research, or discuss it on Facebook".

15 The defendant remembers the reference by the judge to the juror who went onto Facebook and that the judge had told the jury not to discuss the case on Facebook or Twitter or with anyone else. She believed that the manner of the delivery of these words was advice rather than as an order. The judge spoke, according to her account, politely and rather quietly, and formally, with a good accent, but she says that this created difficulties for her in fully comprehending everything that he said. If she had been given an order by the judge she would have expected it to have been said with greater emphasis.

16 On the following day, 5 July, the judge ruled on the Crown's bad character application relating to Medlock's previous conviction for assault occasioning actual bodily harm on 7 April 2009. Medlock had been charged with rape, together with a co-accused. His co-accused was convicted of rape. Medlock was acquitted. The judge allowed the application to a limited extent, following which an admission was made. This referred directly to Medlock having been sentenced in relation to an offence of assault occasioning actual bodily harm committed on 3 November 2007:

"It was a prolonged assault on his then female partner and involved a younger male who played the major role. The defendant accepted that he joined in the assault and kicked his then partner causing her bruising."

17 The evidence unfolded. The jury was informed about the conviction in the limited terms permitted by the judge. After the jury left court for the day, the appellant went home. From what she says in her affidavit, and in her evidence, it was on that evening that she made a search on the internet. Her account was that she looked at the internet because she was unsure of the meaning of the word "grievous". She wanted an exact translation, but rather than ask the judge to explain its meaning, and because she did not want to look a fool, she consulted the internet. She wanted to know exactly what the man was accused of. She looked the word up in Greek and the word was equated with "dangerous". She then moved her search to look up "Luton" and "crime", apparently because of concerns about problems with crime in the town. During this search she came across a link to a Luton newspaper article about Medlock's previous conviction. She recognised his name, and she read it. She did not think she was doing anything she was not allowed to do because a newspaper is in the public domain. The object of the trial was to discover the truth and the whole truth.

18 In her police interview she was asked on three occasions whether she "might" have searched Medlock's name. Three times she said that she might have entered his name. In her affidavit she said that she could not remember if she searched the name "Medlock", adding that she did not think she remembered his name or how to spell it. It was only when she saw the link to the

newspaper report that she realised that it was about the defendant at the trial. When she gave evidence to us on this issue, it was noticeable that, by contrast with much of the remainder of her evidence, she became very hesitant. She said that she did not remember how she found the name, or whether she had put the name into the search engine. She claimed that if she had put his name in, she would have had no specific intention to research it.

19 The trial continued on 6 July. The judge summed up the case. He directed the jury to look at all the evidence presented to them in court: the evidence from witnesses, and the evidence that had been read together with admissions and documents. Having directed the jury to be dispassionate and objective he added:

"What you must not do, however, is speculate or guess about what other evidence there might have been. Do not start worrying when you deliberate about well, what would X have said or what would you have said? That is speculation, guesswork. You simply act upon the evidence that you heard."

After the conclusion of the summing-up, the jury retired to consider their verdict shortly before lunchtime. They were unable to reach a verdict that day. The court did not sit on the following day, and the jury was asked to return to court on Friday 8 July.

20 After the court had risen on 6 July the usher was approached by one of the members of the jury. She was in something of a state, "in a panic". She reported that one of the jurors had been on the internet, had found out about the previous conviction and that it involved rape. She identified the defendant as the juror in question, and continued that as soon as the defendant had started to talk about it she told her to shut up and said she did not want to hear. Other members of the jury were unhappy too, and it had become quite heated in the jury retiring room. The usher made a note of what she had been told. In due course it was drawn to the attention of the trial judge.

21 The court reconvened on Friday 8 July. The defendant and the juror who had reported the problem were kept apart from the rest of the jury and from each other. The judge informed counsel of the report made by the juror.

22 The foreman of the jury was called into court and she was asked about the incident. She confirmed that there had been some reference to the matters reported by the juror, but it was plain that she was reluctant to give any further details.

23 The judge then arranged for the defendant to be provided with legal advice if that became necessary. She was invited into court. He explained the allegation that she had gone onto the internet and found information concerning the defendant's previous conviction which she had shared with other members of the jury panel. In her own interests, he suggested that she should not say anything, but should speak privately with a lawyer, defence counsel, who was available to assist. After their conference, counsel informed the judge that the defendant stated that her behaviour regarding the use of the internet was not deliberate; thus, counsel suggested, she had a defence to any allegation of contempt. The judge then explained that the matter would be referred to the Attorney General. The defendant was bailed unconditionally and discharged from her current and any future jury service.

24 The remaining members of the jury were called into court. They were formally discharged. They were warned that there might be a police investigation. Medlock would be retried.

25 In due course the retrial began on 12 October and concluded on 20 October. The complainant gave evidence again, for an entire day. In due course Medlock was convicted. He is now subject to an eleven year extended sentence.

26 In the meantime the issue was investigated. It is clear from the evidence that while the jury was deliberating in the afternoon of Wednesday 6 July the defendant told her fellow jurors that she had been onto the internet and discovered that the circumstances of Medlock's previous conviction included an allegation of rape.

27 We take the statements of four jurors as representative. The first is the juror who made the initial complaint. She described how during the deliberations a male juror, whom she described in detail, asked whether anyone had looked the case up on the internet. The general response was that they were not allowed to do so because the judge had told them not to. The defendant, however, replied, "I did". She stated that she looked it up on the internet and that it was public knowledge. "She read it on the internet and it was from a newspaper article". The juror said immediately that they were told not to look up anything on the internet and she felt very uncomfortable about what the defendant was saying. Her comments were ignored. The defendant continued to tell the members of the jury what she had read and the juror clearly remembered her telling them that "the defendant had previously been involved in a rape of a female with a third party. He had not raped the female himself, but he had used violence against her". The defendant spoke for about two to five minutes about the information she had read on the internet. The juror was extremely unhappy because there had been evidence about the defendant's bad character but no mention of rape in the information.

28 A second juror described a loud disagreement which arose between the first juror whose account we have just narrated and the defendant. She heard the lady say something about the internet, "something about the previous case between the defendant in our case and another person, and his partner". I heard the word "rape", but did not hear exactly what she said. I interpreted that she meant the previous case for the defendant in our case had been a rape. I heard her say that she had seen or read it on the internet. A lot of people then told her she was not supposed to say that . . . when the lady talked about the defendant's previous case and she mentioned rape, everybody in the jury stopped and listened to what she said. I think it is wrong what she said as it could cloud people's judgment."

29 A third juror understood that the defendant had gone to the Court Service website and obtained information that the defendant in the trial, Medlock, had previously been involved in some capacity in an offence of rape. According to this juror the defendant said that the website had lots of information about the current case and the defendant. It also contains details of the current trial and the barristers involved. As soon as the word "rape" was spoken, "I could see the faces of the other jurors drop". The juror said she did not want to hear it, she did not think they should take any of it into account. The defendant protested that she had obtained the information from the court website and that the information was in the public domain anyway. A male juror said that he had read something similar in the newspaper.

30 A fourth juror described how when they were in the jury room together one female member of the jury asked whether anyone had researched the case, whereupon another female member of the jury who from her accent was believed to be "maybe Cypriot" said "I did", or simply "Yes". She said that she had researched all three people involved in the case and that it was in the news. She had looked on line. She had seen the previous conviction. It was then pointed out that the jury had been made aware of that conviction in court. She said "Yeah, but actually his wife was raped during the assault". This led members of the jury to say that they could not hear this, it was not part of the case.

31 None of this evidence was challenged. It was agreed that the statement of each juror could be treated as his or her evidence. It is clear not merely that the defendant had indeed

consulted the internet, and discussed Medlock's previous conviction and the fact that it involved an allegation of rape, but also that the remaining jurors were extremely disturbed, to put it no higher, by what they had been told. That, if we may say so, is greatly to their credit. They were obviously concerned to ensure that their responsibility as jurors was properly discharged. It also demonstrates that they had fully understood the prohibition against the use of the internet.

32 On 26 July the defendant was interviewed by the police. She was told that she was entitled to legal advice. She was happy for the interview to continue without a solicitor and no interpreter was required. Summarising the effect of her answers, she admitted that she had conducted an internet search and admitted that she had stated to other members of the jury that the previous conviction had also involved an allegation of rape. However, she denied deliberately flouting any instructions and directions regarding misuse of the internet. Something of the flavour of her response can be taken in an early part of the interview:

The defendant: " . . . do you want me to concentrate on what the judge said?"

The defendant said that she "took away",

" . . . that we should not look, we should not publish anything on Facebook or Twitter, we should not tell anybody outside the court about the case . . . and I think he mentioned as well that if we are approached by anybody we should report that outside the court, this is the message I took away. . . . not to publish anything on, on Facebook, on Twitter, and, and not to talk to anybody . . . outside the court . . . about the case."

She could not recall the judge's instruction not to use the internet.

33 Later, discussing the reference to the internet and what she was doing on it, she said:

" . . . you know obviously I'm Greek and, and I always do that, I need to have exact translations, you know, how the things translate and obviously the charge of that defendant was Grievous Bodily Harm, which obviously I wanted to know what it translates to . . . I wanted to see what exactly is the meaning in Greek, I always do that . . . I always do that with, you know, psychology and, and everything all the time. So I put in Greek translation, and obviously it translates as dangerous bodily harm in Greek . . . so to have an idea of, you know, what sort of charge is that and then . . . the frequency of that thing in Luton, because obviously I am aware that Luton is a really bad town and I always wanna really move out this time . . . and it came up . . . obviously the offence."

She then said she looked at many results and then on the internet

" . . . the newspaper was saying it was exactly what the prosecution gave us. However, I mentioned the word rape in it . . . but I did make clear to the jury that that wasn't the defendant's previous conviction . . . that is not related, somebody else . . . charged with that. As for the defendant, the information was what the prosecution gave us."

34 The defendant in her affidavit, and in her evidence, repeated that she had tried to explain to the police that sometimes her grasp of English was not all that good, and that she had not taken the message from the judge that she was to do no research on the internet at all. She wanted to make it clear that she had no intention to influence anybody or somehow to prejudice the jury's decision. She had, she said to us, no idea that she would be disrupting the trial process. She emphasised more than once that if she had not been prompted by a comment by another juror she would have said nothing at all.

35 We have carefully reflected on the defendant's testimony. She struck us as a highly intelligent woman, extremely articulate in English. She skilfully avoided the difficult questions by finding

refuge in carefully prepared answers. Her memory was selective. She was, for example, perfectly well aware that the booklet sent to her as a juror did not include any reference to the internet; nor did the jury video. At the time that she could not recollect references to the internet by the jury officer or the judge, she could nevertheless recollect references to Facebook and Twitter. Notwithstanding the honour she felt at serving on the jury, she was unable to concentrate sufficiently to absorb the information about the internet. She sought to persuade us that there was a significant difference which she as an academic would attach to "search" and "research". During her evidence she referred more than once to the "truth, the whole truth". At one stage she might have been saying that somehow this provided some kind of justification for what she had done, but, as it emerged at the end of her evidence, she appeared to be saying that what she had found on the internet coincided with what the jury had been told, in which case her search would be of no moment. Her attempt to blame another member of the jury for raising the issue of the internet and thereby prompting her disclosure of what she had found, even if true, did not advance her defence.

36 On her account, effectively, she came across the newspaper reference to Medlock's previous conviction in the local newspaper in Luton by following a route from the word "grievous" through to "Luton" and "crime" and in effect, somehow she stumbled across the newspaper entry.

37 We do not believe that the defendant did not seek information about "Medlock" on the internet. Her inability to remember this particular feature of the case, when she has a detailed recollection of so much else, was not credible. We do not believe that she could have just stumbled across the link to Medlock's previous conviction in the way she described.

38 We have no doubt that the defendant knew perfectly well, first, that the judge had directed her, and the other members of the jury, in unequivocal terms, that they should not seek information about the case from the internet; second, that the defendant appreciated that this was an order; and, third, that the defendant deliberately disobeyed the order. By doing so, before she made any disclosure to her fellow jurors, she did not merely risk prejudice to the due administration of justice, but she caused prejudice to it. This was because she had sought to arm and had armed herself with information of possible relevance to the trial which, although not adduced in evidence, might have played its part in her verdict. The moment when she disclosed any of that information to her fellow jurors she further prejudiced the administration of justice. In the result, the jury was rightly discharged from returning a verdict and a new trial was ordered. The unfortunate complainant had to give evidence of his ordeal on a second occasion. The time of the other members of the jury was wasted, and the public was put to additional unnecessary expense. The damage to the administration of justice is obvious.

39 This contempt is proved to the criminal standard.

Sentence

40 This species of contempt of court involves contempt of the jury, and of the jury system. The jury man or woman is vested with the heavy responsibility of doing justice according to law and returning a true verdict in accordance with the evidence produced in court. No more, and no less. We repeat what has already been said in *R v Fraill* [2011] EWCA Crim 1570:

"In every case the defendant and for that matter we add, the prosecution, is entitled as a matter of elementary justice not to be subject to a verdict reached on the basis of material or information known to the jury" (as we would add now for emphasis, or to any individual juror) "but which was not in evidence at the trial".

41 Jurors who perform their duties on the basis that they can pick and choose which principles governing trial by jury, and which orders made by the judge to ensure the proper process of jury trial they will obey, or who for whatever reason think that the principles do not apply to them, are in effect setting themselves up above the jury system and treating the principles that govern it with contempt. In the long run any system which allows itself to be treated with contempt faces extinction. That is a possibility we cannot countenance.

42 Judges are perfectly well aware of the value of modern technology, and the use of the internet as a modern means of communication. Again, we repeat what was said in *Fraill*:

"We emphasise, even if we do so by way of repetition, that if jurors make their own enquiries into aspects of the trials with which they are concerned, the jury system as we know it, so precious to the administration of criminal justice in this country, will be seriously undermined, and what is more, the public confidence on which it depends will be shaken . . . The revolution in methods of communication cannot change these essential principles. The problem therefore is not the internet; the potential problems arise from the activities of jurors who disregard the long-established principles which underpin the right of every citizen to a fair trial."

43 Misuse of the internet by a juror is always a most serious irregularity, and an effective custodial sentence is virtually inevitable. The objective of such a sentence is to ensure that the integrity of the process of trial by jury is sustained.

44 In his submissions to us on behalf of the defendant, Mr Parry acknowledged that a custodial sentence would normally be imposed, but invited us to consider matters by way of mitigation which, he suggested, should lead us to take the merciful course of suspending the effect of the custodial sentence. He drew attention, rightly, to the fact that this was not a case in which the defendant was motivated by any form of possible personal gain; nor indeed for that matter by any personal or political agenda.

45 We acknowledge the point, but if she had been so motivated this would have become a very much more serious crime. As we have already said, the defendant is a woman of positive good character. We acknowledgement her achievements thus far in her relatively young life. We recognise that she has now resigned from her appointment and has undoubtedly put her long-term academic career into jeopardy. We also fully appreciate the stresses of the prolonged proceedings and the understandable concerns about her health. We recognise that she has apologised for the disruption that her contempt has caused, but she lacks any mitigation in the form of an admission of guilt or what would in effect have been a guilty plea.

46 We have considered all these circumstances. We have made due allowance for them, together with the remaining matters drawn to our attention by Mr Parry. We have set them against the very serious features of the case which we have outlined in the judgment we have given. We have come to the conclusion that there is no sufficient basis to comply with Mr Parry's request that the sentence should be suspended. In this case an immediate custodial sentence is the appropriate sentence for the contempt which has been proved.

47 We have considered the length of that sentence and concluded that there should be a sentence of six months' imprisonment. That will be the order of the court.

48 The defendant will serve three months' imprisonment. The defendant will surrender.

[8:13] Roberts, J V and Hough, M, *Public Opinion and the Jury: An International Literature Review*
(2009) Ministry of Justice Research Series 1/09 (at page ii)

Policy briefing
- This report summarises polls that have explored public attitudes towards the criminal jury in England and Wales. Wherever possible and appropriate, comparisons are made between the views of the public here and other jurisdictions. Although the research record is rather limited, a number of conclusions may reasonably be drawn about the state of public attitudes to the criminal jury.
- Polls repeatedly suggest that the public strongly support the concept of the jury. The right to trial by jury is seen as one of the most important rights in a democratic society. The only qualification to this statement is that a significant minority of the public believe that denying the right to trial by jury for people charged with a terrorist-related crime is 'a price worth paying' to counter the terrorist threat.
- The jury attracts high confidence ratings from the public; only the police attract higher confidence or performance ratings than the jury.
- The public also believe that juries are representative of the community from which they are drawn.
- The most recent survey of the public in England and Wales found a very positive reaction to serving on a jury. Over three-quarters of respondents expressed an intention to perform jury service out of a sense of civic duty.
- There is some limited research from another jurisdiction (the United States) that serving on a jury promotes civic engagement.
- The public are opposed to recent proposals to limit the right to trial by jury.
- The results of this literature review suggest that legislators contemplating restricting the right to trial by jury need to consider the strength of public support for the institution of the jury.

Summary
There is a large body of scholarship exploring the jury as a legal institution or the reactions of jurors to the experience of serving on a jury but community reaction to the institution and function of the jury has been less well researched. Major reviews of the jury around the world have ignored the question of public reaction to the institution. The present review fills this void by addressing a number of important questions about public attitudes to the jury. The report summarises findings from a literature review of public attitudes towards the criminal jury, drawing upon polls conducted in Western jurisdictions over the past 40 years. The focus is upon public attitudes to the criminal jury in England and Wales, although limited comparisons are made with public opinion in other jurisdictions.

Aims of the review
This review addresses a number of key questions drawing upon the domestic and international literature on public opinion attitudes to the jury, including the following:

- How much do members of the public know about the jury system or the way in which a jury functions?

- How strong is public support for the criminal jury in England and Wales?
- To the extent that comparisons are appropriate, how much variation is there in levels of support for the jury across different jurisdictions within the common law world?
- Do the public believe that juries are representative of the communities from which they are drawn?
- Are there significant differences between the views of majority and minority respondents with respect to issues such as the fairness and representativeness of juries?

Key findings Confidence in the jury

In recent years, polls in many Western nations have explored public confidence in various branches of criminal justice. Surprisingly, these polls have generally overlooked the jury. However, the few surveys that have explored the issue reveal that in a number of jurisdictions levels of public confidence in the jury are high. When members of the public in England and Wales are asked to rate different components of the criminal justice system such as the judiciary and the police, ratings tend to be higher for the jury than for any other element of criminal justice except the police. In addition, data from Northern Ireland – the only jurisdiction in which polls have tracked the issue over a number of years – suggest that confidence levels have not declined in recent years. The same cannot be said for all other branches of the criminal justice system. For example, public confidence in the police in England and Wales has declined over the past five years.

Support for jury trial as a legal right

One direct way of gauging the level of public support for the jury is to ask people to rate the importance of the right to trial by jury. This approach was adopted in the British Attitudes Survey of 2005. Respondents were asked to rate the importance of six rights in a democratic society, including the right to a jury trial for defendants "charged with a serious crime". They were asked to use a numerical response scale where 1 connoted "not at all important" and 7 meant "very important". Almost three-quarters of the sample (72%) responded with a "7", while a further 15% chose "6". The right to trial by jury in this context was rated as more important than any of the other rights, including the right to protest against the government, the right not to be detained for longer than a week before being charged, the right to privacy, the right not to be exposed to offensive views in public, and the right to free speech in public.

Public reaction to proposals to restrict the right to trial by jury

If the public strongly support the jury, they are likely to oppose any proposals to restrict a defendant's right to trial by jury. The limited research evidence suggests that this is the case. What about the economic argument against the use of juries in the criminal process? Research on a number of issues in criminal justice has demonstrated that the public are sensitive to cost considerations when evaluating criminal justice options. For example, people oppose prison construction in part because of the high cost of this crime control strategy. Respondents to the 2002 Bar Council survey in England were asked whether they would favour a reduction in the number of jury trials "if it would save taxpayers' money". The public was clearly unconcerned about cost savings if it meant restricting the right to trial by jury. Thus only approximately one-quarter of the sample (27%) expressed support for reducing the number of jury trials in order to save money. Over two-thirds (69%) endorsed the alternate response, namely that "I would oppose a reduction in the number of trials by jury in order to preserve my current right to trial by jury" (4% responded "don't know").

Representativeness of juries

Public perceptions of jury representativeness have been explored by surveys conducted in a number of jurisdictions. The general finding is that most people are very confident that juries are representative of the community.

Attitudes to jury service

The most recent and comprehensive analysis of public attitudes to jury service in this country was conducted by the MORI organisation for the recent Ministry of Justice (MOJ) study into the jury in England and Wales (see Thomas, 2007). They reveal a very positive reaction on the part of the public. More than three-quarters of the public expressed an intention to perform jury duty out of a sense of civic duty. When asked about their reaction to the prospect of jury service, attitudes are significantly more positive than negative. Thus over half the sample endorsed the view that they would enjoy jury service; only approximately one-quarter expressed the opposite view. Nor does the public appear to see jury service as a task that would interfere with their family life or result in economic hardship.

Preference for juries over judges

Another way of exploring the nature of public reaction to the jury is to ask members of the public to imagine that they have been charged with a criminal offence and to state whether they would prefer to be tried by a lay jury or a professional judge and two magistrates. When this question was posed to respondents in the Bar Council poll, a clear preference emerged: almost two-thirds of the sample (64%) preferred trial by jury. Only one-quarter of respondents expressed a preference for the judge/magistrate option (4% responded "don't know"; Bar Council, 2002). This finding constitutes further evidence of public confidence in the institution of the jury in England and Wales. Americans react in a similar way when asked to choose between trial by jury and trial by judge alone.

The report concludes by making a number of suggestions for future polling work regarding public knowledge of, and attitudes towards the criminal jury.

Chapter 9

Appeal and Review Decisions

Chapter Contents

The ease and speed with which a decision can be challenged in a higher court is one yardstick by which to measure a criminal justice system. In England and Wales, the role of the Court of Appeal in correcting errors and miscarriages of justice must be scrutinised. In our story, Gerry Good has now been convicted of an offence under the Offences Against the Person Act (OAPA) 1861, section 20 and has been sentenced to two years in prison. This chapter will show how unlikely he is to appeal successfully against either conviction or sentence. The Court of Appeal takes a very cautious approach, reluctant to interpret its powers too widely. And yet the Government has recently attempted to urge yet more caution upon it.

The appeal process has a number of functions. First, and perhaps most obviously, it has to correct mistakes. An appeal court checks that the court of first instance reached an appropriate result, and should put the matter right if it did not. Secondly, it has a due process function. The appellate courts should quash decisions reached unfairly, in order to safeguard the integrity of the criminal justice system as a whole. Finally, it has a consistency function: it allows the judiciary to develop clear legal rules, so providing for the harmonious development of the law.

However, these functions are not always achieved, nor are they all considered to be equally important. Thus, in appeals against conviction, the Court of Appeal is reluctant to interfere with the jury's fact-finding role; and in appeals against sentence it has always held that there is no such thing as a correct sentence – only if the sentence was 'wrong in principle' will the Court of Appeal interfere. The due process function is weighted more strongly by some than by others: Zander's dissent **[9:1]** in the report of the Royal Commission on Criminal Justice (1993) is a strong affirmation of due process values. Note what he says at paragraph 68: 'the moral foundation of the criminal justice system requires that if the prosecution has employed foul means the defendant must go free even though he is plainly guilty'. The consistency function is no more clear-cut, raising many of the fundamental dilemmas facing any legal system: in order to be fair, a legal system must be certain and predictable; but in order to be fair, it must also show some flexibility. Does our criminal justice system correctly balance certainty and flexibility?

(i) Usual appeal routes

(a) After summary trial

Summary appeals, from convictions in the magistrates' courts, are governed by the Magistrates' Courts Act 1980, section 108 **[9:2]** and are heard in the Crown Court. The judge will normally sit with two lay magistrates. The appeal takes the form of a rehearing, with all the witnesses being recalled. Historically, this is because the records of proceedings in the magistrates' court were inadequate, and so there was no option but to hear the case again. But, ironically, this has the effect today that an appeal from a conviction for a summary offence, which normally has less important consequences for the offender than a conviction for an indictable offence, is often dealt with more thoroughly than an appeal from the verdict of a jury. The powers of the Crown Court are governed by the Senior Courts Act 1981, section 48 **[9:3]** (this was originally called the Supreme Court Act 1981 but, unusually, was renamed in 2009 to avoid confusion with the newly established Supreme Court). The court may impose any sentence which was available to the original court and unmeritorious appellants are deterred by the knowledge that the court may (although it rarely does) increase the sentence imposed on the offender.

Less than one per cent of cases dealt with in the magistrates' courts are appealed. Does this reflect satisfaction with summary justice, a lack of legal aid, or a fear of an increased penalty? For Auld **[1:5]** the answer was to remove appeals as of right from the magistrates' courts: but is this really necessary?

Table 9.1 Appeals in the Crown Court

	Number heard	Percentage successful
1993	23,722	47%
1997	16,199	23%
2001	12,679	44%
2005	12,805	43%
2008	12,483	42%
2011	12,767	44%

Source: Judicial Statistics (for 2005, Judicial Statistics Revised, Cm 6903: page 91); Judicial and Court Statistics 2011, Table 4.10

There is no further appeal in summary cases from the Crown Court (except appeals by way of case stated to the High Court: see (ii) below).

(b) After trial in the Crown Court

For those tried in the Crown Court, an appeal lies to the Court of Appeal (Criminal Division). A formal system of criminal appeals was introduced only in 1907. Important reforms were effected, as a result of the Tucker Report (1954), in the Criminal Appeal Act 1966 – which replaced the old Court of Criminal Appeal with the current Court of Appeal (Criminal Division) – and in the Criminal Appeal Act 1968 **[9:4]**. This was then substantially amended in 1995. For a critique of Auld's comments **[1:5]** on the inefficient use of judicial resources in the appellate process, see Malleson and Roberts (2002).

Appeals in the Court of Appeal (Criminal Division) are normally heard by Lords Justices of Appeal and High Court judges. Curiously, these judges may have had little experience of criminal trials. The recommendation of the Royal Commission on Criminal Justice (1993) – that it would be beneficial if senior circuit judges, often with greater experience and knowledge of criminal trials, should be able to sit as members of the court – was adopted in the Criminal Justice and Public Order Act (CJPOA) 1994, section 52. It is also arguable that there should be lay members of the court.

Initially the defendant applies to a single judge for permission (or leave) to appeal, unless the appeal raises a question of law alone. This is a written application, and there is normally no hearing. Even where there is a hearing, witnesses are rarely called. Permission is required when the appeal turns on questions of fact, because of the reluctance of the judiciary to upset jury verdicts. Since most miscarriages of justice hang on questions of fact, such as the alleged police fabrication of evidence or mistaken identification, is this 'permission hurdle' appropriate?

Table 9.2 Applications for leave (permission) to appeal against conviction

	Number of applications	Granted leave by single judge	Application granted by Full Court	Appeals allowed
1997	2,318	589	131	236
2001	1,943	438	150	135
2005	1,661	360	141	228
2009/10	1,114	226	109	171
2013/14	1,148	174	82	142

Source: Judicial Statistics 1997, pages 13–14; 2001, page 14; 2005, pages 17–18; Court of Appeal (Criminal Division) Annual Report 2013–14, pages 27–28

Thus, few defendants make an application to appeal, and many fewer are successful. The role of lawyers is vital: Chapter 5 looked at the need for good quality legal advice throughout the legal process, and an extract from Plotnikoff and Woolfson **[5:10]** described their findings and outlined their recommendations on good practice and the responsibilities of legal advisers in the 28 days following conviction. The Royal Commission (1993) gave considerable space to recommendations for improvements to the practical procedures, in order to help applicants apply for permission to appeal and the grounds of appeal were reformed in 1995, following the recommendations of the majority of the Royal Commission. Malleson **[9:5]** showed how the grounds of appeal overlapped confusingly. The Commission accepted that the Court of Appeal was too narrow in its approach, too heavily influenced by the role of the jury, which led it to concentrate too much on assessing errors of law or procedural irregularities. Note the change to the wording of section 2:

Table 9.3 The wording of section 2 of the Criminal Appeal Act 1968

Old section 2 of the Criminal Appeal Act 1968	Current section 2 of the Criminal Appeal Act 1968 (after Criminal Appeal Act 1995)
Except as provided by this Act, the Court of Appeal shall allow an appeal against conviction if they think: (a) that the conviction shall be set aside on the ground that under all the circumstances of the case it is unsafe or unsatisfactory; or (b) that the judgment of the court of trial should be set aside on the ground of a wrong decision of any question of law; or (c) that there was a material irregularity in the course of the trial; and in any other case shall dismiss the appeal. Provided that the court may, notwithstanding that they are of opinion that the point raised in the appeal might be decided in favour of the appellant, dismiss the appeal if they consider that no miscarriage of justice has actually occurred.	Subject to the provisions of this Act, the Court of Appeal: (a) shall allow an appeal against conviction if they think that the conviction is unsafe; and (b) shall dismiss such an appeal in any other case.

What difference has the change in the law made in practice? Look again at Malleson's conclusions from her research into the Court of Appeal at the beginning of the 1990s. The Court of Appeal remains reluctant to 'upset' a jury's verdict and the question of limited resources is ever more pressing. It is, of course, very difficult for a defendant such as Gerry Good to establish that his conviction is unsafe. He is likely to have to rely on challenging the summing up, and he will bear a heavy burden of proof. The Court of Appeal in *Chalkley and Jeffries* **[9:6]** held that a conviction is safe if there is no possibility that the defendant was convicted of a crime of which he was in fact innocent. But then, shortly afterwards, the Court of Appeal in *Mullen* **[9:7]** seemed to suggest that 'unsafe' bears a meaning wider than simply factually unsafe. Surely if a defendant is convicted following grossly unfair prosecution practices, he should have his conviction quashed? The Court of Appeal in *Togher* [2001] 3 All ER 463 preferred the approach in *Mullen*. That is the position today.

In September 2006, the Government published a consultation paper on 'Quashing Convictions' which proposed modifying the Criminal Appeal Act 1968, section 2 to remove the Court of Appeal's power to quash convictions on 'purely procedural grounds' where the defendant's guilt on the facts is not in question. Note Spencer's critique of this proposal **[9:8]**: he defends the Court of Appeal's record in exercising its discretion, as exemplified by *Mullen* and explores how such cases might be decided had the proposals become law. Do you agree that the Government should refrain from attempting to tie the hands of the Court of Appeal? Despite the proposals being included in the Criminal Justice and Immigration Bill in 2007, they were ultimately removed before it became the Criminal Justice and Immigration Act 2008; section 2 remains unamended since 1995.

Much controversy has surrounded the Court of Appeal's power to hear fresh evidence under the Criminal Appeal Act 1968, section 23 **[9:4]**. This section (amended by the Criminal Appeal Act 1995, section 4) gives the Court of Appeal a wide mandate, but the court remains hesitant about becoming involved. Thus, the Court of Appeal in *McIlkenny* **[9:9]**, the case of the 'Birmingham Six', set out its vision of its role. Is the Court of Appeal construing its role too conservatively? If the Court of Appeal too easily accepts fresh evidence, there is a danger that defendants might 'save up' evidence for the appeal, and the court would be usurping the role of the jury. Yet Pattenden (1996) argues that 'an appellate court genuinely concerned to avoid miscarriages of justice should admit all evidence which could be believed by a reasonable jury, which could have affected the outcome of the case [and] that has not been deliberately saved up for appeal, should the accused be convicted' (at page 138).

There have been a number of legislative attempts to encourage appellate judges to use their powers to order retrials more frequently. Section 43 of the Criminal Justice Act 1988 gave them the power to order a retrial where this appears to be 'in the interest of justice'. Previously, this power had been restricted to cases where there was fresh evidence. But retrials are not a panacea: they are expensive, often impractical, and burdensome on both witnesses and defendants. Perhaps an awareness of these concerns explains why the Court of Appeal is often reluctant to order retrials.

Appeals against sentence are more common than appeals against conviction, because many of those who plead guilty still seek to challenge the sentence imposed by the Crown Court. Although the Court of Appeal will only vary a sentence if it was 'wrong in principle' (and remember that defendants require permission to appeal), appeals against sentence are statistically more likely to be successful than appeals against conviction.

As the Court of Appeal cannot increase a sentence (unless there has been a reference by the Attorney General under the Criminal Justice Act 1988, section 36 (see (iii) below)), why doesn't everyone sentenced in the Crown Court appeal their sentence? They may be deterred by the 'loss of time' rule, developed in two Practice Statements – [1970] 1 WLR 663 and [1980] 1 All ER 555 and now to be found in the Consolidated Criminal Practice Direction, Rule II.16 – which allows the Court of Appeal to order that time spent in prison pending an appeal should not count towards sentence. In *Monnell and Morris v United Kingdom* **[9:10]**, the European Court of Human Rights considered whether the rule infringed the European Convention on Human Rights, and held by a majority that there had been no such infringement. Extracts from both the majority and dissenting judgments are included in order to illustrate how the approach of the European Court of Human Rights to its task is somewhat different from the approach of a domestic appellate court. In practice, it is true, the Court of Appeal rarely orders that time spent on appeal should not count towards sentence, but does this excuse such an erosion of due process rights? And the Court of Appeal has recently emphasised the potential to use 'loss of time' in an attempt to deter 'unmeritorious' appeals: see the strong wording in *R v Gray and others* **[9:11]**.

Table 9.4 Appeals against sentence

	Applications for permission to appeal	Leave granted by single judge	Leave granted by Full Court	Appeal successful
1997	7,160	1,801	391	1,468
2001	5,497	1,551	240	1,101
2005	5,178	1,541	326	1,534
2009/10	4,110	1,156	432	1,484
2013/14	3,841	981	232	1,016

Source: Judicial Statistics 2005, pages 17–18; Court of Appeal (Criminal Division) Annual Report 2013–14, pages 27–28

(ii) Unusual methods of appeal and review

Another way in which a party may appeal is by way of case stated. Under the Senior Courts Act 1981, section 28A, the Divisional Court of the Queen's Bench Division of the High Court may 'reverse, affirm or amend the determination in respect of which the case has been stated, or remit the matter to the magistrates' court, or the Crown Court, with the opinion of the High Court'. This procedure is normally used where magistrates have made an error of substantive law or acted in excess of jurisdiction, and the prosecution states a case for the opinion of the Divisional Court in order that that court (and the Supreme Court, if the decision is further appealed) can stamp on a wrong ruling on a point of law before it spreads dangerously around the lower courts. The procedure is useful for correcting inappropriate rulings on the substantive law, but it may well be time to modernise the procedure and terminology.

Table 9.5 Appeals by way of case stated

	Appeals received from magistrates' courts	Appeals received from Crown Courts	Appeals allowed from magistrates' courts	Appeals allowed from Crown Courts
1997	144	32	62	7
2001	112	24	40	8
2005	98	23	39	6
2009	68	20	44	9
2013	56	10	34	2

Source: Judicial Statistics, 1997, page 17; 2001, page 19; 2005, page 24; Court Statistics Additional Tables, January to March 2014, Table 5.30

Judicial review by the High Court of criminal justice decisions is not common (see Table 9.6), but the importance of judicial review of criminal proceedings is not revealed by the small number of cases involved: look at the number of such cases extracted in this book, which have included reviews of decisions taken by the Home Secretary, the police, the Crown Prosecution Service and the Serious Fraud Office. Judicial review is a vital constitutional safeguard, especially where statutory rights of appeal are inadequate. A further example is provided by the case of R v Secretary of State for the Home Department, ex p Bentley **[9:12]**. (Bentley was convicted and executed in 1952: the case we report is a judicial review hearing – it was not until 1998 that the Court of Appeal eventually quashed his conviction.) Judicial review differs from an appeal in three important ways: first, it is a review of the law and not an investigation of the facts; secondly, judicial review results either in a decision being quashed or upheld (the reviewing court will not substitute its own decision); and thirdly, judicial review is based in common law and is not a creation of statute. Judicial review of court decisions is rare, because where an appeal procedure is available, that will be the appropriate route for the appellant to pursue.

Table 9.6 Applications for judicial review in criminal proceedings

	Applications	Applications allowed
1997	284	45
2001	330	53
2005	251	29
2008	298	31
2011	338	33

Source: Judicial Statistics 1997, page 16; 2001, page 18; 2005, page 23; Judicial and Court Statistics 2008, Table 7.12; Judicial and Court Statistics 2011, Table 7.12

In the past, judicial review was usually only applied for if there had been some illegality, for example, if magistrates had failed to comply with the rules of criminal procedure. Today, despite the greater willingness of the courts to review cases, it remains very difficult to succeed in challenging any alleged misuse of discretion. Lord Diplock summarised the grounds upon which judicial review can be successfully sought as 'illegality, irrationality and procedural irregularity' (*Council of Civil Service Unions v Minister for the Civil Service* [1985] AC 374). Errors of law generally create illegality, and so are challengeable. The scope of irrationality is more difficult: it is difficult to find examples in the criminal context of the High Court quashing a decision for being 'irrational'. Even procedural irregularities will not necessarily lead to the quashing of a decision, since judicial review is itself discretionary. Any matters arising from the trial itself are dealt with through the usual appeal process: because in judicial review proceedings, the court is reviewing the manner in which a decision is taken, and not the merits of the decision, such proceedings are no substitute for a 'real' appeal process.

(iii) The role of the Attorney General

We saw in Chapter 3 how the Attorney General exercises ministerial responsibility for the Crown Prosecution Service (CPS) and the Serious Fraud Office (SFO). His power to enter a plea of *nolle prosequi*, which has the effect of stopping proceedings, was noted in Chapter 4. He also has an important role in the appellate process. In general terms, the Attorney General has three key roles:

(1)   Legal adviser to the Crown (in the wider sense, i.e. to the Government and, on some issues, Parliament and the Queen) and the Crown's representative in the courts. The Attorney General also oversees the Government's in-house legal advisers and is the Minister responsible for the Treasury Solicitor's Department.

(2)   Minister of the Crown with responsibility for superintending the CPS, the SFO, the Service Prosecuting Authority and HM CPS Inspectorate. The Attorney General is also, with the Home Secretary and Secretary of State for Justice, responsible for criminal justice policy.

(3)   Guardian of the public interest, in particular in certain kinds of legal proceedings – such as decisions on the bringing or termination of criminal prosecutions, charity matters, and the appointment of 'advocates to the court' to act as neutral advisers to the court in litigation and 'special advocates' to represent the interests of parties in certain national security cases. The Attorney General's independent public interest role includes consultation by the prosecuting authorities on individual criminal cases as part of the superintendence role.

The prosecution has no general right of appeal in English law. There is an argument for giving the prosecution a right of appeal – for example, where the acquittal is perverse and flies in the face of the evidence, or where the acquittal is due to an error on the part of the prosecution. The Royal Commission on Criminal Justice (1993) rejected such proposals, suggesting only that where it can be shown that the jury was bribed or intimidated, the prosecution should be able to apply for a retrial. However, the Criminal Justice Act 2003 gave the prosecution, in very serious cases (defined in this context as offences which carry a maximum sentence of life imprisonment, and for which the consequences for victims or for society as a whole are particularly serious), the right to apply for a retrial where there is 'new and compelling' evidence against the acquitted person and where a retrial would be 'in the interests of justice'. This undermining of the double jeopardy rule (that no one should stand trial on the same facts twice) has, unsurprisingly, been very controversial. The first person to be convicted under the new provisions was William Dunlop in 2006 who had admitted to the 1989 murder of Julie Hogg after being acquitted in 1991. However, perhaps the best-known application of the provisions was in the case of Gary Dobson in relation to the murder of Stephen

Lawrence in 1993 (see *Dobson* [2011] EWCA Crim 1255). He was convicted, alongside David Norris (who had not previously stood trial for the murder), in January 2012 having been acquitted in a private prosecution in 1996. Dennis (2014) has surveyed the use of the new provisions since their enactment and found that out of 13 applications to the Court of Appeal for a retrial, nine were successful and four were refused. Only one of the nine was acquitted a second time.

Under the Criminal Justice Act 1972, section 36 **[9:13]**, the Attorney General may refer an acquittal for the opinion of the Court of Appeal. Whilst the judgment of the Court of Appeal in the case has no effect on the actual trial or acquittal of the defendant, it is used as a procedure to correct inappropriate rulings on the substantive criminal law. An example is provided at **[9:14]**.

The Criminal Justice Act 1988, sections 35–36 **[9:15]** then gave the Attorney General the power to appeal against an 'unduly lenient' sentence, and in these cases the Court of Appeal may actually increase the sentence. However, the Court of Appeal has again interpreted its role very narrowly here. As Lord Lane CJ said in *A-G's Reference (No 4 of 1989)* 11 Cr App Rep (S) 517, at page 531: 'A sentence is unduly lenient, we would hold, where it falls outside the range of sentences which the judge, applying his mind to all the relevant facts, could reasonably consider appropriate.' Little research has been done into which cases are reviewed, and it may well be that the media exert an improper influence over which cases are referred to the Court of Appeal. Henham (1994) argued that the procedure should either be abolished or replaced by a general prosecution right of appeal free from the limitations of the present system. A long time ago, Thomas (1972) argued that a few prosecution appeals in test cases 'would lead to a more careful articulation of principles in the area of sentencing which would lead in turn to an improvement in the performance of trial courts generally' (at page 306). Can this argument be taken so far as to suggest a mechanism for the review of all sentences, or simply that the CPS should be involved at the trial stage in suggesting a suitable sentence (see Chapter 3)?

(iv) The role of the Home Secretary and the Secretary of State for Justice

We have seen many examples of the powers of both the Home Secretary and the Secretary of State for Justice in criminal justice. Their role in the development of policy is, of course, crucial. They are the driving forces behind most legislative change. But their role in deciding individual cases has been declining fast in recent years, in recognition of the constitutional doctrine of the separation of powers. Parliament may make the law, but it is for judges to apply it.

The royal prerogative of mercy is still granted occasionally. This may take one of three forms: a free pardon, a conditional pardon, or remission of all or part of the penalty imposed by the court. Although a pardon is normally granted because the guilt of the defendant can no longer be accepted beyond all reasonable doubt, the conviction itself stands. This is because only a court can quash a judicial decision. The High Court held that the courts have jurisdiction to review the exercise of the royal prerogative of mercy in *R v Secretary of State for the Home Department, ex p Bentley* **[9:12]**. A person who has been pardoned may, however, be given compensation under the Criminal Justice Act 1988, section 133 **[9:15]**. In *R (Adams) v Secretary of State for Justice* [2012] 1 AC 48, a divided Supreme Court held that entitlement to compensation was not restricted to those who had established beyond a reasonable doubt that they were innocent: a 'miscarriage of justice', for the purposes of compensation, could arise simply where evidence against the defendant had been undermined so that no conviction could possibly be based upon it. However, this decision was essentially nullified by the Government's legislative response: section 175 of the Anti-social Behaviour, Crime and Policing Act 2014 amended the Criminal Justice Act 1988, section 133 to state that compensation will only be paid if it is shown 'beyond reasonable doubt' that the person did not commit the offence. Bailin and Craven **[9:16]** rightly criticise this amendment, arguing that 'the current law on compensation for miscarriages remains contradictory, confused and its compatibility with Article 6 [of the European Convention on Human Rights] is open to question'.

(v) The Criminal Cases Review Commission

Since the Court of Appeal has no power to entertain second applications for permission to appeal, there needs to be a mechanism to reopen cases which turn out to be miscarriages of justice. Until 1995, the Home Secretary could refer a case back to the Court of Appeal. The Home Secretary sat on the horns of a dilemma: on the one hand, he was criticised for his reluctance to use his powers; and on the other he was also criticised, being essentially a political figure, for having a role in the court process at all. In most cases a convicted person had to attract the support of a public figure or a newspaper before the Home Secretary would refer a case back to the Court of Appeal. The power of the media was very clear.

The Royal Commission (1993) **[9:17]** recommended that the Home Secretary's power be given instead to a Criminal Cases Review Authority. This was adopted in the Criminal Appeal Act 1995, section 8 **[9:18]**, though the authority was named the Criminal Cases Review Commission (CCRC). The CCRC is made up of 17 members (12 of whom are Commissioners), and started work in 1997. Its powers are set out in the Criminal Appeal Act 1995, section 13 **[9:18]**: a case may be referred by the CCRC to the Court of Appeal if there is a 'real possibility' that the conviction will be overturned because there exists evidence and/or arguments which were 'not raised in the proceedings which led to it or on any appeal or application for leave to appeal'. Furthermore, section 13(2) of the Act states that the CCRC is not prevented from making a reference 'if it appears to [it] that there are exceptional circumstances which justify making it'. However, Zander (2012) has described this as 'a useless safety valve' which has hardly ever been used.

The CCRC is given powers of investigation by sections 17–21 of the 1995 Act, but its powers are in reality controlled by its budget (£5.47 million in 2013/14). It has faced many problems of case backlog and delay (see James, Taylor and Walker (2000) and Elks (2008)) but Weeden (2012), a former Commissioner, is much more positive about the impact of the CCRC. The annual reports give a clear picture of the sort of cases with which the CCRC deals, and of its working practices. Even if the CCRC was adequately resourced, how can we measure its 'independence' and its 'efficacy'? We saw in Chapter 2 the problems, in relation to the police, of maintaining a force which is simultaneously both independent and truly accountable for its actions. The same issues arise here. Another way forward would have been to enhance the powers of the judiciary to refer cases back to the Court of Appeal, and to strengthen the resolve of the Court of Appeal itself to correct miscarriages of justice.

(vi) The role of the Supreme Court

The Supreme Court plays a relatively minor role in the criminal justice system. Under the Criminal Appeal Act 1968, section 33 **[9:4]** there are two requirements before there can be a further appeal to the Supreme Court (formerly to the House of Lords): (a) the court from which the appeal is brought (either the Divisional Court or the Court of Appeal) must certify that the case involves a point of law of general public importance; and (b) that court, or the Supreme Court itself, must give permission to appeal. Having both hurdles to overcome reflects the priority given to limiting the number of cases that reach the Supreme Court.

Why do we need two levels of appeal in criminal matters? Having reviewed the House of Lords' unimpressive record in clarifying the criminal law, Glanville Williams said, in a letter published at (1981) Crim LR 581, that 'it is a nice question whether, with this sort of balance sheet, the appellate jurisdiction of the House of Lords in criminal cases is worth the expense to the community'. The question is just as pertinent with the Supreme Court today.

Further reading

Cooper, S, 'Appeals, referrals and substantial injustice' [2009] Crim LR 152

Court of Appeal Criminal Division Annual Reports

Criminal Cases Review Commission Annual Reports

Dennis, I, 'Quashing acquittals: applying the "new and compelling evidence" exception to double jeopardy' [2014] Crim LR 247

Elks, L, *The Criminal Cases Review Commission* (2008) Justice

Hamer, D, 'The expectation of incorrect acquittals and the "new and compelling evidence" exception to double jeopardy' [2009] Crim LR 63

Henham, R, 'Attorney-General's References and Sentencing Policy' [1994] Crim LR 499

James, A, Taylor, N and Walker, C, 'The Criminal Cases Review Commission: Economy, Effectiveness and Justice' [2000] Crim LR 140

Malleson, K and Roberts, S, 'Streamlining and Clarifying the Appellate Process' [2002] Crim LR 272

Nobles, R and Schiff, D, 'The Criminal Cases Review Commission: establishing a workable relationship with the Court of Appeal' [2005] Crim LR 173

Pattenden, R, *Judicial Discretion and Criminal Litigation* (1990) Clarendon Press

Pattenden, R, *English Criminal Appeals 1844–1994* (1996) Clarendon Press

Pattenden, R, 'Prosecution appeals against judges' rulings' [2000] Crim LR 971

Smith, A T H, 'Criminal Appeals in the House of Lords' (1984) 47 *Modern Law Review* 133

Spencer, J N, 'Judicial Review of Criminal Proceedings' [1991] Crim LR 259

Spencer, J R, 'Does our present criminal appeal system make sense?' [2006] Crim LR 677

Stevens, R, *Law and Politics: the House of Lords as a judicial body* (1979) Weidenfeld & Nicolson

Thomas, D A, 'Increasing Sentences on Appeal' [1972] Crim LR 288

Weeden, J, 'The Criminal Cases Review Commission (CCRC) of England, Wales, and Northern Ireland' (2012) 80 *U Cin L Rev* 1415

Zander, M, 'Zander on the CCRC' (2012) The Justice Gap, 6 April. Available at: http://thejusticegap.com/2012/04/zander-on-the-ccrc/

Zellick, G, 'The Criminal Cases Review Commission and the Court of Appeal: the Commission's perspective' [2005] Crim LR 937

Documents

[9:1] *Report of the Royal Commission on Criminal Justice*:
Professor Zander's Dissent
(1993) HMSO Cmnd 2263

Professor Zander dissented on three topics: defence disclosure, pre-trial procedures and the powers of the Court of Appeal. Only the third part of his dissent is included here.

(At page 223):

III The Court of appeal's power to quash a conviction (or order a retrial) on account of error at trial or malpractice by the prosecution.

62 When convictions are quashed by the Court of Appeal it is usually because there has been some error or irregularity at the trial or some procedural or legal defect in the pre-trial process, or there has been serious malpractice by the prosecution. Typically, the trial judge misdirected the jury on the law or the evidence, or his summing up was unbalanced, or he wrongly

admitted inadmissible evidence. The Commission is unanimous in believing that the Court of Appeal's past practice of allowing many guilty persons to escape their just deserts simply because there has been a defect in the process leading to their conviction requires consideration. But the Commission is not unanimous as to how the problem should be addressed.

63 The majority of the Commission propose that, where there is an appeal against conviction, the conviction should be upheld unless the ground of appeal is such as to undermine the conviction – in the sense that the Court of Appeal concludes that the verdict is no longer safe. In that event, it would quash the conviction. The gravity of the defect on its own would no longer carry any weight. The question would always be only whether the verdict was safe. If the Court of Appeal thinks the defect may make the conviction unsafe, it would order a retrial. (One of the consequences of such a change of approach would be significantly, perhaps drastically, to reduce the number of successful appeals against conviction.)

64 Two Commissioners and I would go further in regard to errors of law or procedure at the trial, other than minor errors or irregularities. As stated in chapter ten of the Report, paragraph 37, we would in addition give the Court of Appeal the power to order a retrial in such cases even though the error or defect cannot be said to make the verdict unsafe. In our view defendants should not be serving prison sentences on the basis of trials that are seriously flawed. If the court holds that the error at the trial is a serious one but that for any reason a retrial is not a practicable or desirable option, it would have to quash the conviction.

65 Where, however, the basis of the appeal is something that occurred pre-trial the view taken by the minority depends on the gravity of the defect. If the defect is minor or 'harmless' error, we agree with the majority that the appeal should fail. On this the Commission is therefore unanimous. If the defect, though not of the gravest kind, is of the level of gravity that now leads the court to quash the conviction, I and another Commissioner believe that the Court of Appeal should continue to be empowered to deal with such a defect even though it may not render the conviction unsafe. The typical case would be a serious breach of PACE or of its Codes of Practice. Since the introduction of PACE in January 1986 there have been dozens of cases that have gone to the Court of appeal where the substance of the appeal has been that the police broke one or other of the PACE rules. Many have concerned failure to comply with the rules regarding access to a solicitor, or provision of an appropriate adult or with the rules regarding recording of interviews. In a proportion of such cases the Court of Appeal has held that the defect was sufficiently serious to require that the conviction be quashed.

66 The majority would limit the Court of Appeal's power to deal with breaches of PACE to those cases where the breach rendered the jury's verdict unsafe. In my view this is insufficient because it ignores the important role that the Court of Appeal plays in upholding the PACE rules – quite apart from the question whether the breach affected the verdict. Breaches of PACE are automatically breaches of police disciplinary rules but as the Report states 'there are hardly any formal disciplinary proceedings for breaches of PACE'. If any action is taken, even for serious breaches of PACE, it virtually never goes beyond mere 'advice' to the officer concerned. The role of the Court of Appeal in promoting observance of the complex and crucial network of PACE rules is therefore of great importance. The majority's approach would weaken this role. I would however wish to see the Court of Appeal, wherever possible, deal with a serious breach of PACE by ordering a retrial rather than by allowing a guilty person to go free by quashing the conviction. Retrials are not

ideal but where there has been a serious breach of PACE they can be preferable to allowing a guilty person to go free.

67 If, however, the pre-trial malpractice is of the most serious kind, the Court of Appeal must be able not simply to order a retrial but to quash the conviction. This is the only appropriate response where prosecution agencies have fabricated or suppressed important evidence or where the defendant has been subjected to serious violence in the course of interrogation. Obviously, if the fabricated or suppressed evidence or the confession produced by violent means was the only or the main evidence for the prosecution, the Court of Appeal would have no difficulty in quashing the conviction. In such a case the Commission is unanimous as to the outcome. But it may be that there is other, reliable evidence showing that the defendant committed the offence. Nine of my ten colleagues believe that if there is sufficient sound evidence, even the most serious misconduct by the prosecution should not result in the conviction being quashed.

68 I cannot agree. The moral foundation of the criminal justice system requires that if the prosecution has employed foul means the defendant must go free even though he is plainly guilty. Where the integrity of the process is fatally flawed, the conviction should be quashed as an expression of the system's repugnance at the methods used by those acting for the prosecution.

69 The majority's position would, I believe, encourage serious wrongdoings from some police officers who might be tempted to exert force or fabricate or suppress evidence in the hope of establishing the guilt of the suspect, especially in a serious case when they believe him to be guilty. There have unfortunately been some gross examples of such conduct.

70 The position adopted by the majority also seems to me to risk undermining the principle at the heart of section 78 of PACE which explicitly gives the court the power to exclude evidence on the ground that it renders the proceedings 'unfair'. The word 'unfair' expresses the underlying moral principle and the Court of Appeal has repeatedly used this new statutory power very broadly to express its refusal to uphold convictions based on unacceptable police practices even when it could not be said that the misconduct had any impact on the jury's verdict.

71 Section 78 would of course remain – but the majority would in effect be encouraging the Court of Appeal to undercut a part of its moral force by saying that the issue of 'unfairness' can be ignored where there is sufficient evidence to show that the defendant is actually guilty. Any judge concerned to discourage prosecution malpractice would I believe be dismayed by the majority's position. In terms of the message sent to the police service and other prosecution agencies it could undo much of the good effect being achieved by the attitude of the judges to section 78 of PACE.

72 But the matter goes beyond discouraging prosecution malpractice. At the heart of the criminal justice system there is a fundamental principle that the process must itself have integrity. The majority suggest that the answer to prosecution wrongdoing in the investigation of crime is to deal with the wrongdoers through prosecution or disciplinary proceedings. Even were this to happen (and often in practice it would not), the approach is not merely insufficient, it is irrelevant to the point of principle. The more serious the case, the greater the need that the system upholds the values in the name of which it claims to act. If the behaviour of the prosecution agencies has deprived a guilty verdict of its moral legitimacy the Court of Appeal must have a residual power to quash the verdict no matter how strong the evidence of guilt. The integrity of the criminal justice system is a higher objective than the conviction of any individual.

[9:2] Magistrates' Courts Act 1980 (as amended)
Section 108

108 Right of appeal to the Crown Court

(1) A person convicted by a magistrates' court may appeal to the Crown Court –

- (a) if he pleaded guilty, against his sentence;
- (b) if he did not, against the conviction or sentence.

(1A) Section 14 of the Powers of Criminal Courts (Sentencing) Act 2000 (under which a conviction of an offence for which an order for conditional or absolute discharge is made is deemed not to be a conviction except for certain purposes) shall not prevent an appeal under this Act, whether against conviction or otherwise.

(2) A person sentenced by a magistrates' court for an offence in respect of which an order for conditional discharge has been previously made may appeal to the Crown Court against the sentence.

(3) In this section "sentence" includes any order made on conviction by a magistrates' court, not being –

- (b) an order for the payment of costs;
- (c) an order under section 37(1) of the Animal Welfare Act 2006 (which enables a court to order the destruction of an animal); or
- (d) an order made in pursuance of any enactment under which the court has no discretion as to the making of the order or its terms

and also includes a declaration of relevance, within the meaning of section 23 of the Football Spectators Act 1989.

(4) Subsection (3)(d) above does not prevent an appeal against a surcharge imposed under section 161A of the Criminal Justice Act 2003.

[9:3] Senior Courts Act 1981 (as amended)
Section 48

48 Appeals to Crown Court

(1) The Crown Court may, in the course of hearing any appeal, correct any error or mistake in the order or judgment incorporating the decision which is the subject of the appeal.

(2) On the termination of the hearing of an appeal the Crown Court –

- (a) may confirm, reverse or vary the decision appealed against any part of the decision appealed against, including a determination not to impose a separate penalty in respect of an offence; or
- (b) may remit the matter with its opinion thereon to the authority whose decision is appealed against; or
- (c) may make such other order in the matter as the court thinks just, and by such order exercise any power which the said authority might have exercised.

(3) Subsection (2) has effect subject to any enactment relating to any such appeal which expressly limits or restricts the powers of the court on the appeal.

(4) Subject to section 11(6) of the Criminal Appeal Act 1995, if the appeal is against a conviction or a sentence, the preceding provisions of this section shall be construed as including power to award any punishment, whether more or less severe than that awarded by the magistrates' court whose decision is appealed against, if that is a punishment which that magistrates' court might have awarded.

(5) This section applies whether or not the appeal is against the whole of the decision.

(6) In this section "sentence" includes any order made by a court when dealing with an offender, including –

(a) a hospital order under Part III of the Mental Health Act 1983, with or without a restriction order, and an interim hospital order under that Act; and
(b) a recommendation for deportation made when dealing with an offender.

(7) The fact that an appeal is pending against an interim hospital order under the said Act of 1983 shall not affect the power of the magistrates' court that made it to renew or terminate the order or to deal with the appellant on its termination; and where the Crown Court quashes such an order but does not pass any sentence or make any other order in its place the Court may direct the appellant to be kept in custody or released on bail pending his being dealt with by that magistrates' court.

(8) Where the Crown Court makes an interim hospital order by virtue of subsection (2)—

(a) the power of renewing or terminating the order and of dealing with the appellant on its termination shall be exercisable by the magistrates' court whose decision is appealed against and not by the Crown Court; and
(b) that magistrates' court shall be treated for the purposes of section 38(7)of the said Act of 1983 (absconding offenders) as the court that made the order.

[9:4] Criminal Appeal Act 1968 (as amended)
Sections 2; 23; 33

2 Grounds for allowing appeal under section 1
(1) Subject to the provisions of this Act, the Court of Appeal –

(a) shall allow an appeal against conviction if they think that the conviction is unsafe; and
(b) shall dismiss such an appeal in any other case.

(2) In the case of an appeal against conviction the Court shall, if they allow the appeal, quash the conviction.

(3) An order of the Court of Appeal quashing a conviction shall, except when under section 7 below the appellant is ordered to be retried, operate as a direction to the court of trial to enter, instead of the record of conviction, a judgment and verdict of acquittal.

23 Evidence
(1) For the purposes of an appeal, or an application for leave to appeal, under this Part of this Act the Court of Appeal may, if they think it necessary or expedient in the interests of justice –

(a) order the production of any document, exhibit or other thing connected with the proceedings, the production of which appears to them necessary for the determination of the case;

(b) order any witness to attend for examination and be examined before the Court (whether or not he was called in the proceedings from which the appeal lies); and

(c) receive any evidence which was not adduced in the proceedings from which the appeal lies.

(1A) The power conferred by subsection (1)(a) may be exercised so as to require the production of any document, exhibit or other thing mentioned in that subsection to –

(a) the Court;
(b) the appellant;
(c) the respondent.

(2) The Court of Appeal shall, in considering whether to receive any evidence, have regard in particular to –

(a) whether the evidence appears to the Court to be capable of belief;
(b) whether it appears to the Court that the evidence may afford any ground for allowing the appeal;
(c) whether the evidence would have been admissible in the proceedings from which the appeal lies on an issue which is the subject of the appeal; and
(d) whether there is a reasonable explanation for the failure to adduce the evidence in those proceedings.

(3) Subsection (1)(c) above applies to any evidence of a witness (including the appellant) who is competent but not compellable.

(4) For the purposes of an appeal, or an application for leave to appeal, under this Part of this Act, the Court of Appeal may, if they think it necessary or expedient in the interests of justice, order the examination of any witness whose attendance might be required under subsection (1)(b) above to be conducted, in manner provided by rules of court, before any judge or officer of the Court or other person appointed by the Court for the purpose, and allow the admission of any depositions so taken as evidence before the Court.

(5) A live link direction under section 22(4) does not apply to the giving of oral evidence by the appellant at any hearing unless that direction, or any subsequent direction of the court, provides expressly for the giving of such evidence through a live link.

(6) In this section, "respondent" includes a person who will be a respondent if leave to appeal is granted.

33 Right of appeal to Supreme Court

(1) An appeal lies to the Supreme Court, at the instance of the defendant or the prosecutor, from any decision of the Court of Appeal on an appeal to that court under Part I of this Act or Part 9 of the Criminal Justice Act 2003 or section 9 (preparatory hearings) of the Criminal Justice Act 1987 or section 35 of the Criminal Procedure and Investigations Act 1996 or section 47 of the Criminal Justice Act 2003.

(1B) An appeal lies to the Supreme Court, at the instance of the acquitted person or the prosecutor, from any decision of the Court of Appeal on an application under section 76(1) or (2) of the Criminal Justice Act 2003 (retrial for serious offences).

(2) The appeal lies only with the leave of the Court of Appeal or the Supreme Court; and leave shall not be granted unless it is certified by the Court of Appeal that a point of law of general public importance is involved in the decision and it appears to the Court of Appeal or the Supreme Court (as the case may be) that the point is one which ought to be considered by the Supreme Court.

(3) Except as provided by this Part of this Act and section 13 of the Administration of Justice Act 1960 (appeal in cases of contempt of court), no appeal shall lie from any decision of the criminal division of the Court of Appeal.

(4) In relation to an appeal under subsection (1B), references in this Part to a defendant are references to the acquitted person.

[9:5] Malleson, K, *Review of the Appeal Process*
(1993) RCCJ Research Study No 17, HMSO (at page 15)

From these findings, the work of the Court of Appeal can be summarised as follows. Most of its time is spent reviewing the decisions of the trial judge, considering whether his summing up was adequate, whether or not he misdirected the jury as to the application of the law or evidence, or whether he erred in exercising his discretion to include or exclude a piece of evidence. It is rare for the court to hear fresh evidence, consider the existence of a 'lurking doubt' about the conviction or order a retrial. Thus, the court performs, in practice, a relatively limited function. With the exception of the retrial, this cannot be explained as a result of the restrictions of the provisions of the CAA. The rarity of the use of a retrial must, as least party, be explained by the wording of s 7, but the court's interpretation of the grounds set out in s 2(1) and particularly the phrase 'unsafe and unsatisfactory' seems to be quite wide enough to cover a broad range of cases.

The fact that the sample did include fresh evidence cases, lurking doubt and retrial cases shows that the court is quite capable of taking a broad view of its powers and applying them to a wide range of cases if it so chooses. The evidence of both forensic experts and witnesses of fact were considered in cases involving a diverse range of issues and circumstances. The presence of a small number of such cases is evidence that the court considers that it does possess wide powers but that it is reluctant to use them very often.

There are three main explanations which may account for the fact that the court exercises the full range of its powers so infrequently:

(i) The court is very concerned that as far as possible the jury's decision should be final and the trial should not come to be seen as an 'initial skirmish'. The court's anxiety not to undermine the principle of the sovereignty of the jury was referred to directly or indirectly in many of the cases reviewed. When assessing a witness's credibility or the soundness of the conviction the court appeared to be considering questions of fact and placing itself in the position of the jury, so threatening the principle which it claims to be reinforcing.

(ii) The court is keen to limit the flow of cases into the appeal system. A number of the cases reviewed commented on the length of time which the appeal had taken to be heard and the court is conscious that delays can amount to a fresh source of injustice. In limiting the type of cases which it hears, the court contributes to the task of holding closed the 'floodgates' to keep out the tide of cases which it fears will swamp the already overstretched resources of the Court of Appeal. Lawyers and appellants know that they are very unlikely to persuade the court to hear fresh evidence or find that there is a 'lurking doubt' about the conviction. This knowledge may help to ensure that few such cases come into the appeal system. The court's decision that errors of an appellant's legal advisers are not generally valid grounds of appeal is an important example of this process of keeping down the numbers of appeals. The fact that many appeals are submitted on the basis of lawyer's errors, despite the ruling, only to be weeded out by the single judge suggests that many more are kept from appealing by the knowledge that it would be hopeless to do so. This process may also be assisted by fear of the time loss rules which keep many potential appellants out of the system. It is likely that they are so rarely applied because the threat alone is sufficient to keep down the numbers of appeals. Possibly, if it came to be widely known that this power is hardly ever exercised, causing numbers of applications for leave to appeal to rise, its use would increase.

(iii) The resources which the court has at its disposal do not equip it to review all the circumstances of alleged injustice, before during and after trial, which can be raised at appeal. From the papers provided by the CAO the court is relatively well placed to effectively assess the quality of the summing up or the judges decisions on law or procedure but is ill-equipped to look into the surrounding circumstances of the cases. Although it has the power to call for documents, exhibits or other thing connected with the case, this is rarely exercised and it has no facilities for investigating the full range of issues which may be raised at the appeal and is in a weak position to assess the actions and integrity of individuals and institutions such as the police, witnesses, lawyers or forensic experts.

The research findings indicate that the court is reluctant to exercise frequently its full range of powers. Three factors can be identified as affecting the court's approach to reviewing appeals against conviction. These are, firstly, the principle of the sovereignty of the jury which is perceived by the court to limit its role in the criminal justice process, secondly, the limited resources of the appeal system which demands that the court contributes to keeping the 'floodgates' closed and, lastly, the court's limited investigative resources for reviewing individual cases.
[See also **[5:9]**]

[9:6] *R v Chalkley and Jeffries*

[1998] QB 848

Police officers considered that there was a serious threat that the appellants were planning robberies involving firearms. Having obtained permission from an authorising officer, they arrested the first appellant in connection with an unrelated matter, which allowed them to take his keys and let themselves into his home without his knowledge and to install a listening device in his home. Defence counsel submitted that the evidence of the listening device had been obtained unlawfully and should not have been admitted. The trial judge ruled that the police had acted in good faith and that the evidence was therefore admissible. The appellants changed their plea to guilty. They appealed against conviction on the ground that the judge's ruling was wrong.

The Court of Appeal dismissed the appeals.

Auld LJ (at page 98):

In our view, whatever may have been the use by the Court of the former tests of 'unsatisfactor[iness]' and 'material irregularity' (see the penetrating and engaging analysis of Sir Louis Blom-Cooper QC in 'The Birmingham Six' and other cases, Victims of Circumstance, 1997, Duckworth, Cap V), they are not available to it now, save as aids to determining the safety of a conviction. The Court has no power under the substituted section 2(1) to allow an appeal if it does not think the conviction unsafe but is dissatisfied in some way with what went on at the trial. The editors of the third supplement to the current edition of *Archbold* (1997) refer to this as a 'minor, but important, respect' in which the 1995 substitution has done more than just change the wording of the 1968 Act. Whilst we agree that it is an important change, it may not be 'minor', particularly in those cases where, although the Court is of the view that justice has not been seen to be done, it is satisfied that it has been done – that is, that the conviction is safe. All of this is, however, subject to what the Court will make of Article 6(1) of the European Convention on Human Rights, entitling everyone charged with a criminal offence to a fair trial, when it becomes part of our domestic law. Such European Court of Human Rights jurisprudence on the point as there is (see *Murray v United Kingdom* [1996] 22 EHRR 29; *Saunders v United Kingdom* [1996] 1 Cr App Rep 463, [1996] 22 EHRR 313, 342, para 86; *Staines and Morrissey* [1997] 2 Cr App Rep 426, and *Coyne v United Kingdom* 26 September 1997. For a helpful summary of these recent authorities and the light that they may shed on the notion and effect of unsatisfactoriness of a conviction regardless of its safety, see Sir Louis Blom-Cooper QC, op cit pp 74–77) who suggests that procedural unfairness not resulting in unsafety of a conviction may be marked in some manner other than quashing the conviction.

. . .

We hold that the appellants' appeals against conviction fail because, by their pleas of guilty, they intended to admit and have admitted their guilt, and that their convictions are, therefore, safe.

(At page 107):

[W]e consider that the proper course is to make our own decision about the fairness of admitting this evidence. We have no doubt whatever about the fairness of doing so. As we have said, there was no dispute as to its authenticity, content or effect; it was relevant, highly probative of the appellants' involvement in the conspiracy and otherwise admissible; it did not result from incitement, entrapment or inducement or any other conduct of that sort; and none of the unlawful conduct of the police or other of their conduct of which complaint is made affects the quality of the evidence. In the circumstances, we can see no basis for concluding that the admission of this evidence would, in the words of section 78, have had such an adverse effect on the fairness of the proceedings that the Judge should not have admitted it. Accordingly, we would dismiss the appeals on that ground also.

[9:7] *R v Mullen*

[1999] 2 Cr App Rep 143

The defendant, who was wanted by the police in England, was brought back to England from Zimbabwe by a Zimbabwean immigration officer in 1988. He was arrested and in due course convicted of conspiracy to cause explosions and sentenced to 30 years' imprisonment. He was refused permission to appeal against sentence. In 1998, he was granted an extension of time and permission to appeal against conviction. Evidence disclosed revealed that the security services in England and Zimbabwe had colluded in order to procure the defendant's deportation from Zimbabwe in circumstances in which he was denied access to a lawyer, contrary to Zimbabwean law and internationally recognised human rights.

Although there was no complaint about the fairness of the trial itself, the Court of Appeal allowed his appeal.

Rose LJ (at page 159):

This court's jurisdiction is statutory and depends for present purposes on the meaning properly to be attributed to the word 'unsafe'. In particular, is it apt to confer jurisdiction to quash a conviction when no complaint is made about the conduct of the trial and the sole ground of appeal is that no trial should have taken place, because of the prosecution's abuse of the process of the court prior to trial?

In *R v Chalkley* [1998] QB 848, 859, Auld LJ, giving the judgment of the court, referred to the amended test as being much simpler than the old test in the Act of 1968 prior to amendment. At page 869 he expressly agreed with a passage in *Archbold, Criminal Pleading, Evidence & Practice*, 1997 edn, 3rd supplement, page 99, paragraph 7–45, which contains the following:

'Neither the misconduct of the prosecution, nor the fact that there has been a failure to observe some general notion of "fair play" are in themselves reasons for quashing a conviction . . . "unsafe" . . . is clearly intended to refer to the correctness of the conviction (i.e. a conviction is unsafe if there is a possibility that the defendant was convicted of an offence of which he was in fact innocent).'

At first blush, this passage in the court's judgment might be understood as precluding this court from regarding the present conviction as unsafe. But it is to be noted that *R v Horseferry Road Magistrates' Court, ex p Bennett* [1994] 1 AC 42 was not referred to and, in *R v MacDonald* [1998] Crim LR 808 Auld LJ, giving the judgment of a differently constituted division of this court, said:

'Before parting with the matter we express some reservation about the jurisdiction of the Court to quash a conviction where there has been an abuse of process of the *ex parte Bennett* kind, that is, where a fair trial was possible and in the event resulted in a safe conviction, but where, on a proper view of the matter, the prosecution should have been stayed as an affront to justice. The question does not arise for our determination in the light of our conclusion that a fair trial was possible and took place, that it was not unfair to try the defendants and that safe convictions resulted. And the matter was only touched on briefly in argument. However, if our view had been that it was an abuse of the *ex parte Bennett* kind, we do not know where we could have found the power to quash what we regard as a safe conviction. The court's jurisdiction is entirely statutory, and the single criterion for interference with a conviction is now – since its recent amendment of section 2 of the Criminal Appeal Act 1968 – its unsafety. The court seems to have assumed such jurisdiction in *R v Bloomfield* [1997] 1 Cr App Rep 125 and *R v Hyatt* (1977) 3 Archbold News 2, but as the editors of *Criminal Law Week* comment in their Issue 2 of 1998, it is far from obvious as to why this should be so. See the observation of Lord Lloyd in *R v Martin* [1998] AC 917, 928–929, and the judgment of this court in *R v Chalkley* [1998] QB 848, 868–870. It may be that a conviction in a trial which should never have taken place is to be regarded as unsafe for that reason. It may be that, despite the statutory basis of the court's jurisdiction, it has also some inherent or ancillary jurisdictional basis for intervening to mark abuse of process by quashing a conviction when it considers that the court below should have stayed the proceeding. Or it may be that the recent amendment to the Act of 1968 has removed the supervisory role of this court over abuse of criminal process where the affront to justice, however outrageous, has not so prejudiced the defendant in his trial as to render his conviction unsafe. All that is for decision by another court in an appropriate case.'

In the light of these observations, *R v Chalkley* [1998] QB 848 cannot, in our judgment, properly be regarded as having concluded the matter. On the contrary, it is apparent from what he said in the passage cited in *R v MacDonald* [1998] Crim LR 808 that Auld LJ regarded the point as still open. A similar view was expressed in *R v Simpson* [1998] Crim LR 481 by Garland J in the passage cited earlier.

However, in *R v Martin* [1998] AC 917, which was referred to in *R v MacDonald* [1998] Crim LR 808 but not in *R v Simpson* [1998] Crim LR 481, Lord Lloyd of Berwick said [1998] AC 917, 928–929:

> 'Even if the Courts-Martial Appeal Court had been satisfied that there was an abuse of process, it would still have been necessary for the court to dismiss the appeal, unless persuaded that the conviction was unsafe. For the Courts-Martial Appeal Court is a creature of statute, and has no power to allow appeals save in accordance with section 12(1) of the Courts-Martial (Appeals) Act 1968 as substituted by section 29(1) of and paragraph 5 of Schedule 2 to the Criminal Appeal Act 1995.' (These provisions are identical to those amending section 2 of the Act of 1968 in relation to this court).'

Lord Browne-Wilkinson and Lord Slynn both agreed with Lord Lloyd's reasons for dismissing the appeal. Lord Hope of Craighead said, at page 930:

> '... I do not think it can be doubted that the appeal court – in this particular case, the Courts-Martial Appeal Court – have power to declare a conviction to be unsafe and to quash the conviction if they find that the course of proceedings leading to what would otherwise have been a fair trial has been such as to threaten either basic human rights or the rule of law.'

It seems plain that these conflicting observations by Lord Lloyd and Lord Hope were obiter and formed no part of the reasoning which led to the decision in *R v Martin* [1998] AC 917. Furthermore, it does not appear that their Lordships were invited to consider what was said in Parliament when the Act of 1968 was amended or what the pre-amendment practice of this court was, as exemplified by *R v Heston-Francois* [1984] QB 278 and *Attorney-General's Reference (No 1 of 1990)* [1992] QB 630, 643–644. It is also pertinent that Sir John Smith's article in [1995] Crim LR 920 was not before the House of Lords in *R v Martin* [1998] AC 917.

In our judgment the conflicting views expressed in *R v Martin* [1998] AC 917 in themselves afford a sufficient demonstration of the ambiguity of 'unsafe' to permit this court, in accordance with *Pepper v Hart* [1993] AC 593, to have recourse to Hansard. Furthermore, if the construction of Lord Lloyd is correct, it will, with respect, lead to absurdity, which provides a further reason for recourse to Hansard: in relation to a minor offence triable by justices, abuse arguments can lead to redress by judicial review in the Divisional Court, but, in relation to a serious offence tried at the Crown Court, abuse arguments could not lead to appellate success.

Accordingly, we turn to Hansard (HC Debates), 6 March 1995, col 24, the relevant passages from which are conveniently set out in Sir John Smith's article [1995] Crim LR 920, 924. It is unnecessary to rehearse what was said on second reading and in standing committee. But it is apparent that the amended form of section 2 of the Act of 1968 was intended by the Home Secretary, by Lord Taylor of Gosforth CJ and, crucially, by Parliament, to restate the existing practice of the Court of Appeal; although there is nothing to suggest that express consideration was then given by anyone to whether 'unsafe' was apt to embrace abuse of the *Bennett* or any other type. It is common ground that *R v Heston-Francois* [1984] QB 278 and *Attorney-General's Reference (No 1 of 1990)* [1992] QB 630 show the pre-amendment practice of this court, namely that abuse can be a ground for quashing a conviction.

Furthermore, in our judgment, for a conviction to be safe, it must be lawful; and if it results from a trial which should never have taken place, it can hardly be regarded as safe. Indeed the *Oxford English Dictionary* gives the legal meaning of 'unsafe' as 'likely to constitute a miscarriage of justice'.

Sir John Smith's article does not deal with 'unsafe' in relation to abuse, though his commentary on *R v Simpson* [1998] Crim LR 481, raises directly pertinent questions. But, for the reasons which we have given, we agree with his 1995 conclusion that 'unsafe' bears a broad meaning and one which is apt to embrace abuse of process of the *Bennett* or any other kind.

It follows that, in the highly unusual circumstances of this case, notwithstanding that there is no criticism of the trial judge or jury, and no challenge to the propriety of the outcome of the trial itself, this appeal must be allowed and the defendant's conviction quashed.

[9:8] Spencer, J R, 'Quashing Convictions, and Squashing the Court of Appeal'
(2006) 170 JP 790

In its latest consultation paper, entitled 'Quashing Convictions',[1] the Government proposes legislation to curtail the powers of the Court of Appeal, so that it will no longer be able to quash convictions on 'purely procedural grounds' in cases where it is sure that the defendant is factually guilty; and it invites comments on three possible modifications to section 2 of the Criminal Appeal Act 1968 designed to achieve this end.

Painful as it is to have to say so, this paper is marked by two particularly bad qualities: arrogance, and shallowness.

The first emerges from the Home Secretary's foreword, in which he tells readers not to argue about the basic proposal, because the Government has already made up its mind to do it. 'However, whilst the Government is open to suggestions about *how* we achieve the aims, we are not consulting on the aims themselves or therefore *whether* the law should be changed.' And the second emerges from the later pages, in which we find no serious attempt to make the case for the change, and not the slightest recognition that there might be any case against it – let alone an attempt to answer it.[2] The present system, we are simply told, 'risks outcomes which are unacceptable to the law-abiding majority'; the Government is committed 'to rebalancing the criminal justice system in favour of the victim and the law-abiding majority': and that is that.

I believe that the basic proposal set out in this document is objectionable, and for reasons which should be obvious to any member of 'the law-abiding majority' in whose supposed interests this proposal has been made. But as the Home Secretary has made it clear that he is not prepared to listen to arguments of principle, it is presumably a waste of time for me to engage with him in the official consultation process – or with the Lord Chancellor, or the Attorney General, both of whom (surprisingly) have put their names on the document as well. So this response is written for the wider public, in the hope that Parliament may eventually be persuaded to reject the Government's proposal when, having 'consulted', it introduces it as part of its next Bill to 'rebalance' criminal justice.

Put simply, the objection to the proposal is that, in a democratic society which expects certain minimum standards to be respected in the way its citizens are treated, there are values which are higher than inflicting punishment upon the wicked. For this reason, there are limits to the steps that we are prepared to allow the police to take when catching and collecting evidence against criminals, however wicked and however clearly guilty, and there are also limits to the steps that we are prepared to allow the public prosecutor to go in ensuring trial courts convict them. Thus to take some extreme examples, we do not allow the police to put them on the rack, or throw them into rat-infested dungeons without food until at length they talk; and we do not allow the Attorney General or the Home Secretary to threaten jurors if they dare acquit, or intimidate defence witnesses to make them stay away. In a country which respects the rule of law, we simply cannot allow convictions to stand if they have been

---

1 Office for Criminal Justice Reform, September 2006.
2 The attentive reader will also be disquieted to notice that, when discussing the background to the current law, it makes repeated reference to "the 1985 (sic) Royal Commission on Criminal Justice".

obtained by methods such as these, however sure the appeal court is that those concerned are really guilty. And this is for two reasons, one theoretical, and the other practical.

The theoretical reason is that a conviction obtained by such methods is deprived of one of its essential ingredients: moral authority.

> . . . a criminal conviction serves three functions: to make a public finding of the defendant's factual commission of the offence, to make a moral statement of the defendant's guilt and fitness for punishment, and to make a public expression of the continuing validity of the norms of the criminal law and the consequences of its breach. In order for the verdict to discharge these functions it must be factually accurate, morally authoritative, and founded itself on the rule of law.[3]

The practical reason is that, if convictions can be upheld in cases where the authorities have flouted the basic rules of criminal procedure, this will undermine the self-restraint that we expect the authorities to show in keeping to the rules. 'If at the end of the day a conviction obtained by these means will be appeal-proof if it is clear that the defendant committed the offence, why shouldn't we take the risk and break the rules?'
. . ..

The particular butt of the Home Secretary's wrath is the Court of Appeal decision in *Mullen*.[4] In 1990, Mullen was convicted of conspiracy to cause explosions in the context of an IRA bombing campaign in mainland Britain, and sentenced to 30 years' imprisonment. Before arrest he had fled to Zimbabwe, whence the British authorities, unwilling to go through the formalities of extradition, got him back by persuading the Zimbabwe authorities to unlawfully expel him.

In another case four years later, in which the Metropolitan Police had conspired with their South African colleagues to (in effect) kidnap a fugitive suspect and put him on a plane to Heathrow, the House of Lords ruled that where the authorities committed this sort of blatant illegality, the resulting proceedings are irremediably tainted, and cannot go ahead; to prosecute after this illegal start would constitute an 'abuse of process'.[5] It did so because, as Lord Griffiths explained, ' . . . the judiciary accept a responsibility for the maintenance of the rule of law that embraces a willingness to oversee executive action and to refuse to countenance behaviour that threatens either basic human rights or the rule of law.' At this point Mullen appealed, and the Court of Appeal felt obliged to quash his conviction: irrespective of the fact that evidence against him was extremely strong, and had evidently convinced the jury that convicted him. With considerable chuzpah (or its Irish equivalent) Mullen then sued the Home Secretary for compensation for the period he had spent in prison, in which attempt he failed.[6] It seems to have been this unsuccessful attempt that provoked the previous Home Secretary, earlier this year, to announce the immediate abolition of the then-existing discretionary scheme under which the Home Office occasionally (and grudgingly) paid compensation to those whose convictions were quashed upon appeal.[7] And now it is the same case which has led the current Home Secretary to attempt to change the law so that, should the same facts occur in future, the Court of Appeal would be unable to quash the conviction.

If the proposal announced in this Consultation Paper is carried out, then not only would the Court of Appeal be obliged to uphold the conviction of an obviously guilty Mullen in the circumstances of that case; it would also be obliged to uphold the conviction in the following

3   Ian Dennis, "Fair trials and safe convictions", [2003] Current Legal Problems 211, at 235–6.
4   [1999] 2 CrAppR 143.
5   *R v Horseferry Road JJ ex pte Bennett* [1994] AC 42, and [1995] 1 CrAppR 147.
6   *R (Mullen) v Secretary of State for the Home Department* [2004] UKHL 18, [2005] 1 AC 1.
7   See the written Ministerial statement, 19 April 2006, available on the Home Office website.

circumstances, if it was convinced that he had committed the offence for which he had been convicted:

(1) Mullen, instead of being illegally expelled by the authorities in Zimbabwe in collusion with our own, is kidnapped there by our secret service and brought back to London, drugged and shackled, in a crate;

(2) Mullen, when arrested, is interrogated under torture, and confesses; facts discovered as a result of what he said under torture enable his guilt to be established beyond any doubt; at trial the judge, in disregard of sections 76 and 78 of the Police and Criminal Evidence Act 1984, allows the evidence to go to the jury, which convicts;

(3) Mullen, a previously law-abiding citizen, was blackmailed into joining the conspiracy by people posing as members of the IRA, who were in fact agents of the secret service;[8]

(4) at trial, the judge refuses to allow Mullen to have a barrister to defend him, or refuses to allow him to give evidence in his defence (or both);

(5) when summing up, the trial judge directs the jury that on the evidence Mullen is clearly guilty and has no conceivable defence, and it is their duty to return an immediate verdict to that effect – which they promptly do, without retiring;[9]

(6) during the trial, the jurors receive letters from the Home Office warning them that if they acquit this dangerous terrorist, they will be viewed as threats to national security and may find themselves subjected to control orders under the Terrorism Act 2006;

(7) after the trial, it emerges that the judge received a letter from the Prime Minister's office, telling him that the Government believed it to be in the national interest that Mullen should be convicted – to which the judge replied 'You can count on me: but remember that one good turn deserves another.'

Some of these examples are real cases, in which the Court of Appeal, applying the present rules, has actually quashed the conviction – in some cases ordering a retrial, and in other cases not. Some, by contrast, are imaginary. Ten years ago, I would have described the imaginary ones as purely fanciful, but in the oppressive political climate of today I am not so sure they are. Who would have thought, even ten years ago, the President of the USA would publicly admit that terrorist suspects are being held for interrogation in secret prisons – and that when he did so, it would provoke little or no comment? Who would have thought, ten years ago, that we would have a Home Secretary who made a habit of publicly abusing members of the judiciary in the coarsest terms: and that far from being sacked for this, was smiled upon by the Prime Minister, until a scandal about a different matter forced him to resign? Or that his successor-but-one would join the tabloid newspapers in publicly condemning a judge for imposing a sentence which the law required him to impose? Or that, in the land of Magna Carta, a government in time of peace would first try to introduce indefinite administrative detention for suspected terrorists, and when that was struck down by the courts, house-arrest?

To remain the sort of society in which it is safe for the 'law abiding majority' to live, the citizens of this country need to be protected not only from being blown to pieces by the likes of Mullen, but also from being convicted and sent to prison after outrageously illegal conduct by the police and the other agencies of the state. As the law stands at present, happily, they are. But if the Government succeeds in its attempt to 'rebalance' the Criminal Appeal Act, this will no longer be the case.

---

8   c.f. Loosely and A-G's Reference (No.3 of 2000) [2001] UKHL 53, [2001] 1 WLR 2060.
9   Wang [2005] UKHL 9, [2005] 1 WLR 661.

If a Bill is introduced to make the change the Government now has in mind, I fail to see how the Minister will be able truthfully to make the necessary declaration to Parliament that its terms are 'compatible with Convention rights'.[10] And if it is enacted, we shall (I believe) be the only country in Europe in which convictions are not automatically set aside for grave procedural errors, irrespective of the guilt of the accused – and we can expect a further string of embarrassing condemnations from Strasbourg a few years down the line.

Is there really anything to be said for the Government's position?

There is this much: that it is possible to disagree with the Court of Appeal (and indeed the House of Lords) about the details of which procedural irregularities are sufficiently serious to justify the conviction of an obviously guilty person being set aside.

. . .

But the fact that two views are possible about some of the cases in which the higher courts have felt it necessary to quash the conviction of an obviously guilty person is no good reason for abolishing their power to do so altogether. If there is room for argument about the cases mentioned in the previous paragraph, no one, I believe – or at any rate, profoundly hope – would wish to see the Court of Appeal constrained to uphold a conviction in the hypothetical cases numbered (2), (3) (4), (6) or (7) on pages 4–5 above, however convincing the evidence of the defendant's guilt might be.

So if what the Government currently proposes is unacceptable, could the problem (if it is one) be resolved by a watered-down version of it, in which the Court of Appeal's power to quash the conviction of an obviously guilty person is restricted to certain stated cases, or in which certain specific cases are put beyond its reach? I do not think so. Decisions of this sort, I believe, are best made as they are now: by our senior judges, after argument, on a case-by-case basis. As the law stands, I believe they are making a reasonably good job of it. And there is no reason to tie their hands with yet more prescriptive legislation, passed with an eye to reversing particular decisions that happen to have attracted the attention of the tabloid newspapers.

At the beginning of this Consultation Paper, the Home Secretary, Lord Chancellor and Attorney-General did me the honour of quoting from the first page of an article of mine about criminal appeals which was published in the *Criminal Law Review* in August.[11] Had they read to the end, they would have seen that my concluding words were these: 'The message I hope this article has conveyed is that we should stop tinkering with the appeal system, stand back from it, and try to re-plan it as a coherent whole.' If the Government persists with this deplorable proposal, I hope that Parliament will bear these words in mind and resoundingly reject it.

[9:9] *R v McIlkenny*
(1992) 93 Cr App Rep 287

This is the famous judgment of the Court of Appeal in the 'Birmingham Six' case. In 1975 the appellants were convicted of 21 counts of murder, arising out of the IRA bombing of two pubs in Birmingham in which 21 people were killed and 162 injured. Their appeals against conviction were dismissed. In 1987 the Home Secretary referred the case to the Court of Appeal on the ground that there was fresh scientific evidence and fresh evidence that the appellants had been beaten following their arrests, and this was likewise dismissed. On a second reference in 1990, the court held that the convictions were now unsafe and unsatisfactory, as a result

10 As required by s.19 of the Human Rights Act 1998.
11 "Does our present criminal appeal system make sense?", [2006] Crim LR 677–694.

of both the fresh scientific evidence and the fresh investigation into the police evidence. The court stressed that they were saying nothing about the innocence or otherwise of the applicants, and indeed stressed the strengths as well as the weaknesses in the prosecution case.

Lloyd LJ (at page 310):

The Role of the Court of Appeal

Since the present appeal has given rise to much public discussion as to the powers and duties of the Court of Appeal (Criminal Division), and since the Home Secretary has set up a Royal Commission to investigate and report, it may be helpful if we set out our understanding of the present state of the law.

(1) The Court of Appeal (Criminal Division) is the creature of statute. Our powers are derived from, and confined to, those contained in the Supreme Court Act 1981, the Criminal Appeal Act 1968 and the Criminal Justice Act 1988. We have no inherent jurisdiction apart from statute: see *Jeffries* (1968) 52 Cr App Rep 654, [1969] 1 QB 120, *R v Collins* (1969) 54 Cr App Rep 19, [1970] 1 QB 710 and *DPP v Shannon* (1974) 59 Cr App Rep 250, [1975] AC 717. Thus we have no power to conduct an open-ended investigation into an alleged miscarriage of justice, even if we were equipped to do so. Our function is to hear criminal appeals, neither more or less.

(2) Just as we have no powers other than those conferred on us by Parliament, so we are guided by Parliament in the exercise of those powers. Thus by section 2(1) of the 1968 Act we are directed to allow an appeal against conviction if, but only if, (a) we think that the conviction is unsafe or unsatisfactory; (b) there has been a wrong decision on a question of law or, (c) there has been a material irregularity. In all other cases we are obliged to dismiss the appeal. Where we allow an appeal, we are directed by section 2(2) to quash the conviction. Where we quash the conviction, the other operates, by virtue of section 2(3) as a direction to the trial court to enter a verdict of acquittal, except where a retrial is ordered under section 7 of the Act. Nothing in section 2 of the Act, or anywhere else obliges or entitles us to say whether we think that the appellant is innocent. This is a point of great constitutional importance. The task of deciding whether a man is guilty falls on the jury. We are concerned solely with the question whether the verdict of the jury can stand.

(3) Rightly or wrongly (we think rightly) trial by jury is the foundation of our criminal justice system. Under jury trial juries not only find the facts; they also apply the law. Since they are not experts in the law, they are directed on the relevant law by the judge. But the task of applying the law to the facts, and so reaching a verdict, belongs to the jury, and the jury alone. The primacy of the jury in the English criminal justice system explains why, historically, the Court of Appeal had so limited a function. Until 1907, there was no Court of Criminal Appeal at all. If, before then, a point of law arose in the course of a trial, the judge could 'reserve' the point, if he thought fit, for consideration by the Court for Crown Cases Reserved. In the event of the point being decided in favour of the accused, the conviction would be quashed. But there was no right of appeal as such. The Criminal Appeal Act 1907 created the right of appeal for the first time. It also enabled the Court of Criminal Appeal to receive fresh evidence. There was no power to order a retrial, except by way of the writ of venire de novo. But that writ only issued when the trial had been a nullity. There was no general power to order a retrial until the Criminal Appeal Act 1964, and then only in fresh evidence cases. The power has since been greatly extended.

(4) The primacy of the jury in the criminal justice system is well illustrated by the difference between the Criminal and Civil Divisions of the Court of Appeal. Like the Criminal Division, the Civil Division is also a creature of statute. But its powers are much wider. A civil appeal is by way of re-hearing of the whole cases. So the court is concerned with fact as well as law. It is true the court does not re-hear the witnesses. But it reads their evidence. It follows that in a civil case the Court of Appeal may take a

different view of the facts from the court below. In a criminal case this is not possible. Since justice is as much concerned with the conviction of the guilty as the acquittal of the innocent, and the task of convicting the guilty belongs constitutionally to the jury, not to us, the role of the Criminal Division of the Court of Appeal is necessarily limited. Hence it is true to say that whereas the Civil Division of the Court of Appeal has appellate jurisdiction in the full sense, the Criminal Division is perhaps more accurately described as a court of review. In the 1907 Act there was a power to set aside a verdict if the court thought it unreasonable, or that it could not be supported having regard to the evidence. This power was very narrowly construed. The wording has now been changed. We have power to up-set the verdict of a jury on a question of fact if we think a conviction unsafe or unsatisfactory under all the circumstances of the case. These words were substituted by section 4 of the Criminal Appeal Act 1966. We shall return to their meaning later.

(5) Another feature of our law, which goes hand in hand with trial by jury, is the adversarial nature of criminal proceedings. Clearly a jury cannot embark on a judicial investigation. So the material must be placed before the jury. It is sometimes said that the adversarial system leaves too much power in the hands of the police. But that criticism has been met, at least in part, by the creation of the Crown Pros-ecution Service. The great advantage of the adversarial system is that it enables the defendant to test the prosecution case in open court. Once there is sufficient evidence to commit a defendant for trial, the prosecution has to prove the case against him by calling witnesses to give oral testimony in the presence of the jury. We doubt whether there is a better way of exposing the weaknesses in the prose-cution case, whether the witness be a policeman, a scientist or a bystander, than by cross-examination.

(6) A disadvantage of the adversarial system may be that the parties are not evenly matched in re-sources. As we have seen, one reason why the judge expressed his preference for Dr Skuse was that Dr Black had carried out no experiments to prove his theory. Experiments presumably cost money. Whether Dr Black could have carried out any experiments within the limitation of legal aid, or the time available, we do not know. But the inequality of resources is ameliorated by the obligation on the part of the prosecution to make available all material which may prove helpful to the defence. The later history of the present appeal shows how well the prosecution can perform that obligation.

(7) No system is better than its human input. Like any other system of justice the adversarial system may be abused. The evidence adduced may be inadequate. Expert evidence may not have been properly researched or there may have been a deliberate attempt to undermine the system by giving false evidence. If there is a conflict of evidence there is no way of ensuring the jury will always get it right. This is particularly so where there is a conflict of expert evidence, such as there was here. No human system can expect to be perfect.

(8) Just as the adversarial system prevails at the trial, so also it prevails in the Court of Appeal. It is for the appellants to raise the issues which they wish to lay before the court. Those issues are set out in the grounds of appeal. It will be remembered that at the initial application for leave to appeal, virtu-ally the only issue before the court was the fairness of the summing-up. If the appellants had insisted on raising other issues, they could have done so. The same applies when the case was referred back to the court in 1987. A number of distinguished scientists were called on both sides. But as we have seen, the scientific issues before the court in 1987 were not the same as they are now. Thus nobody sug-gested in 1987 that Dr Skuse's results could have been due to nitrite contamination from the soap he was using to clean his bowls. Nobody knew that Dr Drayton would modify her view in the light of later scientific research. Nobody knew that the 'contemporaneous' notes taken by DC Woodwiss of the two McIlkenny interviews were written on four different pads of paper. So the issues were very different.

(9) For an adversarial system to work, there must be an adversary. One of our difficulties in the pres-ent appeal has been that we have listened to the fresh evidence of Dr Scaplehorn and Dr Baxendale,

without the benefit of hearing any cross-examination. We say at once, and as emphatically as we can, that this is not criticism of the Director or Mr Boal. They have acted with perfect propriety. The concluding paragraphs of the Farquharson's Committee's Report on The Role of Prosecuting Counsel, May 1986 (Archbold 43rd ed para 4–47a) deals with prosecution counsel's function in the Court of Appeal in this way:

> 'If prosecution counsel has formed the view that the appeal should succeed he should acquaint the court with the view and explain the reasons for it. If the court disagrees with him counsel is entitled to adhere to his view and is not obliged to conduct the appeal in a way which conflicts with his own judgment. At the same time it remains counsel's duty to give assistance to the court if requested to do so.'

Mr Boal and the DPP had a number of very difficult decisions to take in the abnormal circumstances of the present appeal. Having decided that they could not support the scientific evidence on which the prosecution was based, or the police evidence, it was their duty to. They have since given us every possible assistance. But the effect of their decision was, inevitably, that we have not heard the other side put, if indeed there is another side.

(10) This has led us to consider whether some other system might be devised in the very exceptional class of case, of which this is one, where fresh evidence comes to light long after the conviction. In the ordinary case, not depending on fresh evidence, there is no difficulty. Nor is there any difficulty in fresh evidence cases, where the fresh evidence is discovered soon after the trial. If the evidence is incredible, or inadmissible, or would not afford a ground for allowing the appeal, we decline to receive it. If the fresh evidence surmounts that preliminary hurdle, we first quash the conviction, if we think it unsafe or unsatisfactory, and then order a retrial under section 7 of the Act, if the interests of justice so require. Where new evidence is conclusive, we quash the conviction without ordering a retrial: see R v Flower (1965) 50 Cr App Rep 22, [1966] 1 QB 146. There is a view, put forward notably by Lord Devlin in The Judge, that we should always quash a conviction where fresh evidence has been received, since a conviction is bound to be unsafe, or at least unsatisfactory, where it has not been based on all the evidence. But this view did not find favour with the House of Lords in Stafford and Luvaglio v DPP (1973) 58 Cr App Rep 256, [1974] AC 878.

The difficulty in fresh evidence cases arises where a retrial is no longer practicable, as in the present case. The difficulty becomes acute when there is no contest. For we then have to make up our own minds whether the convictions are unsafe or unsatisfactory without having the benefit of hearing the evidence tested by cross-examination. Where a retrial is still possible, the quashing of the conviction is, as it were, only the first half of a two stage process. Where a retrial is no longer possible, it is the end of the road. This is not the occasion to offer a solution to the difficulty ourselves. No doubt all these problems will be reviewed by the Royal Commission.

[9:10] Monnell and Morris v United Kingdom
(1988) 10 EHRR 205

The two applicants had applied unsuccessfully to the Court of Appeal for leave to appeal against both their convictions and sentences. The Court of Appeal, although neither applicant had been present or represented at the hearing, had ordered that part of the time already spent by the applicants in custody since conviction should not count towards the service of the sentences. The applicants argued that the periods of detention which the court ordered not to count towards their sentence was not covered by any of the categories of permitted detention set out in Article 5(1) of the European Convention on Human Rights (see **[1:13]**), and that the procedure followed did not comply with Articles 6(1), (3)(c) and 14. The court held, by a majority of five to two, that there had been no violation of Articles 5 or 6, and unanimously that there had been no violation of Article 14.

The following extract is taken from the majority judgment (at page 217):

The power of the Court of Appeal to order loss of time, as it is actually exercised, is a component of the machinery existing under English law to ensure that criminal appeals are considered within a reasonable time and, in particular, to reduce the time spent in custody by those with meritorious grounds waiting for their appeal to be heard; this is made patently clear in the 1965 report of the Interdepartmental Committee on the Court of Criminal Appeal and in the two Practice Directions issued by the Lord Chief Justice. In sum, it is a power exercised to discourage abuse of the court's own procedures. As such, it is an inherent part of the criminal appeal process following conviction of an offender and pursues a legitimate aim under sub-paragraph (a) of Article 5(1).

47 It was pointed out in argument that under the law of many of the convention countries detention pending a criminal appeal is treated as detention on remand and a convicted person does not start to serve his or her sentence until the conviction has become final. In such systems, the appellate court itself determines the sentence and, in some of them, exercises a discretion in deciding whether or to what extent detention pending appeal shall be deducted from the sentence. The Delegate of the Commission was of the opinion that such systems, unlike the English system at issue in the present case, would be compatible with Article 5(1).

The difference between the two approaches to sentencing procedures is, however, one of form and not of substance as far as the effect on the convicted person is concerned. Sub-paragraph (a) of Article 5(1), which is silent as to the permissible forms of legal machinery whereby a person may lawfully be ordered to be detailed after conviction, must be taken to have left the Contracting States a discretion in the matter. Sentencing procedures may legitimately vary from Contracting State to Contracting State, whilst still complying with the requirements of Article 5(1)(a). The court considers that the technical and formal difference in the way in which sentencing procedures are arranged in the United Kingdom as compared with other Convention countries is not such as to exclude the applicability of sub-paragraph (a) of Article 5(1) in the present case.

48 In the light of all the foregoing factors, the court finds that there was a sufficient and legitimate connection, for the purposes of the deprivation of liberty permitted under sub-paragraph (a) of Article 5(1), between the conviction of each applicant and the additional period of imprisonment undergone as a result of the loss-of-time order made by the Court of appeal. The time spent in custody by each applicant under this head is accordingly to be regarded as detention of a person under conviction by a competent court, within the meaning of sub-paragraph (a) of Article 5(1).

49 The applicants at certain points in their pleadings appeared to be arguing that their applications for leave to appeal were not in fact hopeless or frivolous. This was a matter of appreciation coming within the discretion conferred on the Court of Appeal by the terms of section 29(1) of the Criminal Appeal Act 1968. Save in so far as is necessary to review the contested measure of deprivation of liberty for compatibility with the Convention, it is not within the province of the European Court to substitute its own assessment of the facts for that of the domestic courts.

50 More generally, the court is satisfied in the circumstances of the present case as to the lawfulness and procedural propriety of the contested periods of loss of liberty. To begin within, it has

been disputed that the relevant rules and procedures under English law were properly observed by the English courts in relation to the making of the loss-of-time orders. Further, contrary to the submissions of the applicants, the court finds that these orders depriving the applicants of their liberty issued from and were executed by an appropriate authority and were not arbitrary.

The contested deprivation of liberty must therefore be found to have been both lawful and effected in accordance with a procedure prescribed by law, as those expressions in Article 5(1) have been interpreted in the court's case law.

51 There has accordingly been no breach of Article 5(1) in the present case in respect of either applicant.

(At page 223):

In the opinion of the Court, Article 6 required that Mr Monnell and Mr Morris be provided, in some appropriate way, with a fair procedure enabling them adequately and effectively to present their case against the possible exercise to their detriment of the power under section 29(1) of the 1968 Act. The court will accordingly review the procedure followed to ascertain whether this condition was satisfied.

62 To begin with, the principle of equality of arms, inherent in the notion of fairness under Article 6(1), was respected in that the prosecution, like the two accused, was not represented before either the single judge or the full Court of appeal.

The principle of equality of arms is, however, only one feature of the wider concept of fair trial in criminal proceedings; in particular even in the absence of a prosecuting party, a trial would not be fair if it took place in such conditions as to put the accused unfairly at a disadvantage.

63 In this connection, it is to be noted that, pursuant to the legal aid scheme, Mr Monnell and Mr Morris had the benefit of free legal advice on appeal. Counsel who had represented them at the trial advised that there were no reasonable prospects of successfully appealing, but both men chose to ignore this advice and pressed ahead with applications for leave to appeal.

64 They were both also aware that, in the absence of arguable grounds of appeal, to lodge and then to renew their applications for leave to appeal might well result in loss-of-time orders. Warnings to this effect were given in the Forms AA and SJ. Nevertheless and despite the fact that the single judge had refused leave, they renewed their applications to the full court of Appeal on the same grounds as in their original applications.

65 As to the possible manner of presenting their case, the system whereby applications for leave to appeal are lodged and then renewed on official forms meant that Mr Monnell and Mr Morris, like all applicants for leave to appeal, were afforded the opportunity to submit written grounds of appeal.

Admittedly, their ancillary applications to be present before the Court of Appeal were unsuccessful, this being a matter within the discretion of the court. Consequently, neither man was able to formulate oral arguments in person before being penalised by an additional loss of liberty.

However, there is no reason why their written submissions should not have included considerations relevant to exercise of the power to direct loss of time, especially in view of the warnings given to them in Forms AA and SJ as to the importance of legal advice and the consequences of pursuing an application without arguable grounds. Indeed, arguments going to the issue of the unmeritorious character of the application will necessarily have been incorporated in their submissions in support of the grounds of appeal.

In accordance with the usual procedure, when considering Mr Monnell's and Mr Morris's applications, both the single judge and the full Court of Appeal had before them all the relevant papers, including the grounds of appeal, a transcript of the trial and, for Mr Monnell, the social inquiry and psychiatric reports prepared on him.

66 Mr Monnell and Mr Morris, like any applicant for leave to appeal, had the right to instruct counsel to appeal on their behalf and present oral argument at a hearing both before the single judge and the full Court of Appeal.

67 It can be presumed that neither Mr Monnell nor Mr Morris could afford to pay counsel out of his own pocket, and under English law they were not automatically entitled to legal aid for the preparation of the written grounds of appeal or for representation through counsel at an oral hearing. Under paragraph 3(c) of Article 6, they were guaranteed the right to be given legal assistance free only so far as the interests of justice so required. The interests of justice cannot, however, be taken to require an automatic grant of legal aid whenever a convicted person, with no objective likelihood of success, wishes to appeal after having received a fair trial in the first instance in accordance with Article 6. Each applicant, it is to be noted, benefited from free legal assistance both at his trial and in being advised as to whether he had any arguable grounds of appeal. In the court's view, the issue to be decided in relation to section 29(1) of the Criminal Appeal Act 1968 did not call, as a matter of fairness, for oral submissions on behalf of the applicants in addition to the written submissions and material already before the Court of Appeal.

68 In short, the interests of justice and fairness could, in the circumstances, be met by the applicants being able to present relevant considerations through making written submissions.

In coming to this conclusion, the court has also borne in mind that, as the power under section 29(1) is exercised in practice, the maximum loss of time risked is in the order of two months and not the whole of the period spent in custody between conviction and determination by the Court of Appeal. It is true, as the applicants' lawyers stressed before the court, that this practical restraint is not brought to the attention of prospective applicants for leave to appeal. However, in view of all the other considerations prevailing, this shortcoming cannot be decisive for present purposes.

69 Finally, the court has no cause to doubt that the Court of Appeal's decision to refuse the applicants leave to appeal and, further, to impose loss of time was based on a full and thorough evaluation of the relevant factors.

70 Having regard to the special features of the context in which the power to order loss of time was exercised and to the circumstances of the case, the court finds that neither Mr Monnell nor Mr Morris was denied a fair procedure as guaranteed by paragraphs 1 and 3(c) of Article 6. There has accordingly been no breach of either of these provisions of the Convention.

The following extract is taken from the dissenting opinion (of judges Pettit and Spielmann):

I Article 5(1) of the Convention

As opposed to the majority, we voted for the violation of Article 5(1) of the Convention.

Quite correctly the court considered that formal differences in the judicial process for ordering detention after conviction cannot render Article 5(1) inapplicable.

In our opinion, however, the majority of the court was wrong in concluding that the aforementioned provision was not violated in the present case.

Generally speaking, it should be observed that, quite significantly, the vast majority of the Member States of the Council of Europe do not possess a system of loss of time similar to the one submitted to the examination of the court.

As a matter of fact, the aforementioned system as regulated by an Act of 1968 provides that when an application for leave to appeal is rejected the single judge may order part or all of the time spent in custody awaiting the determination of the application not to count towards the prospective appellants' sentence. The same applies when the application is renewed before the full court which, moreover, may order a longer loss of time.

This entails a later date of release.

On a purely humanitarian level one may wonder about the validity of an institution which requires authorisation for the lodging of an appeal providing for sanctions in the case of refusal.

More particularly, this being the system of the respondent State, the court had to inquire whether, in the circumstances of the case, such as institution was compatible with the provisions of the Convention.

The Government submitted that the Court of Appeal merely gives directions as to the manner of execution of the sentences of those who persist in lodging an appeal, which the court itself considers as futile.

We cannot share this reasoning.

Even if we were to accept in principle the system of loss of time, it should have been hedged about with a number of elementary guarantees.

We believe that the impugned legislation is in breach of Article 5.

The time lost may comprise the entire period spent in custody between conviction and rejection of the application for leave to appeal.

Within these limits the competent authority decides according to no fixed criteria and no objective reasons.

In the two cases submitted to the court the loss of time at risk was in the range of 8 and 14 months.

The loss of time ordered was 28 and 46 days.

In practice apparently the average time lost would be 64 days.

What is more serious, however, is that the risk run in theory is of a nature to deter even an innocent person, or someone who considers himself to be innocent, from lodging an appeal.

In fact, as the Government itself recognises, the impugned system is used to dissuade convicted persons in custody from lodging appeals in order not unnecessarily to increase the workload of the court.

In our opinion it is inconceivable that the demands of the administration of the courts (shortage of judges, personnel, etc) should be given pre-eminence in a system of penalties involving deprivation of liberty.

Such a deviation, in the short or medium term, runs the risk of exposing the detained person, or anyone amenable to justice, to an instrument of a criminal policy, which is subject to political variations as to what should be, or should have been, the administration of justice.

In these conditions we concur with the opinion of the overwhelming majority of the Commission that there was a violation of Article 5(1) of the Convention.

In fact, as observed by the Commission, we consider that the period of time ordered not to count towards the applicants' sentences imposed by the trial judge cannot be regarded as forming part of their detention after conviction at first instance. The express terms of the loss of time orders exclude this hypothesis.

Quite correctly the majority of the Commission so concluded (. . .) bearing in mind the purpose for which the loss of time orders were made, which was unconnected with the original sentences imposed on the applicants or with the offences for which they were convicted.

In our opinion, the periods of detention which have been ordered not to count towards the service of the applicants' sentence cannot be considered as detention coming within the terms of Article 5 of the Convention.

II Article 6 of the Convention

The court considered, quite wrongly in our opinion, that there was no violation of Article 6 of the Convention.

In fact, even if we were to admit that the impugned system was compatible with Article 5 of the Convention, the additional prison sentence imposed on the two applicants remained the consequence of the refusal of leave to appeal.

In these conditions, we consider that the principle of fair trial would require the applicants to be heard by the competent authorities to enable them to present their arguments in person.

Could one seriously support that a written submission by the applicant – composed in the isolation of a prison – could satisfy the requirements of Article 6?

The importance of an additional prison sentence at stake raises objections to such an argument.

Is it not true that on that score the requirements of Article 6, which were applied in the case of Öztürk – where only a fine was at stake – should also be afforded when several months in prison were in issue?

In accordance with the opinion of the Commission, we consider that the applicants' absence from the determination of their applications for leave to appeal, which resulted in the making of the orders that they lost time in the calculation of their service of sentence, deprived them of a fair hearing in the determination of the criminal charges against them as guaranteed by Article 6(1) and of the right to defend themselves in person as guaranteed by Article 6(3)(c) of the Convention.

We believe that where the liberty of the individual is at stake it is necessary that all decisions are taken in the presence of the person affected in the course of a fully adversarial hearing.

[9:11] *R v Gray and others*
[2014] EWCA Crim 2372 (at paragraph 1)

1 These applications raise yet again the question of when it is appropriate to make a loss of time order. In *R v Jerry Fortean [2009] EWCA Crim 437*, the then Vice President of the Court of Appeal Criminal Division provided useful guidance on the subject. At paragraphs 10 to 17 he observed:

> "10. This court is coping, with considerable effort, with over 6,000 applications each year for leave to appeal. It is anxious to deal promptly with those which raise properly arguable grounds of appeal, whether in the end they are successful or not. It is an important feature of this jurisdiction, unlike some others, that the trial process is concluded with sentence. An appeal is not built into the trial process but must be justified on properly arguable grounds. This also means that the sentence is operative pending appeal. That reinforces the need to attend promptly to those who have appeals of arguable substance. The court's ability to do that is significantly hampered by meritless applications such as the present.
>
> 11. It is for this reason that the court has express statutory power under section 29 of the Criminal Appeal Act 1968 to order that part of the time spent in custody pending appeal is not to count towards the sentence: see *Monnell and Morris v United Kingdom* (1988) 10 EHRR 205.
>
> 12. The applicant, like virtually every other defendant in England and Wales, was represented by independent counsel and solicitors at his trial. In this case, as in most others, that was paid for by the

State's Legal Services Commission. The duty of his representatives towards him extended to providing him with skilled advice upon whether or not there existed arguable grounds of appeal, and to draft them if they existed. He must either have received advice that there were none, or have chosen not to seek it.

13. The form on which an application for leave to appeal is initially made contains a very clear printed warning in bold letters above the place for signature that if the single judge or the court is of the opinion that the application for leave is plainly without merit, an order may be made that time spent in custody as an appellant will not count towards sentence. The single judge did not make such an order, but he expressly indicated that the applicant was at risk if he pursued the application.

14. A further warning to the same effect was contained in the form by which the applicant elected to renew his application. It terms could not be clearer. They read:

"I understand that if an application is renewed after being refused by a judge, and the court comes to the conclusion that there is no justification for the renewal, the court may direct that some or all of the time spent in custody as an applicant shall not count towards sentence (a loss of time order)."

15. This court will exercise this power in order to ensure that applications by those who have some proper basis for making them can be dealt with fully and promptly. It has said so on countless occasions in the past, and we reiterate it today: see, for example, *R v Howitt (1975)* 61 Cr App R 327, the Lord Chief Justice's Practice Direction of 2002 [2002] 1 WLR, and *R v Hart [2007]* 1 Cr App R 31.

16. The present could not be a clearer case. We order that six weeks (that is 42 days) of the time spent in custody by the applicant is not to count towards his sentence.

17. We make it clear that this power may be emphasised in any meritless application which should never have been pursued after due warning. That counsel or solicitors have associated themselves with such a renewal will be relevant, but it will not necessarily avoid such an order if there was no justification for continuing the case."

2 Those observations are as relevant today as there were in February 2009. Unmeritorious renewal applications take up a wholly disproportionate amount of staff and judicial resources in preparation and hearing time. They also waste significant sums of public money, for example in obtaining transcripts, especially in applications for leave to appeal against conviction. The figures for September 2013 to August 2014 show that the total number of applications to the Court of Appeal Criminal Division is now running at nearly 6,500 per year; of those, 1,424 were applications for leave to appeal against conviction. Leave was granted or the application referred to the Full Court in just 245 cases. In the same period 416 applications were renewed and 454 applications refused. The apparent discrepancy in the mathematics is because the figures do not represent the same cases. Nevertheless, a clear picture of a pattern of unjustified renewals of applications for leave to appeal against conviction emerges. The result is that waiting times for conviction cases remain at approximately 12 months. The more time the Court of Appeal Office and the judges spend on unmeritorious cases, the longer the waiting times are likely to be.

3 The only means the court has of discouraging unmeritorious applications which waste precious time and resources is by using the powers given to us by Parliament in the Criminal Appeal Act 1968 and the Prosecution of Offences Act 1985.

4 Section 29 of the Criminal Appeal Act, where relevant, provides:

"(1) The time during which an appellant is in custody pending the determination of his appeal shall, subject to any direction which the Court of Appeal may give to the contrary, be reckoned as part of the term of any sentence to which he is for the time being subject.

(2) Where the Court of Appeal give a contrary direction under subsection (1) above, they shall state their reasons for doing so; and they shall not give any such direction where-

(a)   leave to appeal has been granted; or

(b)   a certificate has been given by the judge of the court of trial under-

    (i)   section 1 or 11(1A) of this Act; or

    (ii)   section 81(1B) of the Supreme Court Act 1981; or

(c)   the case has been referred to them under section 9 of the Criminal Appeal Act 1995."

Thus, if leave has been granted, the trial judge has given a certificate or the Criminal Cases Review Commission has referred the appeal, then a loss of time order cannot be made. If the court does have the power and decides to exercise it, it must give its reasons. They need not be lengthy provided they make it clear to the applicant why the order is being made.

5 The single judge has a similar power to make a loss of time order under section 31(2)(h) of the Criminal Appeal Act. It provides, where relevant:

"(1) There may be exercised by a single judge in the same manner as by the Court of Appeal and subject to the same provisions-

(a)   the powers of the Court of Appeal under this Part of this Act specified in subsection (2) below;

(b)   the power to give directions under section 4(4) of the Sexual Offences (Amendment) Act 1976; and

(c)   the powers to make orders for the payment of costs under sections 16 to 18 of the Prosecution of Offences Act 1985 in proceedings under this Part of this Act.

(2) The powers mentioned in subsection (1)(a) above are the following:—

(a)   to give leave to appeal;

(b)   to extend the time within which notice of appeal or of application for leave to appeal may be given; . . .

(h)   to give directions under section 29(1) of this Act.

    . . .

(3)   If the single judge refuses an application on the part of an appellant to exercise in his favour any of the powers above specified, the appellant shall be entitled to have the application determined by the Court of Appeal."

6 The power to award costs derives from section 18 of the Prosecution of Offences Act 1985. It provides:

"(2) Where the Court of Appeal dismisses-

(a)   an appeal or application for leave to appeal under Part I of the Criminal Appeal Act 1968 ; or

(b)   an application by the accused for leave to appeal to the House of Lords under Part II of that Act;

it may make such order as to the costs to be paid by the accused, to such person as may be named in the order, as it considers just and reasonable, or

(c)   an appeal or application for leave to appeal under section 9(11) of the Criminal Justice Act 1987; or

(d)   an appeal or application for leave to appeal under section 35(1) of the Criminal Procedure and Investigations Act 1996.

(2A) Where the Court of Appeal reverses or varies a ruling on an appeal under Part 9 of the Criminal Justice Act 2003, it may make such order as to the costs to be paid by the accused, to such person as may be named in the order, as it considers just and reasonable.

(3) The amount to be paid by the accused in pursuance of an order under this section shall be specified in the order.

...

(6) Costs ordered to be paid under subsection (2) or (2A) above may include the reasonable cost of any transcript of a record of proceedings made in accordance with rules of court made for the purposes of section 32 of the Act of 1968."

7 The power to award costs is used infrequently and the single judge's power to make an order for loss of time has not been exercised since October 2007. Single judges today faced with what they consider to be a totally unmeritorious application generally prefer to initial a box on the form to indicate that if the application is renewed, the Full Court will consider the making of a loss of time order. However, the fact that the single judge has not initialled the box does not deprive the Full Court of the power to make a loss of time order. The court gave an express warning of this in *R v Hart and others* [2007] 1 Cr App R 31; [2007] 2 Cr App R 34. It also advised that applicants should not consider themselves protected by the advice of counsel. The Vice President at that time suggested that both advocates and applicants should "heed the fact that this court is prepared to exercise its power . . . The mere fact that counsel has advised there are grounds of appeal will not always be a sufficient answer to the question as to whether or not an application has indeed been brought which was totally without merit".

8 If any doubt remained, the Criminal Practice Direction Amendment No 2 issued by the Lord Chief Justice in July 2014 repeats previous warnings about loss of time orders and the fact that renewing an application on the advice of counsel will not necessarily prevent a loss of time order at 68E.1 and 2.

9 The figures suggest that some applicants who might otherwise pursue hopeless applications heed those warnings. There is a significant reduction in the number of renewals, particularly in sentence applications, where the single judge has initialled the box. Nevertheless, a very large number seem to consider they have nothing to lose in renewing their application, often sending yet more voluminous documentation for the attention of the Full Court.

10 In our view, therefore, in every case where the court is presented with an unmeritorious application, consideration should be given to exercising these powers. The single judge should consider whether to initial the box, and if the application is renewed, the Full Court (be it a two or three judge court) should consider whether or not to make a loss of time order or costs order. If it decides to exercise the power, a statement to this effect would suffice:

"Despite being warned of the court's power to make a loss of time order, the applicant chose to pursue a totally unmeritorious application which has wasted the time of the court. Such applications hamper the court's ability to process meritorious applications in a timely fashion."

[9:12] *R v Secretary of State for the Home Department, ex p Bentley*
[1993] 4 All ER 442

Bentley was hanged in 1952 for murder. The Divisional Court held that the Secretary of State's refusal to recommend a posthumous pardon was unlawful.

Watkins LJ (at page 452):

The CCSU case made it clear that the powers of the court cannot be ousted merely by invoking the word 'prerogative'. The question is simply whether the nature and subject matter of the decision is amenable to the judicial process. Are the courts qualified to deal with the matter or does the decision involve such questions of policy that they should not intrude because they are ill-equipped to do so? Looked at in this way there must be cases in which the exercise of the royal prerogative is reviewable, in our judgment. If, for example, it was clear that the Home Secretary had refused to pardon someone solely on the grounds of their sex, race or religion, the courts would be expected to interfere and, in our judgment, would be entitled to do so.

We conclude therefore that some aspects of the exercise of the royal prerogative are amenable to the judicial process. We do not think that it is necessary for us to say more than this in the instant case. It will be for other courts to decide on a case by case basis whether the matter in question is reviewable or not.

(At page 454):

In an earlier part of the announcement of the decision, the Home Secretary, it will be recalled, stated that while he personally agreed that Derek Bentley should not have been hanged, he could not simply substitute his judgment for that of the then Home Secretary, Sir David Maxell Fyfe.

We understand the strength of the argument that, despite the fact that a free pardon does not eliminate the conviction, the grant of a free pardon should be reserved for cases where it can be established that the convicted person was morally and technically innocent. Furthermore, the policy of confining the grant of a free pardon to such cases has been followed by successive Secretaries of State for over a century. We therefore propose to set aside any question of a free (or full) pardon and look at the matter afresh.

The facts as disclosed by the contemporary papers are very striking. (1) Christopher Craig who fired the fatal shot, was not executed. (2) The jury recommended mercy in the case of Derek Bentley. (3) Both Mr Philip Allen, who wrote the memorandum dated 16 January 1953, and Sir Frank Newsam, the Permanent Under-Secretary, advised that effect should be given to the jury's recommendation for mercy. (4) The precedents established by the previous cases to which Mr Allen drew attention supported the argument for a reprieve. (5) Tests which had been carried out indicated that Bentley's mental state was 'just above the level of a feeble-minded person'. He was aged 19. (6) It seems clear from the memorandum initialled by the Secretary of State dated 22 January 1953 that he consulted Lord Goddard CJ, the trial judge, before making his final decision. It will be remembered that in his letter to the Secretary of State dated 12 December 1952 Lord Goddard CJ had said that he could find 'no mitigating circumstances in Bentley's case'.

It is clear from the affidavit of Mr Wilson that one of the ways in which the prerogative of mercy can be exercised is by the grant of a conditional pardon, whereby the penalty is removed on condition that a lesser sentence is served. Had Bentley been reprieved in 1953, the substitution of a sentence of life imprisonment would have constituted a conditional pardon.

These questions, therefore, arise. (a) Is there any objection in principle to the grant of a posthumous conditional pardon? (b) Was the Home Secretary in error in failing to consider the grant of a conditional pardon in this case?

On the first question it may be objected that a conditional pardon is inappropriate where the full penalty has already been paid. The answer to this objection, however, is that it is an error to regard the prerogative of mercy as a prerogative right which is only exercisable in cases which fall into specific categories. The prerogative is a flexible power and its exercise can and should be adapted to meet the circumstances of the particular case. We would adopt the language used by the Court of Appeal in New Zealand in *Burt v Governor General* [1992] 3 NZLR 672 at 681:

'... the prerogative of mercy [can no longer be regarded as] no more than an arbitrary monarchical right of grace and favour.'

It is now a constitutional safeguard against mistakes. It follows, therefore, that, in our view, there is no objection in principle to the grant of a posthumous conditional pardon whew a death sentence has already been carried out. The grant of such a pardon is a recognition by the state that a mistake was made and that a reprieve should have been granted.

We return to the facts of the present case. We can well understand the decision of the Home Secretary in so far as it constituted a response to a free (or full) pardon. But we are far from satisfied that he gave sufficient consideration to his power to grant some other form of pardon which would be suitable to the circumstances of the particular case. It is true, as the Home Secretary pointed out in the announcement of his decision, that in 1953 the then Home Secretary was working in a different climate of opinion. But, as we have already underlined the facts of this case are very striking. There is a compelling argument that even by the standards of 1953 the then Home Secretary's decision was clearly wrong.

In these circumstances the court, though it has no power to direct the way in which the prerogative of mercy should be exercised, has some role to play. The Home Secretary's decision was directed to the grant of a free pardon. In these circumstances we do not think it would be right to make any formal order nor is this an appropriate case for the grant of a declaration. Nevertheless, we would invite the Home Secretary to look at the matter again and to examine whether it would be just to exercise the prerogative of mercy in such a way as to give full recognition to the now generally accepted view that this young man should have been reprieved.

It was submitted to the court that even a limited form of pardon might lead to a flood of other applications seeking to reopen past convictions. No doubt account has to be taken of such a risk. From our examination of the papers in this case, however, and in the light of our understanding of the broad scope of the prerogative of mercy, we are satisfied that the matter is exceptional and requires further consideration. The decision is, of course, one for the Home Secretary and not for the court, but it seems to us that it should be possible to devise some formula which would amount to a clear acknowledgement that an injustice was done.

[9:13] Criminal Justice Act 1972 (as amended)
Section 36

36 Reference to Court of Appeal of point of law following acquittal on indictment

(1) Where a person tried on indictment has been acquitted (whether in respect of the whole or part of the indictment) the Attorney General may, if he desires the opinion of the Court of Appeal on a point of law which has arisen in the case, refer that point to the court, and the court shall, in accordance with this section, consider the point and give their opinion on it.

(2) For the purpose of their consideration of a point referred to them under this section the Court of Appeal shall hear argument –

  (a) by, or by counsel on behalf of, the Attorney General; and
  (b) if the acquitted person desires to present any argument to the court, by counsel on his behalf or, with the leave of the court, by the acquitted person himself.

(3) Where the Court of Appeal have given their opinion on a point referred to them under this section, the court may, of their own motion or in pursuance of an application in that behalf,

refer the point to Supreme Court if it appears to the Court of Appeal that the point ought to be considered by Supreme Court.

(4) If a point is referred to the Supreme Court under subsection (3) of this section, the Supreme Court shall consider the point and give its opinion on it accordingly.

(5) Where, in a point being referred to the Court of Appeal under this section or further referred to the Supreme Court, the acquitted person appears by counsel for the purpose of presenting any argument to the Court of Appeal or the Supreme Court, he shall be entitled to the payment out of central funds of such sums as are reasonably sufficient to compensate him for expenses properly incurred by him for the purpose of being represented on the reference or further reference; and any amount recoverable under this subsection shall be ascertained, as soon as practicable, by the registrar of criminal appeals or, as the case may be, such officer as may be prescribed by order of the Supreme Court.

(5A) Subsection (5) has effect subject to –

(a)   subsection (5B), and
(b)   regulations under section 20(1A)(d) of the Prosecution of Offences Act 1985 (as applied by this section).

(5B) A person is not entitled under subsection (5) to the payment of sums in respect of legal costs (as defined in section 16A of the Prosecution of Offences Act 1985) incurred in proceedings in the Court of Appeal.

(5C) Subsections (1A) to (1C) and (3) of section 20 of the Prosecution of Offences Act 1985 (regulations as to amounts ordered to be paid out of central funds) apply in relation to amounts payable out of central funds under subsection (5) as they apply in relation to amounts payable out of central funds in pursuance of costs orders made under section 16 of that Act.

(6) Subject to rules of court made under section 1(5) of the Criminal Appeal Act 1966 (power by rules to distribute business of Court of Appeal between its civil and criminal divisions), the jurisdiction of the Court of Appeal under this section shall be exercised by the criminal division of the court; and references in this section to the Court of Appeal shall be construed accordingly as references to that division of the court.

(7) A reference under this section shall not affect the trial in relation to which the reference is made or any acquittal in that trial.

[9:14] *A-G's Reference (No 3 of 1994)*
[1997] 3 All ER 936

The defendant stabbed a young woman, who was to his knowledge pregnant with his child. No injury to the foetus was detected and the defendant pleaded guilty to a charge of wounding the woman with intent to cause her grievous bodily harm. A few weeks after the stabbing, and as a result of it, the woman went into labour and gave birth to a grossly premature child who was considered to have only a 50% chance of survival. At the time of the birth it was clear that, contrary to earlier belief, the knife had penetrated the foetus. The child died 121 days later from a lung condition which was due to her premature birth but unconnected with the knife wound and the defendant was thereafter charged with her murder. At the trial, the judge directed an acquittal on the ground that no conviction for either murder or manslaughter was possible in law. The Attorney General subsequently referred to the Court of Appeal under s 36(1) of the Criminal Justice Act 1972 the questions, inter alia, (i) whether, subject to proof of the requisite intent, the crimes of murder and manslaughter could be committed where unlawful injury was deliberately inflicted to a mother carrying a child in utero where the child was subsequently born alive, existed independently of the mother and then died, the injuries while in utero either having caused or made a substantial contribution to the death, and (ii) whether the fact that the child's death resulted from injury to the mother rather than as a consequence of direct injury to the foetus could remove any liability for murder or manslaughter in those circumstances. The Court of Appeal answered the first question in the affirmative, on the ground that the foetus was to be treated as part of the mother until it had a separate existence of its own, but answered the second question in the negative. On the defendant's application the Court of Appeal referred the points to the House of Lords.

Held – (1) Murder could not be committed where unlawful injury was deliberately inflicted to a mother carrying a child in utero in circumstances where the child was subsequently born alive, enjoyed an existence independent of its mother and thereafter died, and where the injuries inflicted while in utero caused or contributed substantially to the death. Notwithstanding the dependence of the foetus on the mother for its survival until birth and the bond between them, the foetus could not be treated as part of the mother but was a unique organism. Accordingly, although there was no requirement that the person who died should be a person in being at the time the act causing the death was perpetrated, in the absence of an intention on the part of the defendant to injure either the foetus or the child which it would become, the required mens rea for murder was not present; it would be straining the concept of transferred malice too far to apply it in the circumstances since it would require the malice to be transferred not once but twice, namely from the mother to the foetus and from the foetus to the child.

(2) In those circumstances, however, manslaughter could be committed since the requisite mens rea to be proved in a case of manslaughter was an intention to do an act which was unlawful and which all sober and reasonable people would recognise as dangerous, i.e. likely to harm another person. Provided the defendant intended to do what he did, it was not necessary for him to know that his act was likely to injure the person who died as a result of it or to intend to injure that person. Since, in the instant case, the defendant intended to stab the child's mother and that was an unlawful and dangerous act, it followed that the requisite mens rea was established and although the child was a foetus at that time, on public policy grounds she was to be regarded as coming within that mens rea when she became a living person. Accordingly, the fact that the child's death was caused solely as a consequence of injury to the mother, rather than injury to the foetus, did not negative any liability for manslaughter, provided the jury were satisfied as to causation.

Decision of the Court of Appeal, Criminal Division [1996] 2 All ER 10 affirmed in part.

Lord Mustill (at page 949):

My Lords, the purpose of this inquiry has been to see whether the existing rules are based on principles sound enough to justify their extension to a case where the defendant acts without an intent to injure either the foetus or the child which it will become. In my opinion they are not. To give an affirmative answer requires a double 'transfer' of intent: first from the mother to the foetus and then from the foetus to the child as yet unborn. Then one would have to deploy the fiction (or at least the doctrine) which converts an intention to commit serious harm into the mens rea of murder. For me, this is too much. If one could find any logic in the rules I would follow it from one fiction to another, but whatever grounds there may once have been have long since disappeared. I am willing to follow old laws until they are overturned, but not to make a new law on a basis for which there is no principle.

Moreover, even on a narrower approach the argument breaks down. The effect of transferred malice, as I understand it, is that the intended victim and the actual victim are treated as if they were one, so that what was intended to happen to the first person (but did not happen) is added to what actually did happen to the second person (but was not intended to happen), with the result that what was intended and what happened are married to make a notionally intended and actually consummated crime. The cases are treated as if the actual victim had been the intended victim from the start. To make any sense of this process there must, as it seems to me, be some compatibility between the original intention and the actual occurrence, and this is, indeed, what one finds in the cases. There is no such compatibility here. The defendant intended to commit and did commit an immediate crime of violence to the mother. He committed no relevant violence to the foetus, which was not a person, either at the time or in the future, and intended no harm to the foetus or to the human person which it would become. If fictions are useful, as they can be, they are only damaged by straining them beyond their limits. I would not overstrain the idea of transferred malice by trying to make it fit the present case.

[9:15] Criminal Justice Act 1988 (as amended)

Sections 36; 133

36 Reviews of sentencing

(1) If it appears to the Attorney General –

   (a) that the sentencing of a person in a proceeding in the Crown Court has been unduly lenient; and
   (b) that the case is one to which this Part of this Act applies, he may, with the leave of the Court of Appeal, refer the case to them for them to review the sentencing of that person; and on such a reference the Court of Appeal may –
   (i)   quash any sentence passed on him in the proceeding; and
   (ii) in place of it pass such sentence as they think appropriate for the case and as the court below had power to pass when dealing with him.

(2) Without prejudice to the generality of subsection (1) above, the condition specified in paragraph (a) of that subsection may be satisfied if it appears to the Attorney General that the judge;

   (a) erred in law as to his powers of sentencing; or
   (b) failed to impose a sentence required by –
   (zi) section 1A(5) of the Prevention of Crime Act 1953;
   (i)   section 51A(2) of the Firearms Act 1968;
   (ia) section 139AA(7) of this Act;
   (ii) section 110(2) or 111(2) of the Powers of Criminal Courts (Sentencing) Act 2000;
   (iii) section 224A, 225(2) or 226(2) of the Criminal Justice Act 2003; or
   (iv) under section 29(4) or (6) of the Violent Crime Reduction Act 2006.

(3) For the purposes of this Part of this Act any two or more sentences are to be treated as passed in the same proceeding if they would be so treated for the purposes of section 11 of the Criminal Appeal Act 1968.

(3A) Where a reference under this section relates to an order under subsection (2) of section 269 of the Criminal Justice Act 2003 (determination of minimum term in relation to mandatory life sentence), the Court of Appeal shall not, in deciding what order under that section is appropriate for the case, make any allowance for the fact that the person to whom it relates is being sentenced for a second time.

(4) No judge shall sit as a member of the Court of Appeal on the hearing of, or shall determine any application in proceedings incidental or preliminary to, a reference under this section of a sentence passed by himself.

(5) Where the Court of Appeal have concluded their review of a case referred to them under this section the Attorney General or the person to whose sentencing the reference relates may refer a point of law involved in any sentence passed on that person in the proceeding to the Supreme Court for its opinion, and the Supreme Court shall consider the point and give its opinion on it accordingly, and either remit the case to the Court of Appeal to be dealt with or itself deal with the case.

(6) A reference under subsection (5) above shall be made only with the leave of the Court of Appeal or the Supreme Court; and leave shall not be granted unless it is certified by the Court of Appeal that the point of law is of general public importance and it appears to the Court of Appeal or the Supreme Court (as the case may be) that the point is one which ought to be considered by the Supreme Court.

(7) For the purpose of dealing with a case under this section the Supreme Court may exercise any powers of the Court of Appeal.

(8) The supplementary provisions contained in Schedule 3 to this Act shall have effect.

(9) In the application of this section to Northern Ireland –

(a) any reference to the Attorney General shall be construed as a reference to the Director of Public Prosecutions for Northern Ireland;
(aa) the reference to section 51A(2) of the Firearms Act 1968 shall be construed as a reference to Article 70(2) of the Firearms (Northern Ireland) Order 2004;
(ab) the reference to section 29(4) or (6) of the Violent Crime Reduction Act 2006 shall be construed as a reference to paragraph 2(4) or (5) of Schedule 2 to that Act;
(b) the references to sections 11 and 35(1) of the Criminal Appeal Act 1968 shall be construed as references to sections 10(2) and 33(1) of the Criminal Appeal (Northern Ireland) Act 1980, respectively;
(c) the reference in subsection (3A) to an order specified in subsection (3B) shall be construed as a reference to an order under Article 5(1) of the Life Sentences (Northern Ireland) Order 2001, and
(d) subsection (2)(b) shall be read as if it included a reference to a sentence required by section 7(2) of the Human Trafficking and Exploitation (Criminal Justice and Support for Victims) Act (Northern Ireland) 2015.

133 Compensation for miscarriages of justice

(1) Subject to subsection (2) below, when a person has been convicted of a criminal offence and when subsequently his conviction has been reversed or he has been pardoned on the ground that a new or newly discovered fact shows beyond reasonable doubt that there has been a miscarriage of justice, the Secretary of State shall pay compensation for the miscarriage

of justice to the person who has suffered punishment as a result of such conviction or, if he is dead, to his personal representatives, unless the non-disclosure of the unknown fact was wholly or partly attributable to the person convicted.

(1ZA) For the purposes of subsection (1), there has been a miscarriage of justice in relation to a person convicted of a criminal offence in England and Wales or, in a case where subsection (6H) applies, Northern Ireland, if and only if the new or newly discovered fact shows beyond reasonable doubt that the person did not commit the offence (and references in the rest of this Part to a miscarriage of justice are to be construed accordingly).

(2) No payment of compensation under this section shall be made unless an application for such compensation has been made to the Secretary of State before the end of the period of 2 years beginning with the date on which the conviction of the person concerned is reversed or he is pardoned.

(2A) But the Secretary of State may direct that an application for compensation made after the end of that period is to be treated as if it had been made within that period if the Secretary of State considers that there are exceptional circumstances which justify doing so.

(3) The question whether there is a right to compensation under this section shall be determined by the Secretary of State.

(4) If the Secretary of State determines that there is a right to such compensation, the amount of the compensation shall be assessed by an assessor appointed by the Secretary of State.

(4A) Section 133A applies in relation to the assessment of the amount of the compensation.

(5) In this section "reversed" shall be construed as referring to a conviction having been quashed –

   (a)   on an appeal out of time;
   (b)   on a reference –
         (i)   under the Criminal Appeal Act 1995; or
         (ii)   under section 194B of the Criminal Procedure (Scotland) Act 1995 (c.46);
   (c)   on an appeal under section 7 of the Terrorism Act 2000;
   (e)   under section 188(1)(b) of the Criminal Procedure (Scotland) Act 1995;
   (f)   on an appeal under Schedule 3 to the Terrorism Prevention and Investigation Measures Act 2011; or
   (g)   on an appeal under Schedule 4 to the Counter-Terrorism and Security Act 2015.

(5A) But in a case where –

   (a)   a person's conviction for an offence is quashed on an appeal out of time, and
   (b)   the person is to be subject to a retrial, the conviction is not to be treated for the purposes of this section as "reversed" unless and until the person is acquitted of all offences at the retrial or the prosecution indicates that it has decided not to proceed with the retrial.

(5B) In subsection (5A) above any reference to a retrial includes a reference to proceedings held following the remission of a matter to a magistrates' court by the Crown Court under section 48(2)(b) of the Supreme Court Act 1981.
(6) For the purposes of this section and section 133A a person suffers punishment as a result of a conviction when sentence is passed on him for the offence of which he was convicted.

(6A) Subject to what follows, in the application of this section in relation to a person ("P") convicted in Northern Ireland of a criminal offence, in subsections (1) to (4) any reference to the Secretary of State is to be read as a reference to the Department of Justice in Northern Ireland.

(6B) If P is pardoned, subsection (6A) applies only if the pardon is a devolved pardon.

(6C) Subsections (6D) to (6H) apply if –

   (a) P's conviction is reversed or P is given a devolved pardon,
   (b) an application for compensation is made in relation to P's conviction,
   (c) the application is made before the end of the period mentioned in subsection (2) or, if it is made after the end of that period, the Department of Justice gives a direction under subsection (2A), and
   (d) the Department of Justice has reason to believe that protected information may be relevant to the application (for example, because the court which quashed P's conviction did not make public (in whole or in part) its reasons for quashing P's conviction).

(6D) The Department of Justice must refer the application to the Secretary of State who must then take a view as to whether or not any protected information is relevant to the application.

(6E) If the Secretary of State takes the view that no protected information is relevant to the application, the Secretary of State must refer the application back to the Department of Justice to be dealt with by the Department accordingly.

(6F) If the Secretary of State takes the view that protected information is relevant to the application, the Secretary of State must refer the application back to the Department of Justice to be dealt with by the Department accordingly unless the Secretary of State is also of the view that, on the grounds of national security, it is not feasible for the Department (including any assessor appointed by the Department) to be provided with either –

   (a) the protected information, or
   (b) a summary of the protected information that is sufficiently detailed to enable the Department (including any assessor) to deal properly with the application.

(6G) If the Secretary of State refers the application back to the Department of Justice under subsection (6F), the Secretary of State must provide the Department with either –

   (a) the protected information, or
   (b) a summary of the protected information that appears to the Secretary of State to be sufficiently detailed to enable the Department (including any assessor) to deal properly with the application.

(6H) If the Secretary of State is not required to refer the application back to the Department of Justice –

   (a) subsections (3) and (4) apply to the application ignoring subsection (6A), and
   (b) any compensation payable on the application is payable by the Secretary of State.

(6I) In this section "protected information" means information the disclosure of which may be against the interests of national security.

(6J) In this section "devolved pardon" means –

(a) a pardon given after the coming into force of the Northern Ireland Act 1998 (Amendment of Schedule 3) Order 2010 in the exercise of powers under section 23(2) of the Northern Ireland Act 1998;

(b) a pardon given before the coming into force of that Order which, had it been given after the coming into force of that Order, would have had to have been given in the exercise of powers under section 23(2) of the 1998 Act (ignoring article 25(2) of the Northern Ireland Act 1998 (Devolution of Policing and Justice Functions) Order 2010).

(6K) The pardons covered by subsection (6J)(a) include pardons given in reliance on article 25(2) of the Northern Ireland Act 1998 (Devolution of Policing and Justice Functions) Order 2010.

(7) Schedule 12 shall have effect.

[9:16] Bailin, A and Craven, E, 'Compensation for miscarriages of justice – who now qualifies?'
[2014] Crim LR 511

The law on compensation for miscarriages of justice is currently in a very unsatisfactory state. One of the hallmarks of any high quality criminal justice system is an acceptance of its own fallibility and a willingness to pay compensation when the system has failed. At the same time, many would say there is an important interest in ensuring that people guilty of serious crimes are not compensated if they fortuitously escape their "just deserts". Some might be willing to countenance the possibility that if a guilty person is convicted following an unfair procedure, and has his conviction quashed only after having spent many years in prison, he should be entitled to some form of compensation – the system has failed by not speedily overturning a wrongful conviction, even if the failure is not as egregious as where the wronged person is innocent. Reconciling these conflicting objectives presents difficult legal challenges. Recent domestic and European Court decisions severely limit the scope for redress for wrongful convictions, but serious uncertainties and contradictions remain.

Compensation for miscarriages of justice – s.133 of the Criminal Justice Act 1988

Section 133 of the Criminal Justice Act 1988 provides a right to compensation for those whose convictions for a criminal offence have been reversed, or who have been pardoned, on the ground that a new or newly discovered fact shows that there has been a "miscarriage of justice". Subsection (1) provides:

> "Subject to subsection (2) below, when a person has been convicted of a criminal offence and when subsequently his conviction has been reversed or he has been pardoned on the ground that a new or newly discovered fact shows beyond reasonable doubt that there has been a miscarriage of justice, the Secretary of State shall pay compensation for the miscarriage of justice to the person who has suffered punishment as a result of such conviction or, if he is dead, to his personal representatives, unless the non-disclosure of the unknown fact was wholly or partly attributable to the person convicted."

The statute applies a criminal standard of proof: the new or newly discovered fact must show "beyond reasonable doubt" that there has been a miscarriage of justice. Section 133 gives effect to the United Kingdom's treaty obligations under art.14(6) of the International Covenant on Civil and Political Rights 1966.

The expression "miscarriage of justice" is one that is heavily used in everyday parlance, and it might be thought that the term has a settled meaning, particularly when compensation for miscarriages has formed part of the United Kingdom's international obligations for over 30 years. Nevertheless, the concept has generated lengthy and conflicting judgments in the highest courts. The leading case is *R. (on the application of Adams) v Secretary of State for Justice* [2011] UKSC 18, in which a nine-judge Supreme Court attempted to provide a clear definition of the meaning of the term. The court eventually held (by a bare majority) that the true meaning of "miscarriage of justice" in s.133 was not restricted to circumstances where conclusive proof of innocence was established. The majority concluded that the phrase included cases where a new or newly discovered fact showed that the evidence against the defendant had been so undermined that no conviction could possibly be based on it; and that, in such circumstances, it could be shown to be beyond reasonable doubt that the defendant had no case to answer and the prosecution should not have been brought.

The court was bitterly divided, with Lord Brown expressing (in Lady Hale's words) a "palpable sense of outrage" that someone who could not prove their innocence might be entitled to compensation for having suffered a miscarriage of justice. The court was polarised by the earlier decision in *R. (on the application of Mullen) v Home Secretary* [2004] UKHL 18, where the applicant did not actively contest his guilt but had his conviction quashed because of gross misconduct by the state prior to his trial. The House of Lords denied him compensation, but Lord Bingham and Lord Steyn disagreed on whether proof of innocence was a pre-condition of eligibility for compensation under s.133. The Supreme Court in *Adams* was unable even to agree on fundamental issues such as whether the Criminal Division of the Court of Appeal has the power to pronounce a successful appellant innocent, or whether its role is merely confined to assessing the safety of convictions.[3]

A person whose conviction is quashed is presumed innocent (whatever the reason for the quashing) but the related question is whether the presumption operates outside the criminal trial so as to entitle the person to compensation for a miscarriage of justice. In *Adams* the Supreme Court unanimously held (albeit for a variety of different reasons) that a refusal to pay compensation following the quashing of a conviction did not violate the presumption of innocence in art.6(2) of the ECHR.

Compensation and retrials

Given the divergence of views in the Supreme Court, further litigation (at home and in Strasbourg) was bound to follow. The first problem concerned retrials: s.133(5A) permits compensation if a person's conviction is quashed at an out-of-time appeal and that person is then acquitted at a retrial. But the Supreme Court's requirement that a new fact must have "so undermined [the case against the defendant] that no conviction could possibly be based on it" would seem to be inconsistent with any notion of a retrial.

The only qualifying scenario falling within s.133(5A) would appear to be where the Court of Appeal allows an appeal, orders a retrial but the trial judge then prevents the case from going to the jury (e.g. by allowing a submission of no case to answer). For example, in the case of Barry George, George was acquitted of the murder of Jill Dando after the Court of Appeal ruled that forensic evidence adduced at his original trial should never have been admitted. The Court of Appeal ordered a retrial, and George was acquitted by a fresh jury. George could not show that no conviction could possibly be based upon the evidence against him and he therefore failed to qualify for any compensation: *R. (on the application of Ali) v Secretary of State for Justice* [2013] EWHC 72 (Admin). The Divisional Court held that only in "the most exceptional circumstances" could an individual obtain compensation under s.133 following a retrial where the case against them was allowed to go before the jury. However applying the formulation in *Adams*, it is difficult to conceive of *any* circumstances that would entitle a person in that position to receive compensation for their wrongful conviction. On appeal, the Court of Appeal said it would be "irrational if entitlement to compensation depended on whether or not a retrial had taken place", suggesting there was no good reason for distinguishing between a situation where a conviction is quashed and no retrial is ordered, and a situation where a conviction is quashed and the individual is then cleared at a subsequent retrial. However, the Court of Appeal did not explain how such a case could satisfy the requirement in *Adams* that "no conviction could possibly be based on" the evidence against the applicant.

The Court of Appeal is surely right as a matter of principle that the existence of a retrial should not prove fatal to a claim for compensation: s.133(5A) expressly permits compensation following retrial. Moreover, it would be inconsistent with the approach adopted by the Grand Chamber of the European Court of Human Rights. In *Allen v United Kingdom* (2013) 36 B.H.R.C. 1 the applicant argued there was a sufficient link between miscarriage of justice compensation proceedings and the anterior criminal proceedings for art.6(2) to apply outside the criminal trial. In other words, because it involves a close appraisal of the *reasons* for the successful out-of-time criminal appeal, a compensation decision itself engages art.6(2). The Grand Chamber accepted that argument (effectively disagreeing with *Adams* to that extent) but went on to hold that unless the acquittal is "an acquittal on the merits" then the presumption of innocence will not be violated by a subsequent refusal to grant compensation. In *Allen's* case, the Court of Appeal had quashed her manslaughter conviction based on the hypothesis concerning "shaken baby syndrome" (which had been accepted at the trial and subsequently discredited) and did not order a retrial. In these circumstances the applicant was unable to establish an acquittal on the merits and was therefore ineligible for redress under art.6(2), despite having served her sentence in full by the time of her appeal.

Precisely what constitutes an acquittal on the merits is unclear. Certainly, a retrial where a defendant is acquitted by a jury falls within the definition; however, it is unclear whether the concept is capable of embracing other circumstances too. In *KF v United Kingdom* (30178/09) Unreported September 3, 2013 ECtHR, the Court of Appeal had quashed the applicant's conviction on the basis that new medical evidence cast doubt on evidence given at the trial and declined to order a retrial. The Strasbourg Court held that although the quashing of the conviction resulted in an acquittal

> "it was not an acquittal 'on the merits' in a true sense: although formally an acquittal, the termination of the criminal proceedings against the applicant might be considered to share more of the features present in cases where criminal proceedings have been discontinued".

Thus, Strasbourg's approach also begs the question of whether the Criminal Division of the Court of Appeal ever has the power to pronounce an appellant innocent (akin to an acquittal on the merits). It is also in conflict with the Supreme Court's formula in *Adams* – if an acquittal on the merits is necessary in order to qualify for compensation, then an order by a judge at a retrial preventing the case from going to the jury would not be an acquittal on the merits.

Section 133 and art.6(2) – squaring the circle

The combined effect of the case law is a bizarre contradiction: a full retrial is almost invariably fatal to a claim for compensation under s.133; while the absence of a full retrial would seem to be fatal to a claim for compensation based on art.6(2). Attempting to reconcile *Adams* and *Allen* therefore requires a case in which: (i) the Court of Appeal orders a retrial (because unless it does so there can be no acquittal on the merits); and (ii) the appellant is acquitted by the jury at that retrial; (iii) in "highly exceptional circumstances" where the decision to leave the case to the jury does not take the applicant outside the scope of *Adams*. The position is complicated further by the fact that in order to qualify for compensation the prior appeal must have succeeded because the new fact had the effect that "the evidence against the defendant had been so undermined that no conviction could possibly be based on it" – precisely a case in which no retrial is likely to be ordered. Moreover, since compensation is not possible following an in-time appeal (that is the system working properly) retrials are correspondingly less likely after an out-of-time appeal (when the appellant may already have served their sentence in full). Satisfying the combined tests of the Supreme Court and European Court seems to produce a "class with no members" – a wholly unsatisfactory outcome for a system intended to remedy serious errors in the criminal justice process.

Tightening the test – legislative proposals

If the position described above were not hard enough for those seeking compensation for a miscarriage of justice, Parliament has decided that the law needs further tightening. Section 175 of the Anti-social Behaviour, Crime and Policing Act 2014 effectively reverses *Adams* by making it a condition of compensation that the new or newly discovered fact "shows beyond reasonable doubt that the person did not commit the offence" of which they were convicted.

The wording of s.175 was the subject of much debate during the Bill's passage through Parliament. An earlier version of the section, cl.161, would have required the new or newly discovered fact to show beyond reasonable doubt that the person "was innocent of the offence". The Joint Committee on Human Rights initially considered that cl.161 would violate the presumption of innocence both at common law and in art.6 of the ECHR. After that Report was published, the Strasbourg Court revisited the question of compensation for miscarriages of justice in the admissibility decisions of *ALF v United Kingdom* and *Adams v United Kingdom* (5908/12 and 70601/11) Unreported November 12, 2013 ECtHR. The applicants challenged the compatibility of s.133 with art.6(2). The Court held that s.133 did not require any assessment of the applicants' criminal guilt and did not call into question the innocence of an acquitted person. The interpretation of s.133 adopted by the Supreme Court was therefore compatible with art.6(2). In *Adams v United Kingdom* the applicant directly challenged the rejection of his presumption of innocence arguments by the Supreme Court. The Strasbourg Court stated that the "clear test" articulated by Lord Phillips in *Adams* established that "questions of guilt and innocence are irrelevant to proceedings brought under section 133". At the same time, in *ALF* the Court suggested that "to avoid . . . bringing into play the presumption of innocence" it would be "prudent" to avoid using the language of guilt and innocence when determining applications for compensation under s.133. The implication seems to be that, if the test does depend on proof of innocence, it would not comply with art.6.

Following those admissibility decisions, the Joint Committee on Human Rights modified its stance in relation to cl.161. The Committee recommended that the reference to "innocence" should be deleted (since its inclusion would be incompatible with art.6(2)) and suggested that the test formulated by Lord Phillips in *Adams* (which was adopted by a bare majority of the Supreme Court) should be elevated to a statutory footing. Neither the Committee nor the Strasbourg Court addressed the issue of retrials.

The House of Lords initially rejected cl.161, instead endorsing a statutory codification of the *Adams* test in an amendment proposed by the crossbench peer and barrister Lord Pannick QC. Ultimately, however, Parliament did not adopt the Committee's proposed formulation, although the language of s.175 appears to have been influenced by the Committee's warning to eschew any express reference to innocence. Nevertheless, there is no difference in substance between "was innocent of the offence" and "did not commit the offence" and decisions applying the new s.175 formulation are bound to give rise to art.6 arguments.

During the 2014 Act's passage through Parliament, the Minister for Policing, Criminal Justice and Victims, Damian Green MP, acknowledged that, "Of course, the substance is not different" between the two formulations, which only differ in a "non-legal" sense. The Minister gave the following rationale for requiring applicants to establish conclusive proof of innocence:

> "The Government believe that a miscarriage of justice arises only when there is in existence a fact which entirely exonerates the accused: in other words, a fact which makes it unquestionable that the accused did not commit the crime. In such cases, it is only the ignorance of this fact that allowed the accused to be convicted in the first place. What we are seeking to define is something far more than merely a failure in the investigative or trial processes. We are seeking to define a clear miscarriage of justice which is – and, in our view, can only be – the wrongful conviction of the innocent."

On that basis, an individual who is in fact innocent must nonetheless forego compensation unless he can prove not merely that the evidence against him was insufficient to sustain any conviction, but that he was unquestionably innocent of the crime in question. It is therefore not enough to establish actual innocence on a balance of probabilities, or even to persuade the Secretary of State there is a high likelihood he did not commit the crime. Instead he must prove his innocence to the criminal standard of proof. However, as Lady Hale explained in *Adams*:

"Innocence as such is not a concept known to our criminal justice system. We distinguish between the guilty and the not guilty. A person is only guilty if the state can prove his guilt beyond reasonable doubt. This is, as Viscount Sankey LC so famously put it in *Woolmington v Director of Public Prosecutions [1935] AC 462*, at p 481, 'the golden thread' which is always to be seen 'throughout the web of the English criminal law'. Only then is the state entitled to punish him. Otherwise he is not guilty, irrespective of whether he is in fact innocent. If it can be conclusively shown that the state was not entitled to punish a person, it seems to me that he should be entitled to compensation for having been punished. He does not have to prove his innocence at his trial and it seems wrong in principle that he should be required to prove his innocence now."

Conclusion

When considering whether compensation ought to be conditional upon proof of actual innocence, it is worth noting that none of the landmark cases on miscarriage of justice involved a formal pronouncement by the Court of Appeal that the applicants were innocent, despite intense public pressure to do so: Birmingham Six; Guildford Four; Maguire Seven; Judith Ward; Cardiff Three; Sally Clark. Despite its consideration by the most senior courts, and notwithstanding the recent intervention of Parliament to tighten the law yet further, the current law on compensation for miscarriages remains contradictory, confused and its compatibility with art.6 is open to question. One thing, however, does seem clear: further litigation at the highest levels is inevitable.

[9:17] *Report of the Royal Commission on Criminal Justice*
(1993) HMSO, Cmnd 2263 (at page 183)

Case for new body

2 In *R v Pinfold* the Court of Appeal held that it had no jurisdiction to entertain a second application for leave to appeal in the same case even where fresh evidence had emerged since the

dismissal of the earlier appeal. The Court of Appeal can only consider such a case again if the Home Secretary uses his power under section 17 of the Criminal Appeal Act 1968 to refer it to the Court of Appeal, when the case is treated for all purposes as an appeal to the court by the convicted person. The power to refer cases in this way is limited to those tried on indictment; it does not include summary convictions by magistrates' courts.

3 If, therefore, an unsuccessful appellant wishes to reopen his or her case in the courts, the Home Secretary must be persuaded to refer it to the Court of Appeal. The only alternative course is to persuade the Home Secretary to recommend to the sovereign that the Royal Prerogative of Mercy be exercised. This alternative, which is described more fully in the next paragraph, is most often used when the case involves a summary conviction in the magistrates' courts. It is very seldom exercised when the option of a reference under section 17 is available, because successive Home Secretaries have been understandably reluctant to reverse a decision of the courts, preferring instead to ask the courts to reconsider the case as the statute envisages. The use of the Royal Prerogative to override convictions on indictment is limited to cases where there are convincing reasons for believing that a person is innocent but a reference to the Court of Appeal is not practicable, for example because relevant material would not be admissible in evidence. The Home Office told us in written evidence that such cases are extremely rare.

4 If the Royal Prerogative of Mercy is exercised by the grant of a free pardon, the effect is that so far as possible the person is relieved of all penalties and other consequences of the conviction. Alternatively, a sentence can be varied so as to give special remission of all or part of the penalty imposed by the court. This may be done for compassionate purposes, for example to give early release to prisoners with terminal illnesses, or in order to reward prisoners who have given exceptional assistance to prison staff, the police, or the prosecuting authorities. The exercise of the Royal Prerogative in this way is not the same as the grant of a free pardon. Nor does the exercise of the Royal Prerogative amount to the quashing of the conviction, even if a free pardon is granted. The conviction stands and can only be quashed by a separate application to the Court of Appeal.

5 The available figures for the number of cases referred by the Home Secretary to the Court of Appeal under section 17 of the Criminal Appeal Act 1968 show that the power is not often exercised. From 1981 to the end of 1988, 36 cases involving 48 appellants were referred to the Court of Appeal as a result of the doubts raised about the safety of the convictions concerned. This represents an average of between 4 and 5 cases a year. In the years 1989–1992, 28 cases involving 49 appellants have been referred, including a number of cases stemming from the terrorist incidents of the early 1970s and inquiries into the activities of the West Midlands serious crimes squad. We were told by the Home Office that it receives between 700 and 800 cases a year which are no longer before the courts and where it is claimed that there has been a wrongful conviction. (The figure for 1992 was 790 of which 634 involved a custodial sentence). Plainly, therefore, a rigorous sifting process is applied, and only a small percentage of cases end in a reference to the Court of Appeal under section 17.

6 There is in theory no restriction on the numbers or categories of cases which the Home Secretary may refer to the Court of Appeal under section 17 since the section gives him discretion to refer cases 'if he thinks fit'. In practice, however, as Sir John May observed in his second report on the Maguire case, the Home Secretary and the civil servants advising him operate within strict self-imposed limits. These rest both upon constitutional considerations and upon the approach of the Court of Appeal itself to its own powers. The Home Secretary does not

refer cases to the Court of Appeal merely to enable that court to reconsider matters that it has already considered. He will normally only refer a conviction if there is new evidence or some other consideration of substance which was not before the trial court. Successive Home Secretaries have adopted this approach, and not only because they have thought that it would be wrong for Ministers to suggest to the Court of Appeal that a different decision should have been reached by the courts on the same facts. They have also taken the view that there is no purpose in their referring a case where there is no real possibility of the Court of Appeal taking a different view than it did on the original appeal because of the lack of fresh evidence of some other new consideration of substance.

7 The effect of this second criterion was examined in depth by Sir John May as part of his inquiry into the case of the Maguires. We cannot do better than quote his conclusion:

'... there is no doubt that the criterion so defined was and is a limiting one and has resulted in the responsible officials within the Home Office taking a substantially restricted view of cases to which their attention has been drawn ... The very nature and terms of the self-imposed limits on the Home Secretary's power to refer cases have led the Home Office only to respond to the representations which have been made to it in relation to particular convictions rather than to carry out its own investigations into the circumstances of a particular case or the evidence given at trial ... the approach of the Home Office was throughout reactive, it was never thought proper for the Department to become proactive.'

8 Sir John May refers later in his second report on the Maguires to the evidence that he heard from Home Office officials and from a former Home Secretary, Mr Hurd, expressing views on alternative machinery for considering alleged miscarriages of justice. This evidence led him to the conclusion that some alternative machinery was indeed required in place of the existing power of the Home Secretary to refer such cases to the Court of Appeal under section 17 of the Criminal Appeal Act 1968. We set out below our view of what the alternative machinery should be. First, however, we give our reasons for recommending (as we do in paragraph 11 below) the creation of a new body independent of both the Government and the courts to be responsible for dealing with allegations that a miscarriage of justice has occurred.

9 Our recommendation is based on the proposition, adequately established in our view by Sir John May's Inquiry; that the role assigned to the Home Secretary and his Department under the existing legislation is incompatible with the constitutional separation of powers as between the courts and the executive. The scrupulous observance of constitutional principles has meant a reluctance on the part of the Home Office to enquire deeply enough into the cases put to it and, given the constitutional background, we do not think that this is likely to change significantly in the future.

10 We have concluded that it is neither necessary nor desirable that the Home Secretary should be directly responsible for the consideration and investigation of alleged miscarriages of justice as well as being responsible for law and order and for the police. The view that these two heavy responsibilities should be divided was expressed to Sir John May's Inquiry by a former Home Secretary and confirmed in oral evidence to us by the then Home Secretary and two of his predecessors.

11 We recommend therefore that the Home Secretary's power to refer cases to the Court of Appeal under section 17 of the Criminal Appeal Act 1968 should be removed and that a new body should be set up to consider alleged miscarriages of justice, to supervise their investigation if further inquiries are needed, and to refer appropriate cases to the Court of Appeal. We

suggest that this body might be known as the Criminal Cases Review Authority. We refer to it in what follows as 'the Authority'.

Role of the authority

12 We recommend that the role of the Authority should be to consider allegations put to it that a miscarriage of justice may have occurred. The applicant's approach to the Authority would normally be made either after his or her conviction had been upheld by the Court of Appeal or after he or she had failed to obtain leave to appeal. In cases which seemed to the Authority to call for further investigation, it would ensure that that investigation was launched. Where the Authority instructed the police to conduct investigations, it would be responsible for supervising the investigation and would have the power to require the police to follow up those lines of inquiry that seemed to it necessary for the thorough re-examination of the case. Where the result of the investigation indicated that there were reasons for supposing that a miscarriage of justice might have occurred, the Authority would refer the case to the Court of Appeal, which would consider it as though it were an appeal referred to it by the Home Secretary under section 17 now. Where, in the Authority's view, the investigation revealed no grounds for such a reference, for example, because it revealed fresh material confirming the correctness of the conviction, an explanation with reasons would be given to the applicant.

Relationships of the authority with government and with Court of Appeal

13 We have already explained why we believe that the Authority should be independent of the Government. It will, however, be necessary for the Government to provide the resources to enable it to operate and a Government Minister will have to be responsible for appointing its members and accounting to Parliament for its activities. We recommend that the legislation which established it gives it operational independence but requires it to submit an annual report to the Minister concerned, who would in turn be required to lay the report before Parliament. The Minister would also be required to answer to Parliament for any suggestion that the Authority was inadequately resourced or not properly constituted for the task it was required to perform. We see these arrangements as necessary in order to ensure that the new system for correcting miscarriages of justice is working properly. We do not see them as compromising its independence.

14 We recommend that the Chairman of the Authority be appointed by the Queen on the advice of the Prime Minister as is done in the cases of Lords Justice of Appeal. Other members might be appointed by the Lord Chancellor. The Home Secretary, as the Minister responsible for criminal justice policy and for law and order, should be responsible for reporting to Parliament for the way in which the new arrangements are implemented.

15 We believe that there are cogent arguments for the Authority to be independent of the Court of Appeal. Their roles are different and, as we have said in the last chapter, we do not think that the Court of Appeal is either the most suitable or the best qualified body to supervise investigations of this kind. We have recommended in chapter ten that the Court of Appeal should be empowered if it thinks fit to refer cases to the Authority for investigation, and that the Authority should be required to report the outcome of any such investigation to the Court of Appeal. But we do not see the Authority as coming within the court structure. Nor, equally importantly, would it be empowered to take judicial decisions that are properly matters for the Court of Appeal.

16 When, therefore, an investigation is completed whose results the Authority believes should be considered by the Court of Appeal, we recommend that it should refer the case to that court, together with a statement of its reasons for so referring it. It should at the same time

provide the court with such supporting material as it believes to be appropriate and desirable in the light of its investigations, and which in its view may be admissible, though without any recommendation or conclusion as to whether or not a miscarriage of justice has occurred. It would be for the Court of Appeal, on receiving a case referred in this way, to treat it as an appeal from the Crown Court. That is to say, it would ensure that the defence and the prosecution received a copy of the statement of reasons and supporting material sent to it, together with any additional material (see paragraph 31) that the Authority thought fit. It would then be for the appellant to present his or her case in whatever manner seemed best. As happens with references by the Home Secretary under section 17 now, it should continue to be open to the appellant to raise before the Court of Appeal any matter of law or fact, or mixed law and fact, as he or she wishes, regardless of whether or not it was included in the papers sent to the court by the Authority. The appellant should also be free to appear before the court if he or she so wishes.

17 As we have explained, we do not see the Home Secretary as continuing to have in general any function in relation to individual cases of miscarriage of justice. We do, however, assume that he or she will retain ministerial responsibility for the exercise of the Royal Prerogative of Mercy. For the reasons that the Home Office gave in oral evidence, and to which we refer above (paragraph 6), it will seldom if ever be necessary or desirable to exercise the Royal Prerogative in cases where it is concluded that a miscarriage of justice may have taken place To do so would be to override the decisions of the courts, whose function it properly is to determine such cases. Nevertheless, we do not entirely rule out the need in the very exceptional case for the Authority to refer the results of its consideration and investigation to the Home Secretary to consider the exercise of the Royal Prerogative. This should only be where the Court of Appeal is unlikely to be able to consider the case under the existing rules.

18 The one category of case that has been drawn to our attention where this might happen is if the Court of Appeal were to regard as inadmissible evidence which seemed to the Authority to show that a miscarriage of justice might have occurred. We have been told by the Home Office in written evidence that these cases are rare and we hope that, following the outcome of the review of the rules of evidence that we have recommended in Chapter Eight, they will become rarer still in the future. We cannot envisage any other circumstances in which the courts would be so far unable to provide a remedy that it ought to be suggested to the Home Secretary that he should recommend the exercise of the Royal Prerogative. There may, however, be unforeseeable circumstances where the need might arise. We therefore recommend that the possible use of the Royal Prerogative be kept open for the exceptional case. We emphasise, however, that it is undesirable for the courts to be deprived of powers to quash a conviction where the evidence, whatever its status, seems clearly to show that the appellant is innocent. We therefore, as we have already said, attach great importance to the Law Commission's review of the rules of evidence which we have recommended.

19 The primary function of the Authority will be to consider and if necessary investigate cases which have already passed through the criminal justice system and in which the right of appeal has been exercised. An applicant who is told by the Authority that it will not intervene in his or her case should always be free to try again, although he or she is likely to need to present flesh evidence or argument to stand any better chance of success. We therefore do not believe that there should be any right of appeal from the Authority's decisions to investigate or not to investigate the cases put to it and to refer or not to refer them to the Court of Appeal. In our view, the Authority's decisions should also not be subject to judicial review. We therefore recommend that there should be neither a right of appeal nor a right to judicial review in

relation to decisions by the Authority, but that it should be free to consider a case more than once if that seems in the circumstances to be an appropriate course.

Composition and accountability of the authority

20 The Authority should consist of several members, the precise numbers depending on its workload at any particular time. Not all need be full-time. We do not favour a single person, however well qualified and eminent, filling the role on the model of the ombudsman, since we believe that the consideration of possible miscarriages of justice will benefit from bringing to bear several different points of view. Both lawyers and lay persons should be represented. We recommend that the Chairman should be chosen for his or her personal qualities rather than for any particular qualifications or background that he or she may have. We recommend, however, given the importance of the Authority being seen to be independent of the courts in the performance of its functions, that the Chairman should not be a serving member of the judiciary.

[9:18] Criminal Appeal Act 1995 (as amended)

Sections 8; 13

8 The Commission

(1) There shall be a body corporate to be known as the Criminal Cases Review Commission.

(2) The Commission shall not be regarded as the servant or agent of the Crown or as enjoying any status, immunity or privilege of the Crown; and the Commission's property shall not be regarded as property of, or held on behalf of, the Crown.

(3) The Commission shall consist of not fewer than eleven members.

(4) The members of the Commission shall be appointed by Her Majesty on the recommendation of the Prime Minister.

(5) At least one third of the members of the Commission shall be persons who are legally qualified; and for this purpose a person is legally qualified if –

- (a) he has a ten year general qualification, within the meaning of section 71 of the Courts and Legal Services Act 1990, or
- (b) he is a member of the Bar of Northern Ireland, or solicitor of the Supreme Court of Northern Ireland, of at least ten years' standing.

(6) At least two thirds of the members of the Commission shall be persons who appear to the Prime Minister to have knowledge or experience of any aspect of the criminal justice system and of them at least one shall be a person who appears to him to have knowledge or experience of any aspect of the criminal justice system in Northern Ireland; and for the purposes of this subsection the criminal justice system includes, in particular, the investigation of offences and the treatment of offenders.

(7) Schedule 1 (further provisions with respect to the Commission) shall have effect.

13 Conditions for making of references

(1) A reference of a conviction, verdict, finding or sentence shall not be made under any of section 9 to 12B unless –

(a) the Commission consider that there is a real possibility that the conviction, verdict, finding or sentence would not be upheld were the reference to be made,

(b) the Commission so consider –

  (i) in the case of a conviction, verdict or finding, because of an argument, or evidence, not raised in the proceedings which led to it or on any appeal or application for leave to appeal against it, or

  (ii) in the case of a sentence, because of an argument on a point of law, or information, not so raised, and

(c) an appeal against the conviction, verdict, finding or sentence has been determined or leave to appeal against it has been refused.

(2) Nothing in subsection (1)(b)(i) or (c) shall prevent the making of a reference if it appears to the Commission that there are exceptional circumstances which justify making it.

Chapter 10

Sentence Management

Chapter Contents

The sentenced offender is more vulnerable to the abuse of power than are most people, particularly if he or she is in custody. A variety of agencies, with different powers, may well be involved in the supervision and management of a sentenced prisoner, usually out of the view of the public, and in this chapter we will look at the role of these various different organisations. In our case study, Gerry Good has been sentenced to two years in prison. The National Offender Management Service, heralded with fanfares by the Government in January 2004, has limped slowly towards a constitutionally acceptable position. In reality, the probation and prison systems are in a state of flux, which has been going for some years. Several private prisons exist outside HM Prison Service. The Probation Service, which became a national service only in 2001, was then, between 2008 and 2010, broken into new component parts (35 self-governing probation trusts), which worked alongside an increasing number of private companies and charities. An even more dramatic change is currently taking place: the probation trusts were abolished in May 2014 and replaced by a National Probation Service and 21 separate Community Rehabilitation Companies which have been sold to a number of private companies. The purpose of this chapter is to raise questions about the powers and accountability of those who have such control over the lives of sentenced offenders. It provides only examples, not a definitive account, of the powers exercised by different bodies within the penal system. Thus, whilst most offenders are fined, fine enforcement – which can result in a fine defaulter serving a sentence of imprisonment – is not dealt with here in any detail. Two developments in recent years should perhaps be noted at the outset.

(a) Procedural openness

The first is an increase in procedural openness. We will see in this chapter that sentence plans are often discussed with offenders and that procedures governing release from prisons or hospital are much more open than they were in recent history. A fundamental question is whether this increased openness has led to increased substantive justice, or whether it sometimes disguises potential and real injustices. Procedural fairness does not necessarily lead to fairer outcomes. And fair hearings can mean very expensive hearings: we will take as an example the work of the Parole Board. The Board can get through a pile of paper hearings in a morning, but rarely more than three oral hearings in a day. Those who do not have the right to an oral hearing often suspect that the process applied to them is less fair, but this is of course not necessarily so. And at the moment, procedural concerns are leading to increased delays, which are certainly not fair. As we have seen elsewhere in this book (Chapter 5, for example), adequate funding is a prerequisite of fair processes. The Parole Board makes a fascinating case study.

(b) Joined up services, or privatisation and fragmentation?

The second development is more difficult to describe. Putting it positively, there has been a huge increase over the last 25 years in co-operation between different agencies, and a commitment by government to 'joined up' thinking in criminal justice. The main example of this must be the creation of the National Offender Management Service. Originally proposed by Lord Carter, who reported in 2003 at the request of the Government (more precisely, at the request of the Prime Minister's Strategy Unit) on more 'effective' ways of managing offenders. In his Report *Managing Offenders, Reducing Crime: a new approach* [10:1] he sought to focus all those involved on the key aim of crime reduction. He made interesting recommendations on sentencing law (which have not been adopted), and put great faith in the 'what works' agenda. But it was his recommendation that, in order to break down the 'silos of prison and probation' it was necessary to create a new National Offender Management

Service (NOMS) responsible for reducing re-offending which caught the Government's imagination. Immediately, in a paper called *Reducing Crime – Changing Lives*, the Government accepted that they would separate the case management of offenders from the provision of prison places, treatment services or community programmes (whether they are in the public, private or voluntary sectors). NOMS started work in the summer of 2004, but, extraordinarily, the Government failed to enact any laws to create the legal basis for these changes. There was a Management of Offenders and Sentencing Bill in 2005, but it failed to get through the parliamentary processes before the Government called the General Election that year: deeply controversial, the Conservative Opposition did not agree that it should rush through the parliamentary process without significant debate (which is what happened to the Serious Organised Crime and Police Act 2005). There were a few abortive attempts to legislate before the Offender Management Act 2007 finally reached the statute book in July 2007. The aim of the Act was to improve the 'delivery of probation services' by creating probation trusts (instead of probation boards); by encouraging the 'commissioning' of probation services; and enabling greater partnership working with voluntary, charitable and private providers.

Central to the Government's vision for NOMS are the concepts of 'commissioning' and 'contestability'. But will small local initiatives survive in this deeply competitive world? Central Government is keeping close control: there are parallels here with our discussion of policing and how to get the balance right between local, central and regional control. Note the Management of Offenders etc (Scotland) Act 2005 which established new Community Justice Authorities in Scotland to co-ordinate services for offenders and monitor joint working between local agencies to tackle re-offending: criminal justice agencies in local government have a duty to consult with partners, share information and draw up plans to reduce re-offending. Is this co-operative structure 'better' than the 'contractual' structure being pursued in England and Wales?

The creation of NOMS came as no surprise: we had already seen two decades of managing criminal justice agencies through performance indicators, audits, framework and strategy documents, and a myriad of other 'performance tools' (see [1:6]). But perhaps it was a step too far. Of course, co-operation is essential at the post-sentence stage, where the different agencies are clearly interdependent. No-one should doubt the need for a formal and standardised system of sentence planning, recognised in the Woolf Report [10:2] as long ago as 1991. This report examined the causes of riots in several prisons in 1990 and remains a valuable tool for those evaluating 'justice' in prisons. It was the Woolf Report which recommended that a national Criminal Justice Consultative Council (CJCC), and 24 area committees, be set up to discuss matters affecting more than one agency. The membership of these committees included representatives of the police, Probation Service, Crown Prosecution Service, Prison Service, judges, magistrates and the legal profession. From 2003 the CJCC became the Criminal Justice Council and the area committees are now 42 local Criminal Justice Boards (CJBs); in addition, a national CJB, chaired by the Minister of State for Policing, Criminal Justice and Victims, was established in February 2013. It is difficult to assess the impact of these bodies: whilst they must indeed open up channels of communication, they may, for example, lead to a greater blurring of the lines of accountability. Look up your local CJB on the internet: you will find performance figures, the minutes of its meetings and so on all available for your study.

Privatisation too is nothing new. It was not until the Prisons Act 1878 that prisons were all brought under the control of a national system run by the Prison Commission (later the Prison Department, then the Prison Service). Many of Charles Dickens' novels paint a picture of the early Victorian (nineteenth century) prison. And throughout the twentieth century many prison services, such as laundries, were run under private contract. It was the Conservative Government, in the Criminal Justice Act (CJA) 1991, which moved towards wholesale privatisation. The Criminal Justice and Public Order Act 1994 allowed the privatisation of prison escort duties (i.e. the delivery of prisoners to and from prison). Under section 94, where a court sentences someone too late in the day for that person to be admitted to prison, he can be held overnight by the escort company instead of by the police. Sections 96 and 99 allowed for the contracting out of part of a prison, or some of the functions within a prison, to the private sector.

The first privately run prison, HMP Wolds, a purpose-built remand prison, was opened in 1992 and there are now 14 private prisons contractually managed by private companies such as Sodexo Justice Services, Serco and G4S Justice Services. While privatisation may lead to improved physical standards in prison, it raises questions of principle, discussed in Logan (1990), Padfield (2005) and Genders and Player (2007). Should the State delegate to private companies its right to punish those who break the law? In practice, the accountability of private prisons continues to be unclear. The Government is represented in the prison by a Controller, whilst the private company employs the Director (the equivalent of the governor in a public sector prison). But despite Government commitments in the 1990s that the Directors of private prisons would not be given powers which should 'properly' be in the hands of the State (the CJA 1991 provided specifically that Directors of private prisons were not allowed to conduct adjudications, segregate prisoners, apply restraints or to order confinement in a special cell, except in emergencies), these provisions were repealed by the Offender Management Act 2007.

(i) Probation

Probation services were set up by the Probation of Offenders Act 1907. Before that, volunteer 'police court missionaries' had worked with offenders, using religion and moral education in an attempt to help people turn away from crime. The 1907 Act encouraged courts of summary jurisdiction to appoint probation officers to 'advise, assist and befriend' offenders, a service to be funded by local authorities. The Criminal Justice Act 1925 made it mandatory for every criminal court to appoint a probation officer. The duties of the 54 separate probation services were laid down in various pieces of legislation, consolidated in the Probation Service Act 1993. The Government published a stream of reports in 1998 and 1999 (*Joining Forces to Protect the Public*, the *Prisons-Probation Review* and the *Correctional Policy Framework*, for example), which led to the creation of a National Probation Service for the first time. The Criminal Justice and Court Services Act 2000 created a unified system, the National Probation Service, based on 42 local areas, matching police areas. This started work in April 2001.

There was then a very short period when it felt as though the Probation Service had 'come of age', standing on an equal footing with the Prison Service (despite a much smaller budget, of course). But any growing confidence within the service was undermined by the slow and uncomfortable birth of NOMS. The Offender Management Act 2007 shook up the organisation of the Probation Service, abolished the existing local probation boards and replaced them with trusts. The Act gives the Secretary of State responsibility for providing 'probation services' and the power to establish probation trusts. Between April 2008 and April 2010, 35 probation trusts were created. However, all ceased to operate on 31 May 2014 and were abolished by statutory instrument in October 2014 (this was despite all 35 probation trusts being rated as either 'good' or 'excellent' by NOMS in 2012/13). As a consequence, the Probation Service is currently undergoing its most radical and controversial reform since its inception in 1907. Since June 2014, the National Probation Service has been responsible for the management of high risk offenders and 21 Community Rehabilitation Companies (CRCs) have been responsible for the management of low to medium risk offenders and all short-sentence prisoners (those sentenced to less than 12 months in prison) after release. On 1 February 2015, the 21 CRCs were all handed over to the private companies who had been the successful bidder in each area – and, at a stroke, the majority of probation services were privatised. It is far too early to assess the impact of this reform but you are advised to keep an eye on the development of probation services in your local area.

Why is all this change necessary? Chris Grayling, the Secretary of State for Justice introducing the *Transforming Rehabilitation* agenda, sets out a strong case against the status quo **[10:3]** but concerns remain about the scale and pace of change (see **[10:4]** and **[10:5]**).

The chief problem facing probation services has been overload and a lack of resources to match their increasing responsibilities. Probation officers have traditionally had two main roles: the provision of a service of social information and advice to the courts (and also to the CPS); and the supervision and rehabilitation of offenders in the community. Now 'probation purposes' are defined (in section 1 of the Offender Management Act 2007, as amended) as providing for:

(a)   courts to be given assistance in determining the appropriate sentences to pass, and making other decisions, in respect of persons charged with or convicted of offences;
(b)   the giving of assistance to persons determining whether conditional cautions should be given and which conditions to attach to conditional cautions;
(c)   the supervision and rehabilitation of persons charged with or convicted of offences;
(d)   the giving of assistance to persons remanded on bail;
(e)   the supervision and rehabilitation of persons to whom conditional cautions are given;
(f)   the giving of information to victims of persons charged with or convicted of offences.

Let us look at each of these in turn.

(a) Court reports

The CJA 1991 required sentencers to consult a pre-sentence report before sentencing someone to imprisonment, but this requirement was watered down by the Criminal Justice Act 1993: the court had a discretion to dispense with a report where it is satisfied that it can properly pass sentence without one. The Criminal Justice Act (CJA) 2003, sections 156–160, develop in detailed and complex language the rules on when a pre-sentence report (PSR) is required. In reality, a well-researched PSR is an invaluable help to the sentencer and as a basis for sentence planning. It should provide general information about an offender's background and some general circumstances surrounding the commission of the offence. In the past, the emphasis might have been on their family circumstances, medical and psychiatric health, and employment situation, but today this information is directed towards assessing risk. A report on Gerry Good might look something like this.

Pre-Sentence Report

This is a Pre-Sentence Report as defined in s. 158 of the Criminal Justice Act 2003 and has been prepared in accordance with the requirements of the National Standard for Pre-Sentence Reports.
    This report is a restricted document

OFFENDER'S DETAILS

Name	Gerry Good		
Date of Birth:	20/06/82	Age:	32
Address:			
Postcode:			

COURT DETAILS

Sentencing Court	Camford
Court Type	Crown Court
Local Justice Area	
Date Report Requested	
Date Report Required	
Purpose of Sentencing	Not stated
Level of seriousness	Not stated

OFFENCE DETAILS

Offence(s) (dealt with in this PSR)	Date of Offence(s)
1 x Unlawful wounding, contrary to section 20 of the Offences Against the Person Act 1861	13/06/14

PSR WRITER'S DETAILS

Name:	Natalie Jones
Office Title:	Probation Officer
Office Location:	Camford Probation Office, Camford

Date report completed and signed:

1. Sources of Information

1.1 For the purposes of writing this report I have interviewed Mr Good on one occasion at the Probation Office. I have read the CPS documents and seen a list of previous convictions. I have also contacted Mr Good's General Practitioner.

This report is underpinned and informed by an Offender Assessment System (OASys) in the identification of the risk of reconviction and the risk of harm presented by this defendant.

2. Offence Analysis

2.1 The Court will be aware of the facts surrounding this case. Gerry Good was found guilty at trial of unlawful wounding, contrary to section 20 of the Offences Against the Person Act 1861. Mr Good was remarkably frank in discussing the circumstances surrounding the offence with me and it is my assessment that he genuinely has little recall of what actually happened. His responses struck me as confused, rather than evasive. He does deny the seriousness of the offence and, although this may indicate a failure to take responsibility, it is also a reflection of the fact that he did not think he had committed an offence. Mr Good acknowledges that the major contributory factor behind this offence is his dependency on alcohol – in particular he tells me he had been drinking for most of the day before the offence took place.

2.2 Clearly the court will view this offence as particularly serious, not only because of its nature, but because it was committed whilst Mr Good was already subject to a Community Order imposed by Bleakham Magistrates' Court on 6 October 2013 for offences of theft. That Order had a requirement attached that Mr Good obtain treatment from the Alcohol Dependency Unit in Camford for his addiction. This offence therefore took place despite Mr Good's access to community resources relevant to his offending. It is my view that the circumstances in this case suggest that a further community disposal would not be effective in preventing re-offending. CPS information suggests that the victim required hospital treatment following the offence. CPS information could not, of course, capture the long-term psychological impact of such an offence, even though physical recovery may have been good. In my view Mr Good minimised the effect of the offence on the victim.

3. Offender Assessment and Likelihood of Re-offending

The OASys Chart below summarises the relevant factors which have been identified as contributing to the defendant's risk of reconviction. The indicators which exceed the mid-way point on the bar chart are those which need to be addressed in order to reduce the likelihood of further offences being committed.

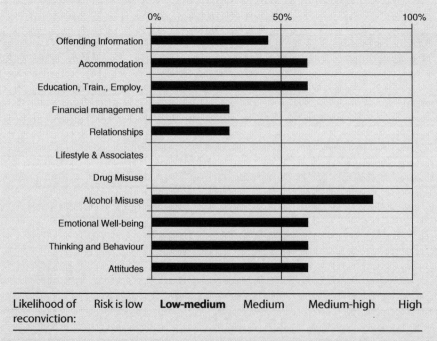

Likelihood of reconviction:	Risk is low	**Low-medium**	Medium	Medium-high	High

3.1 Mr Good has lived in this area for two years. He has led an unsettled and chaotic life for the past five years, since his marriage broke up, when he became homeless. Mr Good does have occasional contact with this mother and with his daughter, who still live in the north of England. He has had no contact with his ex-partner for four years. He has had occasional relationships with women in recent years. He tells me that he had hoped that the victim of the offence was going to become his new partner.

3.2 Mr Good's criminal record reveals that he has previous convictions for dishonesty and minor offences of violence. The court has imposed a number of disposals aimed at reducing the risk of re-offending. None of these has been successful. Mr Good acknowledges that until and unless he addresses his dependency on alcohol he remains at risk of re-offending. At this stage I have not completed a detailed assessment of his attitude to women. His response to supervision has not been positive. He has reported when required during some of the current Order but when he has been drinking heavily he has neglected to fulfil these requirements. Furthermore he has not attended all the appointments offered to him by the Alcohol Dependency Unit.

3.3 At the time of his arrest, Mr Good was not working and was in receipt of Jobseeker's Allowance. The fact that he has not been in employment for more than four years indicates further the effect his addiction to alcohol has had on his ability to lead a responsible lifestyle. He has been offered employment advice by a partnership agency of the Probation Service but did not sustain or take up the advice he was offered.

4. Assessment of the Risk of Harm

4.1 It is apparent that Mr Good deeply regrets what happened between him and the victim of the attack that evening. He considered her a friend, and is deeply hurt that she has, in his eyes, initiated proceedings against him. Although he acknowledges his dependency on alcohol (and occasionally drugs) he failed to complete a treatment programme at the Alcohol Dependency Unit in Camford. My impression is that he has considerable long term personal issues which he attempts to disguise by consuming alcohol. The pessimism he expresses about the future is a reflection of the effects that his long term drinking patterns have had on his ability to take responsibility for his own actions. Until Mr Good addresses his addiction he remains at risk of causing serious harm to members of the public.

4.2 He has previous offences for violence and the Probation Service assessment system assesses him as of low-medium risk of re-offending. He is at high risk of causing harm if he were to be in a similar situation to the one he was in when he committed this offence.

5. Conclusion

5.1 The court will have little option but to give consideration to a custodial sentence given the seriousness of the offence. Such a sentence would protect members of the public from further harm for its duration but it is unlikely that Mr Good would be offered anything other than a nominal introductory programme on the subject of alcohol dependency within the custodial setting. Therefore the likelihood is that he would be released posing a similar risk of harm and re-offending to that which he poses currently.

5.2 Should the court wish to give consideration to a community sentence the options are as follows:

5.3 *Fine or Discharge*:

Neither of these disposals would address the seriousness of the offence.

5.4 *Supervision and Programme Requirements*:

Mr Good could benefit from a general offending behaviour programme. In the course of that programme he would examine his own responses and attitudes to hopefully change his current methods of solving issues. Specific alcohol-related intervention could be sequenced following completion of the initial group work programme.

Mr Good would be expected to:

- report weekly to his supervising officer;
- attend the group work programme;
- be assessed for additional alcohol-related work;
- look at victim and relapse prevention issues;
- be assessed for employment/training.

5.5 If a custodial sentence is inevitable then Mr Good will be assessed for suitability for this programme as part of his licence conditions on release.

5.6 Mr Good could also be made subject to a Community Order comprising an unpaid work requirement with the number of hours appropriate to the court's view of the seriousness of this offence.

5.7 If however the court still judges the offence so serious that it must impose a custodial sentence, it might be possible for a Suspended Sentence to be considered. In that case, I would propose the court impose a Suspended Sentence Order with the same requirements of Unpaid Work and Supervision. I would further request that the amount of hours be reduced in recognition of the more onerous nature of the sentence as a whole.

(b) Assisting in determining whether conditional cautions should be given

As we saw in Chapter 2, a large number of offenders are dealt with out-of-court rather than pros-ecuted. Traditionally probation officers had little involvement in non-court processes, but recently, they have become involved in conditional cautions. Under the CJA 2003, probation officers should give assistance in determining whether conditional cautions should be given and which conditions should be attached, and to provide supervision and rehabilitation to those so cautioned. But the evi-dence seems to suggest that by far the most common condition has been a requirement to pay com-pensation (which accounts for around two-thirds of conditions attached to conditional cautions).

(c) The supervision and rehabilitation of persons charged with or convicted of offences

This is the traditional 'core' probation role. Thus, if Gerry Good had been sentenced to a Community Order, his main contact would have been with a probation officer. The initial appointment with the supervising officer is, whenever possible, held within five working days of the making of the Order, and the appointment is made before the offender leaves court. At the first meeting, the supervising officer gives the offender written information setting out what can be expected from the probation services, and what is expected of the offender. They are given a copy of the court order, with instruc-tions to comply with its terms, and within two weeks a written supervision plan should have been drawn up.

A probation officer is normally required to take breach action after no more than 'one unac-ceptable failure' by the offender to comply with the Order (whereas the National Standards of the early 1990s allowed 'three instances of failure'). This change reflects the pressure to move away from a welfare to a punishment model. The other great pressure is the financial squeeze. The average number of people supervised per main grade officer rose every year from 20.7 in 1992 to 34.6 in 1998, to 40.7 in 2001 (Probation Statistics, 2001). This reflected both rising caseloads and a falling or stable number of fully trained officers. The total annual probation caseload increased by 39 per cent between 2000 and 2008 to 243,434 but has since fallen year on year, reaching 219,588 at the end of 2013 (Offender Management Statistics Quarterly: April to June 2014). Worrall and Hoy **[10:6]** argue for what might be seen as 'traditional' probation values (advice, assistance and befriending), rejecting the prevalent view that community sentences are simply alternatives to imprisonment: for them, prison should be seen as the alternative. We live in uncertain times. Who should be providing probation services: trained probation officers, or private and voluntary sector 'providers'? In the view of these authors, whilst there is scope for innovative contributions from both the private and voluntary sectors, it is professionally well-qualified probation officers who should take a firm lead in work with offenders – particularly if we are concerned about consistency of approach.

As we saw in Chapter 6, the new Community Order introduced under the CJA 2003 replaced all existing community sentences for those aged 18 years and over. The sentencing court must add at least one (but could potentially add all 12) of the following requirements: supervision; unpaid work; specified activities; prohibited activities; accredited programmes; curfew; exclusion; resi-dence/foreign travel prohibition; mental health treatment; drug rehabilitation; alcohol treatment; or attendance centre requirement for under 25s. The CJA 2003 also introduced the new Suspended Sentence Order (SSO) for which the offender is given a custodial sentence suspended for between six months and two years. The court specifies a number of requirements from the set of options available for the Community Order, and these are supervised by the probation services. However, it is clear that certain requirements are used more frequently than others, with unpaid work and/ or supervision being the most commonly used requirements in both Community Orders and SSOs (the next most commonly used standalone requirement is a curfew). Whether these are the requirements which are most likely to have a rehabilitative effect is highly debatable. Many more details about the combinations of requirements is available online in the probation tables to the Offender Management Statistics Quarterly.

According to Mair et al (2007), who studied data from the first 16 months of the new regime, probation officers were worried about the lack of availability of some requirements, and the rise in the use of unpaid work. The use of SSOs was seen not to be diverting offenders from prison, but to be contributing to the prison population (because breaches are much more likely to lead to imprisonment than if a Community Order had been imposed and then breached). Readers are encouraged to read Gelsthorpe and Morgan (2007) and Canton (2011) to learn more on probation practice.

The probation services are of course not only concerned with the supervision of those serving Community Orders. Those released on licence from prison are subject to licence supervision by the probation services. A considerable number of released prisoners are recalled to prison during their licence period: between April 1999 and June 2014, of the total 681,000 people released from prison, 177,229 (26 per cent) were recalled (Offender Management Statistics Quarterly: April to June 2014). Those people who think that early release from prison is a soft option are wrong: release on licence can lead many people swiftly back to prison (Padfield and Maruna, 2006). Padfield [10:7] highlights the stories and impact of procedures which are very difficult for prisoners to understand.

Probation officers are thus increasingly involved in the management of the sentences of imprisoned offenders. In Gerry Good's case, he will be allocated to a supervising probation officer at the start of his sentence, and this officer should be fully involved in devising any sentence plan. Gerry will be automatically due for release at the half way point in his sentence (and perhaps be released earlier under Home Detention Curfew (HDC)). His supervising officer has to provide a pre-discharge report at least one month before release. This will include recommendations to the prison governor on any extra licence conditions felt to be necessary, and will give instructions to Gerry Good on reporting once he is released from custody. Any additional licence condition must be both 'necessary and proportionate' to manage the offender's risk. After release, if the supervising officer wishes to add or delete a licence condition during the supervision period, they will have to apply to the prison establishment from which Gerry was discharged. If the request is approved, the prison issues a new licence (in duplicate) to the supervising officer.

Clearly, problems with the effective flow of information between the probation services, Social Services departments, the police and the Prison Service remain. What happens if the different bodies disagree: if the governor imposes conditions that the probation officer believes to be unduly severe, are they obliged to bring breach proceedings? The picture has been complicated by the introduction of HDC orders by the Crime and Disorder Act 1998. The prison governor may release short-term prisoners on a 'home detention' curfew licence (enforced by electronic monitoring or 'tagging'). Initially this could be for up to two months before the normal date of release, but it was later increased to three months, and then, in 2003, to 135 days. It is clear from the HDC statistics that the power to release early in this way is exercised differently from prison to prison. It obviously makes a mockery of the precise calculation of short sentences by trial judges – now, anyone sentenced to, say, 18 months, may be released at some unpredictable time between five and nine months. There have been huge fluctuations in the use of HDC over the last 15 years and the vast majority of prisoners eligible for HDC are currently not granted it: in the year to June 2014, of the 47,222 eligible prisoners, only 9,317 (20 per cent) were released on HDC (Offender Management Statistics Quarterly: April to June 2014, Table 3.3).

Between June 2007 and March 2010, the Government ran an additional scheme – the End of Custody Licence (ECL) – which introduced a presumption in favour of release on licence for prisoners serving between four weeks and four years for the final 18 days of their sentence subject to meeting strict eligibility criteria and providing a release address. This was to deal with the problem of overcrowding in prisons. Prisoners who would normally be subject to supervision on release were required to meet their probation officer after release and to have regular contact after that in line with their supervision plan. All prisoners released on ECL were liable to recall if they were reported to have misbehaved during the period of the licence. This controversial scheme was abolished just before the 2010 General Election, but it is yet another example of the bewildering complexity of the criminal justice process.

(d) The giving of assistance to persons remanded on bail

One of the most useful ways that probation officers can help defendants likely to be remanded in custody is by providing accommodation to which people who are unable to live in their own homes, or who do not have homes, can be bailed (it is obviously difficult for a court to grant bail to someone who does not have anywhere to go to). Bailees in this position may be housed by the Bail Accommodation & Support Service, privately run under contract by Stonham (Home Group).

(e) The supervision and rehabilitation of persons to whom conditional cautions are given

Despite this being a statutory probation service, the *Code of Practice for Adult Conditional Cautions*, published in April 2013, says little about the involvement of the probation services: merely at paragraph 3.14 that '[a] robust process for demonstrating compliance must be in place' which may include agreements with a number of organisations, one of which are probation and national offender management services. This is an area crying out for further research.

(f) The giving of information to victims of persons charged with or convicted of offences

Where an offender has been sentenced to a custodial sentence of 12 months or more for a violent or sexual offence, the probation services have a statutory responsibility, under the Domestic Violence, Crime and Victims Act 2004, section 35, to take reasonable steps to establish whether the victim of the offence wishes to make representations about whether the offender should be subject to conditions on release and, if so, what these conditions should be. A 2013 inspection by HM Inspectorate of Probation found that contact was usually made with the victim within the target date of 40 working days following sentence and that, overall, victims were positive about the service they had received. This is another thorny area. It is vitally important that victims are supported through the criminal justice process, and it is clear that sometimes they are not treated with the respect they deserve. This is not to suggest that they should have any role in the fixing of the appropriate charges or sentences.

So how should we conclude this brief look at the role of the probation services? Clearly probation officers require discretionary powers: they are often managing difficult people in a problematic environment. What will be the effect of the increased role for the voluntary and private sectors in the supervision of offenders? Considerable uncertainty surrounds issues of accountability when anything goes wrong with private or voluntary sector supervision. These are difficult days for those who work in the probation services, and doubtless therefore also for those that they supervise and 'manage'.

(ii) Prisons

What happens when Gerry is sent to prison? If he were sentenced in Cambridge Crown Court, he would be likely to be sent to HMP Peterborough, which is run by a private company, Sodexo Justice Services. This is one of 14 prisons run by private companies under contract to NOMS. The other 106 prisons are run directly by the Prison Service (this number changes as prisons merge, close and new ones open).

What is the legal status of the Prison Service? In 1993 the Prison Service moved to executive agency status within the Home Office, to be run by a management board, chaired by a Director-General who was directly accountable to the Home Secretary. Whilst agency status may have devolved more decision-making powers to individual prison governors, the audit and performance culture which has developed also led to more central control. Does agency status weaken the political accountability of the Justice Secretary to Parliament? Of course, more controversial than agency status was the decision to privatise the management of individual prisons. In May 2007, the Prison Service became part of the new Ministry of Justice, and it remains an executive agency as well as part of NOMS, which is therefore both its parent organisation and its main commissioner. The Prison Service receives funding from a number of different sources and manages a range of services and establishments. The Prison Service's main commissioner, NOMS, operates through Regional Offender Managers (ROMs) for each of the English regions and a Director of Offender Management for Wales (DOM). The ROMs/DOM commission work regionally both for offenders in custody and for those in the community and have a close dialogue with Prison Service Areas and individual establishments. However, some specialist services, like high security prisons, continue to be provided and purchased on a nationwide basis. ROMs are not the only commissioners of services delivered by the Prison Service. The Skills Funding Agency is responsible, jointly with ROMs, for commissioning education and skills provision for prisoners, the NHS Commissioning Board is responsible for commissioning health services and the Youth Justice Board commissions services for those under 18 years old. The Prison Service also provides services for the Borders and Immigration Agency (BIA), which commissions services at Dover, Haslar, Morton Hall and Verne. So, while the Prison Service is perhaps not feeling quite as fractured as probation services, it is being challenged by the private sector.

A short-term prisoner such as Gerry Good may serve the whole of his sentence in the local prison to which he is initially dispatched. Otherwise, during the initial period of assessment, the observation, classification and allocation units of the prison decide on a classification for him, based on the offences committed and the reports made on him by staff during the period of assessment. This determines to which prison he is allocated. Category A prisoners are those whose escape would be highly dangerous to the public; category B are those for whom the highest degree of security is not necessary but for whom escape must be made very difficult; category C are those who cannot be trusted in open conditions but who do not have the ability or resources to make a determined effort to escape; and category D are those who can reasonably be trusted to serve their sentences in open conditions. A review of categorisation is carried out annually as part of sentence planning and as an incentive to good behaviour. Since this categorisation decision can have a direct impact on the date of a prisoner's ultimate release, the Divisional Court in *R v Secretary of State for the Home Department, ex p Duggan* [1994] 3 All ER 277 held that, when categorisation is reviewed, the gist of reports on which the decision is based should be given to the prisoner, as well as reasons for the decision (followed in *R (Lord) v Secretary of State for the Home Department* [2003] EWHC 2073 (Admin)). A category A prisoner may even have the right to an oral hearing (see *R (Williams) v Secretary of State for the Home Department* [2002] EWCA Civ 498).

It is beyond the scope of this book to look in detail at the profile of the prison population, and life in prison. Students wanting a picture of prison conditions should read the inspection reports of HM Chief Inspector of Prisons. Better still, arrange to spend some time in a prison (voluntarily!).

There are five main types of prison: local prisons; training prisons; young offender institutions; high security prisons; and open prisons. There are currently 13 prisons for women and six of these have mother and baby units (but there are restrictions on how long young children can remain with their mothers in these institutions).

The riots in a number of prisons in April 1990, led to an investigation conducted by Lord Justice Woolf and Judge Stephen Tumin. Their report [10:2] painted a depressing picture and stressed the need for greater 'justice' within prisons. Some issues are only skimmed over by Woolf: for example, the over-representation of ethnic minorities in the prison population.

Table 10.1 Percentage of prison population from ethnic minorities

	Male	Female
1990	15%	23%
1998	18%	24%
2001	21%	26%
2005	25%	29%
2010	26%	25%
2014	26%	18%

Source: Prison Statistics 2001, Chapter 6; Offender Management Caseload Statistics 2005 (HOSB 18/06), Chapter 8; Offender Management Caseload Statistics 2010, Table A1.17; Offender Management Statistics Quarterly: April to June 2014, Table 1.4

The problems facing women prisoners – partly caused, ironically, by their under-representation in the prison population – are not discussed in the Woolf Report, perhaps because the riots did not involve women prisoners. The most recent review of women in prison is the 2007 Corston Report [10:8], which called for a radical change in the way that we treat women throughout the whole of the criminal justice system. Somewhat depressingly, this call is far from original: see also HM Inspector of Prisons *Thematic Review of Women in Prison* (1997), the Prison Reform Trust's report on *Justice for Women* (2000), as well as Eaton (1993). The House of Commons Justice Committee's review of progress since the Corston Report [10:9] suggests that there is still much work to be done.

As a result of the 1990 riots and the Woolf Report that followed it [10:2], there were significant changes in the complaints and disciplinary procedures in prisons. Each prison has an Independent Monitoring Board (known as Boards of Visitors until 2003), composed of lay volunteers, whose prime duty is to act as a watchdog on the prison, with each member having free access to the prison, prisoners and prison records. A prisoner can now formally complain, either orally to the landing officer or the governor, or in writing to the governor or the Independent Monitoring Board. Another Woolf recommendation – that there should be an independent adjudicator at the apex of the system – resulted in the appointment of a Prison Ombudsman. He became the Prisons and Probation Ombudsman in 2001, but unsurprisingly his caseload remains dominated by complaints from those in prison rather than those under the supervision of the Probation Service (according to the Prisons and Probation Ombudsman's Annual Report for 2013/14, 91 per cent of complaints that year were about the Prison Service, eight per cent were about the Probation Service and one per cent were about immigration detention). He also investigates deaths in custody. The reports of the Prisons and Probation Ombudsman are well worth reading, painting a good picture of the many difficulties facing prisoners within the penal system.

The prison disciplinary system underwent major reform in 1992. Until then, the Board of Visitors undertook adjudications over disciplinary matters within the prison. Woolf recommended that those responsible for monitoring conditions should not be responsible for discipline. Since then, the most serious offences against prison discipline, which are also serious criminal offences in themselves, are referred to the police with a view to prosecution in the criminal courts. In

1992, governors were given the power to deal with other offences themselves and to award up to 28 days' (increased to 42 in 1994) deferred release, known as ADAs, or 'additional days awarded'. The European Court of Human Rights, in *Ezeh and Connors v United Kingdom* (2002) 35 EHRR 691, held that disciplinary proceedings constituted criminal proceedings for the purposes of the European Convention on Human Rights, Article 6 **[1:13]**, notwithstanding their classification as disciplinary proceedings. Therefore, prisoners not only had a right to legal representation, but the governor was not an 'independent and impartial tribunal'. As a result, the Prison (Amendment) Rules 2002 (SI 2002/2116) changed the disciplinary process such that serious charges, which may result in ADAs, are referred to an independent adjudicator (normally a district judge). Also controversial are the administrative 'sanctions' available to the governor, such as the incentives and earned privileges scheme, segregation, or transfer to another prison to maintain discipline. Officially not part of the prison discipline system, being segregated or losing privileges feels like punishment: unsurprisingly, there is a large body of 'prison law' largely derived from judicial review proceedings initiated by prisoners (see Owen, Macdonald and Livingstone, 2008).

English prisons in recent years have suffered dreadfully from overcrowding. There was some optimism in the early 1990s that the reforms of the Criminal Justice Act 1991 would lead to a reduction in the total number of prisoners. The male population reached a plateau at around 43,000 between 1990 and 1993. After 1993 it started to rise again and there was another plateau between 1999 and 2001; before it then rose steeply once more (to around 81,500 as we go to press). The female population was at a fairly constant level throughout the twentieth century at around 1,000, until the mid-1980s, when it started to rise. But from the early-1990s it started rising steeply to 4,450 in 2004, before falling below 4,000 in December 2012 for the first time since 2001 since when it seems to have remained more or less constant. (The overall prison population reached a record high of 88,179 prisoners in December 2011.) The changes in release procedures and the continuing pressure on judges to treat 'serious' offenders 'seriously' means that there are an increasing number of long-term prisoners serving increasingly longer sentences.

The Woolf Report **[10:2]** adversely commented on the poor regimes in many local prisons and remand centres: how much has this improved in the last two-and-a-half decades? There have been many improvements, but the rising population of prisoners and financial squeezes have also taken

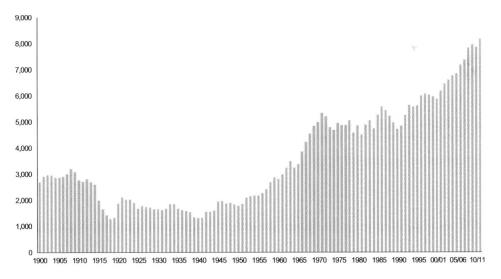

Figure 10.2 The average prison population, England and Wales, 1900–2012

their toll. The regime within prison is often tedious and unconstructive. Prisoners are paid derisory wages and have little incentive to work productively. Educational and work facilities are squeezed in times of financial stringency. However, there can be no doubt that the current political emphasis on reducing offending has led to greater interest on 'what works' in prison, and much greater emphasis is being put on suitable courses, such as the Sex Offender Treatment Programme and other courses designed to encourage prisoners to confront their offending behaviour. However, the inevitable resources problem arises: budgets are limited, and the prison population goes ever upwards (see Liebling and Crewe (2012)).

Clearly, prisoners are in the hands of the prison authorities (and their fellow prisoners) and are vulnerable to the abuse of power. The Prison Act 1952 **[10:10]** lays down the general duties of the prison authorities, and authorises the Secretary of State to make rules for the management of prisons. The Prison Rules for adult prisoners date from 1964, and are regularly amended; the Young Offender Institution Rules are similar to the Prison Rules. The Rules rarely lay down specific rights, but they leave vast discretion to prison governors. Should breaches of the Prison Rules provide the basis for an action for breach of statutory duty? The courts have been reluctant to go this far: the House of Lords in *Hague* **[10:11]** overruled two different decisions of the Court of Appeal, which had allowed prisoners' claims for false imprisonment, based on principles of 'residual liberty' and 'intolerable conditions'. However, this does not mean that prisoners are without rights. The ordinary civil and criminal law applies in prison, even though it may be difficult to enforce. Judicial review is also an avenue available to the prisoner, though Loughlin (1993) warns that we should not assume that 'a greater degree of legalism automatically leads to a better or more enlightened system' (at page 50). Whilst the number of applications for judicial review by prisoners has increased, the breadth of the powers of the prison authorities has meant that the vast majority are unsuccessful (see Valier (2004)). Furthermore, the scope of criminal legal aid in prison law cases was removed in seven important areas in 2013: pre-tariff reviews before the Parole Board; eligibility of women prisoners for mother and baby units; segregation and placement in closed supervision centres; category A reviews; access to offending behaviour courses; resettlement on leaving prison; and disciplinary proceedings where no additional days may be awarded. In the absence of legal aid, of course, many prisoners will be unable to challenge decisions on these issues.

However, the cry for enforceable minimum standards and a new Prison Act will not disappear (see, for example, Owen, Macdonald and Livingstone (2008)). The Human Rights Act 1998 **[1:13]** is having an impact in this area and the European Court of Human Rights remains important, as well. In Chapter 1, we noted the controversial ruling of the European Court of Human Rights in *Dickson v United Kingdom* (2008) 46 EHRR 41 that a prisoner denied the opportunity to inseminate his wife artificially had had his rights under Article 8 breached. Note that the reasoning of the Court is not that the prisoner necessarily has a right to artificial insemination, but that the way it was banned in the UK was unlawful. Of wider importance might be *Hirst v United Kingdom* (2004) 38 EHRR 40 where the European Court held that the blanket ban on prisoners' right to vote was not proportionate. However, a decade on, the blanket ban on sentenced prisoners voting remains.

Who decides when a prisoner comes out of prison? All sentences are now in effect partially suspended sentences, served partly in prison and partly in the community, and all prisoners who commit an imprisonable offence after release but before the end of their original sentences run the risk of being returned to prison to complete their sentence. Since changes introduced by the CJA 2003, all offenders sentenced to a determinate sentence are automatically released at the halfway point in their sentence (with possible earlier release under home detention curfew). (The Criminal Justice and Courts Act 2015 has recently introduced a different release regime for people convicted of certain serious child sex and terrorism offences: these people will no longer be automatically released at the halfway point of their sentence but rather will need to be released by the Parole Board if they are to be released before the expiry of their full determinate term.) The Parole Board decides on the release of those serving indeterminate or extended sentences, and those recalled to prison having earlier been released. The prison authorities play a vital role in all releases, in fixing the terms of licences for those automatically released, and deciding on home detention curfew. They also have a crucial input into the decision-making of the Parole Board by the creation of the prisoner's parole dossier, or file of reports.

(iii) The Parole Board

Parole was first introduced in this country by the Criminal Justice Act 1967. There were originally two main objectives: to reduce the prison population, and to help in the rehabilitation of offenders by releasing them into the community at the 'right' time in their sentence, under the supervision of a probation officer to whom they were required to report regularly. Over the years many changes have been made to the system, both by Parliament (sweeping changes were made by the CJA 1991, the Criminal Justice and Public Order Act (CJPOA) 1994 and the CJA 2003) and change has also been forced on a reluctant Government by a stream of important decisions from the courts.

What is the status of the Parole Board? To give it a semblance of 'independence', in 1994 the Parole Board was made a non-departmental public body (see CJPOA 1994, section 149). But it has never been made a genuinely independent tribunal. In 2008, in R (Brooke and others) v Parole Board and another [2008] EWCA Civ 29, the Court of Appeal upheld the declaration by the High Court that 'the Parole Board does not meet the requirements of the common law and of Article 5(4) of the [European Convention on Human Rights] for a court to have demonstrated objective independence of the executive and of the parties' (R (Brooke and others) v Parole Board and another [2007] EWHC 2036 (Admin) at paragraph 78). In the Court of Appeal, Lord Judge, in giving judgment, stated that '[n]either the Secretary of State nor his Department has adequately addressed the need for the Parole Board to be and to be seen to be free of influence in relation to the performance of its judicial functions' ([2008] EWCA Civ 29 at paragraph 79). In response to this judgment, the sponsorship of the Parole Board was transferred from the NOMS Agency to the Access to Justice Group in the Ministry of Justice in April 2008 which at least meant that the sponsor was no longer also responsible for producing the reports upon which parole decisions are made, but is this enough? Is it time that a 'real' court made these decisions? What constitutes a 'real' court?

The members of the Parole Board include judges, psychiatrists, those with 'knowledge and experience of the supervision or aftercare of discharged prisoners', and those who have 'made a study of the causes of delinquency or the treatment of offenders' (see section 239 of, and Schedule 19 to, the CJA 2003). It carries out its functions in panels: sometimes three, sometimes two and sometimes just one member panels. The work of the Parole Board is well described in its annual reports to Parliament. It used to have an excellent website but unfortunately, like so many criminal justice websites, this has been greatly scaled-back in recent years as part of cost-saving measures. It has, however, encouraged a number of research projects (see [10:12] for example). The task of the Parole Board is to predict and assess risk: it has to balance the need to protect the public from serious harm and to prevent further offending with the benefits of supervision. It seems curious that, while Parliament has attempted to structure judicial discretion in sentencing, the wide powers of the Parole Board – which decides the length of a sentence in practice – should be left wide open. Even if predictions of dangerousness could be made accurately, is it morally justifiable to keep some people in prison longer than others only because of the risk that they represent?

Today, the role of the Parole Board can be seen under three categories of case. First, life or indeterminate sentence cases. For many years, the most controversial parole procedures were those applicable to life sentence prisoners. The European Court of Human Rights in Thynne [10:13] ruled that once the 'tariff' period set by reference to the offence had expired, any subsequent detention on grounds of public protection should be capable of being challenged through proceedings in a court or tribunal that is independent of the executive. As a result, a much more open procedure was introduced in 1991 in relation to discretionary lifers. Slowly the right to an oral hearing was won by other life sentence prisoners. The European Court of Human Rights in *V and T v United Kingdom* (1999) 30 EHRR 121 held that the role of the Home Secretary in fixing the tariff of a juvenile murderer was unlawful; and in *Stafford v United Kingdom* **[10:14]** it struck down the system for adult murderers (mandatory lifers). The House of Lords followed this in R *(Anderson) v Secretary of State for the Home Department* [2003] 1 AC 837.

For a while, all lifers had the right to an oral hearing (see Padfield and Liebling, 2001; Padfield, 2006) however, this was changed by the Parole Board (Amendment) Rules 2009: now, if the decision based on the paper hearing is that release is not recommended, an indeterminate sentence prisoner can only 'request' that an oral hearing is convened rather than, as before this amendment, 'require' that one takes place. When this change was confirmed in the Parole Board Rules 2011, the move was justified by reference to the dramatic increase in the number of oral hearings in the previous decade: in 2000/01 the Parole Board held 272 oral hearings, but this had risen to 3,732 in 2010/11 – an increase of more than 1,270 per cent (Parole Board Rules 2011 Explanatory Memorandum at paragraph 7.2). The key driver of this increased workload were the large number of prisoners serving imprisonment for public protection (IPP) sentences after these sentences came into force in 2005.

In 2013/14, the Parole Board held 2,725 oral hearings for indeterminate sentence prisoners (lifers or IPP sentence prisoners) and granted release in 880 cases (32 per cent) (Parole Board Annual Report, 2013/14 at page 27). Whilst this release rate seems reasonably high, it is important to note that about 1,500 prisoners who are eligible for parole were already filtered out at the paper hearing and did not therefore reach the stage of an oral hearing. If we add these into the total, the release rate drops to around 21 per cent. In the same year, 438 indeterminate sentence prisoners were recalled to prison – either following allegations of further offences or for the breach of their licence conditions.

The second category is a dwindling pool of pre-2005 determinate sentence prisoners and a growing number of extended determinate sentence prisoners. The Parole Board considers (at 'paper' panels) the release of all those sentenced to a fixed term of imprisonment for offences committed before 4 April 2005 (the old Discretionary Conditional Release scheme, studied by Hood and Shute) as well as some of those sentenced to an extended sentence. In 2013/14, the Parole Board considered 514 determinate sentence cases on paper and granted release to 118 of those prisoners, with release granted to a further 28 following an oral hearing (Parole Board Annual Report, 2013/14 at pages 26–27).

Finally, there are the cases of the growing number of released prisoners recalled to prison. The system of recall (or back door sentencing) has undergone a particularly turbulent history. Until 1994, two systems of recall to custody ran in tandem: one operated by the Parole Board and one by the Home Secretary. The system has been changed radically several times. Currently, all decisions to recall people from licence are taken by the Public Protection Casework Section (PPCS) within the NOMS Offender Management and Public Protection Group. The prisoner is then arrested by the police and taken to his nearest local prison. There are three types of recall: fixed term (which results in automatic re-release at the end of a 28-day period beginning on the first day of their return to custody), standard (where the offender is liable to remain in custody until the end of their licence period) and emergency (cases where the offender has been identified as a risk of causing serious harm and/or that the risk of re-offending is unmanageable or imminent). On return to custody, all recalled offenders must be informed of the reasons for their recall within 24 hours of the PPCS being notified of their return to custody. If the recall is fixed term, the offender can make representations to the Parole Board to consider their immediate re-release. If it is a standard recall, then their detention will be reviewed by the PPCS and must be referred to the Parole Board for consideration once they have been in custody for 28 days. They will either:

- order the immediate release of the prisoner on licence; or
- refuse immediate release but order release at a future date; or
- refuse immediate release and set a date for a further review of the case; or
- refuse to release or review the case again (cases where there are less than 12 months to go on the sentence and the prisoner then serves what is left of the sentence in prison).

If dissatisfied, the prisoner can then ask for an oral hearing. In the year to June 2014, 17,383 licensees were recalled to custody (Offender Management Statistics Quarterly: April to June 2014, Table 5.1).

In this book, we can do no more than encourage students to look much more closely at the role of the Parole Board. At a time when much political discourse focuses on 'front door sentencing' (i.e. the decisions of judges and magistrates), it is the probation services, the prison authorities, NOMS and the Parole Board who hold the keys to release, making the more invisible but vitally important 'back door sentencing' decisions **[10:15]** (see also Padfield and Maruna, 2006).

(iv) Mental Health Review Tribunals

Mentally disordered offenders should, wherever possible, receive care and treatment from health and social services rather than from the criminal justice system. But as the number of hospital beds has decreased, community provision has not necessarily expanded: and we continue to see too many people with serious mental health problems in prison. Violent or dangerous mentally disordered offenders may find themselves in one of the three high security hospitals – Ashworth, Broadmoor and Rampton. There are few long-term medium security hospital provisions. The law itself may have little influence on practical decision-making in a system very short of resources.

The Mental Health Act 1983 (as amended by the Mental Health Act 2007) lays down the ground rules for the detention of mentally disordered people. The police are given powers under sections 135 and 136 of the Act and, as Grounds (1992) says, 'the police are often a frontline agency, and may in effect act as a community psychiatric resource' (at page 287). Section 37 authorises the courts to order hospital admission or guardianship, and they may do this even without convicting the accused. In any case where it makes a hospital order under section 37, a court may also make a restriction order under section 41 (see Street (1999)). The effect of a restriction order is that the patient may not be discharged (except by a Mental Health Review Tribunal), granted leave of absence or transferred to another hospital, without the consent of the Secretary of State for Justice. Section 47 allows the transfer of sentenced prisoners who require psychiatric hospital treatment. The Crime (Sentences) Act 1997 inserted into the 1983 Act 'hospital and limitation directions', which allow the court to order that if the offender does not respond to treatment, they be transferred to prison and not simply discharged from hospital. Public (or media?) concern about the need to protect the public from the risks presented by the mentally unstable led to the Home Office's *Managing Dangerous People with Severe Personality Disorder: Proposals for Policy Development* (1999). With its focus on reducing the risks to the public, the document considered the introduction of a 'dangerous severely personality disordered' order, which could be imposed by a civil court (i.e. without the safeguard of the criminal burden of proof, and merely on a balance of probabilities). Controversies continued with the Department of Health's consultation of a draft Mental Health Bill 2002, and more limited changes were eventually introduced in the Mental Health Act 2007. Perhaps the legal structure of the Mental Health Act 1983 needs less reform than the attitudes of those who provide the resources and facilities for them?

Under the European Convention of Human Rights, Article 5(4) **[1:13]**, everyone is entitled to take proceedings 'by which the lawfulness of his detention shall be decided speedily by a court'. In *X v United Kingdom* (1981) 4 EHRR 188 the European Court of Human Rights decided that all people held because they were of unsound mind were entitled to a periodic judicial consideration of the merits of their continued detention. As a result, the role of the Mental Health Review Tribunals (MHRTs) – composed of lawyers, doctors and lay members – was strengthened by the Mental Health Act 1983. The role of MHRTs is to decide who can safely be released from hospital. They will usually meet in the hospital where the patient is detained. It is particularly difficult for a person who is or has been mentally disordered to prove to the satisfaction of the tribunal that their detention is not justified 'with a view to the protection of other persons' (see the Mental Health Act 1983, section 72(1)(a)). Legal aid is available, which is rare in a tribunal: the legal aid provisions were expanded to cover MHRTs largely as a result of a high profile campaign by the pressure group MIND. MHRTs have the advantages, over formal courts, of flexibility and informality, but as a result their performance is all the more difficult to assess. Peay (1989) conducted an important and thorough study. She is concerned by the covert dependence on the 'good sense' of tribunals: should legal criteria be taken more seriously or is the 'welfarist' approach more appropriate? Baker (1993) stressed the risks in using dangerousness as a criterion in decision-making. Predictions of dangerousness, inevitably inaccurate, tend to lead to over-prediction. For this reason, if no other, it is particularly important to evolve clear legal criteria for the detention of those deemed 'dangerous'. Holloway and Grounds **[10:16]** researched the process more recently, and their conclusions include a discussion of the role of the medical member of the MHRT.

The shortcomings of the system continue to be revealed by litigation: the House of Lords in *R (H) v Secretary of State for Health* [2006] 1 AC 441 confirmed once again that Article 5(4) required not only an initial right of access to a court or tribunal to decide whether the criteria for detention were met but also the availability of subsequent review at reasonable intervals, and the European Court of Human Rights in *HL v United Kingdom* (2005) 40 EHRR 32 once again upheld a complaint that a patient's Article 5(1) and (4) rights had been infringed. This case involved an autistic man who was kept at Bournewood Hospital by doctors against the wishes of his carers, and does not concern the criminal justice process, but it shows that there is no room for complacency! It is not the purpose of this section to deal in detail with the role of the MHRT, but readers are encouraged to compare and contrast the different rules concerning the Parole Board with those of the MHRT. More offenders with severe mental health problems should be diverted away from prison and into more appropriate facilities: but it may be as difficult to get released from a mental hospital as it is to be released from prison. Peay (2012) also cautions that mentally disordered offenders are not, and should not, be treated as an isolated category. Treatment needs to be available in prisons, hospitals and in the community.

An underlying concern highlighted in this book has been the need for procedural fairness and political accountability. Offenders need real procedural safeguards from the time of their arrest onwards. Such protections remain vital in a process which allows bodies such as the Parole Board or MHRTs to predict who is fit for release from prison or who is a danger to the public. However, as Lacey (1986) pointed out, the actual and perhaps inevitable powerlessness of the offender at the post-conviction stage may often render effective use of court-like procedures an impossibility. She suggested that it makes more sense, if we are concerned principally with substantive fairness, to concentrate on ensuring fair procedures involving participation and accountability at the policy-making stage. Procedural justice is important, but real, substantive, justice even more so. This book has highlighted some of the tensions evident in the criminal justice process, but it is important to look also at fundamental principles. A system which is under constant pressure to save money is likely to take shortcuts: it is unlikely to value procedural fairness adequately, and even less likely to tackle the underlying causes of crime. The time has now come to invite the student to go back to first principles, to consider the proper functions of the criminal law and to analyse the meaning of criminal justice. Return to Chapter 1, and begin a further evaluation of the criminal justice process!

Further reading

Annual Reports of HM Chief Inspector of Prisons for England and Wales, of the Probation Service, the Prison Service, the Parole Board, etc

Baker, E, 'Dangerousness, Rights and Criminal Justice' (1993) 56 MLR 528

Bottoms, A, Gelsthorpe, L and Rex, S, *Community Penalties: change and challenges* (2001) Willan

Canton, R, *Probation: Working With Offenders* (2011) Routledge

Corston Report, *A review of women with particular vulnerabilities in the criminal justice system* (2007)

Council of Europe Reports to the United Kingdom Government on Visits to the UK carried out by the European Committee for the Prevention of Torture and Inhuman and Degrading Treatment (www.cpt.coe.int)

Coyle, A, *Understanding Prisons: Key issues in policy and practice* (2005) Open University Press

Eaton, M, *Women After Prison* (1993) Open University Press

Gelsthorpe, L, and Morgan, R (eds), *Handbook of Probation* (2007) Willan

Gelsthorpe, L and Padfield, N (eds), *Exercising Discretion: Decision-making in the criminal justice system and beyond* (2003) Willan

Genders, E and Player, E, 'The commercial context of criminal justice: prison privatisation and the perversion of purpose' [2007] Crim LR 513

Grounds, A, 'Mental Health Problems' in Stockdale, E and Casale, S (eds), *Criminal Justice under Stress* (1992) Blackstone

HM Chief Inspector of Prisons for England and Wales, *Women in Prison – a thematic review* (1997) Home Office

HM Inspectorate of Probation, *Victim Contact: An inspection of the victim contact arrangements in Probation Trusts* (2013)

Hulley, S, Liebling, A and Crewe, B, 'Respect in prisons: Prisoners' experiences of respect in public and private sector prisons' (2012) 12 *Criminology and Criminal Justice* 3

Lacey, N, 'Discretion and Due Process at the Post-Conviction Stage' in Dennis, I H (ed), *Criminal Law and Justice* (1986) Sweet & Maxwell

Leibling, A, *Prisons and their Moral Performance* (2004) Oxford University Press

Liebling, A and Crewe, B, 'Prison life, penal power, and prison effects' in Maguire, M, Morgan, R and Reiner, R (eds), *The Oxford Handbook of Criminology* (5th edition, 2012) Oxford University Press

Logan, C H, *Private Prisons, Pros and Cons* (1990) Oxford University Press

Loughlin, M, 'The underside of the law: judicial review and the prison disciplinary system' (1993) 46 *Current Legal Problems* 23

Mair, G, 'The Community Order in England and Wales: Policy and Practice' (2011) 58 *Probation Journal* 215

Mair, G, Cross, N and Taylor, S, *The use and impact of the Community Order and the Suspended Sentence Order* (2007) Centre for Crime and Justice Studies

Morgan, R and Liebling, A, 'Imprisonment: An expanding scene' in Maguire, M, Morgan, R and Reiner, R (eds), *The Oxford Handbook of Criminology* (4th edition, 2007) Oxford University Press

Nash, M, *Police, Probation and Protecting the Public* (1999) Blackstone

Owen, T, Macdonald, A and Livingstone, S, *Prison Law* (4th edition, 2008) Oxford University Press

Padfield, N, *Beyond the Tariff: Human Rights and the Life Sentence Prisoner* (2002) Willan

Padfield, N, 'A Critical Perspective on Private Prisons in England and Wales' in Capus, N, et al (eds), *Public-Prive: vers un nouveau partage du controle de la criminalite?* (2005) Verlag Rüegger

Padfield, N, 'The Parole Board in Transition' [2006] Crim LR 3

Padfield, N (ed), *Who to release? Parole, fairness and criminal justice* (2007) Willan

Padfield, N and Liebling, A, with Arnold, H, *An Exploration of Decision-Making at DLPs* (2000) HO Research Findings No 132

Padfield, N and Maruna, S, 'The Revolving Door at the Prison Gate: Exploring the dramatic increase in recalls to prison' (2006) 6 *Criminology and Criminal Justice* 329

Peay, J, *Tribunals on Trial: A Study of Decision making Under the Mental Health Act 1983* (1989) Clarendon Press

Peay, J, *Decisions and dilemmas: Working with mental health law* (2003) Hart

Peay J, 'Mentally disordered offenders, mental health and crime' in Maguire, M, Morgan, R, and Reiner, R (eds), *The Oxford Handbook of Criminology* (5th edition, 2012) Oxford University Press

Prison Reform Trust (2000) 'Justice For Women: The Need For Reform', The Report of the Committee on Women's Imprisonment, chaired by Professor Dorothy Wedderburn

Raynor, P, 'Community penalties, probation, and offender management' in Maguire, M, Morgan, R and Reiner, R (eds), *The Oxford Handbook of Criminology* (5th edition, 2012) Oxford University Press

Stern, V, *Creating Criminals: Prisons and People in a Market Society* (2006) Zed Books

Street, R, *The restricted hospital order: from court to community* (1999) Home Office Research Study, No 186

Valier, C, 'Litigation as a strategy in penal reform' (2004) 43 *Howard Journal of Criminal Justice* 15

Documents

[10:1] Lord Carter, *Managing Offenders, Reducing Crime: A New Approach*
(2003) Summary (at page 3)

Context of the review
Far greater use is being made of prison and probation, despite the number of people being arrested and sentenced remaining broadly constant.

- The use of prison and probation has increased by a quarter since 1996, whilst the use of fines has fallen by a similar amount. Sentencing practice has become more severe.
- One in four first-time domestic burglars were sent to prison in 1995/96.

  By 2000, this had increased to one in two.

  Tougher sentences have had some limited impact on crime.

- The increased use of prison is estimated to have reduced crime by around 5 per cent, compared to an overall fall of 30 per cent since 1997. Public confidence in sentencing has improved but remains fragile.
- The proportion of people believing sentencing to be "much too lenient" has fallen from one in two to one in three.

  Additional investment in prison and probation since 1998 has improved delivery.

- The Prison Service has dramatically reduced the number of escapes, improved decency and increased the number of offenders achieving basic skills.
- The creation of the National Probation Service has given greater focus to performance management and seen the introduction of a range of new services. The objective now is to ensure that this additional investment is being used to best effect to reduce crime and maintain public confidence.

Current Position

Sentences are poorly targeted and do not bear down sufficiently on serious, dangerous and highly persistent offenders.

- The increased use of prison and probation since 1997 has been concentrated on first time offenders, leading to poor use of additional investment. The variation in sentencing practice between areas remains too large.
- In Merseyside, Magistrates' Courts send one in four burglars to prison, compared to one in two in Staffordshire (despite the areas having the same burglary rates).

Judges and magistrates do not have sufficient information to make the most effective use of prison and probation and to take into account their capacity to deliver.

- This leads to increased overcrowding, reduced time spent by probation staff with offenders and poor transparency in sentencing with increased use of Home Detention Curfew.

The system remains dominated by the need to manage the two services, rather than focusing on the offender and reducing re-offending.

- There remain gaps in the system, with, for example, interventions in prison often not being followed up in the community.

The benefits of competition – from the private and voluntary sector – could be extended further, across both prison and probation.

- The introduction of competition in prisons has provided a strong incentive for improvements in public sector prisons.

Vision

A new approach is needed for managing offenders, to reduce crime and maintain public confidence.

Targeted and rigorous sentences

The Criminal Justice Act provides a platform for major reform and the more effective management of offenders in order to reduce crime and maintain public confidence.

- Judges and magistrates continue to need to have a full range of tough, credible and effective sentences that are enforced.
- Sentences need to reflect the seriousness of the offence and the risk of re- offending – with better targeting of serious, dangerous and persistent offenders.

This means:

- Diverting very low risk offenders out of the court system and punishing them in the community.
- Income-related fines for low risk offenders.
- More demanding community sentences for medium risk offenders.
- Greater control and surveillance (including satellite tracking) of persistent offenders, combined with help to reduce re-offending.
- Custody reserved for serious, dangerous and highly persistent offenders.

New role for the judiciary

Roles and responsibilities need to be clarified for the judiciary.

- Judges and magistrates need to continue to be able to make entirely independent sentencing decisions in individual cases.
- The judiciary needs to ensure the consistent and cost-effective use of prison and probation capacity and to ensure a clear understanding of the link between sentence given and sentence served.

The new Sentencing Guidelines Council provides an immediate opportunity to improve the effectiveness of sentencing.

- Each year the Council should discuss the priorities for sentencing practice with the Home Office. It should then issue guidelines that ensure offences are treated proportionately to their severity, are informed by evidence on what reduces offending and makes cost-effective use of existing capacity.
- The Sentencing Advisory Panel (which works to the Council) should be given responsibility for independently projecting future demand and should produce evidence on the effectiveness of different sentencing options in reducing crime and maintaining public confidence.

If there were new and convincing evidence on interventions that reduce crime then additional resources would need to be found (e.g. if greater use of custody was found to significantly reduce crime, more prisons would need to be built).

A new approach to managing offenders

Building on the significant improvements in delivery over the last seven years, a new approach is needed to focus on the management of offenders.

- Prison and probation need to be focused on the management of offenders throughout the whole of their sentence, driven by information on what works to reduce re-offending.
- Effectiveness and value for money can be further improved through greater use of competition from private and voluntary providers.

This means:

- The establishment of a National Offender Management Service – restructuring the Prison and Probation Services – with a single Chief Executive accountable to Ministers for punishing offenders and reducing re-offending.
- Within the new Service there should be one person – the National Offender Manager – who is responsible for reducing re-offending – supported by Regional Offender Managers. They would supervise offenders and commission custody places, fine collection and interventions – whether in the public, private or voluntary sector.

The Regional Offender Managers would break down the current silos of prison and probation and work across the two services. They would fund the delivery of specified contracts – based on evidence of what reduces re-offending – rather than leaving the services themselves to decide what to deliver.

[10:2] *Woolf Report – Prison Disturbances April 1990*
(1991) HMSO (at page 19)

1.167 Our programme is based on 12 central recommendations. These are that there should be:

(i)   closer co-operation between the different parts of the Criminal Justice System. For this purpose a national forum and local committees should be established;

(ii)   more visible leadership of the Prison Service by a Director General who is and is seen to be the operational head and in day to day charge of the Service. To achieve this there should be a published 'compact' or 'contract' given by Ministers to the Director General of the Prison Service, who should be responsible for the performance of the 'contract' and publicly answerable for the day to day operations of the Prison Service;

(iii)   increased delegation of responsibility to Governors of establishments;

(iv)   an enhanced role for prison officers;

(v)   a 'compact' or 'contract' for each prisoner setting out the prisoner's expectations and responsibilities in the prison in which he or she is held;

(vi)   a national system of Accredited Standards, with which, in time, each prison establishment would be required to comply;

(vii)   a new Prison Rule that no establishment should hold more prisoners than is provided for in its certified normal level of accommodation, with provisions for Parliament to be informed if exceptionally there is to be a material departure from that rule;

(viii)   a public commitment from Ministers setting a timetable to provide access to sanitation for all inmates at the earliest practicable date not later than February 1996;

(ix)   better prospects for prisoners to maintain their links with families and the community through more visits and home leaves and through being located in community prisons as near to their homes as possible;

(x)   a division of prison establishments into small and more manageable and secure units;

(xi)   a separate statement of purpose, separate conditions and generally a lower security categorisation for remand prisoners;

(xii)   improved standards of justice within prisons involving the giving of reasons to a prison for any decision which materially and adversely affects him; a grievance procedure and disciplinary proceedings which ensure that the Governor deals with most matters under his present powers; relieving Boards of Visitors of their adjudicatory role; and providing for final access to an independent Complaints Adjudicator.

1.168 In the following paragraphs and in the remainder of the Report we describe these recommendations more fully. They are central to resolving the problems which have been identified from the April disturbances. They are also a package. They need to be considered together and moved forward together if the necessary balance in our prison system is to be achieved.

[10:3] *Transforming Rehabilitation: A Strategy for Reform*
(2013) Ministry of Justice Response to Consultation CP(R)16/2013 (at page 3)

Ministerial Foreword

Last year, around 600,000 crimes were committed by those who had broken the law before. Nearly half of those released from prison went onto reoffend, in many cases not just once but time and again. Despite increases in spending under the previous Government, reoffending rates have barely changed. This can't go on. I want to ensure that all those who break the law are not only punished, but also receive mentoring and rehabilitation support to get their lives back on track so they do not commit crime again.

It is not a surprise, faced with stubbornly high reoffending rates, that there were important areas of consensus in the response to our recent consultation on 'Transforming Rehabilitation':

- offenders need to be supported 'through the prison gate', providing consistency between custody and community;
- those released from short-sentences, who currently do not get support, need rehabilitation if we are to bring their prolific reoffending under control;
- public protection is paramount, and the public sector must take the key role in keeping people safe;
- the voluntary sector has an important contribution to make in mentoring and turning offenders' lives around;
- nothing we do will work unless it is rooted in local partnerships and brings together the full range of support, be it in housing, employment advice, drug treatment or mental health services.

It is these principles that will act as the foundations of our reform. In order to deliver our shared objectives, we have taken a detailed look at both what the probation service does now, and what needs to change. It is clear that in order to invest in extending and enhancing rehabilitation, we need to free up funding through increased efficiency and new ways of working. I want to bring in the best of the public, private and voluntary sectors to help us achieve this and we will design a competition process which allows a range of organisations, including mutuals, to bid to deliver services; I want to give the front-line professionals the flexibility and resources to innovate and do what works. It is also clear to me that if we are to keep a relentless focus on rehabilitation, providers must have a clear incentive to do so – that is why I am determined the taxpayer will only pay providers in full for those services that actually deliver real reductions in reoffending. When it comes to awarding probation contracts, driving efficiencies will be one factor, but quality of service and the ability to stop the cycle of crime are the central tests. Only by doing this will we bear down on the long-term costs of the criminal justice system.

A new mix of providers with a new set of incentives is essential, but so too are key new services. Through the savings we make, we will extend rehabilitation support to those on short-term sentences, who currently have the highest reoffending rates but who are typically left to their own devices on release. This support will be guaranteed through legislation, which is the only way to ensure we target the hardest to reach and most prolific offenders. In addition to extending rehabilitation to more offenders, we will for the first time create a genuine 'through the gate' service. This has been paid lip-service in the past, so I have ordered the wholesale realignment of our prison service to designate new local resettlement prisons, where the same providers who will be working with offenders in the community will work with them for three months before release too. Combined with the reforms to prison regime we announced last month to incentivise engagement in rehabilitation, this is a significant change. We are, for the first time, creating real continuity between custody and community, easing the transition which at present frequently just leads an offender back to a life of crime.

But again, it is not enough to connect custody and community. We have also got to work with local authorities, Police and Crime Commissioners, and other government departments, joining up our efforts to ensure that offenders can access the broad package of support they need to get their lives back on track. I am keen that the priorities of Police and Crime Commissioners and local agencies are taken into account to inform our commissioning decisions. I am also clear that providers should demonstrate how they will work in and strengthen local partnerships to deliver the results they are incentivised to achieve. There is a role for government leadership here too, so the Ministry of Justice and the Department for Health are coming together to test a 'through the gate' drug treatment programme for offenders, which we intend to roll out alongside the rehabilitation reforms. By fostering this type of partnership, we can bring the full weight of resources to bear as we tackle reoffending.

Breaking the cycle of crime will mean fewer victims in the long term, but we will not forget our primary responsibility for public safety now. This is a key role that is rightly fulfilled by the public sector. We will forge a new National Probation Service, drawing on the expertise and experience of its staff, focused on assessing risk, and managing those who pose the greatest risk of serious harm to the public. We will also recognise the dynamic nature of risk, by ensuring that the public sector has the right to review cases where risk is more volatile or circumstances have changed. At root, I know that protecting the public relies on the judgements of those working with offenders. I understand that it is imperative to sustain and develop the skills of probation professionals whether they are working in the public, private or voluntary sectors. So, as part of our reforms, we will be working with the probation profession to take forward the idea of an Institute of Probation, to recognise and spread best practice.

To conclude, our strategy for reform includes a strong National Probation Service tasked with protecting the public from the most dangerous offenders; a new mix of providers equipped with the flexibility and the right incentives to reduce reoffending; and some important systemic changes to provide effective rehabilitation to those who need it most, and when they need it most, during that crucial transition from custody to community.

I believe we have put together a programme of reform that offers a step change in the way we rehabilitate offenders, and will lead to year-on-year reductions in reoffending. Some of these changes are complex and challenging, but they are necessary nonetheless. Transforming rehabilitation will help to ensure that all of those sentenced to prison or community sentences are properly punished while being supported to turn their backs on crime for good. This will mean lower crime, fewer victims and safer communities. We are determined to deliver, and we are developing detailed plans to do so. I look forward to working with you in the coming months as we make these proposals real.

. . .

Executive Summary

This paper sets out how we will transform the way we rehabilitate offenders, to make progress in driving down reoffending rates. We are clear that the level of reoffending by offenders who have already passed through the justice system has remained unacceptably high for too long.

The case for a new approach is clear. We spend more than £3bn a year on prisons, and almost £1bn annually on delivering sentences in the community. Despite this, overall reoffending rates have barely changed over the last decade and we see the same faces coming back through the system – almost half of all offenders released from custody in 2010 reoffended within a year. Over 6000 offenders sentenced to short custodial sentences of less than 12 months in the year to June 2012 had previously received more than 10 community sentences, yet gaps in the sentencing framework mean little can be done to prevent them from returning to crime once they are released back into the community.

The reasons why offenders turn to crime vary widely. Our reforms are designed to enable flexibility to tailor rehabilitative work, with an emphasis on responding to the broader life management issues that often lead offenders back to crime. We know, for example, that 15%

of prisoners report that they were homeless before entering prison, and around a quarter are thought to suffer from anxiety and depression. Unemployment and substance misuse rates are also high amongst offenders. We also know that we can drive efficiencies in the system to invest in better rehabilitation. We have seen this potential in other parts of the system. The first round of prison competition achieved savings of £216m when compared to current costs and the London Community Payback scheme achieved a 37% reduction in pre competition costs.

By fundamentally reforming the system, and finding efficiencies to extend rehabilitation to more offenders, we can start to make a difference. The reforms we will implement include:

- for the first time in recent history, new statutory rehabilitation extended to all 50,000 of the most prolific group – offenders sentenced to less than 12 months in custody;
- a fundamental change to the way we organise the prison estate, in order to put in place an unprecedented nationwide 'through the prison gate' resettlement service, meaning most offenders are given continuous support by one provider from custody into the community;
- opening up the market to a diverse range of new rehabilitation providers, so that we get the best out of the public, voluntary and private sectors, at the local as well as national level;
- new payment incentives for market providers to focus relentlessly on reforming offenders, giving providers flexibility to do what works and freedom from bureaucracy, but only paying them in full for real reductions in reoffending;
- a new national public sector probation service, working to protect the public and building upon the expertise and professionalism which are already in place.

Our design of this strategy has been guided both by consultation responses, and our commitment to maintain fair and appropriate provision for all groups, including minority offender groups. We have paid early consideration to the likely impacts of our plans on those with protected characteristics and will continue to meet our responsibilities under the Equality Act 2010 as our plans develop further.

We need to stop offenders passing through the system again and again, creating more victims and damaging communities. At a time of financial constraints, it becomes even more important that the money we spend on rehabilitating offenders has the greatest possible impact.

The *Transforming Rehabilitation* Consultation

We consulted on the principles behind the proposals for reform set out in this document from 9 January to 22 February 2013 in the paper *Transforming Rehabilitation: a revolution in the way we manage offenders.*

We received almost 600 formal responses to the consultation and held 14 consultation events which were attended by over 800 stakeholders. We had responses from Probation Trusts and individual officers, Police and Crime Commissioners, private and voluntary and community sector organisations, sentencers through collective and individual responses, Local Authorities and partnerships, other justice system stakeholders, Parliamentarians, members of the public, many of whom worked with offenders, and including some individual offenders.

There was strong support in consultation responses for a drive to reduce reoffending. In particular, respondents agreed that extending rehabilitation to prolific short sentenced offenders and reorganising the prison estate to support continuous rehabilitation from custody into the community were much needed reforms. Other views received have been invaluable in informing the system design and we have made changes to the design proposed in response. For example:

- Many mentioned that by better aligning the prison system with rehabilitative services delivered in the community this could support better outcomes. We will make changes to the way the prison estate is organised and how services delivered there link with those in the community (see Part 1).
- We heard comments that the 'payment by results' payment mechanism must ensure that providers were incentivised to work with all offenders, including the most difficult. We developed our payment mechanism in a way which will ensure this is the case (see Part 1).
- Many respondents were concerned that by retaining responsibility for managing offenders who pose a high risk of serious harm to the public sector probation service, but giving market providers responsibility for others, we might cause fragmentation in delivery. The system design for protecting the public sets out how we will address this, and in particular how we envisage changing risk levels are handled (see Part 2).
- There was also a strong view that we needed to draw on the local expertise of smaller organisations, in particular in the VCSE (Voluntary, Community and Social Enterprise) sector, by ensuring they could participate in bids to deliver services. In response to concerns that the contract package areas over which services would be competed were too large, we have decided to increase the number of areas to maximise the range of providers which can be involved in delivery. Similarly, we have developed a locally responsive commissioning system which, while structured nationally for greatest efficiency, can reflect local and Police and Crime Commissioner priorities and needs (see Part 3).

. . .

A Strategy for Reform

The details of the system design are set out in the following sections of this document:

Part 1: Reducing Reoffending describes how our reforms will tackle reoffending rates head on and describes the system which will underpin this. We will put in place services which work to rehabilitate offenders 'through the prison gate' from custody into the community; we will extend rehabilitation to the most prolific group of re-offenders – those who are released from short custodial sentences; we will open up delivery of rehabilitative services to a wider range of providers, including experts in the voluntary and community sector; we will give providers flexibility to do what works and ability to ensure offenders engage with rehabilitation requirements, introducing legislation where necessary; and we will pay providers according to the reductions in reoffending they achieve.

Part 2: Protecting the Public sets out how we will ensure public protection is at the heart of our reformed system. A new national public sector probation service will retain the management of offenders who pose a high risk of serious harm to the public and who have committed more serious offences; new providers will have contractual obligations to work in partnership with the public sector probation service in managing risk of serious harm; and vital public interest functions will continue to be exercised by the national probation service.

Part 3: Making the System Work explains how we will make sure the new system is effective and efficient in practice. We have designed commissioning arrangements which will be responsive to local and national priorities; a system which can join up funding streams from different Government departments and integrate with existing partnerships; and will put in place effective governance and assurance arrangements over delivery.

Part 4: Implementing Reform sets out a potential timetable for putting this system in place. We will implement our new system in phases, to allow time for providers to prepare bids, for the public sector to restructure while minimising any disruption to business as usual and to allow time for new services to be set up. But we need to make progress towards reducing reoffending now, and it is our aim that new services should begin to operate from the end of 2014.

[10:4] House of Commons Justice Committee, *Crime reduction policies: a co-ordinated approach? Interim report on the Government's Transforming Rehabilitation programme*

(2014) The Stationery Office (at page 3)

Summary

The Ministry of Justice has embarked on a radical and controversial programme to change the scope and structure of community and prison-based probation and rehabilitative services, including opening up the provision of such services to a greater diversity of providers and the introduction of an element of payment for results achieved in reducing reoffending. The Transforming Rehabilitation reforms involve a substantial recasting of the way probation services are provided, and engender sharply differing views both among our witnesses and members of this Committee: some see them as the only means of extending support to short-sentenced prisoners and facilitating innovation through the involvement of private and voluntary sector providers in rehabilitative provision; others believe that the resulting transfer of functions away from the public sector, which will retain responsibility for high risk offenders, is either undesirable in principle, or too risky. We do not seek to resolve this difference in our report but to clarify how the system might operate and how risks will be managed.

We encountered broad support for the programme's aim to use efficiencies in the delivery of existing probation services to provide post-release supervision to short-sentenced prisoners, rectifying a long-standing anomaly in the system whereby those who tend to be the most prolific offenders currently receive no statutory support. We welcome the introduction of services for this group, but consider that care will need to be taken to ensure that any gains made in reducing reoffending by them do not come at the expense of the supervision of offenders on other sentences, and do not diminish the value of community sentences which are proven to be a cost-effective way of dispensing justice for non-violent offenders.

Witnesses in our inquiry, including some supportive of the proposed changes, had significant apprehensions about the scale, architecture, detail and consequences of the reforms – some of which are still to be determined and much of which has not been tested – and the pace at which the Government is seeking to implement them. In particular, our witnesses with professional experience of probation saw potential risks to the effective management of offenders arising from the Government's decision to split the delivery of probation services between a public National Probation Service dealing with the highest-risk offenders and the new providers who will be dealing with low and medium risk offenders. While there is some evidence base for aspects of the reforms, there is a question about how much they are indicative of the potential of the entire programme. The absence of piloting means that some witnesses lack confidence that the particular commissioning model and the novel payment by results mechanism proposed will work better than the existing system. The Government must recognise that any model introduced at the beginning of the new system is likely to require modification in the light of experience and must continue to be open to public and parliamentary scrutiny.

We recognise that, as well as the risks involved in change, there are also risks involved in not taking action to deal with the gaps and weaknesses in the present system. While the Government has undertaken to test the model with shadow state-run companies before contracting the new arrangements out to new providers, there is a lack of systematic information about the risks they might encounter during implementation and full operational conditions and the steps that they will take to mitigate those risks. They also do not appear to have devised clear contingency plans in the event that the competition fails to yield a viable new provider for a particular area, or that a new provider subsequently fails. In such circumstances, it is not clear whether the Government will be able to implement or retain the supervision of short-sentenced prisoners, or whether this element of the programme is contingent on having a complete system in place.

The Ministry has high expectations of what can be achieved in the way of efficiency savings and extension of services through contracting out the management of low and medium risk offenders within existing resources. We wished to examine the affordability of the reforms, the initial costs of which are likely to be considerable but which might, over the longer-term, lessen as demand on the system falls, but we have been unable to determine whether sufficient funding is in place on the limited information that the Government has provided. Furthermore, a key question for the Government is how the focus on reducing reoffending will be maintained while the restructuring of the market that is necessary to create the desired efficiencies takes place.

[10:5] HM Inspectorate of Probation, *Transforming Rehabilitation: 'An independent inspection setting out the operational impacts, challenges and necessary actions', April 2014 — September 2014*

(2014) (at page 4)

Foreword

The Government's *Transforming Rehabilitation* reforms are fundamentally changing the way that adult probation services are organised and delivered. Such a huge shift is inevitably controversial and their likely implications are subject to ongoing debate. It is not for the Inspectorate to engage in such political debate, but to provide the public with a clear evidenced picture of implementation on the ground, to test effectiveness through objective methods and to recommend improvements.

While still too soon to test effectiveness through offender outcomes, a series of inspections completed between April and September 2014 focused on the operational impacts of early *Transforming Rehabilitation* implementation. In particular, Inspectors looked at the newly created interface between the National Probation Service and Community Rehabilitation Companies, while the latter are still publicly operated.

In any type of business, the splitting of one organisation into two separate organisations is bound to create process, communication and information sharing challenges that did not previously exist. This report highlights that challenge for probation services in a fast moving and complex programme of reform. It is clear that many of the issues will not be solved overnight and will remain a challenge for some time to come – but they need close attention and must be addressed in a timely way by all concerned.

It is important to note that a number of the findings set out in this report already existed before the changes on 1 June 2014. We found that the process of implementing change had exposed existing shortfalls in systems, processes, practice quality, consistency, leadership and management. Therefore, in addition to addressing challenges resulting from the introduction of Transforming Rehabilitation, our recommendations also deal with existing issues. We found probation areas that had been struggling to deliver a quality service prior to Transforming Rehabilitation are now finding it hardest to adapt and cope with the challenges brought by the reforms. Conversely, those areas which had performed well in previous inspections were proving most able to implement changes with limited disruption. The correlation between the historical performance of former probation trusts and progress being made with *Transforming Rehabilitation* implementation extended into the important issue of how staff were coping personally with the changes. There were clear differences between organisations we inspected in the confidence felt by those charged with actually delivering services, in the management of the changes. This is an issue that speaks to the urgent and continuing need to support the necessary improvement in the quality of leadership and management.

We were pleased to see that the allocation of cases to the new organisations, the National Probation Service and the Community Rehabilitation Companies, had in the vast majority of cases been achieved in good time for the 1 June 2014 go live date. However, this was despite some concerns raised about the support provided by the Ministry of Justice and the National Offender Management Service.

Some issues identified in court work during the early weeks of implementation were being tackled and were settling over the period of our inspections. Nevertheless, there remains significant challenges in getting the court end processes working as they should. Positively, the quality of reports provided by the National Probation Service to courts supported sentencing proposals appropriately. Negatively, the lack of staff in some areas of the National Probation Service was having a detrimental impact on the delivery of some of the services being provided. This resource issue needs to be addressed in order to ensure an efficient system and avoid potential backlogs.

In fact, there is a need to streamline and speed up processes generally. We found that the majority of organisations we inspected were making progress, but it is clear that the interface between the National Probation Service and Community Rehabilitation Companies will continue to cause challenges that will need to be addressed. The relationships between the two new organisations in each area varied in terms of the extent they worked together to resolve communication issues.

IT continues to provide a predictable challenge. We share the frustration expressed by many staff about the complexities of a number of the new tasks and the lack of integration of IT systems. There is a risk that increased bureaucracy could stifle future innovation, so the issues raised by staff about IT require serious attention. The solution is not straightforward, and in the meantime the continuing impact should not be underestimated.

The speed of the implementation has in itself caused operational problems that could have been avoided, or at least mitigated. A good example of this is the speed at which staff had to learn new processes and systems before being expected to implement them. We sometimes found that new processes were being communicated by email to staff for implementation the next day, with little or no time for training or instruction. We accept that the issue of adopting new procedures is necessarily short-term. However, it is important to recognise the impact that this has had on staff morale, and on the efficiency of the service they were providing. Further process development needs to be handled more efficiently, with each step anticipated, planned and communicated in a timely way. Staff must be supported more appropriately through subsequent implementation of process change.

The matching of resources, particularly staff resources, to the Transforming Rehabilitation workload has been challenging. There were significant gaps, especially in courts, in the early weeks of implementation, and the recovery from that position has often been slow and difficult for staff on the ground. Now we have provided a better understanding of the impact of new systems and the way organisations are working together, it is an appropriate moment for this important issue to be revisited. A full re-evaluation should be carried out to ensure an appropriate match between resources and workload.

Credit should go to staff in Community Rehabilitation Companies and the National Probation Service for the efforts they have put into implementing new processes. However, we are particularly concerned by a significant disconnect between senior managers and frontline staff in understanding and perceptions of the reforms. A key factor in successfully managing change on this scale is the degree to which staff feel well communicated with. But even more important is the degree to which they are engaged in the process. Even allowing for the scale and complexity of these changes we remain concerned that the gap in perception is, in some cases, as wide as it could be. All too often when staff have looked to their senior leaders for reassurance, support and guidance during this period of change to their working environment, they perceive them to be facing in a different direction. That is disappointing, and needs to change quickly. If staff do not feel fully engaged, then the impact on the effectiveness of the service provided is bound to fall short. The nature of communication and staff engagement from the top to the bottom needs urgent attention.

Overall, this report highlights the complexity of the challenges for probation, the operational impact of the Transforming Rehabilitation changes to date, and progress made in addressing them during early implementation. It also exposes the reality of the inconsistency in application of the changes and the shortfalls in quality of service provision, some of which already existed prior to implementation of Transforming Rehabilitation. Consequently, the evidence found points to a mixed picture on the ground.

Probation is on a journey and it is right to point out in this fast paced period of significant change, that during the time lag between the evidence collected by our inspectors and the publication of this report further changes will have been made. Some of the issues we raise here will have been dealt with, and others not. But the fact that progress has been made in the interim must not lead to any complacency on any of our parts. There is no doubt at all that there remains much more to do.

There is now an urgent need for operations and processes to reach a 'steady state' in order for managers and staff to be able think, plan and deliver effectively. What happens in this next period of implementation, and particularly the way it is led and managed, is crucial to ensuring the longer-term development of quality and innovation in Probation that the public expects.

[10:6] Worrall, A and Hoy, C, *Punishment in the Community: Managing Offenders and Making Choices*
(2nd edition, 2005) Willan

The final chapter of this book focuses on the future of punishment in the community (seen through the lens of 2004/5, of course), arguing that it is custody that should be seen as the alternative, and that probation officers "must continue to engage with the social worlds that offenders inhabit" (at page 211).

(At page 205):

Globalization of (community) punishment talk

The English-speaking world of probation and community corrections has been pre-occu-
pied with a model of focused, accountable, standardized intervention in the lives of offenders, based on the actuarial concept of risk assessment, the science of cognitive behavioural
psychology, the morality of individual responsibility and the politics of restorative justice. At
the same time, that world has seen a dramatic rise in the prison population and a blurring
of the boundary between freedom and custody. Offenders increasingly receive sentencing
packages that involve time spent under supervision both inside and outside prison, and
technology now makes it possible for many of the restrictions of imprisonment to be visited on offenders in their own homes and communities. In addition, practitioners are often
overloaded with the bureaucratic demands of 'programme integrity' and evaluation, finding
themselves with less and less time to consider the underlying values and philosophy of their
work and thus making themselves vulnerable to the vagaries of crisis-driven law and order
policy. The globalization of punishment talk has provided comforting prêt a manger solutions in the form of an international trade in penal ideas, of which 'What Works' is but one –
the fast food of punishment in the community. Little account, it seems, need be taken of
regional, let alone local differences of demography, culture or economy. So how do we make
sense of these developments in the context of the globalization of crime and punishment
discourses? How do we take advantage of the insights offered by global knowledge while at
the same time taking account of national, regional and local differences? How can we learn
from each other without being forced into adopting a bland and simplistic language which
we *think* we all recognize but which may, in reality, mean very little to any of us? If the 'What
Works' agenda is to be more than just a 'phase' in the treatment of offenders, then it needs to
demonstrate that it has within it the seeds of its own development and adaptation to changing social, political and economic circumstances.

The question of *practice wisdom* involves national and international comparative
research, in order to learn about approaches and programmes that are successful with particular types of offenders, in particular locations at particular times. Some will be cognitive-
behavioural programmes that lend themselves to conventional forms of evaluation. But many
more will have grown out of locally identified needs and resources, not the least of which
will be enthusiastic and skilful individual workers. Not all will immediately reduce recidivism
in any measurable way, but all will be aiming to influence offenders' attitudes, behaviour
and circumstances, making them 'stop and think' before offending next time and thus offering the greatest hope of long- term protection for the public. In this search for practice wisdom, there is also a need to explore what *doesn't* work. It is part of the received wisdom of
'What Works' that intervention which focuses only on insight-giving or the therapeutic relationship and which does not include a problem-solving dimension is not successful with
offenders. But what is less well publicised is that there is plenty of research on other things
that don't work (Trotter 1999). These include approaches which focus on blame and punishment, those where the goals are set only by the worker rather than collaboratively, lack of
clarity on the part of the worker about his or her role and authority, pessimism and a negative
attitude by the worker and, finally, failing to see the offender in their family and social context.

The question of *political awareness* involves asking why the simple phrase 'What Works'
has become so invested with meaning. Or is it precisely because it lacks meaning that it has
become so ubiquitous? There are at least four interest groups whose purposes might be
served by the 'What Works' agenda and whether those interests are to be viewed positively or
negatively will depend entirely on one's standpoint:

- The interests of *governance* are served to the extent that the 'What Works' agenda demonstrates to a sceptical public that community sentences can be tough, demanding and based on scientific premises which can be tested and evaluated.
- The interests of *management* are served to the extent that the agenda demonstrates accountability – showing that resources are being used efficiently, effectively and, above all, economically – and giving managers confidence that they know exactly what their workers are doing and why.
- The interests of *professionalism* are served to the extent that the agenda reassures individual workers that they are doing something worthwhile with the minimum of risk to their own status – that the areas in which they have to exercise their own judgement are limited and consequently so is the potential for error, thus reducing the otherwise stressful nature of the job.
- Finally, the interests of *restorative justice* are served to the extent that the offender, victim and, possibly, the wider community believe that the agenda delivers on its promises. Whatever the content of any particular intervention, it can be argued that 'What Works' aims to instil in the offender a sense of responsibility towards the community in general and empathy for the victim in particular. But in return, the offender has the right to expect to be *reintegrated* into that community and unless that right is respected, 'What Works' becomes little more than a sophisticated form of the stocks – as indeed it is for many sex offenders who, no matter what programmes they have co-operated with, remain irredeemable and non-reintegratable in the eyes of the community.

[10:7] Padfield, N, *Understanding Recall 2011*
(2013) University of Cambridge Faculty of Law Research Paper No 2/2013

Summary

The primary aim of this small project was to increase understanding of the recall process. The two specific research questions were

- Are the reasons for recall clearly understood (both by prisoners and those who work in the criminal justice system)?
- What can be done to reduce the number of prisoners recalled to prison?

Forty-six prisoners (36 men and 10 women) were interviewed in two local prisons about their experience of being recalled to prison. These prisoners were serving a wide variety of sentences, from life (3), extended sentences (9), to less than 2 years (10). At the same time, a wider 'snap-shot' of recall was obtained by a review of 129 prisoners' files, and context-setting interviews were held with a number of probation and NOMS staff.

In interview, several prisoners felt that they had been 'set up to fail' by unreasonable licence conditions, which had been inadequately discussed with them. Their relationship with their probation officers varied, and several showed real sympathy with their probation officers for the difficult decisions they had to make. However, many felt 'let down' by probation officers. They told powerful stories about the difficulties of building law-abiding lives when on licence. Some accepted why they had been recalled, but could not understand why it was taking so long for them to be re-released. Most seemed to think that their probation officer had far too much power, and many argued for a more judicialised process.

Thirty-three of the 46 prisoners (including the 7 fixed term recalls) interviewed had been recalled for allegations of fresh offences. For some this was a 'fair cop', but many strenuously denied the offences, some suggesting that they had been 'stitched–up'. Several were not subsequently charged, or the charges were later dropped. Others were acquitted at court. None of these prisoners could understand why they remained in prison as recalled offenders. Even those who had pleaded guilty, or intended to do so, were angry at some of the perceived injustices of the process: for example, the fact they did not have remand prisoner status, or the period spent on recall after a short fresh sentence had been completed.

Thirteen of the 46 had been recalled for breaching conditions of their licence, not for allegations of further offending. These 'unacceptable failures' included being expelled from Approved Premises, failing to demonstrate motivation to deal with drug addiction, associating with known offenders, using a computer, and not making contact or losing contact with their probation officers.

All prisoners had received a 'recall pack' or 'recall dossier' after they had been returned to prison. For many, this was too complicated, and many were irritated by the negative and outdated account of them given in the dossier, and by the reliance on risk predictors, which seemed impossible to challenge. The overwhelming impression given by the prisoners was that they had little knowledge or understanding of what was being done to progress their case. The invisibility of those empowered to make the decision to release them, and the uncertainty which surrounds the release process were both enormously debilitating. Parole Board panels were perceived as part of a distant bureaucracy which takes unreasonable and uncertain time to reach decisions. The different roles of the Ministry of Justice's PPU and the Parole Board were not understood. Prisoners felt that they were not given reliable information. Prison staff were seen as uninformed, or at worst, deliberately unhelpful. There was widespread misunderstanding of the process: for example, the criteria for the somewhat rare 'fixed term' recall; or whether a 'standard' recall is for a fixed or indefinite term. Even those who understood the process were deeply frustrated by it.

Many of the offenders interviewed in this study did not appear to need to be in prison for public protection, certainly not in the sense of being a vivid 'danger' to society. Whilst there was a risk of them re-offending, for many this risk seemed to be exacerbated, rather than reduced, by some licence conditions and particularly by further imprisonment.

Possible policy implications:

- Sentence management: 'beginning to end' sentence management should include the transition of offenders from prison to the community (and, if necessary and appropriate, back to prison). There needs to be a review of the way prisoners progress from prison to the community, for example, via Approved Premises. Probation officers should actively supervise 'their' offenders who are in custody. Their role as both licence enforcer and sympathetic supporter of released offenders needs review.
- The role of the courts in the management of offenders. The law and practice on bail and recall, in the light of what is clearly inconsistent current practice, needs review. Priority should also be given to the codification of sentencing law, to include the law on release and recall, including the powers and practice of the Parole Board (a review should consider whether sentence review courts would work better to encourage offenders to earn their way out of prison and off supervision, and also to encourage NOMS to provide swift, well prepared support packages).
- Human rights and fairness issues. Prisoners should be provided with better general advice on recall (leaflets, video etc), as well as with better individual advice (oral practical

advice on the wings, as well as confidential legal advice, perhaps by way of 'champions' on the wings); they should receive reliable and regular updates on the progress of their applications for re-release.

Future research should explore:

- the perceptions of recall by other criminal justice professionals and participants, including other offenders, and not only those currently in prison.
- the ways different sentences are implemented in practice (exploring, for example, the realities of serving an extended sentence, as well as life and IPP sentences).
- the current use of recall, including the different forms of recall, the use of non-disclosed 'intelligence', and other 'sanctions' apart from recall.
- whether there are better ways to stimulate good behaviour, to increase individual motivation, and to prepare prisoners prior to release.
- the role of the probation officer, in the light of the development of MAPPA, PPO schemes, and the changing role of the police in the supervision of offenders.
- comparative research (particularly in European jurisdictions) on both the law and practice in this area.

Many of the prisoners in this study felt they had had little support whilst on licence. Back in prison, they could pass weeks, or months, wondering what was happening to their 'case'. Prisoners described a level of support in prison which often seemed almost non-existent. This could appear inhumane, unfair and counter-productive. It was also a wasted opportunity. What this small study would suggest is that, if the 'system' of recall is to be perceived as fair and legitimate, prisoners deserve more information, more advice, more certainty and much less delay.

[10:8] Corston Report, *A review of women with particular vulnerabilities in the criminal justice system*
(2007) Home Office (at page 2)

Executive summary and recommendations

1. This has been a short and economic review, not an in-depth lengthy resource intensive commission. In nine months I have held five consultation events, visited six women's prisons, three women's community centres and one medium secure women's hospital. I have had over 40 meetings with individuals and groups and over 250 people have contributed in some way to my review. There is much more that could be done but I am confident that I have seen and heard enough to enable me to draw conclusions and make recommendations. I have interpreted my terms of reference liberally and sought to include all those women whom I regard as either inappropriately located in prison and all those outside who are at risk of offending. I consider these women in terms of their "vulnerabilities", which fall into three categories. First, domestic circumstances and problems such as domestic violence, child-care issues, being a single-parent; second, personal circumstances such as mental illness, low self-esteem, eating disorders, substance misuse; and third, socio-economic factors such as poverty, isolation and unemployment. When women are experiencing a combination of factors from each of these three types of vulnerabilities, it is likely to lead to a crisis point that ultimately results in prison. It is these underlying issues that must be addressed by helping women develop resilience, life skills and emotional literacy.

2. There are three important and very positive points that I want to make at the outset. First the number of self-inflicted deaths of women in prison custody has fallen. No one wishes to be complacent about this and every single death is one too many. Nevertheless, it is encouraging that the numbers have fallen from 14 in 2003 and 13 in 2004 to four in 2005 and three in 2006. I have no doubt that this reduction is in part due to the determined efforts of many staff and greatly improved drug treatment services in all women's prisons. The dark days of Waite Wing are, I hope, gone forever. Second, the provision of all types of health services within women's prisons has improved in recent years with prison health having been absorbed into the NHS and this is welcome. Third, I pay tribute to the many dedicated, caring staff working throughout all of the criminal justice agencies, who strive every day to provide a decent environment and improve the well-being of the women in their care. I have been very impressed by much of what I have seen.

3. I have, however, concluded that it is timely to bring about a radical change in the way we treat women throughout the whole of the criminal justice system and this must include not just those who offend but also those at risk of offending. This will require a radical new approach, treating women both holistically and individually – a woman-centred approach. I have concluded that there needs to be a fundamental re-thinking about the way in which services for this group of vulnerable women, particularly for mental health and substance misuse in the community are provided and accessed; there needs to be an extension of the network of women's community centres to support women who offend or are at risk of offending and to direct young women out of pathways that lead into crime.

4. Women have been marginalised within a system largely designed by men for men for far too long and there is a need for a "champion" to ensure that their needs are properly recognised and met. There is also a need for an integrated approach across government demonstrated by the creation of an Inter-Departmental Ministerial Group for women who offend or are at risk of offending supported by a Commission for this group of women as a visible, strategic lead. I have also concluded that there needs to be a re-design of women's custody introduced in parallel with other gender specific workable disposals and sanctions. I summarise below the main conclusions of my review. I also set out chapter-by-chapter all of my recommendations, which build into my Blueprint which can be found in Chapter 8 of my report.

Chapter 2. Men and women; equal outcomes require different approaches – the need for a distinct approach.

5. My first recommendation concerns the treatment of men and women within the criminal justice system. From April 2007 the government will have a statutory duty to take positive action to eliminate gender discrimination and promote equality under the Equality Act. I have seen little evidence that much preparatory work is in hand in respect of the imminent statutory duty or of any real understanding that treating men and women the same results in inequality of outcome. Equality does not mean treating everyone the same. The new gender equality duty means that men and women should be treated with equivalent respect, according to need. Equality must embrace not just fairness but also inclusivity. This will result in some different services and policies for men and women. There are fundamental differences between male and female offenders and those at risk of offending that indicate a different and distinct approach is needed for women. For example:

- Most women do not commit crime;
- Women with histories of violence and abuse are over represented in the criminal justice system and can be described as victims as well as offenders;

- The biological difference between men and women has different social and personal consequences;
- Proportionately more women than men are remanded in custody;
- Women commit a different range of offences from men. They commit more acquisitive crime and have a lower involvement in serious violence, criminal damage and professional crime;
- Relationship problems feature strongly in women's pathways into crime;
- Coercion by men can form a route into criminal activity for some women;
- Drug addiction plays a huge part in all offending and is disproportionately the case with women;
- Mental health problems are far more prevalent among women in prison than in the male prison population or in the general population;
- Outside prison men are more likely to commit suicide than women but the position is reversed inside prison;
- Self-harm in prison is a huge problem and more prevalent in the women's estate;
- Women prisoners are far more likely than men to be primary carers of young children and this factor makes the prison experience significantly different for women than men;
- Because of the small number of women's prisons and their geographical location, women tend to be located further from their homes than male prisoners, to the detriment of maintaining family ties, receiving visits and resettlement back into the community;
- Prison is disproportionably harsher for women because prisons and the practices within them have for the most part been designed for men;
- Levels of security in prison were put in place to stop men escaping;
- The women's prison population suffers disproportionately because of the rapidly increasing male prison population and the pressure to find places for men, leading to re-roling of female prisons;
- 30% of women in prison lose their accommodation while in prison; and
- Women and men are different. Equal treatment of men and women does not result in equal outcomes.

Recommendation

Every agency within the criminal justice system must prioritise and accelerate preparations to implement the gender equality duty and radically transform the way they deliver services for women.

Chapter 3. Life and death. How women experience prison – the need for a *radically different* approach.

6. These were the women I saw in prisons:

- Most were mothers. Some had their children with them immediately prior to custody, others had handed them to relatives or their children had been taken into care or adopted. Some were pregnant. Some discovered they were pregnant when they had no idea that that could be a possibility.
- They were drug users. It was not uncommon to have £200 a day crack and heroin habits disclosed.
- They were alcoholics.
- They often looked very thin and unwell.

- They had been sexually, emotionally and physically abused.
- They were not in control of their lives.
- They did not have many choices.
- They were noisy and at first sight confident and brash but this belied their frailty and vulnerability and masked their lack of self-confidence and esteem. They self-harmed.
- They had mental health problems.
- They were poor.
- They were not all the same, they were individuals.
- There were significant minority groups, including BME and foreign national women.

7. A soon-to-be published report of women in custody explains how women recounted the stress that came from newly encountering the prison environment, with crowding, noise and a threatening atmosphere. They were alarmed at sharing cells with women with mental health problems and who self-harmed; they were frightened and unprepared when confronted with women who were suffering severe drug withdrawal or seizures. They complained that the prison environment was dirty with unhygienic sharing of facilities. Five women in a dormitory could be sharing one in-cell sink, which was being used for personal washing as well as cleaning eating utensils. There was a lack of fresh air and ventilation. Some women reported that vermin were present in the areas where they ate, slept and stored their personal food items. Prison facilities hindered them from maintaining self-care, including limited access to personal hygiene products and restricted access to bathing. Shower facilities were often dirty. I too was dismayed to find that in some of the prisons I visited there were toilets, often without lids, in cells and dormitories, sometimes screened by just a curtain, sometimes not screened at all. It is humiliating for women to have to use these facilities in the presence of others, most particularly during menstruation.

8. The following describes a typical ten-day period in a women's local prison:

- A woman had to be operated on as she had pushed a cross-stitch needle deep into a self-inflicted wound.
- A woman in the segregation unit with mental health problems had embarked on a dirty protest.
- A pregnant woman was taken to hospital to have early induced labour over concerns about her addicted unborn child. She went into labour knowing that the Social Services would take the baby away shortly after birth.
- A young woman with a long history of self-harm continued to open old wounds to the extent that she lost dangerous amounts of blood. She refused to engage with staff. A woman was remanded into custody for strangling her six-year old child. She was in a state of shock.
- A woman set fire to herself and her bedding.
- The in-reach team concluded that there was a woman who was extremely dangerous in her psychosis and had to be placed in the segregation unit for the safety of the other women until alternative arrangements could be made.
- A crack cocaine addict who displayed disturbing and paranoid behaviour (but who had not been diagnosed with any illness) was released. She refused all offers of help to be put in touch with community workers.

9. We must find better ways to keep out of prison those women who pose no threat to society and to improve the prison experience for those who do. One example is the regular,

repetitive, unnecessary overuse of strip-searching in women's prisons which is humiliating, degrading and undignified and a dreadful invasion of privacy. For women who have suffered past abuse, particularly sexual abuse, it is an appalling introduction to prison life and an unwelcome reminder of previous victimisation. It is also clear that prison is not the right place for many women. They need help and caring, therapeutic environments to assist them rebuild their lives. This is not an easy option; it is demanding a great deal of women to delve into issues they prefer to block out. For those with drug addictions clinical detoxification does not stop the habit. Those women for whom prison is necessary would clearly benefit from being in smaller units closer to home or more easily accessible for visitors, such as in city centres. The existing system of women's prisons should be dismantled and replaced by smaller secure units for the minority of women from whom the public requires protection.

Recommendations

The government should announce within six months a clear strategy to replace existing women's prisons with suitable, geographically dispersed, small, multi-functional custodial centres within 10 years.

Meanwhile, where women are imprisoned, the conditions available to them must be clean and hygienic with improvements to sanitation arrangements addressed as a matter of urgency.

Strip-searching in women's prisons should be reduced to the absolute minimum compatible with security; and the Prison Service should pilot ion scan machines in women's prisons as a replacement for strip-searching women for drugs. The work underway in respect of foreign national offenders should take account of the views expressed in my report. The strategy being developed should include measures designed to prevent prison becoming a serious option.

Deaths in custody and bereaved families

10. In Chapter 3 of my report I describe the circumstances of some recent self-inflicted deaths of women in prison and the grief these tragedies cause to their families. Most depressing was the familiarity of these events, which followed the same patterns time and again with little indication that lessons were being learned to prevent further deaths. I make a recommendation concerning families' access to public funding for legal representation at inquests. The state has unlimited access to legal funding and will always have legal representation and Counsel at inquests that engage Article 2 of the European Convention on Human Rights, the right to life. It is inequitable that families whose close relatives have died whilst being cared for by the state should undergo means testing when applying for legal funding to represent their interests.

Recommendation

Public funding must be provided for bereaved families for proper legal representation at timely inquests relating to deaths in state custody that engage the state's obligations under Article 2 of the European Convention on Human Rights. Funding should not be means tested and any financial eligibility test should be removed whenever Article 2 is engaged. Funding should also cover reasonable travel, accommodation and subsistence costs of families' attendance at inquests.

Chapter 4. Who's in charge? The need for visible leadership and a strategic approach

. . .

Seven pathways to resettlement

13. I considered work in hand in connection with the seven resettlement pathways which I fear are leading to fragmentation of services and funding streams. Many of the small voluntary agencies working with women do not fit exclusively into a sole pathway and these artificial divisions risk putting an intolerable administrative burden on these small bodies. I looked closely at the pathway on accommodation because that is women's greatest resettlement concern on release and it seems to me to be the pathway most in need of speedy, fundamental gender specific reform. I also spent some time during my review considering education, learning, training and skills because this is a subject in which I have a particular interest and which seemed to me during my visits and meetings very sadly lacking in the concept of emotional literacy, the base from which all learning must start. Respect for one another, forming and maintaining relationships, developing self-confidence, simply being able to get along with people without conflict must come before numeracy and literacy skills. Life skills, for example, how to live as a family or group, how to contribute to the greater good, how to cook a healthy meal, are missing from the experiences of many of the women in modern society who come in contact with the criminal justice system. The chaotic lifestyles and backgrounds of many women result in their having very little employment experience or grasp of some very basic life skills. Two additional pathways for women have been developed to the credit of the Prison Service Women and Young People's Group and I recommend that they should be mandatory in every regional resettlement plan for women, namely:

- Pathway 8: support for women who have been abused, raped or who have experienced domestic violence.
- Pathway 9: support for women who have been involved in prostitution.

. . .

And finally

28. An additional 8,000 places for men are planned and a reported £1.5 billion is being sought to fund them. Unless the current sentencing trend can be reversed, more must follow. A much smaller level of funding would provide an opportunity for government to do something innovative for women. I do not pretend that my proposals will free up hundreds of prison places overnight. It will take time and determination and persistence but I do believe that, if my package of recommendations is implemented, over time the women's prison population will decrease. Another factor that makes this the right time to take action is that new commissioning arrangements are currently being worked up by the National Offender Management Service. The time is right to adopt a new approach to women in the criminal justice system, with central drive and direction at the highest level of a long-term strategy, coupled with a sound structure for commissioning services.

[10:9] House of Commons Justice Committee, *Women offenders: after the Corston Report*
(2013) Second Report of Session 2013–14 (at page 3)

Summary

Baroness Corston's report *A review of women with particular vulnerabilities in the criminal justice system* made a series of recommendations to bring about improvements in the women's criminal justice system. Now, six years after her report, we found that it is well recognised that women face very different hurdles from men in their journey towards a law abiding life, and that responding appropriately and effectively to the problems that women bring into the criminal justice system requires a distinct approach. Our examination of developments in policy and practice over this period indicates that in the first two years of the Coalition Government there was a hiatus in efforts to make headway on implementing such an approach. We welcome the fact that, after we announced our inquiry, the Secretary of State recognised the importance of these issues, and assigned particular Ministerial responsibility for women offenders. We consider that clear leadership and a high level of support from other Ministers will be essential in restoring lost momentum. The Minister has set out four strategic priorities, which we support, and has created a new Advisory Board to work across Government and with key stakeholders in order to further these priorities. We would like to see these commitments, which appear to have been produced in haste, given greater substance and accompanied by measures of success.

A key lesson still to be learnt is that tackling women's offending is not just a matter for the justice system. We believe that there must be much more explicit recognition, including by the Parliamentary Under Secretary for Justice, Women and Equalities, of the need to focus as much on those women and girls at the periphery as those who are already involved in the system. We welcome the commitment to generate a 'whole system' approach to these issues but there is little to signal a radical shift in thinking about what this means. We suggest some additional safeguards to broaden cross-departmental accountability including extending full representation on the newly created Advisory Board to other relevant Government Departments and the inclusion of matters relating to women's offending as a standing item on the agenda for the Inter-Ministerial Group on Equalities. We recommend that, once adopted, these governance arrangements are subsequently reviewed to consider whether responsibility for the overall strategic approach should transfer to the Department for Communities and Local Government.

There is little evidence that the equality duty, and its forerunner the gender equality duty, have had the desired impact on systematically encouraging local mainstream commissioners to provide services tackling the underlying causes of women's offending, or on consistently informing broader policy initiatives within the Ministry of Justice and the National Offender Management Service (NOMS). Both struggle to reflect fully the distinct needs of female offenders. We are extremely disappointed that there is still not sufficient evidence about what those needs are, or how best to address them. There have been improvements in the provision for women, notably the development of a network of women's community projects. We believe these projects must be maintained as they are central to providing a distinct approach to the treatment of women offenders, as well as playing an integral role in supporting women at risk of criminality.

We urge NOMS to consider gender as a matter of course, rather than seeking to reduce any detrimental impact on women of their general approach after the event. The most striking incidence of this is the likely impact of the Transforming Rehabilitation reforms which have clearly been designed with male offenders in mind. We welcome the Government's extension of "through the gate" support to prisoners sentenced to less than 12 months, which should benefit many women offenders. The concentration on reducing reoffending seems likely to reinforce the loss of generic funding for women's community centres that has occurred since NOMS gained oversight of their funding. It is also uncertain whether there will be sufficiently strong data about what is effective for women offenders to enable new providers to make sensible commissioning decisions. We consider that there is a compelling case for commissioning services for women offenders separately and for applying other incentive mechanisms that would also encourage the diversion of women from crime.

We make a series of recommendations about the Government's review of the female custodial estate, which we welcome. Taking the size of the women's prison population as a given when recent legislative changes may create some headroom represents a missed opportunity to address wider concerns, including that: the women's prison population has not fallen sufficiently fast; over half of women continue to receive ineffective short custodial sentences; and appropriate community provision which would arrest the use of custody, such as mental health and substance misuse treatment, remains unavailable to the courts in sufficient volume. We propose that the custodial estate review should examine in particular: the impact of recent, and planned cost savings and staff headcount reductions; means of encouraging women to take more responsibility; support for the development and sustainability of family ties; resettlement support for foreign national prisoners; staff training and competencies; and alternative forms of community-based residential provision for women who have committed offences of lesser seriousness but who might benefit from constructive regimes and support.

Prison is an expensive and ineffective way of dealing with many women offenders who do not pose a significant risk of harm to public safety. We revisited Baroness Corston's suggestion that those women who have committed serious offences should be held in smaller, more dispersed, custodial units. Having considered this carefully we recommend a gradual reconfiguration of the female custodial estate, coupled with a significant increase in the use of residential alternatives to custody as well as the maintenance of the network of women's centres, as these are likely to be more effective, and cheaper in the long-run, than short custodial sentences.

[10:10] Prison Act 1952 (as amended)

Sections 1; 47

1 General control over prisons

All powers and jurisdiction in relation to prisons and prisoners which before the commencement of the Prison Act 1877 were exercisable by any other authority shall, subject to the provisions of this Act, be exercisable by the Secretary of State.

47 Rules for the management of prisons, remand centres and young offender institutions

(1) The Secretary of State may make rules for the regulation and management of prisons, remand centres, young offender institutions or secure training centres respectively, and for the classification, treatment, employment, discipline and control of persons required to be detained therein.

(2) Rules made under this section shall make provision for ensuring that a person who is charged with any offence under the rules shall be given a proper opportunity of presenting his case.

(3) Rules made under this section may provide for the training of particular classes of persons and their allocation for that purpose to any prison or other institution in which they may lawfully be detained.

(4) Rules made under this section shall provide for the special treatment of the following persons whilst required to be detained in a prison, that is to say –

(d) any person detained in a prison, not being a person serving a sentence or a person imprisoned in default of payment of a sum adjudged to be paid by him on his conviction or a person committed to custody on his conviction.

(4A) Rules made under this section shall provide for the inspection of secure training centres and the appointment of independent persons to visit secure training centres and to whom representations may be made by offenders detained in secure training centres.

(5) Rules made under this section may provide for the temporary release of persons detained in a prison, remand centre, young offender institution or secure training centre not being persons committed in custody for trial before the Crown Court or committed to be sentenced or otherwise dealt with by the Crown Court or remanded in custody by any court.

[10:11] *Hague v Deputy Governor of Parkhurst Prison*
[1991] 3 All ER 733

Hague was deemed to be a trouble-maker, and was transferred to another prison, where he was removed from association under rule 43 of the Prison Rules. The Court of Appeal had granted a declaration that, because of errors of procedure, the removal had been unlawful, but refused *certiorari* and damages. Weldon alleged that he had been forcibly dragged downstairs and detained without clothes overnight in a strip cell. The (differently constituted) Court of Appeal had refused to strike out that part of the statement of claim which was based on false imprisonment. The House of Lords in both cases was concerned not with judicial review, but only with civil actions for breach of statutory duty and false imprisonment.

Lord Bridge (at page 737):

My Lords, there are two appeals before the House. I shall refer to them as *Hague's* case and *Weldon's* case respectively. They raise important questions with respect to the rights of convicted prisoners.

Introduction

The decisions of the Court of Appeal in *R v Hull Prison Board of Visitors, ex p St Germain* [1979] 1 All ER 701, [1979] QB 425 and of this House in *Leech v Deputy Governor of Parkhurst Prison* [1988] 1 All ER 485, [1988] AC 533 established that the courts have jurisdiction to entertain applications for judicial review of disciplinary awards made by boards of visitors and by prison governors respectively under the Prison Rules 1964, SI 1964/388. In both cases it had been contended, in effect on behalf of the Home Office, that jurisdiction should be declined on the ground that any interference by the courts in the management of prisons would be subversive of prison discipline. In *Leech's* case [1988] 1 All ER 485 at 499, [1988] AC 533 at 566, as I record, Mr Laws had urged that, if jurisdiction were accepted in relation to awards by prison governors, this would 'make it impossible to resist an invasion by what he called 'the tentacles of the law' of many other departments of prison administration'. In deciding the appeal your Lordships faced that prospect without undue alarm and I believe that the circumstances of *Hague's* case now before the House show that it was right to do so. In *Hague's* case both courts below held that they had jurisdiction to entertain an application for judicial review which questioned the legality of Hague's segregation under r 43 of the Prison Rules and the Court of Appeal declared that the procedure followed pursuant to the terms of a Home Office circular issued in 1974 (Circular Instruction 10/1974) was not warranted by the terms of the rule and was accordingly unlawful. In your Lordships' House the Secretary of State, acting by Mr Laws, has chosen, very sensibly if I may say so, not to pursue any challenge either to the assumption of jurisdiction or to its exercise by the declarations granted. Instead the Home Office have issued a new circular prescribing a new procedure to be followed in future in the relevant circumstances which conforms to the requirements of r 43 as construed by the Court of Appeal. I believe this confirms the view that the availability of judicial review as a means of questioning the legality of action purportedly taken in pursuance of the Prison Rules is a beneficial and necessary jurisdiction which cannot properly be circumscribed by considerations of policy or expediency in relation to prison administration. Those considerations only come into play when the court has to consider, as a matter of discretion, how the jurisdiction should be exercised. But the issues which it is necessary to resolve in the present appeals relate neither to the scope of the courts' public law jurisdiction in judicial review nor to the exercise of discretion in that jurisdiction. The appeals raise the wholly different question whether a convicted prisoner who, in the course of serving his sentence, has been treated in a way which the rules do not permit has in any and what circumstances a cause of action in private law sounding in damages against the prison governor or the Home Office on the ground either of a breach of statutory duty or of the tort of false imprisonment.

(At page 739):

Breach of statutory duty

It was not open to counsel for Hague in any court below your Lordships' House to advance a claim to damages for breach of statutory duty because of the decision of the Court of Appeal in *Becker v Home Office* [1972] 2 All ER 676, [1972] 2 QB 407, where one of the grounds on which it was held that the plaintiff failed was that a breach of the Prison Rules does not, per se, give rise to a cause of action. But Mr Sedley has now put the claim for damages in *Hague's* case on this alternative basis in the forefront of his argument and I think it logical to consider it first.

In *Becker v Home Office* [1972] 2 All ER 676, [1972] 2 QB 407 both Lord Denning MR and Edmund Davies LJ expressed their conclusion that a breach of the Prison Rules 1964 creates no civil liability in equally general terms. Mr Sedley submits that such a general approach is erroneous and that each provision in the rules must be considered separately. Whilst I do not accept this criticism of the earlier authorities, I do accept that we may properly be invited in asking the question whether the breach of a particular provision of the rules gives rise to a cause of action to examine that provision in its context. Adopting that course, I can find nothing in r 43 or in any context that is relevant to the construction of r 43 which would support the conclusion that it was intended to confer a right of action on an individual prisoner. The purpose of the rule, apart from the case of prisoners who need to be segregated in their own interests, is to give an obviously necessary power to segregate prisoners who are liable for any reason to disturb the orderly conduct of the prison generally. The rule is a purely preventive measure. The power is to be exercised only in accordance with the procedure prescribed by sub-r (2). But where the power has been exercised in good faith, albeit that the procedure followed in authorising its exercise was not in conformity with r 43(2), it is inconceivable that the legislature intended to confirm because of action on the segregated prisoner.

(At page 742):

False imprisonment

The Court of Appeal in *Weldon's* case approached the question whether a prisoner serving his sentence can ever sustain a claim for false imprisonment, as they were invited to do so by Mr Laws, as a single question which must admit of the same answer irrespective of the identity of the defendant. Ralph Gibson LJ, delivering the leading judgment, with which both Fox and

Parker LJ agreed, said ([1990] 3 All ER 672 at 681, [1990] 3 WLR 465 at 474): 'There is no reason, apparent to me, why the nature of the tort, evolved by the common law for the protection of personal liberty, should be held to be such as to deny its availability to a convicted prisoner whose residual liberty should, in my judgment, be protected so far as the law can properly achieve unless statute requires otherwise. If, however, as [Mr Laws] submits, the tort of false imprisonment is not available to a convicted prisoner against a prison officer, I accept his sub-mission that it could not, for the same reasons, be available to a convicted prisoner against a fellow prisoner.'

Ralph Gibson LJ had also delivered the judgment of the Divisional Court in *Hague's* case in which he expressed the view that the segregation of a prisoner would not constitute the tort of false imprisonment if the order for segregation, although not lawfully authorised under r 43, was given in good faith. Giving the judgment in *Weldon's* case he found it unnecessary to express a final conclusion on this point since, if want of good faith were a necessary ingre-dient of the tort, he held that it was sufficiently alleged in the pleading against the officers concerned. The pleading, he held, also alleged circumstances capable of amounting to 'intol-erable conditions of detention' such as would sustain a claim of false imprisonment on the au-thority of the decision of the Court of Appeal in *Middleweek v Chief Constable of the Merseyside Police* [1990] 3 All ER 662, [1990] 3 WLR 481. It was on these grounds that the Court of Appeal declined to strike out the pleading of false imprisonment in *Weldon's* case. Parker LJ, in adding his own reasons to his agreement with those given by Ralph Gibson LJ, was clearly much con-cerned with the problem of the rights of prisoners as against fellow prisoners or prison officers acting in bad faith. He said ([1990] 3 All ER 672 at 686, [1990] 3 WLR 465 at 480):

'Although the plaintiff may, in the end, fail to establish the facts, we must proceed for the moment on the basis that he was kept locked up naked overnight in a cell known as a strip cell. It is said that as he was lawfully detained in the prison this cannot amount to false imprisonment. If this be right it must I think follow that he could have had no claim for false imprisonment if his detention naked in that cell had continued for weeks. It would also seem to me to follow that if he had been locked up in a similar condition, not by prison officers, but by fellow inmates, he would have no such claim. It would follow, too, that, if a convicted criminal were confined in a prison which he and his fellows were permitted, within the confines of a perimeter fence enclosing some acres of ground, to lead normal lives he would have no such claim if he were locked up, with or without clothes, in a shed in some remote part of the grounds, whether by fellow inmates or prison officers. To hold that such treatment could not amount to false imprisonment offends in my judgment against common sense.'

In so far as the Court of Appeal's reasoning in these judgments proceeds from the prem-ises urged upon them by Mr Laws that a prisoner's 'right to liberty' is either totally abrogated or partially retained in the form of a 'residual liberty', I think, with all respect, that it is errone-ous. To ask at the outset whether a convicted prisoner enjoys in law a 'residual liberty', as if the extent of any citizen's right to liberty were a species of right in rem or a matter of status, is to ask the wrong question. An action for false imprisonment is an action in personam. The tort of false imprisonment has two ingredients: the fact of imprisonment and the absence of lawful authority to justify it. In *Meering v Grahame-White Aviation Co Ltd* (1919) 122 LT 44 at 54 Atkin LJ said that 'any restraint within defined bounds which is a restraint in fact may be an impris-onment'. Thus if A imposes on B a restraint within defined bounds and is sued by B for false imprisonment, the action will succeed or fail according to whether or not A can justify the restraint imposed on B as lawful. A child may be lawfully restrained within defined bounds by his parents or by the schoolmaster to whom the parents have delegated their authority. But if precisely the same restraint is imposed by a stranger without authority, it will be unlawful and will constitute the tort of false imprisonment.

I shall leave aside initially questions arising from the situation where a convicted prisoner serving a sentence is restrained by a member of the prison staff acting in bad faith, by a fellow prisoner or any other third party, or in circumstances where it can be said that the conditions of his detention are intolerable. I shall address first what I believe to be the primary and fundamental issue, viz whether any restraint within defined bounds imposed upon a convicted prisoner whilst serving his sentence by the prison governor or by officers acting with the authority of the prison governor and in good faith, but in circumstances where the particular form of restraint is not sanctioned by the Prison Rules, amounts for that reason to the tort of false imprisonment. The starting point is s 12 (1) of the Prison Act 1952 which provides: 'A prisoner, whether sentenced to imprisonment or committed to prison on remand pending trial or otherwise, may be lawfully confined to any prison.'

This provides lawful authority for the restraint of the prisoner within the defined bounds of the prison by the governor of the prison, who has the legal custody of the prisoner under section 13, or by any prison officer acting with the governor's authority. Can the prisoner then complain that his legal rights are infringed by a restraint which confined him at any particular time within a particular part of the prison? It seems to me that the reality of prison life demands an alternative answer to this question. Certainly in the ordinary closed prison the ordinary prisoner will at any time of day or night be in a particular part of the prison, not because that is where he chooses to be, but because that is where the prison regime required him to be. He will be in his cell, in the part of the prison where he is required to work, in the exercise yard, eating meals, attending education classes or enjoying whatever recreation is permitted, all in the appointed place and at the appointed time and all in accordance with a more or less rigid regime to which he must conform. Thus the concept of the prisoner's 'residual liberty' as a species of freedom of movement within the prison enjoyed as a legal right which the prison authorities cannot lawfully restrain seems to be quite illusory. The prisoner is at all times lawfully restrained within closely defined bounds and if he is kept in a segregated cell, at a time when, if the rules has not been misapplied, he would be in the company of other prisoners in the workshop, at the dinner table or elsewhere, this is not the deprivation of his liberty of movement, which is the essence of the tort of false imprisonment, it is the substitution of one form of restraint for another.

Mr Harris seeks to surmount these difficulties by submitting that whenever there is a breach of the rules which is sufficiently 'fundamental' this converts an otherwise lawful imprisonment into an unlawful imprisonment. This, as I understand it, is quite a different concept from that of an infringement of residual liberty. The submission is that any breach of the rules which is sufficiently far reaching in its effect on the prisoner, for example the failure to supply him with clothing 'adequate for warmth and health' pursuant to r 20(2), undermines the legality of his imprisonment. Logically this would lead to the conclusion that the prisoner who has not been supplied with proper clothing would be entitled to walk out of the prison, but Mr Harris understandably disclaims any such extravagant proposition. It follows that the authority given by s 12(1) for lawful confinement of the prisoner cannot possibly be read as subject to any implied term with respect to compliance with the Prison Rules and this is fatal to any submission which seeks to make the lawfulness of the imprisonment depend in any sense on such compliance.

In my opinion, to hold a prisoner entitled to damages for false imprisonment on the ground that he has been subject to a restraint upon his movement which was not in accordance with the Prison Rules would be, in effect, to confer on him under a different legal label a cause of action for breach of statutory duty under the rules. Having reached the conclusion that it was not the intention of the rules to confer such a right, I am satisfied that the right cannot properly be asserted in the alternative guise of a claim to damages for false imprisonment.

(At page 745):

There remains the question whether an otherwise lawful imprisonment may be rendered unlawful by reasons only of the conditions of detention. In *R v Metropolitan Police Comr, ex p Nahar* (1983) Times, 28 May, two applicants for habeas corpus who had been remanded in custody were held pursuant to the provisions of s 6 of the Imprisonment (Temporary Provisions) Act 1980 in cells below the Camberwell Green Magistrates' Court which were designed only to enable persons to be held in custody for a few hours at a time and which were obviously deficient in many respects for the purpose of accommodating prisoners for longer periods. They sought their release on the ground that the conditions of their detention rendered it unlawful. The applications were rejected, but Stephen Brown J said in the course of his judgment: 'There must be some minimum standard to render detention lawful . . . ' McCullough J said: 'Despite the temporary nature of the detention there contemplated, there must be implied into s 6 of the 1980 Act some term which relates to the conditions under which a prisoner may lawfully be detained. I say so because it is possible to conceive of hypothetical circumstances in which the conditions of detention were such as would make that detention unlawful. I do not propose to offer any formulation of that term. Were it broken in any particular case I would reject emphatically the suggestion that the matter would not be one for the exercise of the court's jurisdiction to grant the writ of habeas corpus.'

These observations were considered by the Court of Appeal in *Middleweek v Chief Constable of the Merseyside Police* [1990] 3 All ER 662, [1990] 3 WLR 481. The plaintiff has been awarded damages for false imprisonment by the jury on the basis that his otherwise lawful detention at a police station has been rendered unlawful because it was unreasonable in the circumstances to keep him in a police cell. The defendant successfully appealed, but Ackner LJ, delivering the judgment of the court, said ([1990] 3 All ER 662 at 668, [1990] 3 WLR 481 at 487):

> 'We agree with the views expressed by the Divisional Court that it must be possible to conceive of hypothetical cases in which the conditions of detention are so intolerable as to render the detention unlawful and thereby provide a remedy to the prisoner in damages for false imprisonment. A person law fully detained in a prison cell would, in our judgment, cease to be so lawfully detained if the conditions in that cell were such as to be seriously prejudicial to his health if he continued to occupy it, e.g. because it became and remained seriously flooded, or contained a fractured gas pipe allowing gas to escape into the cell. We do not therefore accept as an absolute proposition that, if detention is initially lawful, it can never become unlawful by reasons of changes in the conditions of imprisonment.'

I sympathise entirely with the view that the person lawfully held in custody who is subjected to intolerable conditions ought not be to left without a remedy against his custodian, but the proposition that the conditions of detention may render the detention itself unlawful raises formidable difficulties. If the proposition be sound, the corollary must be that when the conditions of detention deteriorate to the point of intolerability, the detainee is entitled immediately to go free. It is impossible, I think, to define with any precision what would amount to intolerable conditions for this purpose. McCollough J understandably and perhaps wisely abstained from any attempt of definition in *Ex p Nahar*. The examples given by Ackner LJ of a flooded or gas-filled cell are so extreme that they do not, with respect, offer much guidance as to where the line should be drawn. The law is certainly left in a very unsatisfactory state if the legality or otherwise of detaining a person who in law is and remains liable to detention depends on such an imprecise criterion and may vary from time to time as the conditions of his detention change.

The logical solution to the problem, I believe, is that if the conditions of an otherwise lawful detention are truly intolerable, the law ought to be capable of providing a remedy directly related to those conditions without characterising the fact of the detention itself as unlawful. I see no real difficulty in saying that the law can provide such a remedy. Whenever one person is lawfully in the custody of another, the custodian owes a duty of care to the detainee. If the custodian negligently allows, or a fortiori, if he deliberately causes, the detainee to suffer in any way in his health he will be in breach of that duty. But short of anything that could properly be described as a physical injury or an impairment of health, if a person lawfully detained is kept in conditions which cause him for the time being physical pain or a degree of discomfort which can properly be described as intolerable, I believe that could and should be treated as a breach of the custodian's duty of care for which the law should award damages. For this purpose it is quite unnecessary to attempt any definition of the criterion of intolerability. It would be a question of fact and degree in any case which came before the court to determine whether the conditions to which a detainee had been subjected were such as to warrant an award of damages for the discomfort he had suffered. In principle I believe it is acceptable for the law to provide a remedy on this basis, but that the remedy suggested in the *Nahar* and *Middleweek* cases is not. In practice the problem is perhaps not very likely to arise.

Conclusion

For the reasons I have given I conclude that a claim for damages either for breach of statutory duty or for false imprisonment is not sustainable in either of the cases before the House.

[10:12] Hood, R and Shute, S, *Parole Decision-making: Weighing the Risk to the Public*

(2000) HO Research Findings No 114 (at page 2)

The research aimed to assess the effectiveness and efficiency of the parole system. It examined:

- how the Parole Board assessed applications
- whether interviews conducted by Parole Board members made a difference to the decisions reached
- the relationship between parole decisions and actuarially-based risk assessment scores
- reasons given for refusing or granting parole
- how probation officers' recommendations influenced parole decisions.

There are various stages in parole decision-making. In addition to the information in a prisoner's dossier (which includes details of the offence, previous convictions and reports from prison and probation officers), Parole Board Interviewing Members (PBIMs) visit prisons to interview prisoners about their parole application. Their reports are added to prisoners' dossiers and forwarded to the Parole Board. Three-member panels of the Board meet in London and on each occasion consider the dossiers of 24 parole applicants. Dossiers are read in advance and at the meeting members take it in turns to 'lead' the discussion, having prepared reasons for their decision which may be amended after discussion.

Research Methods

The research was carried out in two linked phases:

- 151 PBIM interviews were observed in 14 prisons and the prisoners and PBIMs concerned were interviewed

- interviews with 63 seconded probation officers, 112 prison officers and 103 prisoners who had recently been refused parole
- questionnaires were sent to the prisoners' home probation officers.

In addition, 20 Parole Board panel meetings were observed where the applications of the 151 prisoners were discussed along with others. Information was gathered on decisions made about 437 prisoners. Panel members were asked about the value of the PBIM report. They were also asked to make an assessment of the risk of reconviction posed by each prisoner.

Decision-Making

Members of panels rarely disagreed. The lead member's opinion was confirmed in 82% of cases. In a further 10%, the lead member's opinion was confirmed after some dissent and discussion. The final decision differed from that initially expressed by the lead member in only 8% of the cases observed. A prediction model of parole decision-making was calculated on the basis of data extracted from the prisoners' dossiers but not including the PBIM report. The model correctly predicted both Yes and No decisions in 85% of cases:

- 49% of the prisoners had a very low probability of release (between 0%–20%); only 4% of them were released
- at the other end of the scale, 17% had a very high probability of parole (80% and above); 89% were paroled
- taking these together, Parole Board decisions for 65% of prisoners were predicted by the statistical model with 94% accuracy.

With so many decisions correctly predicted from other information in the dossier, there was little room for the PBIM report to have a substantial impact on the decisions made. Indeed, those who drafted the reasons for the panel's decision said that their decision had been changed by something contained in the PBIM report in only 8% of cases.

The Parole Rate

Power to release on parole is now called Discretionary Conditional Release (DCR) and applies to those prisoners sentenced to four years or longer. The only valid comparison that can be made between the parole rate before and after the introduction of DCR is the proportion of prisoners in both periods who received parole at some time prior to having served two-thirds of their sentence. Of those serving four years or more who were reviewed between June 1992 and May 1995, under the old system, 69.7% were released on parole. By comparison, the latest Report of the Parole Board for 1998–99 shows that 47.7% of prisoners dealt with under the DCR system from its inception in October 1992 until March 1999 were granted parole. Thus, 22% fewer prisoners are now paroled during their sentence – equivalent to a 32% decline in the use of parole.

Reasons that might explain this decline are:

- the introduction of the Directions, which gave priority to risk, and the way that Board members have interpreted these Directions
- that under the new DCR system all prisoners are supervised after release whether paroled or not, whereas formerly prisoners only received supervision if granted parole
- that most prisoners now only get one parole review, whereas under the old system they had at least two.

Granting or Refusing Parole

As required by the Directions, panels, in their written reasons, placed great emphasis on risk factors and on whether or not prisoners had 'satisfactorily addressed their offending behaviour' – by completing an offending behaviour treatment course, for example.

When the panel refused parole, specific indicators of risk were mentioned in 84% of cases. These were mostly based on the prisoner's past history – factors such as the seriousness of the offence, previous history of sexual or violent offending, previous failure to respond to supervision and breaches of bail.

Progress, or lack of progress, made by the prisoner in addressing offending behaviour was the reason mentioned in 96% of refusals and 98% of cases where parole was granted. In a third of the cases refused, the panel stressed that 'more work' should be done, or should be 'consolidated' in prison, rather than while under parole supervision in the community.

Panels mentioned in their reasons that 73% of prisoners granted parole had 'satisfactory release plans'. However, in only one-third of cases where parole was granted did the panel state in their reasons that risk would be further reduced by a period on parole supervision. This perhaps suggests that members of the Board do not have a great deal of confidence in the effectiveness of parole supervision as a method of containing or reducing risk.

More than 80% of the refused prisoners who were interviewed said that the reasons they had been given were 'unfair'. Three-quarters said that the reasons given had not made them change their behaviour, and nearly all the rest said they had responded negatively to the 'knock back'.

Licence Conditions

The average period of parole licence granted to the paroled prisoners was 330 days. Before the introduction of DCR, 44% of prisoners were paroled with further conditions attached to their licence (see Hood and Shute, 1994 and 1995). In this study, 87% had conditions attached. For example, of those paroled, 52% had a residence condition in comparison with 15% under the old system. 82% were released on condition they continued to deal with their offending behaviour (including drugs, alcohol, anger and sexual behaviour) in comparison with 32%. Furthermore, 44% of those paroled had three or more conditions attached. All prisoners are now supervised on release from prison whether paroled or not. 60% of those not paroled (who formerly had no conditions at all) had at least three conditions attached on release from prison. Thus, the degree of control over prisoners after release has increased and widened.

Parole Related to Reconviction Risk

The risk of a prisoner committing further offences if released on parole licence is the main consideration of the Board. Parole decisions can be compared with actuarial, objectively determined risk of reconviction data. A risk of reconviction score (ROR) has been calculated by Copas et al., 1996, on the basis of a follow-up study of a large number of prisoners. Parole decisions in this study were analysed, separately for non-sex and sex offenders, in relation to the ROR for a serious offence (one likely to lead to imprisonment) during the period available for parole. The findings for non-sex offenders are shown in Table 1.

As can be seen in Table 1, there was a strong and statistically significant correlation between actuarial ROR and the parole decision so far as non-sex offenders were concerned. Although half of the sex offenders had a ROR of 7% or less (average 3.7%), 40% of them were denied parole, demonstrating the Board's considerable caution.

The Board was even more cautious in relation to sex offenders. Only 22% of those with a risk of reconviction rate of 7% or less (average 3.2%) were paroled. As the ROR was not a major factor

Table 1 Relationship between ROR for a serious offence on parole licence and parole decision (for non-sex offenders)

Actuarial risk of reconviction	No. of cases observed	Cases paroled (No.)	Cases paroled (%)	Percentage of cases in each risk group
0%–2%	52	43	83	15%
3%–7%	115	58	50	33%
Total (to 7%)	**167**	**101**	**61**	**48%**
8–16%	100	22	22	29%
17%	78	6	8	23%
Total (8%+)	**178**	**28**	**16**	**52%**

explaining which sex offenders did and did not get parole, a different prediction score was calculated drawing on the formula devised by Dr David Thornton of HM Prison Service. This categorises prisoners into three risk levels and takes into account whether or not the prisoner has completed a Sex Offender Treatment Programme. The findings showed that the statistical risk of reconviction according to the Thornton scale was a less strong predictor of parole than whether the prisoner had successfully completed a Sex Offender Treatment Programme. Amongst those who had done so, the parole rate was virtually the same whatever their risk category.

'Clinical' assessments of risk compared with 'actuarial' risk

Panel members have to rely on their own 'clinical' assessment as the actuarially-based ROR score for each prisoner is not available to them. Their assessment of risk was compared with the actuarial risks calculated by Copas et al. The findings showed that panel members were making decisions on the basis of unduly pessimistic 'clinical' estimations of risk when compared with the actuarial risk calculation:

- 85% of prisoners had a statistical rate of reconviction of a serious offence during parole period in the 'low' category (0–19%). Half of them had a ROR of 7% or less. Yet, Board members estimated risk of reconviction to be 20% or higher for more than half the prisoners they assessed
- 73% of the sex offender cases fell into the lower Levels I and II of the Thornton sex offender predictor. Yet, Board members assessed the risk to be equivalent to Level III in more than half the cases.

Probation Officers' Reports

There was a strong correlation between parole decisions and the recommendations made by both seconded probation officers in the prison and home probation officers (see Table 2). If probation reports were negative the chances of getting parole were close to zero. However, over 40% of prisoners recommended by both probation officers were refused parole. This may partly explain why half of the prisoners interviewed said they found the reasons they had been given 'hard to take'.

Low-Risk Offenders and Parole

The study assessed what the consequences would be if the parole rate for low risk offenders was increased. Estimates were made of what the effect would have been if the Parole Board

Table 2 The relationship between probation officers' (seconded probation officers in prison and the prisoner's home probation officer) recommendations and parole decisions

Recommendation	Paroled		Total	
	No.	%	No.	%
Both recommended parole	133	54	247	56
Only one recommended parole	11	18	60	14
Neither recommended parole	3	2	131	30

had released on parole all prisoners who had both a low actuarial risk of reconviction (ROR of 7% or less) for a serious offence while on parole licence and a recommendation from both probation officers.

The average risk of these prisoners being reconvicted of an offence while on parole for which they would be likely to receive a further prison sentence was less than four in a 100. Because they have such a low risk of reconviction, their inclusion amongst all parolees would actually reduce the average rate of reconviction from 6.2% to 5.7%.

If this group of prisoners had been released, the parole rate in the sample would have risen from 33.6% to 43.2%, which is equivalent to an increase of 29%. Translating this into a national estimate, this would mean that approximately 550 more prisoners would be released on parole annually. Of these, about 500 could be expected to complete parole without a conviction of any kind. Given the expense of imprisonment compared with supervision in the community, the cost of not granting parole to these low risk offenders is considerable.

Policy Implications

Procedural implications

- Both the degree of unanimity in decision-making and the ease of predicting parole decisions on the basis of recorded information raise the question of whether a formal meeting of three Board members in London is necessary for every case and, if not, how best the resources available might be used.
- The time and expense involved in the use of Parole Board Interviewing Members could be reassessed in view of the marginal role played by their reports in decision-making. Perhaps the prisoner's case could be communicated to the Board in a different way.
- There appears to be a strong argument for including an updated ROR score in parole dossiers. In a system that gives priority to risk, it is essential that risk should be assessed as accurately as possible, both to protect the public and to ensure that the liberty of low-risk prisoners is not unnecessarily restricted.

Wider implications

The 1988 Parole Review Committee (Carlisle Committee), whose recommendations led to the reform of the system by the 1991 Act, expected that, by moving the eligibility date forward from one-third to a half a sentence, and by providing supervision for all prisoners whether paroled or not, a higher, not a lower, proportion of prisoners would be granted parole. This has not happened. While the findings of this research show that parole decisions are in line with the Home Secretary's Directions, these Directions, together with the Board's interpretation of them, have undoubtedly created a more risk-averse approach than originally expected by the Carlisle Committee.

It will always be necessary to strike a balance between the risk to the public and the liberty that might be accorded the individual prisoner. These findings question whether the right balance has been found.

References

Copas, J.B., Marshall, P. and Tarling, R. (1996) *Predicting reoffending for Discretionary Conditional Release*. Home Office Research Study No. 150. London: Home Office.

Hood, R.G. and Shute, S.C (1994, 1995) *Evaluating the impact and effects of changes in the Parole System*. University of Oxford, Centre for Criminological Research. Occasional Papers Nos. 13 and 16. Oxford: University of Oxford.

[10:13] *Thynne, Wilson and Gunnell v United Kingdom*
(1991) 13 EHRR 666

The three applicants had been separately convicted of serious offences and sentenced to discretionary life sentences. All three applicants complained about the lack of regular judicial scrutiny of the lawfulness of their detention and, in the cases of the second and third applicants, re-detention. The court held, by a majority of 18 to 1, that there had been a violation of article 5(4) European Convention on Human Rights, and in the case of the third applicant, also a violation of article 5(5).

(At page 693):

73 As regards the nature and purpose of the discretionary life sentence under English law, the Government's main submission was that it is impossible to disentangle the punitive and 'security' components of such sentences. The court is not persuaded by this argument: the discretionary life sentence has clearly developed in English law as a measure to deal with mentally unstable and dangerous offenders; numerous judicial statements have recognised the protective purpose of this form of life sentence. Although the dividing line may be difficult to draw in particular cases, it seems clear that the principles underlying such sentences, unlike mandatory life sentences, have developed in the sense that they are composed of a punitive element and subsequently of a security element designed to confer on the Secretary of State the responsibility for determining when the public interest permits the prisoner's release. This view is confirmed by the judicial description of the 'tariff' as denoting the period of detention considered necessary to meet the requirements of retribution and deterrence.

74 The court accepts the Government's submissions that the 'tariff' is also communicated to the Secretary of State in cases of mandatory life imprisonment; that the Secretary of State in considering release may not be bound by the intimation of the 'tariff'; and that in the assessment of the risk factor in deciding on release the Secretary of State will also have regard to the gravity of the offences committed.

However, in the court's view this does not alter the fact that the objectives of the discretionary life sentence as seen above are distinct from the punitive purposes of the mandatory life sentence and have been so described by the courts in the relevant cases.

75 It is clear from the judgments of the sentencing courts that in their view the three applicants, unlike Mr Weeks, had committed offences of the utmost gravity meriting lengthy terms of imprisonment. Nevertheless, the court is satisfied that in each case the punitive period of the discretionary life sentence has expired.

In the case of Mr Thynne, it was accepted that by the end of 1984 risk was the sole remaining consideration in his continued detention.

In addition to the life sentence imposed on him for the offence of buggery, Mr Wilson was sentenced in 1972 to seven years' imprisonment for each of the nine other counts to be served concurrently. In the circumstances of his case it would seem reasonable to draw the conclusion that the punitive period of his life sentence has expired when he was released in

1982 and that thereafter his re-detention pursuant to that sentence depended solely on the risk factor.

In Mr Gunnell's case, too, it may be taken that, notwithstanding the gravity of his offences on which the courts laid particular emphasis, the applicant had served the punitive period of his sentence by March 1982, the date fixed for his provisional release.

76 Having regard to the foregoing, the court finds that the detention of the applicants after the expiry of the punitive periods of their sentences is comparable to that at issue in the *Van Droogenbroeck* and *Weeks* cases – the factors of mental instability and dangerousness are susceptible to change over the passage of time and new issues of lawfulness may this arise in the course of detention. It follows that at this phase in the execution of their sentences, the applicants are entitled under Article 5(4) to take proceedings to have the lawfulness of their continued detention decided by a court at reasonable intervals and to have the lawfulness of any re-detention determined by a court.

(At page 695):

79 Article 5(4) does not guarantee a right to judicial control of such scope as to empower the 'court' on all aspects of the case, including questions of expediency, to substitute its own discretion for that of the decision-making authority; the review should, nevertheless, be wide enough to hear on those conditions which, according to the Convention, are essential for the lawful detention of a person subject to the special type of deprivation of liberty ordered against these three applicants.

80 The court sees no reason to depart from its finding in the *Weeks* judgment that neither the Parole Board nor judicial review proceedings – no other remedy of a judicial character being available to the three applicants – satisfy the requirements of Article 5(4). Indeed, this was not disputed by the Government.

C Recapitulation

81 In conclusion, there has been a violation of Article 5(4) in respect of all three applicants.

[10:14] *Stafford v United Kingdom*
(2002) 35 EHRR 1121

This case concerned the power of the Home Secretary not to accept a recommendation of the Parole Board to release on licence an offender subject to a mandatory life sentence whose previous licence had been revoked. The court accepted that all life sentences are made up of two parts: the first, the punishment element of the sentence, is a sentencing exercise, not the administrative implementation of the sentence of the court. The second part, imposed for the protection of the public because of the offender's dangerousness, should be reviewed regularly by a body with a power to release, and under a procedure with the necessary judicial safeguards, including, for example, the possibility of an oral hearing. The court held unanimously that there had been a violation of both Article 5(1) and Article 5(4) of the European Convention on Human Rights in the case before it. The Home Secretary should not have the power to detain post-tariff lifers against the recommendation of the Parole Board. The Court acknowledged that the Convention is a dynamic tool.

(At paragraph 58):

58 The applicant disputed that the true objective of the mandatory life sentence was life-long punishment. He remained the only mandatory life prisoner who had been

detained post-tariff on the basis that the Secretary believed that he might commit a non-violent offence if released. Different considerations might apply where a risk of drug trafficking was concerned as such activity was clearly capable of causing physical or psychological harm to others. To justify indefinite imprisonment by reference to a belief that he might on release commit a non-violent crime involving no conceivable physical harm to others, was arbitrary, encompassing matters wholly unrelated in nature and seriousness to the reasons for the prisoner being within the power of the State in the first place.

2. The Government

59 The Government submitted that the imposition of a mandatory life sentence for murder satisfied Article 5(1) of the Convention. In its view, this continued to provide a lawful basis for his detention after the expiry of the six-year sentence for fraud offences as his life licence had been revoked. It rejected the applicant's argument that this detention, on the basis of a concern that he might commit serious non-violent offences of dishonesty bore no proper relationship to the object of the original mandatory life sentence. It argued that the original sentence was imposed because of the gravity of the offence of murder. A mandatory life sentence for murder fell within a distinct category, different from the discretionary life sentence, as it was imposed as punishment for the seriousness of the offence. It was not governed by characteristics specific to a particular offender which might change over time, factors such as dangerousness, mental instability or youth. A trial judge was required by Parliament to impose a life sentence for murder whether or not the offender was considered dangerous.

60 The object and purpose of the punishment was to confer power on the Secretary of State to decide when, if at all, it was in the public interest to allow the applicant to return to society on life licence and to empower the Secretary of State to decide, subject to the applicable statutory procedures, whether it was in the public interest to recall the applicant to prison at any time until his death. Whether or not the concern was about risk of further offences of violence or further non-violent offences, a refusal to release on life licence, or a decision to revoke the life licence, was closely related to the original mandatory life sentence by reason of the gravity of the offence and to ensure that the prisoner could only be released when the public interest made it appropriate to do so. The sentence also provided flexibility since it allowed reconsideration of the tariff if such had been set in ignorance of relevant factors, a possibility not available to a judge.

61 The Government submitted that, in deciding whether it was in the public interest to release the applicant, the Secretary of State was therefore entitled to have regard to the risk of serious non-violent offending. It would not be logical or rational if he was unable to refuse to order the release of a prisoner where there was an unacceptable risk of his committing serious non-violent offences such as burglary or trafficking in heroin, which attracted far longer prison sentences than some offences of a violent nature and which caused far more harm to the public interest. The Government referred to the previous case law of the Court which found that continued detention of life prisoners was justified by their original trial and appeal proceedings. The fact that the applicant had been released on life licence and had been living for some time at liberty had no relevance to the lawful basis of his detention after revocation of that licence. Nor had there been any relevant developments in either domestic or Convention case law which altered the statutory basis of the mandatory life sentence or its proper meaning and effect.

B. The Court's assessment

1. Preliminary considerations

62 The question to be determined is whether, after the expiry on 1 July 1997 of the fixed term sentence imposed on the applicant for fraud, the continued detention of the applicant under the original mandatory life sentence imposed on him for murder in 1967 complied with the requirements of Article 5(1) of the Convention.

63 Where the 'lawfulness' of detention is in issue, the Convention refers essentially to national law and lays down the obligation to conform to the substantive and procedural rules of national law. This primarily requires any arrest or detention to have a legal basis in domestic law but also relates to the quality of the law, requiring it to be compatible with the rule of law, a concept inherent in all the Articles of the Convention. In addition, any deprivation of liberty should be in keeping with the purpose of Article 5, namely to protect the individual from arbitrariness.

64 It is not contested that the applicant's detention from 1 July 1997 was in accordance with a procedure prescribed by English law and otherwise lawful under English law. This was established in the judicial review proceedings, where the Court of Appeal and House of Lords found that the Secretary of State's decision to detain the applicant fell within his discretion as conferred by section 35(1) of the 1991 Act. This is not however conclusive of the matter. The Court's case law indicates that it may be necessary to look beyond the appearances and the language used and concentrate on the realities of the situation.[5] In the case of Weeks v. United Kingdom, which concerned the recall to prison by the Secretary of State of an applicant who had been released from a discretionary life sentence for robbery, the Court interpreted the requirements of Article 5 as applying to the situation as follows: The lawfulness required by the Convention presupposes not only conformity with domestic law but also, as confirmed by Article 18, conformity with the purposes of the deprivation of liberty permitted by the sub-paragraph (a) of Article 5(1) (see as the most recent authority the Bozano judgment of 18 December 1986, Series A No. 111, p. 23 (54)). Furthermore, the word 'after' in sub-paragraph (a) does not simply mean that the detention must follow the 'conviction' in point of time: in addition, the 'detention' must result from, 'follow and depend upon' or occur 'by virtue' of the 'conviction' (ibid., pp. 22–23, (3), and the Van Droogenbroeck judgment . . . p. 19, (35)). In short, there must be a sufficient causal connection between the conviction and the deprivation of liberty at issue (see the abovementioned Van Droogenbroeck judgment, p. 21 (39)).

65 The Court recalls that in the Weeks case it was found that the discretionary life sentence imposed on the applicant was an indeterminate sentence expressly based on considerations of his dangerousness to society, factors which were susceptible by their very nature to change with the passage of time. On that basis, his recall, in light of concerns about is unstable, disturbed and aggressive behaviour, could not be regarded as arbitrary or unreasonable in terms of the objectives of the sentence imposed on him and there was sufficient connection for the purposes of Article 5(1)(a) between his conviction in 1966 and recall to prison in 1977.

66 Much of the argument from the parties has focused on the nature and purpose of the mandatory life sentence as compared with other forms of life sentence and whether the detention after 1 July 1997 continued to conform with the objectives of that sentence. And since the procedures applying to the varying types of life sentences have generated considerable case law, both on the domestic level and before the Convention organs, there has been extensive reference to the judicial dicta produced as supporting the arguments on both sides.

67 Of particular importance in this regard is the Wynne case decided in 1994, in which this Court found that no violation arose under Article 5(4) in relation to the continued detention after release and recall to prison of a mandatory life prisoner convicted of an intervening offence of manslaughter, the tariff element of which had expired. This provides strong support for the Government's case while the applicant sought to argue that this decision did not succeed in identifying the reality of the situation for mandatory life prisoners which subsequent developments have clarified still further. The Court in Wynne was well aware that there were similarities between the discretionary life and mandatory life sentences, in particular that both contained a punitive and a preventive element and that mandatory life prisoners did not actually spend the rest of their lives in prison. The key passage states: However the fact remains that the mandatory life sentence belongs to a different category from the discretionary life sentence in the sense that it is imposed automatically as the punishment for the offence of murder irrespective of considerations pertaining to the dangerousness of the offender. (p. 14, (35))

68 While the Court is not formally bound to follow any of its previous judgments, it is in the interests of legal certainty, foreseeability and equality before the law that it should not depart, without cogent reason, from precedents laid down in previous cases. Since the Convention is first and foremost a system for the protection of human rights, the Court must however have regard to the changing conditions in Contracting States and respond, for example, to any emerging consensus as to the standards to be achieved. It is of crucial importance that the Convention is interpreted and applied in a manner which renders its rights practical and effective, not theoretical and illusory. A failure by the Court to maintain a dynamic and evolutive approach would risk rendering it a bar to reform or improvement.

69 Similar considerations apply as regards the changing conditions and any emerging consensus discernible within the domestic legal order of the respondent Contracting State. Although there is no material distinction on the facts between this and the Wynne case, having regard to the significant developments in the domestic sphere, the Court proposes to re-assess 'in the light of present-day conditions' what is now the appropriate interpretation and application of the Convention.

2. Legal developments

70 The mandatory life sentence is imposed pursuant to statute in all cases of murder. This position has not changed, though there has been increasing criticism of the inflexibility of the statutory regime, which does not reflect the differing types of killing covered by the offence from so-called mercy killing to brutal psychopathic serial attacks.

71 The inflexibility of this regime was, from a very early stage, mitigated by the approach of the Secretary of State, who in all types of life sentences – mandatory, discretionary and Her Majesty's pleasure detention adopted a practice of setting a specific term known as the 'tariff' to represent the element of deterrence and retribution. This was generally the minimum period of detention which would be served before an offender could hope to be released. It was never anticipated that prisoners serving mandatory life sentences would in fact stay in prison for life, save in exceptional cases. Similarly, the decision as to the release of all life prisoners also lay generally with the Secretary of State. The tariff-fixing and release procedures applicable to life sentences have however been modified considerably over the past 20 years, to a large extent due to the case law of this Court. It is also significant that the domestic courts were frequently called upon to rule on lawfulness issues arising out of the Secretary of State's role in fixing the tariff and in deciding the appropriate moment for release, the courts

requiring the establishment of proper and fair procedures in his exercise of those functions. Between Strasbourg and the domestic courts, a steady erosion on the scope of the Secretary of State's decision-making power in this field may be identified.

72 The first examination of the Court in this area focused on the situation of discretionary life prisoners. In the cases of Weeks and Thynne, Gunnell and Wilson, the Court analysed the purpose and effect of the discretionary life sentence, imposable for very serious offences such as manslaughter and rape. It was held that since the grounds relied upon in sentencing to a discretionary life term concerned risk and dangerousness, factors susceptible to change over time, new issues of lawfulness could arise after the expiry of the tariff which, in the context of Article 5(4), necessitated proper review by a judicial body. As a result, the Criminal Justice Act 1991 provided that the question of release, after expiry of tariff of a discretionary life prisoner, was to be decided not by the Secretary of State but by the Parole Board in a procedure with judicial safeguards. The same Act also gave statutory force to the Secretary of State's policy of accepting the judicial view of the tariff in discretionary life cases. The judges then took on the role, in open court, of setting the punishment element of the sentence. Though no significant changes were made by statute to the regime of mandatory life sentences, the procedure whereby the tariff was fixed was shortly afterwards modified following the House of Lords decision in the Doody case, where it was found that procedural fairness required that mandatory life prisoners be informed of the judicial view of the tariff in order that they could make written representations to the Secretary of State before he reached his decision. This reflected a growing perception that the tariff-setting function was closely analogous to a sentencing function.

73 It was at this stage that the Court directly addressed the position of mandatory life prisoners in the Wynne case and took the view that the mandatory life sentence was different in character from the discretionary life sentence. In reaching that decision, it concentrated on the automatic imposition of the mandatory life sentence, which was perceived as pursuing a punitive purpose.

74 Not long afterwards, the situation of post-tariff juvenile murderers (Her Majesty's pleasure detainees) was the subject of applications under the Convention. Though this type of sentence, as with the adult mandatory life sentence, was imposed automatically for the offence of murder, the Court was not persuaded that it could be regarded as a true sentence of punishment to detention for life. Such a term applied to children would have conflicted with United Nations instruments and raised serious problems under Article 3 of the Convention. Considering that it must be regarded in practice as an indeterminate sentence which could only be justified by considerations based on the need to protect the public and therefore linked to assessments of the offender's mental development and maturity, it therefore held that a review by a court of the continued existence of grounds of detention was required for the purposes of Article 5(4).

75 The issues arising from the sentencing process for juvenile murderers at the tariff-fixing stage were then examined both in the domestic courts and in Strasbourg. In Ex parte T and V the House of Lords made very strong comment on the judicial nature of the tariff-fixing exercise and quashed a tariff fixed by the Home Secretary which, inter alia, took into account 'public clamour' whipped up by the press against the offenders in the case. This Court found that Article 6(1) applied to the fixing of the tariff, which represented the requirements of retribution and deterrence and was thus a sentencing exercise. The fact that it was decided by

the Secretary of State, a member of the executive and therefore not independent, was found to violate this provision.

76 By this stage therefore, there were further statutory changes, which assimilated the position of juvenile murderers to that of discretionary life prisoners in giving the courts the role of fixing the tariff and providing the Parole Board with decision-making powers and appropriate procedures when dealing with questions of release.

77 While mandatory life prisoners alone remained under the old regime, the coming into force on 2 October 2000 of the Human Rights Act 1998 provided the opportunity for the first direct challenges to the mandatory life regime under the provisions of the Convention in the domestic courts. In the case of Lichniak and Pyrah the prisoners' arguments that the mandatory life sentence was arbitrary due to its inflexibility were rejected. It may be observed, as pointed out by the applicant, that the Government in that case contended that the mandatory life sentence was an indeterminate sentence by which an individualised tariff was set and that after the expiry of the tariff the prisoner could expect to be released once it was safe to do so. They expressly departed from the position that the mandatory life sentence represented a punishment whereby a prisoner forfeited his liberty for life. On that basis, the Court of Appeal found that there were no problems of arbitrariness or disproportionality in imposing mandatory life sentences. Then in the case of Anderson and Taylor, which concerned a challenge under Article 6(1) to the role of the Secretary of State in fixing the tariffs for two mandatory life prisoners, the Court of Appeal was unanimous in finding that this was a sentencing exercise which should attract the guarantees of that Article, following on from clear statements made by the House of Lords in the cases of *Ex parte T and V* and *Ex parte Pierson*.

78 The above developments demonstrate an evolving analysis, in terms of the right to liberty and its underlying values, of the role of the Secretary of State concerning life sentences. The abolition of the death penalty in 1965 and the conferring on the Secretary of State of the power to release convicted murderers represented, at that time, a major and progressive reform. However, with the wider recognition of the need to develop and apply, in relation to mandatory life prisoners, judicial procedures reflecting standards of independence, fairness and openness, the continuing role of the Secretary of State in fixing the tariff and in deciding on a prisoner's release following its expiry, has become increasingly difficult to reconcile with the notion of separation of powers between the executive and the judiciary, a notion which has assumed growing importance in the case law of the Court.

79 The Court considers that it may now be regarded as established in domestic law that there is no distinction between mandatory life prisoners, discretionary life prisoners and juvenile murderers as regards the nature of tariff-fixing. It is a sentencing exercise. The mandatory life sentence does not impose imprisonment for life as a punishment. The tariff, which reflects the individual circumstances of the offence and the offender, represents the element of punishment. The Court concludes that the finding in Wynne that the mandatory life sentence constituted punishment for life can no longer be regarded as reflecting the real position in the domestic criminal justice system of the mandatory life prisoner. This conclusion is reinforced by the fact that a whole life tariff may, in exceptional cases, be imposed where justified by the gravity of the particular offence. It is correct that the Court in its more recent judgments in T and V, citing the Wynne judgment as authority, reiterated that an adult mandatory life sentence constituted punishment for life. In doing so it had, however, merely sought to draw attention to the difference between such a life sentence and a sentence to detention during Her Majesty's pleasure, which was the category of sentence under review in the cases

concerned. The purpose of the statement had therefore been to distinguish previous case law rather than to confirm an analysis deriving from that case law.

[10:15] Padfield, N, '"Back door sentencing": is recall to prison a penal process?'

(2005) Camb LJ 276

While much effort has gone into training judges and advocates in the intricacies of the new sentencing regime introduced in the Criminal Justice Act 2003, and implemented in large measure in April 2005, it is refreshing to see the House of Lords turn its attention to what might be considered an area of equal importance: executive recall to prison, or 'back door sentencing'. The Parole Board's Annual Reports reveal the huge increase in recall cases in recent years: from 2,457 in 2000–01, to 9,031 in 2003–04, for example. The prison population is thus increasingly shaped by those who enter by the 'back door'.

The facts of the two cases before the House of Lords in *R v Parole Board, ex parte Smith; R v Parole Board, ex parte West* [2005] UKHL 1; [2005] 1 WLR 350; [2005] 1 All ER 755 were not untypical. Justin West was released at the halfway stage of his three-year sentence for affray on 6 August 2001, subject to the standard licence conditions. Ten days after his release, he had allegedly assaulted his former partner in a hostel, but the victim would not confirm the incident. He then failed to keep an appointment with his supervising officer, and on 22 August the Home Secretary revoked his license, under s. 39(2) of the Criminal Justice Act 1991. He was arrested on 24 August and returned to prison. The Home Secretary referred the case to the Parole Board under s. 39(4)(b) and his solicitors made written representations urging an urgent oral hearing to be attended by witnesses whose evidence should be heard on oath. The Parole Board rejected these representations in a letter of 2 October and Mr West remained in prison until 9 May 2002.

The Parole Board's decision was unsuccessfully challenged in the High Court and the Court of Appeal. The majority of the Court of Appeal concluded that Article 6 (the right to a fair trial) had no application because of 'the critical fact that when a parole licence is revoked and its revocation is subsequently confirmed this is solely with a view to the prevention of risk and the protection of the public and not at all by way of punishment' (Simon Brown LJ). Only Hale LJ recognised, in her dissenting judgement, that 'to the person concerned it is experienced as punishment, whatever the authorities may say'. However, the House of Lords (Lords Bingham, Slynn, Hope, Walker and Carswell) decided unanimously that he should have been allowed an oral hearing:

> In his representations against revocation the appellant West offered the Board explanations, which he said he could substantiate, of his failure to keep an appointment with his probation officer and of the incident at his ex-partner's hostel. The Board could not properly reject these explanations on the materials before it without hearing him. He admitted spending one night away from his approved address, staying (he said) with a cousin. While this was a breach of his licence conditions, it is not clear what risk was thereby posed to the public which called for eight months' detention. His challenge could not be fairly resolved without an oral hearing and he was not treated with that degree of fairness which his challenge required (per Lord Bingham).

The other case was that of Trevor Smith, who was released on license from a 6 1/2 year extended sentence for rape on 7 November 2001, which was his 'non-parole date', the date on which he was entitled to be released. Having tested positive for cocaine whilst living in a probation hostel, he was moved at his request to another hostel, but again tested positive to cocaine, and three days later to cocaine and opiates. His probation officer referred the case to the Parole Board under s. 39(1) of the Act of 1991. The Board supported the recommendation that he should be recalled, which he was, on 4 February 2002. Smith made written representations under s. 39(3), but these were rejected in a letter which explained that his drug use presented too great a risk to public safety. His original application for judicial review was turned down. At an oral renewal of the application, he was granted permission to seek judicial review, but only in relation to Article 6 and the common law. The case was listed before a third judge who refused to allow him to rely also on Article 5 (right to liberty). He appealed against that refusal, and the Court of Appeal (led by Lord Woolf CJ) ordered that he be permitted to rely on Article 5, as well as Article 6 and common law. The Court also ordered that the case be heard in the Court of Appeal, where the case was heard by Kennedy, Brooke LJJ, Holman J, who held that Mr Smith had no right to an oral hearing, and that there was no objective need for an oral hearing, as there was no dispute on the primary facts. Smith was eventually released on 3 December 2003, having served 22 months during the period of recall.

The House of Lords also unanimously allowed this appeal:

> The resort to class A drugs by the appellant Smith clearly raised serious questions, and it may well be that his challenge would have been rejected whatever procedure had been followed. But it may also be that the hostels in which he was required to live were a very bad environment for a man seeking to avoid addiction. It may be that the Board would have been assisted by evidence from his psychiatrist. The Board might have concluded that the community would be better protected by encouraging his self-motivated endeavours to conquer addiction, if satisfied these were genuine, than by returning him to prison for 2 years with the prospect that, at the end of that time, he would be released without the benefit of any supervision. Whatever the outcome, he was in my opinion entitled to put these points at an oral hearing. Procedural fairness called for more than consideration of his representations, on paper, as one of some 24 such applications routinely considered by a panel at a morning session (per Lord Bingham).

Much of the analysis in the House concerns the relationship between the appellants' common law and their Convention rights. They agreed that the common law demanded, in these cases, an oral hearing: 'the prisoner should have the benefit of a procedure which fairly reflects. . . the importance of what is at stake for him, as for society' (per Lord Bingham). Lord Hope explicitly identifies the breach of Article 5(4). Controversially they appear to conclude that recall is not a punishment, and that therefore the criminal due process rights of Article 6 are not engaged (though Lord Bingham thought it unnecessary to resolve this question). Lord Hope adds that Article 6 civil rights are not infringed by proceedings of this kind so long as the individual has access to the domestic courts to assert his right to liberty. Doubtless these conclusions will be challenged, but there are more fundamental points to question: is the Parole Board really 'an independent and impartial tribunal'? Who should bear the burden of proof before the Parole Board? (And is the Parole Board adequately resourced for the inevitable flood of applications?)

The statutory provisions and subordinate rules governing the release, licensing and recall of prisoners have, as Lord Bingham points out, been the subject of 'ceaseless change' over the past 10–15 years. Under ss. 254 and 255 of the Criminal Justice Act 2003, in force for all prisoners subject to license conditions on or after 4 April 2005 irrespective of the date of their offence, recall becomes more obviously an executive decision. This removes the previous anomaly whereby the Parole Board both advised on recalls and acted as an appeal body against those same recalls. It is time that lawyers, both academic and practising, paid much closer attention to the fairness (or otherwise) of these 'back door sentencing' decisions.

[10:16] Holloway, K and Grounds, A, 'Discretion and the Release of Mentally Disordered Offenders'

in Gelsthorpe, L and Padfield, N (eds), *Exercising Discretion: Decision-making in the criminal justice system and beyond* (2003) Willan (at page 158)

Conclusions and proposals for reform

The results of this research raise questions about the quality of Mental Health Review Tribunal decision-making in restricted cases and suggest that Tribunals are failing in their fundamental duty to safeguard some patients from unjustified detention in hospital. This failure, however, is not solely a response to the current climate of heightened concern for public safety. The majority of problems were observed in the decision-making *process*, but problems were also noted with the Tribunals' powers, the rules governing the Tribunal process, and the evidence upon which their decisions were to be based.

Although many doubtful practices were evident, the broad approach to decision-making was generally highly conscientious. Tribunal panels could spend hours ensuring that reasons were accurately and appropriately phrased. Medical members were heard persuading patients to try new courses of treatment in an effort to help them make progress. Annoyance and frustration were observed because of Tribunals' inability to transfer patients out of maximum security and efforts were regularly made to help improve the patient's situation. It was notable that the Tribunal members experienced real pleasure when granting discharges. Successful patients were usually invited back to the hearing room to be told the good news in person and to be congratulated on their success. In cases where no discharge was authorized the Tribunals endeavoured to emphasise progress that had been made rather than highlighting problems and failures. The members were anxious not to damage a patient's future chances of discharge or transfer.

In September 1998 the government appointed an Expert Committee to conduct a review of the Mental Health Act 1983. The Committee, chaired by Professor Genevra Richardson, was commissioned to inquire into 'how much mental health legislation should be shaped to reflect contemporary patterns of care within a framework which balances the need to protect the rights of individual patients and the need to ensure public safety' (Department of Health 1999a). In response to the Expert Committee's report a Green Paper was issued outlining the government's initial proposals for reform of the Mental Health Act (Department of Health 1999b). Following a consultation period the government published a White Paper in December 2000 (Department of Health 2000). These proposals have important and far-reaching implications, particularly for the Mental Health Review Tribunal system.

One of the main recommendations is to establish a new Tribunal system. This would extend the Tribunal's function to include the task of confirming an initial compulsory treatment order[1] and for renewing that order at regular intervals.[2] Patients would also be entitled to apply to the new Tribunals for a review of their case once during the currency of each order. The new system would, therefore, require Tribunals to review the need for a compulsory order that in some cases they themselves had confirmed.

---

1 Offender patients would be subject to compulsory care and treatment on the decision of the court rather than the new Tribunal.
2 The new Tribunals would be required to renew orders after six months, after a second six months and thereafter annually.

As noted above, the White Paper does not remedy the lack of Tribunal powers to effect hospital transfers in restricted cases. It also appears possible that the influence of Tribunals will be further restricted by limitations in their ability to order deferred conditional discharges. Whilst a Tribunal would be able to order discharge from hospital that is conditional on co-woperation with a community care plan, such an order could only be made if the necessary forms of care are available.

In addition to the change in the Tribunals' fundamental role, proposals are also made for an alteration in the composition of the Tribunal panel. The medical member's role as both an expert adviser and a decision-maker is viewed as incompatible and contrary to natural justice. Recommendations have therefore been made to separate these roles, so that the patient is assessed by a medical member of an independently appointed expert panel. The White Paper does not make clear, however, whether the patient would have access to this assessment. The Tribunal would have a clinical member (not necessarily medical). The loss of medical members from the Tribunal panels may have serious consequences for the quality of Tribunal decision-making. The observational research demonstrated that the medical members were crucial in the deliberations of Tribunals: they guided the members through the medical evidence, they explained key concepts and terms, and helped in the formulation of reasons that accurately described patients' conditions. It is likely, therefore, that the absence of a medical member would result in even greater reliance on the views of the patient's consultant or clinical supervisor, thereby compromising the 'independence' of the Tribunal system still further.

Index

Printed in Great Britain
by Amazon